A Companion to William Faulkner

Blackwell Companions to Literature and Culture

1. *A Companion to Romanticism* — Edited by Duncan Wu
2. *A Companion to Victorian Literature and Culture* — Edited by Herbert F. Tucker
3. *A Companion to Shakespeare* — Edited by David Scott Kastan
4. *A Companion to the Gothic* — Edited by David Punter
5. *A Feminist Companion to Shakespeare* — Edited by Dympna Callaghan
6. *A Companion to Chaucer* — Edited by Peter Brown
7. *A Companion to Literature from Milton to Blake* — Edited by David Womersley
8. *A Companion to English Renaissance Literature and Culture* — Edited by Michael Hattaway
9. *A Companion to Milton* — Edited by Thomas N. Corns
10. *A Companion to Twentieth-Century Poetry* — Edited by Neil Roberts
11. *A Companion to Anglo-Saxon Literature and Culture* — Edited by Phillip Pulsiano and Elaine Treharne
12. *A Companion to Restoration Drama* — Edited by Susan J. Owen
13. *A Companion to Early Modern Women's Writing* — Edited by Anita Pacheco
14. *A Companion to Renaissance Drama* — Edited by Arthur F. Kinney
15. *A Companion to Victorian Poetry* — Edited by Richard Cronin, Alison Chapman, and Antony H. Harrison
16. *A Companion to the Victorian Novel* — Edited by Patrick Brantlinger and William B. Thesing
17–20. *A Companion to Shakespeare's Works: Volumes I–IV* — Edited by Richard Dutton and Jean E. Howard
21. *A Companion to the Regional Literatures of America* — Edited by Charles L. Crow
22. *A Companion to Rhetoric and Rhetorical Criticism* — Edited by Walter Jost and Wendy Olmsted
23. *A Companion to the Literature and Culture of the American South* — Edited by Richard Gray and Owen Robinson
24. *A Companion to American Fiction 1780–1865* — Edited by Shirley Samuels
25. *A Companion to American Fiction 1865–1914* — Edited by Robert Paul Lamb and G. R. Thompson
26. *A Companion to Digital Humanities* — Edited by Susan Schreibman, Ray Siemens, and John Unsworth
27. *A Companion to Romance* — Edited by Corinne Saunders
28. *A Companion to the British and Irish Novel 1945–2000* — Edited by Brian W. Shaffer
29. *A Companion to Twentieth-Century American Drama* — Edited by David Krasner
30. *A Companion to the Eighteenth-Century English Novel and Culture* — Edited by Paula R. Backscheider and Catherine Ingrassia
31. *A Companion to Old Norse-Icelandic Literature and Culture* — Edited by Rory McTurk
32. *A Companion to Tragedy* — Edited by Rebecca Bushnell
33. *A Companion to Narrative Theory* — Edited by James Phelan and Peter J. Rabinowitz
34. *A Companion to Science Fiction* — Edited by David Seed
35. *A Companion to the Literatures of Colonial America* — Edited by Susan Castillo and Ivy Schweitzer
36. *A Companion to Shakespeare and Performance* — Edited by Barbara Hodgdon and W. B. Worthen
37. *A Companion to Mark Twain* — Edited by Peter Messent and Louis J. Budd
38. *A Companion to European Romanticism* — Edited by Michael K. Ferber
39. *A Companion to Modernist Literature and Culture* — Edited by David Bradshaw and Kevin J. H. Dettmar
40. *A Companion to Walt Whitman* — Edited by Donald D. Kummings
41. *A Companion to Herman Melville* — Edited by Wyn Kelley
42. *A Companion to Medieval English Literature and Culture c.1350–c.1500* — Edited by Peter Brown
43. *A Companion to Modern British and Irish Drama: 1880–2005* — Edited by Mary Luckhurst
44. *A Companion to Eighteenth-Century Poetry* — Edited by Christine Gerrard
45. *A Companion to Shakespeare's Sonnets* — Edited by Michael Schoenfeldt
46. *A Companion to Satire* — Edited by Ruben Quintero
47. *A Companion to William Faulkner* — Edited by Richard C. Moreland

A COMPANION TO

WILLIAM FAULKNER

EDITED BY **RICHARD C. MORELAND**

Blackwell
Publishing

© 2007 by Blackwell Publishing Ltd
except for editorial material and organization © 2007 by Richard C. Moreland

BLACKWELL PUBLISHING
350 Main Street, Malden, MA 02148-5020, USA
9600 Garsington Road, Oxford OX4 2DQ, UK
550 Swanston Street, Carlton, Victoria 3053, Australia

The right of Richard C. Moreland to be identified as the Author of the Editorial Material in this Work
has been asserted in accordance with the UK Copyright, Designs, and Patents Act 1988.

All rights reserved. No part of this publication may be reproduced, stored in a retrieval system, or
transmitted, in any form or by any means, electronic, mechanical, photocopying, recording or
otherwise, except as permitted by the UK Copyright, Designs, and Patents Act 1988, without the
prior permission of the publisher.

First published 2007 by Blackwell Publishing Ltd

1   2007

Library of Congress Cataloging-in-Publication Data

A companion to William Faulkner / edited by Richard C. Moreland.
    p.   cm.—(Blackwell companions to literature and culture ; 47)
        Includes bibliographical references and index.
        ISBN-13: 978-1-4051-2224-5 (hardcover : alk. paper)
        ISBN-10: 1-4051-2224-2 (hardcover : alk. paper)
1. Faulkner, William, 1897–1962—Criticism and interpretation—Handbooks, manuals, etc.
            I. Moreland, Richard C.   II. Series.
                PS3511.A86Z7585 2007
                    813´.52—dc22
                    2006012584

A catalogue record for this title is available from the British Library.
Set in 11 on 13 pt Garamond 3
by SNP Best-set Typesetter Ltd, Hong Kong
Printed and bound in Singapore
by COS Printers Pte Ltd

The publisher's policy is to use permanent paper from mills that operate a sustainable forestry policy,
and which has been manufactured from pulp processed using acid-free and elementary chlorine-free
practices. Furthermore, the publisher ensures that the text paper and cover board used have met
acceptable environmental accreditation standards.

For further information on
Blackwell Publishing, visit our website:
www.blackwellpublishing.com

Contents

Notes on Contributors   viii
Acknowledgments   xiv

Introduction   1
Richard C. Moreland

PART I   *Contexts*   5

1   A Difficult Economy: Faulkner and the Poetics of Plantation Labor   7
     Richard Godden

2   "We're Trying Hard as Hell to Free Ourselves": Southern History and
     Race in the Making of William Faulkner's Literary Terrain   28
     Grace Elizabeth Hale and Robert Jackson

3   A Loving Gentleman and the Corncob Man: Faulkner, Gender,
     Sexuality, and *The Reivers*   46
     Anne Goodwyn Jones

4   "C'est Vraiment Dégueulasse": Meaning and Ending in *A bout de souffle*
     and *If I Forget Thee, Jerusalem*   65
     Catherine Gunther Kodat

5   The Synthesis of Marx and Freud in Recent Faulkner Criticism   85
     Michael Zeitlin

6   Faulkner's Lives   104
     Jay Parini

PART II   *Questions*   113

7   Reflections on Language and Narrative   115
     Owen Robinson

8   Race as Fact and Fiction in William Faulkner   133
    Barbara Ladd

9   "Why Are You So Black?" Faulkner's Whiteface Minstrels,
    Primitivism, and Perversion   148
    John N. Duvall

10 Shifting Sands: The Myth of Class Mobility   165
    Julia Leyda

11 Faulkner's Families   180
    Arthur F. Kinney

12 Changing the Subject of Place in Faulkner   202
    Cheryl Lester

13 The State   220
    Ted Atkinson

14 Violence in Faulkner's Major Novels   236
    Lothar Hönnighausen

15 An Impossible Resignation: William Faulkner's Post-Colonial
    Imagination   252
    Sean Latham

16 Religion: Desire and Ideology   269
    Leigh Anne Duck

17 Cinematic Fascination in *Light in August*   284
    Peter Lurie

18 Faulkner's Brazen Yoke: Pop Art, Modernism, and the Myth of
    the Great Divide   301
    Vincent Allan King

PART III   *Genres and Forms*   319

19 Faulkner's Genre Experiments   321
    Thomas L. McHaney

20 "Make It New": Faulkner and Modernism   342
    Philip Weinstein

21 Faulkner's Versions of Pastoral, Gothic, and the Sublime   359
    Susan V. Donaldson

22 Faulkner, Trauma, and the Uses of Crime Fiction   373
    Greg Forter

23 William Faulkner's Short Stories 394
Hans H. Skei

24 Faulkner's Non-Fiction 410
Noel Polk

25 Faulkner's Texts 420
Noel Polk

PART IV *Sample Readings* 427

26 "By It I Would Stand or Fall": Life and Death in *As I Lay Dying* 429
Donald M. Kartiganer

27 Faulkner and the Southern Arts of Mystification in *Absalom, Absalom!* 445
John Carlos Rowe

28 "The Cradle of Your Nativity": Codes of Class Culture and Southern
Desire in Faulkner's Snopes Trilogy 459
Evelyn Jaffe Schreiber

PART V *After Faulkner* 477

29 "He Doth Bestride the Narrow World Like a Colossus": Faulkner's
Critical Reception 479
Timothy P. Caron

30 Faulkner, Latin America, and the Caribbean: Influence, Politics, and
Academic Disciplines 499
Deborah Cohn

31 Faulkner's Continuance 519
Patrick O'Donnell

Index 528

Notes on Contributors

Ted Atkinson serves as assistant professor of English at Augusta State University. His primary areas of research and teaching interest are modern American literature and culture and Southern studies. His publications include *Faulkner and the Great Depression: Aesthetics, Ideology, and Cultural Politics* (2005), as well as essays in the *Faulkner Journal* and *Mississippi Quarterly*.

Timothy P. Caron is professor of English at California State University, Long Beach, where he teaches courses in nineteenth- and twentieth-century American literature. His research and teaching interests include religion and literature, particularly in the works of writers such as William Faulkner, Flannery O'Connor, Richard Wright, Zora Neale Hurston, Ralph Ellison, Toni Morrison, and Cormac McCarthy. He is currently working on a book on the critical reception of William Faulkner.

Deborah Cohn is associate professor of Spanish at Indiana University. She has published essays in *Comparative Literature Studies, CR: The New Centennial Review, Latin American Research Review, Southern Quarterly*, and elsewhere. She co-edited *Look Away!: The U.S. South in New World Studies* with Jon Smith (2004). She recently received a National Endowment for the Humanities fellowship to work on a book entitled *Creating the Boom's Reputation: The Promotion of the Boom in and by the U.S.*

Susan V. Donaldson is National Endowment for the Humanities Professor at the College of William and Mary, where she has taught American literature and American studies since 1985. She is the author of *Competing Voices: The American Novel, 1865–1914* (1998), which won a *Choice* Outstanding Academic Book award, and of over three dozen essays on Southern literature and culture. She has co-edited, with Anne Goodwyn Jones, *Haunted Bodies: Gender and Southern Texts* (1997); guest-edited two special issues of the *Faulkner Journal* on sexuality and masculinity respectively; and co-edited, with Michael Zeitlin, another special issue on memory and history. Her works in progress include a book on the politics of storytelling and visual culture in the US South and a book-length study of William Faulkner, Eudora Welty, Richard Wright, and the demise of Jim Crow.

Leigh Anne Duck is an assistant professor of English at the University of Memphis. Her essays have appeared in *American Literary History*, the *Journal of American Folklore*, and *Mississippi Quarterly*, as well as the books *Faulkner in the Twenty-First Century* (2003) and *Look Away!: The U.S. South in New World Studies* (2004). Her book *The Nation's Region: Southern Modernism, Segregation, and U.S. Nationalism* is forthcoming.

John N. Duvall is professor of English and editor of *Modern Fiction Studies* at Purdue University. He is author of *Faulkner's Marginal Couple: Invisible, Outlaw, and Unspeakable Communities* (1990) and *The Identifying Fictions of Toni Morrison: Modernist Authenticity and Postmodern Blackness* (2000), and editor or co-editor of *Productive Postmodernism: Consuming Histories and Cultural Studies* (2002), *Faulkner and Postmodernism* (2002), and *Approaches to Teaching DeLillo's White Noise* (2006). He is currently finishing a study of racial figuration in Southern fiction.

Greg Forter is associate professor of English at the University of South Carolina. He is the author of *Murdering Masculinities: Fantasies of Gender and Violence in the American Crime Novel* (2000) and, among other essays, "Against Melancholia: Contemporary Mourning Theory, Fitzgerald's *The Great Gatsby*, and the Politics of Unfinished Grief" (*differences* 2003). His current project traces the links among gender identity, racial fantasy, and socially induced loss in American modernism.

Richard Godden teaches American literature in the Department of American Studies at the University of Sussex. He has published *Fictions of Capital* (1990) and *Fictions of Labor* (1997); a study of Faulkner's later work, *William Faulkner: An Economy of Complex Words*, is forthcoming. He currently works on the relationship between narrative poetics and the economic forms of Flexible Fordism.

Grace Elizabeth Hale is associate professor of American studies and history at the University of Virginia. The author of *Making Whiteness: The Culture of Segregation in the South* (1999) and the forthcoming *Rebel, Rebel: Outsiders in Postwar America*, she has also written about American culture for *American Scholar*, *Southern Cultures*, *Southern Exposure*, *Radical History Review*, the *Journal of Southern History*, the *Journal of American History*, and the *American Historical Review*. Her new project traces non-poor Americans' cyclical discoveries of American poverty from the Great Depression to the present.

Lothar Hönnighausen is professor emeritus of English and North American Studies at the University of Bonn. Among his Faulkner publications are *William Faulkner: The Art of Stylization in his Early Graphic and Literary Work* (1987), *William Faulkner: Masks and Metaphors* (1997), and many essays. He is the editor of the series Transatlantic

Perspectives and co-editor of *Space – Place – Environment* (2004) and *Regionalism in the Age of Globalism* (2004).

Robert Jackson is an instructor of history at the University of Virginia, where he currently is completing a dissertation on the history of early Southern filmmaking. His work in American literature has explored the late nineteenth- and twentieth-century South, African American literature, and ecocriticism. His book *Seeking the Region in American Literature and Culture: Modernity, Dissidence, Innovation* was published in 2005.

Anne Goodwyn Jones has taught as an itinerant professor at the University of Missouri-Rolla, the Mississippi University for Women, and the University of Mississippi. She is now in Oxford, Mississippi, a good spot for writing about Faulkner. Author of several essays on Faulkner, she is completing a book on Faulkner's masculinities, working on Southern masculinity for the 2007 Lamar Lectures at Mercer University, and preparing courses on representations of slavery.

Donald M. Kartiganer holds the William Howry Chair in Faulkner Studies at the University of Mississippi. He is the author of *The Fragile Thread: The Meaning of Form in Faulkner's Novels* (1979), and co-editor of eight collections of critical essays on American literature and Faulkner. He has recently completed a book-length study, "Repetition Forward: The Ways of Modernist Meaning."

Vincent Allan King is associate professor of English at Black Hills State University, where he teaches American literature and creative writing. He has written scholarly essays on Robert Penn Warren, Dorothy Allison, Tony Crunk, William Gilmore Simms, Thomas Pynchon, and William Faulkner.

Arthur F. Kinney is the Thomas W. Copeland Professor of Literary History at the University of Massachusetts. He is the author of *Faulkner's Narrative Poetics: Style as Vision* (1978) and *Go Down, Moses: The Miscegenation of Time* (1996). He has edited four volumes on Faulkner's families with long historical introductions, and co-edited, with Lynn Z. Bloom and Francis L. Utley, *Bear, Man, and God: Eight Approaches to William Faulkner's The Bear* (1971) and, with Stephen Hahn, the MLA's *Approaches to Teaching "The Sound and the Fury"* (1996). He has also published a book and several essays on Flannery O'Connor; his essays have appeared, among other publications, in *Southern Review*, *Virginia Quarterly Review*, and the *Mississippi Quarterly*.

Catherine Gunther Kodat is associate professor of English and American studies, chair of the English Department, and director of the Program in American Studies at Hamilton College. She is finishing a book on the uses of culture during the Cold War.

Barbara Ladd teaches at Emory University in Atlanta, Georgia. Her publications include "Literary Studies: The Southern United States, 2005" (*PMLA* 2005); "Faulkner, Glissant, and a Creole Poetics of History and the Body in *Absalom, Absalom!* and *A Fable*," in *Faulkner in the Twenty-First Century* (2003); and *Resisting History: Gender, Modernity, and Authorship in William Faulkner, Zora Neale Hurston, and Eudora Welty* (forthcoming).

Sean Latham is associate professor of English at the University of Tulsa, where he serves as editor of the *James Joyce Quarterly* and director of the Modernist Journals Project. He is a specialist in modernist literature, and his publications include *"Am I A Snob?" Modernism and the Novel* (2003) and *Joyce's Modernism* (2005) as well as articles in *PMLA*, *New Literary History*, *Modern Fiction Studies*, and the *Journal of Modern Literature*. He is president-elect of the Modernist Studies Association and a trustee of the International James Joyce Foundation.

Cheryl Lester is associate professor of American studies and English and director of American studies at the University of Kansas, where she has served as a faculty member since 1987. She is the author of numerous articles on migration, race, and place in the writings of William Faulkner, and is currently completing a book-length study on Faulkner and co-editing a collection of essays on applications of Bowen Theory, emotional process, and counter-hegemony. With Alice Lieberman, she is the co-editor of *Social Work Practice with a Difference: A Literary Approach* (2003). With Philip Barnard, she is the translator and co-editor of *The Literary Absolute: The Theory of Literature in German Romanticism* (1988) by Philippe Lacoue-Labarthe and Jean-Luc Nancy.

Julia Leyda teaches in the Department of English Literature at Sophia University in Tokyo. Her research interests include US literature and culture, cinema studies, and the role of space and place in the construction of identity. She has published articles in *Arizona Quarterly*, *Cinema Journal*, the *Japanese Journal of American Studies*, and *Comparative American Studies*. She is currently writing a book with Sheila Hones tentatively entitled "Geographies of American Studies."

Peter Lurie is an assistant professor of English at the University of Richmond. He has taught in the History and Literature Program at Harvard and was the News International Research Fellow in Film Studies at Keble College, Oxford. He is the author of *Vision's Immanence: Faulkner, Film, and the Public Imagination* (2004) and of articles on Faulkner, cultural studies, and Hart Crane.

Thomas L. McHaney is an editor of the 25-volume *William Faulkner Manuscripts* (1986) and *Mosquitoes: A Facsimile and Transcription of the Holograph Manuscript* (1997), and author, most recently, of a short biography of Faulkner, a critical guide to *The Sound and the Fury*, and a history of the Southern Renaissance.

Richard C. Moreland is professor, director of undergraduate studies, and former director of graduate studies in English at Louisiana State University. He is the author of *Faulkner and Modernism: Rereading and Rewriting* (1990) and *Learning from Difference: Teaching Morrison, Twain, Ellison, and Eliot* (1999). He is currently working on questions of learning in modern American literature and culture.

Patrick O'Donnell is professor and chair of the English Department at Michigan State University. He is the author of a number of books and essays on modern and contemporary literature and film, including *Latent Destinies: Cultural Paranoia in Contemporary U.S. Narrative* (2000), *Echo Chambers: Figuring Voice in Modern Narrative* (1992), and *Passionate Doubts: Designs of Interpretation in Contemporary American Fiction* (1986). He is currently working on book-length projects about the novels of Henry James and contemporary film, contemporary American fiction since 1980, and a co-edited MLA volume, *Approaches to Teaching As I Lay Dying*.

Jay Parini is Axinn Professor of English at Middlebury College. He is a poet, novelist, and biographer. A volume of his new and selected poems, *The Art of Subtraction*, appeared in 2005. His biography of Faulkner, *One Matchless Time*, came out in 2004. He has also written lives of John Steinbeck and Robert Frost. He edited *The Oxford Encyclopedia of American Literature* (2004).

Noel Polk is editor of the *Mississippi Quarterly* and professor of English at Mississippi State University. He has published and lectured widely on William Faulkner, Eudora Welty, and other American authors. He has recently completed the editing of all of Faulkner's novels for the Library of America. Recent books include *Eudora Welty: A Bibliography of Her Work* (1994), *Children of the Dark House: Text and Context in Faulkner* (1996), and *Outside the Southern Myth* (1997).

Owen Robinson is lecturer in US literature at the University of Essex. He is the author of *Creating Yoknapatawpha: Readers and Writers in Faulkner's Fiction* (2006), and, with Richard Gray, has co-edited *A Companion to the Literature and Culture of the American South* (2004). He is currently working on writing centered on New Orleans, as part of the AHRC-funded project American Tropics: Towards a Literary Geography.

John Carlos Rowe is University of Southern California Associates' Professor of the Humanities at the University of Southern California. He is the author of numerous books, including *Literary Culture and U.S. Imperialism: From the Revolution to World War II* (2000) and *The New American Studies* (2002), and the editor of *"Culture" and the Problem of the Disciplines* (1998) and *Post-Nationalist American Studies* (2000). His current scholarly projects are: *Culture and U.S. Imperialism since World War II*, *The Rediscovery of America: Multicultural Literature and the New Democracy*, and Blackwell's *Companion to American Studies*.

Evelyn Jaffe Schreiber is associate professor of English at the George Washington University in Washington, DC. Her book *Subversive Voices: Eroticizing the Other in William Faulkner and Toni Morrison* (2002) examines identity and race via the theory of Jacques Lacan and cultural studies, and was awarded the Toni Morrison Society book prize, 2003. Her literary articles appear in *Mississippi Quarterly*, the *Faulkner Journal*, *Literature and Psychology*, *Style*, and the *Journal of the Fantastic in the Arts*. Her current research analyzes Morrison's novels using trauma theory.

Hans H. Skei is professor of comparative literature at the University of Oslo. He is the author of *William Faulkner: The Short Story Career* (1981), *William Faulkner: The Novelist as Short Story Writer* (1985), and *Reading Faulkner's Best Short Stories* (1999), and has translated into Norwegian Faulkner's Snopes trilogy as well as *Intruder in the Dust* and *The Sound and the Fury*. He is the editor of *William Faulkner's Short Fiction: An International Symposium* (1997), and is on the editorial board of the *Faulkner Journal*. He has published a number of essays on other Southern writers, including Shelby Foote, Eudora Welty, Walker Percy, and Mary Chesnut.

Philip Weinstein is Alexander Griswold Cummins Professor of English at Swarthmore College. His books that focus on Faulkner include: *Faulkner's Subject: A Cosmos No One Owns* (1992), *What Else But Love?: The Ordeal of Race in Faulkner and Morrison* (1996), and *Unknowing: The Work of Modernist Fiction* (2005).

Michael Zeitlin teaches American literature at the University of British Columbia. He has published a number of essays on Faulkner's fiction and is the co-editor, with André Bleikasten and Nicole Moulinoux, of *Méconnaissance, Race, and the Real in Faulkner's Fiction* (2004). He is also co-editor, with Edwin Arnold, of the *Faulkner Journal*.

Acknowledgments

I am extremely pleased that so many accomplished and talented contributors agreed to participate in this project, from which I have learned so much about Faulkner, current criticism, and writing. I also want to thank a series of research assistants for their crucial help and advice – Tameka Cage, Elizabeth Cowan, Marla Grupe, Anthony Hoefer, Eric Lundgren, and Alicia Ringuet – as well as the students in my Faulkner seminars in 2004 and 2005, who helped me imagine how so many different ideas might converge in readings and discussions. It has been a pure pleasure to work with Emma Bennett, Karen Jones, Jennifer Hunt, and Astrid Wind at Blackwell, all of whom have been both patient and persistent with me and the other contributors, and I owe a special debt to the skill and good judgment of copy-editor Fiona Sewell. As always, I have also relied on the personal support of Ed, Irv, Wayne, Allison, my parents Joe and Joyce, Gavin, Luke, and Susan.

Introduction

Richard C. Moreland

William Faulkner has received more critical attention than any other American writer, and since the 1980s that critical attention has dramatically changed. At first either ignored or considered scandalous or insufficiently engaged, Faulkner was then long championed by the New Critics for his formal experiments and his focus on apparently universal themes of tradition, community, and individual moral consciousness. Now, however, his writing is more often appreciated for raising unwieldy questions about the legacies of ongoing economic change, historical violence, and intractable social tensions, both within the US South and in related contexts such as urbanization and mass culture in other parts of the US and Europe, plantation economies in the Caribbean, and civil wars and racial codes in Latin America. His readers have also returned to questions of social and aesthetic forms, especially the formation of gnarled cultural consciousness and uneasy critique, both in his subject matter and in his adaptations of existing literary styles and popular culture genres. This dynamically changing state of Faulkner criticism is what this volume proposes to represent.

The chapters are grouped in five parts. The first part, "Contexts," emphasizes recent critical attention to various dimensions of the world within which Faulkner's work is situated – reflecting, exploring, and interrogating that world. The chapters in this part demonstrate how various contexts precede and surround Faulkner's work, not merely figuring as backdrops or subject matter but thoroughly informing everything that is done, said, heard, or written in his novels and stories. This part begins with Richard Godden's study of powerfully persistent, underlying economic structures in the US South and slow, faltering changes in the relations between laborers and their masters, debtors, and employers. Grace Elizabeth Hale and Robert Jackson place Faulkner's work within a history of regional and national thinking about race and civil rights that changed almost as slowly as economic structures, while Anne Goodwyn Jones closely links Faulkner's life and work with changing "beliefs about gender and sexuality contemporary to both." Catherine Gunther Kodat shows how Faulkner, like Jean-Luc Godard, struggled with art's place in a more rapidly shifting twentieth-century world of cinema, pulp fiction, and mass-market commerce. Michael Zeitlin's focus is yet another context in which Faulkner's writing has been read and reread, a Western intellectual history dominated by Marx and Freud, and Jay Parini reflects on his own and others' approaches to Faulkner biography as "historical context of a particular kind."

Turning from "Contexts" to "Questions," the second part considers certain common issues, problems, and debates in recent Faulkner criticism somewhat less as aspects of the surrounding world than as questions posed within Faulkner's fiction. Owen Robinson's chapter traces how Faulkner's distortions of language and narrative tend to defamiliarize certain fundamental but unstable constructions of reality, and to implicate his readers in these constructions, both as individual readers and as members of choruses like those represented in the fiction. Barbara Ladd shows Faulkner exploring a more conscious moral imperative articulated by Ralph Ellison – "the necessity for white writers to represent black characters in all their human complexity not only as a way to understand black humanity but as a way for whites to come to understand 'the broader aspects' of their own humanity." John N. Duvall's chapter considers some of these broader aspects of both race and sexuality in Faulkner's use of "whiteface" male characters to underscore the "otherness and alienation that result from their fundamental inability to assimilate to the values of their community." The class dimension of this alienation is emphasized in Julia Leyda's attention to the ways Faulkner's fiction challenges "the liberal and paternalist ideas that naturalize and legitimize inequality." Although such questions of race, gender, sexuality, and class figure throughout the fiction, Arthur F. Kinney demonstrates how thoroughly Faulkner frames them within family relationships that seem to define and haunt his characters. Cheryl Lester's chapter stresses instead the importance of geography and place, reviewing critical treatments of place in Faulkner to assess "the limits of Faulkner's hold on his world and its diverse peoples, material life, historical formation, geopolitical location, struggles, and possibilities." The question addressed by Ted Atkinson is how Faulkner responds to the profound change during his career in the relation between the individual and the state, as the philosophy of liberalism was transformed in the US "from its nineteenth-century roots as a philosophy of individual liberty and laissez-faire economics into a twentieth-century agent for collective identity and decisive federal action." Lothar Hönnighausen's topic is the variety of ways the fiction represents violence – in individual cases and in recurring patterns of racial, class, family, and mob violence. In at least one period of his career, according to Sean Latham, Faulkner was engaged with the violent aftermath "not of the Civil War, but of the original colonization of the Americas" as he attempted a post-colonial "perspective skewed not by tragedy but by a liberating impulse to escape the anguish of a South turned hopelessly inward on itself." Leigh Anne Duck reflects on more intimate versions of anguish and escape in the "often idiosyncratic interactions" in Faulkner's fiction "between the Southern religious context and individuals' spiritual perceptions." Peter Lurie's chapter traces how Faulkner's *Light in August* addressed the growing influence of cinema in his time: in permitting the historical traumas of Southern history "to remain traumatized, 'unhistorical,' *fascinating*, Faulkner allows a way to distinguish his novel from narratives of the South, like *Birth of a Nation*, that present this history so falsely." And Vincent Allan King discusses Faulkner's self-conscious relationship with both modernism and the popular culture industry.

Chapters in the third part focus on the main "Genres and Forms" in which Faulkner found many of these worldly contexts and questions articulated, and the different ways he attempted to reshape these genres and forms in his own writing. His experiments in poetry, drawing, hand-made books, letters, drama, romance, prose sketches and other short fictions, screenplays, essays, and speeches are the subject of this part's first chapter, by Thomas L. McHaney. Philip Weinstein considers the influence of "some modernist precursors without whose work it is difficult to imagine Faulkner becoming Faulkner," including Conrad, Freud, Eliot, and Joyce; then he "compares Faulkner's practice with that of his most compelling peers," especially Proust, Woolf, Hemingway, and Mann. Susan V. Donaldson places Faulkner at the intersection of older traditions of pastoral, gothic, and the sublime, including a shift "from the erotic sublime to something like a racial sublime," while Greg Forter sees Faulkner negotiating in different ways "the tension between authorial invention and generic formula" in his engagement with the conventions of the contemporary detective story and the psychological suspense story or *roman noir*. Hans H. Skei surveys Faulkner's long career as a writer of short stories, a form he took seriously for both financial and artistic reasons, sometimes easily accepting editors' suggestions but often also rewriting stories as better stories, as parts of story collections or cycles, or as imported parts or adapted and expanded germs of novels. Noel Polk's two chapters end this part by considering first Faulkner's non-fiction writing, not as a guide to his fiction, "but rather as emerging out of a more discursive and public part of his character," especially his sense of his responsibilities as a citizen, friend, and father. Then Polk reviews the textual record of Faulkner's writing in the forms of holographs, typescripts, tear-sheets, and galley proofs as another resource for understanding his life and the different public appearances of his work.

Criticism focused on contexts, questions, genres, and forms in the first three parts is combined in the fourth part's "Sample Readings" of particular works. Donald M. Kartiganer reads *As I Lay Dying* as a self-reflexive novel of and about compromise, "combining private need with family duty, lyric meditation with narrative action – conceived by a writer who has reached a moment in his career when these conflicting drives have become the terms of his own personal and professional situation." In John Carlos Rowe's reading of *Absalom, Absalom!*, the novel's narrative unreliability and literary self-consciousness about genres and forms such as lies, fables, chronicles, parables, yarns, odes, epitaphs, gossip, allegory, as well as realism, avant-garde modernism, and postmodern metafiction, raise the question of how these different forms of storytelling serve or disserve the political and moral criticism of social reality. Evelyn Jaffe Schreiber's reading of the Snopes trilogy – *The Hamlet*, *The Town*, and *The Mansion* – combines cultural studies with Lacanian psychoanalysis to help explain how the men in these novels, both collectively and individually, either force, resist, or adapt to cultural change in a stratified society.

The fifth and final part, "After Faulkner," considers three different legacies of Faulkner's writing. Timothy P. Caron reviews the critical response to Faulkner from early and New Critical readings through the theory boom to a new attention to Faulkner's later writing and a turn toward comparative Faulkner studies. Discussing one of the most important areas of this recent comparative work, Deborah Cohn analyzes Faulkner's literary influence on Spanish American authors, the political implications of his relationship with Latin America, and the current scholarly interest in "commonalities shared by the South, Latin America, and the Caribbean, including the legacies of slavery and the plantation; cultural mixing and hybridity; and the experience of US colonialism and imperialism." Finally, Patrick O'Donnell reflects on even broader commonalities suggested by Edouard Glissant's sense of Faulkner's "continuity, his ongoing presence in a [postcolonial] world of historical contingency and brutal contact, whose narrative is a multiplicity of conflicting and converging narratives."

This volume is itself a multiplicity of narratives both conflicting and converging with each other. Most of the conflicts result from the very different questions asked by each contributor. How might Faulkner's work reflect the history of economic conditions in the US South? Where does his writing fit in the twentieth century's changing ways of thinking and writing about race, sexuality, Marx, or Freud? How does Faulkner's fiction itself address these questions, or other questions about class, family, the state, colonization, religion, cinema, or pulp fiction? Comparing Faulkner to other modernist writers produces a different picture than analyzing his adaptations of pastoral, the sublime, or crime fiction. But of course many of the questions asked in different chapters also intersect and overlap in various contributors' references to some of the same novels, even some of the same incidents in those novels, and different questions converge again in the chapters designated as sample readings. Perhaps this multiplicity of narratives comes together most dramatically in the strong sense throughout this volume that all these questions are parts of an ongoing critical dialogue, a trans-historical, transnational, trans-cultural, trans-sexual dialogue among different readers learning from and building upon each other's different readings. In multiplicity, then, and what some of Faulkner's contemporaries and characters might fear as a kind of miscegenation, this attentive, continuing dialogue suggests a healthy future for Faulkner studies.

PART I
Contexts

1

A Difficult Economy: Faulkner and the Poetics of Plantation Labor

Richard Godden

Preface: A Labor Parable

The bound man carries in his hands the means to his unbinding, at least according to Hegel (1910: 180–9), whose argument runs as follows: the master, seeking to ensure the independence of his mastery, consigns the slave to chattel status, or that of a thing capable of acting only as a dependent extension of his master's will. No human, no matter how peculiar the institution which binds him, is without will. Slaves who assume will-less-ness by playing Sambo make a choice in barely possible circumstances: more typically, they adopt the available means of limited resistance – they go slow, sick, silent, or they steal – activities registered as a delay in or reticence over the provision of the master's goods. Consequently, the master, at the moment of his mastery and in receipt of those goods that amount to his substance, may recognize that those who render him supreme do so with reservation. Furthermore, since the objects through which he represents that mastery to himself derive from labor that is not his own, he needs must at some level know that his authority, the authority in the antebellum South of a labor lord rather than a landlord, depends on the labor of the bound man. Or, as Hegel would have it: "just when the master had effectively achieved lordship, he really finds that something has come about quite different from an independent consciousness. It is not an independent consciousness but rather a dependent consciousness that he has achieved" (1910: 184). Such recognition involves him in an impassable contradiction: the lord must extract from his lordship the very materials that define it. Put tersely, he must deny who he is (a man made by slaves) in order to be who he is (a slave-empty, masterful master).

Meanwhile, the bound man, contemplating his hands and the goods that they have made, exists in an equally problematic relation to those objects of labor. Having experienced himself as little more than an extension of his lord's will (or as a negation, one "whose essence of life is for another" [Hegel 1910: 182]), he too is troubled because he recognizes, in the independent existence of the goods made by him, the negation of his own prior negation by the lord: "Shaping and forming the object has . . . the positive significance that the bondsman becomes thereby the author of himself as factually and objectively self existent" (p. 186). Such a moment is uncomfortable in that it requires the slave to experience his hands as both the instruments of his own death (as a dependent self) and of the subsequent manufacture of a nascent, independent, and radical self. "Precisely in labor, where there seems to be some outsider's mind and ideas involved, the bondsman becomes aware, through his rediscovering of himself by himself, of having and being a mind of his own" (p. 187). Where the master risks his masterful self in the appreciation that the objects of his desire are the products of the slave's hand, the slave risks his abject self in the consciousness that his labor not only postpones the master's satisfaction, but also produces an object "that is permanent" and "remains after the master's desire is gratified" (p. 186). Judith Butler notes that Hegel's discussion of labor "begins to show how the world of substance becomes . . . the world of the subject" (Butler 1987: 58); though one should add that since slaves are subjects subjected to systemic coercion, they are likely to live in dread of that freedom which the substance of their labor might reveal to them. Nonetheless, within the parable, a parable peculiarly applicable to the slaveholding South, goods and persons radically divide – split on a structural contradiction: that the plantocracy is simultaneously independent (or the world the masters made) and yet dependent (or the world the slaves made). From which it would follow that white should be black; or, more accurately, that white planters are blacks in whiteface.

An Historical Interlude

The applicability of Hegel's "Lordship and Bondage" to Faulkner's major plantation fiction (*The Sound and the Fury* [1929], *Absalom, Absalom!* [1936], and *Go Down, Moses* [1942]) derives from a continuity of labor use within the Southern economy, a continuity bridging the ante- and postbellum periods. Jay Mandle, historian of African American labor, notes that Confederate defeat notwithstanding, black labor in the plantation South remained bound, or more accurately, "not slave, not free" (Mandle 1992: 21–32), during the second half of the nineteenth and the first third of the twentieth centuries. As W. E. B. Du Bois put it, after the war, "the slave went free; stood a brief time in the sun; then moved back again toward slavery" (1935: 30). The brevity of that free-time under the sun was ensured by a failure of Northern nerve in the matter of land redistribution. When the Emancipation Proclamation of 1863 decreed over three million slaves "free," Lincoln effectively transformed a war into "a social revolution in the South." The revolution remained "unfinished" (Foner 1988: 7) in large part because 40 acres and a mule, per freedman, were not forthcoming. No matter that ex-slaves might protest, "[t]he property which they hold was nearly all earned by the sweat of *our* brows" (Foner 1988: 105), Congressional Republicans, while prepared to deprive planters of their illegitimate property in persons, were unprepared to dispossess them of what were held to be their legitimate property rights in land. As Eric Foner observes: "Without land there could be no economic autonomy, for African American labor would continue to be subject to exploitation by its former owners" (Foner 1988: 104).

Non-redistribution ensured a protracted stand-off between a labor force on the brink of translation into a class of free workers, and planters unwilling to transform themselves into a managerial class; that is, to reconceive themselves as rentiers rather than labor lords (see Wright 1986: 17–50). Landowners sought prewar levels of control but had to reorganize production fast or face bankruptcy. "Southern planters emerged from the Civil War in a state of shock. Their class had been devastated – physically, economically and psychologically . . . The loss of the planters' slaves and life savings (to the extent that they had invested in Confederate Bonds) wiped out the inheritance of generations" (Foner 1988: 129). Freedmen wanted autonomy but had as a lever only their capacity to work. Consequently, Northern hopes for the development of wage labor in the South proved fragile; freedmen were sufficiently "free" to resist gang labor and vagrancy acts, but lacking capital they were not "free" enough to avoid being bound in yet another peculiar institution – the institution of sharecropping.

Share wages differ substantially from free wages. The owner contracts to pay his laborer at the close of the growing season; payment takes the form of a predetermined share of the crop. Should the yield be low, or the international price of cotton drop, or the market be glutted, the cropper may not make enough to pay the merchant who has "furnished" his seed and sustenance on credit for the year – in which case, the tenant becomes a peon insofar as he is bound to labor to pay the debt (see Wright 1986: 81–123). A study of black tenants in Alabama in 1932 estimated that only 10 percent received any cash for their year's work, with the remainder "breaking even" or "going into the hole" (Rony 1971: 159). With labor immobilized by such means, the debt holder – be he the merchant, or the planter, or both as one – exerts an absolute author-ity over the laborer. Jonathan Wiener argues that because owners maintained "invol-untary servitude" as "the special form of Southern wage" from Reconstruction to the New Deal, they cannot be spoken of as "classical capitalists" (Wiener 1979: 992). Eric Foner, less emphatic, speaks of the South as "a peculiar hybrid – an improvised colonial economy integrated into the capitalist market place yet with its own distinctive system of repressive labor relations" (Foner 1988: 596). Mandle specifies the distinction, arguing that "the plantation mode of production" (turning on labor "confinement") is a better analytic device for interpreting postbellum economic underdevelopment and racial eti-quette than "the capitalist mode of production" (Mandle 1992: 23). He emphasizes how much of capitalism was missing from the South, at least until the early forties. The South was not a free labor market, nor did "bourgeois individualism" (shadowed by "merit" and "universalist principle") carry much weight in a region where "subordina-tion and paternalism typify relations between white and black" (Mandle 1992: 67).

Because the laborer could not realize his "wage" until he cashed in his crop (what Gerald Janes called "the long pay"; quoted by Mandle 1992: 21), he was bound to the land for at least a year, during which time the landlord sought unlimited power over the productive energies of the cropper and his family, or, in the words of Charles Johnson, writing in 1934, the planter "demands an unquestioning obedience to his managerial intelligence . . . the right to dictate and control every stage of cultivation; [he] cannot and does not tolerate the suggestion of independent status" (Johnson 1966: 127). What Johnson misses is that this level of "policing" also ensured that the knower knew little else, thereby rendering himself liable to the damaging insight that he depended upon his dependents.

Whether one views Johnson's "tradition of dependence" (Johnson 1966: 104) as the result of a distinctive system of production or as the remnant of an archaic regime, it *is* clear that "dependency" was both all pervasive and much disputed within the agricultural South from Redemption to the New Deal. I would reiterate that dependency cuts two ways, though tacitly: that is to say, within such a regime, the white landowning class, owing their substance to black labor, are in essence black. The same claim could not be made of capitalist employers, that is, that they are in essence their workers, since under wage labor, employer–employee relations are "partial" in that the wage payer pays for, and assumes power over, only the working part of the workers' day. In contradistinction, the notion of dependency grows out of what Mark Tushnett calls the "total relations" of slavery – relations between binder and bound that extend to the whole life of the slave or tenant, and to the whole life of the master or landlord (Tushnett 1981: 6). The co-dependence of the white landowning Southern class and black labor must be denied, though during the teens and early twenties shifting demographic patterns ensured that black did not rest quite so quiet and easy within white. As portions of the tenantry mobilized, so structures enforcing dependency necessarily relaxed: in Jay Mandle's terms, "dependency" weakened toward "deference" as economic circumstances indicated that the bound black body might just unbind (1978: 71–83). Where the properties of the selfhood of the owning class – from face, to skin, to sex, to land – are determined by the laboring other, any looseness of the other threatens that self's best parts. In Joel Williamson's terms, commenting on disruptions within the legacy of Southern black–white relations in the first half of the twentieth century, for white to release black may involve the declaration, "I'm not going to be me anymore":

> Southern white identity . . . was intimately bound up with the Southern white image of the Negro, however unreal that image might have been. To let that image go, to see black people as people, was a precarious and exceedingly dangerous venture that exposed the individual to alienation from his natal culture and the loss of his sense of self. (Williamson 1984: 499)

At which point figures for demographic change condition the corporeality – the face, sex, skin, and land – of an owning class as it negotiates the retention within itself of that which has made it what it is, the increasingly unsettled body of African American labor.

If the extended counter-revolution of the planter class from 1865 may be thought to involve the retention of the black within the white, US entry into the Great War finally triggered a long-deferred whitening of whiteness by way of steady out-migration. What has become known as the Great Migration involved many migrations into Southern towns as well as into Northern cities. But always the migrants moved away from rural lands. The rate of drift depended on the readiness of Northern capital to draw low-cost labor out of the South. For as long as European immigration served Northeastern labor needs, the planters retained their entrapped workforce. World War I cut the labor supply to the North, with a consequent and drastic increase in out-migration from the South. Between 1916 and 1919, half a million blacks left the region, and Mississippi recorded its first-ever decline in black population (Litwack 1998: 487). During the twenties, Mississippi alone lost over 14 percent of its black males aged between 15 and 34 – that is, ready to move and employable: the figure gains in dimension with the recognition that in 1910 over 10 percent of American blacks were Mississippians. Neil McMillen, historian of African American Mississippi, notes of the wartime phase of the great migration: "To the reader who followed early local press accounts of this mass movement, it surely seemed that an entire people were abandoning the state for the packing houses and steel mills of Chicago, Detroit and St Louis as fast as the railroad could carry them" (McMillen 1989: 262). Rates of abandonment slowed during the twenties and thirties, though migration figures remained consistent with those recorded during the 1910s, that is, at levels higher than in any previous decade. Creative rejection of that economy in daily practice might involve a considered refusal of deference, or taking the time to go to the railhead to find a copy of the *Chicago Defender*,[1] but most typically it turned on the idea of motion – "a persistent and overriding theme in [Southern black] conversations (as in their songs) was movement away from where they were living and working, if not always towards a clearly defined destination" (Litwack 1998: 482). Motion remained for the majority conceptual, in that the depression, with its attendant news of the immiseration of urban blacks, ensured that Northern capital no longer needed to draw on the Southern labor reserve. In effect the breakdown of the plantation economy stalled, though the influx of federal funds, associated with the New Deal, set in place a capitalization of the Southern owning class, which allowed a new regime of accumulation to emerge.

In 1933, responding to a world market for cotton glutted with twelve and a half million unsold bales, the federal government (by way of the Agricultural Adjustment Act) offered Southern landowners between $7 and $20 an acre (depending on estimated yield) to plow their crops under. Fifty-three percent of the South's cotton acreage went out of production. Since a sharecropper, cropping on a half-the-crop agreement, would by rights receive half the federal payment for the sacrifice of his acres, it paid the land-owner not to sign sharecropping contracts for the following year. Instead, he might hire the same cropper on a wage, pay him to plow the crop under, and reap the entire subsidy himself. Between 1933 and 1940 the Southern tenantry declined by more than 25 percent, while the number of hired laborers increased, though not proportionately, since landowners might simply evict any unnecessary "dependents," enclosing their farms to produce larger units, more viable for mechanized agriculture: "The first stage of the consolidation of the plantations was the wholesale eviction of tenants of all classes, especially sharecroppers. The process was protracted but it seems to have been underway

all over the South by 1934, the first full crop year following the creation of the AAA"
(Kirby 1987: 64). Eviction, enclosure, and drastically increased tenant mobility were
the visible marks of this structural change, as sharecroppers (bound by debt) were made
over into cash workers, "free" to be under- or unemployed in a region where dependency
was slowly ousted by autonomy as a cultural dominant.

From Subsemantics Toward Semantics: Three Phases of
Labor Withdrawal

Phase I: Hiding

In *The Sound and the Fury*, the Compson household, founded on plantation wealth, comes
apart. The father drinks; the mother sickens, and the children are variously given to
idiocy, suicide, promiscuity, and commerce. Yet, from the perspective of 1929, the house
coheres; at least to the point at which a rotting gutter, or a black boy practicing on a
musical saw in the cellar, are symbolic indices rather than structural factors. Coherence,
albeit precarious, depends upon the domestic labor of Dilsey and her extended black
family. That family also has its flaws: Versh, Dilsey's eldest son, departs for Memphis,
intimating the force of Neil McMillen's observation that the "dark journey" of diaspora
seldom involved a single, one-way trip, but instead featured regional stages . . . maybe
from Jefferson to Memphis, and so, via New Orleans, to St Louis or Chicago. Similarly
restless, Dilsey's daughter Frony's youngest son, Luster, longs to go to the circus – ever
an image of mobile modernity for Southern writing.[2] Nonetheless, according to Faulkner's
1945 "Appendix: Compson, 1699–1945," Dilsey, her family, and her white dependents
"endured," at least in 1929.

   I would suggest that the Compson house retains its form despite dilapidation not
simply because Dilsey works to exhaustion, but because the male children of the household continue to perceive themselves through the substantiating and disguised body of
the black worker: that is to say, without the recovery within themselves of intimations
of the bound man's displaced presence, they, to echo Williamson, would come apart,
ceasing to be what they are – the failing inheritors of an archaic regime of accumulation, founded on coerced labor. My claims are large and abstract: my evidence, constrained by space, will necessarily be narrow and concrete: "concrete" in Brecht's sense
of that term, for whom an attribution of "concreteness" involves the recognition that
the reality of things and persons is simply the coming to materiality of "causal com-
plexes," whose determinants (of class, race, gender . . .), however various, are in the last
instance subject to motivation by patterns of labor (Brecht et al. 1980: 82).

   The first of my evidential contractions involves taking Quentin Compson to stand
for his brothers in the matter of a shared habit of mind; the second identifies that habit
of mind (perceived finally as an ur-structure, generative of the three fraternal monologues), through close attention to the subsemantics of a single passage – Quentin's
recovery of an incident at the branch, in 1909, when he and Caddy (his sister), came

close to engaging in incest. Prior to the analysis, the context: on June 2, 1910, the date of the Quentin section, Quentin drowns himself in the Charles River, his freshman year at Harvard having been paid for by the sale of ex-plantation land. His preparations for suicide (letters, clocks, tram trips, and a purchase of flatirons) decorate his abiding preoccupation with his sister's virginity and its loss – central to which concern would seem to be his own trial for the abduction of a speechless Italian child, who adopts him during his preparatory location-scouting journey to the river Charles. Tried in an ad hoc country court, on the outskirts of Boston, for "meditated criminal assault" (Faulkner 1987: 85) on the sister of an Italian immigrant, Quentin is fined six dollars. The justice accounts precisely for the sum – one dollar to Julio for "taking him away from his work" (p. 87); five dollars to the marshal for his two-hour pursuit. Apprehended for child molestation, Quentin receives a fine for theft of labor time. Incest, since the Italian girl is emphatically a "sister" and has been critically understood to replicate Caddy, and labor, albeit Northern industrial labor, are therefore tacitly aligned within the six dollars. I shall return to the silent co-presence of desire and labor within split signs later.

The conversation at the branch (my focal passage) directly follows not the trial, but Quentin's subsequent beating by Gerald Bland. The two events may be understood as forming a linked frame. Released from a court in which his Southern familial tragedy, concerning a sister's honor, has been rerun as Northern farce, Quentin comes close to seeing double: himself (a "Galahad," if "half baked" [p. 67]) within Julio (a migrant worker); Caddy (what W. J. Cash calls "the lily-pure maid" [Cash 1971: 89]) as a "dirty" Italian girl; sexual soiling extending into coal-dust; a hymen lost as expenditure of labor-time. Yet, invited to doubt the coherence, desirability, or relevance of his own subject position, Quentin reverts singularly to type. He strikes Bland over the matter of "sisters" (p. 101) and is knocked semi-conscious. At which point the reader encounters an abrupt tonal transition from opacity to transparency. Direct report conceals what Eric Sundquist and Richard Gray have characterized, respectively, as "chaotic first-person effusions" (Sundquist 1983: 12) or "intensely claustrophobic prose" of "an almost impenetrable nature" (Gray 1986: 211). On which grounds it might be argued Bland's punch levels Quentin physically and intellectually, disarming those habits of perception through which he has previously preserved a version of himself. If so, culturally impaired, Quentin does not "recall" the incident of his attempted incest at the branch; rather, he finds it for the first time, discovering a very different brother and sister, and becoming, in effect, the revisionist historian of his own pathologies, and of those of his class insofar as they turn on incest and the hymen. I run ahead of myself, providing the conclusions to a reading without the reading. But, prior to an offer of evidence, I should add that having traced patterns of desire, I shall seek to discern, within the subsemantics of those desires, the whispered presence of African American labor, as that labor structures a cultural erotics founded on the sister's hymen.

The evidence: Quentin comes to the branch in order to call his sister a whore. Instead they talk, and motives emerge; the brother is physically jealous of Dalton Ames and wishes to take his place. Impotence prevents him and provokes the substitution of a childish suicide pact for the sexual act about which he knows so little:

> I held the point of the knife at her throat
> it wont take but a second just a second then I can do mine
> I can do mine then
> all right can you do yours by yourself
> yes the blades long enough Benjys in bed by now
> yes
> it wont take but a second Ill try not to hurt
> all right
> will you close your eyes
> no like this youll have to push it harder
> touch your hand to it (p. 92)

One detail is particularly revealing; Caddy, ever practical, asks if Quentin will be able to cut his own throat. Quentin's reply involves an apparent non sequitur: "yes the blades long enough Benjys in bed by now." Several elements are involved: Quentin invokes his resentment of Benjy, who slept with Caddy until he was 13; fears of sexual inadequacy, tied up with the innuendo that all idiots are sexual giants; and a glimmer of self-recognition. The evocation of Benjy's howl has been one of Quentin's customary ways of voicing his own confusion, and that all-obscuring noise is now silent. The knife, like the howl, is a substitute. Like the howl, the knife falls away.

> dont cry poor Quentin
> but I couldn't stop she held my head against her damp hard breast I could hear
> her heart going firm and slow now not hammering and the water gurgling
> among the willows in the dark and waves of honeysuckle coming up the air
> my arm and shoulder were twisted under me
> what is it what are you doing
> her muscles gathered I sat up
> its my knife I dropped it
> she sat up
> what time is it
> I dont know
> she rose to her feet I fumbled along the ground (pp. 92–3)

Lulled by Caddy's firm, slow heart, Quentin rests. The startling disjunction between the smell of honeysuckle and a cramped arm can be simply explained as an interval of sleep; Caddy's sudden "what time is it" may indicate an interrupted stillness. I propose that Quentin's sexual response energizes this scene, that sleep relieves him of guilt and restores his potency, and that he wakes with an erection. Caddy [reacts] in a way that balances between objection and response:

> what are you doing
> her muscles gathered

The line-break could be understood conventionally, as marking a division between speech and action; however, a passage that conspicuously omits the marks whereby such divisions are negotiated – marks of punctuation and capital letters – may well foreground the spacing of the text, causing readers to make meanings from textual items (such as spaces) that are not otherwise particularly meaningful. In which case, this break could be read as signaling a significant pause, during which Caddy's body adjusts to changes in Quentin's body – it appears that she is not gathering herself to sit or stand, since Quentin rises first. "I sat up" is at once an embarrassed male reaction and an attempt to disguise an erection. The duplicity is contained in the knife play. Sleep renders the symbol unnecessary, so he "dropped it" and woke to discover the absolute redundancy of the substitute. However, the symbol is easier than the reality of standing straight and of his sister's gathering muscles; consequently, Quentin fumbles. As they walk away Caddy seems sexually stimulated: "she walked into me . . . she walked into me again" (p. 93). Her arousal probably derives from an intermingling of thoughts about her lover and brother. What is clear is that Caddy (aged 17) departs to meet Dalton Ames in the woods, and that her 18-year-old brother goes with her. Whether she wants him there or thereabouts depends on how "sat up" and "gathered" are disposed: she may bump into him because he blocks her path to the woods, or because she is flirting with him – both readings are possible and may even be simultaneous. To stress a mutual and confused arousal, as I do, is to appreciate that the physical actions and reactions of the brother and sister constitute an erotics that both find troubling yet exciting.

The details cumulatively prompt a simple question: why, with all controls down, does an erection command faulty encryption within a knife-play and a line-break? I have time only to sketch an abbreviated answer, which in the first instance must return to Benjy's performance of a similar entry on a similar occasion: confronting Caddy, back from a liaison at the branch, Benjy bellows:

> Caddy came to the door and stood there. . . . I went toward her, crying, and she shrank against the wall and I saw her eyes and I cried louder and pulled at her dress. She put her hands out but I pulled at her dress. Her eyes ran.
>
> *Versh said, Your name Benjamin now. You know how come your name Benjamin now. They making a bluegum out of you. Mammy say in old time your granpaw changed nigger's name, and he turn preacher, and when they look at him he bluegum too. Didn't use to be bluegum, neither. And when family woman look him in the eye in the full of the moon, child born bluegum.*
> (pp. 42–3)

Late in the summer of 1909, Caddy lost her virginity, and Benjy intuits that loss. (His intuition need not be considered mysterious. He does not stare at eyes because he has insight but because, like fire and glass, the eye moves and reflects light, and at this moment Caddy's eyes are probably moving far too fast.) Benjy's recollection goes back almost nine years to November 1900, when his name was changed. The shift appears to have no mechanical trigger, yet there is evidence of a narrow imagination producing partially conscious comparisons. Caddy's sexual change is associated with Benjy's name change, in an essentially cultural analogy likening loss of virginity to loss of a first or maiden name. Prior to recognition of his retardation, Benjy had been named Maury for his mother's brother. In effect, Benjy counters his disturbing insight by recalling a particular story about multiple names. A Mississippi bluegum is a black conjuror with a fatal bite. Versh's bluegum has the additional gift of magic eyes. Simply by being looked upon at a certain time, the bluegum preacher can make his congregation all, even the pregnant women's unborn children, bluegum too. According to Benjy's analogical use of Versh's story, he, care of a black body, is the surrogate father of Caddy's child. I beg a lot of questions about Benjy's cognitive capacity for analogy: they must remain begged (see Godden 1997: 9–21 for an argument attributing a limited temporal sense and a capacity for association to Benjy). Instead, I am reminded that for Quentin any and all of Caddy's suitors were "blackguards." The epithet is carefully chosen and much repeated: meaning "scoundrel," "blackguard" or "black guard" contains the implication that those who would take Caddy's virginity are the guardians of what they take. In 1933, in an introduction to the novel which he did not see published, Faulkner tries to characterize the "ecstasy," "nebulous" yet "physical" (*his* terms in Faulkner 1987: 219), that writing the Benjy section gave him. He likens the manuscript to "unmarred sheet[s] beneath my hand inviolate and unfailing" (Faulkner 1987: 219) – a complex innuendo forms in which paper turns into the white space of a bed (Benjy's pristine consciousness), while language (so black) "mar[s]" that original purity by "marrying" it. Since in 1956, Faulkner was famously to claim, "it began with a mental picture . . . of the muddy seat of a little girl's drawers" (Faulkner 1987: 240), writing "it" – *The Sound and the Fury* – becomes densely synonymous with a barely traceable act of miscegenous entry into a sister ("bluegum," "blackguard", "marred") – almost without trace because the paper appears to absorb the black marks of the carressive script. Unpicking puns from linked similes may strain credibility, but remains necessary in order to establish a submerged affinity between Benjy (as "bluegum"), Quentin (erect at the branch), and Faulkner in "physical . . . ecstasy . . . waiting for release" as he wrote the manuscript (Faulkner 1987: 219).[3]

It would I think be a mistake to cast these black marks ("bluegum," "blackguard," "marred") simply as stains generated by racial anxiety, though a cultural case might be made in the following terms. During the Radical era (1890–1915), the era of both Faulkner and the Compson boys' childhoods, the South "capitulated to racism" (McMillen 1989: 7). As McMillen stresses, the years between 1889 and 1915 saw the most repressive Jim Crow activity in Mississippi's history: that activity was designed to keep a low-wage labor force in place. High among its forms was the sexual threat stemming from a forged link between the white hymen and the black phallus. In the antebellum South, white males of the owning class idealized white womanhood, building pedestals to lift the female gentry above the reality of interracial sex between slave women and slave owners. As the color line was crisscrossed in the quarters, so the pedestals soared at the plantation house. In the words of Cash, the white woman became:

"the South's Palladium . . . – the shield-bearing Athena gleaming whitely in the clouds, the standard of its rallying. . . . She was the lily-pure maid of Astolat. . . . And – she was the pitiful mother of God" (Cash 1971: 89). By means of her propriety, husbands, fathers, and sons whitewashed their property and its sustaining institutions. However, the cult of Southern Womanhood raised the standard of the unbreachable hymen precisely because miscegenation breached the color line throughout the prewar South. Plainly, if the iconic item was to withstand the iconoclastic force of the evidence, it needed support that white males found in the incest dream. Where the hymen quarantines the family "blood," protecting it from risk of contamination through crossing, incest ensures that where crossing has occurred it shall be between like "bloods."

Emancipation changed the obsessional map; freeing the slaves blocked automatic white entry to the quarters, while, in the mind of the planters, because the "freed" man would necessarily seek the white women earlier denied him, he must be restrained. Within this pervasive fantasy, white men, having impeded their own intimacy with white women (cast as the hymen), project onto the black male extravagant and guilt-free versions of the sexual behavior whose ordinary forms they were declaring guilty and denying to themselves. Ergo, the cultural hymen – at once a color line and a device for keeping labor in its place – depends for its coercive vitality on the presence of that which threatens it: since all rhetorical appeals to purity needs must anxiously elicit a threat to that purity, the hymen is necessarily shadowed by the black.

Simply to apply such a model to these textual instances would be to ignore the degree to which "bluegum," "blackguard," "marred" contain an amatory as well as an anxious imperative. In exploring their secrets, in order to establish the foundation of Quentin's covert erection, I am reminded of Malcolm Bull's account of hiddenness: "If something is hidden, it is not because the truth has eluded you and is unobtainable, but because the truth is flirting with you, simultaneously offering and withholding" (Bull 2000: 19–20). Behind the knife and in the gap, an erection of questionable color "flirts": like "blackguard," "bluegum," "marred," that member, coming into hiding on the white space of the page, is released as a whispered semantic valency by motions within the body of Southern labor, from which body, the body of the owning class takes its very particular substance.

"Shadows" typically darken the branch, gathering with intensity around Ames, so that Caddy, Ames, and Quentin eventually unite as "one shadow" (p. 94), and Caddy, "her shadow high against his shadow" (p. 94), will lean down from Ames's "shadow" to kiss Quentin, who "drew back," retreating into the "gray light" among the "dark willows" (p. 95): Quentin literally becomes the dark body that in economic terms he already is. Consequently, his flirtatious hard-on (now you glimpse it, now you don't), spotted among the "shadows," stands as an exact (and exact hidden) class essence. In effect, Quentin all but takes the increasingly archaic and anxious emblem of his class (the hymen as color line and labor-control device); furthermore, he all but takes it from within a darkening and amatory body (the black within the white), which, as it emerges toward the emergency of recognition, embodies the true form and substance of his class.

Phase II: Secretion

In 1929, recognition remains covert, a matter largely of the subsemantic. Not until the agricultural revolution initiated by the New Deal and renewed tenant displacement will the profile of black labor rise more overtly through the whiteface of Faulkner's planters, their children, and their grandchildren. Even in 1936, after the first phase of the Great Migration and the structural transformation initiated by the Agricultural Adjustment Act (1933), the whiteness of Sutpen's very white Hundred (despite its designation as "A Dark House" in Faulkner's working title) retains its intimations of contested entitlement beneath the semantic surfaces of its representation. Those surfaces exhibit a semantic and political leeway which in effect secretes (as in "secretion") that which they make secret. Witness the capacity of a single and central pun to operate as the novel's displaced key, a key lying hidden in plain sight within Bon's name.

Quentin, citing his father and his father's father, notes: "Father said he probably named him himself. Charles Bon. Charles Good. . . . Grandfather believed, just as he named them all – the Charles Goods and the Clytemnestras" (pp. 213–14). Bon: Good: Goods . . . the pun is cruelly obvious and apt within a tradition whose authority over labor extended to the naming of new slaves, whether new by birth or purchase. Planters were entitled to declare their title or property within a slave by naming that slave as they wished, and in so doing they deadened the slave's right by birth to human connection. Orlando Patterson describes this renaming as "natal death" (Patterson 1982: 8). Sutpen does not deny his son his patronym, since Eulalia does not give birth to a "son" but to "goods," and in naming him as such Sutpen declares Bon dead and himself an "owner," not a "father." In effect, the choice of name seeks to contain the central and debilitating contradiction of slave production, that the master's body is made by the slave's work: a fact that casts ethnic interdependency as white dependency, ensuring that from the planter's white body black "goods" must come. It should be stressed that in the antebellum South sexual production literally resembled cotton production, insofar as both yielded a crop that could be taken to market. The banning of the overseas trade in slaves (1808) transformed miscegenation into another way in which slaves made goods for masters. By setting his first ("Spanish") wife aside, Sutpen effectively ascribes Bon's "natal death" to her, on the grounds that she and her father lied to him in the matter of "Spanish blood" (p. 203), presuming on his innocence as to the euphemism whereby "Spanish" contains in displaced form "black." Nonetheless, "Bon," while proprietorial in purpose, may be thought to allude residually, and within a secretive complexity, to that structure of feeling within which the planter both recognizes and denies that his own "good" (that which makes him and his class what they are) resides exactly in what he must not be – the body of African American labor. A non-proprietorial trajectory for the pun might be described as – Bon: Good: Bonheur.

Much here depends on whispered paths running through a single albeit central pun. A pun involves speakers or readers hearing their voices buckle, interrupting the pattern of their speech, to release a second word from a first. Because the second appears to be saying more than the first intended, a semantic excess results, stalling the narrative trajectory of the utterance. Puns are caesural sounds; by breaking a word across an acoustic they produce two words ("good" and "goods" from "Bon"), which sound the same but whose occurrence "one after another . . . lacks connecting words." Henry Krips follows Freud in linking puns to "an anxiety with no apparently appropriate object" (Krips 1999: 37). He suggests that those who pun, overcome by what has sprung from their mouths (materials appearing to derive from somewhere else, quite other than their intentions), tend to reassess their words: "Speakers are thus transformed into listeners to their 'own' alienated utterances, and correspondingly a wedge is driven between the 'I' producing speech and the 'I' reflexively listening to what is being said" (Krips 1999: 38). If so, Sutpen heard his selfhood split as he chose the name "Bon." Arguably and contra Krips, since that choice conceals an attempt to declare white black (by designating his son as property, in translation), Sutpen remains, in some sense, aware of the anxious "object" from which he derives the chosen name. In effect, he hears his voice tear on a real contradiction, the contradiction that planters are blacks in whiteface. Indeed, the word "Bon" reminds Sutpen, from beneath the masking sound of a second language, of the actual condition of things and persons under slavery.

The return of the named to the namer is, for Sutpen, the return of his "face" within the "face" of the other. On seeing Bon ride up to the Hundred in 1859, he witnesses his own features on a male slave: "– saw the face and knew . . . and Father said that even then, even though he knew that Bon and Judith had never laid eyes on one another, he must have felt and heard the design – house, position, posterity and all – come down like it had been built out of smoke" (pp. 214–15). The form of the reported encounter directly recalls Sutpen's childhood experience (circa 1820) of approaching a Virginia planter's door only to be turned from it by a black butler. The coexistence of the two incidents, along with the tacit invitation that we read the latter through the former, ensures that, seeing as Sutpen saw (in 1859 as in 1820), we see the irrepressible recurrence of an economy's founding and recurrent impasse, even as that recurrence revises the status and position of the subjects involved. The "child" come again who *is* and *plays* Sutpen is a slave (black goods); the master who *is* and *plays* the "monkey nigger's" part is, despite his name (Sutpen), black goods. Faced with this, Sutpen has no option – he must turn the boy (and the insight) from the door, or lose the door. To extend the logic of the insight is to appreciate the impossibility either of Sutpen's acknowledging Bon as his son, or of his living with the insight in undisplaced form: should Bon marry Judith, not only will the Hundred be a materialization of black work but its inheritors will lose the euphemistic patronym (Sutpen), becoming goods (Bon) in name as well as in fact. As a result, the white master's nominal authority along with his nominal irony ("Bon") will vanish "like smoke." Sutpen meets revolutionary recognition with counter-revolutionary violence. Henry will kill Bon at his father's bidding, but in so doing he will kill that which manufactures mastery. Consequently, Henry vanishes to all intents and purposes as he pulls the trigger. He returns to a diminished Hundred *"to die"* (p. 298), a "wasted yellow face" with "wasted hands" who is "already a corpse"

in 1909, because, as a planter who has killed his own most vital part (labor), he has
been a corpse since that act in 1865.

In order to unmask a pun, I have ignored its masked status and effect in the text.
Given that Sutpen senses the term's duplicities (else why chose it?), his choice is an act
of secretion, in both senses of the verb "to secrete": "to place in concealment, to keep
secret" or "to produce by means of secretion" (*Shorter Oxford English Dictionary*), where
"secretion" involves the "extraction and elaboration of matter from blood or sap" as a
prelude to "emission [as] waste" . . . or perhaps, in intertextual terms, as excess. "Bon"
secretes, or conceals what it reveals, in a manner which exemplifies the ur-structure of
the plantocracy. To reiterate: since black labor constituted the substance of the labor
lord, that lord and his class had to retain the black body, while denying the formative
centrality of its presence in their own race, skin, sex, land, and language. The contradiction, white is black, had both to be recognized, else what is Southern about the Southern
landowner, and to be denied, else how does the Southern landowner "remain me some
more"? The means to denied recognition in *Absalom, Absalom!* is, in effect, a poetics of
aporia or doubt, through which each of the five narrators who retell Sutpen's story replicate, with variations, the duplicity of Sutpen's pun. Faulkner's aporetics[4] ensures difficulty, the sheer opacity of which draws into hiding (or secretes) the real contradiction
from which the plantocracy takes and retains its particularity. Since each of the five,
with the exception of Shreve, is either a planter or the inheritor of plantation lands, to
do less would be to jeopardize the integrity of their class.

Phase III: Emergency

Yet during the late thirties and early forties, the conceptual habits shared by Sutpen
and his narrators incline to redundancy as the transformation of their base and motive
– a singular regime of labor – required that a class of labor lords become a class of
landlords. With African American labor federally forced from the land onto roads and
into cities, landowners no longer found blacks so corporally in their whiteface. In
effect, government subsidies, administered by local elites, sponsored the dispossession
of rural blacks, and laid the land fallow for capital. Even as black Mississippians were
displaced, federal funds restored the state: "As a result of the AAA and other related
programs, bank deposits, farm values, and farm incomes all doubled. Between 1993
and 1939, the federal government's direct expenditure in Mississippi totalled $450
million, while an additional $260 million entered state banks through ensured loans"
(Woods 1998: 143). With blacks less and less in their laboring place, and capital more
and more in that place, the substance of plantation land and of its owners is transformed. The historian Jonathan Wiener notes that the influx of federal subsidy checks
induced greater transformation than the influx of federal troops (Wiener 1979: 970–
1006). And Donald Grubbs continues the trope by describing the Farm Security
Administration's 1937 attack on "tenancy['s] . . . version of slavery" as a Second Reconstruction (Grubbs 1971: 135).

Go Down, Moses (1942) as a whole can be read as a response to a moment of acute structural change. I have space only to outline a reading of one element of the novel, "Pantaloon in Black," a story apt to the argument in its manifest concern for the emergent body of autonomous labor, in the shape of Rider. "Pantaloon in Black," set in 1941, opens with Rider burying his young wife of six months (Mannie), and closes two days later with his lynching.

For the two days between Mannie's funeral and his death, Rider is characterized as rogue labor. We first see him filling Mannie's grave:

> Soon he had one of the shovels himself. . . . Another member of his sawmill gang touched his arm and said, "Lemme have hit, Rider." He didn't even falter. He released one hand in midstroke and flung it backward, striking the other across the chest, jolting him back a step, and restored the hand to the moving shovel, flinging the dirt with that effortless fury so that the mound seemed to be rising of its own volition, not built up from above but thrusting visibly upward out of the earth itself. (Faulkner 1994: 102)

I cannot improve on Michael Toolan's reading of the passage (Toolan 1990: 119): he notes that Rider is not, syntactically, the stable subject of the verbs "striking," "jolting," and "flinging," the first two of which find their subject in "one hand" and not "He"; while "flinging" displaces the pronoun for "the moving shovel" as subject. Agency, as a result, is ascribed to a body part and a shovel. The grammatical strategy contributes to the conclusion that the mound has an independent will, "thrusting . . . upward out of the earth itself." I would merely add that, drawn to Mannie in the earth, Rider's body and the objects of his hand are animate with purposes beyond the purpose of those who customarily hire his manual labor. The "earth," albeit briefly, has more than one proprietor. Confronted on every side with artifacts no longer singly owned (or available for rent), Rider experiences a form of body loss. His physique, that of a giant, the very type of heroic labor, is temporarily beyond his own and his employer's control, in the sense that it is doubly occupied or at cross-purpose. Something else, encrypted as Mannie, exerts a pressure.

Faulkner details Rider's grief as a sequence of labor infractions; he shovels when he should mourn; he goes to work when he should absent himself; having started his shift, "he walks off the job in the middle of the afternoon" (p. 118); he buys too much liquor at an inappropriate time. Rider's final violation of labor practice is to cut the throat of Birdsong, the night watchman and gambler who, working out of industrial premises, in the boiler shed tool-room (pp. 114, 115), takes back, on a nightly basis, a portion of black earnings. Like the deputy who partially frames the story, Birdsong is what Rider calls him, "boss-man" (p. 115), evidence of the extent of the informal networks of control that constrain black work.

Yet it would be a mistake to cast Rider as the master of his own infringements. His is a body out of control, mastered neither by himself, nor by his employers. Faulkner scrupulously records how the loss of Mannie takes Rider apart, and to what end. Mannie's ghost is promiscuous and specific. She makes one appearance and her instructions are clear. Unable to prevent her fading from the kitchen's threshold, Rider, "talking as sweet as he had ever heard his voice speak to a woman," asks, "Den lemme go wid you, honey": "But she was going. She was going fast now; he could actually feel between them the insuperable barrier of that very strength which could handle alone a log which would have taken any two other men to handle" (p. 106). If Rider is to attend her as a lover, he must lose not just his body, whose very strength blocks its passage into the earth, but his body defined as an instrument of labor, twice as productive as that of any of his co-workers.

In that Mannie's presence remains tangibly within those objects that she so recently used, external reality, during the days following her death, solicits Rider with her breath, eye, and touch, "his body breasting the air her body had vacated, his eyes touching the objects – post and tree and field and house and hill – her eyes had lost" (p. 103). In effect, Rider experiences his body as a faulty aperture into that which it is not (literally, into Mannie), rather than as an entity or tool. She, who is now quite "other" to him, in her death, exerts a dispossessive power, drawing his perceptions toward self loss. At the risk of gilding the grave, Mannie occupies the earth as an exquisite corpse,[5] offering herself through the body of the land, as a site of unworkable desire into which Rider must pass. He "breast[s]" her "air" (p. 103), elsewhere "breasting aside the silver solid air which began to flow past him" (p. 112): Rider is subject to that object (the air) which, in that it has passed through her as breath, takes erotic form as a skin whose touch calls his skin into felt existence (breast to breast). At times Rider feels that his spaces are so packed with memories of his six-month marriage that "there was no space left for air to breathe" (p. 105). To inhale such scant air, "solid" and promise-crammed, is to be overcome with desire.

On the day after the funeral, Rider seeks to rejoin Mannie by translating labor into an industrial accident: he lifts a log no one man should lift:

> He nudged the log to the edge of the truck-frame and squatted and set his palms against the underside of it. For a time there was no movement at all. It was as if the unrational and inanimate wood had invested, mesmerised the man with some of its own primal inertia. Then a voice said quietly: "He got hit. Hit's off de truck," and they saw the crack and gap of air, watching the infinitesimal straightening of the braced legs until the knees locked, the movement mounting infinitesimally through the belly's insuck, the arch of the chest, the neck cords, lifting the lip from the white clench of teeth in passing, drawing the whole head backward and only the bloodshot fixity of the eyes impervious to it, moving on up the arms and the straightening elbows until the balanced log was higher than his head. "Only he aint gonter turn wid dat un," the same voice said. "And when he try to put hit back on de truck, hit gonter kill him." But none of them moved. Then – there was no gathering of supreme effort – the log seemed to leap suddenly backward over his head of its own volition, spinning, crashing and thundering down the incline. (p. 110)

Faulkner so focuses our attention on the slow lift of the log that "its," in "its own volition," is oddly apt (logs are not volitional), reducing the more likely "his" to an antonymic inference. Further, by subordinating the personal to the impersonal pronoun, "its" mimes Rider's desire to move from animacy to inanimacy. Since Mannie is mesmerically latent in most of the objects Rider encounters, her presence complicates the issue of "volition," allowing "its" to retain "her" ("her volition") within its redistribution of industrial agency. If Mannie is in the log, lifting that log is an erection. Faulkner engages in erotic writing, offering a segment-by-segment account of Rider's "straightening" body ("legs," "belly," "chest," "head"). Rider's "brace," "lock," "insuck," "arch," and "fix" leave him most erect when most laborful. Straightening until literally a column of muscle, he figures desire and yet remains excessive and unreadable, not least because his body is simultaneously engaged in suicide, gainful labor, an assault on the means of production, and tumescence. Semantic excess results from the clash of two discourses as they vie for possession of the same object. Read through the optic of labor, the lift is either an accident about to happen ("hit gonter kill him") or a particularly productive use of labor time. However, Rider's slow-motion straightening is surely intended, in its anatomical transposability, to make plain why he is called Rider – a name understood by Faulkner as a synonym for a sexual athlete.[6] Neither discursive option ousts the other; instead Rider stands available for a profit or loss *and* for desire, and consequently as a real contradiction beyond our or Faulkner's semantic control. The variables latent in Rider's working erection are triggered by Mannie, gone into the ground, but still active therein.

The nature of her activity lies encrypted in her name. Mannie summons Rider into the earth. Through her he enters a conceit which casts the soil as a black vagina containing a black phallus. Entry may be read as signatory: given that Mannie suggests the conjunction of a male term and a first person pronoun, Rider's death, in admitting him to the ground, admits him to a full identity (Man – I). Since Rider's reclaimed body will doubtless be laid in Mannie's grave, their reunion is tacitly proprietorial. The grave, containing the embodiment of independent black work and desire, will be marked by "shards of pottery and broken bottles and old brick," unreadable by whites and "fatal to touch" (p. 102). The space is narrow and the dedication an assemblage of refuse, but encryption declares the place black and privately owned. Furthermore, Faulkner tacitly and intratextually names the grave as the resting place of Moses. *Go Down, Moses* makes only one reference to the patriarch: in the opening story "Was," dogs pursue a semi-domesticated fox through the McCaslin cabin (circa 1859). Eventually, at the story's close, the lead dog ("old Moses" [p. 25]), in his keenness to catch the fox, enters its cage head-first, to emerge "wearing most of the crate around its neck" (p. 25). The taking apart of a cage recurs at the close of "Pantaloon in Black," where old Moses's collar is revised during Rider's dismantling of a Jefferson jail cell. Rider, who has been systematically associated with or likened to animals, grabs the "steel barred door," rips it from the wall and walks from the cell "toting the door over his head like it was a gauze window-screen" (p. 120). Rider, circa 1941, by analogy a *new* Moses, keeps to the letter of the chorus of Faulkner's titular song ("Let my People Go. A Song of the Contrabands"):

> – O go down, Moses
> Away down to Egypt's land,
> And tell King Pharaoh
> To let my people go!

For Egypt, read the South (also a place of bondage); for Pharaoh, read the owning class; for Jews read blacks, and for Exodus read the Great Migration. This much is critical commonplace. Less so, for Moses read Rider, in that he, as the song instructs, "go[es] down" to obtain release and partial recovery of "Egypt's spoil."[7]

On which ground (Mannie's ground), Rider as the Mosaic embodiment of black labor, circa 1941, *is* independent. Yet such autonomy does not gel with the manner of his death, lynched by the Birdsongs. "Hanging from a bell-rope in the Negro schoolhouse" (p. 116), his corpse makes their educative point that "extra legal violence" continues to operate as "an instrument for social discipline" in ways "guaranteed to serve the needs, and particularly the labor needs, of the white caste" (McMillen 1989: 242). Emergent autonomy or dependent archaism – neither option covers Rider's excessive tumescence in the timber yard. My route to a fuller reading of that image passes again through Rider's name, directed there by an ambiguity in the story's title. The term "pantaloon" refers to "a kind of mask on the Italian stage, representing the Venetian" (*Shorter Oxford English Dictionary*), for whom Pantalone was a nickname.[8] But who masks in black? "Pantaloon" might be thought to trip "Rider" into "Writer," as Faulkner assumes the guise of a black character. Since "pantaloon" refers more generally to "trousers," the conjunction of terms permits the momentary and curious implication that Faulkner masks himself in Rider's trousers; curious, that is, until one recognizes the homoerotic potential of Rider's erection.

As already argued, Rider's laborious tumescence involves a contradictory meeting of seemingly incompatible worlds: the world of labor in which black work yields white substance, and the world of desire in which a black male tumesces for a "Man," that is for "Man̶n̶i̶e̶," as the name is refocused through the optic of the story's title. Incompatibility, so stated, seems startlingly compatible, since both elements are liable to a single summary, whereby white absorbs black by taking black into itself either as property or as phallus. But, in 1941, and thereafter throughout the forties, white ownership of black bodies grew increasingly redundant. Structurally speaking, whites, at least those raised with habits of mind deriving from an archaic regime of accumulation, had to find alternative modes for retention of the black body, even as they studied its departure. Rider's phallus figures a fantastical solution: "love," imaged in the eminently deniable form of homoerotic desire.

Reread, as a figure for the writer's desire rather than for Rider's, the focus of the timber-yard scene shifts from the log to he who raises it. The black body as phallus recedes as he who desires Mannie, and emerges as he who is manifestly desirable – the embodiment of Faulkner's grieving desire. The extent to which a black member draws a white member from hiding (and I would stress that both are merely inferential) is the extent to which Mannie ceases to be a wife and becomes a gender caption, whose second syllable now nominates one who must not speak his name.

I have switched bodies in the crypt, or at least in the encryption, by extracting "Man-I" from "Mannie," where, in this inflection, "I" refers not to Moses but to an aroused white male. My purpose has not been to identify instances of homoeroticism veiled in work place and name play. Rather, I seek to characterize structural arousal: if, after Freud, mourning may result from the loss of an idea (be it that of nation or region) (Freud 1981: 243), then Faulkner's immersion in Rider's grief may be understood as possibly occurring in response to radical economic change, particularly where that change implies an abrupt break in the social relations of production – involving a severance of white from black. Confronted with the necessary loss of the black body, and thrown into disarray by the recession of that object, Faulkner mourns through the mask of Rider's mourning: finding the black in his own face, he fears and loves the resultant profile.

NOTES

1 "In the absence of local press that met their needs, some blacks turned to black newspapers in the North. By World War I the favourite had become the *Chicago Defender*, virtually smuggled into the region by Pullman porters working the North–South lines. In Mississippi a prominent black observed, 'Negroes grab the defender like a hungry mule grabs fodder,' and in its pages they would find not only a graphic description of white atrocities in the South, but also news of opportunities awaiting them in the North" (Litwack 1998: 429).

2 See Mark Twain (1999: 133–7), particularly for the "drunk" horse rider, as emblematic of spectacular mobility in the cause of social transformation ("and away he went like the very nation," p. 136). See also Jayne Anne Phillips's use of elephants in "Bess" (1987: 135) and Helen Stoddard (2000: 3–5).

3 For Jason, entering a sister in displaced form, through a darkening word, involves entering that sister's daughter (Miss Quentin), through the word "slave": in his case, "slave," triggered by the insistence that Miss Quentin is of his "flesh and blood" (pp. 110, 126), grants him masked access. Jason is associated with a "slave" because he works so hard, though the epithet develops additional associations. Jason is attracted to his niece, whom he likens to "a nigger wench" (p.114), believing that she "act[s] like [a] nigger" (p.110) because it's in her blood (p.140). Since he shares her blood, it

is a short step from his claim that "blood always tells" (p.110) to the recognition that what it tells may be a tale of mixed race. He does not take this step, however, perhaps because the blood that beats in his head gives him blackouts. On which grounds "slave" joins "blackguard," "bluegum," and "marred."

4 The formal aspects of an aporetics might be thought to consist of those stylistic features which foreground divided perception: parataxis, alterity, ellipsis. Central, in relation to *Go Down, Moses*, would be free indirect discourse, as a narrative mode whereby an author, by identifying with yet retaining distance from a creation, allows "two differently orientated voices" to interfere with one another. Since "author and character speak at the same time," their utterances are "double faced," yielding words whose "double orientation" results in split referents, split addressers, and split addressees. Where doubling and division compound, a poetics of doubt (aporetics) may form. See Vološinov (1973: 144) and Bakhtin (1981: 304–5).

5 Maria Torok uses the phrase of "[a]ll those who admit to having experienced . . . an 'increased libido' when they lost an object of love," arguing that they respond in "shame, astonishment and hesitation" to the lost object, as though to an "exquisite corpse" capable of eliciting erotic response. See Maria Torok, "The Illness of Mourning and the Fantasy of the Exquisite

Corpse," in Nicolas Abraham and Maria Torok, *The Shell and the Kernel*, ed. and trans. Nicholas Rand (Chicago: University of Chicago Press, 1997), p.109.

6 In *If I Forget Thee, Jerusalem* (1939), Charlotte Rittenmeyer, requesting that her lover and abortionist, Harry Wilbourne, apply his scalpel, links blade, phallus, and black masculinity with her observation, "What was it you told me nigger women say? Ride me down Harry" (Faulkner 1990b: 645).

7 The third verse of the song reads, "No more shall they in bondage toil / Let my people go, / Let them come out with Egypt's spoil / Let my people go." For full lyrics and tune see http://my.homewithgod.com/heavenlymidis/songbook/moses.html.

8 Judith L. Sensibar first alerted me to the potential significance of the names Mannie and Rider. For Sensibar, "Mannie" crucially goes to "Mammy," and so to "MAMMY[,] CAROLINE BARR," to whom the novel is dedicated. I can see little of the maternal in Mannie's tie to Rider. Nonetheless, Sensibar's essay is striking. See Sensibar (1996: 101–27).

REFERENCES AND FURTHER READING

Bakhtin, M. M. (1981). *The Dialogic Imagination* (trans. C. Emerson and M. Holquist). Austin, TX: University of Texas Press.

Blotner, J. (1974). *Faulkner: A Biography* (vol. 1). New York: Random House.

Brecht, B., E. Bloch, G. Lukács, W. Benjamin, and T. Adorno (1980). *Aesthetics and Politics*. London: Verso.

Bull, M. (2000). *Seeing Things Hidden*. London: Verso.

Butler, J. (1987). *Subjects of Desire*. New York: Columbia.

Cash, W. J. (1971). *The Mind of the South*. London: Thames and Hudson.

Davis, R. (1982). *Good and Faithful Labor*. Westport, CT: Greenwood Press.

Du Bois, W. E. B. (1935). *Black Reconstruction in America, 1860–1880*. New York: Harcourt Brace.

Faulkner, W. (1987). *The Sound and the Fury*. New York: Norton. (Original pub. 1929.)

Faulkner, W. (1990a). *Absalom, Absalom!* New York: Random House. (Original pub. 1936.)

Faulkner, W. (1990b). *If I Forget Thee, Jerusalem*. In *William Faulkner: Novels 1936–1940*. New York: Library of America. (Original pub. 1939.)

Faulkner, W. (1994). *Go Down, Moses*. In *William Faulkner: Novels 1942–1954*. New York: Library of America. (Original pub. 1942.)

Foner, E. (1988). *Reconstruction*. New York: Harper.

Freud, S. (1981). Mourning and Melancholia. In *The Standard Edition of the Complete Psychological Works of Sigmund Freud* (trans. and ed. J. Strachey), vol. 14 (pp. 239–58). London: Hogarth Press.

Genovese, E. (1979). *From Rebellion to Revolution*. Baton Rouge: Louisiana State University Press.

Godden, R. (1997). *Fictions of Labor*. Cambridge: Cambridge University Press.

Gray, R. (1986). *Writing the South*. Cambridge: Cambridge University Press.

Grubbs, D. (1971). *Cry from the Cotton*. Chapel Hill, NC: University of North Carolina Press.

Hegel, G. W. F. (1910). *The Phenomenology of Mind* (trans. J. B. Baille). New York: Macmillan.

Johnson, C. S. (1966). *Shadow of the Plantation*. Chicago: University of Chicago Press. (Original pub. 1934.)

Kirby, J. T. (1987). *Rural Worlds Lost*. Baton Rouge: Louisiana State University Press.

Krips, H. (1999). *Fetish: The Erotics of Culture*. London: Cornell University Press.

Litwack, L. F. (1998). *Trouble in Mind*. New York: Alfred A. Knopf.

Mandle, J. R. (1978). *The Roots of Black Poverty*. Durham, NC: Duke University Press.

Mandle, J. R. (1992). *Not Slave, Not Free*. Durham, NC: Duke University Press.

Matthews, J. T. (1996). Touching Race in *Go Down, Moses*. In L. Wagner-Martin (ed.). *New Essays on Go Down, Moses* (pp. 21–48). Cambridge: Cambridge University Press.

McMillen, N. (1989). *Dark Journey*. Champaign, IL: University of Illinois Press.

Patterson, O. (1982). *Slavery and Social Death*. Cambridge, MA: Harvard University Press.

Phillips, J. A. (1987). *Fast Lanes*. London: Faber.

Rony, V. (1971). The Organization of Black and White Farm Workers in the South. In T. R. Frazier (ed.). *The Underside of American History* (vol. 2) (pp. 153–74). New York: Harcourt and Brace.

Sensibar, J. (1996). Who Wears the Mask? Memory, Desire and Race in *Go Down, Moses*. In L. Wagner-Martin (ed.). *New Essays on Go Down, Moses* (pp. 101–28). Cambridge: Cambridge University Press.

Stoddard, H. (2000). *Rings of Desire*. Manchester: Manchester University Press.

Sundquist, E. (1983). *Faulkner: The House Divided*. Baltimore, MD: Johns Hopkins University Press.

Toolan, M. (1990). *The Stylistics of Fiction*. London: Routledge.

Tushnett, M. (1981). *The American Law of Slavery, 1810–1860*. Princeton, NJ: Princeton University Press.

Twain, M. (1999). *The Adventures of Huckleberry Finn*. Oxford: Oxford University Press.

Vološinov, V. N. (1973). *Marxism and the Philosophy of Language* (trans. L. Matejka and I. R. Titunik). New York: Seminar Press.

Wiener, J. (1979). Class Structure and Economic Development in the American South, 1865–1955. *American Historical Review*, 84: 970–1006.

Williamson, J. (1984). *The Crucible of Race*. New York: Oxford University Press.

Woods, C. (1998). *Development Arrested*. London: Verso.

Wright, G. (1986). *Old South: New South*. New York: Basic Books.

2

"We're Trying Hard as Hell to Free Ourselves": Southern History and Race in the Making of William Faulkner's Literary Terrain

Grace Elizabeth Hale and Robert Jackson

It was a different time, the late 1950s, in Mississippi, in the South, and in America. In a series of multiple births, a new mass movement for civil rights emerged, in the Supreme Court's *Brown v. Board of Education* decision and the Emmett Till case and the Montgomery bus boycott. At last, the accumulated weight of decades of *de jure* segregation and its rituals of discrimination – black men and women humiliated, cheated out of the fruits of their labor, and even killed – became visible to people outside the region. In the carrying out of court victories and in non-violent mass protest, African Americans exposed the violence of segregation. The visual mass media, the slick photo magazines like *Life*, *Look*, and even *Time* but also the new medium of television, circulated these images in a political context shaped by the Cold War and the growing importance of black voters in the North. At last, the Southern culture of segregation became a critical political issue, for whites as well as blacks.

Sometimes William Faulkner knew these changes were coming. "We speak now against the day," Faulkner told the 1955 annual meeting of the Southern Historical Association in a speech reprinted in the Memphis *Commercial Appeal*, "when our Southern people who will resist to the last these inevitable changes in social relations, will, when they have been forced to accept what they at one time might have accepted with dignity and goodwill, will say, 'Why didn't someone tell us this before? Tell us this in time?'" (Faulkner 2004: 151). A few months later, obsessed with events surrounding the forced admission of African American student Autherine Lucy to the University of Alabama, Faulkner corresponded with a young man there who had written him for advice about what students should do in the wake of the rioting in Tuscaloosa. "Segregation," he insisted, "is going, whether we like it or not. We no longer have any choice between segregation and un-segregation. The only choice we now have is by what means." White Southerners, he argued, should choose to "abolish" segregation, "if for no other reason than, by voluntarily giving the Negro the chance for whatever equality he is capable of, we will stay on top; he will owe us gratitude" (Faulkner 1978: 395).

Many white "Southerners," Faulkner wrote in his widely read "Letter to a Northern Editor" have been willing to face insults and threats "because we believed we were helping our native land which we love accept a new condition which it must accept whether it wants to or not" (Faulkner 2004: 86). He never said publicly that he liked the changes, and privately, he often argued that he and other black and white Southerners did not want "integration" but simply a guarantee of justice and freedom from violence. But the history Faulkner was living, he seemed to sense with the same ambivalence that made his best fiction so rich, was different from the time so recently past.

Still, Faulkner wanted the impossible – to stop the flow of time, to suspend historical change, to preserve a moment, a space between segregation and civil rights. Faulkner's suggestions for how the South – always meaning the white South – should proceed, as a hundred years of civil rights activism finally became a mass movement in the 1950s, contradicted his repeated admissions that change was unavoidable. In "A Letter to the North," published in *Life* on March 5, 1956, he praised Southern whites and blacks who "by still being Southerners, yet not being a part of the general majority Southern point of view; by being present yet detached, committed and attainted neither by Citizens' Council nor NAACP [National Association for the Advancement of Colored People]; by being in the middle, being in position to say to any incipient irrevocability: 'Wait, wait now, stop and consider first,'" could preserve this past. "Where will we go," he wailed in lament, "if that middle becomes untenable? If we have to vacate in order to keep from being trampled?" (Faulkner 2004: 86–7). It was too late, of course, in the late 1950s for this kind of thinking. Faulkner was lost, like his character Quentin Compson in *The Sound and the Fury* and *Absalom, Absalom!* Quentin had not lived long enough to find a South where loving and hating were both possible, a space where he could somehow magically, simultaneously, be both the region's judge and critic, lover and son. But Faulkner had experienced this South – he had imagined Quentin from just this kind of place. Faulkner, like the segregationists, wanted to halt time, to live in a past both mythical and historical, but his past was neither the Confederates' Lost Cause antebellum pastoral nor the segregationists' vision of 1920s Jim Crow paradise before the creeping intervention of the federal government began. His South was a place where white Southern liberalism grew in a middle ground between white Southern investment in a culture of segregation and black resistance. Faulkner's past was the integrated white space of the 1930s and his best fiction.

An Integrated White Space

The 1930s and the early 1940s were the Golden Age – perhaps the only age – of white Southern liberalism. Liberals then, not to mention radicals and even some conservatives, talked not about race but about class. Liberal thinkers viewed "the race problem" as a subset of class inequality, linking the Southern system of segregation, and more vaguely, black oppression across America, as symptoms of a greater Depression-era malady.

Radicals and liberals disagreed on the ultimate goal, whether Americans should work to do away with capitalism or reform it through government regulation of corporations and government-administered redistributive programs. But they agreed that economic change, confronting the problem of class inequality, would solve the race problem as well. President Franklin D. Roosevelt and his closest advisors, with the possible exception of his wife Eleanor, saw racial inequality as secondary in the face of the nation's economic collapse: an unemployment rate in 1933 of over one quarter of American workers, waves of business closings, foreclosures, and bank failures, the bankruptcy of state governments, and the breakdown of the private system of charity and social services. In the South, which was poor well before the 1929 stock market crash, economic problems were particularly acute. Cotton cost more per pound to grow than it brought at the gin. Public schools across the region, already inadequate by national standards, shut down completely for lack of funds. Thousands of people, black and white share-croppers, tenants, and small farmers, lost the limited employment they had as banks foreclosed on small farmers and the new government agricultural programs paid remaining owners not to plant crops. At the peak of the misery, 1933, the poorest white and black Southerners struggled with starvation. The need to focus on economic problems seemed obvious (Pells 1984; Denning 1996; Kennedy 1999).

With the exception of the fight to pass the Dyer anti-lynching bill, major New Deal-era efforts to transform the South focused on the economy and on the problem of poverty. White Southern New Dealers Clifford Durr and Clark Foreman believed the weight of Southern political conservatism and poverty was drowning the nation's recovery from the Depression. They directed the research and writing of the FDR administration's major statement on the region, the 1938 *Report on the Economic Conditions of the South*. The South, the introduction to the report frankly stated, was "the nation's number one economic problem." Mobilizing a sleeping majority of liberal voters in the region would help elect governments that could solve Southern economic problems – the too-heavy dependence on cotton, the lack of manufacturing jobs, the anti-unionism. Since most Southern blacks were poor, the report implied, eliminating poverty would ease the region's racial problem as well.

Everywhere in the New Deal era, liberals minimized the importance of race. A. Philip Randolph, the president of the all-black union The Brotherhood of Sleeping Car Porters and the most powerful African American of the period, was a labor leader, and not strictly a race man in the sense of those old rivals Booker T. Washington and W. E. B. Du Bois. Du Bois himself quit the NAACP in 1934 and became a Communist. In a way that reveals the centrality of economics to 1930s thought, even the most directly racial reform effort of the period, the fight to pass the Dyer anti-lynching bill, was hawked as an essential aspect of the South's economic improvement. Lynching, white New Dealers argued, was bad for Southern businesses and, by extension, bad for white Southerners. University of North Carolina sociology professor Howard Odum's theory of "regionalism," an important scholarly effort to analyze the meaning of the South in the period, downplayed older ideas about the region as distinct in its history and its devotion to white supremacy and focused instead on geographic and economic factors. A more literary cohort based at Vanderbilt University chose the terms "industrial" and "agrarian" – thus earning them the nickname "Agrarians" – to characterize the economic and cultural, though decidedly not racial, conditions of the South in their 1930 collection *I'll Take My Stand* (Twelve Southerners 1977). Even African American activists placed race in the larger context of New Deal reform that would benefit white Southerners. Charles Houston, Howard University law professor and leader of the NAACP's legal battle for civil rights, warned white liberals in 1934 that the race problem could "yet be the decisive factor in the success or failure of the New Deal." The goal, he stated plainly, should be to "free white America." The white South, Houston added, "when it squeezes Negro wages and as a consequence cuts down his consuming power in the community," was "cutting off its nose to spite its face" (Sullivan 1996: 86; Singal 1982).

Partly, these efforts to minimize the racial implications of white Southern liberalism were strategic. Liberals could not prevail, many believed, by attacking African American oppression directly. Even many segregationists spoke out against lynching, but the Dyer anti-lynching bill still failed in Congress. Southern white liberals in the 1930s were thought radicals, rebels in their hometowns, and pariahs in their families; they wielded little power even in Southern cities. But no matter how hard they tried to skirt the topic of racial inequality, white Southern liberals could not dismiss the way segregation oppressed black workers and consumers without exposing the inconsistency between their fundamental liberal beliefs in the economic, legal, and social equality of rights for all American citizens and the lived experience of Southern blacks. For many of these liberals, subsuming race into other discourses – particularly that of class – seemed to offer the path of least resistance.

And that resistance, to say the least, was vigorous. Conservative white Southerners certainly perceived, and attacked, this strategic sleight of hand in white liberal rhetoric. The Southern Conference on Human Welfare (SCHW), the most important liberal organization in the region at the time, began in 1938 with an integrated membership – one delegate in five at the founding conference in Birmingham was black. SCHW faced persecution because it held integrated meetings even as it pushed for broad reforms like anti-poll tax legislation. In fact, the organization only decided to support racial equality in response to Birmingham's young police chief Eugene "Bull" Connor, who denied the conference permission to hold integrated meetings in the city auditorium. Eleanor Roosevelt, there to address a plenary session, refused to comply with the segregation order. Forced out of her seat in the black section, she famously sat straddling the line that ran down the center aisle to divide the races. In its early years, however, SCHW focused on economic issues and on broadening the franchise while supporting anti-lynching legislation and equal salaries for black and white teachers, a program far short of calling for racial equality. Even these modest aims, however, drew the ire of white conservatives who argued that liberals like the members of SCHW were just using black rights as a means to their real end, Communist revolution. Hoover's FBI listed the mere holding of integrated meetings as evidence that an organization was run by Communists. The House Un-American Activities Committee investigated the

SCHW for years, ruling finally in 1947 in exasperation that the group was "perhaps the most deviously camouflaged communist front organization" in America. Race was never about race during the two decades before World War II. Instead, to white liberals and conservatives alike, it was always a stand-in or a medium for some other meaning, for class or Communism. Sensing the overdetermined but obfuscatory quality of blackness in this environment, Ralph Ellison saw Southern political and social conditions at work in more individual and aesthetic terms when he wrote, with Faulkner in mind, that "for the Southern artist the Negro becomes a symbol of personal rebellion, his guilt and his repression of it" (Ellison 1964: 42). That blackness should function so powerfully as a symbol in the personal realm discerned by Ellison – and Faulkner – is hardly surprising in light of its ubiquitous political and social significations.

The middle ground carved out in the thirties and early forties by white Southern liberals was an integrated white space, not an integrated space. The distinction was crucial. In this historical moment, any white Southerner who publicly recognized African American humanity and admitted that any part of the South's culture of segregation would have to change was a liberal. The definition brought together people whose political positions and even degree of political involvement varied greatly, from transplanted Southerners working in Washington, DC, like Clifford and Virginia Durr, labor activists like Lucy Randolph Mason, and academics like Odum to ministers like Billy Graham and artists like William Faulkner. They were, even in the middle to late thirties New Deal heyday, a tiny group. But they created a space that had not existed in the region since the late nineteenth century, a position between unwavering support for segregation, with its insistence on absolute racial difference and white supremacy, and belief in racial equality. African American activists in this era – New Dealers John P. Davis and Mary McLeod Bethune, for example, both served as SCHW officers – often avoided denouncing Southern segregation directly and suggested that blacks simply wanted to make separate truly equal. NAACP lawyer Thurgood Marshall used this argument in the early years of the NAACP's fight against segregated schools. Still, black activists' very existence attacked the central premise of segregation no matter what they actually said. African American liberals could not really inhabit, as agents or actors, the middle ground white Southern liberals were fashioning in the thirties and forties. Southern liberalism was always a white space, a place run by white leaders and defined by white strategic choices according to whites' sense of what was possible. African Americans could have little visible agency here. Just to have black members, as SCHW did, made it difficult for an organization to accomplish anything in the region (Sullivan 1996).

African Americans were present, however, in this middle ground, only as members and officers of organizations, as signs manipulated by both liberals and segregationists and as characters in their competing narratives. They were not present as people. The "we" of Southern liberalism – the first person plural who mattered, who spoke for the region, suffered its backward reputation, and worried about its future – remained white. Seeing African Americans as more than symbols, as actors in their own right, was beyond the capacity of most Americans, much less most white Southerners. Indeed, blacks as the carriers of white hopes and white fears were terrifying enough to most white people. New Deal liberalism did not create a truly integrated space, a Southern politics in which whites and blacks were both actors, in which blacks initiated and planned and led reform efforts as well as whites, in which blacks could be the voice of the region.

When Faulkner made one of his most liberal public statements about "the race problem" in the South in 1950, he was still speaking out of that peculiarly integrated white space of the thirties and early forties. In a public letter to the Memphis *Commercial Appeal*, he responded to the sentencing of three white men – two to life in prison, one to 10 years – found guilty of murdering three black children in Attala County, Mississippi. Faulkner lamented:

> And those of us who were born in Mississippi and have lived all our lives in it, who have continued to live in it forty and fifty and sixty years at some cost and sacrifice simply because we love Mississippi and its ways and customs and people; who because of that love have been ready and willing at all times to defend our ways and habits and customs from attack by the outlanders who we believed did not understand them, we had better be afraid too. Afraid that we have been wrong; that what we have loved and defended not only didn't want the defense and the love, but was not worthy of the one and indefensible to the other. (Faulkner 2004: 204)

Here, in what had become by then a well-worn white liberal ritual, Faulkner claimed for himself and other white Southern liberals the role of regional saviors. They had suffered the sins of their region, they had loved its white and black inhabitants, and they were in danger of being rendered irrelevant by the actions of white extremists. The ritual, however, was wrong. Black civil rights activists, leaving behind the middle ground, the integrated white space of Southern liberalism, would make white Southerners like Faulkner irrelevant in the new politics of the region. The history African Americans created in the fifties and early sixties would force white Southern liberals to abandon their peculiar "middle" and to side, finally, with segregation or integration. White violence simply gave Faulkner something to agonize over as he put off making his choice.

Sole Owner and Proprietor: Faulkner in the 1930s

There is little in Faulkner's early writings – poetry or fiction, published essays or private correspondence – to suggest the importance race would assume as he matured into a great novelist. By the end of 1930, the same year the Agrarians published *I'll Take My Stand*, Faulkner had published five novels of broadly uneven (and roughly ascending) quality: *Soldiers' Pay* (1926), *Mosquitoes* (1927), *Sartoris* (1929), *The Sound and the Fury* (1929), and *As I Lay Dying* (1930). None of these dealt with race in any sustained fashion, with the possible exception of *The Sound and the Fury*, whose final section

counterpoints the endurance, service, and faith of Dilsey Gibson with the tragic corruption of the white Compson family. Indeed, Dilsey's is the sole black presence in these
works that threatens to move beyond the flattened backdrop of local color to demand
thematic and critical attention on its own terms. In the same novel, too, Quentin
Compson, newly arrived at Harvard, makes an analytical observation about race that
is remarkable in part because it is so rare in Faulkner's early work, and in part because
it foreshadows Faulkner's treatment of race in later writings: "That was when I realised
that a nigger is not a person so much as a form of behavior; a sort of obverse reflection
of the white people he lives among" (Faulkner 1990c: 86). The next several years would
include the revision and publication of *Sanctuary* (1931), Faulkner's most commercially
successful novel of the period, which brought lucrative offers of screenwriting work from
Hollywood; and a deluge of short stories that, despite their enormous range from throw-
away exercises to minor masterpieces, gave Faulkner the chance to work toward the
larger ideas of his major phase that would culminate in 1936 with *Absalom, Absalom!*
Among these stories was "Dry September," written in early 1930, a lynching tale that
indicts both individual aggression and communal complicity (among whites; there is
no black community to speak of in the story) for the racial violence of the small-town
South. This sort of story, for all its indignation still a fairly isolated example, contextualized Faulkner's consciousness of racial injustice within the larger constellation of
themes he was addressing during this period – among them, primarily, a deep concern
with individual human identity in the face of two overwhelming forces: society and
history. But it was not until *Light in August*, the major novel that Faulkner completed
in an astonishing six months and published in October of 1932, that this humanistic
concern would be wedded to a more rigorous social and psychological analysis of race.
Light in August also exemplifies how Faulkner's aesthetic forms during this period reflect
his deep investment in the integrated, white middle ground of Southern liberalism as
he seeks a complex understanding of human identity and social relations in the segregated 1930s South. In a manner strikingly parallel to how Southern liberal politics
remained at all times white – with blacks as signs and symbols of white political structures, as subsidiary figures but never as independent actors – Faulkner's novel utilizes
Joe Christmas, a character whose blackness is always invoked but never actually established definitively, in the service – indeed, the *redemption* – of a white community that
misunderstands him, alienates him, and finally kills him.

Such a white perspective is dramatically rendered in Faulkner's portrayal of the
young Percy Grimm. Many readers have generally missed the sympathy and depth of
characterization with which Faulkner perceives the young man he would later dismiss,
in a 1957 University of Virginia interview, as "a Nazi Storm Trooper" (Gwynn and
Blotner 1959: 41); but they have also failed to register the crucial symbolic connection
between Grimm and Christmas himself, and the more complex implications of this
connection in Faulkner's best fiction of the 1930s (Gwynn and Blotner 1959: 41).

Percy Grimm's sense of alienation from the community of Jefferson is nearly as acute
as that of Christmas, the possibly mixed-race figure whose mystery – for the whites of
Jefferson as well as Faulkner's readers – lies at the center of the novel. "Too young to

have been in the European War," Grimm harbors a grudge because of all this lost experience and glory, a grudge made more painful because "he had no one to tell it, to open his heart to" (Faulkner 1990b: 450). Grimm suffers from not having any way of confirming his own identity, like Christmas, and from the distance this creates between himself and the military culture of the post-World War I South. Not surprisingly, then, Grimm experiences the solution to his existential and social crisis with a profound sense of relief. Working such an otherwise conventional coming-of-age process into a crucially overdetermined and socially loaded gesture, Faulkner makes this lifting of Grimm's burden indistinguishable from the young man's adoption of the martial, racist values of his time and place. "Saved" by "the new civilian-military act" of the postwar years, Grimm for the first time feels liberated from the isolation of the "wasted years" of his youth (p. 451).

> He could now see his life opening before him, uncomplex and inescapable as a barren corridor, completely freed now of ever again having to think or decide, the burden which he now assumed and carried as bright and weightless and martial as his insignatory brass: a sublime and implicit faith in physical courage and blind obedience, and a belief that the white race is superior to all other races and that the American is superior to all men, and that all that would ever be required of him in payment for this belief, this privilege, would be his own life. And . . . he walked among the civilians with about him an air half belligerent and half the selfconscious pride of a boy. (p. 451)

In upholding these values and taking them to such dramatic extremes, Grimm's over-compensating ambition is to gain the acknowledgement and respect of his community. His impulse is not for chaos or disruption, but for the strictest kind of order. Much as the tragedy of Joe Christmas was, as Faulkner said years later, "not to know what he is and to know that he will never know," Grimm's own crisis of uncertainty pushes him to a different but comparably desperate demand for order (Gwynn and Blotner 1959: 72). Grimm's crisis, of course, is a recognizable aspect of white efforts to maintain segregation. In making this crisis a necessary part of the culmination of *Light in August*, Faulkner displays his investment in the integrated white space of Southern liberalism, providing a critique of white Southern extremism entirely from within – that is, playing against the damning perspective of Grimm himself, and without recourse to any explicit black voices or perspectives beyond the mere invocation of blackness as a problematic presence. At this moment Faulkner even seems a bit unclear about whose existential crisis in the novel is more pressing – Grimm's or Christmas's.

But Faulkner oversees another transformation of Grimm, a more important one than this new social identity. After Christmas escapes custody in the crowded square on Monday morning, Grimm's single-minded pursuit and eventual killing of the fugitive in the Rev. Gail Hightower's kitchen transport him into another realm of experience altogether. During the chase, Faulkner's language suggests an intensely spiritual quality of Grimm's new state: "His face was rocklike, calm, still bright with that expression of fulfillment, of grave and reckless joy" (p. 461). Indeed, joy comes to define Grimm; elsewhere he is described as having "a kind of fierce and constrained joy" and "that quiet joy," as though his chase is not primarily a violent, murderous hunt but somehow also a spiritual quest for immanent communion with providence (pp. 460, 462). Faulkner's strategy is not to disown one or the other but to link these seemingly opposed principles of violence and sacredness, as he does effectively in a single sentence when he writes of the perverse Grimm: "Above the blunt, cold rake of the automatic his face had that serene, unearthly luminousness of angels in church windows" (p. 462).

Faulkner continues the link between violence and sacredness even more directly when he self-consciously connects Grimm and Christmas. Much as Keats preserves the eternity of a single moment in his "Ode on a Grecian Urn" – a poem Faulkner admired enormously and referenced implicitly and explicitly throughout his writing career – so Faulkner stops time's passage at one point in the narrative in order to present a kind of tableau of the two men locked into one another's attention (Sundquist 1983: 137–8). "For an instant they glared at one another, the one stopped in the act of crouching from the leap, the other in midstride of running, before Grimm's momentum carried him past the corner" (p. 461). This instant, this suspended, mirroring glance between unlikely antagonists, is Faulkner's device for envisioning a special and deepening intimacy between Grimm and Christmas; it is, disturbingly, the same instant that gives way to a strange sort of communion, Grimm's killing and emasculation of Christmas. Coming so soon after the elaborate description of Grimm's identity crisis and newfound, purposeful "joy" at the prospect of his own hatred and violence, such a moment again suggests that Faulkner is at least as concerned here with Grimm's spiritual condition as with Christmas's very survival. Indeed, Faulkner's treatment of the scene of the killing makes it clear that even Grimm's explicitly racist last words to the dying fugitive – "Now you'll let white women alone, even in hell" – cannot alter what is portrayed as a deep metaphysical connection between them, a connection that will defy time itself (p. 464). Christmas's non-violent submission, a kind of surrender that leaves him, finally, with a tragic dignity, articulates a response to Grimm's words that evokes the crucifixion of Jesus, and thus the Christian ideals of selflessness, compassion, and unconditional love. "For a long moment," Faulkner writes, again bringing time to a halt in order to imagine the sacredness, the singularly invested presence, of the setting, "he looked up at them with peaceful and unfathomable and unbearable eyes" (pp. 464–6). At the moment of his death, Christmas reveals to Grimm a presence that cannot be desecrated, cannot be killed away. The solution to Grimm's violently racist existential struggle, Faulkner seems to suggest at this moment, is something like divine love. Of course, the disturbing irony in this revelation lies not just in the fact that it only comes in the moment of Grimm's commission of such an archetypally Southern act of racial violence, but also, and just as fundamentally, that it is only revealed to white people. Faulkner makes it clear, too, that the mystical connection he has conjured between Grimm and Christmas will not fade away as a merely momentary phenomenon, but will remain ever-present in the world of Grimm and his white neighbors:

> Then his face, body, all, seemed to collapse, to fall in upon itself, and from out the slashed garments about his hips and loins the pent black blood seemed to rush like a released

breath. It seemed to rush out of his pale body like the rush of sparks from a rising rocket; upon that black blast the man seemed to rise soaring into their memories forever and ever. They are not to lose it, in whatever peaceful valleys, beside whatever placid and reassuring streams of old age, in the mirroring faces of whatever children they will contemplate old disasters and newer hopes. It will be there, musing, quiet, steadfast, not fading and not particularly threatful, but of itself alone serene, of itself alone triumphant. (p. 465)

Faulkner lyrically unites violence and peace in this climactic passage. In doing so he uses memory to bridge past and future, "old disasters" and "newer hopes," death and birth, the fading visage of Joe Christmas with the "mirroring faces" of still unborn children. Importantly, too, he alludes to both the Old Testament of the just, unforgiving, distant God and the New Testament of the compassionate, redemptive, human God. Thus advancing a more broadly biblical and mythical sense of time over any local or historical one, Faulkner veers away from the present – which is to say, the *political* – implications of Grimm's violence against Christmas in order to imagine a sense of the wholeness (and holiness) of creation and time itself. The "peaceful valleys" and "placid and reassuring streams of old age" allude to Psalm 23, whose speaker cites the protection of God in "green pastures" and "still waters" and again, of course, in "the valley of the shadow of death" (Psalm 23: 2, 4). Joe Christmas, who upon his death "seemed to rise soaring into their memories," takes on the symbolism of Christ's resurrection and ascension into heaven.

It is crucial to note that the supposedly black Christmas takes on this identity not simply by dying, but by claiming a new life and presence in the memory of Percy Grimm and the other white men who stand over his dead body in Hightower's kitchen. In yoking Christmas's horrifying death to the racist white community's experience of the Christian mystery of redemption, Faulkner invokes blackness – indeed, a particularly stoic or long-suffering model of blackness – as a key resource upon which the redemption of the whites depends. And it is this bizarre vision of white redemption that constitutes the dividend, the long-awaited return, on Faulkner's headlong investment in the integrated white space of 1930s Southern liberalism. In an era when white liberals like Clifford Durr and Clark Foreman were subsuming the morass of race into a more serviceable discourse of Southern economic uplift in hopes of rescuing the South from its own poverty and backwardness, Faulkner was busy transposing even the suggestion of blackness in Joe Christmas into a literary and spiritual force with extraordinary utility and meaning – for whites.

Later, describing Gail Hightower's final delirium, Faulkner suggests the deepest meaning of Christmas's death for Grimm. Contemplating the face of "the man called Christmas" among many others in a giant wheel-shaped halo, Hightower sees that "it is two faces which seem to strive . . . in turn to free themselves one from the other, then fade and blend again" (pp. 491–2). Hightower then places the vague second face: "Why, it's that . . . boy. With that black pistol, automatic they call them. The one who . . . into the kitchen where . . . killed, who fired the –" (p. 492). Beyond Christmas's mere *symbolism* as Christ, Hightower discerns that Christmas *is* Grimm, and Grimm Christmas. Their *agon*, which, again, is grounded by a mythical rather than merely local conception of time, ensures that the two men begin to resemble one another, until, finally, they blend into one composite visage. This vision completes Hightower's own spiritual quest, at which point "some ultimate dammed flood within him breaks and rushes away" (p. 492), making Hightower's bottomless despair indistinguishable from, and simultaneous with, his final fulfillment. But Faulkner's vision, from the integrated white space he inhabited as a Southern artist, resides in the fact that despite their blending and fusing, white and black are never precisely equal and interchangeable; black infuses and animates white, symbolically, mystically, in order to facilitate white redemption.

This culminating episode in *Light in August* offers in compressed form Faulkner's treatment of race during his most productive period from 1929 to 1936. In the latter year, the publication of *Absalom, Absalom!* would represent Faulkner's most radical statement about race, the germ of which is already apparent in the amalgamation of Percy Grimm and Joe Christmas. Conflating the history of the Sutpen family with that of the entire South, the greatest of Faulkner's novels presents Henry Sutpen's racially overdetermined murder of his mixed-race half-brother Charles Bon as the stroke that brings down the entire design of a great Southern civilization whose originary flaw is racism itself – not the black race, as many segregationists feared, but a racism traceable to Thomas Sutpen's disavowal of his mulatto wife and infant son. The novel implies the most advanced position on race Faulkner would ever take. Essentially, it is the vision of a mulatto South. Critic Frederick R. Karl sums up this view by noting that in *Absalom* Faulkner "appears on the edge of suggesting that the resolution of the South's (and the nation's) racial dilemma was in a single race, one that would transcend black and white by becoming black-and-white" (Karl 1989: 558). As a political or social vision, such a proposal would have been unthinkable for most white Southerners and indeed Americans in the 1930s and afterwards. For Faulkner, though, it represented the unbearable but inexorable solution to America's identity crisis, the only honest response to the dilemma of his time articulated in non-negotiable humanistic rather than political terms. Like the Grimm–Christmas union envisioned by Hightower, though, this single race remains for Faulkner imaginable only from the white perspective, and its redemptive power comes from the invocation of blackness in an integrated white space. "And so in a few thousand years," a non-Southern white prophesies at the end of the book, piecing together his own interpretation of the fall of the house of Sutpen, "I who regard you will also have sprung from the loins of African kings" (Faulkner 1990a: 302). At such moments, it is almost tempting to see Faulkner as a kind of white liberal Moses figure, leading his people to the edge of the Promised Land but not entering with them; Faulkner's death in the summer of 1962, which prevented him from witnessing the University of Mississippi's integration in his hometown, only makes this comparison more suggestive. Such a reading would mix what for Faulkner were the very distinct roles (especially during the 1930s, but less so after *Brown*) of artist and private citizen. Such a reading would also obscure the fact that Faulkner's design in *Absalom* no less than in *Light in August* depends on the integrated white space of 1930s Southern liberal thought, appropriating such figures as Charles Bon and the mulatto slave Clytie in the service of the white Sutpens' tragic arc.

Fictions of the Middle Ground

Around the time his Nobel Prize (awarded in 1949, although the ceremony took place in 1950) made him an internationally celebrated writer expected to comment on events in the South, William Faulkner lost his way. By the mid-1950s, Faulkner's middle ground, both the historical space out of which he worked and the imaginative space his fiction helped create and expand, was gone. Grasping desperately for some place to stand, he made ever more evasive and convoluted statements in an increasingly passive voice. His famous *Life* piece "A Letter to the North" in 1956 may have been his most coherent comment on life in a different South.

> So I would say to the NAACP and all the other organizations that would compel imme-
> diate and unconditional integration: "Go slow now. Stop for a time, a moment. You have
> the power now; you can afford to withhold for a moment the use of it as a force. You
> have done a good job, you have jolted your opponent off-balance and he is now
> vulnerable."

This power, of course, was *Brown v. Board of Education,* Thurgood Marshall and the NAACP's finest victory, the 1954 Supreme Court decision that ruled "separate but equal," the legal foundation of racial segregation, unconstitutional. Faulkner ignored the history he had mined with such complexity and depth in *Light in August* and *Absalom, Absalom!,* the violence at the core of a land of equality founded on slavery and segrega-tion, the rapes and murders and lynchings. Unwilling or perhaps unable to recall any such litany of injustices, Faulkner pointed instead to the *Brown* decision itself as "the first implication . . . even promise, of force and violence" (Faulkner 2004: 87, 88).[1]

Faulkner's middle ground was never a thoroughly integrated place, a space between white and black that defied segregation's insistence on absolute racial difference. At best, in novels like *Light in August* and *Absalom, Absalom!,* it was a ground where liberal whites could turn blacks into symbols not of white supremacy but of white moral fail-ings and even inhumanity, which in turn held out the opportunity for white redemp-tion. Still, Faulkner tried to hold onto this vanishing middle ground by claiming that many black Southerners agreed with his stand. In "A Letter to the North," he claimed that "Southern Negroes" had written him and asked him politely as a white liberal to "stop talking and be quiet . . . you are not helping us." "Our solidarity," he argued about his region, "is not racial, but instead is the majority white segregationist plus the Negro minority . . . who prefer peace to equality" (Faulkner 2004: 89, 90). In a 1955 letter to the president of a Mississippi Lions Club that had condemned a local white man's murder of a black man, Faulkner wrote, "I have always said that the 'best' Negroes, I believe most, nearly all Negroes, do not want integration with white people any more than the best, nearly all, white people want integration with Negroes." Southern blacks, Faulkner continued, "do not want integration but just justice, to be let alone by NAACP and all other disruptive forces, just freedom from threat of violence" (Faulkner 1978: 389–90). Such remarks represented, rather than any black consensus, the projection of the common desire on the part of Southern whites to avoid any substantive change to the racial status quo, particularly if that change came from public and not private – which is to say, white – sources.

Even more desperately, Faulkner took a step beyond the strategy he employed in his fiction and in essays like his 1954 piece "Mississippi" for *Holiday* magazine, in which he identified black characters as carriers of white Southern morality and domestic unity across the white generations. The title of the piece Faulkner published in *Ebony* in 1956 described his more direct racial ventriloquism perfectly: "If I Were a Negro." "Go slow," Faulkner claimed, in response to criticism of his *Life* piece, meant "be flexible." Filling the piece with bizarre, repetitive requests that blacks practice "cleanliness," Faulkner mused on the repeated refrain of what he would do if he were a black man. In what stands out as some of the most incomprehensible writing of his career, he insisted:

> So if I were a Negro, I would say to my people: "Let us be always unflaggingly and inflexibly flexible. But always decently, quietly, courteously, with dignity and without violence. And above all with patience. The white man has devoted three hundred years to teaching us to be patient: that is one thing at least in which we are his superiors. Let us turn it into a weapon against him." (Faulkner 2004: 111)

"If I were a Negro," Faulkner argued again and again, I would do just what many white Southern moderates want; I would worry less about rights and more about not scaring the white folks. Even Faulkner's prose, capable at its best of staking out a moral or humanistic vision with startling precision, could not rescue this disappearing middle ground, the integrated white space, of white Southern liberalism. More honest about this vanishing middle ground – not in the sense of Faulkner's actually preparing for battle but in the public admission that despite all his evasive musings he had already chosen a side – were his infamous comments in an interview in February of 1956:

> As long as there's a middle road, all right. I'll be on it. But if it came to fighting I'd fight for Mississippi against the United States even if it meant going out into the street and shooting Negroes . . . I will go on saying that the Southerners are wrong and that their position is untenable, but if I have to make the same choice as Robert E. Lee made then I'll make it. (Blotner 1984: 618)

And *Brown*, like the firing on Fort Sumter in 1861, did force everyone in the region to take a side. Many white Southerners previously considered liberals, like Faulkner, found themselves without a place to stand. Arkansas governor Orval E. Faubus won election in 1954 as a liberal who minimized racial issues and promised to spend more money on education and old-age pensions for both blacks and whites; later he would become famous for using the state's National Guard forces to stop the integration of Little Rock high school. The popular Alabama governor "Big Jim" Folsom clung to his liberalism in the *Brown* era, refusing to sign a statement issued by other Southern governors condemning the Supreme Court decision. His crushing defeat in the 1958 Democratic gubernatorial primary served notice that no Southern politician could remain a racial moderate after *Brown* and expect to defeat a hard-line segregationist (Sims 1985). George Wallace, in his first campaign for governor in the 1958 election to replace Folsom, ran on a liberal platform promising improved roads and schools and more industrial jobs and offering a moderate defense of segregation. Wallace finished ahead of Folsom but lost to John Patterson, a candidate who had the backing of the Ku Klux Klan. "Well boys," the runner-up Wallace told a group of his advisors as the incoming election returns registered his defeat, "no other son of a bitch will ever outnigger me again" (Carter 2000: 96). Few white liberals had the courage to condemn the South's culture of segregation publicly. Most of those who did, like Clark Foreman, did not live in the region. Only a few, like Clifford and Virginia Durr and Lillian Smith, continued to live in the South, enduring years of threats, social ostracism, and financial ruin. Supreme Court justice Hugo Black, Virginia Durr's brother-in-law, predicted that *Brown* would destroy Southern liberalism. He was right (Sullivan 1996).

Brown and the successful Montgomery bus boycott in 1955–6 made it clear that African Americans intended to make a new South and indeed, a new America. Charles Houston's NAACP legal team, led in the fifties by Marshall, had been winning in the courts since 1938, when the Supreme Court ruled that the University of Missouri law school had to accept African American student Lloyd L. Gaines. The victories just kept coming – most importantly, *Smith v. Allright* in 1944 outlawing segregated Democratic party primaries, and the monumental *Brown* decision itself. Ralph Ellison, in a long letter to his friend Albert Murray in March of 1956, captured this new time. Something had happened to "Mose," Ellison's and Murray's play on the minstrel-show character as average black man, an amalgamation of white fantasy, stereotype, and actual African American, their name for a figure most writers called "the Negro." "Mose is fighting and he's still got his briarpatch cunning," Ellison wrote.

> He's just waiting for a law, man, something solid under his feet; a little scent of possibility. In fact, he's turned the Supreme Court into the forum of liberty it was intended to be, and the Constitution of the United States into a briarpatch in which the nimble people, the willing people, have a chance. And that's what *it* was intend[ed] to be. (Murray 2000: 116–17)

"Bill Faulkner can write a million letters to the North as he recently did in LIFE," Ellison argued,

> but for one thing he forgets that the people he is talking to are Negroes and they're everywhere in the States and without sectional allegiance when it comes to the problem.

African Americans in the 1950s were not speaking from a middle ground of white Southern liberalism, or from any position of deference to white paternalism; increasingly, they were demanding nothing more or less than the rights of full American citizenship. Ellison continued,

> The next thing [Faulkner] forgets, is that Mose isn't in the market for his advice, because he's been knowing how to "wait-a-while" – Faulkner advice – for over three hundred years, only he's never been simply waiting, he's been probing for the soft spot, looking for the hole, and now he's got the hole.

Ellison, who acknowledged publicly and often his deep appreciation for Faulkner as a writer, next made a cutting – and accurate – assessment of Faulkner's fiction as well as his disastrous public comments about race:

> Faulkner has delusions of grandeur because he really believes that he invented these characteristics which he ascribes to Negroes in his fiction and now he thinks he can end this great historical action just as he ends a dramatic action in one of his novels with Joe Christmas dead and his balls cut off by a man not nearly as worthy as himself; Hightower musing, the Negroes scared, and everything, just as it was except for the brooding, slightly overblown rhetoric of Faulkner's irony. Nuts! He thinks Negroes exist simply to give ironic overtone to the viciousness of white folks, when he should know very well that we're trying hard as hell to free ourselves . . .

Historical time was not a narrative device Faulkner could simply play with in his writing, nor were blacks products of his prodigious imagination. Ellison simply revealed the limits of Faulkner's reach; for in late 1950s America, Mose, not Faulkner, was setting the pace.

By the late fifties, many African Americans had grown weary of white Southern liberals', moderates', or any other Americans' attempts to stop time. Angry over Faulkner's "go slow" comment in *Life*, W. E. B. Du Bois challenged Faulkner to debate integration. Insisting again on the need for more time, Faulkner replied by telegram:

> I do not believe there is a debatable point between us. We both agree in advance that the position you will take is right morally legally and ethically. If it is not evident to you that the position I take in asking for moderation and patience is right practically then we will both waste our breath in debate. (Faulkner 1978: 398)

In 1956 James Baldwin questioned Faulkner's sense of both pace and time. "After more than two hundred years in slavery and ninety years of quasi-freedom, it is hard to think very highly of William Faulkner's advice to 'go slow,'" Baldwin insisted. "They don't mean go slow," he quoted Thurgood Marshall as saying. "They mean don't go." And Baldwin declared Faulkner's sense of place just as dishonest. "Faulkner – among so many others! – is so plaintive concerning this 'middle of the road' from which 'extremist' elements of both races are driving him that it does not seem unfair to ask just what he had been doing there until now," Baldwin argued. "Why – and how – does one move from the middle of the road where one was aiding Negroes into the streets – to shoot them?" Faulkner wanted a place in which he could save white Southerners from yet another monumental moral error and the time to accomplish the task. But "the time Faulkner asks for does not exist," Baldwin concluded, "and he is not the only Southerner who knows it. There is never time in the future in which we will work out our salvation. The challenge is in the moment, the time is always now" (Baldwin 1985: 148, 149, 152). Over and over, Faulkner was reminded that the chance to stop time – that moment of suspended motion in which the perfection of form and action could be shaped, apprehended, contemplated – did not exist, and would never present itself. African American voices demanded an accounting of the past and modeled a vision of the future in historical time, rejecting Faulkner's sense of a mythical time too eternal to be measured by a clock or a court docket.

Seven years later, sitting in a jail cell in Alabama, Martin Luther King felt it necessary to make this point yet again. He had hoped, he wrote, "that the white moderate would reject the myth of time," the "tragic misconception" that the flow of history alone will solve society's problems. Time, King argues, is actually "neutral." Freedom must be demanded. "Frankly, I have never yet engaged in a direct action movement that was 'well-timed' according to the timetable of those who have not suffered unduly from the disease of segregation," King claimed. "For years now I have heard the word 'Wait!' It rings in the ear of every Negro with a piercing familiarity. This 'Wait' has almost always meant never." "Too long," King laments, turning Faulkner and other white Southerners' professed love of their region back against them, "has our beloved Southland been bogged down in the tragic attempt to live in monologue rather than dialogue" (King 1986: 296, 290, 292). While white Southern liberalism was stronger in the thirties than it had ever been or ever would be again, it had never managed to create dialogue, only an integrated white space, a more honest and searching reflection, surely, but still a monologue, a conversation between and about whites who had their own timetable for redemption. This integrated white space was the time and space of Faulkner's best work. By the mid-fifties, both the time and the space were gone.

Again, in the new space of the late fifties and early sixties, Faulkner and many other white Southerners were lost. Some, like the fictional Percy Grimm from a generation earlier, found certainty, identity even, in extreme racism and violence. Many Southern white liberals, after the model of the Reverend Hightower, instead fell through space, unable to see blacks as Americans, as individuals free to make their own lives, to pursue their own desires, to act to achieve things not only not wanted but not even imagined by whites.

One of Faulkner's few black characters from this period is Chick Mallison's boyhood companion Aleck Sander in *The Town* (1957). Aleck Sander appears briefly in order to collect four one-dollar debts owed him by Chick and three other 12- and 13-year-old white boys in payment for his jumping into a frozen creek on a bet during a hunting trip. Narrated by Chick himself, the anecdote has virtually nothing to do with the novel's larger story of the Snopes clan, but expresses in atrophied form the kind of integrated white space that Faulkner staked out in such depth several decades earlier. After the others have performed increasingly challenging stunts to pay their shares of the debt, John Wesley Roebuck agrees to the most challenging deal yet:

> John Wesley borrowed my hunting coat to put on top of his because we had already proved that mine was the toughest, and he borrowed Ashley's sweater to wrap around his head and neck, and we counted off twenty-five steps for him and Aleck Sander put one shell in his gun and somebody, maybe me, counted One Two Three slow and when whoever it was said Three Aleck Sander shot John Wesley in the back and John Wesley gave me and Ashley back the sweater and my hunting coat and (it was late by then) we went home. (Faulkner 1957: 55)

Telling the story from adulthood, Chick admits, "I wonder how any boys ever live long enough to grow up" (p. 53). Ignorance, or at least a kind of childlike innocence, is a bliss no longer available to Faulkner's too-old South of the late 1950s; Chick hints at this impossibility in looking back on the shooting: "Because when you are just thirteen you don't have sense enough to realize what you are doing and shudder" (p. 53). White guilt and black vengeance define this fictional space, a tame version of segregationists' worst nightmare. And time for Faulkner here moves forward in a deadly countdown to violence, in which one of the unnamed white boys counts to three and Aleck Sander pulls his shotgun's trigger. Nevertheless, the settlement is privately negotiated instead of publicly litigated, and the fact that these are young boys who hunt together regardless of race mitigates the scene's severity. Even as race looks like such a determinant and explosive factor on the surface, Faulkner seems to suggest, the event is less a signifier of racial antagonism than a harmless bonding ritual among friends – a kind of pastoral tableau of timelessness in which any possible trauma is negated by the unknowing simplicity of childhood. But here again, and with almost none of the depth and tension of his work of the 1930s, Faulkner remains unable to envision black identity apart from white needs – even, finally, the need for punishment and a simultaneous need to evade punishment through recourse to a more innocent time. In this short parable, the era is recognizably post-*Brown*; Faulkner's towering ambivalence, of course, has a much earlier vintage.

To the last, William Faulkner expressed the burden of segregation not only in terms of the black agency he denied, but also in terms of a fictional space that suggests the limits of the white imagination under the sign of Jim Crow. Whether by historical accident or artistic freedom (or both), Faulkner largely remained in that circumscribed space of Hightower's reverie in *Light in August* – gazing with ironic but tortured longing at an imagined communion between Percy Grimm and Joe Christmas – without ever moving beyond that vision. Not even *Absalom*'s audacious implication of a single Southern race could tempt Faulkner from the garden of his integrated white space into a truly integrated world. To the last, Faulkner preferred the careful designs of his art to the contingencies of history in the present moment, which may partly explain how a man who saw so much could also miss so much, especially "Mose" on the move, "talking sense and acting," in Ellison's phrase, making a new history.

NOTE

1   The shift in terminology used by contemporaries to describe the middle ground (often reproduced by historians in their work on these distinct periods of the thirties and early forties versus the postwar era) from the term "white liberal" to the term "white moderate" is itself a sign of the disappearance of this middle ground. White liberals offer some critique of "the [white] Southern way of life," without taking a direct stand on the future of segregation. *Brown* made this maneuver impossible.

White moderates were white southerners who defended segregation but were not willing to resort to violence or court federal intervention. They would, for example, accept limited integration – a few selected black students at white schools – in order to save the public school system. The difference here is significant. White liberals believed change in the culture of segregation was positive. White moderates thought change was bad but necessary to preserve the larger structures of segregation.

REFERENCES AND FURTHER READING

Baldwin, J. (1985). *The Price of the Ticket: Collected Non-Fiction, 1948–1985.* London: Michael Joseph.

Blotner, J. (1984). *Faulkner: A Biography.* New York: Random House. (Original pub. 1974.)

Carter, D. T. (2000). *The Politics of Rage: George Wallace, the Origins of the New Conservatism, and the Transformation of American Politics.* Baton Rouge: Louisiana State University Press. (Original pub. 1995.)

Denning, M. (1996). *The Cultural Front: The Laboring of American Culture in the Twentieth Century.* London: Verso.

Ellison, R. (1964). *Shadow and Act.* New York: Random House.

Faulkner, W. (1957). *The Town.* New York: Random House.

Faulkner, W. (1978). *Selected Letters of William Faulkner* (ed. J. Blotner). New York: Vintage. (Original pub. 1977.)

Faulkner, W. (1990a). *Absalom, Absalom!* New York: Vintage. (Original pub. 1936.)

Faulkner, W. (1990b). *Light in August.* New York: Vintage. (Original pub. 1932.)

Faulkner, W. (1990c). *The Sound and the Fury.* New York: Vintage. (Original pub. 1929.)

Faulkner, W. (2004). *Essays, Speeches and Public Letters* (ed. J. B. Meriwether). New York: Modern Library.

Gwynn, F. L. and J. Blotner (eds.) (1959). *Faulkner in the University: Class Conferences at the University of Virginia, 1957–58.* Charlottesville: University of Virginia Press.

Karl, F. R. (1989). *William Faulkner: American Writer.* New York: Weidenfeld and Nicolson.

Kennedy, D. M. (1999). *Freedom from Fear: The American People in Depression and War, 1929–1945.* Oxford: Oxford University Press.

King, M. L., Jr. (1986). Letter from Birmingham City Jail. In J. M. Washington (ed.). *A Testament of Hope: The Essential Writings of Martin Luther King, Jr.* (pp. 289–302). San Francisco: Harper and Row.

Murray, A. (ed.) (2000). *Trading Twelves: The Selected Letters of Ralph Ellison and Albert Murray.* New York: Modern Library.

Pells, R. H. (1984). *Radical Visions and American Dreams: Culture and Social Thought in the Depression Years.* Middletown: Wesleyan University Press. (Original pub. 1973.)

Sims, G. E. (1985). *The Little Man's Big Friend: James E. Folsom in Alabama Politics, 1946–1958.* University, AL: University of Alabama Press.

Singal, D. J. (1982). *The War Within: From Victorian to Modernist Thought in the South, 1919–1945.* Chapel Hill, NC: University of North Carolina Press.

Sullivan, P. (1996). *Days of Hope: Race and Democracy in the New Deal Era.* Chapel Hill, NC: University of North Carolina Press.

Sundquist, E. J. (1983). *Faulkner: The House Divided.* Baltimore: Johns Hopkins University Press.

Twelve Southerners (1977). *I'll Take My Stand: The South and the Agrarian Tradition* (ed. L. D. Rubin, Jr.). Baton Rouge: Louisiana State University Press. (Original pub. 1930.)

3

A Loving Gentleman and the Corncob Man: Faulkner, Gender, Sexuality, and *The Reivers*

Anne Goodwyn Jones

Meta Carpenter, William Faulkner's Hollywood lover, called her memoir of their affair *A Loving Gentleman* (Wilde and Borsten 1976). Her description of a passionate, courtly, tender man provides a clear (and probably intentional) contrast to the public nickname that came to identify Faulkner after the publication of his shocking 1931 novel *Sanctuary*: the "corncob man." In the novel, readers are led to believe that an impotent Memphis bootlegger named Popeye has vaginally raped a college flapper, Temple Drake, using a corncob. Near the end of the novel, a lynch mob anally rapes the man falsely convicted of the crime: "Only we never used a cob," one says. "We made him wish we had used a cob" (1993: 296).

In fact, Faulkner also imagined sexually anxious young white men, feminine or gay military men, love- and grief-stricken black men, sexual murderers, white spinsters with violent sexual fantasies, young boyish girls who look like saplings, maternal prostitutes, pregnant questers, vindictive bitches, and moralistic ladies along with rapists like Popeye. He questioned accepted beliefs about gender and sexuality with what seems an almost untrammeled sense of freedom. In his own life, too, he occupied risky and unconventional gender positions and geographies of desire. In his twenties, he masqueraded his way into the RAF in Canada and then circulated within what today we might call gay communities in New Orleans and New York. He married – with some reluctance – the woman who had been the girl of his dreams, Estelle Oldham, now divorced with two young children; the marriage, by all accounts, was unhappy. During the marriage he had affairs with younger women, one of them Meta Carpenter, and one a college student he met in his middle age. With just this sampling, we begin to see the complexities of his encounters with gender and sexuality, as a writer and as a person during an especially critical time in the history of American genders and sexualities.

Only since Faulkner's death in 1962 have gender and sexuality emerged as clear and useful categories and methods of analysis for historians and literary critics. The wealth of publication on these issues helps to make sense of Faulkner's range of imaginative and literal experiences; what remains, though, is the sense that at least as a writer the questions he asked and possibilities he entertained constitute one of the most radical and even today least understood explorations of sexuality and gender in the twentieth century.[1]

A look at reviews published during his lifetime provides an entry into the conventions William Faulkner challenged. Here are a few:

- Katherine Anderson, 1938: Faulkner's typical "morbid concern in sexual aberrations and evil [is] not evident in *The Unvanquished*" (Bassett 1972: 118).
- Murray Bonnoitt on *The Hamlet*, 1940: "Sex and slime that is Faulkner at his best and worst" (Bassett 1972: 140).
- Maxwell Geismar on the theme of *The Sound and the Fury*, 1956: "The disenchantment of an evil maturity" (Bassett 1972: 36).
- Aubrey Williams on Temple Drake in *Sanctuary*, 1960: "The development of sin in children is a major theme" (Bassett 1972: 68).

Even as late as 1986, the first essay in Harold Bloom's Faulkner collection – taken from *William Faulkner: The Yoknapatawpha Country* by Cleanth Brooks (1963) – is called "Discovery of Evil."

Anyone new to Faulkner's texts might be led by these quotations from reviews and articles written during his lifetime to expect something rather different from what she or he will find. Even a person familiar with the texts and with Faulkner criticism as well might raise an eyebrow in surprise at the moralistic virulence of responses like these to Faulkner's work. Yet these reviews not only characterize the reaction of many to his works over several decades (in this case from 1938 to 1960) but give a glimpse into the tenor of the times of his life.

Because the concepts are rarely, if ever, defined in these contexts, the pervasiveness of terms like "evil" and "sin" in the reviews must assume a homogeneity of belief – Judeo-Christian belief, to be specific – between writers and audiences that today seems almost unthinkable. Unspoken as well are the specific scenes and characterizations that lead the writers to these conclusions. Yet all four refer directly or indirectly to "sex" as the key component in Faulkner's fictional "sin" and "evil." Sex outside of marriage is central to Caddy's and Jason's "evil maturity" in the review of *The Sound and the Fury* (1929); Temple's initiation into "sin" is an initiation, in the review of *Sanctuary*, to sexual pleasure, again outside of marriage. *The Hamlet* (1940), for Murray Bonnoitt, offers not only sex but slime, each term with no apparent irony reinforcing the other's sleaziness. Only *The Unvanquished* (1938) escapes Faulkner's "morbid" fascination with "sexual aberrations," perhaps because the protagonists are children not yet matured into "sin." Further, reviewers during his lifetime implicitly or explicitly see evil and sin in his work, insofar as they involve sex (or alcohol, or gambling on the cotton market, or mistreating family members) as personal issues, not collective or political or social issues, and believe they have to do with the individual and the individual's need for personal salvation or at the least moral correction.

How distant we are now from those times can be measured by the differences in the unspoken assumptions of reviewers and critics. No longer are those assumptions theological or personally moralistic; frequently they assume a political valence for texts, sometimes with an unspoken moral tone, or seek out cultural context as a way of understanding in preference to judging. Nor are acts of "sex" in Faulkner's work judged by the same standards. Take the narrative of rape and molestation followed by the development of sexual desire in Temple Drake: understanding better how people react to rape has exposed as naïve older criticism that blames the victim. Overdetermined heterosexual romances like that of Joe Christmas and Joanna Burden are examined with an eye to multiple points of view and methods of determination. Homoeroticism and homosexuality in stories like "Turnabout" (1932) and "Divorce in Naples" (1931) are read now in the context not of judgment but of a history that is still being written. A romance with a cow like Ike's in *The Hamlet* (1940) finds readers responding with not just humor but a range of emotions. In short, the enormously various "sex acts" and gender performances present within Faulkner's texts are read now in an enormous variety of ways, but rarely as signs of authorial evil, morbidity, or sin.

In this chapter, I hope to show certain intersections linking Faulkner's life, his work, and the beliefs about gender and sexuality contemporary to both. I will first outline those beliefs, insofar as they are now understood, and then use a reading of his last novel, *The Reivers* (1962), as a sort of template with which to compare his earlier work.

"American" Sexuality and Gender

In recent years, historians have been seeking out and writing the history of gender and sexuality in the USA. Beginning with histories of women and femininity, and more recently moving to histories of men, masculinity, and (hetero- and homo-)sexuality, the resources for Faulkner scholars are generous. To date, however, most of the studies of American gender and sexual history in the twentieth century have relied on models that work only partially for the South, for Mississippi, and thus for Faulkner. In *Born for Liberty*, her history of American women, for example, Sara M. Evans writes that "modern America – urban, industrial, bureaucratic – came of age between 1890 and 1920" (1989: 145). For Michael Kimmel, too, in *Manhood in America: A Cultural History*, at the beginning of the twentieth century "rapid industrialization, technological transformation, capital concentration, urbanization, and immigration – all of these created a new sense of an oppressively crowded, depersonalized, and often emasculated life" (1996: 83). Peter Filene agrees: "By 1900 the middle-class economy was becoming corporatized and bureaucratized. . . . [A man] lost touch with the product of his work . . . Moreover, the operations of a large firm aspired toward efficiency and specialization, in deference to 'economy of scale'" (1986: 73).[2] The current model shared by these historians depends on the assumption that the modernization of American life – economic, cultural, social – had taken hold by the turn of the twentieth century. By the time of Faulkner's birth in 1897, according to this model, Americans lived crowded together in multiple cultures and ethnicities in cities, worked for corporations on the factory line, in mills, in the secretarial pool, or in middle management, and occupied a world that had effectively shifted from an emphasis on production to a focus on consumption. The consequences of these changes affected both gender and sexuality in complex ways, so the argument goes. Separate spheres for middle-class men and women, for example – men leaving for work away from home, women keeping the home – had meant widening gulfs in understanding between the sexes. Laboring without seeing the product of one's labor, working in mass, and being forced to work by a clock all reduced the sense of control that men, especially, had over their work, and threatened to erode confidence in manhood. Urban freedoms made it easier for women and men, gay and straight, to find and enjoy sex.

According to these national narratives, enormous changes took place during the period of Faulkner's life (1897–1962) in the relations among race, class, gender, and sexuality and in the meanings of personal and communal identity. For Kimmel, during this period American manhood tried, tested, and failed at the project of Self-Made Manhood, a manhood based on self-control, independence, and individualism, all virtues useful for the new corporate economy. For Filene, the extreme individualism produced by late Victorian "excesses of capitalism" was countered nationally by Progressivism's ethical agenda and industrial anonymity, producing an impossible conflict for men's identities similar to the one they faced sexually: "be pure" but "sow your wild oats" (1986: 73, 78).

But this national narrative and these assumptions describe neither the material conditions nor the conventions of gender and sex in Oxford, Mississippi, during Faulkner's time there, nor in his imagined Yoknapatawpha County. News of modernization did not escape either Oxford or Jefferson, Mississippi, of course, as Jason Compson demonstrates in his obsessions with cars, money, and the New York market. But the timing of modernization and, more importantly, the culture it modernized differed in key and dramatic ways from the Northern norm. Insofar as Southern understandings of gender and sexuality stem from differing economic, social, and cultural realities, then, we can expect differences from historians' national norms. Despite remarkable work on specific periods and locales, general histories of Southern sexuality and Southern gender like Kimmel's of American manhood and d'Emilio and Freedman's of American sexuality have yet to appear. We can, however, piece together evidence to come to some understandings especially of Southern dominant masculinity and femininity. We can then look at those gender constructions in Faulkner's texts and life. Key studies over several decades (see note 1) have paved the way for seeing how Faulkner treats Southern women and femininity. Studies of his representations of sexuality are well underway, as are studies of his representations of men and masculinity. What then were the changes Faulkner faced in the American South?

Southern Sexualities and Genders

Southern genders and sexualities during this period, it is becoming clear, were neither simply varieties of nor belated expressions of American manhood and womanhood.

Dominant notions of Southern gender emerged from a significantly different history, a history of slaveholding and enslavement, of bloody battle on home ground, of military loss (for whites) or constitutional victory (for blacks), of sudden or sustained poverty, of transatlantic connections, and of visions of masculinity and femininity that traced their roots not to Puritan but to other British, European, and African cultural sources. Albeit with important exceptions, the rapid growth of cities, factories, corporation life, and layers of bureaucracy lay decades in the future of the South, after World War II. To think historically about Faulkner's life as a man and about his fictional representations of sexuality, of men and women, and of masculinity and femininity, thus requires revising the major current models of dominant American gender and sexuality insofar as they depend on the grounding assumption of an economic reality that is missing in the South. Meanwhile, most historical work on gender and sexuality in the South has been limited to the nineteenth century and earlier. While we await a cultural history of gender and sexuality in the twentieth-century South, it is possible to see some of the narratives that shaped Faulkner's life and work, and to the shaping of which his own work still contributes. And we can make some general observations about the conventions he faced in the South, with the help especially of d'Emilio and Freedman.

In the North, conditions of labor and living changed from rural to urban, agrarian to industrial. The growth of cities and factories meant reduced fertility as well as less community input into sexual behavior. Contraception and abortion meant fewer children and opened the way to a focus on sex as a bond of intimacy, spiritual or romantic, separable from its role in reproduction, and on sex as a form of pleasure for both women and men. As the home narrowed to the nuclear family, and neighbors became strangers, the traditional power of the community to regulate directly its members' sexual behavior vanished, replaced by the notion of individual self-control that accompanied the individualism rewarded by the market economy. But in the South both whites and blacks kept high rates of childbirth. Abortion and contraception, though practiced, were generally condemned there; children were needed for labor, marriages were made with an eye to their economic and political implications, and the work place – especially on the plantations – was virtually identical with the home. Similarly, the Southern planter family kept its patriarchal structure with the white man on top, and continued to serve as the model for many non-planter families. The "community" retained its powers of surveillance (d'Emilio and Freedman 1997: 58 ff.).

Throughout the nation, not only in the South, sexuality was entwined with race and used to establish and maintain white supremacy. Those with darker skins – Mexicans or Indians or blacks or immigrants – became fair game, almost literally, for white predatory sex. If they married a "white," people of color increasingly were refused assimilation to the dominant community, while traditionally open sexual practices of these "other" groups (such as premarital sex and childbirth or cross-dressing) were increasingly repressed. Missionaries in the West converted Indians to the "missionary" position, man on top and woman on the bottom. The South differed from these other regions not in its enforcement of white supremacy – all the nation participated in this – but in its historical and continuing proximity to the "other." White women's sexuality was more precisely regulated than it was in other regions, in part because of the proximity of black men. The proximity of black women to white men, on the other hand, meant these women were sexually available. As d'Emilio and Freedman put it, "relations with black women provided white men with both a sexual outlet and a means of maintaining racial dominance"(1997: 94). Thus the ethos of self-control, already made unlikely by the absence of a developing competitive economy, lost its chances in the face of increased sexual privilege for white men.

The terms "homosexual" and "heterosexual," and the identities associated with them today, did not exist in cities like New York until late in the nineteenth century, and probably later in the South. In the South, to draw from John Howard's title (1999), even now gay men are called, discreetly, "men like that." Though records are hard to find, there is evidence that young men in the South felt neither guilt nor shame about the sex that could result when they spent the night together in a bed (see, e.g., Duberman 1999). For men in the South, sexual acts with other men, though most likely common enough, did not constitute one's identity, as would come to be the case more clearly outside the South in the twentieth century. Prostitution, a longstanding American institution, grew with the cities, and red-light districts like the one in Memphis that Faulkner knew and represented in his fiction could be found even in towns in the South; judging from his fictional representation, such districts may have lasted longer in the South than in other regions where women's organized health campaigns were more likely to be found. Intense friendships and "Boston marriages" between women were often erotic but were not understood as sexual or categorized as a sexual identity; however, as a product of schools and cities, these relationships were perhaps less likely in the South.

As the century continued, politics and medicine began to intervene in the sexual lives at least of Northerners: reformers challenged prostitution and drinking in saloons; doctors challenged the spread of venereal disease. Anthony Comstock made war on sexual representations, whether in visual images or in words, and Congress passed an anti-obscenity law in 1873. The desire for control worked together with the new economic patterns to separate the growing urban middle class from other classes in terms of their gender – the middle class featured masculine self-control – and to make new forms of competitive labor possible (d'Emilio and Freedman 1997: 142). Again, the South differed. To Northern eyes, white Southerners were sensualists, intemperate emotionally and sexually, made reckless by their history of slaveholding power. And certainly the economic incentives to sexual reform that characterized other regions did not apply so early or so clearly to the South. Other forces, however, kept the language and images of Southerners inoffensive: a "don't ask, don't tell" practice maintained the sexual privilege of the ruling white men. Rarely did a white privileged woman – one exception was Mary Boykin Chesnut, whose "diary" is deservedly well known (1981) – even acknowledge the presence of mulatto children, much less consider, in print, their parentage. White women, languishing untouchable on imaginary pedestals, lost their association with sexual desire, whether as object or subject, while black women were culturally assumed to be forever desirable and desiring. Black men were represented increasingly as oversexed and out of control, a risk to the frail white woman; sex was identical to rape in ideologically imagined relationships between white women and black men. This assumption bolstered white supremacy and undergirded the practice of lynching, public rituals of disfigurement, dismemberment, and death inflicted primarily on black men on the charge of raping white women. Ida B. Wells was run out of Memphis when in 1892 she published in her paper *Free Speech* arguments that some sexual relationships between white women and black men were voluntary (d'Emilio and Freedman 1997: 219). Indeed, as Jacquelyn Hall has written, "rape and rumors of rape became a kind of acceptable folk pornography in the Bible Belt" during this time (quoted in d'Emilio and Freedman 1997: 220).

In the year *The Sound and the Fury* was published, 1929, Katharine Bement Davis published a ten-year study of the sex lives of 2,200 American women. Her study, along with Clelia Mosher's in California (conducted 1892–1920, but not published until 1980), demonstrated that women felt sexual "emotions" and desire but struggled to express them and to negotiate them in relationships with men. Men, meanwhile, were torn between the imperative to self-control and their "natural" explosiveness (d'Emilio and Freedman 1997: 179). They did have access to red-light districts, however, where they learned about "speedy orgasm, the lack of emotional connection, and the absence of any expectation of mutuality" (d'Emilio and Freedman 1997: 182), certainly not the best training for them as husbands and lovers. These patterns may have characterized some Southern men and women as well, but it was kept quiet. The pattern of official belief in white women's untouchability spread from the planter class to other white women, while white men were learning about sex, if not from prostitutes, from black girls and women (d'Emilio and Freedman 1997: 186). In *Killers of the Dream* (1949) Lillian Smith discusses the implications of practicing this pattern in the South: in her world, white mothers are emotionally severed from their children and their own bodies, black women nurse white and black together, white boy-children seek yet despise their first love, the black mammy, and the black man is an impotent beast as long as he is controlled.

By the time Faulkner was old enough to understand such matters, across the nation Freud and sexology had begun to replace more traditional explanatory systems for sexuality. Freud visited Clark University in 1909; news of his theories about the deep and wide power of sexuality spread quickly and widely. Sexologists like Havelock Ellis identified gender with sexuality, so that "inverts" took on both the gender and the sexual object choice of the opposite sex. Gay culture developed; enclaves in most major cities shared meeting places, cruising streets, clubs, and entertainment. Greenwich Village, where Faulkner would live as a man in his twenties, stood out as the best-known location for "eccentricities" of all sorts, including sexual. George Chauncey's *Gay New York* (1994) details the geography, language, culture, and changes in that gay scene. Here he comments on the ways convention collapsed homosexuality and artistic tendencies: "Although not everyone thought their queer tastes extended to sexual matters, the bohemian men of the Village were often regarded as unmanly as well as un-American, and in some contexts calling men 'artistic' became code for calling them homosexual"

(1994: 229). Malcolm Cowley recalled that the literary journal *Broom* received letters at its 45 King Street office addressed to "45 Queer Street" or mentioning Oscar Wilde (Chauncey 1994: 230). The Village's "reputation as a gay neighborhood solidified throughout the 1920s." A novel set in the New York gay scene of the 1920s and published first in Paris was co-authored by another Mississippian, Charles Henri Ford from Columbus (Ford and Tyler 1933). He and Faulkner communicated about Faulkner's submission of writing to one of Ford's magazines; Ruth Ford, the actress for whom Faulkner would later write *Requiem for a Nun* (1951), was Charles Henri Ford's sister. George Chauncey writes that during the first part of the twentieth century, before the categories of "homosexual" and "heterosexual" became dominant, men who had same-sex experience would have recognized no "homosexual" category in which they all could be placed.

> In the very different sexual culture that predominated at the turn of the century, they understood themselves – and were regarded by others – as fundamentally different kinds of people. To classify them [as we might today] would be to misunderstand the complexity of their sexual system, the realities of their lived experience [as variously] fairies, punks, their husbands, trade, wolves, or customers. (1994: 96)

In the Village, womanlike gender status meant a man was a "fairy"; simple sexuality, the desire for sex with men, meant a man was "queer" (p. 101). The world in general was ignorant of the existence of a "hidden middle-class gay world – a world that did not fit the fairy stereotype" (p. 103). It is perhaps for these reasons that we know so little of Faulkner's life there.

As popular culture spread throughout the nation – movies, dance halls, magazines, amusement parks – the mores and styles of the working class were accepted into the middle class. A "white slavery panic" in the teens brought out the reformers again, this time to tell young women to stay at home rather than risk being snatched away in the streets. One 1913 play about white slavery was called *Little Lost Sister* (d'Emilio and Freedman 1997: 209), suggesting, if not a direct influence, a cultural connection to Quentin Compson's view of his sister Caddy. "By 1920 the red-light district had passed into history" according to d'Emilio and Freedman. Again the South – at least Memphis – may have been an exception. The Memphis red-light district was still there after 1920, at least for Popeye and Jason Compson.

Bill(y) Faulkner's Sexualities and Genders

In his life, from boyhood through adultery, Faulkner flouted the expectations of both dominant American and dominant Southern gender expectations. As the first son of a semi-aristocratic family well known in the community, he would have been expected to carry on a tradition of mastery despite his own father's lacks. Yet he failed courses, dropped out of school, worked in a post office until he was fired, dressed oddly, and bummed around town seeming both arrogant and indolent: "Count No 'Count" became his nickname. Perhaps in an effort to compromise between the town's expectations and his own sense of true masculinity, which had to do with the glamour, risk, and danger of war, he managed to join the Canadian Air Force, write home about the dangers he faced, and later write fictions such as the short story "Landing in Luck" (1919) exposing the masquerade he played out. At the same time, his near obsession with clothing, evident in his letters to his mother, his closeness with her both as an artist and as an indulged child who seemed to find it easy to ask for what he wanted from her, and his attraction to the dandy style in the art and manners of the British Decadents suggested a counter and resistant femininity. As numerous feminist critics have shown from a variety of theoretical positions, Faulkner had, heard, and articulated a female voice. Gender for him was no simple matter, particularly in his youth.

The story of Faulkner's sexuality before his marriage, insofar as it has been told, has focused on his infatuations with women, Estelle Oldham, of course, and Helen Baird, among others, and on the works he wrote for them. But he also had a bohemian life shared primarily with gay friends and possibly lovers. Faulkner had been reading modernist prose and poetry, as well as some philosophy, with Phil Stone, who, unlike his friend, had made it through school and to Yale, and who developed with Faulkner an intense and complex friendship. Faulkner found a special fondness for Aubrey Beardsley, which he articulated in his own drawings of dances at Ole Miss and aviators in airplanes, and for Oscar Wilde, both of whom figured publicly in discussions of homosexuality as well as gender "inversion." When he moved to New Orleans, Faulkner joined socially with a group of artists including several gay men, with one of whom, William Spratling, he shared quarters, painted Sherwood Anderson's son's penis green, among other antics, and traveled to and through Europe. The European trip by ship generated material for the short story "Divorce in Naples" about a gay couple who split up when they land in Italy. Faulkner lived for a while in New York, in Greenwich Village, in some of the neighborhoods George Chauncey mapped as the best-known gay enclave in America. There he stayed for a while in a household headed by gay Southern writer Stark Young, who welcomed other gay Southern artists. Faulkner eventually shared a one-room, one-bed apartment with a young painter whom he years later met, once, in Hollywood.

After his apparently difficult decision to marry Estelle, and as Billy Faulkner became William, Faulkner's range of gender and sexual positions narrowed. Now the husband of a woman who herself had been rather indulged, and soon a father, Faulkner's gender identifications solidified into the then-familiar masculine forms: provider and head of household. Nor does he seem to have pursued his connections with a gay world or possible homosexual relationships; so far as we know, his extramarital sexual relationships were all with women. It may have been a decision he made before the wedding; whatever the conscious process, material conditions and traditional gender and sexual conventions did their work very powerfully indeed.

This is not to say that Faulkner's imagination narrowed with his experience. On the contrary, for the rest of his career he was to explore the complexities of genders and sexualities, ideologies and bodies, in his fiction. In their behavior and in their subjectivity, Faulkner's male and female characters cross conventional boundaries of gender and sex, sometimes eagerly and sometimes reluctantly, sometimes with great pain, sometimes defiantly, and sometimes with relish and even joy.

William Faulkner's Fictional Sexualities and Genders

How did those experiments turn out? One possible answer will be found in turning to Faulkner's last novel, *The Reivers*. It recounts the story told (apparently in the present and apparently to a grandson) by the grandfather, Lucius Priest. In the story he tells, Priest was 11; the year was 1905, and the "reminiscence" focuses on four wild days in Memphis with Boon Hogganbeck, Ned McCaslin, and a host of others: gamblers, race track habitués, prostitutes, trainmen, horses, aristocrats, and a mud-farmer. The outlaw journey clarifies but does not change Lucius's quite traditional Southern enactment of a gender and sexual identity: he was raised to be and in the novel's present tense remains a loving gentleman. The meanings of that gender and sexuality in Faulkner's South unfold throughout the story.

The Reivers has not drawn the critical attention that most of Faulkner's earlier works have elicited. A recent MLA search pulled up 38 references; the only novels attracting less attention were *Pylon* (1935) and *Soldiers' Pay* (1926), while the "major" novels – *The Sound and the Fury* (1929), *As I Lay Dying* (1930), *Light in August* (1932), *Absalom, Absalom!* (1936), *Go Down, Moses* (1942) – have roughly ten times the number of references. Even *A Fable* (1954), that late and contested novel, has twice the references of *The Reivers*. One reason for this lack of interest may be the novel's apparent simplicity. Its narrative moves for the most part in a straight chronological line. Its tone is forgiving, humorous, kind even when satirical. Its characters live in a world in which people from all classes, sexes, genders, and races know and accept one another. Not surprisingly, it was made into a movie; Steve McQueen stars as Boon Hogganbeck.

Perhaps Faulkner wrote *The Reivers* with the market in mind. Perhaps Faulkner as a writer was, in the words of *Intruder in the Dust* (1948), "carrying into manhood only the fading tagend of that old once-frantic shame and anguish and need not for revenge, vengeance but simply for . . . reaffirmation of his masculinity" (1991: 26). Perhaps Faulkner was simply past his prime. Or perhaps the novel represents, like Shakespeare's late romances, a form of resolution. Whatever the critical judgment, it is a useful text through which to recall and against which to contrast Faulkner's more complex and more experimental earlier narratives' imaginings of gender and sexuality.

If to reive, a word Faulkner half-invented, is to steal, then *The Reivers* tells the story of multiple thefts. In the plot, the white aristocratic boy Lucius, the black working man Ned, and the white working (sometimes) man Boon reive a stolen car, a stolen horse, and a stolen holiday. The novel also enacts a theft in its very telling: Grandfather Priest's tale alludes to, quotes, and signifies on Faulkner's own writing past. Faulkner fans can entertain themselves endlessly decoding the allusions; more relevant for this chapter is the notion of code itself. The novel is about hiding, encoding, and decoding as much as it is about theft. Learning how to read codes is a key task for the young Lucius. On the most obvious level, he asks what words mean:

"What's pugnuckling?" Lucius asks of the prostitute Miss Corrie's small son Otis. Otis has been comparing the sales in Reba's house of prostitution to the sales in saloons. Ned intervenes to stop Otis's answer; during the remaining conversation, Otis simply repeats "___t." The reader is expected to be able to decode Otis's code as "shit" rather than asking for the answer directly. But the young and trusting Lucius asks directly about pugnuckling. He is not given the answer (1969: 140).[3]

In the same scene, after saying "Twenty-three skiddoo" repeatedly, Otis states "This town is where the jack's at" (1969: 141). Ned misunderstands it as "jacks": "In course they has jacks here. Dont Memphis need mules the same as anybody else?" This time Otis explains. "Jack" means "Spondulicks. Cash" (p. 142). Later, another meaning for "Jack" familiar to Faulkner readers and students of the period will appear when Boon calls an unnamed "man with a lantern" the generic and semi-pejorative masculine appellation "Jack."

The need to decode has come up earlier for the reader in a more explicitly sexual encoding. Boon, who is in love with Miss Corrie, has just taunted another man, Sam, in one of what will be many fits of jealousy. Miss Reba starts by calling Boon "You bas –" but then switches to an explanatory tone, finally ordering Boon to apologize.

> "All right," Boon said. "Forget it."
> "You call that an apology?" Miss Reba said.
> "What do you want?" Boon said. "Me to bend over and invite him to –"
> "You hush! Right this minute!" Miss Corrie said.
> "And you dont help none neither," Boon said. "You've already got me and Miss Reba both to where we'll have to try to forget the whole English language before we can even pass the time of day." (1969: 138)

The act to which Boon's reference is truncated is anal intercourse. He was about to say something like "invite him to fuck my ass."[4] This coded reference to sodomy is not the only allusion to homosexuality in the text; the other scene, however, is more deeply hidden in codes, and will be discussed below. For now, the point is simply the need for decoding and its relation to sexuality and gender.

Decoding threads through several themes in the novel. Failure to decode as a result of ignorance, naïveté, or gentility is a source of humor. Yet the ability to decode is no guarantee of anything other than superficial knowledge. The young (and evil) Otis is excellent at decoding popular language but his acquisitive, unfeeling attitudes prevent him from understanding (and following) the codes of the gentleman his mother wants him to be. The novel itself finally takes a serious position on masculinity that redeems the gentleman as the norm for all men and women, and the funded white male aristocracy as the rightful "top" of this society. Though "othered" people – blacks, women, and working-class whites – can be true gentlemen, the novel never addresses the economic base that provides lasting public and private power to the white aristocratic men who own the horses and have named the town (Parsham, or "Possum") as well as the venerated black gentleman Uncle Parsham.

At the end of the scene with Otis described earlier, Otis speaks a word to Ned that Lucius understands but rejects: nigger. Lucius thinks: "something Father and Grandfather must have been teaching me before I could remember because I dont know when it began, I just knew it was so: that no gentleman ever referred to anyone by his race or religion" (1969: 143). Instead of giving Lucius up as hopelessly naïve in his morals as well as his knowledge, the novel will show that Lucius's values effectively change the world for what the reader is led to believe is the better.

For starters, Lucius saves Corrie from a life of prostitution through his chivalric treatment of her. This narrative becomes clear when, under the influence of what she sees as Lucius's ideal masculinity, Corrie refuses to sleep with any of her customers, even the man she loves: "Boon!" Miss Corrie said. "I'm not going home with anybody! Come on, Lucius, you and Otis" (1969: 151).[5] When they are in his bed that night, Otis tells Lucius his mother Corrie's real name – Everbe Corinthia – which she wants no one else to know, and recounts the story of the fine business he had back home selling looks at Corrie with her clients through his peephole above her room.

For this, Lucius hits Otis: he wants not to "just hurt him but to destroy him" for debasing Corrie's privacy (1969: 157). The smaller Otis scrabbles for his "discarded trousers" to get his pocket-knife, which, because it equalizes the two in Lucius's eyes, serves as his "carte blanche" to be violent. Lucius takes the knife away but is cut, and downed, in the process. Alerted by the ruckus, Boon, clad only in pants, lifts him up; Corrie, in a kimono and with her hair down, orders Otis to her room. Lucius then learns "what was wrong about Otis," he recalls in his tale-telling grandfatherly role: despite his small size, Otis is already 15 years old. How this is "wrong" is not exactly clear yet. Later that night, Miss Corrie kneels beside Lucius's mattress to tell him that he's "the first one ever fought [not over her but] for me." She then makes him a promise: "It [prostitution] won't be my fault any more" (p. 160). She will keep this promise, she says, just as he has kept his promise to his father about drinking alcohol, the promise he "told Mr. Binford about before supper tonight." When Boon comes to get her to go back to bed, Corrie insists "I cant! I cant!" (p. 161), and she keeps this promise almost to the end of the novel, breaking it only for what are represented as acceptable reasons. Now, she says, "I've quit! Not any more. Never!" (p. 197).

Miss Reba notices Lucius's effectiveness at sexual reform: "Boon Hogganbeck brings one [child] that's driving my damned girls into poverty and respectability" (1969: 209). But this is not enough. Once again Lucius is set off by an insult to Miss Everbe Corinthia: Boon hits her after she has had sex with another man, Butch. "She's quit," Lucius says. "She promised me" (p. 259). Lucius now tries to "strike at [Boon's] face" to defend Corrie's person and her honor (p. 260); then he cries, bawls, says he wants to go home. Ned tries to explain what turns out to be an alternative set of rules about hitting women: "Hitting a woman dont hurt her because a woman dont shove back at a lick like a man do; she just gives [in] to it and then when your back is turned reaches for the flatiron or the butcher knife. [And] what better sign than a black eye or a cut mouf can a woman want from a man that he got her on his mind?" (p. 263). Finally, Lucius inspires Boon to marry Everbe: "If you can go bare-handed against a knife defendin her, why the hell cant I marry her?" Boon asks Lucius rhetorically. "Aint I as good as you are, even if I aint eleven years old?" (p. 299).

Lucius learns how to be a Southern gentleman, then, by feeling the emotions for a woman that lead him to risk his own safety to defend her honor. Like Ike with his cow in *The Hamlet*, what could be read as parody is rendered instead as a wise grandfather's story told for a grandchild, about how he himself became a man.

Within the tale Lucius is telling in the present, his grandfather sums up what it means to be a man. When Lucius the boy comes home again after the Memphis adventure, his father seems about to beat him with a razor strop (1969: 300); his mother is crying. Was this the right response to his son's behavior? "'It was wrong,'" says Lucius's grandfather, "and Father and I both knew it. I mean, if after all the lying and deceiving and disobeying and conniving I had done, all he could do about it was to whip me, then Father was not good enough for me" (p. 301). Lucius's grandfather stops them and sends Lucius's parents away. Lucius then asks him to "do something" about his lying. Grandfather says he can't do anything; only Lucius can. And what can Lucius do? He can "live with it." "A gentleman always does. A gentleman can live through anything. He faces anything. A gentleman accepts the responsibility of his actions and bears the burden of their consequences." Hearing this, Lucius cries, bawls, again (p. 302). And Grandfather says "A gentleman cries too, but he always washes his face." Grandfather concludes that "your outside is just what you live in, sleep in, and [it] has little connection with who you are and even less with what you do" (p. 304). Since it has been established earlier that anyone – Uncle Parsham is the model – can be a gentleman, though not a moneyed aristocrat, it's clear to the reader that even Everbe is a true gentleman: she has taken responsibility for her actions and bears the burden – her children – of their consequences. This gender(less) "message" challenges Kimmel's Self-Made Man. Instead of excluding others such as women and blacks in order to shore up masculinity, as do Kimmel's men, it offers a definition of masculinity that is open to anyone.

The material conditions in the story, however, undercut this message. Lucius refuses the money won on the horse race because he didn't do it for the money; in fact, that was the least of his concerns. But he is able to refuse it because he knows he has a "home" to return to, a business owned by his father and grandfather, even a car he might continue to drive. Ned is less confident in the ability to live only with his ideals. After the initial series of races is over, Grandfather and the legal owners of the two horses gather for toddies in "the old Parsham place." It is "big, with columns and porticoes and formal gardens and stables and carriage houses and what used to be slave quarters," reminiscent of the mansion to which Sarty Snopes attributes gentlemanly values in the short story "Barn Burning" (1939). Grandfather, Col. Linscomb, and Mr. van Tosch are inside drinking toddies and Ned is sitting on the back steps. Though later Ned is offered a toddy in the living room with the white men (1969: 293), the gesture cannot erase the obvious and sustained differences in wealth and power, nor does it address institutionalized racism. One moment of individual cross-race male bonding does not mean Ned will live in this, or any, big house or make the decisions concerning it. Faulkner's gentleman, then, suffers a limitation similar to the individualism of the Self-Made Man: he may respond to a given situation with generosity, but he does not plan to move into collective action. It is no wonder that the more obscured text of Lucius's growth during the novel, the level hidden by "gentleman," is that of "master."

The women of *The Reivers* occupy gender positions and characterizations familiar to Faulkner readers. Of Diane Roberts's (1994) helpful categories – the Confederate Woman, the Mammy, the Tragic Mulatta, the New Belle, the Night Sister, and Mothers – the two most obvious in *The Reivers* are the Night Sister and Mothers. In fact, Faulkner's strategies merge the two. Readers will remember the night sister madame, Miss Reba, from *Sanctuary*, set after the action in *The Reivers* when Mr. Binford has died and been replaced by a yapping little dog with his name. Miss Corrie's real name, Everbe Corinthia, is taken from a much earlier short story, "The Leg" (1934). Here, Everbe Corinthia – Miss Corrie – represents both the night sister and the heart of the mother: she cares for her unappealing son Otis through all his escapades and escapes, washes Lucius's clothes in the middle of the night, and looks at him in tender ways that belie her "plain" face. There is very little, if any, recognition of her as a sexually desiring person, despite (or because of) her job. Lucius's love for Miss Corrie is primarily that of a boy who misses his mother, overdetermined by a romantic reaction to the sexual ambience of the house so that it feels like he is falling in love. Miss Reba is the mother of mothers as well as the queen of prostitutes; she runs her domestic space with authority and intelligence, and cares for her "girls" while "employing" them in her business. Mr. Binford plays the roles of the pimp and the dominating, patriarchal father: his rules about dining cannot be disobeyed. In these representations, Faulkner challenges the period's stereotypes of white slavery, of nymphomaniac prostitutes, of hardened women in a whorehouse, and – importantly – of unmitigated patriarchal power.

But gender trouble, insofar as these inventions accomplish that through these characters, comes more easily to Faulkner in this novel than does sexual trouble. Lucius awakens not only to romantic love of a maternal figure, but to sexuality and desire as well, including homosexual desire. The story is buried, but its traces can be decoded.

When Otis tells Lucius that he has made money spying on his mother having sex with clients, Lucius is repelled, not only because he loves and wants to defend Everbe. He is repelled by the very idea of (hetero)sex: he hates "that such not only was, but must be, had to be if living was to continue and mankind be a part of it" (1969: 175). Like a young Quentin Compson, he is not capable of accepting the idea of sexuality into his construction of the body of a woman he loves, or of allowing himself to feel sexual desire for her. Yet clearly something has happened to him as a result of hearing Otis's story. Thus when he immediately thereafter feels "anguished with homesickness, wrenched and wrung and agonised with it: to be home, not just to retrace but to retract, obliterate" (p. 175), it is because at home he need not think of his own mother in relation to sex.

Less easily decoded are Lucius's anxieties about homosexuality. Numerous references to, and scenes of, sleeping in bed with men – from Grandfather to Boon to Uncle Parsham to Lycurgus to Otis – appear in the novel, for no apparent thematic reason. Most of the scenes include detailed representations of removing clothes before getting into bed, with particular focus on Lucius's lack of nightclothes (he left home without them). In this context, the scene with Uncle Parsham is comforting in every way. Uncle Parsham finds Lucius a shirt to sleep in, to cover his nakedness, tells him to say his prayers, and falls asleep himself almost instantly. This scene serves, I think, as an effort to revise and recover from a disturbing earlier scene in bed with Otis. Here is that scene:

> Otis had a nightshirt but . . . he went to bed just like I had to [without clothes]: took off his pants and shoes and turned off the light and lay down too. There was one little window and now we could see the moon and then I could even see inside the room because of the moonlight; there was something wrong with him; I was tired and coming up the stairs I had thought I would be asleep almost before I finished lying down. But I could feel him lying there beside me, not just wide awake, but rather like something that never slept in its life and didn't even know it never had. And suddenly there was something wrong with me too. It was like I didn't know what it was yet: only that there was something wrong and in a minute now I would know what and I would hate it; and suddenly I didn't want to be there at all . . . : I wanted to be at home. (1969: 153)

What is wrong? After Otis tells him how he makes money selling sights of Bee's sex, Lucius is certain that what is wrong with Otis is that he is too old for his size. Lucius doesn't explain any further. Literally, Otis is older, 15, than the larger 11-year-old Lucius. Figuratively, he is too old in his superficial knowledge of sex and finance. Physically and emotionally, he is too old to be talking and thinking about his mother in relation to sex. And perhaps there is another problem. It seems plausible that the most basic meaning Lucius has for "something wrong with Otis" has more to do with (homo)sex than it does with size, age, sophistication, or his relation to his mother. As Lucius narrates, the friendly, even intimate "we" he uses to describe the scene from their bed almost immediately separates into "he" and "I," as if it risked too much. If being in bed naked with another adolescent boy stirred up sexual feelings, Lucius would certainly interpret them as "something wrong." And it's likely that he – if not Faulkner – would have been unable and unwilling to decode the "wrongness" in this way. But the proliferation of scenes of undressing and sleeping with another male is so clear that the reader must undertake that very process. Confused about heterosexuality in familiar Faulknerian ways – how can the virgin be a whore? how can the mother desire? how can I desire the mother? – Lucius seems, if more opaquely, equally troubled by homoerotic possibilities.

Homosociality, however, if not homosexuality, is Faulkner's career-long forte, and this novel offers scene after scene of homosocial pleasure and drama. The trip to Memphis brings together three unlikely males; the horse and the races bring more into the scene; and the scene of toddies in the big house near the end shows that

homosociality is still the way to be a man. Tellingly, the "office" (like Kimmel's "den")
in Parsham Hall is Lucius's favorite room. He remembers it in loving detail:

> "We'll go to the office," Colonel Linscomb said. It was the best room I ever saw. I wished
> Grandfather had one like it. Colonel Linscomb was a lawyer too, so there were cases of
> law books, but there were farm-and horse-papers too and a glass case of jointed fishing
> rods and guns, and chairs and a sofa and a special rug for the old setter to lie on in front
> of the fireplace, and pictures of horses and jockeys on the walls, with the rose wreaths
> and the dates they won, and a bronze figure of Manassas (I didn't know until then that
> Colonel Linscomb was the one who had owned Manassas) on the mantel, and a special
> table for the big book which was his stud book, and another table with a box of cigars
> and a decanter and water pitcher and sugar bowl and glasses already on it, and a French
> window that opened onto the gallery above the rose garden so that you could smell the
> roses even in the house, and honeysuckle too and a mockingbird somewhere outside.
> (1969: 284)

The breathlessness of the prose represents the excitement of a child, even though the
voice is also Lucius's as a grandfather. This is Lucius's idea of real manhood, even as an
adult, we surmise: to be in a room, a space, a world like this. It is filled with signs of
masculinity – drinks, stud book, prizes, the dog – yet open to the natural world. It
lacks any sign of woman, femininity, or, worst of all, feminine sexuality. Even the
honeysuckle that so troubles Quentin Compson in *The Sound and the Fury* has no effect
at all on Lucius; he is safe with men in a manly space, an interior that is neither a
boudoir nor a bedroom. Nor are there signs or signals of homoerotic desire in this space.
Manhood without sex at all is the answer.

How then does Faulkner cap his career of exploration? As suggested earlier, this
last novel ultimately returns to a traditional rendering of gender and sexuality for both
men and women. Miss Corrie marries Boon and has his baby. Lucius returns home to
occupy the space of the aristocratic heir, the loving gentleman, presumably with many
of the anxieties about sex that Lillian Smith analyzes as part of that role in *Killers
of the Dream* (1949). As a young man, and in his earlier fiction, Faulkner defied –
deliberately or not – both national and regional prescriptions for masculinity, femininity, and sexuality, sometimes opposing, sometimes exaggerating, sometimes rendering
them with detachment. At the end, he raises the specters again, particularly the specter
of complex and contradictory male sexual desire. Yet by leaving them in code, perhaps
hidden even from himself, and by omitting the story of Lucius's adult sexual life, by
leaving us with the idealized image of a homosocial space, he fails to lay those ghosts
to rest.

It is hard to imagine how that would be done, in fact. How could the contradictions
inherent in Southern genders and sexualities be resolved without erasing Southern
culture? I can't think of a novel that does so. Rather, it is a mark of Faulkner's honesty
as a writer that in even as "light" a novel as *The Reivers*, he left traces of the cultural
and personal ambivalences about gender and sex – particularity about masculinity and
male desire – that continue to pervade the South.

Notes

I would like to thank Rick Moreland for his help in the writing of this chapter in the forms of remarkable generosity and patience as well as gifted insight and editing.

1   Three issues of the *Faulkner Journal* alone (vols. 4, 9, and 15) have been dedicated to sexuality, masculinity, and feminism. The Faulkner and Yoknapatawpha conferences have produced collections of essays on Faulkner and gender and Faulkner and women (Fowler and Abadie 1986; Kartiganer and Abadie 1996). The catalogue of other essays, collections, and books on gender and sexuality in Faulkner is enormous; a search of the MLA online bibliography can be overwhelming. I recommend Caroline Carvill's useful and brief history of feminist and gender criticism in Peek and Hamblin's *A Companion to Faulkner Studies* (2004: 215–32), as well as Peter Lurie's survey of cultural studies (pp. 163–95) and Doreen Fowler's survey of psychological criticism (pp. 197–214) in the same volume, which summarize a number of works on Faulkner, gender, and sexuality in the process of articulating those chapters' main concerns. Work on masculinity, male characters, and gay representations is more recent and more scattered; important works in Faulkner criticism not mentioned in the Peek and Hamblin collection or included in the three *Faulkner Journal* issues and the two Faulkner and Yoknapatawpha collections include Richard Godden and Noel Polk's collaborative and controversial "Reading the Ledgers" (2002) as well as several essays (including one by Polk) in Jones and Donaldson (1997), in Howard (1997), and in Dews and Leste Law (2001).

2   On the other hand, John d'Emilio and Estelle Freedman in their history of sexuality in America, *Intimate Matters* (1997), take pains to include the South and to note its key differences. Their insights are extremely helpful. Kimmel, too, accounts for his study's regional and other limitations: "Manhood means different things at different times to different people. . . . At the same time, though, all American men must also contend with a singular vision of masculinity, a particular definition that is held up as the model against which we all measure ourselves. . . . I do not tell the story of these 'others' [working class men, gay men, men of color, immigrant men, presumably Southern men] from their point of view nor in their own voices; rather, I trace the ways that they [these 'other' men] were set up as everything that 'straight white men' were not, so as to provide public testimony and private reassurances that those 'complete' men were secure in their gender identity. Thus, this book describes only one version of 'Manhood in America' – albeit the dominant version" (1996: 6–7).

3   But this author will hazard one. Remove the pug and the l, change the n to an f, and you have it.

4   This is also, I believe, a plausible decoding of Popeye's final "Fix my hair" in *Sanctuary*.

5   The apparent hopelessness of Lucius's developing crush on the woman he then knows as Miss Corrie is indicated by this seemingly simple statement. She is clearly going home with Lucius and Otis; unfortunately, they aren't "anybody." Later, though, Lucius changes her life.

References and Further Reading

Bardaglio, P. W. (1995). *Reconstructing the Household: Families, Sex, and the Law in the Nineteenth-Century South.* Chapel Hill, NC: University of North Carolina Press.

Bassett, J. (1972). *William Faulkner: An Annotated Checklist of Criticism.* New York: David Lewis.

Bercaw, N. (ed.) (2000). *Gender and the Southern Body Politic.* Jackson: University Press of Mississippi.

Bleser, C. (ed.) (1991). *In Joy and in Sorrow: Women, Family, and Marriage in the Victorian South, 1830–1900.* New York: Oxford University Press.

Blotner, J. (1984). *Faulkner: A Biography*. One-vol. edn. New York: Random House.

Brooks, C. (1986). Discovery of Evil. In H. Bloom (ed.). *Modern Critical Views: William Faulkner* (pp. 7–26). New York: Chelsea House.

Chauncey, G. (1994). *Gay New York: Gender, Urban Culture, and the Making of the Gay Male World, 1890–1940*. New York: Basic Books.

Chesnut, M. B. (1981). *Mary Chesnut's Civil War* (ed. C. V. Woodward). New Haven, CT: Yale University Press.

Clarke, D. (1994). *Robbing the Mother: Women in Faulkner*. Jackson: University Press of Mississippi.

Clinton, C. (1982). *The Plantation Mistress: Woman's World in the Old South*. New York: Pantheon.

d'Emilio, J. and E. B. Freedman (1997). *Intimate Matters: A History of Sexuality in America*. 2nd edn. Chicago: University of Chicago Press. (Original pub. 1988.)

Dews, C. and C. Leste Law (eds.) (2001). *Out in the South*. Philadelphia: Temple University Press.

Donaldson, S. V. (guest ed.) (1994). *Faulkner Journal: Faulkner and Sexuality*, 9(1, 2).

Donaldson, S. V. (guest ed.) (2000). *Faulkner Journal: Faulkner and Masculinity*, 15(1, 2).

Duberman, M. (1999). "Writhing Bedfellows" in Antebellum South Carolina. In J. Howard (ed.). *Men Like That: A Southern Queer History* (pp. 15–33). Chicago: University of Chicago Press.

Duvall, J. N. (1990). *Faulkner's Marginal Couple: Invisible, Outlaw, and Unspeakable Communities*. Austin, TX: University of Texas Press.

Evans, S. M. (1989). *Born for Liberty: A History of Women in America*. New York: Free Press.

Faulkner, W. (1969). *The Reivers: A Reminiscence*. New York: New American Library. (Original pub. 1962.)

Faulkner, W. (1991). *Intruder in the Dust*. New York: Norton. (Original pub. 1948.)

Faulkner, W. (1993). *Sanctuary: The Corrected Text*. New York: Norton. (Original pub. 1931.)

Filene, P. G. (1986). *Him/Her/Self: Sex Roles in Modern America*. 2nd edn. Baltimore: Johns Hopkins University Press.

Ford, C. H. and P. Tyler (1933). *The Young and Evil*. Paris: Obelisk Press.

Fowler, D. and A. J. Abadie (eds.) (1986). *Faulkner and Women: Faulkner and Yoknapatawpha, 1985*. Jackson: University Press of Mississippi.

Fox-Genovese, E. (1988). *Within the Plantation Household: Black and White Women of the Old South*. Chapel Hill, NC: University of North Carolina Press.

Friend, C. T. and L. Glover (eds.) (2004). *Southern Manhood: Perspectives on Masculinity in the Old South*. Athens, GA: University of Georgia Press.

Godden, R. and N. Polk (2002). Reading the Ledgers. *Mississippi Quarterly*, 55: 301–59.

Gwin, M. (1985). *Black and White Women of the Old South: The Peculiar Sisterhood in American Literature*. Knoxville, TN: University of Tennessee Press.

Gwin, M. (1990). *The Feminine and Faulkner: Reading (Beyond) Sexual Difference*. Knoxville, TN: University of Tennessee Press.

Hine, D. C. and E. Jenkins (1999). *A Question of Manhood: A Reader in U. S. Black Men's History and Masculinity*. Vol. 1. Bloomington: Indiana University Press.

Holditch, W. K. (1998). William Spratling, William Faulkner, and Other Famous Creoles. *Mississippi Quarterly*, 51: 423–34.

Howard, J. (ed.) (1997). *Carryin' On in the Lesbian and Gay South*. New York: New York University Press.

Howard, J. (ed.) (1999). *Men Like That: A Southern Queer History*. Chicago: University of Chicago Press.

Irwin, J. T. (1975). *Doubling and Incest/Repetition and Revenge: A Speculative Reading of Faulkner*. Baltimore: Johns Hopkins University Press.

Jones, A. G. (1982). *Tomorrow Is Another Day: The Woman Writer in the South, 1859–1936*. Baton Rouge: Louisiana State University Press.

Jones, A. G. and S. V. Donaldson (eds.) (1997). *Haunted Bodies: Gender and Southern Texts*. Charlottesville: University of Virginia Press.

Kartiganer, D. M. and A. J. Abadie (eds.) (1996). *Faulkner and Gender: Faulkner and Yoknapatawpha, 1994*. Jackson: University Press of Mississippi.

Kimmel, M. S. (1996). *Manhood in America: A Cultural History*. New York: Free Press.

Kimmel, M. S. (2000). *The Gendered Society*. New York: Oxford University Press.

Kimmel, M. S. (2005). *The History of Men: Essays on the History of American and British Masculinities*. Albany, NY: SUNY Press.

Leverenz, D. (1989). *Manhood and the American Renaissance*. Ithaca, NY: Cornell University Press.

Matthews, J. T. and J. B. Wittenberg (eds.) (1989). *Faulkner Journal: Faulkner and Feminisms*, 4(1, 2).

Minter, D. L. (1980). *William Faulkner: His Life and Work*. Baltimore: Johns Hopkins University Press.

Mortimer, G. L. (1983). *Faulkner's Rhetoric of Loss: A Study in Perception and Meaning*. Austin, TX: University of Texas Press.

Ownby, T. (1990). *Subduing Satan: Religion, Recreation, and Manhood in the Rural South, 1865–1920*. Chapel Hill, NC: University of North Carolina Press.

Parini, J. (2004). *One Matchless Time: A Life of William Faulkner*. New York: HarperCollins.

Peek, C. A. and R. W. Hamblin (eds.) (2004). *A Companion to Faulkner Studies*. Westport, CT: Greenwood Press.

Reid, P. (ed.) (2000). *Conversations with Ellen Douglas*. Jackson: University Press of Mississippi.

The Reivers (1969). Dir. Mark Rydell. National General.

Roberts, D. (1994). *Faulkner and Southern Womanhood*. Athens, GA: University of Georgia Press.

Rotundo, A. (1993). *American Manhood: Transformations in Masculinity from the Revolution to the Modern Era*. New York: Basic Books.

Sears, J. T. (2001). *Rebels, Rubyfruit, and Rhinestone: Queering Space in the Stonewall South*. New Brunswick, NJ: Rutgers University Press.

Smith, L. (1949). *Killers of the Dream*. New York: Norton.

Summers, M. (2004). *Manliness and its Discontents: The Black Middle Class and the Transformation of Masculinity, 1900–1930*. Chapel Hill, NC: University of North Carolina Press.

Watson, J. G. (1992). *Thinking of Home: William Faulkner's Letters to his Mother and Father, 1918–1925*. New York: Norton.

Weinstein, P. M. (ed.) (1995). *The Cambridge Companion to Faulkner*. Cambridge: Cambridge University Press.

Wilde, M. C. and O. Borsten (1976). *A Loving Gentleman: The Love Story of William Faulkner and Meta Carpenter*. New York: Simon and Schuster.

Williamson, J. (1993). *William Faulkner and Southern History*. New York: Oxford University Press.

4

"C'est Vraiment Dégueulasse": Meaning and Ending in *A bout de souffle* and *If I Forget Thee, Jerusalem*

Catherine Gunther Kodat

A plea for an America that is guilty gives me the chance of a better hearing.
Eric Rohmer, in Hillier (1985: 91)

About halfway through Jean-Luc Godard's *A bout de souffle*, Patricia Franchini, the American in Cold War Paris, asks her charming, thuggish French boyfriend, Michel Poiccard, if he's ever read *The Wild Palms*. The two are sitting on Patricia's bed in her tiny hotel room, and their conversation up until this point has centered on love, so Michel's response – "Take your jersey off" – is not an absolute non sequitur, especially given that his answer to her earlier question ("Do you know William Faulkner?" "No, who is it? You've slept with him?") has already indicated to the film's viewers (if not to Patricia) that Michel is something less than *un homme des lettres*. Undeterred, however, Patricia (played by Jean Seberg) reads aloud to her lover: "Listen," she says, "the last sentence [la dernière phrase] is beautiful. 'Between grief and nothing I will take grief.'" Having read the line in its original English, she turns to Michel (played by Jean-Paul Belmondo) and repeats it in French ("entre le chagrin et le néant c'est le chagrin que je choisis"), then asks him which he would choose. Michel's first response follows from his initial reaction to Faulkner's eleventh novel (and to Faulkner himself): "Show me your toes; a woman's toes are most important." When Patricia insists on an answer, Michel's reply is impatient and categorical: "Grief is idiotic. I'd choose nothingness. It's not any better, but grief's a compromise. You've got to have all or nothing" (Andrew 1987: 88).[1]

This intertextual moment – one of many in a film that also cites Louis Aragon, Guillaume Apollinaire, Lenin, Dylan Thomas, and Maurice Sachs – has received little attention in the body of work that has grown up around Godard's now-classic film (shot in 1959, released in 1960, and known to English-speaking viewers as *Breathless*), but it has not gone completely unnoticed. In his study on Faulkner and film, Bruce Kawin claims that the double-stranded novel of sex, death, flood, and imprisonment is centrally

important not only to the meaning and structure of *A bout de souffle* but also to much
of Godard's later work, though he avers that "in *Breathless*, [Godard] appears to have
in mind only the title novella [that is, the "Wild Palms" narrative] and not the entire
work" (Kawin 1977: 151). According to Kawin, *If I Forget Thee, Jerusalem* (as the novel
has been known since the 1990 corrected text restored Faulkner's original title) has a
plot that "clearly parallels" the film, even though *A bout de souffle* is "just as clearly at
pains to render those correspondences as ironic as possible," and in much the same way
that it renders ironic its correspondences to the movies of the American B-film company,
Monogram Pictures, to which it is dedicated (Kawin 1977: 151). However, Kawin does
not see the quotation itself functioning ironically in *A bout de souffle*, for, at the end of
the film, "Michel gets 'nothing' and Patrice [sic] is left with the burden of remembering
him, of trying to understand him, and of having caused his death"; he names two
of the novel's chief characters to indicate how Faulkner's book, in his view, helps us
interpret Godard's heroine: Patricia is "Harry with a difference, and Charlotte as a
coward" (Kawin 1977: 151). In his study of intertexuality in French New Wave cinema,
T. Jefferson Kline takes a different approach: though the quotation is useful for helping
us understand the relationship between Patricia and Michel, that relationship is best
understood not in terms of individual psychology but rather as a local example of the
film's true subject: the post-World War II "rapprochement franco-américain" (as Michel
jokingly calls sex with Patricia) that saw France flooded with American films, American
books, and American music, all of which clearly influenced Godard's film practice. By
citing the novel, Kline argues, Godard invites viewers to interpret the film not simply
through the immediate quotation but also through the entire work, and he finds the
"Old Man" narrative a fruitful, if silent, intertext. The tall convict, imprisoned after
his failed attempt to stage a train robbery like those he'd read of in "the paper novels
– the Diamond Dicks and Jesse Jameses and such" (Faulkner 1990: 20), "resembles no
one so much as Jean-Luc Godard in his attempt to construct his own enterprise on the
basis of literary and cinematic models. . . . Both convict and filmmaker have constructed their work on the basis of quotation, and in both cases the quotation has an
uncanny way of betraying the erstwhile imitator" (Kline 1992: 199). Kline cites
Godard's later repudiation of the film as proof of his thesis: "*A bout de souffle* is a film
that I just can't look at without beginning to perspire, to feel, I don't know, as if I'd
been forced to strip naked at a moment that I didn't feel like it, and that's always seemed
a bit strange to me. . . . It's a film that came out of fascism and that is full of fascist
overtones" (Kline 1992: 185). If Kawin sees Faulkner's contribution to Godard's artistic
practice as largely enabling and liberatory (a perspective that repeats, on the literary
critical level, the view Eisenhower-era Americans had of their relationship to postwar
France), Kline is less sanguine: *A bout de souffle*'s engagement with American modernism
signals its dalliance with "fascist" aesthetics, its dangerous liaison with forms and modes
of cultural expression more complacent than critical. That each mounts his reading by
privileging a different aspect of Faulkner's text – for Kawin the crucial intertext is
"Wild Palms," while for Kline it is "Old Man" – perhaps signals that the reasons for
Godard's interest in Faulkner are less obvious than might at first appear.

As contradictory as they are, Kline's and Kawin's discussions of Godard's purposes in quoting Faulkner resemble each other in one odd, and I think revealing, particular. They both fall silent on a rather obvious mistake Godard makes in his use of Faulkner: the line Patricia reads is *not*, in fact, "la dernière phrase" of the novel, but rather the last sentence of the "Wild Palms" narrative. It is true that "Wild Palms" ends with Harry's famous vow (and accompanying, if somewhat less frequently cited, masturbation); but the novel itself goes on for another dozen or so pages, wrapping up the details of "Old Man" by explaining how the tall convict's heroic "escape" gets him an extended prison sentence. As Faulkner scholars know, the actual last words of *If I Forget Thee, Jerusalem* contain an expletive – " 'Women, shit,' the tall convict said" (Faulkner 1990: 287) – that Faulkner's publishers refused to print, and Faulkner chose to accept the traditional sign of censorship rather than change the objectionable word. Thus the novel the journalist Van Doude gives to Patricia, and from which she reads aloud to Michel, almost undoubtedly concludes with " 'Women, – !' the tall convict said" (Faulkner 1939: 339), a last sentence that ends the novel at the brink of aporia, closing on a "nothing" somewhat other than the opposite of grief (unless, as may have been the case, Godard had in mind the 1952 French translation of the novel, which offers yet a third last sentence: "– Ah! les femmes!» dit le grand forçat" [Faulkner 1952: 348]). The film's confusion (or disingenuousness: viewers can clearly see that Patricia is not at the end of the book as she reads the passage aloud) over the novel's true last words could be attributed either to Godard's indifference to the facts of his intertext (not impossible) or to the French publication history of the novel Godard knew as *Les palmiers sauvages*, a publication history that may have led him to believe he had accurately quoted "la dernière phrase," were it not for the fact that mistaken last words (and women) have a crucial role to play in *A bout de souffle*, as well. Gunned down by the detective to whom Patricia has betrayed him, Michel looks up at his lover as he lies on a Parisian street and quietly mutters an assessment of his fate – "C'est vraiment dégueulasse" ("It's really disgusting") – before dying. Patricia, though, doesn't quite hear him. "What did he say?" she asks the policemen gathered around the body, and Inspector Vital (undoubtedly named for Jean-Jacques Vital, a French film producer whose projects Godard strongly disdained [Milne 1986: 99]) responds, "He said, 'You are really a bitch' " ("Il a dit: Vous êtes vraiment une dégueulasse"). Throughout the film, however, Patricia's American college French never has been quite a match for Michel's slangy argot, and the case is no different here. "What is 'dégueulasse'?" she asks, ending the film with a last sentence that poses both a question and a translation problem (Andrews 1987: 146).

I bring up this subject of improper, or misconstrued, last words because it seems to me that the questions it raises are linked to the larger issue of the relationship between commercial value and artistic worth that is engaged in Faulkner's novel and in Godard's film, an issue that both texts address directly (indeed, the confluence of commerce and art is a concern central to both novel and film) but that neither is able to satisfactorily settle. My project here, then, is not simply to explain an intertext (that is, to interpret Godard's reasons for quoting Faulkner), but to uncover the common expressive practices and artistic interests subtending these two works: not only to read *A bout de souffle* through *If I Forget Thee, Jerusalem* but also to read Faulkner's novel through Godard's film. Both *If I Forget Thee, Jerusalem* and *A bout de souffle* articulate their concerns through references to expressive media similar to, and yet different from, their own: cinema and pulp fiction in the case of Faulkner's novel, literature and American genre movies for Godard's film. Faulkner wrote *If I Forget Thee, Jerusalem* after a stint of Hollywood screenwriting, his third (and at that point his longest) period of employment in the film industry and one that saw the beginning of an intense, highly erotic, but also emotionally fraught affair with Howard Hawks's secretary and sometime "script girl," Meta Carpenter, an affair that lasted for over 15 years and that seems to have progressed along lines not so different from a classic Hollywood melodrama (" 'Bear with me, Meta,' he implored once again and I kissed him and put up a brave Irene Dunne–Ann Harding face" [Wilde and Borsten 1976: 166]). Godard shot *A bout de souffle* after several years' apprenticeship as a film critic for *Cahiers du Cinéma*, where he and other future members of the New Wave group of filmmakers (François Truffaut, Eric Rohmer, Claude Chabrol) developed their *politique des auteurs*, essentially an assertion (it could not be called a theory) that great films, like great literature, were expressions of an individual artistic vision. Faulkner would later claim that he wrote *If I Forget Thee, Jerusalem* "to try to stave off what I thought was heart-break" (Blotner 1977: 338) over what he believed was the conclusive end of his affair with Carpenter (their relationship, however, would see intermittent revivals in the years after the book appeared), but the novel is at least as much engaged with the vexed entanglements of mass and "high" art production and consumption as with the complications of love; in fact, and as Richard Gray has pointed out, relations between the sexes in *If I Forget Thee, Jerusalem* are thoroughly enmeshed in the expressive structures of Hollywood and pulp fiction, structures that the novel itself does not entirely escape (Gray 1994: 247). Likewise, years after the release of his first feature film, Godard, one of the most vociferous champions of an independent *auteur* film practice, characterized *A bout de souffle* as "a picture that I've done for others. . . . [Y]ou don't make a movie, the movie makes you" (McCabe 1980: 45). I want to suggest that the complications at play here (Faulkner claiming he was writing out of love when, of course, he also was writing for the market; Godard discovering that "self"-expression is always shaped by "outside" forces) reveal the difficulty Faulkner and Godard experienced in attempting to make a neat separation between art and commerce that would allow them to safeguard the former even as they exploited the latter – a difficulty that made it impossible for them to pronounce the last word on the relationship between the two.

Cunning

I have lived for the last six months in such a peculiar state of family complications and back complications that I still am not able to tell if the novel is all right or absolute drivel. To me, it was written just as if I had sat on the one side of a wall and the paper was on the other and my hand and the pen thrust through the wall and writing not only

on invisible paper but in pitch darkness too, so that I could not even know if the pen
still wrote on paper or not.

William Faulkner, in Blotner (1977: 106)

The composition and publication history of the novel that would first appear under the
title *The Wild Palms* is well known, but it is worth reviewing that history, as well as
salient aspects of the novel's appearance and reception in France. As he would recollect
during class conferences at the University of Virginia, Faulkner began writing the novel
with "Wild Palms," the story of the extravagant, doomed love affair of Harry Wilbourne
and Charlotte Rittenmeyer, but found

> that it needed a contrapuntal quality like music. And so I wrote the other story ["Old
> Man"] simply to underline the story of Charlotte and Harry. I wrote the two stories by
> alternate chapters. I'd write the chapter of one and then I would write the chapter of the
> other just as the musician puts in – puts in counterpoint behind the theme that he is
> working with. (Gwynn and Blotner 1959: 171)

Faulkner's appeal to musical counterpoint to describe a novel that proceeds through
two alternating and seemingly unrelated narratives is more metaphorical than exact, of
course; but Thomas L. McHaney's study of the manuscript leads him to conclude that
Faulkner did, indeed, write the novel as he claimed (McHaney 1975: xiv–xv, 37), and
the musical analogy does convey not only the novel's effect on readers but also the
critical interrelatedness of the two narratives, an interrelatedness expressed at levels both
formal and thematic. However, that interrelatedness was quite blithely ignored in the
years following the novel's initial appearance, first in 1946 when Malcolm Cowley
scissored out "Old Man" for inclusion in his *Portable Faulkner*. Two years later New
American Library, treating the Mississippi convict's narrative as a novel, issued a paper-
back edition entitled *The Old Man*, following up later in the year with a paperback
edition of *The Wild Palms* that contained only Harry and Charlotte's story. Then, in
1954, they published yet another edition, this time including both stories, but printing
them as individual wholes, abandoning the interleaved, "contrapuntal" form in which
Faulkner constructed the novel. Finally, two years later, "Old Man" appeared yet again
by itself as one of the *Three Famous Short Novels* published by Modern Library. The effect
of these various editions, McHaney notes, "was that most readers first came to only half
of the novel in one of these divided texts, an experience that caused them to ignore
altogether the question of Faulkner's meaning and the purpose of the intricately related
plots" (McHaney 1975: xv).

Faulkner's novel received a similar, though not so long-lasting, disaggregation in
France: "Les palmiers sauvages" was printed through the first four numbers of the 1951
volume of Sartre's *Les temps modernes*, a redaction that, among other things, did indeed
make Harry Wilbourne's vow "la dernière phrase" of the work for its first French
readers. This was also the first "new" work of Faulkner's to appear in France after the
Nobel Prize, which fact made the novella's publication in Sartre's journal very much

an event. In 1952, the year Éditions Gallimard brought out the complete work, an essay on the novel by its translator, Maurice-Edgar Coindreau, appeared in the January issue of *Les temps modernes*, and it strongly urged readers to accept the challenge presented by such a seemingly disjointed text:

> The two sections of *The Wild Palms* . . . illuminate each other, and without their alternation the deepest meaning of each would remain concealed. But this meaning is the only one which matters. To say that "Old Man" gains by being printed and read independently of "Wild Palms" is to pretend that a fugue would be more beautiful if the answer and the counter-subject were detached from the subject. I realize that the separation of the two stories makes them easier to read. But if William Faulkner is occasionally obscure, he is not willfully so. His complexities, whether of content or form, are never gratuitous. Consequently, they ought to be respected. (Coindreau 1971: 62)

That this essay also appeared as the preface to the French edition of the novel perhaps accounts for the fact that, after its first, partial appearance in *Les temps modernes*, *Les palmiers sauvages* was subjected to none of the editorial indignities visited on its American counterpart: the French reading public apparently accepted Coindreau's assertion that the novel worked as an organic whole despite its bifurcated appearance.

McHaney and Coindreau are of course both correct in asserting that Faulkner's original intentions for the novel are lost if its two narratives are separated from each other, but it is worth keeping in mind that these editorial shenanigans proceeded with Faulkner's approval, usually grudging but always given. It is not always easy, in fact, to divine Faulkner's feelings about proposals to "excerpt" his work: sometimes he objected strenuously, other times he acquiesced almost carelessly. A 1946 letter to Random House senior editor Robert N. Linscott, written to cover *The Sound and the Fury* "Appendix" Faulkner had just produced for Cowley's *Portable*, is exemplary in this way. Faulkner objects strongly to treating the new piece as a kind of foreword to the novel (the idea "seems bad . . . a deliberate pandering to those who won't make the effort to understand the book"), yet he goes on to propose a new edition of *The Sound and the Fury* that would bind it together with the excerpted "Wild Palms" section of *The Wild Palms* (Blotner 1977: 228). Faulkner also gave his approval to what was one of the most flagrant examples of editorial meddling in his career, the aforementioned 1954 New American Library edition of *The Wild Palms* that printed the two stories back to back as self-contained units rather than as interlocked narratives. He admitted to his agent, Saxe Commins, that "[d]ismembering *The Wild Palms* will in my opinion destroy the over-all impact which I intended," but, now post-Nobel, he seems to have concluded that his artistic reputation was finally such as to "not need petty defending" (Blotner 1977: 352). Faulkner appeared willing, in other words, to tolerate a fairly high level of potential misunderstanding of his work so long as the various publishing schemes inviting such misunderstanding kept his books selling. Here, the seductive allurements of the market trumped the rigorous demands of art.

Add to this publication history developments of the recent past – the appearance of the corrected text, which turned *The Wild Palms* into *If I Forget Thee, Jerusalem*, and the adoption of that text as the basis for a revised French translation, *Si je t'oublie, Jérusalem* (which offers yet a fourth candidate for the novel's last words: "– Les femmes. Font chier!» fit le grand forçat" [Faulkner 2001: 351]) – and we find ourselves faced with a novel quite remarkably protean, even by the standards of an author who perpetually revisited and revised his material. Partly because of this odd publication history, a body of scholarship on *If I Forget Thee, Jerusalem* has only begun to take shape since the mid-1970s. McHaney's study was in fact among the first to recognize the novel as the serious and complex work it is, pointing out the multiple connections between the narratives, drawing out its allusions to the work of Dante and Hemingway (not only *A Farewell to Arms* but also "Hills Like White Elephants"), finding parallels in the novel's "philosophy" (if it can be called that) to the work of Schopenhauer and of Nietzsche, and going so far as to offer an interpretation of Harry's masturbation as he chooses grief over nothingness (McHaney 1975: 172–4). As valuable as McHaney's study is, however, it is limited by its insistence on passing judgment on Harry and Charlotte, dressing out the text with a poorly fitting "sin and redemption" schematic that reads the novel as an instantiation of the "endure and prevail" ethos of the Nobel Prize speech, an interpretive gambit common to a great deal of Cold War Faulkner scholarship. McHaney also gives "Old Man" a decidedly secondary status; though he adopts Faulkner's term, "counterpoint," to describe the relationship between the two stories, his reading treats "Old Man" more as an accompaniment to "Wild Palms." Most discomfiting for contemporary scholars, however – and not unrelated to the study's moralistic, myth-critical framework – is McHaney's strong condemnation of Charlotte, a condemnation that at times seems nearly misogynist in its intensity: Charlotte is "a female love buccaneer whose high regard for what she calls 'bitching' approaches an implied nymphomania"; she is "false and commercial," producing a debased art that provides the model for Harry's later brief career as an author of "primer-bald . . . sexual gumdrop[s]" (Faulkner 1990: 104); she is "deceived by notions of romantic love" (which McHaney assumes come from the sentimental counterparts of the convict's detective fiction, though Charlotte's reading matter is never specified), "and snar[es] the innocent Wilbourne into her scheme" (McHaney 1975: 11, 8, 31); she is, in short, a veritable Emma Bovary-*cum*-Mata Hari. McHaney's connecting of Charlotte's romanticism with the erotic titillations and deceptions of mass culture (Harry's onanism, however, signifies "a symbolic elevation of the object of procreation . . . the will to live" [McHaney 1975: 173]), and his condemnation of this self-involved, sentimental womanhood as simultaneously cloying and vicious, can be seen as a manifestation of the sort of modernist anxiety diagnosed by Andreas Huyssen in *After the Great Divide* (1988), and, as is to be expected, much recent scholarship on the novel has drawn on the tools of feminist analysis to take issue with McHaney's view. Anne Goodwyn Jones has gone so far as to praise *If I Forget Thee, Jerusalem* as "one of the few places in Faulkner's fiction where one can find not only popular culture but also an adult woman who is both actively and happily sexual and also appears to have intelligence, imagination, and a certain independence of spirit" (Jones 1990: 145), but other feminist analyses of the novel have been less sanguine, linking Charlotte's "painful, messy, sordid, and significantly 'female' death in a failed abortion" (Roberts 1994: 207) to the novel's last words in order to speculate that, far from celebrating or even mourning Charlotte's desire, *If I Forget Thee, Jerusalem* means to punish her for it and to show that women are, indeed, shit.

A middle space within these extremes has been carved out by scholars attending to how the novel seems to interrogate the gender norms that nonetheless are so important to the narrative (Jones promotes a version of this view, as well). Thus John Duvall and Minrose Gwin, in formulations indebted to the theoretical positions developed by French feminism, see the novel as questioning "binary construction[s] of gender" (Duvall 1990: 37) and as revealing the "bisexual nature of Faulkner's art" (Gwin 1990: 126). The difficulty with these readings is that, like McHaney's, they downplay the importance of "Old Man": Duvall and Jones write off the tall convict as the foil to Faulkner's cherished couple, an avatar of the patriarchal gender norms that Harry and Charlotte seek to evade and that, it is implied, take revenge on them; Gwin grounds her discussion of artistic bisexuality almost exclusively in "Wild Palms." In addition to paying so little attention to the issues highlighted in "Old Man," a narrative that blends Buster Keaton-style slapstick with highly wrought descriptions of a natural world gone haywire, these readings tend to render distinctly secondary (even as they acknowledge) the novel's concern with the entangled relationship between lowbrow mass culture and high art.

In recent years scholarship on the novel has redressed this lack of interest in "Old Man" by turning strongly toward this question, following Matthews's (1992) lead in his work on Faulkner's relationship to the culture industry (and the term coined by Theodor Adorno [Adorno and Horkheimer 1989] to describe the work of film, radio, publishing, and television manufactured under a capitalist regime of mass production is apropos here, since much of this scholarship reads Faulkner through Adorno). Though gender issues appear only rarely in this criticism, it is nonetheless the case that the central claim about the purpose of the novel's engagement with mass culture maps almost exactly (ideologically speaking) onto the gender readings of Gwin and Duvall (and other advocates of the novel's "androgynous" aesthetic). *If I Forget Thee, Jerusalem* seems to employ the tropes and techniques of the culture industry in much the same fashion that it employs the tropes and techniques of misogyny: in order to hollow out an inhuman, despotic power and thereby engender readers who are more critically aware of the social and political consequences of certain practices of cultural production and consumption. Thus over the course of several interrelated essays on the novel Richard Godden claims that Harry and the convict both appear as "prisoners" of "the same 'objective' reality, where reification touches every sphere of life" (Godden 1997: 221), a reification exemplified through the novel's echoing of the discourses of hard-boiled fiction (particularly the work of James M. Cain and Horace McCoy) and Hollywood films in a tissue of intertextuality that points to the completely prefabricated nature of the protagonists' experiences: "intertexuality . . . is a contentless principle of structure that allows all literature, indeed all discourse, to intersect. Intertextuality could be read as literary criticism for advanced capitalism" (Rhodes and Godden 1985: 97). For Godden, "Old Man" produces scenes and language that force the text's "reified 'specta-cle'... open, as Adorno said, 'irradiated by the light of its own self-determination'"; the convict's sojourn in the swamp, where he first appears to enjoy his unexpected freedom, "explodes with meanings, perceptual, judgmental, and economic, purging them of appropriation" (Rhodes and Godden 1985: 104–5). Even though this liberatory moment is "as rare as it is brief," the convict's release from the reified terms of his exis-tence serves to "nudge" readers along a "dialectical habit of mind" that cracks both "Old Man" and "Wild Palms" along the seams of their narrative fashioning, making readers critically aware of the novel's reliance elsewhere on the modes and forms of the culture industry and so, presumably, critically aware of those modes and forms when they encounter them on the screen or between soft covers (Godden 1997: 231). Peter Lurie likewise traces out the novel's engagement with the culture industry, but his reading departs from Godden's in a striking particular. He agrees that "Old Man" clearly treats ironically the world of culture industry melodrama evoked by the narrative of "Wild Palms," but he privileges the narrative differently: in casting the flooded Mis-sissippi as a two-dimensional mirror or movie screen that offers "no realist account of the landscape in which readers can place themselves," Faulkner "avoids the harbingers of novelistic 'verisimilitude and authenticity' such as realist description.... [T]he convict (despite his centrality in 'Old Man') possesses little interior life, depth, or psy-chology whereby readers are encouraged to (falsely) identify with him" (Lurie 2004: 133, 134). Thus for Godden readers must identify with the convict in his brief idyll of "free labor" (in every sense: like the Polish miners of "Wild Palms," he's never paid) in order to win critical purchase on the rest of *If I Forget Thee, Jerusalem*; for Lurie, however, it is the novel's persistent denial of the comforts of identification that makes it a sub-versive text. Lurie and Godden, then, like Gwin and Duvall, see *If I Forget Thee, Jerusalem* as working to reverse the terms of the discourse that bears it forward (in other words, to make the narrative flow backwards); all four readings grant that *If I Forget Thee, Jerusalem* is deeply implicated in some rather distasteful, even disgusting, rhetorical modes, but insist that the novel's posture toward its material saves it from being com-pletely engulfed by it, pointing to the text's implicit reliance on a classically modernist approach to the sentimental subject – irony – as the key to their readings. The fact that they locate this irony in wildly differing aspects of the novel, however, indicates that further critical work remains to be done.

As is frequently noted, Faulkner's original title for the novel was drawn from the 137th Psalm. Following is the King James translation, the one Faulkner almost cer-tainly knew best:

> By the rivers of Babylon, there we sat down, yea, we wept when we remembered Zion,
> We hanged our harps upon the willows in the midst thereof.
> For there they that carried us away captive required of us a song; and they that
> wasted us required of us mirth, saying, Sing us one of the songs of Zion!
> How shall we sing the Lord's song in a strange land?

If I forget thee, O Jerusalem, let my right hand forget her cunning.

If I do not remember thee, let my tongue cleave to the roof of my mouth; if I
  prefer not Jerusalem above my chief joy.

Remember, O Lord, the children of Edom in the day of Jerusalem; who said, Rase
  it, rase it even to the foundations thereof.

O daughter of Babylon, who art to be destroyed; happy shall he be, that rewardeth
  thee as thou hast served us.

Happy shall he be, that taketh and dasheth thy little ones against the stones.

McHaney has connected the psalm to the novel's concern with issues of freedom and
captivity, exemplified in the attempted escapes and fated imprisonments experienced
by Harry and the tall convict; though he gestures toward a reading that would link
the "cunning" hand of the psalm to Harry's hand as he masturbates in memory of
Charlotte, he doesn't pursue the analogy. François Pitavy, in his foreword to the revised
French translation of the corrected text, also notes the novel's concern with "cunning"
hands, even though, as he points out, the French translation of the psalm does not speak
of manual "cunning" ("Si je t'oublie, Jerusalem, que ma droite m'oublie!" [Faulkner
2001: 16) and even though the multiple English meanings of the homophone "palm"
do not translate (French relies on two different words, *palmier* and *paume*, to indicate
tree and hand; however, Pitavy believes that French readers understand as well, or
poorly, as their English counterparts the action accompanying Harry's last words [per-
sonal communication]). For many Faulkner scholars, the invocation of the psalm,
combined with the novel's engagement with the products of the culture industry, invites
an analogy linking Faulkner's Hollywood screenwriting "exile" to the captivity of the
Israelites; in this view, the cherished, never-to-be-forgotten "cunning" of the right hand
is novel writing, even though the hand of the "cunning" writer allows him to produce
work that satisfies the demands of Babylon. Vincent King's (1998) reading of the novel
draws out and develops precisely this point: Faulkner, like the psalmist of the Old
Testament, employs a double strategy in order to sing the song demanded of Babylon
while remaining true to his own artistic vision, and, as we have seen, much the same
view subtends those analyses of the novel that see it as critical of its own discourse.

If I Forget Thee, Jerusalem is indeed obsessed with what King (1998) calls the "use
and abuse of fiction," that is, the degree to which fictions of all brows and media – high,
low, and middle, literature and film – not only shape but confuse the conditions of
freedom and imprisonment. In being arrested for attempting a crime modeled on his
reading in the *Detectives' Gazette*, the tall convict is the novel's most frequently cited
avatar of the cultural dupe, but, as the readings of Lurie and Godden make clear, no
one in *If I Forget Three, Jerusalem* works without a script, and especially not Faulkner.
As compelling as this line of analysis is (and it is extraordinarily useful not only for
interpreting *If I Forget Thee, Jerusalem* but also for understanding Godard's later discomfort with *A bout de souffle*), these readings of the novel's "cunning" falter in adopting
a highly moralistic view of Harry's final act: for Godden, Harry's "sealed onanistic
chamber typifies the closed and rigid thought forms of commodity production, presenting themselves as immovable and eternal" (Rhodes and Godden 1985: 101); for Lurie,

the scene "offers a model of the way commercial film, like all commodity culture, stimulates consumers' desire, only to frustrate (but then sustain) it by refusing satisfaction" (Lurie 2004: 155). Thus the scene links Hollywood films to pornography, both

> [g]eneric, commodified forms of pleasure . . . [that] are underpinned by a common motive: to manipulate audience's desires for the sake of profit. Faulkner's larger concern . . . is that generic forms such as melodrama, the historical film, pulp fiction, and pornography all rely on a pleasure that is produced by the culture industry and whose nature is, finally, the same: projective, solipsistic, and melancholy [*sic*]. (Lurie 2004: 155)

Such interpretations of Harry's last gesture are appealing not least because they set the novel down firmly on the side of the culturally righteous; but the recent emergence of queer theory, which among other things has prompted reconsideration of representations of sex once deemed obvious in their import, should lead us to question what seem, on further consideration, rather conventional (if not vaguely Victorian) notions of proper sexual economy. It appears, in other words, that there remains something in *If I Forget Thee, Jerusalem*'s engagement with the culture industry that a redemptive reading of the novel finds irredeemably disgusting, and for reasons not so dissimilar, ultimately, to those McHaney gives for condemning Charlotte: the novel serves up as art material that, by rights, should only be shit. Harry's final words may well savor of the melodramatic, but they are also (as Patricia Franchini points out) quite beautiful, and in a way typically Faulknerian. In other words, it is possible that Faulkner's aim in *If I Forget Thee, Jerusalem* was not simply diagnostic but also interrogatory, in the sense that its production of pleasure forces us to examine not only our blind acceptance of reified experience as "natural" but also our "natural" revulsion. This is not to claim that *If I Forget Thee, Jerusalem* exonerates or valorizes those modes of cultural expression so damaging as to be killing; it is, though, to take seriously the possibility that the novel is a kind of plea for the guilty:

> "This case is closed," the judge said. "The accused is waiting sentence. Make your statement from there." Rittenmeyer stopped. He was not looking at the judge, he was not looking at anything, his face calm, impeccable, outrageous.
> "I wish to make a plea," he said. For a moment the judge did not move, staring at Rittenmeyer, the gavel still clutched in his fist like a sabre, then he leaned slowly forward, staring at Rittenmeyer: and Wilbourne heard it begin, the long in-sucking, the gathering of amazement and incredulity.
> "You what?" the judge said. "A what? A plea? For this man? This man who wilfully and deliberately performed an operation on your wife which he knew might cause her death and which did?" (Faulkner 1990: 269)

Francis Rittenmeyer is not allowed to speak, so his plea is never heard; we must look elsewhere for our sense of what a plea for the guilty might sound like. Though, as I have noted, Psalm 137 is the most widely cited intertext of the novel, it is also true that its last three lines are generally not allowed to speak in the scholarship (the exception is Grimwood 1987: 89–90), even though the prediction that the Lord's revenge upon the daughter of Babylon will entail the destruction of her and her "little ones" bears a gruesome parallel to Charlotte's fate; it may be precisely because the parallel can be drawn that scholars have been reluctant to engage it. The daughter of Babylon is guilty insofar as she abets the captivity of the Israelites; and it could be said that Meta Carpenter abetted Faulkner's "captivity" in Hollywood – indeed, the evidence suggests that she transformed it into an idyll of erotic pleasure whose contours bore a striking resemblance to that of Harry and Charlotte (the relationship was marked not only by intense sex but also by a "pattern of isolation and frugality" [Wilde and Borsten 1976: 60]), and to the extent that he surrendered to this captivity (and then sought to dash against stones the "little ones" it produced – perhaps the more sentimental, commercial aspects of his novel?), Faulkner was "guilty," too. Faulkner's own recollection of the link between the "ending" of the affair and the writing of the novel further complicates the relationship between psalm and text insofar as it admits to double casting: Carpenter, and by extension Hollywood (which Carpenter remembers Faulkner calling "this good ol' place" [Wilde and Borsten 1976: 277]), may be, no less than Yoknapatawpha and Oxford, the blissful, lost "Jerusalem" to be remembered. Along these lines, it is worth considering the possibility that it was in learning to appreciate the passions of his lover – Carpenter was an accomplished musician, and their two best friends in Hollywood were likewise musical – that Faulkner first got his idea for a "contrapuntal" novel. Thus the very structure of *If I Forget Thee, Jerusalem*, a crucial piece of evidence for those readings of the novel that see it as only critical of the culture industry (since the narrative alternation interrupts a potentially mesmerizing flow), may itself bear a guilty connection to Hollywood.

Taken together, Rittenmeyer's silent plea and the contradictory web of correspondences indicated by the conclusion of the psalm point to the importance of what is probably the novel's least attractive rhetorical feature, its discourse of "meat," a trope registering simultaneous disgust and affection. Charlotte's sculpted Falstaff is "gross with meat" (Faulkner 1990: 77); Charlotte and Harry's bourgeoisification in Chicago is "the mausoleum of love . . . the dead corpse borne between the olfactoryless walking shapes of the immortal unsentient demanding ancient meat" (Faulkner 1990: 118); the convict resentfully describes the pregnant woman as "female meat" (Faulkner 1990: 126, 144). The novel's obsession with "meat" reaches its apotheosis in Harry's musings on memory, musings that begin in a meditation on Charlotte's grave and end in his masturbation:

> he could imagine it, it would be a good deal like the park where he had waited, maybe even with children and nurses at times, the best, the very best; there would even be a headstone soon, at just exactly the right time, when restored earth and decorum stipulated, telling nothing; it would be clipped and green and quiet, the body, the shape of it under the drawn sheet, flat and small and moving in the hands of two men as if without weight though it did, nevertheless bearing and quiet beneath the iron weight of earth. *Only that cant be all of it* he thought. *It cant be. The waste. Not of meat, there is always plenty of meat. They found that out twenty years ago preserving nations and justifying mottoes – granted*

the nations the meat preserved are worth the preserving with the meat it took gone. But memory. Surely memory exists independent of the flesh. But this was wrong too. *Because it wouldn't know it was memory* he thought. *It wouldn't know what it was it remembered. So there's got to be the old meat, the old frail eradicable meat for memory to titillate. . . . So it is the old meat after all, no matter how old.* (Faulkner 1990: 265, 272)

The "old meat" that memory titillates is Harry's penis (another, littler "old man"), which, once taken in hand, "remembers" Charlotte in a way that makes Harry's body a kind of fleshly sonnet. As this passage implies, Harry concludes that total escape from the encumbrances of "meat" entails unacceptable "waste." One view of *If I Forget Thee, Jerusalem*, then, would take seriously the novel's economic refusal to let anything go to waste, no matter how repellent. This rejection of "waste" is, however, undertaken in service to a most wasteful (indeed, some might even say self-abusive) economy of "high" literary art, and in fact the self-involved, densely allusive quality of much modernist literature can itself seem more than slightly onanistic. The gratifications of "high" modernist expression are, too, guilty pleasures, and not only for Marxist reasons (i.e., the guilt involved in producing art while others suffer). Indeed, Faulkner's description of the experience of producing the novel as a kind of alienated writing in the dark describes *both* Hollywood screenwriting *and* Oxford novel writing. Thus one might say that *If I Forget Thee, Jerusalem* doesn't so much finally acquiesce to, or critique, a capitalist mode of mass production as weasel its way through it, and the work's sign for this cunning negotiation is the homophone (or pun), "palm," whose multiple meanings (as noun [a type of tree, the inside of the hand] and verb [to stroke with the inside of the hand, to trick, to defraud]) ramify through the text as a central revelation of the novel. On the one hand (so to speak), Faulkner produced despite moral censure a moving and dramatic narrative of boundless love and remarkable heroism in the face of natural disaster; on the other, he produced an extended, ruthless parody that ridiculed and pressed to the limits the pretensions not only of just such a narrative but also the equally highly stylized, putatively non-sentimental "art" literature of the prison world of "men without women" (among other things, Charlotte's fate reads beyond a prior fictional assurance that a matter of a woman's "meat" is "really not anything. It's just to let the air in" [Hemingway 1931: 75]). The scandal at the heart of *If I Forget Thee, Jerusalem*, then, is that it fuses together high and low, art and commerce, in a common expressive project such that they illuminate each other, and transform each other, *equally*, in the manner of true counterpoint. Faulkner couldn't tell whether his novel was "all right or absolute drivel" because, like the pun, it signifies in two directions at once in a manner most unruly — a manner wild, even savage.

Con

The cinema . . . can be everything at once, both judge and litigant.

Jean-Luc Godard, in Milne (1986: 208)

As we have seen, Bruce Kawin claims a central importance for *If I Forget Thee, Jerusalem* in Godard's *A bout de souffle*, but for Kawin Faulkner's centrality extends far beyond the moment of quotation in this single film and even beyond Godard: it encompasses the emergence of the New Wave itself. Kawin sees the 1952 publication of *Les palmiers sauvages* as a crucial moment for the development of New Wave cinema, insofar as its parallel but seemingly unrelated stories propose a model of narrative composition eschewing the long-dominant, Hollywood-based embrace of continuity editing in narrative film. Agnès Varda's 1956 *La pointe courte* "had placed together two separate plots . . . in an imitation of Faulkner's novel"; as Kawin notes, the film, which was edited by Alain Resnais, has been identified as "the first New Wave picture" (Kawin 1977: 147). Though *A bout de souffle* is concerned with only one narrative, its famous jump cuts and *faux raccords* can be seen likewise to signal the discontinuity and "unresolution" of Faulkner's fiction (Kawin 1977: 150). Thus Kawin asserts a central place for Faulkner not only in literary history but in film history, a place that depends "not on Faulkner's films [that is, his screenplays] but on the influence of his fiction. . . . [H]e used such unusual tropes as montage, freeze-frames, superimposition, flashback, and perspective distortion, as well as sound-overlap and sound/image conflict" such that his work

> kept the traditions of radical subjectivity, of montage, and the "metaphysics of time" alive during the period when the coming of sound had rendered montage unfashionable and the economics of the film industry had militated against "visionary" experimentation. Although it remains to be established whether Faulkner hit on these techniques through the films he might have seen in Paris in 1925–26, or conceived them in strictly literary terms (finding most of them in *Ulysses*), it is clear that he is one of the central figures in cinema's rediscovery of its own narrative – and *anti*-narrative – potential. . . . Godard has been putting Faulkner on film throughout his career. (Kawin 1977: 147–8, 153)

There is much merit in Kawin's analysis, but his desire to make a case for Faulkner's influence leads him to disregard other developments within cinema itself that cannot be traced directly to Faulkner but that nonetheless had a strong effect on Godard's first picture (and on his subsequent cinematic practice). Not least of these is the unprecedentedly wide circulation of American films in France in the years immediately following World War II.

Before the war, France protected its domestic film industry with quotas restricting the importation of foreign films, especially American films. But in 1946, and almost certainly as a condition of access to Marshall Plan funds, France approved the Blum/ Byrnes accord, an agreement that revoked the prewar quotas and established France as "a free market as far as the American [film] industry was concerned" (Guback 1969: 21). Rather than an import quota, the accord established a screen-time quota: just four weeks out of the year were set aside for the screening of French films. The particulars of this treaty combined with what Motion Picture Association of America then-President Eric Johnston called a "tremendous backlog of pictures that had not been shown in most foreign countries" during the war to result in "these pictures flood[ing] in, even more than the countries could absorb" (Guback 1969: 16). Thus within a year of the signing of the accord French film production fell by 23 percent; by the end of 1947, "more than half of the French studios were said to have suspended operation, and unemployment reportedly rose to more than 75 percent in some branches of the industry" (Guback 1969: 22). According to Guback, the outcry was such that in 1948 a new five-year agreement was signed that reinstated import quotas and raised the portion of screen time that exhibitors were required to devote to French films – though American films continued to enjoy preferential import treatment compared to that granted other countries (Guback 1969: 22).

It was against this volatile and hardly romantic "rapprochement franco-américain" that Godard and his cohorts at the *Cahiers du Cinéma* began their reassessment of the state of French cinema, and it was a reassessment that proceeded largely by comparing French and American films (with crucial detours into Italian neo-realism). The hegemony of the American film industry, which enjoyed an economy of scale that the much smaller, war-damaged industries of Europe could never hope to match, was a sore point, and to some degree the championing in the pages of *Cahiers* of directors like Howard Hawks, Nicholas Ray, Alfred Hitchcock, Anthony Mann, Robert Aldrich, and Samuel Fuller (to offer a list indicating the catholic range of the *Cahiers* critics' enthusiasms) was deliberately provocative. Still, and as Jim Hillier points out, the upward revaluation of American film undertaken by the *Cahiers* crowd was not entirely unprecedented; André Bazin's work on Hollywood preceded his affiliation with the journal, and the critics at the more left-leaning *Positif* were embarked on a similarly revisionist project (Hillier 1985: 1–2). What distinguished the *Cahiers* view was the journal's willingness to take seriously films other critics wrote off as lightweight fluff or trash, and to see those films as having been *authored*:

> If the *politique des auteurs* caused ripples, and more, in French film culture and beyond, it was not because of the idea itself but because the idea was used in *Cahiers* with polemical brio to upset established values and reputations. There was nothing new or scandalous in . . . discussing, say, Murnau, Buñuel, Dreyer, Eisenstein, Renoir, Cocteau or Bresson or, from the USA, Stroheim or Welles or Chaplin, as the *auteurs* of their films. It was a slightly different matter – but only slightly – to propose, say, Howard Hawks as an *auteur*, mainly because, unlike Stroheim, Welles, or Chaplin, Hawks had not been noticeably in conflict with the production system. It was perhaps a significantly different matter when the cultural perspectives brought to bear on the proposal of Hawks as *auteur* of Westerns, gangster movies and comedies derived their terms from classical literature, philosophy or the history of art. It verged on positive outrage when, at the end of the 1950s and the beginning of the 1960s, such perspectives were brought to bear on, say, Vincente Minnelli or Samuel Fuller, not to mention Don Weis or Edward Ludwig. In other words, the closer *Cahiers* moved to what had been traditionally conceived as the "conveyor belt" end of the cinema spectrum, the more their "serious" discussion of film-makers seemed outrageously inappropriate. As it happens . . . the more they outraged in this way, the more acutely they raised crucial questions, however unsystematically, about the status and criticism

appropriate to film as an art form in which unsystematic divisions were constantly being made between art and commerce. If *Cahiers* came to be associated primarily with American cinema and a revaluation of its status, it was not because they talked about American cinema more than about other cinema – quite simply, they did not – but because American cinema as a whole, so generally ignored, misunderstood or undervalued, provided the most obvious site for engagement with these critical questions. (Hillier 1985: 7)

As an example of the dramatic, and swift, effect *Cahiers* criticism had on the European reception of Hollywood films, Hillier gives a striking "before and after" example in the *Guardian* reviews of Howard Hawks's *Rio Bravo*. At its first release in 1959, the film was described as "a typical Western of this age of the long-winded, large screen. . . . a soporofic 'blockbuster.' " On its re-release in 1963, however, it was hailed as a "gem": "*Rio Bravo* is . . . first and last a Howard Hawks film. For those who know Hawks this should be enough; for those who don't, it means that *Rio Bravo* is an example of the classical, pre-Welles school of American film-making at its most deceptively simple: broad lines, level glances, grand design, elementary emotions" (Hillier 1985: 11–12).

It is undoubtedly the case that more than a portion of this revaluation was driven less by the quality of the films themselves than by an effort to find some way to live with the postwar "flooding" of American films into European theaters – to deliberately look away from the social, economic, and political issues in Gaullist France that the American invasion betokened. But Godard's film, produced in the moment of ascendancy of what some have termed *Cahiers'* "culturally conservative, politically reactionary attempt to remove film from the realm of social and political concern" (Hillier 1985: 6), shows that the implications of the *politique des auteurs* were at least as interrogative as they were recuperative. Indeed, Annette Michelson has argued that, far from promoting a culturally conservative agenda, the *politique des auteurs* was "a concerted attempt to stem the advancing tide of American hegemony in the international market of the film industry, and in the domination of the studio system, whose model . . . had been the automotive industry's total rationalization and perfection of the principle of the division of labor" (in Milne 1986: vi).

It is a commonplace in the criticism to note that *A bout de souffle* is stitched together out of quotations from American gangster pictures (what the French, in a renaming that has stuck, termed film noir), Westerns, and melodrama: like *If I Forget Thee, Jerusalem*, *A bout de souffle* is an intertextual text. The usual view of this use of allusion and quotation in Godard's film grants that it tends toward a cultural conservatism, but also praises its highly artistic (i.e., ironic) practice as a kind of cheeky *hommage* to genre pictures that has a certain philosophical point. As Dudley Andrew has observed,

[t]he theme of the film, like the essence of its hero, is precisely the futile struggle to be original "in the manner of" something or someone else. The notion of individuality and of forthrightness is as American as the movies, and as fully processed. Since there can be no escaping genre, since freedom is attainable only within or against genre, Godard the *cinéphile* embraces it. And he chooses the genre that most promoted and problematized freedom, the *film noir*. (Andrew 1987: 12)

Though he is more interested in Godard's later meditations on the problem of freedom imagined through psychological coherence, and so less sanguine than Andrew, Kline too asserts that the film is imprisoned in its "free" expressive mode: "Michel, as character, enjoys a nonproblematical status guaranteed him by the warmed-over American essentialism of the film" (Kline 1992: 202); that is, Michel assumes a "liberty" that the canny critic recognizes as completely prefabricated (in Andrew's words, the "fully processed" American belief in "individuality" and "forthrightness"). This is not a surprising view given Kline's (rather odd) assertion that Faulkner, for Godard, presents an ultimately false model of American psychological "coherence" (Kline 1992: 220), but it is one deserving interrogation.

If I have suggested that Faulkner's novel is somewhat less subversive of the seductions of the culture industry than might be wished, I would like to propose also that Godard's film is less complacent in the face of those seductions than has been asserted. In the first spoken line of the film, Michel identifies himself as an idiot driven by compulsion ("All in all, I'm a dumb bastard. [Après tout, j'suis con.] All in all, if you've got to, you've got to!" [Andrew 1987: 33]), and through the course of the film he largely lives up to that self-description. Belmondo's undeniable charm, which Godard put to more than good use (the engaging way he addresses the camera while telling those who dislike France to go fuck themselves is a case in point), has worked to turn critics away from a too-careful exploration of the gap that opens up precisely between Michel's triumphalist American belief in absolute individual freedom and his deeply circumscribed postwar French reality, a disjunction that is crucial to the meaning of the film. Or rather, critics have preferred to trace that disjunction to Jean Seberg's Patricia, who is no less of a US mass-culture dupe than Michel (he wants to be "Bogie," she wishes her name were Ingrid) but who, precisely by virtue of her Americanness, manages to escape the deadly consequences of this fantasy (*après tout*, *her* national fantasy, not Michel's) and so can be made out to be the target of all of the film's meditations on inauthenticity; in other words, many critics read Patricia in much the same way McHaney reads Charlotte (there is something of this in Kawin's interpretation). But a *cherchez la femme* reading of cultural reification is no more satisfying for Godard's film than it is for Faulkner's novel, and for much the same reasons: *A bout de souffle*'s relationship to the culture industry is as disturbingly unsettled as that of *If I Forget Thee, Jerusalem*, with tropes both of complicity and of resistance attaching themselves to nearly every available surface.

As Pamela Falkenberg has pointed out, *A bout de souffle* "might be described as a simultaneous and double rewriting: the rewriting of the French commercial cinema (conceived of as a transformation) through the rewriting of the Hollywood commercial cinema (conceived of as a reproduction): the real art cinema as Hollywood" (Falkenberg 1985: 44). I cannot do justice here to Falkenberg's suggestive essay, which adopts Baudrillard's work on simulation in order to explore the relationship between Godard's "art" film and, on the one hand, the American crime melodramas that it cites and, on the other, Jim McBride's 1983 Hollywood remake, *Breathless*. Falkenberg's central claim, however – "The art cinema is both without and within the commercial cinema and

exists on both sides of the difference that its vacillation secures" (Falkenberg 1985: 48)
– captures exactly the point I mean to make here about the expressive complications
Godard's film and Faulkner's novel face in attempting to produce a "successful" critique
of the culture industry (i.e., one that sells) by adopting expressive modes peculiar to it.
Much as Faulkner's novel turns on the disquieting attributes of the homophone,
Godard's film is marked by a pun – *c'est pareil* (it's the same) and *séparé* (separated) – that
literalizes the vacillation Falkenberg identifies. The pun unfolds over two widely separated (though parallel) scenes, the first in Patricia's hotel room:

> Michel: Why did you slap me when I looked at your legs?
> Patricia: It wasn't my legs.
> Michel: It's exactly the same. [C'est exactement pareil.]
> Patricia: The French always say things are the same [sont pareil] when they aren't at all.
> Michel: I've found something nice to say, Patricia.
> Patricia: What?
> Michel: I want to sleep with you because you're beautiful.
> Patricia: No, I'm not.
> Michel: Then because you're ugly.
> Patricia: It's the same? [C'est pareil?]
> Michel: Sure, my little girl, it's the same [c'est pareil]. (Andrew 1987: 76)

the second in the model's apartment:

> Patricia: It's sad to fall asleep. You have to . . . sepa . . . [sépa . . .]
> Michel: . . . rate [. . . ré]
> Patricia: . . . to separate [séparé]. They say, "sleep together," but it's not true. (Andrew 1987: 134)

Along with *con* and *dégueulasse*, the words that open and close *A bout de souffle* and that
are repeated throughout in varying contexts, this play of *c'est pareil/séparé* signals the
central concern of the film: how are two ostensibly similar things nevertheless deemed
separate? How do the separate become similar? What's truly idiotic, or disgusting? The
pun in *A bout de souffle* works much as Faulkner's wild and cunning palm does in *If I
Forget Thee, Jerusalem*: it opens up simultaneous and mutually contradictory possibilities
of meaning precisely around the problem of determining "proper" (sexual, cultural,
aesthetic) expression and gratification.

   Thus the importance of Faulkner's novel to Godard's film lies less in the way the
narrative of *If I Forget Thee, Jerusalem* aligns (whether sincerely or ironically) with that
of *A bout de souffle* than in the fact that author and *auteur* were embarked on similar
projects of cultural interrogation. What Godard saw in Faulkner's novel, and what he
put into his film, were not only its technical innovations in structure and expression,
not only the "story line" of sex and death (separate, yet somehow the same), but also
the work's problematic – indeed, tortured – effort to find a place to stand in a cultural

landscape that had seen once-obvious distinctions between the high ground and the low flooded over and flattened out into a puzzling sameness. Godard's decision to combine high with low (Picasso, Renoir, Klee, Bach, Mozart – and Faulkner; Bogart, Aldrich, Fuller, Radio Luxembourg, *Paris Flirt* comics, and Preminger) illuminates that landscape in a manner he imagined both serious and substantive. Two years after the release of the film, though, Godard would describe *A bout de souffle* as *"Alice in Wonderland"* (Milne 1986: 175); later still, it would be "a film I've always been ashamed of . . . a film that came out of fascism" (Kline 1992: 185).

Michel may be a dumb bastard, but he is Godard's dumb bastard, and in one crucial respect he did in fact speak for his creator: in the wake of the movements of 1968, Godard embraced a Maoist politics and turned his back on commercial film production, choosing, over a career of compromising "grief," a life in cinema that for many years would be, at least commercially speaking, close to "nothing." As is well known, this is not the path that Faulkner chose: though he complained about invasions of privacy in the post-Nobel period, Faulkner nevertheless enjoyed the acclaim and increasingly wrote, in the twilight of his career, works that were quite consonant with the demands of the market, both formally and ideologically (*The Town, The Reivers*). Both artists, in other words, turned away from an aesthetic practice that would persist in reading high art and mass culture in terms of each other in favor of producing work more clearly "legible" on the cultural landscape. Which turn is courageously liberatory, which delusionally complicit, is actually harder to say than may at first appear: clearly, in the political realm, an unforgiving insistence on "all or nothing" can be as much terrorist as noble and, as Falkenberg makes clear, commerce and art are not so easily separated to begin with. Which is to say, finally, that though Faulkner and Godard moved on from (or rather, abandoned) the flooded fun-house cultural landscapes of *If I Forget Thee, Jerusalem* and *A bout de souffle*, they did so without having enjoyed a last word on the relationship between high and low. For those of us who persist in some final verdict, some summative judgment, both texts have the same non-answer: art, shit.

NOTE

1   English translations are drawn from Andrew (1987). French dialogue is taken from the Winstar DVD.

REFERENCES AND FURTHER READING

Adorno, T. and M. Horkheimer (1989). *Dialectic of Enlightenment* (trans. J. Cumming). New York: Continuum. (Original pub. 1944.)

Andrew, D. (1987). *Breathless*. New Brunswick, NJ: Rutgers University Press.

Blotner, J. (1977). *Selected Letters of William Faulkner*. New York: Random House.

Coindreau, M.-E. (1971). *The Time of William Faulkner: A French View of Modern American Fiction* (trans. G. M. Reeves). Columbia: University of South Carolina Press.

Duvall, J. (1990). *Faulkner's Marginal Couple: Invincible, Outlaw, and Unspeakable Communities.* Austin, TX: University of Texas Press.

Falkenberg, P. (1985). "Hollywood" and the "Art Cinema" as a Bipolar Modeling System: *A bout de souffle* and *Breathless. Wide Angle*, 7(3): 44–53.

Faulkner, W. (1939). *The Wild Palms.* New York: Random House.

Faulkner, W. (1952). *Les palmiers sauvages* (trans. M.-E. Coindreau). Paris: Éditions Gallimard.

Faulkner, W. (1990). *If I Forget Thee, Jerusalem.* New York: Vintage. (Original pub. 1939.)

Faulkner, W. (2001). *Si je t'oublie, Jérusalem* (trans. M.-E. Coindreau and F. Pitavy). Paris: Éditions Gallimard. (Original pub. 1952.)

Godard, J.-L. (1960). *A bout de souffle.* Impéria Films, Société de Vouvelle de Cinéma. (Winstar Video DVD, 2001.)

Godden, R. (1997). *Fictions of Labor: William Faulkner and the South's Long Revolution.* Cambridge: Cambridge University Press.

Gray, R. (1994). *The Life of William Faulkner: A Critical Biography.* Oxford: Blackwell.

Grimwood, M. (1987). *Heart in Conflict: Faulkner's Struggles with Vocation.* Athens, GA: University of Georgia Press.

Guback, T. H. (1969). *The International Film Industry: Western Europe and America since 1945.* Bloomington: Indiana University Press.

Gwin, M. C. (1990). *The Feminine and Faulkner: Reading (Beyond) Sexual Difference.* Knoxville: University of Tennessee Press.

Gwynn, F. L. and J. Blotner (1959). *Faulkner in the University: Class Conferences at the University of Virginia, 1957–1958.* Charlottesville, VA: University Press of Virginia.

Hemingway, E. (1931). *Men Without Women: Stories.* London: Jonathan Cape. (Original pub. 1928.)

Hillier, J. (1985). *Cahiers du Cinéma: The 1950s: Neo-Realism, Hollywood, The New Wave.* Cambridge, MA: Harvard University Press.

Huyssen, A. (1988). *After the Great Divide: Modernism, Mass Culture, Postmodernity.* London: Macmillan. (Original pub. 1986.)

Jones, A. G. (1990). "The Kotex Age": Women, Popular Culture, and *The Wild Palms.* In D. Fowler and A. J. Abadie (eds.). *Faulkner and Popular Culture: Faulkner and Yoknapatawpha, 1988* (pp. 142–62). Jackson: University Press of Mississippi.

Kawin, B. (1977). *Faulkner and Film.* New York: Frederick Ungar.

King, V. A. (1998). The Wages of Pulp: The Use and Abuse of Fiction in William Faulkner's *The Wild Palms. Mississippi Quarterly*, 51(3): 503–25.

Kline, T. J. (1992). *Screening the Text: Intertextuality in New Wave French Cinema.* Baltimore: Johns Hopkins University Press.

Lurie, P. (2004). *Vision's Immanence: Faulkner, Film, and the Popular Imagination.* Baltimore: Johns Hopkins University Press.

Matthews, J. T. (1992). Shortened Stories: Faulkner and the Market. In E. Harrington and A. J. Abadie (eds.). *Faulkner and the Short Story: Faulkner and Yoknapatawpha, 1990* (pp. 3–37). Jackson: University Press of Mississippi.

Matthews, J. T. (1995). Faulkner and the Culture Industry. In P. Weinstein (ed.). *The Cambridge Companion to William Faulkner* (pp. 51–74). Cambridge: Cambridge University Press.

McCabe, C. (1980). *Godard: Images, Sound, Politics.* London: Macmillan.

McHaney, T. L. (1975). *William Faulkner's The Wild Palms: A Study.* Jackson: University Press of Mississippi.

Milne, T. (1986). *Godard on Godard.* Cambridge, MA: Da Capo Press. (Original pub. 1972.)

Rhodes, P. and R. Godden (1985). *The Wild Palms*: Degraded Culture, Devalued Texts. In M. Gresset and N. Polk (eds.). *Intertextuality in Faulkner* (pp. 87–113). Jackson: University Press of Mississippi.

Roberts, D. (1994). *Faulkner and Southern Womanhood.* Athens, GA: University of Georgia Press.

Wilde, M. C. and O. Borsten (1976). *A Loving Gentleman: The Love Story of William Faulkner and Meta Carpenter.* New York: Simon and Schuster.

5

The Synthesis of Marx and Freud in Recent Faulkner Criticism

Michael Zeitlin

In his influential essay, "What is an Author?," Michel Foucault describes Marx and Freud as modernity's central cultural theorists, its "founders of discursivity,"

> unique in that they are not just the authors of their own works. They have produced something else: the possibilities and the rules for the formation of other texts. . . . Freud is not just the author of *The Interpretation of Dreams* or *Jokes and Their Relation to the Unconscious*; Marx is not just the author of the *Communist Manifesto* or *Das Kapital*: they both have established an endless possibility of discourse. (Foucault 1984: 114)

In the work of such figures as Foucault himself, Jacques Derrida, Louis Althusser, Jacques Lacan, Mikhail Bakhtin, Fredric Jameson, Raymond Williams, Theodor Adorno, Max Horkheimer, Walter Benjamin, and Herbert Marcuse (the list could be extended considerably of course), and in such broader intellectual formations as "cultural studies," "new historicism," "historical materialism," "post-Marxism," "post-Freudianism," and "postmodernism," Marx and Freud have shown themselves to be nearly inexhaustible sources of new theoretical and textual production. Refusing, in other words, to remain locked away within the historical scenes of their founding intellectual acts, Marx and Freud have continued to be present participants in the dialogical transformation of their own thought, regenerating the "possibility for something other than their discourse, yet something belonging to what they founded" (Foucault 1984: 114).

In this process of often heated engagement and revision, unfolding over a period of well over one hundred years and counting, certain concepts and propositions in their work have been judged to be false, dead, obsolete, or damaging, but for Foucault, "when trying to seize the act of founding, one sets aside those statements that are not pertinent, either because they are deemed inessential, or because they are considered 'prehistoric' and derived from another type of discursivity" (Foucault 1984: 116). In the case of feminism's engagement with Freud, this process of "setting aside" has not always been deemed possible or even desirable (a comprehensive dismissal of his thought, in extreme cases, being preferred), yet at least since Simone de Beauvoir's *The Second Sex* (1953) and Betty Friedan's *The Feminine Mystique* (1963), the question of what is dead, and what might still be valuable, in Freud's thought has remained polemically urgent. In de Beauvoir and Friedan, as in the work of Luce Irigaray, Hélène Cixous, Julia Kristeva, Judith Butler, Jacqueline Rose, and Juliet Mitchell, among many others, psychoanalysis continues to drive the developing theories of identity and gender formation. In the words of Rose, psychoanalysis

> gives an account of how the status of the phallus in human sexuality enjoins on the woman a definition in which she is simultaneously symptom and myth. As long as we continue to feel the effects of that definition we cannot afford to ignore [it]. . . . Psycho-analysis does not produce that definition. It gives an account of how that definition is produced. (Rose 1985: 57)

In the case of Marx, such slogans as "the dictatorship of the proletariat" or "the withering away of the state" have taken on an uncanny, grotesque quality (to all except any current apologists of Stalin and Mao). Yet for all that may be characterized as merely historic (or "prehistoric") in their work, Freud and Marx, as "founders of discursivity" in Foucault's sense, continue to generate "the possibilities and the rules for the formation of other texts" (Foucault 1984: 114), including the possibility that genuine theoretical insight – into the material and historical conditions of social conflict, or into the formation of subjectivity amidst the libidinal and ideological pressures of family life – can be achieved.

In the discussion which follows, my goal is not to enter into debates about the vitality or obsolescence of Freudian and Marxian thought but merely to define some of the ways in which it has assumed a significant place in recent Faulkner criticism. As read by Faulkner critics, or as mobilized through a series of mediating figures and exegetes, or merely as a felt source of conceptual pressures or political commitments, Marx and Freud have generated a series of key questions driving a series of significant explorations into Faulkner's fictional domain and the historical and biographical contexts into which it extends (across its sometimes resistant and refractive, sometimes permeable and porous borders).

Many Faulkner critics have been drawn to Freud's texts and theories in the recognition that psychoanalysis was a pervasive cultural force during the time of Faulkner's development as a novelist who would himself become a "founder of discursivity" in *The Sound and the Fury* (1929) and the succeeding novels of his great central period. As John T. Irwin claims,

> In dealing with Freud's writings as literary/philosophical texts, I have tried to present certain structures like the Oedipus complex, the death instinct, and the repetition compulsion in . . . their classically Freudian form, devoid of later clinical revision. I have done this because my approach to these structures is, in part, historical as well as literary and

philosophic. . . . I have tried to evoke the general understanding of certain major psycho-analytic structures contemporary with the writing of Faulkner's novels. (Irwin 1996: 4)

If Faulkner critics like Irwin, Bleikasten (1990), Gresset (1989), Polk (1996), and Weinstein (1992) sometimes organize Faulkner's texts according to classical Freudian categories and concepts, that is because those texts, as a strict matter of cultural history, compositional structure, and narrative content, explicitly deal with or implicitly act out scenes of incest, narcissism, the Oedipus complex, the castration complex, and so on. To the extent that such psychoanalytic scenes are invariably rooted in the conflicts and calamities of a social life understood as being resolutely historical, Faulkner critics have equally been drawn to Marxian theory to help show how Faulkner's human subjects are shaped and constrained by their laboring condition and those material, economic, and political forces which define it. Faulkner's fiction itself, that is, has helped to determine the methods and critical modes with which the critics have approached it.

Marx

For Marx, "The history of all hitherto existing society is the history of class struggles" (Marx and Engels 1969: 13):

> Freeman and slave, patrician and plebeian, lord and serf, guild-master and journeyman, in a word; oppressor and oppressed, stood in constant opposition to one another, carried on an uninterrupted, now hidden, now open fight, a fight that each time ended, either in a revolutionary re-constitution of society at large, or in the common ruin of the contending classes. (Marx and Engels 1969: 14)

The pre-revolutionary struggles of contending groups over power and property have produced "manifold graduations of social rank" ("in ancient Rome we have patricians, knights, plebeians, slaves; in the Middle Ages, feudal lords, vassals, guild-masters, journeymen, apprentices, serfs; in almost all of these classes, again, subordinate gradations" [Marx and Engels 1969: 14]). Yet in the "epoch of the bourgeoisie" (i.e., modernity, the Industrial Revolution), class antagonisms have become radically simplified: "Society as a whole is more and more splitting up into two great hostile camps, into two great classes directly facing each other: Bourgeoisie and Proletariat" (Marx and Engels 1969: 15). These two great classes, whether they fully realize it or not, are at war, the one profiting nakedly from the labor, misery, and oppression of the other. "By bourgeoisie is meant the class of modern Capitalists, owners of the means of social production and employers of wage-labor. By proletariat, the class of modern wage-laborers who, having no means of production of their own, are reduced to selling their labor-power in order to live" (Marx and Engels 1969: 13).

A major trend of recent Faulkner criticism has sought to transpose Marx's scheme of urban class struggle in nineteenth-century Europe to the complicated economic, class, and racial caste systems of Faulkner's South, primarily the South of the 1920s to 1940s as the place from which the Old South is remembered and mythologized. For Myra Jehlen's *Class and Character in Faulkner's South*, the first sustained Marxian inquiry into Faulkner's novels, "the underlying organizing principle in their social structure is class, more precisely the division between two classes of white society, the planters and the 'rednecks'" (Jehlen 1976: 9). More recent criticism has been committed to exploring how the division between planters and rednecks is prodigiously complicated by divisions between, on one hand, planters and slaves and, on the other, slaves (and newly freed slaves) and poor whites. All these divisions, and the "legacy of violently maintained labor relations" (Godden 1997: 2) which sustains them, are obscured by contorted ideological alliances between the owners and those whom they oppress (such alliances marked, for example, by the image of the liveried black servant, or the story of Wash Jones's worship of Thomas Sutpen in *Absalom, Absalom!*). In turn, the black servants and poor whites, despite whatever interests they might "objectively" have in common, are sustained in a relation of mutual antagonism by a vicious ideology of racial contradiction magnified by a system of "economic rivalry . . . which was to send Snopes in droves into the Ku Klux Klan" (Faulkner 2004c: 19).

Thus in a Marxian sense, the Civil War did not bring slavery to an end. In accordance with the market imperatives of the emergent "bourgeois epoch," which "resolved personal worth into exchange value, and in place of the numberless indefeasible chartered freedoms . . . set up that single, unconscionable freedom – Free Trade" (Marx and Engels 1969: 19), the agrarian poor, black and white, were transformed into wage slaves. In Richard Godden's formulation, Faulkner's major novels are thus *Fictions of Labor* representing (whether directly or indirectly) the historical passage of Southern agrarian workers "through forms of bondage to waged 'freedom'" (Godden 1997: 3). "These laborers, who must sell themselves piecemeal, are a commodity, like every other article of commerce, and are consequently exposed to all the vicissitudes of competition, to all the fluctuations of the market" (Marx and Engels 1969: 27), including the market for cotton sown in "fields where the cotton is mortgaged in February, planted in May, harvested in September and put into the Farm Loan in October in order to pay off February's mortgage in order to mortgage next year's crop" (Faulkner 2004c: 36–7). The landlords themselves, threatened by the "disappearance of a traditional South and . . . the emergence of a modern, deregionalized America" (Zender 1989: x), find their own land-based wealth and status under siege by "the rise of the redneck," the loss of black labor to "the Great Migration" (Lester 1995), and the augmenting pressures emanating from an industrializing North with its staggering concentrations of capital. As Faulkner noted in his 1933 introduction to *The Sound and the Fury*,

> But the South, as Chicago is the Middlewest and New York the East, is dead, killed by the Civil War. There is a thing known whimsically as the New South to be sure, but it is not the south. It is a land of immigrants who are rebuilding the towns and cities into replicas of towns and cities in Kansas and Iowa and Illinois, with skyscrapers and striped canvas awnings instead of wooden balconies, and teaching the young men who sell the

gasoline and the waitresses in the restaurants to say O yeah? and to speak with hard r's. (Faulkner 1994: 229)

In *The Sound and the Fury: Faulkner and the Lost Cause*, John T. Matthews situates the novel within this large-scale scene of economic and cultural transformation, focusing attention on the "conversion of the former planter class (in the generation of Jason's grandfather) into the new mercantile class" (Matthews 1991: 6) which Jason Compson, the narrator of the third section of the novel, is now in danger of falling out of altogether. As Marx and Engels observed in 1848,

> The low strata of the middle-class – the small tradespeople, shopkeepers, and retired tradesmen generally, the handicraftsmen and peasants – all these sink gradually into the proletariat, partly because their diminutive capital does not suffice for the scale on which Modern Industry is carried on, and is swamped in the competition with the large capitalists, partly because their specialized skill is rendered worthless by new methods of production. Thus the proletariat is recruited from all classes of the population. (Marx and Engels 1969: 29)

In exploring the complex social history of Faulkner's South, recent critics have been drawn to a number of crucial sites, or "primal scenes," in Faulkner's novels, scenes representing the sudden revelation of an essentially traumatic reality. For Godden, the essential trauma in Faulkner "is a labor trauma, centered on a primal scene of recognition during which white passes into black and black passes into white along perceptual tracks necessitated by a singular and pervasively coercive system of production" (Godden 1997: 1). For Richard Moreland the "primal scene" drives the tragic repetitions of history, its legacy of "violent social exclusions" (Moreland 1990: 9). Among the key primal scenes in Faulkner's fiction would be young Thomas Sutpen's humiliation by the black servant at the front door of the owner's mansion in *Absalom, Absalom!*, and the short story, "Barn Burning," which Moreland reads as a "compulsive repetition" of the earlier scene. In "Barn Burning," a young, poor white boy, Sarty Snopes, sees the de Spain plantation for the first time and is staggered – indeed traumatized and "mystified" – by its physical and symbolic magnificence. Sensing this, the boy's father, Ab Snopes, exposes the imposture which sustains the beautiful plantation house and its "Old South" ideological aura: " 'Pretty and white, ain't it?' [Ab] said. 'That's sweat. Nigger sweat. Maybe it ain't white enough yet to suit him. Maybe he wants to mix some white sweat with it' " (Faulkner 1977: 12). Stolen from the poor whites and black servants, labor is somehow magically transformed into the leisure of the owning classes and the opulent "surplus value" of their houses.

As the scene unfolds from this point, it "concentrates and intensifies" (Williams 1977: 100) "a generative social trauma constituting its formal core" (Godden 1997: 1): blocked by a black servant at the front door, Ab Snopes barges past him (thus "undoing" the earlier paralysis of young Thomas Sutpen) in order to deface the owner's pale rug with a smear, or "signature," of manure. The story reveals how "the now nostalgically idealized myth of the plantation" (Moreland 1990: 13), what Faulkner himself called the "makebelieve region of swords and magnolias and mockingbirds which perhaps never existed anywhere" (Faulkner 1994: 229), "effectively holds within it the place of what this imaginary scene must 'repress,' exclude, force out, in order to constitute itself" (Žižek 1991: 52) – that is, the "other" scene of stolen labor, rape, lynching, or miscegenation (as in Ike McCaslin's traumatic discoveries in the fourth part of "The Bear" and in "Delta Autumn" of *Go Down, Moses*).

(Counter-)Hegemony

Moreland marks the presence of a major trend in recent Faulkner criticism by noting its commitment to recovering "the repeatedly repressed and excluded voice of human suffering, desire, and grief" (Moreland 1990: 11), voices muted or erased by oppressive social classifications and categorical divisions of labor. For Moreland, opening a space for "blacks' and women's critically different voices" (Moreland 1990: 7) is central to the moral and political thrust of Faulkner's overall narrative project, and it is marked by the movement from "compulsive" to "revisionary repetition" of the primal scene (as the story of the "Barn Burning" recurs, now comically transmuted, in *The Hamlet*). Moreland's concept of revisionary repetition implies not so much Marx's celebrated sense of historical irony ("Hegel remarks somewhere that all facts and personages of great importance in world history occur, as it were, twice. He forgot to add: the first time as tragedy, the second as farce" [Marx 1972: 8]) as the transformation of historical determinations by acts of creative praxis, here marked as Faulkner's "working through" of the tragic repetitions driven by the primal scene "in order somehow to alter [its] structure and its continuing power, especially by opening a critical space for what the subject might *learn* about that structure in the different context of a changing present or a more distant or different past" (Moreland 1990: 4).

What the subject might learn: here "the subject" is the given reader of Faulkner's novels, but it is also Faulkner himself as an author, and the series of white focal characters in his fiction who live in the town of Jefferson (as Thomas McHaney observes, "almost invariably the characters' stories are told, and the novels written, from the point of view of a narrative intelligence based in Jefferson" [McHaney 2004: 528]) and are associated with established families in decline. For Kevin Railey, in *Natural Aristocracy*, Faulkner is a historical subject more or less aligned with the ideology of a residually surviving "aristocracy" caught within "the larger historical conflict between paternalism and liberalism" (Railey 1999: xi). Railey's project seeks to understand "the development of this authorial ideology as a working through of [Faulkner's] identifications with these forces" (Railey 1999: xi). For James Snead, in turn, in *Figures of Division*, Faulkner's great novels from *The Sound and the Fury* to *Go Down, Moses* "primarily concern the white mind and its struggles with the systems of division it has created" (Snead 1986: xiv). John Matthews underlines "how many scenes in Faulkner's writing involve young men shocked by the revelation that the world they inhabit rests on racial, class, and gender oppression. Faulkner's writing is the very activity that forces him to confront the contradictions of his world" (Matthews 1991: 10), a struggle marked by the prototypical trauma of Quentin Compson, who "remains resistant to fully confronting that history; instead, he enshrouds himself in nostalgia, denial, and ambiguity" (Matthews 1991: 121). In Philip Weinstein's formulation, the essential narrative subject of Faulkner's fiction is therefore

> [n]ot the undivided subjectivity of liberal Western thought – the (white, male) autonomous self-knowing individual – but rather the subject in process, the subject in contestation. Beleaguered, charged with Imaginary desires, immersed from infancy within conflicting alignments of the Symbolic field, this subject is more likely to be a site of interior disturbance than a locus of concerted action. Who better than Faulkner has delineated the pathos and value of such a figure? (Weinstein 1992: 10)

For Diane Roberts, in *Faulkner and Southern Womanhood*, Faulkner stages the scene of the white male subject's struggle against his own unconscious complicity in discursive, economic, and imaginary systems of domination. Thus as Faulkner "confronts the representations of women he inherits from southern culture" he "makes fiction out of the struggle" between those "political and social forces [which] were trying to reinscribe" such representations and those forces trying to "tear them apart" (Roberts 1994: xv). Along such lines Deborah Clarke, in *Robbing the Mother*, observes that "as a product of white bourgeois society Faulkner himself is necessarily inscribed by our dominant ideology of gender and family" (Clarke 1994: 17); as an artist, however, he "questions the beliefs which underlie his . . . culture and analyzes both the power and the limitations of such a paradigm" (Clarke 1994: 17), drawing attention, in John Duvall's formulation, "to what is available in [his fiction], namely, a recurring scrutiny of the uses and abuses of patriarchal authority through characters warped by the will of the father" (Duvall 1990: 132).

As read by recent Faulkner criticism, then, Faulkner is an "author who would both describe and write against large-scale ideological concepts encoded" in the hegemonic, "rhetorical narratives" of his time, narratives fraught with "systematic paradoxes" and "statutory divisions" reflecting related paradoxes and divisions in society as a whole (Snead 1986: ix). Thus the project of recovering the voices of the marginalized is accompanied by a critical recognition and analysis of what post-Marxian and post-Freudian theory has tended to call "the Logos," that pervasive complex of symbolic categories, imaginary systems of representation, and real, material divisions of labor and culture "whereby blacks, poor whites, and women have been classified, separated, and dominated" (Snead 1986: xii). This (phal)logocentric system finds its support both in the institution of "the law" itself – in what Jay Watson formulates as "a deeply normative cultural system, a vehicle of ideology . . . a force of social stability and control, an entrenched and often blindly self-interested institution" (Watson 1993: 3) – and in the "lived system of meanings and values . . . [whose] assignments of energy" (Williams 1977: 110) express themselves in colloquial language and general social practices. Thus, for example, as Theresa Towner suggests, "With Frederick Douglass and W. E. B. Du

Bois, Faulkner understood the destructive power of racialized language – knew how racial epithets, to take an obvious example, erase an individual name and identity and replace them with a categorizing insult" (Towner 2000: 16). As Snead summarizes the matter:

> Yoknapatawpha's major classifications – "white/black," "poor/rich," "male/female" – depend on polar thinking. The reality of the human beings thus classified remains absent. Faulkner's narratives mainly concern the effects of these classifications on human sensibilities, white and black, rich and poor, male and female: how can we ever know each other, if our society works through a forced organization into distinct groupings? (Snead 1986: xii)

The reality of the human beings thus classified remains absent: yet it is of course the dynamic force of recent Faulkner criticism (including Snead's own argument explicitly) to show how these figures of division persistently *fail*. This failure can be understood in the Marxian sense as reflecting the force of "counter-hegemonic" resistance, those social forms of "alternative or directly oppositional politics and culture [which always] exist as significant elements in [any] society" (Williams 1977: 113). Thus the Logos, whether incarnated as the Constitution's "three-fifths" equation or the overall legacy of Jim Crow, is "also continually resisted, limited, altered, challenged by pressures not all its own" (Williams 1977: 112). In this way Thadious Davis, in *Games of Property*, shows how *"Go Down, Moses* can be deconstructed in terms of political action, of the assertion of civil rights, and of resistance to the domination of ideological tyrants" (Davis 2003: 20).

As it has developed over the last few decades, Faulkner criticism has become more attuned to hearing the plurality of "counter-hegemonic" voices inhabiting Faulkner's complex narratives. According to Charles Hannon,

> Faulkner's novelistic language is shot through with voiced conflicts of the 1930s South. . . . as his novelistic style developed, and particularly as he made his "great discovery" of Yoknapatawpha, such representations became more dialogized and less ruled by the fictions of white fantasy. His novels still would be replete with the dominant languages of his time, but increasingly these intersect with the languages of resistance and opposition, making the novels more fully representative of the discursive atmosphere of the modern South. (Hannon 2005: 5, 8–9)

As a writer Faulkner not only hears and records the "other" voices from an objective, historical distance but projects himself into "the danger zones such others may represent" for him (Morrison 1992: 3), perennially rediscovering that "every narrative allows its teller to embody (not simply to express) an identity" (Matthews 1982: 10). While for Snead "Faulkner's narratives utter a truth of merging across social boundaries that his contemporaries found unspeakable" (Snead 1986: x), for André Bleikasten, this process of imaginary merging lies at the deepest layer of Faulkner's creativity: "is not writing, at least writing with any claim to originality, also – with all the ambiguities of the reflexive, all the deceptions of doubling – writing oneself? . . . Whatever our theoretical premises, we cannot do without the tacit belief that every literary text conceals somewhere in its folds the secret of its production" (Bleikasten 1990: vii, ix). It is this "secret" place from which Faulkner extends himself as a writer into that astounding plurality of lives which his fictional cosmos, in Yoknapatawpha and beyond, represents. As generations, now, of readers have seemed to testify, his fiction renders what it *feels like* to be another human being, to be "an *is* different from my *is*" in Vardaman's formulation (Faulkner 1990b: 56), and thus to be enclosed by a mind, body, and self both intimate and foreign. Yet Faulkner shows that identifying in this way with another is not a transcendence but a repositioning of the self: one remains a *given* human being, encircled by a "blood meridian" (McCarthy 1992) through which "the secret and selfish life" (as Addie puts it [Faulkner 1990b: 170]) of the other, of all the others, is felt as an insistent pressure. In giving us a multiplicity of fictional lives with which to re-embody ourselves, Faulkner extends our range prodigiously, but what we experience, again and again, is a singular mode of existence dominated by an uncanny sense of familiarity and alienation.

One might think in this respect of Faulkner's representation of Joe Christmas or Lucas Beauchamp, whom Doreen Fowler reads as "doubles of the white male protagonist" (Fowler 1997: ix); or of Faulkner's unmistakably "creative and powerful" (Gwin 1990: 31) explorations of cross-gendered embodiment. As Minrose Gwin has suggested, Faulkner in the process of writing "permits his own subjectivity to become entangled with [women's], thus blurring the boundaries of what is male and what is female, who writes and who is written" (Gwin 1990: 31). In all these explorations, Faulkner's subjects are invariably traversed by powerful symbolic and material forces, some converging from the "outside" (as imperatives of labor, economy, politics, law), some irrupting from the "inside" (as emphatic sexual or aggressive drives, unconscious fantasies, or the intimidation of consciousness itself, i.e., the Super-Ego as the internalization of "the gaze," of proscriptive social forces).

I, Myself

In much recent Faulkner criticism, Freud (as a "founder of discursivity") is being read and understood as an essentially post-Marxian materialist of psychosexual existence, and it is indeed under the sign of "the personal" that the essential synthesis of Marx and Freud might be said to occur. Yet to put things in this way is to animate, perhaps, a debate that has tended to orient itself according to a *polarity* of terms: the individual *versus* the social. As Raymond Williams has observed, "one dominant strain in Marxism [is] its habitual abuse of the 'subjective' and the 'personal'," that is, the "bourgeois" (Williams 1977: 129). Thus one encounters in the criticism a sometimes explicit, sometimes implicit valorization of an approach stressing "social relations" over "individual lives," since a concern solely with the latter might be deemed to obscure the larger frameworks of social history and politics. As if to ward off the charge that one is concerned too narrowly with the individual and the personal, recent Faulkner criticism has reiterated an insistent social and material emphasis. We are reminded, persistently, that "cultural structures of race, gender, and class [are] powerfully deter-mining forces in the construction of individual subjectivity" (Dussere 2003: 9); that "all individuals are radically conditioned by the historical and material realities of their eras" (Matthews 1990: 277); that Faulkner's "people are made of the stuff of class dis-tinctions: they are planter or poor-white (some few in between and defined by that too) and become individual by being a variant of their type" (Jehlen 1976: 10). At the same time, one encounters a profound recognition, as Faulkner shows us again and again, as in, for example, the figure of Joe Christmas, that "the individual" is the essential place where massive, and often shattering, social and historical forces converge.

Insofar as subjectivity in Faulkner is the site of lived contradictions and ceaseless contestation between "personal" and "social" pressures, Faulkner criticism has been drawn to

> the theories of Marxist critics who have studied the process by which various languages of the social formation are inscribed upon the individual unconscious, and thus become one's "own." . . . There is always this tense reciprocity between the individual subjects who are the "authors" of discourse and the discourses themselves, which, to the degree that they are a function of the entire social formation, actually produce the subjects who "speak" them. (Hannon 2005: 2, 11)

Thus Faulkner's novels provide the means of deconstructing a false and reductive binary: "Though man is a *unique* individual – and it is just his particularity which makes him an individual, a really *individual* social being – he is equally the *whole*, the ideal whole, the subjective existence of society as thought and experienced" (Marx 1956: 76). After Marx, then, Faulkner's characters become more easily understood as "living evidence of a continuing social process, into which individuals are born and within which they are shaped, but to which they then also actively contribute, in a continuing process. This is at once their socialization and their individuation: the connected aspects of a single process which the alternative theories of 'system' and 'expression' had divided and dissociated" (Williams 1977: 37).

The scene of social struggle in Faulkner, even as it is structured by the categorical divisions of class, gender, and race, tends to be depicted as one version or another of individualized human beings living "together" (though not on equal terms) in families, houses, plantations, towns. And as Engels put the matter in a letter to J. Bloch in 1890, "what each individual wills is obstructed by everyone else, and what emerges is some-thing that no one willed" (quoted in Williams 1977: 86). One might recognize the echo of this concept in that stunning moment of Faulknerian insight as expressed by Judith Sutpen in *Absalom, Absalom!*:

> you are born at the same time with a lot of other people, all mixed up with them, like trying to, having to, move your arms and legs with strings only the same strings are hitched to all the other arms and legs and the others all trying and they don't know why

either except that the strings are all in one another's way like five or six people all trying
to make a rug on the same loom only each one wants to weave his own pattern into the
rug. (Faulkner 1990a: 100–1)

It is this sense of being caught up in the social struggle with myriad others that may
give perspective to what André Malraux has called the "powerful, and savagely
personal" dimension of Faulkner's fiction (Malraux 1966: 272–3), the dialectical
process by which "the I, myself, that deep existence which we lead" (Faulkner 1990a:
109), "the citadel of the central I-Am's private own" (Faulkner 1990a: 112), comes
into being.

False Consciousness

Yet from the sense of a central Marxian (and Lacanian) paradox, what the individual
subject may live as "deep existence," as "the fullest, most open, most active kind of
consciousness" (Williams 1983: 127) or as "full, central, immediate human experience" itself (Williams 1977: 46), may also signify his constitutive blindness, for the
subject is, typically for Marx, "a product of social conditions or of systems of belief or
of fundamental systems of perception . . . which by definition [the subject] cannot
itself explain" (Williams 1983: 128). The intensely felt personal realm is thus often
to be understood as "the ideological reflex and echo" (Marx 1956: 75) of the larger
processes of historical reification which have produced "the individual" as an "integer"
(Faulkner 2004e: 63, 71) within the socio-economic system. This is the poignant
predicament of what Carolyn Porter has defined as "the plight of the participant
observer" in Faulkner's novels:

> The reifying process endemic to capitalism produces a new kind of world and new kind
> of man. It generates, on the one hand, a "new objectivity," a "second nature" in which
> man's own productive activity is obscured, so that what he has made appears to him as
> a given, an external and objective reality operating according to its own immutable laws.
> On the other hand, it generates a man who assumes a passive and "contemplative" stance
> in the face of that objectified and rationalized reality – a man who seems to himself to
> stand outside that reality because his own participation in producing it is mystified.
> (Porter 1981: xi)

The realm of false consciousness and ideology designates the systems of thought which
block the (often unconsciously alienated) subject's understanding of his own materiality,
of the conditions that have helped produce him as a socially situated, racially marked
(whether as white or black), and emphatically gendered subject (forms of social definition, that is, with respect to which the subject may feel misaligned and against which
he or she may struggle). This sense of "false consciousness" lies at the nucleus of
Althusser's well-known definition of ideology as designating "the imaginary relationship
of individuals to their real conditions of existence" (Althusser 1989: 87). Yet lest it

always be the *other person* whose consciousness is mystified, Erik Dussere suggests that we ourselves, "[l]ike the characters in [Faulkner's] novels . . . never grasp in their whole- ness, in their subtlety, the historical forces we inherit and by which we are often led; we are never sure what contracts were signed, what debts incurred, before we arrived" (Dussere 2003: 2).

In Freudian terms, "false consciousness" and "ideology" belong in that constellation of concepts including "repression," "negation," "denial," and "disavowal," modes of psychic defense which consist in the subject's refusal to recognize the reality of outra- geous or traumatic perceptions. For Freud, *"the essence of repression lies simply in turning something away, and keeping it at a distance, from the conscious"* (Freud 1966c: 47; emphasis in original), and it is this agency of "turning away" that is deemed by Lacan to be "the most constant attribute of the ego, namely, *Verneinung* [negation]" (Lacan 1977: 15), which encompasses "everything that the ego neglects, scotomizes, misconstrues in the sensations that make it react to reality, everything that it ignores, exhausts, and binds in the significations that it receives from language" (Lacan 1977: 22). The agency of negation and misrecognition ("méconnaissance") is further "organized in those reactions of opposition, negation, ostentation, and lying that our experience has shown us to be the characteristic modes of the agency of the ego in dialogue" (Lacan 1977: 15). Thus the subject's chronic misrepresentations, distortions, "condensations and displacements" (in Freud's dreamwork terminology [Freud 1966b]), along with the passionate intensi- ties of affect with which they are invested, point us in the direction of those truths which cannot be borne and which must be negated. (A given truth or a particular reality, in this sense, is the dialectical "other" which gives mystified consciousness its unique form.) For Marx, that is, "the phantoms of the human brain also are necessary sublimates of men's material life-process, which can be empirically established and which is bound to material preconditions" (Marx 1956: 75).

It has often been observed that the mobilization of such terms as "false conscious- ness," "ideology," or "repression" often implies the hypocrisy inherent in "the distinction between (my) *ideas* or *principles* and (your) *ideology* or *dogma*" (Williams 1983: 109). As T. H. Adamowski elaborates, "if there be 'ideology,' understood as 'false consciousness,' a corruption of thought by one's material interests, how do the analysts of ideology (Marxists) escape it?" (1994: 389). Yet, to be sure, as Faulkner's novels show, ideological thinking – let alone ignorance, blindness, stupidity, and what Freud called "obstinate misunderstanding" (Freud 1966b: 53) – exists, and to be an ideological subject in this sense is to be implicated in the politics of pointing this out to one another: "every man is tabernacled in every other and he in exchange and so on in an endless complexity of being and witness to the uttermost edge of the world" (McCarthy 1992: 141). Thus recent criticism has focused on Faulkner's complex representations of subjectivity as situated within pressing and turbulent scenes of social and historical duress, the focus as much on Faulkner's representation of American history per se as on the inability of his characters – the individual human subjects *in* history – to grasp and comprehend their social realities without telling distortions and evasions. Given this situation, in which the subject simultaneously knows and refuses to know, in which he hesitates in face of what he "knows and dares not admit to himself" (Faulkner 2004d: 96), often the most that can be hoped for is therefore "not resolution but perhaps, at times, just that extra edge of consciousness" (Williams 1983: 24). Or as Freud put the matter in a characteristically metapsychological mode, "the ego must observe the external world, must lay down an accurate picture of it in the memory-traces of its perceptions, and by its exercise of the function of 'reality-testing' must put aside whatever in this picture of the external world is an addition derived from internal sources of excitation" (Freud 1966a: 75). Thus might "the classical terms of epistemology: knowledge, truth, corre-spondence, representation" (Adamowski 1994: 397) be reclaimed in "a conscious com-mitment to understanding and describing real forces (a commitment that at its best includes understanding the processes of consciousness and composition that are involved in any such attempt)" (Williams 1983: 262). There can be no doubt that Faulkner's *representation* of ideology – the fundamental epistemological mode of his fictional sub-jects – epitomizes this commitment.

Faulkner and the Frankfurt School

The most extensively developed syntheses of Marx and Freud are to be found in the work of the Frankfurt School, primarily the writings of Walter Benjamin (who died in France in 1940) and his fellow refugees from Hitler's Europe, Theodor Adorno, Max Horkheimer, and Herbert Marcuse, who became naturalized American citizens in 1940. The latter three figures produced a body of work contemporaneous with Faulkner's emergence (in the period following *The Portable Faulkner* [1946]) as a public figure who felt his privacy to be increasingly under siege (Schwartz 1988; Urgo 1989; Matthews 1995; Zender 2002: 32–52; Lurie 2004). In terms uncannily similar, both Faulkner and these Frankfurt School thinkers understood the essential crisis of the 1950s as defined not so much by the Cold War antagonism between immense power blocks intent on collision, as by the collapse of any distinction at all between "the individual" and "society," the former losing his or her power to meaningfully resist the coercive seductions of the latter. The former Marxian understanding of "the social" as the site of class conflict and latent revolutionary forces had increasingly to come to terms with the transformation of "the people" into a newly formed, and paradoxically atomized, mass, that is, in Don DeLillo's memorable formulation, "the TV audience. . . . The crowd broken down into millions of small rooms" (DeLillo 1993: 290). It was this mass that was held in thrall by "the whole apparatus of assimilation" (DeLillo 1993: 290), that is, the state, the media, the "culture industry," and its powerful technologies of broadcasting and projection.

In his preface to *Eros and Civilization: A Philosophical Inquiry into Freud* (1955), Marcuse therefore declared that "psychological categories . . . have become political categories":

The traditional borderlines between psychology on the one side and political and social philosophy on the other have been made obsolete by the condition of man in the present era: formerly autonomous and identifiable psychical processes are being absorbed by the function of the individual in the state – by his public existence. Psychological problems there turn into political problems. . . . The era tends to be totalitarian even where it has not produced totalitarian states. (Marcuse 1966: xxvii)

Psychology, designating the realm of private and personal interiority, has become a political category, that is, precisely because the private and personal domain is under siege by the penetrative and imperializing forces of monopoly capitalism, governmental control, and the media – an alliance of powers that the Frankfurt School has referred to as "the culture industry."

A decade earlier Adorno had already asserted that "the sphere of private existence" had become that of "mere consumption, dragged along as an appendage of the process of material production, without autonomy or substance of its own" (Adorno 1978: 15). Reading Faulkner's essays and public letters published in the 1950s, during the McCarthy period and after, certainly suggests that Faulkner, like Adorno and Marcuse, understood "the individual" to be not so much a "separate but an *opposing* term" (Williams 1977: 12; emphasis added), since "the totality" seemed intent on transforming that individual into "one more identityless integer in that identityless anonymous unprivacied mass which seems to be our goal" (Faulkner 2004e: 71). In "On Privacy (The American Dream: What Happened to It?)" Faulkner sketches out a brief history of "the American individual" in opposition to powerful sources of authority emanating from beyond the self. In seventeenth-century New England this individual believed that he "could be free not only of the old established closed-corporation hierarchies of arbitrary power which had oppressed him as a mass, but free of that mass into which the hierarchies of church and state had compressed and held him individually thralled and individually impotent" (Faulkner 2004e: 63). Now this unique version of American freedom was disappearing. "It is gone now. We dozed, slept, and it abandoned us" (Faulkner 2004e: 65). In one sense the outlines of the crisis could still be sketched with a degree of clarity: the private individual was, again, pitted vehemently against "powerful federations and organizations and amalgamations like publishing corporations and religious sects and political parties and legislative committees" (Faulkner 2004e: 73). Yet this vast conglomeration of powerful institutions was (like the amplifier in *Pylon*) "sourceless, inhuman, ubiquitous" (Faulkner 1985: 801) and hence mappable only in terms of an almost hallucinatory inflation of figures pitting the "puny" human form against

that furious blast, that force, that power rearing like a thunder-clap into the American zenith, multiple-faced yet mutually conjunctived, bellowing the words and phrases which we have long since emasculated of any significance or meaning other than as tools, implements, for the further harassment of the private individual human spirit, by their furious and immunised high priests: "Security." "Subversion." "Anti-Communism." "Christianity." "Prosperity." "The American Way." "The Flag." (Faulkner 2004e: 73)

(See also "An Innocent at Rinkside," where Faulkner wonders "just what a professional hockey-match, whose purpose is to make a decent and reasonable profit for its owners, had to do with our National Anthem" [Faulkner 2004b: 51].)

In Joseph Urgo's reading of the late fiction, Faulkner is therefore "a far more politically challenging and politically radical writer" (Urgo 1989: 4) than we've come to appreciate. Indeed the "pattern of human defiance and rebellion" (Urgo 1989: 42) is fundamental to Faulkner's "apocrypha," which, "in its entirety . . . stands as a political and ideological alternative to what Faulkner considered to be the totalitarianism of modern society" (Urgo 1989: 4): "The human spirit, as Faulkner would come to define it in his apocrypha, is inherently rebellious, or else it is doomed" (Urgo 1989: 42). (And as Faulkner's essay "A Guest's Impression of New England" [2004a] suggests, Faulkner's rebelliousness cannot be comprehensively aligned with that of the Southerner's resistance to "Yankee" interference – though naturally this complex issue remains very much alive in contemporary Faulkner criticism.)

In Karl Zender's reading, Faulkner "clearly foresaw both the homogenizing power of the mass media and the impending emergence of a popular culture founded largely on amplified sound, and he developed a powerful array of images with which to express his understanding of these matters" (Zender 1989: 22). The problem so conceived concerns the subject's radical openness, the failure of "insulation": "If the imagination could not control external reality, then alien aspects of the world – alien sounds – could at their own discretion enter and overwhelm the mind. . . . In his unequal struggle with these voices, smells, and sounds, we see his inability to defend himself against the invasive power of his culture" (Zender 1989: 11, 16). For Peter Lurie, Faulkner was always especially wary of "the enormous and at times destructive power of the new medium" of film: "Accompanying the broad distribution of a centrally produced, standardized product . . . was film's capacity to shape the consciousness of millions of spectators, an aspect of film that for many, including Faulkner, was both a fascination and a concern" (Lurie 2004: 11, 10). Lurie points out, for example, that insofar as *Birth of a Nation*, "the most widely viewed film in history," exercised a pernicious effect upon the visual shaping of popular "attitudes about race as well as gender" (Lurie 2004: 11, 15), *Absalom, Absalom!* "amounted to a literary alternative to cinematic approaches to southern history epitomized by Griffith's film" (Lurie 2004: 20).

By the 1950s, the contest between "the individual" and what Zender designates, in a significative condensation, as "the power of sound" (Zender 1989: 3–42) had become a master theme linking "liberals" and "radicals." In *Freud and the Crisis of Our Culture*, for example, Lionel Trilling's composure belies a barely restrained sense of panic:

> One does not need to have a very profound quarrel with American culture to feel uneasy because our defenses against it, our modes of escape from it, are becoming less and less adequate. One may even have a very lively admiration for American culture, as I do, and yet feel that this defenselessness of the self against its culture is cause for alarm. . . . We must, I think, recognize how open and available to the general culture the individual has become, how little protected he is by countervailing cultural forces, how unified and demanding our free culture has become. (1955: 49–50, 53–4)

For Marcuse, the subversion of the autonomy of the individual subject or ego prepares "the ground for the formation of masses. The mediation between the self and the other gives way to immediate identification" (Marcuse 1989: 235) with the projected *imagos* of authority ("leaders"). This is precisely how Faulkner understood the matter in the 1950s, as Urgo cites Faulkner's letter to Muna Lee of the State Department (March 4, 1959): "All evil and grief in this world stems from the fact that man talks. I mean, in the sense of one man talking to a captive audience" (Urgo 1989: 36). Faulkner continues:

> Except for that, and its concomitants of communication – radio, newspapers, such organs – there would have been no Hitler and Mussolini. I believe that in the case of the speaker and his captive audience, whatever the reason for the captivity of the audience, the worst of both is inevitably brought out – the worst of the individual, compounded by the affinity for evil inherent in people compelled or persuaded to be a mass, an audience, which in my opinion is another mob. (Blotner 1978: 424).

The problem now, as it was in the Fascist 1930s and 1940s, concerned the impoverishment of the resistant ego from which something like genuine privacy, creative resistance, and praxis (whether personal or collective) might flow. As Marcuse elaborates:

> The shrinking of the ego, its reduced resistance to others appears in the ways in which the ego holds itself constantly open to the messages imposed from outside. The antenna on every house, the transistor on every beach, the jukebox in every bar or restaurant are as many cries of desperation – not to be left alone, by himself, not to be separated from the Big Ones, not to be condemned to the emptiness or the hatred or the dreams of oneself. (Marcuse 1989: 235)

Much is at stake, then, in whether one considers "the individual" to be a conservative or a radical term. Lawrence Schwartz suggests that "Faulkner became universalized as an emblem of the freedom of the individual under capitalism, as a chronicler of the plight of man in the modern world" (Schwartz 1988: 4), but perhaps there was more at play here than "the bourgeois tactic of heroizing the alienated artist and mystifying his productions under the sign of the Imagination" (Porter 1981: 292). Recent discussions of what Faulkner produced affirm (whether explicitly or not) "that some extraordinary human beings struggle, against overwhelming odds" (Snead 1986: xiv), to oppose "the monstrosity of absolute production. . . . Only by virtue of opposition to production, as still not wholly encompassed by this order, can [we] bring about another more worthy of human beings" (Adorno 1978: 15).

Marx and Freud have helped to shape the dominant intellectual contexts of recent Faulkner criticism, which has sought to illuminate Faulkner's representation of the social and individual dimensions of historical existence in Yoknapatawpha County and beyond. Marx offers linguistic and conceptual tools with which to analyze the realities of labor, class, politics, and economics, and the ways of resistance to and transformation of those realities. Freud helps define the logic with which fantasy and repression become entangled with Faulkner's narrative modes, plots, and characters. The synthesis of Marx and Freud in the work of the Frankfurt School and in contemporary cultural theory represents a force that will generate new forms of insight and discursivity as Faulkner criticism continues to unfold.

REFERENCES AND FURTHER READING

Adamowski, T. H. (1994). Radical Ingratitude: Mass-Man and the Humanities. *University of Toronto Quarterly*, 63: 381–407.

Adorno, T. (1978). *Minima Moralia: Reflections from Damaged Life* (trans. E. F. N. Jephcott). London: Verso. (Original pub. 1951.)

Althusser, L. (1989). Ideology and Ideological State Apparatuses (trans. B. Brewster). In D. Latimer (ed.). *Contemporary Critical Theory* (pp. 60–102). San Diego: Harcourt Brace Jovanovich. (Original pub. 1970.)

Bleikasten, A. (1990). *The Ink of Melancholy: Faulkner's Novels from* The Sound and the Fury *to* Light in August. Bloomington: Indiana University Press.

Blotner, J. (ed.) (1978). *Selected Letters of William Faulkner*. New York: Vintage. (Original pub. 1977.)

Clarke, D. (1994). *Robbing the Mother: Women in Faulkner.* Jackson: University Press of Mississippi.

Davis, T. M. (2003). *Games of Property: Law, Race, Gender, and Faulkner's* Go Down, Moses. Durham, NC, and London: Duke University Press.

DeLillo, D. (1993). The Art of Fiction CXXXV. Interview. *Paris Review*, 128: 274–306.

Dussere, E. (2003). *Balancing the Books: Faulkner, Morrison, and the Economies of Slavery*. New York and London: Routledge.

Duvall, J. N. (1990). *Faulkner's Marginal Couple: Invisible, Outlaw, and Unspeakable Communities.* Austin, TX: University of Texas Press.

Faulkner, W. (1977). Barn Burning. In *Collected Stories of William Faulkner*. New York: Vintage International. (Original pub. 1939.)

Faulkner, W. (1985). *Pylon*. In *William Faulkner: Novels 1930–1935*. New York: Library of America. (Original pub. 1935.)

Faulkner, W. (1990a). *Absalom, Absalom!* New York: Vintage. (Original pub. 1936.)

Faulkner, W. (1990b). *As I Lay Dying.* New York: Vintage. (Original pub. 1930.)

Faulkner, W. (1994). An Introduction to *The Sound and the Fury*. In *The Sound and the Fury* (ed. D. Minter) (pp. 228–32). New York: Norton.

Faulkner, W. (2004a). A Guest's Impression of New England. In *Essays, Speeches and Public Letters* (ed. J. B. Meriwether) (pp. 44–7). New York: Modern Library. (Original pub. 1954.)

Faulkner, W. (2004b). An Innocent at Rinkside. In *Essays, Speeches and Public Letters* (ed. J. B. Meriwether) (pp. 48–51). New York: Modern Library. (Original pub. 1955.)

Faulkner, W. (2004c). Mississippi. In *Essays, Speeches and Public Letters* (ed. J. B. Meriwether) (pp. 11–43). New York: Modern Library. (Original pub. 1954.)

Faulkner, W. (2004d). On Fear: Deep South in Labor: Mississippi (The American Dream: What Happened to It?). In *Essays, Speeches and Public Letters* (ed. J. B. Meriwether) (pp. 92–106). New York: Modern Library. (Original pub. 1956.)

Faulkner, W. (2004e). On Privacy (The American Dream: What Happened to It?). In *Essays, Speeches and Public Letters* (ed. J. B. Meriwether) (pp. 62–75). New York: Modern Library. (Original pub. 1955.)

Foucault, M. (1984). What is an Author? In P. Rabinow (ed.). *The Foucault Reader* (pp. 101–20). New York: Pantheon.

Fowler, D. (1997). *Faulkner: The Return of the Repressed.* Charlottesville, VA, and London: University Press of Virginia.

Freud, S. (1966a). The Dissection of the Psychical Personality. In *The Standard Edition of the Complete Psychological Works of Sigmund Freud* (trans. and ed. J. Strachey), vol. 22 (pp. 57–80). London: Hogarth Press. (Original pub. 1933.)

Freud, S. (1966b). *The Interpretation of Dreams*. In *The Standard Edition of the Complete Psychological*

Works of Sigmund Freud (trans. and ed. J. Strachey), vols. 4 and 5. (Original pub. 1900.)

Freud, S. (1966c). Repression. In *The Standard Edition of the Complete Psychological Works of Sigmund Freud* (trans. and ed. J. Strachey), vol. 14 (pp. 141–57). London: Hogarth Press. (Original pub. 1915.)

Godden, R. (1997). *Fictions of Labor: William Faulkner and the South's Long Revolution*. Cambridge: Cambridge University Press.

Gresset, M. (1989). *Fascination: Faulkner's Fiction, 1919–1936* (adapted from the French by T. West). Durham, NC, and London: Duke University Press.

Gwin, M. C. (1990). *The Feminine and Faulkner: Reading (Beyond) Sexual Difference*. Knoxville: University of Tennessee Press.

Hannon, C. (2005). *Faulkner and the Discourses of Culture*. Baton Rouge: Louisiana State University Press.

Irwin, J. T. (1996). *Doubling and Incest/Repetition and Revenge*. Baltimore and London: Johns Hopkins University Press. (Original pub. 1975.)

Jehlen, M. (1976). *Class and Character in Faulkner's South*. New York: Columbia University Press.

Lacan, J. (1977). Aggressivity in Psychoanalysis. In *Écrits: A Selection* (trans. A. Sheridan) (pp. 8–29). (Original pub. 1948.)

Lester, C. (1995). Racial Awareness and Arrested Development: *The Sound and the Fury* and the Great Migration (1915–1928). In P. M. Weinstein (ed.). *The Cambridge Companion to William Faulkner* (pp. 123–45). Cambridge: Cambridge University Press.

Lurie, P. (2004). *Vision's Immanence: Faulkner, Film, and the Popular Imagination*. Baltimore and London: Johns Hopkins University Press.

Malraux, A. (1966). A Preface for Faulkner's *Sanctuary*. In R. P. Warren (ed.). *Faulkner: A Collection of Critical Essays* (pp. 272–4). Englewood Cliffs, NJ: Prentice Hall. (Original pub. 1933.)

Marcuse, H. (1966). *Eros and Civilization: A Philosophical Inquiry into Freud*. Boston: Beacon Press. (Original pub. 1955.)

Marcuse, H. (1989). The Obsolescence of the Freudian Concept of Man. In S. E. Bronner and D. MacKay (eds.). *Critical Theory and Society: A Reader* (pp. 233–46). New York: Routledge. (Original pub. 1963.)

Marx, K. (1956). Existence and Consciousness. In *Karl Marx: Selected Writings in Sociology and Social Philosophy* (eds. T. B. Bottomore and M. Rubel, trans. T. B. Bottomore) (pp. 67–87). New York: McGraw-Hill.

Marx, K. (1972). *The Eighteenth Brumaire of Louis Bonaparte*. Moscow: Progress Press. (Original pub. 1869.)

Marx, K. and F. Engels (1969). *Communist Manifesto* (trans. S. Moore). Chicago: Henry Regnery. (Original pub. 1848.)

Marx, K. and F. Engels (1970). *The German Ideology*. Part One (trans. and ed. J. Arthur). New York: International Publishers. (Original work written 1845.)

Matthews, J. T. (1982). *The Play of Faulkner's Language*. Ithaca, NY, and London: Cornell University Press.

Matthews, J. T. (1990). The Autograph of Violence in Faulkner's *Pylon*. In J. Humphries (ed.). *Southern Literature and Literary Theory* (pp. 247–69). Athens, GA: University of Georgia Press.

Matthews, J. T. (1991). *The Sound and the Fury: Faulkner and the Lost Cause*. Boston: Twayne.

Matthews, J. T. (1995). Faulkner and the Culture Industry. In P. M. Weinstein (ed.). *The Cambridge Companion to William Faulkner* (pp. 51–74). Cambridge: Cambridge University Press.

McCarthy, C. (1992). *Blood Meridian, or The Evening Redness in the West*. New York: Vintage. (Original pub. 1985.)

McHaney, T. L. (2004). First Is Jefferson: Faulkner Shapes His Domain. *Mississippi Quarterly: The Journal of Southern Cultures*, 58: 511–34. Special Issue: William Faulkner and Yoknapatawpha (guest ed. M. Kreiswirth).

Moreland, R. C. (1990). *Faulkner and Modernism: Rereading and Rewriting*. Madison: University of Wisconsin Press.

Morrison, T. (1992). *Playing in the Dark: Whiteness and the Literary Imagination*. New York: Vintage.

Polk, N. (1996). *Children of the Dark House: Text and Context in Faulkner*. Jackson: University Press of Mississippi.

Porter, C. (1981). *Seeing and Being: The Plight of the Participant Observer in Emerson, James, Adams, and Faulkner*. Middletown, CT: Wesleyan University Press.

Railey, K. (1999). *Natural Aristocracy: History, Ideology, and the Production of William Faulkner*. Tuscaloosa and London: University of Alabama Press.

Roberts, D. (1994). *Faulkner and Southern Womanhood*. Athens, GA, and London: University of Georgia Press.

Rose, J. (1985). Introduction II. In J. Mitchell and J. Rose (eds.). *Feminine Sexuality: Jacques Lacan and the École Freudienne* (trans. J. Rose) (pp. 27–57). New York: Norton.

Schwartz, L. H. (1988). *Creating Faulkner's Reputation: The Politics of Modern Literary Criticism*. Knoxville: University of Tennessee Press.

Snead, J. A. (1986). *Figures of Division: William Faulkner's Major Novels*. New York and London: Methuen.

Towner, T. (2000). *Faulkner on the Color Line: The Later Novels*. Jackson: University Press of Mississippi.

Trilling, L. (1955). *Freud and the Crisis of Our Culture*. Boston: Beacon Press.

Urgo, J. R. (1989). *Faulkner's Apocrypha: A Fable, Snopes, and the Spirit of Human Rebellion*. Jackson and London: University Press of Mississippi.

Watson, J. (1993). *Forensic Fictions: The Lawyer Figure in Faulkner*. Athens, GA, and London: University of Georgia Press.

Weinstein, P. M. (1992). *Faulkner's Subject: A Cosmos No One Owns*. Cambridge: Cambridge University Press.

Williams, R. (1977). *Marxism and Literature*. New York: Oxford University Press.

Williams, R. (1983). *Keywords: A Vocabulary of Culture and Society*. New York: Oxford University Press. (Original pub. 1976.)

Zender, K. F. (1989). *The Crossing of the Ways: William Faulkner, the South, and the Modern World*. New Brunswick, NJ, and London: Rutgers University Press.

Zender, K. F. (2002). *Faulkner and the Politics of Reading*. Baton Rouge: Louisiana State University Press.

Žižek, S. (1991). *Looking Awry: An Introduction to Jacques Lacan Through Popular Culture*. Cambridge, MA: MIT Press.

6

Faulkner's Lives

Jay Parini

William Faulkner said many times that he wanted no biography, that he hoped the man would vanish behind the work, as if it were written by nobody. He wrote in frustration to Malcolm Cowley, who in editing *The Portable Faulkner* (1946) probed for biographical details:

> It is my ambition to be, as a private individual, abolished and voided from history, leaving it markless, no refuse save the printed books; I wish I had had enough sense to see ahead thirty years ago and, like some of the Elizabethans, not signed them. It is my aim, and every effort bent, that the sum and history of my life, which in the same sentence is my obit and epitaph too, shall be them both: He made the books and he died. (Cowley 1966: 126)

Other modernist writers shared Faulkner's distaste for biography, including T. S. Eliot and W. H. Auden, both of whom refused to condone an "authorized" life. Of course, given the interest, and interests, of readers, there was little chance that these important writers would escape the biographer's gaze. Literary studies would certainly be poorer without the resource of biography, and Faulkner scholarship is no exception. One might say that Faulkner, in particular, has been lucky in the quantity and quality of biographical energy expended on his behalf in the half century since his death in 1962.

As soon as Faulkner won the Nobel Prize for Literature in 1949, hopeful biographers began to swirl around him, intruding on his life. First, there was *Life*, the most popular magazine in the USA in the fifties. It sent Robert Coughlin to interview and write about the elusive author. Coughlin poked around Oxford for some days, talked directly to Faulkner, and secretly colluded with Faulkner's boyhood friend, Phil Stone, to write a two-part biographical feature. Inaccuracies and caricatures abounded in this piece, infuriating Faulkner and his family. Not surprisingly, Faulkner's mother, Miss Maud, cancelled her subscription to the magazine when this was published. Faulkner himself actually took the trouble to write an essay for *Harper's*, "On Privacy," subtitled: "The

American Dream: What Happened to It?" It was about the invasion of privacy, which he regarded as a sign of the decline of the modern world. "It's not what the writer said," Faulkner explained, "but that he said it."

Horrified by the *Life* business, Faulkner hoped to foil future biographers. This was futile, of course. The Faulkner industry was now fully underway, and local friends (such as John B. Cullen) soon began to assemble their own recollections of the great man in a parade of memoirs that has continued until quite recently. Faulkner's two surviving brothers, John and Murry, weighed in immediately after his death with *My Brother Bill* (1963) and *The Falkners of Mississippi* (1967), two early volumes. These works, though entertaining, only skimmed the surface of their brother's life, providing a good deal of irrelevant information in addition to some useful things.

More substantial biographical work followed quickly. Carvel Collins had for some time been amassing material, although he never managed to bring off a biography before his death. He did, however, supply helpful and informative introductory essays to volumes of Faulkner's early prose and poetry. In addition, Collins left behind a substantial trove of material about Faulkner, now stored at the University of Texas. In 1966, Michael Millgate published a fine early study, *The Achievement of William Faulkner*, which made considerable strides in the direction of solid biographical writing in one chapter devoted to the author's career. Another sturdy survey of Faulkner's progress as a writer appeared in *William Faulkner: The Journey to Self-Discovery* (1969) by H. Edward Richardson. Both of these volumes are still worth reading.

There is no such thing as a definitive biography, although the fantasy of such persists in the popular culture, even among book reviewers. The notion itself is a myth that belongs to an earlier era, when pure objectivity and completeness seemed both desirable and possible. One of the (few) advantages to the age of poststructural theory has, perhaps, been the release of biographical writing from fantasies of completeness and totality. Biography is (and has been from the ages of Plutarch or Suetonius) a form of fiction, as in the root meaning of the term (*fictio*), meaning a careful selection and arrangement of facts, assembled with an eye toward narrative drive. One must never mistake the figure conjured in a biography for the man himself; art (biography) is not life, and never can be. A biographer creates a kind of verbal holograph, assembling a picture from a vast number of possible facts, selecting and *shaping* this material.

The tradition of Faulkner biography has much in common with the biographical trail of other modern writers. In each case, rather tentative and sketchy books (often in the form of memoirs) were followed by a major foundational biography. These were produced during the heyday of the New Criticism, when biographical approaches to an author were suspect, and so the biographer tended to overwhelm the subject with research, as a way of establishing credibility. One need only look back to I. A. Richards and his *Practical Criticism* to see that professional criticism of the sort practiced in the universities leaned stiffly away from biography. Yet biographical context is nothing more than historical context of a particular kind; the New Critic, however, wished to remove the text from its context, including the author's life, preferring to examine the poem or novel in its own right, producing a very special kind of "knowledge."

Biographical knowledge was not knowledge at all. (The prejudice against biography has, in fact, continued in the age of theory, with many poststructuralist critics, such as Stanley Fish (1999), expressing a distaste for biography.)

To this day, biography remains one of the most popular genres (among ordinary readers) but the least theorized form of narrative. One need only look at reviews of literary biographies to see that a good deal of hostility exists for this genre among critics (book reviewers are usually New Critics, even today, although they would shrink from the use of the term). Again and again, reviewers write some version of this formulation: *Forget the biography and read the work.* Of course there is a good deal of truth in this: one should always read the work first, and return to the work as soon as possible. But one can surely enhance one's knowledge of the work by reading about the context from which it emerged. The more you know about the conditions under which a text was produced, the more you know about the text itself. Biographical knowledge, in other words, enhances and deepens one's reading.

The biographer in the age of New Criticism was placed in a difficult position. Richard Ellmann, for example, had been a professor at Yale during the apogee of New Critical theory. He plunged into his canonical life of James Joyce in the fifties, producing a model text of sorts in a biography that depended heavily for its value on a formidable amount of research, on facts derived from the biographer's wide travels to places where the author lived, on his access to letters and interviews, and on his close observation of original manuscripts, which allowed him to talk in detail about the evolution of Joyce's stories and novels. Ellmann also brought to bear on the texts themselves his formidable powers of analysis, much in the vein of New Critical writing. He had previously demonstrated these powers on Yeats, writing a two-fold study of the master that began with *Yeats: The Man and the Masks* (1948) and concluded with *The Identity of Yeats* (1964). These are fascinating works, summoning immense resources. They paved the way for the Joyce biography.

Another critic at work at this time was Lawrance Thompson, who had written a strong New Critical study of Robert Frost in the early forties. He began, soon after the war, to gather material for a massive life of Frost, whom he knew as a friend for over twenty years. He pursued his subject with a vengeance, publishing three hefty volumes after the author's death. This biography takes Frost from cradle to grave and everywhere in between with an almost obsessive interest in the subject's "darkness." Thompson combed the facts one way and not another, producing a Frost who was anything but the loveable old farmer-poet whom readers had come to adore. His Frost was a man prone to jealous rages against all competitors, willing to do whatever it took to succeed. He was a father who could behave with unbelievable cruelty toward his children, and – most damning – a husband willing to ride roughshod over his poor wife, Elinor, in order to promote his career. In his old age, he became a thirsty ego, desperate for attention, for public recognition of any sort.

I read Thompson's biography in one fell swoop in the mid-seventies, soon after the publication of the third volume. I was terribly upset by this harsh portrait of a poet I admired, and I suspected that Thompson had chosen to create a monster (a word he applied often to Frost) for inexplicable personal reasons. I certainly did not accept that his portrait was "truth," although I believed that Frost had a very dark side, one revealed in many of his best poems, such as "Desert Places," "Acquainted with the Night," and "Design." Many years of research on the life of Frost led me to understand that Frost was, indeed, more complex than Thompson's one-dimensional monster. He was, in fact, a depressive, prone to great anxieties, beset by horrific personal and familial problems, many of them not altogether of his making. He was, at times, a loving husband and father as well. He was also a difficult husband and father, and the cruel streak that Thompson underscored in his biography was just that – a streak. It was hardly the whole of Frost, and it does not define the man.

Thompson stayed rather far from the poems, and that also seemed to me quite a bad choice on his part. What is Frost if not a poet, first and foremost? To understand his motivation, one would have to understand what drove him to the desk, from poem to poem. How did he manage, over a lifetime, to assemble such a magnificent body of work? What interests me as a reader of literary biography is just that: the progress of a writer from text to text. It seems worth studying the evolution of a literary career in the context of certain agreed-upon facts, within the context of chronology. If possible, a good biographer should ask over and again: why was this work written at this time? What elements, personal and otherwise, played a role in the creation of a given text? How do the life and work interact? What does an understanding of the context or circumstances of composition of a given work add to our reading of the work itself?

The case of William Faulkner is perhaps less complicated in some ways than that of Frost, but – much like Frost – Faulkner had an obsessive biographer who wrote what anybody would consider a foundational biography. Joseph Blotner's two-volume *Faulkner* appeared in 1974, and it represents a labor of intense affection and considerable skill. Unlike Thompson, who had personal reasons for disliking Frost (they were both in love with the same woman at one point), Blotner was an unabashed admirer without an ax to grind. He obviously wished his subject well, and approached the difficult material of Faulkner's life – including the heavy drinking and the bad marriage – with tact. If anything, he was at times a little too tactful and gentlemanly, although I admire him for this. He understood that, given his relationship with Faulkner's family and friends, who provided access to so much good material, he could not press too hard in sensitive places or subject the material to harsh scrutiny. He stayed remarkably above the fray, keeping a certain distance from the darker regions, although nobody would come away from this biography thinking that Faulkner had been happy in his marriage or that his drinking was not suicidal.

Blotner enjoyed wonderful access to Faulkner's wife and daughter, to his stepchildren and extended family, to the author's friends in Oxford and elsewhere. He had, more importantly, a thorough firsthand knowledge of Faulkner's extensive correspondence. As with most biographies before the advent of email, letters played a crucial role in organizing the "life" of the subject, in giving the biographer a basic grid. Faulkner was not, it should be said, a massively gifted correspondent, although his early letters to his mother, in particular, are revealing; they are even, at times, poetic – something that can rarely be said for his later letters. One exception here would be his correspondence with his lovers, such as Meta Carpenter or Joan Williams, which are wonderfully intimate, eccentric, and revelatory. But Faulkner was fairly businesslike in the main, and most of his surviving letters consist of publishing details and travel arrangements. One cannot easily discern the state of the author's mind as he wrote them. Only rarely does he speak in a personal way.

Blotner's life of Faulkner, which appeared in a revised single-volume edition in 1984, has been admired, criticized, and mulled over for three decades. For all its faults, which include a hesitance to push deeply into problematic areas of the author's life and a lack of sustained critical analysis of the novels or stories, there is nevertheless something majestic about the book, not only in its sheer size but in the old-fashioned effort to write a definitive life. This cannot be done, as I have said, but the attempt remains a noble one; Blotner sought to gather as much information in such a volume as was possible. He also laid a useful grid of sorts, looking at the life in terms of certain key developmental stages, divided by him into comprehensible chunks with apt titles, such as "Soldier, Student, and Public Servant (1918–1925)" or "Husband and Father (1929–1932)." Blotner's subdivisions gave a coherence to this vast body of material that it would otherwise not possess: that is the function of biography, part of its fiction.

For the most part, Blotner opened a good deal of ground for the first time. Others would soon follow in his wake, correcting minor details, reinterpreting the material at hand, adding their own analyses of the work, making fresh connections. There was, indeed, a lot to be done, and many fascinating books appeared shortly after. Judith B. Wittenberg was able to read the fiction in fresh ways, taking into account Blotner's biographical insights, expanding on them in brilliant ways in *Faulkner: The Transfiguration of Biography* (1979). Only a year after Wittenberg's book came David Minter's succinct but wholly admirable *William Faulkner: His Life and Work*. Minter's book is written in an accessible, crisp, almost aphoristic style. It's a pleasure to read, and it remains a useful introduction to the life and work. Although it relies utterly on Blotner for the facts, it reassembles them in fresh, insightful ways, and it has a swift narrative drive. Minter wrote with immense sympathy for his subject, and with a powerful grasp of the region of Yoknapatawpha County.

In 1987, Stephen B. Oates published a strange, impressionistic biography called *Faulkner: The Man and the Artist*. This slight volume was attacked by Faulkner scholars for its unacknowledged reliance on Blotner and its crude attempt to blend fact and fiction. It has largely disappeared from the scene. But three more substantial volumes soon came out, and each of these has added something of value to Faulkner studies.

Frederick R. Karl published *William Faulkner: American Writer* in 1989. Known for an impressive biography of Joseph Conrad, Karl brought to bear on Faulkner biography an almost encyclopedic knowledge of literary modernism. His book, however, is considerably flawed. To begin with, it's badly written: repetitive in the extreme, vague, often boring. Karl frequently relies on crudely Freudian concepts. He looks for homoeroticism in odd places, suggesting (for example) that Faulkner preferred boyish women, those with small breasts. The evidence does not bear this out. His readings of the novels put them too firmly into the modernist camp, where they sit uneasily. Faulkner did, of course, read Joyce and Conrad; he understood something of modern art. Cubism interested him. But his innovations, especially in the crucial period of the late twenties and thirties, when he wrote his masterworks (*The Sound and the Fury* [1929], *As I Lay Dying* [1930], *Light in August* [1932], *Absalom, Absalom!* [1936]), are *sui generis*, and one can easily overplay the modernist hand. Karl does, neglecting other sources and traditions (such as that of Southern humor and regional writers) that were a huge part of Faulkner's inheritance.

Among the best of the biographical studies after Blotner was *William Faulkner and Southern History* (1993) by Joel Williamson. Williamson has a solid understanding of regional history, and he brings all of this knowledge to bear on Faulkner's life and, to a lesser extent, his work. He carefully examined the Blotner Papers, now part of the Louis Daniel Brodsky Collection in the Kent Library at Southeastern Missouri State University. As Williamson explains: "These materials were gathered over a span of twenty years during which Professor Blotner became something of a lightning rod attracting new information concerning the famous writer, some of which was highly charged." (In a fascinating parallel case, Leon Edel – biographer of Henry James – served as a lightning rod for his subject as well, making his work on James an unavoidable touchstone for later scholars of James and his circle.)

Williamson's research yielded a windfall of fresh evidence, making his book an invaluable source for Faulkner readers. In particular, he looked at Faulkner's ancestry, discovering elements of miscegenation in his slaveholding forebears, such as the Old Colonel, William Falkner, "an emotional, highly romantic, willful man who insisted on getting what he wanted" (p. 26). These elements played out, imaginatively, in such novels by Faulkner as *Light in August* and *Absalom, Absalom!* One could argue that Williamson was able to use material unconsciously (perhaps) suppressed by Blotner, such as details about Estelle's first marriage to Cornell Franklin and her troubled marital history with Faulkner. This study examines the explosive combination of sexual desire, racial prejudice, and violence in Faulkner's life and work in ways that transfigure our understanding of how these elements worked together.

Only a year after Williamson's book came Richard Gray's *Life of William Faulkner* (1994), part of a series of biographies of major authors commissioned by Blackwell. An English academic, writing at a moment when literary theory had suddenly gained a huge foothold in the academy, his biography draws on Blotner and other biographers for the facts, but it reinterprets the life through the fiction itself, pulling into play the language of theory, looking for junctures in the texts where historical experience intrudes and transforms the language itself. In this sense, history "writes" Faulkner. Indeed, Gray suggests that Faulkner's individual "stemmed, as ours does, from occupying a special moment in history." The particular web of history that ensnared Faulkner connects to the "web" of the text, spun from the author's gut, no doubt, but deriving from the substance around him. Gray sees Faulkner as a revisionist at heart, involved in a constant rewriting, replaying, retelling of his own past, and the imagined past of his family and Southern history itself. Remarkably free from theoretical jargon (although deeply informed by theory), Gray's biographical study reaches deftly into the language of Faulkner's fiction, finding the man himself in the interstices, hiding in the syntax, beneath the folds of prose.

In the decades after Faulkner's death, friends and acquaintances stepped forward to add their recollections of the man, swelling the shelf of memoirs. Among the crucial memoirs was that by Meta Carpenter Wilde, whose account of her love affair with Faulkner added astonishing details to the story and revealed a good deal about this passionate, troubled, covert relationship that Blotner had either not known or chose not to reveal. *A Loving Gentleman: The Love Story of William Faulkner and Meta Carpenter* (1976) was co-authored by Orin Borsten, and it remains a seminal text for biographers, one that gives us a vivid sense of the author's time in Hollywood in the thirties, when he was lonely and miserable, cut off from his roots in Oxford, spiritually adrift. In 1977, Faulkner's stepson, Malcolm Franklin, published his own recollections of life in Oxford: *Bitterweeds: Life with William Faulkner at Rowan Oak*. Malcolm's sister, Victoria, contradicts some of her brother's memories in her own recollections, which appeared in an interview with Louis Daniel Brodsky that was published in Brodsky's *Life Glimpses* (1990).

Ben Wasson was an early friend who also acted as literary agent for Faulkner at various times; he published his amusing *Count No 'Count* in 1983. This is a folksy book with a good deal of interesting material in its pages. Other books of interest for Faulkner scholars followed, some of them converging on Faulkner in tangential but fascinating ways, as in Susan Snell's *Phil Stone of Oxford: A Vicarious Life* (1991), which adds significant details about a crucial (if troubled) early friendship between the author and a local figure who became his first literary mentor. Faulkner's nephew, Jimmy Faulkner, also added an appealing volume of recollections in *Across the Creek: Faulkner Family Stories* (1986). While many stories and specific details in these various memoirs overlap, each of them adds an element to the larger life-narrative; a few of them actually deepen our sense of the man and his work.

My own biography, *One Matchless Time: A Life of William Faulkner*, appeared in 2004. As I suggested earlier, no biography is definitive, and mine certainly pretends to be no such thing. A major author, such as Faulkner, benefits from the attention of many biographers, and his life – on paper – becomes the sum of all biographies, a layering of portraits, each of them partial and subjective. The first generation of biography was written by those, especially Blotner, who had access to Faulkner's immediate circle of family and friends, even Faulkner himself. For this reason, Blotner's and other biographies of that period will always remain useful, even indispensable. I was, however, lucky enough to interview Jill Faulkner Summers, the novelist's daughter, and to talk with a fair number of his surviving relatives and friends, including Joan Williams. I also had the advantage of nearly half a century of Faulkner criticism, and drew selectively but with due respect on that tradition.

Since the time of Blotner, who edited a valuable selection of Faulkner's letters in 1977, many new letters have become available, such as the correspondence between Faulkner and Joan Williams. Faulkner revealed himself in an intensely personal way in those letters, and I benefited from reading them and being allowed to quote from them. Quite recently, Faulkner's correspondence with his parents – Miss Maud in particular – became widely available, and my portrait of Faulkner in his early twenties benefits from access to those letters. I also came across interesting letters by others, such as a revealing portrait of Faulkner in Paris by W. H. Auden.

I was able to correct or augment many anecdotes from the author's life. For example, his period as postmaster at Ole Miss has become legendary. The impression left by Blotner and Karl, among others, was that Faulkner was fired by his supervisors for negligence. Yet as Joan St C. Crane has shown, Faulkner more or less engineered his own downfall, and delighted in exaggerating the stories about his uselessness and dereliction at the post office. This was part of the personal mythmaking in which he engaged from first to last. His own life was, indeed, one of his great fictions, more legend than reality in many cases.

None of the earlier biographers attempted a critical biography except for Richard Gray. In contrast to the other biographies, I have commented in some detail on each of the major novels and many of the stories, drawing on the vast body of criticism now available on this work, always trying to ask the crucial question that confronts the biographical critic: What does the fact that Faulkner wrote this novel or story at a particular point in his career say about where his mind was at this time? For example, in writing about *The Wild Palms* (1939), I note that Charlotte Rittenmeyer, a sculptor, teaches Harry Wilbourne how "to be alive and know it." She pulls Harry from his normal life, tears him away from his marriage and his familial responsibilities, bestowing (to a degree) the gift of existential knowledge. She is a Siren of sorts, calling him from the day-to-day worries about money and relationships that are the common stuff of life. I suggest that Faulkner was talking to himself in this regard, trying to coax himself into living as an artist, without regard for money and responsibility. He was also – in his own life – experiencing deep conflicts in his marriage, and was having the first of many affairs with a younger woman. He wondered at times if he should abandon his wife and child, but chose – unlike Harry – to remain at home. I write that "Faulkner somehow managed to balance life and art, staying true to his artistic vision while, as a true gentleman, denying himself the freedom of the artist that Charlotte demands for herself" (2004: 240).

Faulkner was not, like Joyce or Lawrence, Fitzgerald or Hemingway, a straightforwardly autobiographical writer; nevertheless, his fictions emerged, however indirectly, from his life, and from the circumstances of his life. Critics have, of course, been teasing out the correspondences between Lafayette and Yoknapatawpha Counties for many decades. One can, in fact, learn a good deal about the man from reading the work respectfully, understanding that life and art never correspond exactly, especially in Faulkner.

In my biography, I attempted to address the Common Reader, as Virginia Woolf famously called the intelligent non-professional reader. In doing so, I shied away from technical or theoretical jargon, preferring a more casual and straightforward approach. But I remain only too painfully aware of the limitations of biographies, how they can, at best, capture only a piece of an author, can summon only one of several figures who might credibly be called William Faulkner. Any writer – like any human being – has multiple selves, and Faulkner seems quite extraordinary in the number of selves he presented to the world over six decades. He was, in succession, the obedient son, the frustrated young lover, the helmeted airman, the uniformed limping veteran, the indifferent college student, the romantic poet, the apprentice novelist, the town drunk, the world traveler, the married man and father, the Hollywood hack, the famous novelist, the farmer and countryman, the hunter, the equestrian, the dandy, the world-famous figure and ambassador-at-large, the public man of letters. This list catches only a few of the obvious personae worn by Faulkner.

Needless to say, biographers will sketch Faulkner again and again. Each generation of readers demands a fresh angle of vision, one that takes into account changing approaches to criticism and new information. A single life of Faulkner will never supplant all of those that went before it, and no amount of criticism or biographical energy will ever fundamentally alter the author's unique relationship with grateful readers, who will always open his books with excitement, will always find in his pages a remarkable world, one that exists in a parallel universe, utterly familiar yet always strange as well.

References and Further Reading

Blotner, J. (1974). *Faulkner: A Biography*. New York: Random House.

Brodsky, L. D. (1990). *Life Glimpses*. Austin, TX: University of Texas Press.

Cowley, M. (1966). *The Faulkner–Cowley File: Letters and Memories 1944–1962*. New York: Penguin.

Crane, J. St C. (1989). "Case No. 1337-C": The Inspector's letter to Postmaster William Faulkner. *Mississippi Quarterly*, summer: 228–45.

Cullen, J. B. (1961). *Old Times in the Faulkner Country*. Chapel Hill, NC: University of North Carolina Press.

Ellmann, R. (1959). *James Joyce*. New York: Oxford University Press.

Falkner, M. C. (1967). *The Falkners of Mississippi: A Memoir*. Baton Rouge: Louisiana State University Press.

Faulkner, J. (1963). *My Brother Bill: An Affectionate Remembrance*. New York: Trident Press.

Faulkner, J. (1986). *Across the Creek: Faulkner Family Stories*. Jackson: University of Mississippi Press.

Fish, S. (1999). Just Published: Minutiae Without Meaning. *New York Times*, September 7.

Franklin, M. (1977). *Bitterweeds: Life with William Faulkner at Rowan Oak*. Irving, TX: Society for the Study of Traditional Culture.

Gray, R. (1994). *The Life of William Faulkner: A Critical Biography*. Oxford: Blackwell.

Karl, F. R. (1989). *William Faulkner: American Writer*. New York: Weidenfeld and Nicolson.

Millgate, M. (1966). *The Achievement of William Faulkner*. New York: Random House.

Minter, D. (1980). *William Faulkner: His Life and Work*. Baltimore: Johns Hopkins University Press.

Oates, S. B. (1987). *Faulkner: The Man and the Artist*. New York: Harper and Row.

Parini, J. (2004). *One Matchless Time: A Life of William Faulkner*. New York: HarperCollins.

Richardson, H. E. (1969). *William Faulkner: The Journey to Self-Discovery*. Columbia: University of Missouri Press.

Snell, S. (1991). *Phil Stone of Oxford: A Vicarious Life*. Athens, GA: University of Georgia Press.

Thompson, L. (1966). *Robert Frost: The Early Years, 1874–1915*. New York: Holt, Rinehart and Winston.

Thompson, L. (1970). *Robert Frost: The Years of Triumph, 1915–1938*. New York: Holt, Rinehart and Winston.

Thompson, L. and R. H. Winnick (1975). *Robert Frost: The Later Years, 1938–1963*. New York: Holt, Rinehart and Winston.

Wilde, M. C. and O. Borsten (1976). *A Loving Gentleman: The Love Story of William Faulkner and Meta Carpenter*. New York: Simon and Schuster.

Williamson, J. (1993). *William Faulkner and Southern History*. New York: Oxford University Press.

Wittenberg, J. B. (1979). *Faulkner: The Transfiguration of Biography*. Lincoln, NE: University of Nebraska Press.

PART II
Questions

7

Reflections on Language
and Narrative

Owen Robinson

During his time as writer-in-residence at the University of Virginia (1957–8), William Faulkner inquired of a student, "I believe I'm paraphrasing Whitman, didn't he say, 'To have good poets we must have good readers, too,' something like that?" (Gwynn and Blotner 1995: 52). His own work's demands upon those "good readers" are considerable, and constantly changing from book to book. To a great extent Yoknapatawpha County comes about through the shifting, intense relationships between the writer and the readers of the novels. In this chapter, I shall consider some of the narrative systems that Faulkner employs, and how these systems reflect upon the malleability and the sometimes destructive power of language; I will also look at some examples of analogous situations represented within the writer–reader construct that is Yoknapatawpha. Needless to say, this discussion will be far from exhaustive, but should give some indication of the many functions and implications of Faulkner's language and narrative.

The opening section of *The Sound and the Fury* (1929) poses perhaps the most famous Faulknerian challenge to the reader, offering a complex narrative constructed of disarmingly simple language:

> Through the fence, between the curling flower spaces, I could see them hitting. They were coming toward where the flag was and I went along the fence. Luster was hunting in the grass by the flower tree. They took the flag out, and they were hitting. Then they put the flag back and they went to the table, and he hit and the other hit. Then they went on, and I went along the fence. Luster came away from the flower tree and we went along the fence and they stopped and I looked through the fence while Luster was hunting in the grass.
>
> "Here, caddie." He hit. They went away across the pasture. I held to the fence and watched them going away. (Faulkner 1967a: 11)

The defamiliarization of what we recognize to be the observation of a game of golf is deeply disconcerting, alerting the reader to the eccentricity of the account. The strangeness in the description is its very *exactness*; alien though the mode of illustration may be, the "curling flower spaces" and the "flags" and "hitting" of the game are actually highly realistic. It is the lack of framing terms like "golf" that in fact makes this narrative strange. By telling us as exactly as possible what Benjy sees, the narrator alienates the audience. Furthermore, the use of the incorrect framing term "pasture" to refer to what we have taken to be a golf course confuses matters even more.

It is only through the words of others that we eventually learn the name of the narrator, Benjy Compson, and through the ensuing shifts and clashes of the narrative that we begin to understand the reasons for the strange nature of his account. Benjy is 33 today, but has the mental age of a child; he has virtually no notion of cause and effect, no awareness of the movement of time, and no power of language. As such, he neither has nor needs any explanation for the actions of the men in the field – these actions simply *happen*; Benjy is unable to conceive of the binding idea that makes these people behave as they do. To borrow Ferdinand de Saussure's (1988) linguistic terminology, Benjy has a "*parole*," but has little understanding of a "*langue*" to give it easily recognizable meaning.[1] Time and again through the first section of the novel we see this principle, or, rather, lack of principle, in action. Likewise, Benjy's wild shifts between various episodes from his life are presented as a "continual present," his lack of awareness of time and inability to control his thoughts rendering his entire history as one apparently aimless mass of paradoxically factual (or very oddly framed) description.

Benjy's impression of the nature of things is produced by this almost exclusively descriptive mode, with Faulkner's language approximating nearly a lack of interpretation:

> We went into Mother's room, where she was lying with the sickness on a cloth on her head.
> "What is the matter now." Mother said. "Benjamin."
> "Benjy." Caddy said. She came again but I went away.
> "You must have done something to him." Mother said. "Why won't you let him alone, so I can have some peace. Give him the box and please go on and let him alone."
> Caddy got the box and set it on the floor and opened it. It was full of stars. When I was still, they were still. When I moved, they glinted and sparkled. I hushed. (Faulkner 1967a: 43)

As Benjy associates the cloth on his mother's head with her sickness, he has no means for realizing that this is his association and that the sickness is not intrinsic to the cloth itself. The lack of awareness of his own perspective in his perceptions, however, makes his unwitting transformation of the scene a creation of a truth. As far as Benjy is concerned, there is no way to dispute the cloth's culpability, so this association becomes a truth; in the same way, the sedative jewelry box becomes not metaphorically but literally a box of "stars." Benjy recognizes that their appearance is different when he moves, but he has no way of knowing his own "cause-and-effect" relationship with this change in their appearance (or for him, their behavior), and is thus spellbound by their changes. This dominance of "fact" in the narrative is even carried through to the transformation of his mother's question into a statement: questions have no place in a world without awareness of perspective or ambiguity. Not that Benjy has any understanding of what are, in effect, *his* facts – he lives in a world of his own unconscious creation, but he does not understand how, why, or what this creation is, often resulting in an incomprehensible terror expressed by his howling.

But for all Benjy's "writing" of his world in this way, his lack of awareness of doing so is absolute, calling attention to our own more relative lack of awareness of how our language and stories create our own realities. Faulkner requires us to recognize what is happening in Benjy's world, and then to take into account Benjy's own unconscious rules of creation to understand the scenes and experiences he relates. Our juxtaposition of this alien conception of the world with our own corresponding understanding of reality defines the space that Benjy inhabits, and is the key factor in the author and reader's collaborative creation of the character/narrator himself. Benjy's psyche is, in effect, a personification of what Pierre Macherey refers to as an "area of shadow" around a work (Macherey 1990: 215), the vital "unspoken" component of the text, or "the juxtaposition of several meanings which produces the radical otherness which shapes the work: this conflict is not resolved or absorbed, but simply displayed. . . . In its every particle, the work *manifests*, uncovers, what it cannot say. This silence gives it life" (p. 217). The character that emerges through the reader's involvement with Faulkner's structural techniques *is* this silence, a silence filled with myriad voices – prominently including the reader's own – but which itself, literally, has no voice.

As the voices cannot be heard, so the silence cannot provide the "life" (and in this case, *be* the very represented life of the narrative) without a receptor to understand or interpret it. And as Faulkner exploits the necessary silence intrinsic to the text in the conception of the character of Benjy, so he exploits the cognitive activity of the reader to realize the silence, to grant the silence its eloquence. Understanding the relationship of the reader to the text as vital to its fruition, Faulkner plays with the operations he establishes to challenge the reader to perform his or her allotted task, to turn Benjy from being a difficult character merely understood, however effectively, to one actually living, moving through time and space in ways which Benjy himself cannot know. The timbres, moods, and states of Benjy's mind are evoked by means of the linguistic filter through which his observations are transmitted. While the mode avoids veering from the strictly descriptive, the things being described are called up by our recognition of what they signify beyond the realm of description. For example, we recognize the importance of key images in evoking a certain frame of mind, and we use motifs like "Caddy smelled like trees" (Faulkner 1967a: 13 and passim) to establish footholds in Benjy's confused chronology.

The creation of Benjy Compson serves as an extreme example of how Faulkner's language requires the reader to take a highly active role in the narrative processes, and to be more self-conscious of this activity than usual. The reader's involvement is used in a rather different, but still disarming way, in *Sanctuary* (1931): here, we are not asked to become the deciphering interlocutor of the narrative, but to be complicit in its violating gaze. The chief object of the gaze is, of course, Temple Drake:

> Townspeople taking after-supper drives through the college grounds or an oblivious and
> bemused faculty-member or a candidate for a master's degree on his way to the library
> would see Temple, a snatched coat under her arm and her long legs blond with running,
> in speeding silhouette against the lighted windows . . . vanishing into the shadow
> beside the library wall, and perhaps a final squatting swirl of knickers or whatnot as she
> sprang into the car waiting there with engine running on that particular night. (Faulkner
> 1993: 28)

Temple is not so much introduced as lusted after: both we and observers within the
scene are treated to an intimate and covert glance up her skirt as her frantic activity
prevents her guarding against this violation. Of course, the onlooker is painted as male
by Faulkner ("his way"), one of the many observations or constructions of the male gaze
that, along with "the aggression the narrative voice seems to feel toward [Temple],"
contributes to the severe male/female dichotomy that contributes to the novel's notoriety
(Gray 1994: 167). But whatever the reader's identity in this instance, he or she engages
in the same activity as those figures on the Oxford campus: staring at a vulnerable
young woman. We might question the degree of this complicity: just as the narrative
seems to imply that the townspeople or academics have this view foisted upon them,
so the reader's view seems led by the narrator up Temple's skirt with little choice but
to follow. But the narrative is subtler than it may first appear: we "perhaps" see "a final
squatting swirl of knickers or whatnot." That use of "perhaps" and "whatnot" is enough
to encourage the reader to consider the possibilities, and in doing so we are immediately
relieved of our moral rectitude. This is not simply a case of being shown an indecent
image: rather, the narrative forces us to recognize our own application of imagination.
This is another manifestation of Faulkner's manipulation of the reader's cognitive
engagement, but applied with a purpose different to that in *The Sound and the Fury*.

But can the reader really be blamed for our part in the voyeuristic process taking
place here? After all, it is the narrator who unequivocally tells us that Temple is "[l]ong
legged, thin armed, with high small buttocks" (Faulkner 1993: 89), who places us
almost on her shoulder as she desperately searches for a private space in which to defe-
cate: "When she rose she saw . . . the squatting outline of a man" (p. 91), a man who
is never identified and as such is worryingly analogous to the reader, again being
involved in basically the same activity. Is this not, as some early reviews claimed, merely
Faulkner being deliberately shocking, leading the gentle reader into a moral underworld
more or less regardless of his or her own feelings? This might be the case were it not
for the challenge implicit in the narrative: *what are you doing?* On the most basic level,
we (presumably) keep reading the book, refusing to be swayed by our outrage from
finding out more. This may seem rather a truism at first, but the very nature of the
novel plays with these impulses. Faulkner's identification of his "cheap idea" may be
disingenuous, but *Sanctuary* is, in many respects, a thriller, a page-turner, and much of
its tension comes from its encouraging of both excitement and fear in the reader. Therefore, we cannot honestly condemn Faulkner for cruelty without acknowledging our own
tacit complicity: the book is a thriller because we are thrilled, and the application of
hard-boiled narrative elements to such terrible material is chillingly effective in making

us question our motivations for reading. Once again, form and content are wholly intertwined, refusing to provide answers to the disturbing questions raised, but situating those questions in narrative points of view mirroring those of figures like Tommy who watch "the movement of Popeye's hand" "[b]eneath the raincoat on Temple's breast" (p. 61).

These examples of the ways in which Faulkner's language places different narrative demands upon the reader are just two of many. But rather than present a list of other such processes, we might examine some potentially analogous narrative situations within the fiction itself. Consider, for instance, this description of the Civil War hero Colonel John Sartoris:

> Then I began to smell it again, like each time he returned . . . that odor in his clothes and beard and flesh too which I believed was the smell of powder and glory, the elected victorious but know better now: know to have been only the will to endure, a sardonic and even humorous declining of self-delusion which is not even kin to that optimism which believes that that which is about to happen to us can possibly be the worst which we can suffer. (Faulkner 1967b: 11)

This account of Sartoris's return from battle is given by his son Bayard near the beginning of *The Unvanquished* (1938), and neatly establishes both the tensions apparent within him with regard to his father and what he represents, and the relations between the figure of the child protagonist and his more mature textual presence as narrator. In calling attention to the differences between what he believed in the past and "knows" now, Bayard immediately sets up a narrative distance within which conflicting views can be fielded. Thus, the myth of "the elected victorious" does battle with "the will to endure" in an engagement which never finds adequate resolution in Bayard's mind. The juxtaposition of the two readings within the single description of his father's return, as well as actively interpreting the relationship between myth and reality, is vitally constitutive of the Colonel and his son as we perceive them, and, to a degree, of their perceptions of themselves and each other. For within the tableau of the father–son reunion presented there are at least four figures involved: Bayard the young protagonist, Bayard the older narrator, and the two John Sartorises that are the projections of each of these. Somewhere between the various elements that we see here lurks John Sartoris himself, but, of course, any attempt to pin him down exactly would be extremely difficult. As well as the Colonel himself, the character of Bayard is being fundamentally constructed primarily through consideration of his relationship with the heroic myth of his father, and, more broadly, the myth of the Old South itself. In this context, Bayard serves as an embodiment of one of the chief concerns of the Yoknapatawpha novels, the tensions between the South's past, its conceptions of that past, and its present. As a young man on the cusp of change in his family and regional history, Bayard's mentality and life enact many aspects of Yoknapatawpha's struggles with itself, and these tensions and struggles appear both in the novel's story and in the novel's language and narrative processes, as in the passage excerpted above.

A far more complex narrative consideration of narrative functions and implications takes place in *Absalom, Absalom!* (1936), wherein we are not really told the story of Thomas Sutpen itself, as such, but rather its *telling*. Even Quentin's telling Shreve of Sutpen's background is couched wholly in terms of Sutpen's relating it to General Compson, not to mention the intermediary narration that has taken place in order to get it to Massachusetts in 1909:

> And I reckon Grandfather was saying "Wait, wait for God's sake wait" about like you are, until he finally did stop and back up and start over again with at least some regard for cause and effect even if none for logical sequence and continuity . . . and still it was not absolutely clear – the how and the why he was there and what he was – since he was not talking about himself. He was telling a story. He was not bragging about something he had done; he was just telling a story about something a man named Thomas Sutpen had experienced, which would still have been the same story if the man had had no name at all, if it had been told about any man or no man over whiskey at night. (Faulkner 1969: 247)

Notwithstanding all the distorting layers of narrative involved in the eventual relaying of Sutpen's early life to us – some of which we see, some of which is implied and continued in the reader's mind – Sutpen's own directly authorial role is established here, not only in terms of his actual life but in the relaying of it into the public domain. We might say that he is apparently rather inefficient as a storyteller, necessitating inquiry and a need for order on the part of his audience – a role which, of course, continues down the line all the way to the reader of Faulkner's novel. It is important to note that the formative events of Sutpen's childhood, despite coming from the horse's mouth, are never related as any kind of fact but rather, in this manner, as a fireside yarn, joining the "rag-tag and bob-ends of old tales and talking" that constitute the Sutpen legend (p. 303). What is more, this is a story highly contingent in itself on the circumstances of its telling: Sutpen has little regard for the niceties of "logical sequence and continuity." As a result the story is shaped by the machinations and instincts of the teller's mind as he tells it. For instance, he moves on to the episode of the Haitian slave revolt seemingly by accident: "This anecdote was no deliberate continuation of the other one but was merely called to his mind by the picture of the niggers and torches in front of them" (p. 246). Similarly, the tale stops when Sutpen decides that enough has been told for one night (and in the narrative present, Quentin reflects that it would take the 30 years it took Sutpen to tell it to do so properly, an indicator of how important, to Quentin at least, the process of storytelling is to the story). Furthermore, as Richard Godden has discussed, Sutpen's Haitian period constitutes a troubling anachronism: by the time he claims to have arrived there, slavery had long since ended, rendering the uprisings he suppresses an "unreadable revolution" (Godden 1997: 49). As well as the class- and race-related questions posed by Sutpen's narrative here, treated at valuable length by Godden, we are forced to recognize that empirical "truth" is never the motivating force – the suggestion is that the story creates its own momentum, regardless of whether it is about Sutpen, "any man or no man." What this means, at root, is that the jungle of fictions that comes to surround Sutpen is itself growing from what is more or less fiction in itself – "he was telling a story" – however "true" his account may or may not be.

These rather important qualifications noted, Sutpen's account is the nearest to truth that we have, be it created or otherwise, and so, in terms of his story at least, we are in a similar position to the readers within the book: in order to come to any conclusions at all, we have to take some things more or less on trust, whilst all the time being disturbingly aware that such an attitude has no real viability. Most of the story is not, of course, related by Sutpen himself, but in the context this does little to alter narrative reliability one way or the other. Even assuming that Sutpen's partial account is an accurate one, his authorship here is perhaps most powerful as a reminder, or indicator, of the extent to which he is responsible for the events of his own destiny, notwithstanding its many outside influences, even down to the possible fictive creation of the circumstances from which he shapes it. Thomas Sutpen attempts to write a grand Southern text that he hopes will compete with his previous state of innocence and exclusion, but which creates its own parameters of innocence, corruption, and continued exclusion. In his appropriation of the old order as he sees it, he and those who respond to it create their own, one whose paradoxically subversive determinism replaces the destiny apparently apportioned to him with a self-ordained and ultimately self-destroying fervor. To paraphrase his daughter Judith, he has left his mark on the stone, woven his pattern into the rug, existentially *humanized* himself through narrative in a world that is structured effectively to muzzle that humanity (Faulkner 1969: 127–8). Indeed, he has inscribed the retrospective statement of intent "*I was here*," which Faulkner himself held so central to the creative impulse, on the walls of Yoknapatawpha (Gray 1994: 372; King 1980: 143).

The various narrators obsessively attempt to piece together the life of Thomas Sutpen and the motivations behind it, a painstaking process of sifting through fragmented evidence and trying to fill in the gaps through interpretation and reason. The reader of *Absalom, Absalom!* engages in much the same activity in trying to understand the unity of the text. Our awareness of this, and its importance, is made all the more intense by each narrator's acute awareness of the others' machinations, and by the explicit likening of their activities to the act of reading, not least in Mr. Compson's frustration at the elusiveness of his subject:

> It's just incredible. It just does not explain. Or perhaps that's it: they dont explain and we are not supposed to know. We have a few old mouth-to-mouth tales; we exhume from old trunks and boxes and drawers letters without salutation or signature . . . ; we see dimly people. . . . They are there, yet something is missing; they are like a chemical formula exhumed along with the letters from that forgotten chest, carefully, the paper old and faded and falling to pieces, the writing faded, almost indecipherable, yet meaningful, familiar in shape and sense, the name and presence of volatile and sentient forces; you bring them together in the proportions called for, but nothing happens; you re-read, tedious and intent, poring, making sure that you have forgotten nothing, made no miscalculation; you bring them together again and again nothing happens: just the

words, the symbols, the shapes themselves, shadowy inscrutable and serene, against that turgid background of a horrible and bloody mischancing of human affairs. (Faulkner 1969: 100–1)

As well as articulating the sheer difficulty of constructing the saga of Sutpen's Hundred, Mr. Compson here captures much of the experience of the reader of *Absalom, Absalom!* As such, the above passage is a telling, not to mention brave, self-reflexive comment to place in a novel so apparently concerned with making things difficult for the reader. It also points out that this is no mere literary contrivance for its own sake, but synonymous with the fundamental need to understand ourselves and our contexts. If the work of literature requires effort on the part of its reader, effort that will frequently be frustrated, then so does its object: life, conceived as the "turgid background of a horrible and bloody mischancing of human affairs."

All the major narrators in *Absalom, Absalom!* make explicit reference to their own conscious creation of the scenes and people they describe, quite aside from the implicit ways in which the reader can see their dispositions color the narrative. We can detect a certain cynical enjoyment in Mr. Compson's self-appointed role of scribe of the Sutpen saga: he frames things in willful conjecture – "perhaps (I like to think this) . . ." – thereby adding elements that he has constructed himself through his admitted desire to have them there (p. 95). What makes this blatant fictionalizing all the more ironic in terms of the alleged attempt to find the "truth" is the leitmotif of "doubtless" to be found in his narrative, a word whose meaning is perpetually undermined by being juxtaposed with scenarios that are quite clearly open to doubt. Indeed, it is only because there *is* so much doubt that Mr. Compson feels the need to fictionalize consciously and to substantiate his findings by dismissing the doubt that originally allowed for them. Miss Rosa, the only one of the present-day narrators to have actually known Sutpen firsthand, and indeed to have been part of the story as it occurred, recognizes her own potential invention of people and events. At the same time as her passion seems to insist upon the correctness of her portrayal of Sutpen and his progeny, she points out, about one of the novel's central characters (Charles Bon) and events that she and others try to explain (his death), that *"(I never saw* him. *I never even saw him dead. I heard a name, I saw a photograph, I helped to make a grave: and that was all)"* (p. 146). Miss Rosa is fully aware that Bon is, in effect, a fictional character for herself as a reader as well as for her audience, a character whose very realization depends upon her interpretation: the godlike overtones of her writerly actions do not escape her. None of this stops her from believing her account to be the correct one, and, indeed, it does not necessarily discount it from being so; again, however, this is largely irrelevant. Whatever the basis of her picture in empirical "truth," she has, like Mr. Compson, brought a scenario into being and acted on it through her interpretations.

Some early reviews of *Absalom, Absalom!*, perhaps unwilling to consider it on the terms suggested here, accused Faulkner of a failure to distinguish stylistically the characters of his individual narrators. Such narrow readings of Faulkner's use of language are rendered somewhat obsolete by the intervening decades of Faulkner criticism and literary theory, but it is this very narrowness that makes these views interesting. Far from constricting either character or story, the linguistic "limitation" that these reviews identify is what marks its freeing of voice: what is seen as a damagingly singular vision is, in textual terms at least, rather the result of the exact opposite. *Absalom, Absalom!* is constructed of voice upon voice upon voice speaking simultaneously and eternally, layered not on top of one another, but rather in and around and through each other, voices that merge and mingle together to the point where they escape from any one discernible speaker and take on a creative life of their own. That the narrators' voices often appear to be constructed through recognizably Faulknerian diction and structure is not, when one considers the novelistic purpose behind their apparent similarity, a sign of technical weakness, but rather of Faulkner's virtuosity in controlling his theme. Rather than an overbearing omniscience that dehumanizes his characters, what actually occurs is a transcription of narrative itself, built up from its numerous sources and unified in the consciousness of Quentin Compson and, of course, the reader, both of whose voices become haunted by previous voices and stories, much as Sutpen's "own" story is shown to be thoroughly haunted by the very stories he decided to challenge with his "own."

Flem Snopes is another character who attempts to inscribe himself upon a world which would deny him, and is the primary focus of a trilogy with other subtle narrative complexities, two volumes of which I will discuss here. *The Hamlet* (1940) is delivered by an authorial voice, though it is one that is frequently inhabited by the eager contributions of others, most notably V. K. Ratliff. As always with Faulkner's use of such a voice, its position can never be taken for granted – it would be a mistake, for instance, to assume omniscience in any Faulkner narrative, however external its voice may seem. In the early stages of *The Hamlet*, Ratliff takes over the narrative to tell the tall tale of Ab Snopes and Pat Stamper. After many pages of the story, we suddenly and briefly leave Ratliff's voice and swing out to see the scene of its telling.

> "'Sho now,' Stamper says. 'That horse will surprise you.'
>
> "And it did," Ratliff said. He laughed, for the first time, quietly, invisible to his hearers though they knew exactly how he would look at the moment as well as if they could see him, easy and relaxed in his chair, with his lean brown pleasant shrewd face, in his faded clean blue shirt, with that same air of perpetual bachelorhood which Jody Varner had, although there was no other resemblance between them and not much here, since in Varner it was a quality of shabby and fustian gallantry where in Ratliff it was that hearty celibacy as of a lay brother in a twelfth-century monastery – a gardener, a pruner of vines, say. "That horse surprised us . . ." (Faulkner 1940: 48–9)

Ratliff is talking here to the apparently ever-present group of poor white Frenchman's Bend men assembled on the porch of Varner's store, a chorus with whom he is frequently seen and, more importantly, heard throughout the novel. Part of the effect of this passage is to make us newly aware of this: it is important that we do not treat his rambling account in isolation, but rather as part of the scene in which its teller is present – one is reminded, perhaps, of Sutpen's campfire telling of his early life during the hunt for the French architect. Ratliff's tale, his telling of it, is necessarily full of his readings, and this authorial step back in the middle of the narrative reminds us of its contingency. More than this, though, Faulkner carefully contextualizes Ratliff himself here: he is presented in terms of his intimates, largely through that familiar Faulknerian technique of describing in the negative – they can't see him, but we are treated to their under-standing of how he looks despite this. This also represents a prime example of one of the great achievements of *The Hamlet*'s narrative voice, in its subtle yet inextricable combination of the chorus's thoughts and interpretations with the diction and broader world-view of the authorial voice. Factual description is tinged with slight value judg-ments (Ratliff's "lean brown pleasant shrewd face") and willfully speculative analogy ("a gardener, a pruner of vines, say") that serve to accommodate the views of Ratliff's audience at the same time as allowing authorial freedom to suggest. This in turn reminds us that the interactivity between Ratliff as writer/reader and his audience, and that between Faulkner and ourselves, are essentially engagements in the same process.

This passage is typical of much of the handling of material in *The Hamlet*, and is itself contextualized and qualified a little later when we are told of Will Varner's first encounter with Flem Snopes:

> Then at last, on Friday afternoon, Will Varner himself appeared. Perhaps it was for this Ratliff and his companions had been waiting. But if it was, it was doubtless not Ratliff but the others who even hoped that anything would divulge here. So it was very likely Ratliff alone who was not surprised, since what did divulge was the obverse of what they might have hoped for; it was not the clerk who now discovered at last whom he was working for, but Will Varner who discovered who was working for him. (p. 61)

Again, what could be a simple description of a meeting is turned into a multi-leveled analysis of the scene in all its narrative relevance. Everything is couched in uncertainty here – even the uncertainty. The authorial voice gives us a detailed and indeed plausible account of the thinking of the porch-chorus, while at the same time registering Ratliff's at least partial distinction from them, and even goes further to posit probable ramifica-tions of the meeting of expectation and event. But despite the description of the scene through fine psychological detail, it is undercut throughout by acknowledgement of the portrait's own basis in supposition.

At first glance, this kind of writing seems a long way from the intense interiority of, for example, *The Sound and the Fury* and parts of *Absalom, Absalom!*, wherein we gain access to individuals' thought-patterns, and partake in their fictive construction. Surely the very uncertainty of this authorial voice sets it at the opposite end of the scale, as a voice so *exterior* that precise understanding is impossible, and indeed recognized as such? But closer analysis suggests that, in fact, something rather similar is occurring, though seen from another perspective. For all their sophistication, the dominant char-acteristic of such earlier Faulknerian voices is their utter subjectivity and, therefore, their inability to do anything further than speculate, however constructively, upon the scene or people occupying them. In this passage from *The Hamlet*, the subtly ironic use of the word "doubtless" hauntingly echoes the same word's use as a leitmotif in *Absalom, Absalom!*, wherein it registers attempts by narrators to validate what is, pointedly, full of doubt. The assertion of certainty serves to indicate the very lack of it. The tone of this authorial voice, like the tone of those more subjective, interior narrative voices, suggests a similar position: like the relationship of Quentin to Sutpen, the relationship of the authorial voice – and the reader – to the chorus is one founded on a series of assumptions, explorations, deductions, and presentations in a hopefully coherent form. If the dominant narrative mode is exterior here, we are asked to remember that this is *necessarily* so, and that for all the turmoil of internalized subjectivity in such books as *Absalom, Absalom!*, the readers themselves are in the same position as this authorial voice – all they can do is read, however "doubtlessly," and it is their readings that become the written story. If a major effect of *Absalom, Absalom!* is to assert the analogous natures of readers and writers within and of texts by focusing attention on the characters' acts of reading and writing, then passages such as this one achieve a similar purpose by focusing attention instead on our acts of reading and writing characters. We observe Ratliff and the chorus reading the "text" of Snopes, but our own necessary uncertainty with regard to reading *them* reminds us of the doubt at every level from writer to character to narrator to reader.

This represents a double-edged narrative approach, using the shiftiness of free indirect discourse with characters or groups, most poignantly and parodically in the astonishing romance of Ike and the cow, interspersed with wider-angled, more apparently stable meditations upon problems of social and personal readership. Adding to this the heady, unpredictable element of conversation, *The Hamlet* is steeped in what Richard Gray has called "narrative plenitude" (Gray 1994: 254). "The talking of the people of Frenchman's Bend," Gray continues, is

> a system of verbal collusion that implies its own gaps and omissions. . . . The talking that incorporates and surrounds these people – that is, the talking of *The Hamlet* as a whole – is something quite different: an exchange of voices which challenges the idea that any relationship is fixed and stable, and invites us to see all relationships – between, say, character and narrator and reader, or personality and environment – as existing in a medium of change. (pp. 268–9)

This presence within the text of different levels of "talking" brings to mind certain dynamics of *The Sound and the Fury*, wherein voices form and are formed by personal conceptions of truth, while our privileged position as reader allows us to witness and partake of the unstable relationships between them. The perspective is different here, however, this unstable relationship among the varying levels of voice being acknowledged within the text itself, while we constitute another stage. And while the voices in the earlier novel were striking for their painful isolation, their intermingling rather a process of invasion only realized at the level of our readership, here that intermingling forms a kind of linguistic foundation for such fragile social cohesion as exists in the village.

Ratliff plays an important part in the narration of *The Mansion* (1959), as well, and here becomes a vocal theorist of narrative processes; in discussing his own machinations as a creative reader of the ongoing Snopes scenarios he also offers candid observations upon the writerly presumptions of, for instance, his fellow narrators, including Faulkner. In giving his version of the village boys' humiliation and jealousy over the union of Eula Varner and Hoake McCarron – a situation already familiar to us from *The Hamlet* – Ratliff considers one of the injured:

> it was Theron Quick; for a week after it you could still see the print of that loaded buggy whip across the back of his skull; not the first time naming him Quick turned out to be what the feller calls jest a humorous allusion – laying cold in the weeds beside the road. And that's when I believe it happened. I don't even insist or argue that it happened that way. I jest simply decline to have it any other way except that one because there ain't no acceptable degrees between what has got to be right and what jest can possibly be. (Faulkner 1962: 120)

This passage is full not only of loaded references to recognizable scenes from the trilogy, but of slyly self-referential jokes about the meditations upon narrative throughout Faulkner's career. In the fictive terms of Yoknapatawpha itself, Quick is a family name like any other, and Ratliff is free to laugh about its inaptitude on these grounds alone. But in the wider sphere in which the county is a construct of the writers and readers of books, it is, of course, Faulkner who has decided both to name a particular character Quick, and to make it that character who ends up in the ditch – at least as far as we can gather from Ratliff. Ratliff himself, of course, is unaware of Faulkner, but is keenly alert to the humor in such an apparent half-wit being "named Quick." The remark works both as the sort of literary in-joke we have encountered previously in *Absalom, Absalom!*, for instance, and as a vernacular aside on the spuriousness of creation – such voices being every bit as profound, in Faulkner, as any more allegedly "proper" voices. This would be rich enough in itself, but the creation motif is continued into Ratliff's analysis of his own interpretive actions. Having, in effect, referred to a godlike, writerly force dictating events, he then goes on to identify just such an arbitrary trait in his own readership of the situation. It happened like this, he says, simply because he "decline[s] to have it any other way." Of course, if the best of Faulkner's work shows us anything, it is those very "degrees" that Ratliff so blithely dismisses here. Again, this works both as a joke and as a more serious reflection upon fictive creation on Faulkner's part, but also on Ratliff's. For Ratliff himself is self-deprecating and somewhat sardonic here, freely admitting his own willful creative bigotry by declining to argue his point and telling us this. Ratliff, as well as Faulkner, is pointing to the constructive power of interpretation. The implication of this passage as a whole is that the authorial, godlike figure sensed in the "humorous" naming of Quick is in fact those who identify him by interpreting him, his readers both within Yoknapatawpha and outside it, thereby implicating Ratliff, Faulkner, ourselves, and so on. In fact, just before this passage, Ratliff offers another observation by which to contextualize his apparent assumption of absolutism:

Naturally they never brought no bystanders with them and after the first two or three minutes there wasn't no witness a-tall left, since he was already laying out cold in the ditch. So my conjecture is as good as yourn, maybe better since I'm a interested party, being as I got what a feller calls a theorem to prove. (p. 119)

Again, here, Ratliff undercuts his own reading, and its professed "truth," by admitting its conjectural premise. He also, however, points to one of the most important dynamics of "Snopeswatching": that those engaging in it are contemporaneous "interested parties," and that this has a crucial effect on their writerly construction of character and event. The processes by which the readers in the work read and co-construct Flem Snopes are not merely akin, as in *Absalom, Absalom!*, to their experience in life – they are one and the same. The story that they are fascinated by for so long is not only another man's tale, but to a great extent their own. Ironically, perhaps, they ultimately fail to tell Flem's story: he remains an enigma whom we can never firmly say we "know," much as we can speculate – and see others speculate – about the inner workings of Sutpen without ever being able to lay claim to his psyche. Flem himself remains tight-lipped throughout his life: for a man so studied, we hear remarkably little from him.

A look at *Light in August* (1932) should pull some of these concerns of language and narrative together. This novel consists not only of its numerous voices, but also of the explicit and necessary consideration of their effects and interaction. Each voice present applies itself in particular to Joe Christmas, bringing a potentially infinite battery of connotations with words like "Christmas" or "nigger," and immediately and automatically entering and contributing to the endless dialogic web that is the linguistic world. Joe's first entrance into the novel is through another man's memory of what others said about him in the past:

Byron Bunch knows this: It was one Friday morning three years ago. And the group of men in the planer shed looked up, and saw the stranger standing there, watching them. . . . He did not look like a professional hobo in his professional rags, but there was something definitely rootless about him, as though no town or city was his, no street, no walls, no square of earth his home. And that he carried his knowledge with him always as though it were a banner, with a quality ruthless, lonely, and almost proud. "As if," as the men said later, "he was just down on his luck for a time, and that he didn't intend to stay down on it and didn't give a damn how much he rose up." (Faulkner 1964: 25)

This is character-creation, and indeed history, in the form of multiple recollection, and in its style is perhaps similar to the narrative voice used in sections of *The Hamlet* and *The Mansion*, wherein the authorial voice merges with a social collective consciousness. Joe's appearance here is also similar to Thomas Sutpen's arrival in Jefferson in *Absalom, Absalom!*, taking the form of a kind of oral legend, before we are allowed near the man himself. Just as Sutpen seems to grow out of the "steady strophe and antistrophe" of voices (Faulkner 1969: 32) – the intrinsic call-and-response process that Bakhtin posits as fundamental to language – so Joe here is founded in the reader's consciousness in the spaces between the men's initial conception of him as "definitely rootless" (an evocative oxymoron) with a particular kind of "knowledge" and pride, their *later* words about him, and Byron's memory of these stages. This approach is important: rather than just tell us about Joe, the authorial voice tells us about an individual perception of a collective consciousness of him, immediately foregrounding his existence in dialogue. The reader is probably inclined to come from this passage with an initial impression of Joe, but we are not "given" this by the authorial voice: rather, we are presented with a dialogue out of which we must come to our own conclusions. We might say that our impression is validated by the men's words, but the "rootlessness" we sense is all the more striking through our inability even to place Joe firmly in this narrative construct. Faulkner's decision to give *ideas* of Joe, rather than Joe himself, is a recognition that this is necessarily all he *can* do, as well as pointing to his own role as a reader as well as writer.[2]

Joe himself is alert to the power of language from the start. Even while he is unsure, as a young child, of the meaning and resonance of his name, he unconsciously identifies it as an essential facet of his being as he hears McEachern announce his intention to give his own surname along with his religion to Joe:

> The child was not listening. He was not bothered. He did not especially care, anymore than if the man had said the day was hot when it was not hot. He didn't even bother to say to himself *My name aint McEachern. My name is Christmas* There was no need to bother about that yet. There was plenty of time. (Faulkner 1964: 111)

Later, Joe will say these italicized words out loud to his lover Bobbie in a vocal expression of his self-identity. Here, however, the self represented by the name "*Christmas*" is the very core of his largely inarticulate being, and McEachern's protestations to the contrary are as irrelevant and inane to him as Joe's own individuality is to his foster-father. This, of course, is on a level deeper even than that usually suggested by Faulkner's use of italics, through being presented in the negative: despite his immaturity and lack of advanced comprehension as to his situation, he is subconsciously claiming the identity, the difference, embodied in the name he was given when he was delivered to the orphanage. Alfred Kazin famously suggests that " 'Joe Christmas' is worse than any real name could be" because it indicates the sheer extent of his rootlessness and lack of identity (Kazin 1960: 248), but surely the important point here is that Joe takes the negative implied by his name and claims it for himself. True, it is a name arbitrarily given by strangers – any child turning up that night would probably have been called "Christmas" – but in identifying himself with it he embraces all that this emptiness allows. His name may signify a lack of identity, or a nebulous identity imposed by others, but his adherence to it and to the ambiguities and connotations it has is another conspicuous example of the various ways language turns even formlessness into defining characteristics.

On the night before he kills Joanna Burden, Christmas lights a cigarette in his cabin, and flings the match into the darkness:

Then he was listening for the light, trivial sound which the dead match would make when it struck the floor; and then it seemed to him that he heard it. Then it seemed to him, sitting on the cot in the dark room, that he was hearing a myriad sounds of no greater volume – voices, murmurs, whispers: of trees, darkness, earth; people: his own voice; other voices evocative of names and times and places – which he had been conscious of all his life without knowing it, which were his life, thinking *God perhaps and me not knowing that too* He could see it like a printed sentence, fullborn and already dead *God loves me too* like the faded and weathered letters on a last year's billboard *God loves me too.* (Faulkner 1964: 80)

In the apparently trivial act of throwing a match to the floor, Joe experiences a kind of linguistic epiphany. He is keenly aware of the "myriad" elements that constitute his life and history, and furthermore becomes aware at this point of his own previously unnoted consciousness of them. Joe's reflections here encompass virtually all the participants in his make-up, whether explicitly or otherwise: himself, others, places, God – we might add to the list the author and the reader of *Light in August*. Joe is aware of his life as a kind of linguistic democracy, a product of voices, including his own, all of whom are contingent in themselves and none of which has individual authority. To consider the identity of Joe Christmas, therefore, is to engage with a network of voices each trying to "write" him, and each consciously and unconsciously "reading" him simultaneously, receiving the influence of other elements of his dialogic presence.

Faulkner's narrative devices in *Light in August* perhaps come most tellingly to bear in its treatment of race as linguistic construct, and particularly in the disturbing position of the reader in the racial discourse. Joe is "black" because he is said to be so, and the reader is arguably as involved in the saying as anyone. James A. Snead points to our conundrum:

In *Light in August* Faulkner diverges from Fielding's omniscient narrators or Conrad's or James's unreliable ones by exposing omniscience as unreliability. The unreliability is an active deception. There is no deficiency, of either intelligence or perspicacity: the narrator is actively creating error. Society here turns arbitrary codes of dominance into "fact." To make matters worse, the reader helps to accomplish the entire process. (Snead 1986: 85)

While this is directed at such narrative complexities as I have mentioned, Snead also, rightly, challenges some of the authorial voice's more overt racial stereotyping – its frequent references to the smells, jobs, mentality of African Americans. This, of course, is never as simple as it may initially appear, and presents the reader with a further challenge beyond our realization of complicity in Jefferson's racism. "Faulkner gives us the choice to be racists in a very cunning way," says Snead. "[D]o we passively accept the truth of the narrator's judgment and thereby ourselves join the town's consensus? Or do we suspend our own judgment for the sake of fairness?" (p. 83). There is no denying the discomfort one is liable to feel when faced with an authorial description of a black nursemaid with "the vacuous idiocy of her idle and illiterate kind" (Faulkner 1964: 45), and Snead is probably right to suggest that Faulkner shares the town's "conservative compulsion to impose order," but surely our duty goes further than merely measuring our own politics against those of the narrator (Snead 1986: 82)? I would suggest that even at points such as this, the authorial voice is far from singular: in this instance it is following the consciousness of Gail Hightower. In the controversial description of Joe's journey through Freedman Town, the racial attributes expressed must be read in the context of the narrative's close following of Christmas's consciousness, thereby prominently including his voice. This is neither to deny nor to excuse the racism in Faulkner: crucially he attempts to do neither himself. Faulkner's keen awareness of himself as a product of his environment is evident throughout his work: even as he rails against the South's atrocities he makes no attempt to deny his own culpability as a Southerner, however comparatively liberal he may be. The linguistic and narrative problem that Snead identifies is, of course, all part of the novel's conceit. Nobody escapes interrogation, and that very much includes the author and the reader.

The men at the mill in *Light in August* and the porch-chorus in *The Hamlet* are essential components of Faulkner's narrative strategies, their world of speech largely constituting the psychological framework of Frenchman's Bend. Such talkers appear throughout the series, especially in those novels more structurally dominated by outright speech. *As I Lay Dying* (1930), for instance, as well as featuring the voices of the Bundren family themselves, is partially made up of a chorus of observers, figures such as Vernon and Cora Tull, Dr. Peabody, and Moseley. Not only does the interaction of such commentators with the action and each other constitute much of that particular novel's narrative power, it also contextualizes their own appearances in other novels, in different roles. The Tulls, for instance, are the family whose telephone Ruby uses to report Tommy's death in *Sanctuary*: they are hardly mentioned themselves in that novel, but their role in *As I Lay Dying* allows for a much richer picture of their reactions to such revelations as they try to eat their Sunday dinner. Peabody, similarly, has previously featured as a somewhat comic character in *Sartoris* (1929), an appearance that makes his minor part in *As I Lay Dying* all the more humorous and desperate. It is in small, fragile details such as this, and the fundamental role of the reader in realizing them, that the characters and the world which they inhabit come to life, both within and outside their immediate novelistic place.

If anything, Yoknapatawpha can be seen as a state of mind – or, rather, a convergence of many states of mind exercising themselves both toward and within the series of novels. The need for people to work together, whether harmoniously or otherwise, is fundamental not only to the processes of fictional practice but also to the building of the environments in which we live. The fictive nature of Yoknapatawpha, and the requirement for everybody involved to participate with full involvement in its creation, is central to the investigations into the "real-world" issues with which Faulkner is so concerned. Realizing and acting upon this sometimes demands a great deal of us, but if we are willing to take up Faulkner's writerly challenges, we will have a reading experience with quite extraordinary rewards.

NOTES

1 Saussure's focus is specifically linguistic — *langue* referring to an overall language system, and *parole* to an individual speech act — but we can easily see the principle at work in Benjy's particular mode of comprehension (or, often, lack of one). Indeed, the linguistic tenor of this model is ironically appropriate for a discussion of Benjy, a character constructed through language yet possessing almost none of his own.

2 Arthur F. Kinney gives a subtle, extended close reading of this passage, focusing on the perspective of Byron Bunch, his ordering of his vision of "the stranger," and the other men's relative knowledge and distance (Kinney 1978: 15–30).

REFERENCES AND FURTHER READING

Bakhtin, M. M. (1981). *The Dialogic Imagination: Four Essays* (ed. M. Holquist, trans. C. Emerson and M. Holquist). Austin, TX: University of Texas Press.

Barthes, R. (1974). *S/Z* (trans. R. Miller). London: Cape. (Original pub. 1970.)

Barthes, R. (1993). *Mythologies* (trans. A. Lavers). London: Vintage. (Original pub. 1957.)

Beck, W. (1961). *Man in Motion: Faulkner's Trilogy.* Madison: University of Wisconsin Press.

Cullick, J. S. (1996). "If I Had a Design": Sutpen as Narrator in *Absalom, Absalom! Southern Literary Journal*, 28(ii): 48–57.

Faulkner, W. (1929). *Sartoris.* New York: Harcourt, Brace. (Original pub. 1929.)

Faulkner, W. (1940). *The Hamlet.* New York: Random House. (Original pub. 1940.)

Faulkner, W. (1962). *The Mansion.* London: Reprint Society. (Original pub. 1959.)

Faulkner, W. (1964). *Light in August.* London: Penguin. (Original pub. 1932.)

Faulkner, W. (1967a). *The Sound and the Fury.* London: Penguin. (Original pub. 1929.)

Faulkner, W. (1967b). *The Unvanquished.* London: Chatto and Windus. (Original pub. 1938.)

Faulkner, W. (1969). *Absalom, Absalom!* London: Chatto and Windus. (Original pub. 1936.)

Faulkner, W. (1993). *Sanctuary.* New York: Vintage. (Original pub. 1931.)

Faulkner, W. (1996). *As I Lay Dying.* London: Vintage. (Original pub. 1930.)

Godden, R. (1997). *Fictions of Labor: William Faulkner and the South's Long Revolution.* New York and Cambridge: Cambridge University Press.

Godden, R. (1999). Earthing *The Hamlet*, an Anti-Ratliffian Reading. *Faulkner Journal*, 14(ii): 75–109.

Gray, R. (1994). *The Life of William Faulkner: A Critical Biography.* Oxford: Blackwell.

Gwynn, F. L. and J. L. Blotner (eds.) (1995). *Faulkner in the University.* Charlottesville, VA, and London: University of Virginia Press.

Hoffman, F. and O. W. Vickery (eds.) (1960). *William Faulkner: Three Decades of Criticism.* New York and Burlingame: Harbinger.

Holland, N. N. (1980). Unity Identity Text Self. In J. P. Tompkins (ed.). *Reader-Response Criticism: From Formalism to Post-Structuralism* (pp. 118–33). Baltimore: Johns Hopkins University Press.

Irwin, J. T. (1975). *Doubling and Incest/Repetition and Revenge: A Speculative Reading of Faulkner.* Baltimore: Johns Hopkins University Press.

Iser, W. (1980). The Reading Process: A Phenomenological Approach. In J. P. Tompkins (ed.). *Reader-Response Criticism: From Formalism to Post-Structuralism* (pp. 50–69). Baltimore: Johns Hopkins University Press.

Kartiganer, D. M. (1979). *The Fragile Thread: The Meaning of Form in Faulkner's Novels.* Amherst: University of Massachusetts Press.

Kazin, A. (1960). The Stillness of *Light in August.* In F. Hoffman and O. W. Vickery (eds.). *William Faulkner: Three Decades of Criticism* (pp. 247–65). New York and Burlingame: Harbinger.

King, R. H. (1980). *A Southern Renaissance: The Cultural Awakening of the South, 1930–1955.* New York: Oxford University Press.

Kinney, A. F. (1978). *Faulkner's Narrative Poetics: Style as Vision.* Amherst: University of Massachusetts Press.

Macherey, P. (1990). The Text Says What It Does Not Say (trans. G. Wall). In D. Walder (ed.). *Literature in the Modern World: Critical Essays and Documents* (pp. 215–22). Oxford: Oxford University Press.

Matthews, J. T. (1982). *The Play of Faulkner's Language.* Ithaca, NY: Cornell University Press.

Moreland, R. C. (1990). *Faulkner and Modernism: Rereading and Rewriting.* Madison: University of Wisconsin Press.

Reed, J. W., Jr. (1973). *Faulkner's Narrative.* New Haven, CT: Yale University Press.

Robinson, O. (2001a). Monuments and Footprints: The Mythology of Flem Snopes. *Faulkner Journal,* 17(1): 69–85.

Robinson, O. (2001b). "That Florid, Swaggering Gesture": Faulkner's Thomas Sutpen as Southern Writer. *European Journal of American Culture,* 20(2): 100–11.

Robinson, O. (2003a). Interested Parties and Theorems to Prove: Readership in Faulkner's Snopes Trilogy. *Southern Literary Journal,* 36(1): 58–73.

Robinson, O. (2003b). "Liable To Be Anything": The Creation of Joe Christmas in Faulkner's *Light in August. Journal of American Studies,* 37(1): 119–33.

Saussure, F. de (1988). The Object of Study. In D. Lodge (ed.). *Modern Criticism and Theory: A Reader* (pp. 2–9). London: Longman.

Snead, J. A. (1986). *Figures of Division: William Faulkner's Major Novels.* New York: Methuen.

Tompkins, J. P. (ed.) (1980). *Reader-Response Criticism: From Formalism to Post-Structuralism.* Baltimore: Johns Hopkins University Press.

Végsö, R. (1997). Let Me Play a While Now: The Hermeneutics of Heritage and William Faulkner's *Absalom, Absalom! Amerikastudien/ American Studies,* 42(4): 625–36.

Walder, D. (ed.) (1990). *Literature in the Modern World: Critical Essays and Documents.* Oxford: Oxford University Press.

8

Race as Fact and Fiction in William Faulkner

Barbara Ladd

At this late date, most of us realize that "race," understood as a matter of genetic differentiation, is a fiction, with little scientific currency – the genetic differences between any two races are minuscule compared to the genetic differences one might find within racial groups. Yet "race" remains a fact of our lives, one of the most powerful signifiers in Western culture. As a concept it has a long history in Western thought, having served to distinguish people on the basis of family, community, nation, language, gender, color and other physical features, even profession (e.g., the race of farriers) at least since the fifteenth century. It was not until the nineteenth century, however, with the coming of pseudoscientific theories of heredity and mutation, that race became essentialized and took on many of its modern significations. Only then could we attribute to black persons a "natural" affinity for the performative or aesthetic sensibility, or envision Caucasians as "master organizers" of civilization, charged with bringing order where "chaos reigned" (Tuveson 1968: vii). William Faulkner, born in 1897 in Mississippi, grew up in a nation deeply rooted in ideologies of racial difference. The color line was sharply drawn – drawn more sharply in fact than it had ever been before. Prior to 1863, slavery itself had contained and segregated most of the black population in the US South, and "one-drop rules," those legal standards that determined how much African ancestry an individual could have and still be "white," were more lenient than they were after the Civil War. Before the Civil War, the fatal drop was often considered to be one-fourth or one-eighth part African ancestry or more; after the Civil War a more vigilant racism replaced slavery as a means of black containment. The one-drop rules became stricter: in some states in the early twentieth century (and on into the 1980s in Louisiana), the "fatal drop" could be as small as one-thirty-second (Williamson 1984: 109). These laws had serious implications for legal matters, such as inheritance of property.

The disputes that arose from these increasingly stringent one-drop rules as segregation became law at the turn of the twentieth century – many having to do with rights of inheritance, one of Faulkner's central concerns – make it clear that the social fact of race and the fictions upon which race-consciousness was built were very real matters of daily life in Southern cities, towns, and rural areas where the memory of slavery and racism was not only alive but very personal. It still is. It should not be surprising that Southern white writers have written so much, although sometimes very badly, about race – it is more surprising that twentieth-century white writers from elsewhere in the United States have written so little about it. There is no issue in William Faulkner's work that is more pervasive or more compelling.

In 1946, Ralph Ellison placed Faulkner in what he calls the "great 19th century moral tradition" which sought to understand the Negro as "a rounded human being" and a "symbol of man" (Ellison 1972: 33). Since that time many have questioned Ellison's assessment of Faulkner (and of nineteenth-century American literature), and a good deal of academic work has turned away from Ellison's framing of race as a moral issue – that is, as a question of individual or community conscience and action – to reframe it in terms of systems and ideologies, in terms of questions of production and reproduction. Despite this turn, which has illuminated previously obscure facets of the functioning of race and racism (and certainly has moral implications), the moral imperative Ellison articulates – the necessity for white writers to represent black characters in all their human complexity not only as a way to understand black humanity but as a way for whites to come to understand "the broader aspects" of their own humanity – remains one of the most urgent issues in Faulkner studies.

The novel that has emerged as the central text in Faulkner's exploration of race from a moral perspective is *Go Down, Moses* (1942), a book until recently often dismissed as "the beginning of the end" for Faulkner by interpreters who saw in the slight hope for redemption the book holds out an unearned appeal to the reader, or who took the measure of Faulkner's achievement primarily in terms of his construction of the voice of modern suffering around young white male desire (Quentin Compson's most notably). In *Games of Property: Law, Race, Gender, and Faulkner's Go Down, Moses* (2003a), Thadious M. Davis turns once again to this book to assess Faulkner's limitations as well as his achievement. Davis reads the book from an African Americanist perspective, historicizing and amplifying black voices, pointing to "white shame" as a central issue, and identifying cross-racial recognition and racial justice as the book's moral imperatives (Davis 2003a: 4).

A study like Davis's would have been virtually impossible even as recently as the mid-1980s. The ability to historicize and amplify black voices in Faulkner is one very specific consequence of the monumental project of excavation and interpretation undertaken over the past half-century in the areas of African American culture and history. And prior to the appearance in the 1990s of academic interest in "whiteness" as a racial category, "white shame" would hardly have been a focal point in any race-based inquiry. Until that time, any proposed discussion of race in Faulkner's work was almost certain to be a discussion of "the Negro question," turning on the "meaningful depiction of the Southern black" (Terry 1985: 308). Ellison, who sometimes had very harsh words for Faulkner's representation of black characters, also quite famously credits him with the ability to represent Southern blacks meaningfully: he is "more willing perhaps than any other artist to start with the stereotype, accept it as true, and then seek out the human truth which it hides" (Ellison 1972: 42).

For Ellison, however, *The Unvanquished* (1938) is an exception; he describes the friend-ship between a black and a white boy, Ringo and Bayard, in *The Unvanquished*, as "obscene," based as it is on what he sees as Ringo's complete identification with the perspective and values of the slaveholder (Ellison 1972: 43). Recent critical opinion agrees with Philip M. Weinstein that the book is "a racially retrograde text," but the issue is complicated. Weinstein acknowledges that the text "does recurrently and power-fully signal a racial disturbance." The problem, for him and for many others, is that Faulkner "will not explore [that disturbance] directly" (Weinstein 1996: 43, 45). This is true. *Go Down, Moses*, appearing four years later, will be the first book in which Faulkner undertakes a "direct" and sustained exploration of racial conflict; *Intruder in the Dust* (1948) would follow. Major works on race though they be, neither *Light in August* (1932) nor *Absalom, Absalom!* (1936) contains any black voice: Joe Christmas is not so much black as he is a white man who fears he might be black, and in *Absalom, Absalom!* Clytie speaks as a Sutpen, Jim Bond is prelinguistic, and Charles Bon's racial identity (like Joe Christmas's) remains indeterminate. The moral judgment of Faulkner by contemporary readers rests upon whether one can locate black voices as distinct from that of the slaveholder or former slaveholder in his work: are there black voices unmedi-ated by white ideology, and what impact do those voices have on narrative discourse?

With these questions in mind, *The Unvanquished* is a much more interesting text than many have realized. It is here, in a book David Minter characterizes as the model for *Go Down, Moses*, that Faulkner undertakes his first sustained effort to access black voices for their capacity to challenge the white perspective (Minter 1980: 186). *The Unvanquished* has been most often read as little more than a collection of conventional Civil War stories written for the *Saturday Evening Post* reader; in preparing the book for publication, however, Faulkner undertook significant revisions to the published stories, adding the final story to bring the action of the previous six to dramatic closure, with Bayard's implicit critique of his father's intolerance and misplaced pride in his own refusal to challenge the man who shot his father in a fair fight. Faulkner also pays considerably more attention to slavery and Emancipation. These revisions resulted not only in the inclusion of Uncle Buck and Uncle Buddy McCaslin's plan for freeing their own slaves but also the inclusion of several powerful lyrical scenes of former slaves on the road in search of freedom. These are sounds of motion itself, a chorus of murmuring and chanting that adds dramatic weight and tension to the first two stories, "Ambus-cade" and "Retreat."

Nevertheless, hearing a black voice in this narrative does require some suspicion of the white voice on the part of the reader. Bayard and Rosa comment on the flight of former slaves in predictably racist ways, and Faulkner constructs a black subplot in the story that provides a basis for a critique of the slaveholder's perspective. But the black chorus in *The Unvanquished* has more often than not been read in the terms in which Rosa and Bayard present it, as pathos, an accompaniment to the unpurposed and dream-like movement of newly emancipated slaves without leadership or preparation for freedom. Faulkner has been charged with being unable or unwilling to imagine African American agency in history. Craig Werner, building on Robert Stepto's work in African American literary history, writes that Faulkner "consistently interpreted Afro-American behavior in static rather than kinetic terms, substituting 'endurance'" for the two major tropes of African American literary and cultural historiography, i.e. for 'ascent' [to literacy and freedom] and 'immersion' [return to the black community]" (Werner 1987: 37). Yet *The Unvanquished* and *Go Down, Moses* belie this assessment. In the following passage, we are provided with a commentary on the movement of former slaves from Ringo's perspective:

> the rushing locomotive which [Ringo] hoped to see symbolised [to Ringo] . . . the motion, the impulse to move which had already seethed to a head among his people . . . one of those impulses inexplicable yet invincible which appear among races of people at intervals and drive them to pick up and leave all security and familiarity of earth and home and start out, they don't know where, emptyhanded, blind to everything but a hope and a doom. (Faulkner 1938: 92)

This passage clearly inscribes the freedpersons as possessed of historical agency, one of those "races of people" akin here to the ancient Israelites and to those white populations who did (and continued to do) the same thing in their own migrations to America. It is very likely that Faulkner knew of the figurative significance of the Israelites' exodus from Egypt in African American culture, and it is highly unlikely that the migration of white persons to America under the same conditions is insignificant to a reading of the above passage.

What critical attention there has been to black voice in *The Unvanquished* has centered not so much on the collective chorus but on a subplot concerned with a more individualized character who goes by the name of Loosh. Over the years many readers have been troubled or intrigued by Loosh and his dream of freedom. When *The Unvanquished* opens, he is about 30 years of age, Joby's son and uncle to Ringo, who is about 12. One afternoon in the summer of 1862, as the young Ringo and his white playmate Bayard, the novel's point-of-view character, sit building a miniature Vicksburg with woodchips in their ongoing game of Confederate generals, Loosh approaches, watches them for awhile, and then "swept the chips flat. . . . 'There's your Vicksburg.'" He laughs, an expression on his face, of triumph, which the young Bayard does not recognize: "'And I tell you nother un you ain't know,' he said. 'Corinth.'"

> "Corinth?" I [the child Bayard] said. . . . "That's in Mississippi too. That's not far. I've been there."
> "Far don't matter," Loosh said. Now he sounded as if he were about to chant, to sing; squatting there with the fierce dull sun on his iron skull and the flattening slant of his nose, he was not looking at me or Ringo either; it was as if the red-cornered eyes had reversed in his skull and it was the blank flat obverses of the balls which we saw. "Far don't matter. Case hit's on the way!" (Faulkner 1938: 5–6)

Bayard refuses to discuss Loosh's remarks with Ringo, asserting loudly that Loosh could not know anything that Bayard's father John Sartoris had not already told them. But, even as he says this, he has his doubts, because "niggers know, they know things" (Faulkner 1938: 5). Folk superstitions about black prescience aside, Quentin Compson, in *The Sound and the Fury*, is the first to sound the note of what that "nigger knowing" might actually be when he speculates that "a nigger is not a person so much as a form of behaviour; a sort of obverse reflection of the white people he lives among" (Faulkner 1990c: 86). In Faulkner's description of Loosh's eyeballs – "the red-cornered eyes had reversed in his skull and it was the blank, flat obverses of the balls which we saw" – he references Quentin's remark and signals that what Bayard may find most disturbing, even stupefying, is the suggestion of Loosh's possession of "personhood." To this point, Bayard's awareness of the human mystery associated with subjectivity and separateness has been limited to his fascination with his own swashbuckling father, John Sartoris. But here Loosh wears expressions that Bayard cannot read, he possesses in his abstracted inward gaze an interiority that Bayard does not recognize. Loosh's possession of information he has not been given by John Sartoris together with his opacity point to an ability to "think otherwise," and, by extension, to resist, that even Ringo, as devoted as he presumably is to Bayard's white vision, acknowledges: "Loosh laughed," Ringo replies to Bayard's assertion that Loosh meant "nothing." "He say Corinth too. He laughed at Corinth too. What you reckon he know that we ain't?"

Overhearing John Sartoris tell Louvinia (Loosh's mother) to "watch Loosh," Bayard himself comes to understand that Loosh does possess some potentially dangerous knowledge; he and Ringo both undertake to watch Loosh. They discover that he has traveled, without a pass, to Corinth and back for information. Thanks to their eavesdropping upon Loosh's return, the reader shares Bayard's voyeuristic glimpse into the slave quarters, into a black interior ordinarily unavailable in Faulkner's work:

> standing in front of the fire . . . with that look on his face again which resembled drunk-enness but was not, as if he had not slept in a long time and did not want to sleep now, and Joby and Philadelphy leaning into the firelight and looking at him and Philadelphy's mouth open too and the same look on her face. . . . "You mean they gwinter free us all?" Philadelphy said. "Yes," Loosh said, loud, with his head flung back; he didn't even look at Joby when Joby said. "Hush up, Loosh!" "Yes!" Loosh said, "Gin'ral Sherman gonter sweep the earth and the race gonter all be free!'" (Faulkner 1938: 25–26)

The impact of the scene is built on the discrepancy between what Bayard sees and hears and what the reader sees and hears. Hearing Loosh's words, Bayard, with no developed sense of any separate black community (even though he has seen a couple of signs of it recently), runs to Granny to announce that the Union Army is on the way to set them *all* free – himself, Granny, and everyone else. Although Bayard's misunderstanding is humorous, it is also telling, amounting to an ironic evocation of the plantation myth of innocence upon which *The Unvanquished* with its children and its Cavalier heroics rests, drawing Faulkner's implied reader's attention all the more to "black interiors," the cabin interior to be sure but more so to a black scene of separateness and subjectivity as Loosh, Joby, and Philadelphy, all adults, speak to each other unaware of any white mediating presence.

Loosh speaks loudly in this small interior space, excitedly; his raised voice oratorical as he speaks as a part of and *to* an invisible black world beyond the cabin interior, that population from which the singing, chanting road-walkers will soon begin to come, as if in response to his oratorical call. In a famous letter to Malcolm Cowley, Faulkner characterizes his own style in studbook terms as the product of "Southern Rhetoric" – which he describes as "an inherited regional or geographical (Hawthorne would say, racial) curse" – "out of Solitude" (Cowley 1966: 78). Loosh's mode of speech might be described in the same way, as Oratory out of his own black Solitude, a move that gives him some narrative agency.

Joby's efforts to hush Loosh signal how dangerous that oratorical voice is within the context of a quiet night-time exchange of contraband information among three members of an enslaved family. It might so easily be overheard, interpreted by John Sartoris and other slaveholders as incendiary, reminiscent of the battle-cries of past slave rebellions. Of course it is an echo of those battle-cries, even though the slaveholders never recognize it as such.

When Emancipation does come, Loosh packs up to leave the Sartoris place despite appeals from Philadelphy, his wife. And, in a direct hit at the conventional plantation novel's predilection for the slave who remains behind to protect the white family's wealth, he shows the Union soldiers where the silver is buried:

> [Loosh] was coming up from his cabin with a bundle on his shoulder tied up in a bandanna and Philadelphy behind him, and his face looked like it had that night last summer when Ringo and I looked into the window and saw him after he came back from seeing the Yankees. Granny stopped fighting. She said "Loosh."
>
> He stopped and looked at her; he looked like he was asleep, like he didn't even see us or was seeing something we couldn't. But Philadelphy saw us; she cringed back behind him, looking at Granny. "I tried to stop him, Miss Rosa," she said. " 'Fore God I tried."
>
> "Loosh," Granny said, "are you going too?"
>
> "Yes," Loosh said, "I going. I done been freed; God's own angel proclamated me free and gonter general me to Jordan. I don't belong to John Sartoris now; I belongs to me and God."
>
> "But the silver belongs to John Sartoris," Granny said. "Who are you to give it away?"
>
> "You ax me that?" Loosh said. "Where John Sartoris? Whyn't he come and ax me that? Let God ax John Sartoris who the man name that gave me to him. Let the man that buried me in the black dark ax that of the man what dug me free." He wasn't even looking at us; I don't think he could even see us. He went on. (Faulkner 1938: 85–6)

Previously Loosh has been both visible and audible to Bayard, although Bayard was yet too young to understand black separateness. In this scene, one year after the cabin scene,

Bayard has crossed the threshold to adolescence and seems to have lost his capacity to hear Loosh. (He may register what Loosh says, but Loosh's words here are not weighted as they were in the cabin scene.) Although Loosh *speaks* eloquently, neither Bayard nor Granny remarks his words at all. Granny is interested in the silver; Bayard is, if anything, even more fascinated by the "blank" and "flat" expression on Loosh's face, apparently mesmerized by its challenge to his own visibility and that of Granny. He will remark on being "unseen" a couple of times over the next few pages. But once again, despite the inability or unwillingness of either of the white characters to respond to black speech in this scene, Faulkner's implied reader can both *see* and *hear* Loosh. The conjunction of sight and hearing is a very important one for a moral reading of race in Faulkner's work, in that it disrupts the presumed identification between reader and white narrator, and amounts to a challenge to the radical interiority of stream-of-consciousness on the one hand and, more relevant here, to objectifying specularization on the other.

In this scene the oratory of Loosh's demand is even more resonant, although so completely ignored *within* the scene that one wonders once again where that oratorical power is actually directed. Lee Jenkins, who has provided a lengthy commentary on the black subplot in *The Unvanquished*, reads Loosh in this scene as exemplary of "Faulkner's presentation of blacks in moments of intense emotional transport" as possessed of an "abstract and otherworldly quality of abandon, as if they were removed from the very crisis of the moment to which they give expression," which Jenkins attributes to the "social conditioning that demands passivity" (Jenkins 1981: 118–19). Such a reading hardly describes the Loosh who rides to Corinth and back for information, or who undertakes an oratorical role in speaking beyond his identity as a "nigger" and a slave both in the intimate setting of Joby's cabin and in the openness of the plantation yard. In each place we witness an instance of a dynamic interplay between narrative and oratory – a dynamic interplay that characterizes so much of Faulkner's work – and in the plantation yard Faulkner gives Loosh's oratorical voice an even further reach by giving it an extra-diegetic resonance, a capacity to speak beyond the story, to offer judgment and commentary on the story for the implied reader. In the scene in the plantation yard, Loosh does not so much speak *to* Granny or Bayard (who seem unable to understand, or even hear, him) but *via* Granny and Bayard presumably to the absent slaveholder. Yet his proper audience is no more John Sartoris than it is Bayard or Rosa Millard; the oratorical register of his words suggests that they are intended for a larger audience: "Let God ax John Sartoris who the man name that gave me to him," Loosh demands in rage; "Let the man that buried me in the black dark ax that of the man what dug me free." In directing the slaveholder to examine his conscience, Loosh gives voice to the most central question of his life: who gave the slaveholder the right to take his humanity, to bury him "in the black dark"? "Why?" Loosh is thus the first black character in Faulkner's work to articulate the moral imperative that will face the white man in *Go Down, Moses*.

This interchange between the world of dramatic prose narrative and the world of oratory, between the diegetic world of story and the extra-diegetic world of commentary and judgment, points to Faulkner's interest in the dramatic possibilities inherent in a black voice uncircumscribed by the world of the story. When Loosh assumes, however briefly, an oratorical voice, he is able both to represent and to critique the discursive economy of slavery which assesses the relative value (and therefore meaning) of black bodies against the devaluation (and meaninglessness) of black voices. The eloquence with which Loosh directs the slaveholder to consult his conscience and asks the most important question of his life points to Faulkner's discomfort with the containment of black voices as well as black bodies in the white plantation tradition.

Here Faulkner is hardly trying to "fix," or stabilize, blacks in the places allotted to them in Southern tradition, as some have argued (see, for example, Terry 1985: 308). Instead he seems more interested in using Emancipation to destabilize the familiar relationship of white and black as master and slave and to suggest a black humanity capable of challenging – within the story and beyond it – the presumptions of whiteness. In short, Faulkner has constructed a scene that "slips," that releases its grip on the conventional register of interracial seeing, speaking, and hearing as it operated in 1863 to slide into a register associated with exhortation and moral judgment in the mid-twentieth century. Even Granny, Bayard, Ringo, and Drusilla are carried along on the tide of freedpersons who have been figuratively if not literally constructed in the book as responding to Loosh's voice in the cabin scene. When they reach the river, the revolutionary potential of this "free" black voice is rendered (quite literally this time) in the conjunction of what the white characters can see, hear, and feel: "We might not have even been there" Bayard says again, still obsessed with his own invisibility. "They made a kind of long wailing sound, and then I felt the whole wagon lift clear of the ground and begin to rush forward . . . And we couldn't stop anymore than if the earth had tilted up and was sliding us all down toward the river" (Faulkner 1938: 84).

When Loosh and Philadelphy become part of that swelling chorus of freedpersons on the roads of the South, that is the last we see of them until a few years later, when, in "An Odor of Verbena," Loosh is back on the Sartoris plantation, still working with the horses (Faulkner 1938: 279). Faulkner never says anything about how he gets there or what his presence there means. All of that is left up to the reader. For some readers, his return is evidence of his degeneration to type. Others read it as evidence that Loosh's departure amid the exodus of former slaves in the aftermath of Emancipation signifies nothing more than the pathos of a futile dream or the mindless movement of a mob, nothing more than what the adult Bayard remembers, as he walks the grounds with Drusilla talking about John Sartoris, only as "the tide of crazed singing niggers as we went down into the river" (Faulkner 1938: 257). His inability to grasp the significance of that immersion is an index of his narrative limitations.

Arguably black characters, once presented in some tension with the stereotype, are never again entirely hidden and the potential for black resistance and return remains in the text. Drusilla, interrupting Bayard's ruminations on "the tide of crazed singing niggers" as she picks up on their conversation about John Sartoris, says that "A dream is not a very safe thing to be near." Her conversation with Bayard, of course, is not actually about the dream of freed slaves; it is about John Sartoris's dream. Drusilla herself has become a priestess of the Lost Cause, the cult of John Sartoris as it were. But when Faulkner places her line just after Bayard's recollection of that day in 1863, he references, again primarily for the reader, the other dream running alongside and usually, but not always, muted by the plantation narrative. "If it's a good dream, it's worth it," Drusilla concludes (Faulkner 1938: 257).

Faulkner tells us nothing at all about Loosh's time on the road, how far he went, to what purpose, and what brought him back. But Faulkner's most unqualified achievement in the field of racial representation is undoubtedly his exploration of *white* racial consciousness. As audible as black voices are on occasion, the reader never sees very far into the lives of Faulkner's black characters. For all his oratorical power, Loosh, like most other major black characters in Faulkner, is inscribed chiefly as an instrument for white self-recognition, as an instrument for posing the question of "tragic responsibility" that Ralph Ellison would soon (in 1946) identify as the most important question facing white men in so many of Faulkner's novels, the question of one's "personal responsibility in the condition of society"(Ellison 1972: 33).

Faulkner's inability to fully imagine the subjective experience of his African American characters does not mean that traces of that experience are not inscribed in his texts for us to read. Whatever kind of "white knowing" we can credit Faulkner with – conscious or unconscious, analytical or intuitive – the fact remains that his capacity for observation and witnessing – not the same thing as a capacity for imagining and understanding in this context – is remarkable. Today, in the wake of a half-century of recovery and interpretation of African American history and culture, in the aftermath of the Civil Rights Act and the arrival of African Americanist studies in well-funded research universities in the United States, we are in a better position to read Faulkner than we were before. As national and regional histories and cultures are reassessed and redefined in light of this work, Faulkner can be reread through the lens of a new cross-racial perspective that may uncover facets of his work invisible to past readers. For example, although Bayard, like the many white historians and cultural commentators of the past, sees the exodus of freedpersons from farms and plantations around the South in the wake of Emancipation as the movement of a mob, more recent work in African American history and culture has revealed that exodus to have been something else. Many of the road walkers knew where they were going, and if they were "blind to everything but a hope and a doom," that "hope" often had to do with the urgent desire to reunite with family and friends, and that "doom" with the impossibility of undoing history, of bringing the dead back to life (see Williamson 1984: 44–50). As we learn to read this book (and others) in the light of African American histories and cultures, we will certainly read differently: Loosh may have gone in search of extended family, and he may have found them or not. Or he may have gone in nothing less than a spirit of grieving postponed for too long and a new capacity to hope. The Emancipation journey in *The Unvanquished* alludes repeatedly to a ritual of grieving in the face of the burial of black persons in the "black dark" and the rebirth of hope in being "dug free." Today we can see more clearly than before that what brings Loosh back is in all likelihood the economic and social reality of the post-Reconstruction return to power of the white man in the South, that is, the historical context of "Skirmish at Sartoris" and "An Odor of Verbena" from a black perspective.

The presence of a black subplot in a book otherwise devoted to the story of the Sartoris and Millard penchant for grandiose self-destructive gestures raises the possibility that the meaning of the Civil War is not to be found in the derring-do of John Sartoris, or in Grandmother Millard's audacious offensive against those who would threaten "the Southern way of life," or even in the *freeing* of men and women who had been held in slavery, but in the new presence, in the South and in the nation, of a free black population and, in what was of most significance for Faulkner's future work, the new narrative potentialities of black voices. It is here, in the black voices of *The Unvanquished*, that Faulkner discovered *Go Down, Moses*. Loosh's challenge to the slaveholder to look to his conscience structures the thematics of virtually every story in the latter book. Whether that challenge is restated in the form of Tomey's Turl's dealing of the cards that will determine the shape of the future in "Was," or in "Aunt Mollie's" demand that Roth Edmonds accept responsibility for the death of her grandson in "Go Down, Moses," it is Loosh's challenge taken up again. Lucas, Molly, and Henry Beauchamp are defined by resistance and challenge; so is the unnamed woman of "Delta Autumn" who, in the face of Ike's ideological admonitions to "go" and to "forget," has the last word: "Old man . . . have you lived so long and forgotten so much that you don't remember anything you ever knew or felt or even heard about love?" (Faulkner 1990b: 346).

In *Go Down, Moses*, the post-Emancipation imperative issued to the slaveholder by African Americans comes down to white recognition – white recognition of black humanity and, in that, white *self*-recognition. Self-recognition proves to be especially problematic for many of the white men in *Go Down, Moses* (and with few exceptions, they are all men) because it requires acknowledgment that one's own humanity, both during and after slavery, had been and would continue to be wrapped up in that of the African American, and that to deny the humanity of African Americans constitutes a betrayal of one's own humanity. There, as anyone knows who has studied the issue, lies the problem: whiteness is supposed to mean freedom and autonomy. Faulkner likes the word "immunity," which evokes not only a state of special racial privilege but a state of spiritual invulnerability. Self-recognition, in the terms in which it is presented in *Go Down, Moses* as an acceptance of *shared* humanity, undermines that immunity. Given what whiteness is in Faulkner, the imperative of recognition is a challenge to the white man to find some way of living with honor and pride without immunity (Ellison 1972: 43).

One of the most relentless scenes of white self-recognition and its almost immediate denial appears in "The Fire and the Hearth." Here the 7-year-old Roth Edmonds, who has been, like Bayard in *The Unvanquished*, sharing a pallet with Henry Beauchamp, the son of Lucas and Molly Beauchamp, suddenly and mysteriously comes to an awareness of his identity as white. In his new race pride he refuses to share bed or pallet with Henry (Faulkner 1990b: 108–9). For Thadious M. Davis, the child Roth, assuming that his birthright means freedom of choice and unconditional acceptance from the

world around him, never anticipates what his own white identity will actually entail –
isolation from the only mother he has ever known, grief, and shame (Davis 2003a:
200–1, 204–6). When he realizes the extent of his own loss, when he comes to recognize
grief and to believe (mistakenly) that he is ready to "admit shame," he returns to the
Beauchamp cabin. There, "he said it the best he could for that moment," "it" being his
intended admission of grief and shame, believing that "later he would be able to say it
all right, say it once and forever so that it would be gone forever, facing her before he
entered her house yet, stopping, his feet slightly apart, trembling a little, lordly, peremp-
tory: 'I'm going to eat supper with you all tonight.'" Seeing that Molly betrays no
emotion, he lets himself off the hook: "He could say it almost any time now, when the
time came." Molly sends him out to find Henry. "Then it was as if it had never happened at all," we are told:

> Henry came almost at once; he must have seen him from the field, and he and Henry
> killed and dressed the chicken. Then Lucas came and he went to the barn with Henry
> and Lucas while Henry milked. Then they were busy in the yard in the dusk, smelling
> the cooking chicken, until Molly called Henry and then a little later himself, the voice
> as it had always been, peaceful and steadfast: "Come and eat your supper."
>   But it was too late. The table was set in the kitchen where it always was and Molly
> stood at the stove drawing the biscuit out as she always stood, but Lucas was not there
> and there was just one chair, one plate, his glass of milk beside it, the platter heaped
> with untouched chicken, and even as he sprang back, gasping, for an instant blind as the
> room rushed and swam, Henry was turning toward the door to go out of it.
>   "Are you ashamed to eat when I eat?" he cried.
>   Henry paused, turning his head a little to speak in the voice slow and without heat:
> "I aint shamed of nobody," he said peacefully. "Not even me." (Faulkner 1990b:
> 109–10)

Having spoken, and with a definitive *black* voice, Henry walks out of the room and out
of the book. It is not until this moment of humiliation, when Roth discovers that he
has shown a desire for something that can be denied to him and realizes that "it was
too late . . . , forever and forever too late" for innocence, that Roth can be credited with
anything in the way of self-recognition. As the text sets it up, recognition of self requires
that one recognize others (which Roth is certainly forced to do, however briefly, here),
and white self-recognition in this scene is not so much his recognition that his pride
has hurt others but the more devastating recognition – implicit in the question he asks
Henry – that his "old haughty ancestral pride" itself "stemmed not from courage and
honor but from wrong and shame." "So he entered his heritage. He ate its bitter fruit"
(Faulkner 1990b: 107,109–10).

For Roth Edmonds, race pride has made any real acceptance of his own "personal
responsibility in the condition of society" virtually impossible. Almost immediately
following his moment of self-recognition, we witness the displacement of his memory
of this originary moment of "wrong and shame" by something that is not even memory,
but a patriarchal ideology, a fiction of race:

He listened as Lucas referred to his father as Mr. Edmonds, never as Mister Zack; he watched him avoid having to address the white man directly by any name at all with a calculation so coldly and constantly alert, a finesse so deliberate and unflagging, that for a time he could not tell if even his father knew that the negro was refusing to call him mister. At last he spoke to his father about it. (Faulkner 1990b: 110)

His father is not much help, claiming that he and Roth are, as descendants of a female McCaslin and carrying another name, "usurpers," while Lucas is a McCaslin, like Ike McCaslin to whom the land actually belongs. At once closed away by pride from memory and yet compelled toward a neurotic retracing of the fault-lines in his self-image, Roth figures out eventually that "*it was a woman. . . . My father and a nigger, over a woman. My father and a nigger man over a nigger woman. . . .*" Roth's ideology of race pride entitles him to "forget" the identity of the woman who was the only mother he ever knew: "*He didn't even think Molly's name. That didn't matter*" (Faulkner 1990b: 110). He does not recognize her when she comes to see him in the commissary. When he visits her, as he does once a month for a half hour to deliver a sack of candy, it is with pride and arrogance: "[h]e called it a libation to his luck, as the centurion spilled first a little of the wine he drank" (Faulkner 1990b: 97).

When he agrees to help her with Lucas, who has been spending all his time in a search for buried treasure, "[i]t was not just concern, and, if he had told himself the truth, not concern for her at all. He was raging – an abrupt boiling over of an accumulation of floutings and outrages covering not only his span but his father's lifetime too," floutings and outrages in the person of Lucas Beauchamp (Faulkner 1990b: 101). When the adult Roth Edmonds looks at Lucas Beauchamp he does not remember the occasion that marked his irreparable separation from the Beauchamp family and certainly not Molly's central role in it; instead, he ruminates on Lucas's descent from the male McCaslin line and his priority in being born a generation before Roth. This seems to be the only shame the adult Roth can admit to himself. Roth's whiteness – and by implication the whiteness of his paternal forebears – demands a substitution of ideology for memory where shame or grieving is concerned (Faulkner 1990b: 111–15).

The exchange does not work. Ideology is no viable substitute for memory, even though memory is ideological. *Go Down, Moses* is about the stand-off between memory and ideology, grief and pride (see Fowler 1996: 165–6). As such, it is Faulkner's most ambitious critique of white supremacist ideology and his most direct treatment of what needed to be done in order for the Southerner (and the American more broadly) to be redeemed. In *Go Down, Moses*, what needs to be done is fundamentally a moral issue, that is, an issue involving individual action, and the act repeatedly called for is the admission of shame and the grieving of the originary loss, the wrong and shame, that pride is intended to hide. The "long wailing sound" that Bayard heard at the river in *The Unvanquished*, the sound of mourning into which he was tumbled, returns with a vengeance at the end of *Go Down, Moses* as Molly (identified as "Aunt Mollie" in this story), her brother Hamp Worsham, and Miss Worsham (no doubt the descendant of the family that once owned Molly's ancestors) mourn the death of Butch Beauchamp,

Molly's grandson whom Roth Edmonds sent away from his home and who has been executed in Chicago. Her mourning ritual is a calling-out of Roth Edmonds comparable to Loosh's calling-out of John Sartoris in the earlier book: "Roth Edmonds sold my Benjamin. Sold him in Egypt. Pharoah got him" (Faulkner 1990b: 353). But Roth Edmonds is not among the mourners, leaving Gavin Stevens, a poor substitute, to hold his place. And Gavin *is* simply a place-holder here, without the memory that would enable him to understand that Molly's demand for proper notice and proper burial is something much more than a desire for show.

Typically, the male protagonist in Faulkner who is faced with the necessity of grieving will displace grief with fury and/or violence rather than succumb to a kind of emotional expression associated with vulnerability – that is, shame – and with women. Ike, confronted by Roth's black lover and their son in "Delta Autumn," falls into a rage and tries to send the woman away. Gavin Stevens in the title story flees the scene of black and female grieving as fast as he can. Roth is no exception. Even at 7 years old, he responds to "the grief he could not explain, the shame he would not admit" with "rigid fury" (Faulkner 1990b: 109). The adult Roth is still choleric, still unable to explain or admit, to free himself from the black family (now represented by Lucas rather than by Molly), or to believe that he belongs to the white one, involved in a conflicted romantic relationship with one of Molly's and Lucas's granddaughters, at one point living openly with her outside the South and planning marriage; at another point, betraying her to return to the South where he can take his place among other propertied and respectable white men; and, finally, in an indisputable act of cowardice, hiding from her and their son in the woods when he hears of her presence on the property. Grieving can be revolutionary, as all of these men who resist it so fiercely know. When it leads, as it is supposed to lead, to the acceptance of loss, acknowledgement of a shared humanity, and the readiness to take up the demands of the present and the promise of a future, it can be earth-shaking.

In the absence of the admission of shame and grieving, Loosh's metaphor of burial and return becomes one of the governing tropes of *Go Down, Moses*, with most of the stories having something to do with the return of what has supposedly been buried, whether it is the possibility of a "return" of buried treasure in "The Fire and the Hearth," the haunting of Rider by his just-buried wife in "Pantaloon in Black," the return of the "Spirit Buck" in "The Old People," the return of the unnamed woman of "Delta Autumn" with her skin "dead-looking" but still "ineradicably alive" with her newborn son (Faulkner 1990b: 343–4), or the return and burial of Butch Beauchamp in "Go Down, Moses" as a testament to a still living memory.

The question of inheritance remains. Who inherits? At present the most ambitious literary revisionings of Faulkner come from African American writers. Craig Werner wrote in the mid-1980s that one of the best ways to study Faulkner and race is to read his work in conjunction with the post-Civil Rights generation of African American writers who are "pursuing his [Faulkner's] possibilities." In this group, he included Ernest Gaines, David Bradley, Sherley Anne Williams, Gloria Naylor, and Leon Forrest (Werner

1987: 48). He did not mention Toni Morrison, in all probability because *Beloved*, the book that established her as one of the major voices in the African American dialogue with Faulkner, was published in 1987, one year after Werner's essay first appeared. Since the publication of *Beloved*, however, Faulkner has often been paired or juxtaposed with Morrison in the classroom. Comparative critical studies of Faulkner and Morrison have proliferated. We have seen fewer studies that examine Faulkner through the lens of other black authors of the post-Civil Rights era. A more complete assessment of Faulkner and race awaits those studies, as well as other kinds of race-based inquiry. We will better understand Faulkner and race as we continue to explore the implications of African American legacies in the modern world. We will understand race in Faulkner better when we can bring contemporary discourses about racial hybridities to our reading of his texts, when we can better understand the complex positioning of his US South as both part of the US and part of a transnational region of post-plantation cultures that extends from Virginia to South America and into Africa and Asia. Faulkner may have associated modernity itself more with Emancipation and black migration than we have realized. It is unlikely that Faulkner will always be as significant to the African American literary imagination as he has been over the past generation or two, but the racial imaginary itself will no doubt remain central to any reading of Faulkner for some time to come.

REFERENCES AND FURTHER READING

Cowley, M. (1966). *The Faulkner–Cowley File: Letters and Memories, 1944–1962.* New York: Viking.

Davis, T. M. (1983). *Faulkner's "Negro": Art and the Southern Context.* Baton Rouge: Louisiana State University Press.

Davis, T. M. (1987). From Jazz Syncopation to Blues Elegy: Faulkner's Development of Black Characterization. In D. Fowler and A. J. Abadie (eds.). *Faulkner and Race: Faulkner and Yoknapatawpha 1986* (pp. 70–92). Jackson: University Press of Mississippi.

Davis, T. M. (2003a). *Games of Property: Law, Race, Gender, and Faulkner's* Go Down, Moses. Durham, NC: Duke University Press.

Davis, T. M. (2003b). The Signifying Abstraction: Reading "the Negro" in *Absalom, Absalom!* In F. Hobson (ed.). *William Faulkner's* Absalom, Absalom!: *A Casebook* (pp. 69–106). New York: Oxford University Press.

Ellison, R. (1972). Twentieth-Century Literature and the Black Mask of Humanity. In *Shadow and Act* (pp. 24–44). New York: Random House. (Original pub. 1953.)

Faulkner, W. (1938). *The Unvanquished.* New York: Random House.

Faulkner, W. (1990a). *Absalom, Absalom!* New York: Random House. (Original pub. 1936.)

Faulkner, W. (1990b). *Go Down, Moses.* New York: Random House. (Original pub. 1942.)

Faulkner, W. (1990c). *The Sound and the Fury.* New York: Random House. (Original pub. 1929.)

Fowler, D. (1996). *The Return of the Repressed.* Charlottesville, VA: University Press of Virginia.

Genette, G. (1980). *Narrative Discourse: An Essay in Method.* Ithaca, NY: Cornell University Press.

Jenkins, L. (1981). *Faulkner and Black–White Relations: A Psychoanalytic Approach.* New York: Columbia University Press.

Kartiganer, D. M. (1988). William Faulkner. In E. Elliott (ed.). *The Columbia Literary History of the United States* (pp. 887–909). New York: Columbia University Press.

Kolmerten, C. A., S. Ross, and J. B. Wittenberg (eds.) (1997). *Unflinching Gaze: Faulkner and Morrison Re-Envisioned*. Jackson: University Press of Mississippi.

Minter, D. (1980). *William Faulkner: His Life and Work*. Baltimore: Johns Hopkins University Press.

Nicholaisen, P. (1995). "Because We Were Forever Free": Slavery and Emancipation in *The Unvanquished*. *Faulkner Journal*, X(2): 81–91.

Ross, S. (1989). *Fiction's Inexhaustible Voice: Speech and Writing in Faulkner*. Athens, GA: University of Georgia Press.

Rowe, J. C. (1995). The African-American Voice in Faulkner's *Go Down, Moses*. In J. G. Kennedy (ed.). *Modern American Short Story Sequences: Composite Fictions and Fictive Communities* (pp. 76–97). New York: Cambridge University Press.

Skei, H. H. (1999). *Reading Faulkner's Best Short Stories*. Columbia: University of South Carolina Press.

Terry, E. A. (1985). For "Blood and Kin and Home": Black Characterization in William Faulkner's Sartoris Saga. In A. F. Kinney (ed.). *Critical Essays on William Faulkner: The Sartoris Family* (pp. 303–17). Boston: G. K. Hall.

Tuveson, E. (1968). *Redeemer Nation: The Idea of America's Millennial Role*. Chicago: University of Chicago Press.

Weinstein, P. M. (1987). Marginalia: Faulkner's Black Lives. In D. Fowler and A. J. Abadie (eds.). *Faulkner and Race: Faulkner and Yoknapatawpha 1986* (pp. 170–91). Jackson: University Press of Mississippi.

Weinstein, P. M. (1995). Diving into the Wreck: Faulknerian Practice and the Imagination of Slavery. *Faulkner Journal*, X(2): 23–54.

Weinstein, P. M. (1996). *What Else But Love? The Ordeal of Race in Faulkner and Morrison*. New York: Columbia University Press.

Werner, C. (1987). Minstrel Nightmares: Black Dreams of Faulkner's Dreams of Blacks. In D. Fowler and A. J. Abadie (eds.). *Faulkner and Race: Faulkner and Yoknapatawpha 1986* (pp. 35–69). Jackson: University Press of Mississippi.

Williamson, J. (1984). *The Crucible of Race: Black–White Relations in the American South Since Emancipation*. New York: Oxford University Press.

9

"Why Are You So Black?" Faulkner's Whiteface Minstrels, Primitivism, and Perversion

John N. Duvall

> A book is the writer's secret life, the dark twin of a man: you can't reconcile them.
>
> William Faulkner, *Mosquitoes*

While Joseph Blotner has laid out connections between the characters in *Mosquitoes* (1927) and their probable real-life counterparts (1984: 183–5), the novel is more than a *roman à clef* of the New Orleans literati. Long derided as one of William Faulkner's weaker efforts, his second novel has undergone a decided resurgence of critical interest since the 1990s, thanks largely to the work of feminist scholars who have shown how significant this novel's engagement with matters of gender and sexuality is to Faulkner's subsequent development as an artist. For Frann Michel (1988–9), Faulkner is a lesbian author, who, terrified of cultural emasculation, ultimately uses lesbian sexuality to avoid representing male–male desire; for Minrose Gwin (1996), Michel misses instances of homoerotic possibility between male characters; for Lisa Rado (1993–4), Gwin and Michel overlook the fundamental androgyny of Faulkner's artistic imagination. And Meryl Altman argues for the unhinging of "'homosexuality' or 'lesbianism' from 'effeminacy,' 'inversion,' even 'gender dysphoria,' in order to observe the conjunctions and disjunctions that occur historically between the two sets of ideas" (1993–4: 51). *Mosquitoes*, we now know, openly portrays sexual multiplicity and dissonances in a fashion that the later Faulkner tends to address more obliquely.

In the novel Mrs. Maurier, an aging New Orleans socialite and self-styled patron of the arts, puts together a yachting party, imagining it will be an occasion for several day trips filled with uplifting conversation about the arts. Her plans go awry, however, when the *Nausikaa* runs aground the first night out. Many of the conversations over the next three days do center on the production of art, but they are far from the respectable and conventional sentiments Mrs. Maurier hopes to have confirmed. In addition to her nephew and niece, Theodore (Josh) and Patricia Robyn, Mrs. Maurier's party consists of a small artistic band – the poets Mark Frost and Eva Wiseman (accompanied by her brother Julius); the painter Dorothy Jameson; the novelist Dawson Fairchild; the sculptor Gordon; and the aesthete Ernest Talliaferro – as well as a British entrepreneur, Major Ayres, and a working-class couple, the voluptuous Jenny Steinbauer and her bootlegger boyfriend, Pete, whom Patricia meets the morning the trip begins and impulsively invites to come along.

Faulkner's material often has the feel of a Noel Coward farce. Gordon is attracted to Patricia; Patricia is attracted to Gordon's art but tries to run off to Mandeville with the boat's steward; Ernest ineffectually seeks to seduce Jenny; Dorothy desperately tries to seduce Pete, Mark, and Josh, Patricia's brother; Pete tries to kiss Patricia; Patricia shares a bunk one evening with a naked Jenny; Eva is interested in Jenny; Major Ayres asks Jenny to run off to Mandeville for a tryst; Josh and Jenny have a petting session; and Ernest accidentally ends up in Mrs. Maurier's bed. None of the shipboard romance is consummated, and the only sex act occurs after the trip when Gordon goes to a whorehouse in New Orleans.

From my brief description of Faulkner's novel, it is easy to see why the recent critical conversation about *Mosquitoes* has focused on matters of gender and sexuality. Race, however, is entirely absent from this sophisticated discussion. And with apparent good reason. Race seems to fall outside of *Mosquitoes'* field of vision. African American characters in the novel's portrayal of New Orleans and the four-day yacht cruise on Lake Pontchartrain are so minor as to be merely decorative. And yet race, I wish to argue, is actually quite important to the novel through recurring figurations of blackness, figurations that provide one of the earliest indications of the imbricated relation between racial and sexual otherness that would come to characterize Faulkner's major fiction. In Faulkner's second novel, blackness, artistic production, and non-normative sexuality all meet in a strange hall of mirrors in which the novelist appears to be everywhere (and thus finally nowhere) in the text.

Philip Weinstein, writing about Faulkner's depiction of African Americans, quite reasonably claims that, although the author's black characters are crucial for understanding whiteness, they are "largely deprived by the narrative of interior voice, of point of view, of a sense of their own past and future (their memories and desires)"; as a result Faulkner's "blacks . . . are truncated figures" (1992: 44). While not wishing to gainsay the correctness of this assertion about Yoknapatawpha's blacks of African descent, I would nevertheless argue that Weinstein's point becomes less transparent if one acknowledges that not all of Faulkner's black lives are lived by African Americans. These other black figures (Caucasians tropologically linked to blackness), whose inner lives are fully and complexly rendered and whose identities emerge precisely through a struggle with history, suggest that blackness may be more crucial to an understanding of Faulkner's white Southern masculinity than has been previously imagined.

Even before Faulkner turned to fiction, his early work gives strong indications of the black presence shadowing his conception of the white artist. In particular, his use of the Pierrot figure, as Judith Sensibar has pointed out, over and above the contemporary vogue of Pierrot poems, was deeply personal and spoke to a sense of the self as a multiplicity rather than an identity:

> Pierrot's paralyzing duality of vision, his doubleness, was something Faulkner recognized. It sprang from a dilemma almost eerily familiar. Pierrot was Faulkner's fictional representation of his fragmented state. In pretending simultaneously to be the wounded war hero, the great airman, the British dandy, the poet-aesthete, and the tramp, Faulkner too was playing forms of Pierrot. (Sensibar 1984: xvii)

Building on Sensibar's biographical characterization of Faulkner's Pierrot, I would add a consideration of racial masquerade and minstrelsy. John T. Matthews argues that "Faulkner evokes the minstrel tradition to signal his own complex alienation from the South's dominant social and cultural traditions" (2000: 80). Matthews, however, is speaking exclusively of the American tradition of blackface minstrelsy. While blackface does resonate with certain instances in Faulkner's work, a different tradition of minstrel masking may more fully express the author's alienation from Southern culture by opening a complex epistemology of self and Other.

In the pen-and-ink drawings accompanying his hand-produced verse and prose play *The Marionettes* (1920), Faulkner evokes a long European tradition of Pierrot. First developed in commedia dell'arte toward the end of the seventeenth century, Pierrot, Faulkner's poet figure, was reimagined in the early nineteenth century for French pantomime by Jean-Gaspard Deburau. Deburau established Pierrot as the ineffectual lover, represented on stage as a clown in baggy white clothes and stylized whiteface make-up. Descendants of Pierrot include mimes and whiteface circus clowns. Deburau's is certainly the Pierrot embraced by fin-de-siècle European culture and subsequently modernist art. (Pablo Picasso and many other modernist artists represented Pierrot.) French pantomime came to England in 1891 and spawned numerous Pierrot troupes that entertained at English seaside towns through the 1920s. These troupes of male and female performers in Pierrot costume presented shows that mixed music, dancing, and comic sketches (Green and Swan 1986: 1–24). The Pierrot shows bear an uncanny resemblance to American blackface minstrelsy, but Faulkner chose the European rather than the American minstrel tradition to express his most complicated understanding of an always divided artistic identity.

If blackface minstrelsy raises one set of questions about racial figuration, whiteface minstrelsy immediately poses a question about what is at stake when a Caucasian attempts to pass as white. Faulkner's Pierrot appears in whiteface, but his double, Shade of Pierrot, is always in silhouette. Pierrot, to follow Sensibar, is a drunken, impotent dreamer, while Shade of Pierrot is "the Rake . . . a fictionalized ideal, a fantastically successful poet and lover" (1984: xvii). But Faulkner's fashioning of an idealized sexual and aesthetic self, as I will argue, appropriates blackness in a way that plays on stereotypes of "primitive" sexual license. In Faulkner's third illustration for *The Marionettes*, Pierrot stands before the viewer as a tall clown with eyes closed and hands crossed just below his waist. What his stylized eyebrows, bowed lips, and cap-like hair (all black) make clear is that he is not simply white but in whiteface. In Faulkner's eighth illustration, Shade of Pierrot (again, a silhouetted figure), standing in the background and facing the viewer, plays his lute for Marietta, who is positioned in the foreground with her back to the viewer; perspectively, Shade of Pierrot appears as a little black man.[1] What Faulkner suggests through these drawings is that the real artist is not the one who presents a white face to the world but rather is the poet's interiority, which turns out to be black. The duality of Pierrot/Shade of Pierrot is crucial to understanding Faulkner's subsequent development of a whiteface minstrelsy.

The most obvious instance in *Mosquitoes* of Faulkner's use of blackness as a way of imagining a kind of male identity comes in an apparently minor metafictional moment, one that ultimately helps to link race and sexual difference precisely by opening a gap between blackness and race. Together in the same bunk, the naked Jenny tells Patricia about being at Mandeville; while her boyfriend and another couple go swimming, Jenny meets someone: "I was waiting for them, and I got to talking to a funny man. A little kind of black man —"; Patricia asks if he was "a nigger?" (Faulkner 1955: 144) and Jenny explains, "No. He was a white man, except he was awful sunburned and kind of shabby dressed — no necktie and hat. . . . I think he was crazy. Not dangerous: just crazy" (p. 145). Jenny finally remembers that this clownish little man, whose racial identity is less immediate to her than the way in which he is in some deep but undefined way "black," is named Faulkner. At one level, the real-life Faulkner pokes fun at his artist aspirations by identifying novel writing as professional lying and his obscurity through Patricia's response: "Never heard of him." More important to my argument, however, is that the character named Faulkner points to a semantic difference in which an individual can be black without being African American, a situation that ultimately makes whiteness more contingent and less a given. (For the sake of clarity, I will refer to Faulkner the author without quotation marks but to the character as "Faulkner.") This metafictional moment takes a more complicated turn when Jenny tells the rest of her brief story about "Faulkner"; returning to New Orleans from their day trip, she notes

> That crazy man was on the boat coming back. He got to talking to Pete and Roy while me and Thelma was fixing up downstairs, and he danced with Thelma. He wouldn't dance with me because he said he didn't dance very well, and so he had to keep his mind on the music while he danced. He said he could dance with either Roy or Thelma or Pete, but couldn't dance with me. I think he was crazy. Don't you? (pp. 145–6)

This crazy white "black" man who imposes himself on the two couples seems intimidated only by Jenny's voluptuous body, but is ready to dance with (and as?) the other female member of the party. Neither tough-talking Pete nor Roy, presumably, would be interested in coupling with "Faulkner" on the dance floor. But a fictional, trickster "Faulkner" who is willing to "dance" both ways — with male or female partners — hints at the ways blackness becomes a trope for sexual dissonance throughout Faulkner's fiction, even his later fiction that explicitly takes race as its central matter.

This is not to say that Faulkner was not attempting to think about the dynamics of racial difference in his Southern community; however, Faulkner's figurations of blackness also frequently carry an extra valence that speaks to his struggle to imagine a way to perform an identity as a Southern white male. Fictional "Faulkner's" craziness, for

Jenny at least, arises from his refusal to play gender roles straight. Although he appears only in the brief story that Jenny tells, the presence of black "Faulkner" looms over the whole of *Mosquitoes* through his figurative parallels to several other characters.

To the extent that Faulkner does implicitly conflate racial and sexual otherness, he employs blackness to figure certain white characters' (and perhaps his own) fantasized relation to otherness. As an aspiring poet, the young Faulkner could hardly be unaware that his own performance of masculinity differed from the norm of Oxford, Mississippi; his pilgrimage in 1925 to Oscar Wilde's grave, his college drawings in imitation of Aubrey Beardsley (whose illustrations for Ernest Dowson's *The Pierrot of the Minute: A Dramatic Phantasy in One Act* [1897] may well have inspired Faulkner's illustrations of Pierrot), as well as his friendship with men whom Frederick Karl (1989) identifies as homosexual (including Stark Young, Ben Wasson, and Bill Spratling) are just a few indications of Faulkner's awareness of alternative masculinities. Growing up white in the South in the first quarter of the twentieth century, Faulkner found blackness to be an immediately available and flexible trope to serve as a hinge between racial and sexual otherness. Since black women were viewed as promiscuous (thus available to white men) and black men were seen as sexually obsessed with interdicted white women, small wonder that a racially inflected blackness should come to serve Faulkner as a figure for delineating fissures in sexual identities. One result in Faulkner's fiction, then, is that the interdiction of mixed-race sexuality (even as miscegenation between black women and white men was an open secret) could signify taboos in other realms of sexual behavior (homo- and bisexuality, as well as incest) that define culture.

In the South, then, the African American served the role of the primitive other in the terms that Marianna Torgovnick has laid out in *Gone Primitive*. If for the West, "Africa is the quintessential locus of the primitive," in the American South, African Americans could serve a similar role in which "to study the primitive brings us always back to ourselves, which we reveal in the act of defining the Other" (Torgovnick 1990: 11). To seek the primitive is, in one sense, to search for what is primal and authentic to our human being prior to the distortions of civilization, since the primitive implies both origin and simplicity (Torgovnick 1990: 18). But because the primitive takes us back to a liminal moment, the transition from nature to culture, the primitive also reveals what in Freudian terms needs to be repressed in civilized society, most notably sexual license prior to cultural taboos. Faulkner's fiction often channels a primitivist discourse in which the African American serves as the primitive; perhaps no better instance of this occurs than in the conversation between Ike McCaslin and McCaslin Edmunds in part 4 of "The Bear." Ike's positive assertions about blacks are always countered by McCaslin:

> "[African Americans] are better than we are. Stronger than we are. Their vices are vices aped from white men or that white men and bondage have taught them: improvidence and intemperance and evasion – not laziness: evasion: of what white men had set them to . . ." and McCaslin

"All right. Go on: Promiscuity. Violence. Instability and lack of control. Inability to distinguish between thine and mine" (Faulkner 1990: 281)

For Ike, African Americans are superior because they are pure, and whatever limitations they exhibit represent the corrupting evils of white civilization, while for McCaslin, African Americans are subhuman, incapable of ethical reasoning, akin more to mules and dogs than to white people. Although these perspectives are apparently at odds, Ike's positive and McCaslin's negative characterizations of blacks share a central premise that resonates with primitivism. Both men agree that African Americans are different because they are prior to the effects of white civilization; it's just a question of how they spin "black" simplicity and spontaneity. For Ike, blacks retain primitive virtues that whites have lost, while for McCaslin their primitive, precultural status means that it makes no more sense to ascribe virtue to African Americans than it does to animals. Ike too is implicated in seeing African Americans as more animal-like, as his word choice to describe blacks' mimicry of white culture ("aped") reveals.

Torgovnick's linking of modernism with primitivist discourse bears a resemblance to Toni Morrison's thinking about racial figuration and the Africanist presence in American literature. For Morrison, white writers, in a fashion akin to blackface minstrel entertainers, have been able to deploy images of blackness "in order to articulate and imaginatively act out the forbidden in American culture" (1992: 66). Even though Faulkner works with a European minstrel tradition, he is nonetheless using blackness as a trope, which means Morrison's point is still germane. Morrison's sense of the minstrel possibilities of white writing has been engaged in broader cultural contexts by Susan Gubar, Michael Rogin, and Eric Lott. Gubar terms all forms of racial metamorphosis in art "racechange" and sees it emerging in the twentieth century as a "crucial trope of high and low, elite and popular culture, one that allowed artists from widely divergent ideological backgrounds to meditate on racial privilege and privation as well as on the disequilibrium of race"; "racechange" includes a variety of symbolic behavior, such as "racial imitation and impersonation, cross-racial mimicry or mutability, white posing as black or black passing as white, pan-racial mutuality" (1997: 5).[2] Lott points out that prior to the Civil War, the Irish found a path to whiteness through blackface (1994: 94–6), just as Rogin details the way Jewish entertainers in the 1920s, such as Al Jolson, were able to effect their assimilation into American culture – to become "white" – precisely by donning blackface (1996: 73–119). Faulkner's use of blackness in *Mosquitoes*, however, seems quite different. Rather than as a way to normalize himself in white Southern culture, Faulkner often uses his "whiteface" males to underscore their otherness and alienation that result from their fundamental inability to assimilate to the values of their community.

From the example of *Mosquitoes*' black "Faulkner," I would like to propose a semiotic square that expands the opposition between "white" and "Negro" in order to suggest the cultural differences in play in the racial masquerade of Faulkner's whiteface minstrelsy. If the mixture of the races, however repressed, reveals the white/Negro opposition to be a continuum rather than a true binary, the sharper oppositions can be represented diagonally:

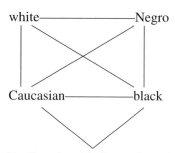

Faulkner's whiteface minstrels:
Pierrot/Shade of Pierrot, *The Marionettes*
"Faulkner" and Gordon, *Mosquitoes*
Quentin Compson, *The Sound and the Fury*
Ike McCaslin, *Go Down, Moses*

The relations outlined here show the differences between and among "white" (the privileged term A); its contrary, the presumptive cultural opposite, "Negro" (non-A); its contradictory, the logical opposite, "black" (not-A); and "Caucasian" (not-non-A). While the relationships between the contraries (white–Negro) and the contradictories (white–black and Negro–Caucasian) are the clearest, there are also important relations of implication vertically between the subcontraries and the contraries, in which to be black implies one is Negro and to be Caucasian implies whiteness, but these are implications only. In other words, being a Caucasian is a necessary but finally insufficient condition of whiteness, and being black does not definitively equate with Negro. Stated differently, all whites are Caucasian but not all Caucasians finally qualify as white in Faulkner's South. (Faulkner's poor whites, such as the Snopes, exemplify this dynamic.) What I'm particularly interested in is the conjunction of the subcontraries where "Caucasian" and "black" meet, since this is what I take to be the site of Faulkner's whiteface minstrelsy.

The urge in Southern culture to oppose whiteness to the Negro turns out to be a kind of category mistake, one Faulkner's figurative use of blackness helps to illuminate. The Southern male who says "I am white and you are Negro" assumes he has only made a claim about race, but by invoking whiteness he has in fact made a metaphysical claim of privilege with broad class, sexual, and theological implications. My semiotic square does not begin to address the connotative cultural associations of blackness and whiteness; however, one trajectory away from this square takes us to the realm of sexual difference. In Faulkner, blackness is associated with a kind of undisciplined libidinal energy producing a variety of non-heteronormative possibility that defies cultural taboos. Although characters such as McCaslin Edmonds and Isaac McCaslin, as we have seen, want to essentialize this form of blackness as a biological difference of the Negro, Faulkner's whiteface artist figures unhinge this presumption by revealing Caucasians who are as black as or blacker than any African American.

"Faulkner's" blackness, staged as a kind of playful bisexual orientation, is directly linked to his "crazy" gender performance that embraces either male or female dance partners. If "Faulkner" were the only artist figure linked to blackness in *Mosquitoes*, my discussion might seem overwrought. But blackness recurs elsewhere in relation to the possibilities of artistic production.

Although neither one of them is among the novel's "blacks," Dawson Fairchild and Julius Wiseman have the most to say about the relation of darkness to artistic and literary production. In another metafictional passage, late on the evening of the fourth day aboard ship, Eva, Julius, and Dawson discuss art and artists. Eva claims that "all artists are insane," to which Fairchild says, "It's a kind of dark thing. It's kind of like someone brings you to a dark door" (Faulkner 1955: 248). During their discussion, Fairchild pages through a book of poems Eva has published and claims to have trouble "reconcil[ing] her with this book." Fairchild's problem, Julius claims, arises from innocence regarding recent theories of sexuality, "this park of dark and rootless trees which Dr. Ellis and your Germans have recently thrown open to the public." Fairchild may recognize "emotional bisexuality" in what he reads, but Julius suggests that the relation of poet to poem is something more intimate: "A book is the writer's secret life, the dark twin of a man: you can't reconcile them" (p. 251). This moment, which calls attention to the act of reading Faulkner's book, invites the reader to wonder how *Mosquitoes* might serve as Faulkner's dark twin. As John Irwin points out, Eva's poem "Hermaphroditus" is one that Faulkner would publish under his name in *The Green Bough* in 1933 (Irwin 1975: 167), evidence Michel (1988–9) later uses as an indication of Faulkner's lesbian identification. But as the poem speaks of the sly smiling figure with "boy's hand" and "woman's breast," desire is always unfulfilled: "canst thou bride / Thyself with thee and thine own kissing slake?" (Faulkner 1955: 252). No, says the poem, and the result is "thy twinned heart's grief." While the hermaphrodite clearly suggests androgyny, the completed twinning of this figure is, for Dawson, "a kind of dark perversion" (p. 252), and Havelock Ellis's review of the literature on hermaphrodites shows a considerable degree of confusion between the terms "bisexual" and "hermaphroditism," especially when considered in light of such "sexoesthetic inversion" as transvestism and cross-dressing (1924: 313–15). The implication here is that if art is a perversion, artists themselves are perverts. This implication finds its direct statement in an earlier section of the novel deleted from the typescript prior to publication. In this deleted material, there is a holographic addition in which Julius tells Fairchild, "Art is against nature: those who choose it are perverts" (Faulkner 1987: t.s. 43), adding (now back to typeface): "You don't think it is natural for a man to spend his life making little crooked marks on paper, do you?" (t.s. 43). For a reader trying to decipher Faulkner's cramped and crooked additions on paper, the passage becomes highly self-reflexive.

Turning back to the long conversation on art growing out of Eva's poem, one notes the references to Freud and Havelock Ellis, both of whom frankly discussed homosexuality, although in ways that look less progressive now than they did a hundred years ago. In particular, Ellis's treatment of sexual inversion, while unquestionably arguing for a more enlightened treatment of homosexuals, also clearly participates in the minoritizing taxonomy that Sedgwick has argued ultimately perpetuates homophobia (Sedgwick 1990: 20–1). Although Faulkner later would claim only a second-hand knowledge of Freud, his characters, as Irwin notes (1975: 5), certainly seem familiar with Freud and, one might add, with Ellis as well. Ellis's *Sexual Inversion* is at pains to show the universality of homosexuality – that it occurs in other animal species, throughout human history, and in all cultures. But Ellis singles certain groups out as having particularly high incidences of homosexuality: geniuses ("homosexuality is especially common among men of exceptional intellect" [1924: 26]), literary artists, and primitives. As Ellis elaborates on his claim regarding literature as one of the chief avocations of inverts, it is almost impossible not to speculate on how Faulkner might have experienced such an assertion, especially in light of his pose as the failed poet: "[homosexuals] especially cultivate those regions of *belles-lettres* which lie on the borderland between prose and verse. Though they do not usually attain much eminence in poetry, they are often very accomplished verse writers" (Ellis 1924: 294). Ellis's first two categories, geniuses and artists, would seem to overlap, which makes his third category all the more anomalous. If homosexuality in European nations is practiced by a discrete (and discreet) minority, Ellis speaks of the commonness of inversion in a variety of primitive peoples, from American Indians and Tahitians to Africans:

> Among the negro population of Zanzibar forms of homosexuality which are believed to be congenital (as well as acquired forms) are said to be fairly common. . . . Among the Bangala of the Upper Congo sodomy between men is very common, especially when they are away from home, in strange towns, or in fishing camps. (p. 19)

"On the whole," Ellis summarizes, "the evidence shows that among lower races homosexual practices are regarded with considerable indifference, and the real invert . . . generally passes unperceived or joins some sacred caste which sanctifies his exclusively homosexual inclinations." Ellis's following paragraph significantly adds class to the mix: "Even in Europe today a considerable lack of repugnance to homosexual practices may be found among the lower classes. In this matter . . . the uncultured man of civilization is linked to the savage" (p. 21). What Ellis misses here is that his extremes meet, for it is not just the uncultured man of civilization who is paired with the primitive (lower races/lower classes) but also the overcultured man (genius/artist) who takes his sexual pleasure in primitive fashion.

In keeping with Ellis's views of homosexuality, Faulkner's self-portraits in *Mosquitoes*, both ironic and idealized, seem to merge the under- and overcultured. If "Faulkner," the professional liar, seems like the author's wry gesture toward one of his youthful poses as the tramp, the sculptor Gordon represents Faulkner's serious artistic ambition.[3] The tall Gordon, who we are repeatedly told has a hawk's face, is the 5' 5" Faulkner's idealized version of himself as a hardworking masculine artist. Gordon (hawk-man/falconer/Faulkner), the dedicated artist as genius, seems opposed to the licensed fool "Faulkner"; however, they share a similar ambiguous relationship to whiteness, since both are merely Caucasians in whiteface. This ambiguity is signaled by the very space in which we meet Gordon. Accessible only by a "darkling corridor" (Faulkner 1955: 13) leading to "dark tortuous stairs" (p. 21), Gordon's attic studio/apartment, with its "unevenly boarded floor," "rough stained walls," and "ruined pitch of walls," one learns "had housed slaves long ago" (p. 11).

Early in the novel, Mrs. Maurier, accompanied by her niece Patricia and Mr. Talliaferro, drops by Gordon's studio to try to persuade the sculptor to join her yachting party. Patricia openly admires the statue of the female torso and asks Gordon if he will give or sell it to her. When he refuses, she asks, "Why are you so black?" Since Gordon clearly does not understand her meaning, she elaborates: "Not your hair and beard. I like your red hair and beard. But you. You are black. I mean . . ." (Faulkner 1955: 25). Although Patricia is unable to fully identify what constitutes Gordon's blackness, she, like Jenny, identifies the white male artist as black. Like "Faulkner," then, Gordon is not white, which places him in implied relationship to racial otherness. At the same time, as a starving artist, Gordon oddly combines both of Ellis's extremes for inverted tendencies: he is simultaneously overcultured (as artist) and undercultured (economically lower-class). Living in poverty in a space where blacks had lived, Gordon is perceived by Mrs. Maurier in a way that oddly suggests Southern attitudes toward race. Because he's an artist, he must be "so spiritual": "He's one of these artists who never have much, lucky people" (p. 30). Mrs. Maurier's attitudes reveal that the dark artist is little different than the happy-go-lucky darkies, who must be equally lucky not to have much either. When Gordon walks out on her, Mrs. Maurier tries to blame Patricia's behavior, but Patricia points out that in fact it is her aunt who has been rude by barging into his studio unannounced. Mrs. Maurier's response is telling: "These people are different," her aunt told her coldly. "You don't understand them. Artists don't require privacy as we do: it means nothing whatever to them" (p. 30). What I hope my discussion to this point has made clear is how easily one might, in the context of the South in the 1920s, substitute "Negroes" for "artists" in the previous sentence. Mrs. Maurier's fascination with artists, her desire to decorate her party with them, reveals that she's slumming for the primitive in much the same way that wealthy New Yorkers went to Harlem's Cotton Club.

And though "black" himself, Gordon sets out to craft whiteness. As initially described, his statue is "passionately eternal – the virginal breastless torso of a girl, headless, armless, legless, in marble temporarily caught and hushed yet passionate still for escape, passionate and simple and eternal in the equivocal derisive darkness of the world." This statue, which "trouble[s] the very fibrous integrity of your being" (Faulkner 1955: 11), is explicitly marked as a double for Patricia, who when she first encounters it immediately remarks, "It's like me." Gordon's "growing interest [in] her flat breast and belly, her boy's body which the poise of it and the thinness of her arms belied" nearly reproduces the imagined viewer's response to Gordon's statue: "Sexless, yet somehow vaguely troubling" (p. 24). The statue's marble (linked to the eternal and purity) is knowable primarily by its relation to the world's (and Gordon's) "darkness." Early on the third morning of the yacht party, Patricia goes skinny dipping and the description of her body makes her the animated version of Gordon's statue: "Her legs and arms were so tan that naked she appeared to wear a bathing suit of startling white" (p. 164). To the extent that Patricia is delineated in relation to the marble statue, she is raced "white," but this whiteness, as we shall see, is contingent.

As a coded primitive and Africanist presence, Gordon struggles with his desire for Patricia, which it turns out is prohibited in more ways than one. Gordon's blackness, in one sense, marks him as artistic primitive, giving him the ability, for example, to see past the layers of civilization to what is elemental and authentic in Mrs. Maurier. Mrs. Maurier may have wished to surround herself with artists, but in bringing Gordon along, she gets much more than she bargained for. Seeing Gordon alone at night on the second day aboard ship, she thinks, "there was that queer, shy, shabby Mr. Gordon, mooning alone, as usual" (Faulkner 1955: 151) and goes over to him to do her duty as hostess. She tries to talk about art but becomes discomfited by his "uncomfortable stare," which produces "a queer cold feeling within her"; his stare makes her think Gordon is "like an animal, a beast of some sort" (p. 153). Although I don't mean to suggest that Mrs. Maurier's use of the word "queer" means that she thinks Gordon is a homosexual (after all, he's not effeminate), by the 1920s "queer" had become a way to name homosexuals (Chauncey 1995: 13–23). If Patricia experiences Gordon's difference as his blackness, Mrs. Maurier experiences it as his "queerness," and she has a direct encounter with blackness/queerness/primitivism when he abruptly lays his sculptor's hands on her face to examine her, a moment she experiences as a kind of sexual violation.

I would like to turn the claim that Julius Wiseman makes about artistic twinning back on Faulkner's representation of Gordon as artist. If a book is the writer's secret life and dark twin, how might that pertain to artists and their work more generally? In sculpting the marble statue of the sexually ambiguous yet still female torso, has Gordon created his own "dark twin"? Gordon suggests as much when Julius and Dawson visit his studio. Dawson admires the statue and begins to idealize it as something to allow one to forget grief. Gordon contradicts Fairchild: "She's not blonde. . . . She's dark, darker than fire. She is more terrible and beautiful than fire" (Faulkner 1955: 329). Early in the novel, as he contemplates his desire for Patricia, Gordon seems to merge her back into his work and to see himself in relation both to Jesus and to the maternal: "christ by his own hand an autogethsemane carved darkly out of pure space but not rigid no no an unmuscled wallowing fecund and foul the placid tragic body of a woman who conceives without pleasure and bears without pain" (p. 48). One should recall that when Gordon lays his hands on Mrs. Maurier's face, his demand for information about Patricia turns to maternity again: "Why aren't you [Patricia's] mother so you could tell me how conceiving her must have been, how carrying her in your loins must have been?" (p. 154). Gordon's obsession with Patricia queerly positions his desire as a series of crossings. To the extent that his sacrifice to art (the sublimation of desire) has allowed him to produce a white (yet "really" dark) marble statue that is Patricia's twin, he is simultaneously the young woman's mother (artistic production being analogous to female reproduction), her brother (the statue is his dark twin and she's the statue's double), and even, it seems, her father.

Given all the kissing and fondling in the novel, it is striking that Gordon and Patricia have very little physical contact. Although Gordon desires Patricia, she does not reciprocate his desire. His desire for her, then, is coded metaphorically as father–daughter incest inasmuch as she's only 18 while he's 36 – in other words, old enough to be her father. The prohibited nature of their relationship is made clear by the two main things that pass between them physically: he swings her around and he spanks her when she uses a naughty word. The father–daughter relationship is particularly underscored when, after she's been swimming, Gordon asks her to give him her hands and begins to swing her around. She admires and touches his muscular forearms and asks him to "do it again." As he obliges her, one sees that in "her taut simple body, almost breastless with the fleeting hips of a boy, was an ecstasy in golden marble, and in her face the passionate ecstasy of a child" (Faulkner 1955: 82). After Gordon spanks Patricia, he comforts her by holding her and then places his hands on her face, not as sexual caresses but, as he tells her, to learn her face that he might sculpt it. Gordon apparently sublimates his sexual (and culturally incestuous) desires, but in some sense the threat of incest is a screen for the more profound prohibition. If he's black and she is white, then he is equally prohibited from acting on his desire by the cultural and legal prohibitions against miscegenation. Here we see how prohibition in one sphere serves to displace another perhaps more disruptive prohibition in the Southern imaginary. This is certainly an important facet of Faulkner's major fiction, as in *Absalom, Absalom!* (1936) where a story of incest masks a story of miscegenated incest, which in turn may mask the imagined threat of homosexual miscegenated incest.

The only other physical contact Gordon has with Patricia is on the final night of the cruise when she accepts his request to dance with her. Remembering that Gordon earlier told her aunt that he couldn't dance, Patricia tells him he doesn't look like he can dance. His response, "I can't" (Faulkner 1955: 284), reminds us of another dancer with oddly constrained ability, black "Faulkner," who is willing to dance with Pete, Roy, Thelma, but not full-figured Jenny. If "Faulkner" can't dance with Jenny, Gordon, unlike the other men on the *Nausikaa*, simply won't because he's not attracted to Jenny. What this later scene of dancing confirms in relation to the earlier one is that even male–female pairings on the dance floor may bespeak the range of non-normative desires suggested by Gordon's attraction to Patricia.

It is in the context of my foregoing discussion that I want to examine Gordon's trip through New Orleans' red-light district with Dawson and Julius in section 9 of the Epilogue. Everything about the men's drunken excursion is dark – dark rooms on a dark street in a dark city. It should be noted that the space of purchased sex and that of art are themselves doubles. Just as the part of New Orleans that the prostitutes inhabit is figured through multiple images of darkness, so too (as I pointed out earlier) is the space leading up to Gordon's studio that had once housed slaves; hence, illicit sex and artistic practice again constitute each other as the "dark doors" leading to "dark perversions."

From an external perspective, Gordon's sex with a prostitute could only be described as a conventionally heterosexual (if illegal) act. Gordon's sexual act, however, enacts a variety of crossings and certainly hinges on an explicit moment of racechange. Interspersed in the narrative of Julius, Fairchild, and Gordon's drunken ramblings is a different, primitivist narrative that tells of another mythic time and place. Recounting the death of a beggar, the indifference of the priests, and the lamentations of captive women in bondage, the italicized portions of the narrative link up finally to Gordon's claim (made just prior to their trip to the red-light district) that his marble statue is actually black. These italicized passages, however, rather than being simply a freestanding counterpoint to the men's wanderings, suggest Gordon's troubled and alcohol-impaired interiority. The fantasy narrative juxtaposes *"a young naked boy daubed with vermilion"* with "the *headless naked body of a woman carved of ebony, surrounded by women wearing skins of slain beasts and chained one to another, lamenting"* (Faulkner 1955: 337). The boy painted with vermillion suggests Gordon's desire for Patricia, the girl with a boy's body and twin to his statue. This statue, however, has become a racechange totem – instead of marble, the female figure is now carved in ebony. The primitive women, potential sacrifices to the black statue, are doubles for the lower-class prostitutes and their solicitations, offerings of proscribed sexuality. The fantasy scene in which is heard *"the clashing hooves of centaurs"* builds to a crescendo in which *"the headless black woman becomes a carven agony beyond the fading placidity of the ungirdled maiden"* (p. 338). It is at this point that Gordon demands money from Julius and enters a door, lifting a woman seemingly at random, "smothering her squeal against his tall kiss." But in Gordon's interiority, the physical contact with the actual woman is overwhelmed by *"voices and sounds, shadows and echoes change form swirling, becoming the headless, armless, legless torso of a girl, motionless and virginal and passionately eternal before the shadows and echoes whirl away"* (p. 339). This image, of course, matches exactly the description of Gordon's passionate and eternal statue that one encounters at the beginning of the novel. Black Gordon, it seems, can only steel himself for his encounter with the prostitute if he drinks himself into a near stupor and casts himself as a rapist centaur (man-beast) copulating under the sign of a black totem. Through this fantasy of violation and this fantasy only is Gordon able to consummate his desire for Patricia.

But what exactly does this episode say about Gordon's "heterosexuality"? Black Gordon, whose sole sexual performance conflates the body of his epicene marble statue (which simultaneously points to its black racechanged double in ebony and the naked boy marked by red) with that of Patricia, engages in behavior coded in primitivist and Africanist terms. If Patricia stands in a series of metaphorical and metonymical substitutions, what is she but a figure (both rhetorical and psychosexual) of the reification of desire's multiplicity that goes by the inappropriate name "sexual identity"? In the dizzying chain of substitutions, where can any form of sexual identity claim to ground itself or find its original? Looked at from the psychic interiority of this "black" man, Gordon's "heterosexual" act simultaneously consummates desire all over the map: miscegenation (he's "black"), father–daughter incest, brother–sister incest (she's his dark twin's double), mother–daughter incest (he's her twin's "mother"), even pedophilia (he's a middle-aged man imaginatively having sex with a sexless boy-girl). Perhaps all of these possibilities taken together answer Patricia's question, "Why are you so black?" One is black if one's desires transgress culture's sexual taboos, because one is then primitive (prior to the repressions of civilization) and implicitly racially other. Even a heterosexual act, I would argue, can constitute a decidedly queer moment in Faulkner's text. Recalling Eva Wiseman's poem, Gordon may be the true hermaphrodite. He has, in displaced fashion, brided himself through and to his double(s).

In addition to "Faulkner" and Gordon, Eva Wiseman is another artist figure delineated by darkness. If Eva Wiseman's poetry is a high-cultural expression of primitive "emotional bisexuality," then her lesbian orientation doubles her poetry as a marker of her "blackness." In another of the deletions from the typescript, Eva walks in and turns the light on the naked Jenny and Patricia while Patricia is in the act of demonstrating on Jenny how to kiss in a refined manner. This girl-kissing-girl scene leaves Eva "staring at them with a dark intent speculation" (Faulkner 1987: t.s. 207). And if her poetic words will later be claimed directly by William Faulkner, she already shares another word with black "Faulkner," the character who appeared to be so minor and yet who repeatedly reappears as a subliminal presence in the text. At one point Jenny tries on some of Patricia's clothes, but Mrs. Wiseman warns her that she can't wear these around the men because the effect is "devastating." Jenny repeats the word and notes "There was a kind of funny little man at Mandeville that day . . ." (p. 203). Although Jenny doesn't complete the thought, clearly the reason she repeats the word "devastating" is that she's heard it about herself before from "Faulkner." Whatever the exact relationship between Eva and William Faulkner as poets, we know that Eva and "Faulkner" have identical perceptions of Jenny but that Eva is more capable of effecting physical contact with Jenny than "Faulkner." Eva in a sense mediates between "Faulkner" and Faulkner in terms of linguistic and libidinal identity. If "Faulkner" first speaks the word that Eva repeats to describe Jenny's sexual presence, Eva will first be identified as the author of the poem about hermaphrodism that Faulkner will later claim as his own.

There is another way in which "Faulkner" inhabits the novel even in his absence. If he shares qualities of artistry and blackness with Gordon and Eva, "Faulkner" also is linked to the aesthete Ernest Talliaferro in a particular way. If "Faulkner" is the funny little black man, Talliaferro is "that funny talking little man . . . that dreadful polite one" (Faulkner 1955: 141). Little men both, "Faulkner" and Ernest both represent sides of the youthful William Faulkner. If "Faulkner" stands in for Faulkner's tramp persona, Talliaferro's affected English accent and changed spelling of his patronymic both suggest self-parody of Faulkner's pose as the dandy (Arnold 1989: 5). Talliaferro may self-identify as a heterosexual, but everything about his attempted seductions of women works to ensure that he does not have to actually perform as a heterosexual. For all of his stratagems of seduction aimed toward Jenny, when she takes him to a secluded space in order to kiss him, Ernest feels an "unbearable lightness" moving through him, but once it reaches his feet, he runs away from her (Faulkner 1955: 189). His status as heterosexual, then, is all public performance, literally an act, one undertaken so that he will be taken as a man by other men. As Gwin points out, Ernest even views his impending marriage to Mrs. Maurier as a way to avoid having to perform as a heterosexual (1996: 128–9).

Ernest is also oddly related to that professional liar "Faulkner" because so many of the prefatory sections to the various days of the novel are voiced through a poetic discourse that is strangely close to Talliaferro's own overblown rhetoric. The opening of "The Third Day," for example, exhibits this quite clearly:

> The yacht was a thick jewel swaddled in soft gray wool, while in the wool somewhere dawn was like a suspended breath. The first morning of Time might well be beyond this mist, and trumpets preliminary to a golden flourish; and held in suspension in it might be heard yet the voices of the Far Gods on the first morning saying, It is well: let there be light. (Faulkner 1955: 164)

This purple prose captures precisely Meryl Altman's point: "it is impossible to tell when [Faulkner] is parodying this discourse and when he believes it, or what he does believe, which of the clichéd pontifications about beauty are meant as clichéd pontifications and which are supposed to represent Beauty" (1993–4: 44). But even if the irony spins out of control in *Mosquitoes*, Faulkner's much later and clearly ironic "Afternoon of a Cow" (1943) has another Ernest T. who speaks to what is at stake discursively in his second novel. In this short story set at Faulkner's home, Rowan Oak, Ernest Trueblood reveals that he has "been writing Mr. Faulkner's fiction for years" (Faulkner 1979: 424) through a kind of unstable collaboration. The overtly masculine, hard-drinking, taciturn Mr. Faulkner generates the broad outlines and plots, but the effeminate, sensitive Trueblood fleshes them out with the actual words. Strikingly, the story is told through a poetic, euphemistic prose that is unmistakably "Faulknerian," but that rhetoric is here attributed to the fussy and prudish Trueblood. Is Faulkner's story a wry way of acknowledging his own "emotional bisexuality," of allowing, as it were, E. T. to come home? One can only speculate, but these "Ernest" characters oddly point to a biographical enigma – what is the "E. T." that has its own small marker at the foot of Faulkner's grave in the Oxford cemetery?

This figure of the black white man (and by now every time I use these coloring terms they seem to cry out for problematizing quotation marks) recurs throughout Faulkner's subsequent fiction: Popeye in *Sanctuary* (1931), whom Temple identifies as a black man; Quentin in *The Sound and the Fury* (1929), who is identified by the boys fishing by the bridge as speaking like a colored man; and Uncle Ike McCaslin in *Go Down, Moses* (1942), who can never claim his proper white identity as a "Mister" after he repudiates his property. All of these characters, "blacks" in whiteface, suggest a non-normative performance of Southern masculinity, the full scrutiny of which is beyond the scope of this chapter.[4] But from this study of *Mosquitoes* one can perhaps make some preliminary conjectures.

When performing "What Did I Do To Be so Black and Blue?" Louis Armstrong would intone the line "I'm white inside." Faulkner's whiteface minstrels, however, seem to be saying, "I'm black inside." This claim, as I have argued, unhinges black primitivism from the racial category of the Negro by suggesting that Caucasians too could be the primitive other. This use of figurative blackness, I believe, signals the extent to which Faulkner struggled to become an envoy of otherness. But his attempt is fraught always with the ethical problem of how to speak legitimately for (or indeed as) the other. Moreover, Faulkner's racially inflected use of blackness as a way to critically delineate Southern whiteness always faces another problem: once white has mixed with black, it ceases to be white. Faulkner's personal relation to whiteness becomes rhetorically imperiled, hybrid, and even miscegenated by his very attempt to imagine non-normative masculine identity. Faulkner's male artists are "black" in some essential way that certain women can immediately recognize. These artists are, then, a kind of photographic negative to blackface minstrelsy: they are "blacks" in whiteface and therefore experience the world in a way analogous to the racial passer – always in danger of having their whiteness exposed as fraudulent. If the book is an individual's "dark twin," then rather like black "Faulkner," William Faulkner himself is metaphorically (part) black to the extent that he can repeatedly imagine the queerly proliferating multiplicity of desire.

NOTES

1 The illustration of Pierrot appears between pp. 6 and 7 of Noel Polk's facsimile edition of *The Marionettes* (Faulkner 1977); the illustration of Shade of Pierrot appears between pp. 45 and 46 of that same edition. Much smaller versions of these images can also be seen in Wilhelm (2004: 9, 19). I planned to reproduce the two illustrations in my chapter; however, Lee Caplin, Esq., who manages the William Faulkner Estate, required a licensing fee of $3,500 for permission to use the illustrations. I apologize for any inconvenience to the reader.

2 See especially Gubar's chapter 6, "Psychopathologies of Black Envy: Queer Colors," in which she argues for a reflexive relationship between racial and sexual crossings such that "the blurring of normative categories of eroticism contributes to the permeable boundaries of racial borderlines" (1997: 176).

3 Appendix A of *Sexual Inversion*, "Homosexuality among Tramps," posits that an unusually high percentage of American tramps engage in homosexuality. As a particular instance of the lower class, this obviously fits Ellis's scheme, but casts a curious light on Faulkner's self-fashioning posture as the tramp.

4 In "Was Ike Black?" (Duvall 2004) I address Isaac McCaslin's role as the secret "black" man of *Go Down, Moses*.

REFERENCES AND FURTHER READING

Altman, M. (1993–4). The Bug That Dare Not Speak Its Name: Sex, Art, Faulkner's Worst Novel, and the Critics. *Faulkner Journal*, 9(1–2): 43–68.

Arnold, E. (1989). *Annotations to Faulkner's* Mosquitoes. New York: Garland.

Blotner, J. (1984). *Faulkner: A Biography*. New York: Random House.

Brooks, C. (1978). *William Faulkner: Toward Yoknapatawpha and Beyond*. New Haven, CT: Yale University Press.

Chauncey, G. (1995). *Gay New York: Gender, Urban Culture, and the Making of the Gay Male World, 1890–1940*. New York: Basic Books.

Duvall, J. N. (2004). Was Ike Black? Avuncular Racechange in *Go Down, Moses*. In M. Zeitlin (ed.). *Misrecognition, Race and the Real in Faulkner's Fiction*. Special issue of *Etudes Faulkériennes*, 4: 39–51.

Ellis, H. (1924). *Sexual Inversion. Vol. 2: Studies in the Psychology of Sex*. 3rd ed. Philadelphia: F. A. Davis.

Faulkner, W. (1955). *Mosquitoes*. New York: Liveright. (Original pub. 1927.)

Faulkner, W. (1977). *The Marionettes* (intro. and textual apparatus N. Polk). Charlottesville, VA: University Press of Virginia. (Written 1920.)

Faulkner, W. (1979). Afternoon of a Cow. In *Uncollected Stories of William Faulkner* (ed. J. Blotner) (pp. 424–34). New York Random House. (Original pub. 1943.)

Faulkner, W. (1987). *William Faulkner Manuscripts 4: Mosquitoes* (ed. J. Blotner). New York: Garland.

Faulkner, W. (1990). *Go Down, Moses*. New York: Vintage International. (Original pub. 1942.)

Green, M. and J. Swan (1986). *The Triumph of Pierrot: The Commedia dell'Arte and the Modern Imagination*. New York: Macmillan.

Gubar, S. (1997). *Racechanges: White Skin, Black Faces in American Culture*. New York: Oxford University Press.

Gwin, M. C. (1993–4) *Mosquitoes* Missing Bite: The Four Deletions. *Faulkner Journal*, 9(1–2): 31–42.

Gwin, M. C. (1996). Did Ernest Like Gordon?: Faulkner's *Mosquitoes* and the Bite of "Gender Trouble." In D. M. Kartiganer and A. J. Abadie (eds.). *Faulkner and Gender* (pp. 120–44). Jackson: University Press of Mississippi.

Irwin, J. T. (1975). *Doubling and Incest/Repetition and Revenge*. Baltimore: Johns Hopkins University Press.

Karl, F. (1989). *William Faulkner: American Writer*. New York: Weidenfeld and Nicolson.

Kartiganer, D. M. and A. J. Abadie (eds.) (1996). *Faulkner and Gender*. Jackson: University Press of Mississippi.

Lott, E. (1994). *Love and Theft: Blackface Minstrelsy and the American Working Class*. New York: Oxford University Press.

Matthews, J. T. (2000). Whose America? Faulkner, Modernism, and National Identity. In D. M. Kartiganer and A. J. Abadie (eds.). *Faulkner at 100: Retrospect and Prospect* (pp. 70–92). Jackson: University Press of Mississippi.

Michel, F. (1988–9). William Faulkner as a Lesbian Author. *Faulkner Journal*, 4(1–2): 5–20.

Morrison, T. (1992). *Playing in the Dark: Whiteness and the Literary Imagination*. Cambridge, MA: Harvard University Press.

Rado, L. (1993–4). "A Perversion That Builds Chartres and Invents Lear Is a Pretty Good Thing": *Mosquitoes* and Faulkner's Androgynous Imagination. *Faulkner Journal*, 9(1–2): 13–30.

Rogin, M. (1996). *Blackface, White Noise: Jewish Immigrants in the Hollywood Melting Pot*. Berkeley: University of California Press.

Sedgwick, E. K. (1990). *Epistemology of the Closet*. Berkeley: University of California Press.

Sensibar, J. L. (1984). Introduction to *Vision in Spring*. In W. Faulkner. *Vision in Spring* (pp. ix–xxviii). Austin, TX: University of Texas Press.

Torgovnick, M. (1990). *Gone Primitive: Savage Intellects, Modern Lives*. Chicago: University of Chicago Press.

Weinstein, P. (1992). *Faulkner's Subject: A Cosmos No One Owns*. New York: Cambridge University Press.

Wilhelm, R. (2004). Faulkner's Big Picture Book: Word and Image in *The Marionettes*. *Faulkner Journal*, 19(2): 3–24.

10

Shifting Sands: The Myth of Class Mobility

Julia Leyda

In much of American literary study, and indeed in American culture more generally, class remains an underexamined or taboo issue. As Renny Christopher and Carolyn Whitson argue, "'Class' is almost always ignored in the contemporary critical discourse of 'race, class, and gender'" (1999: 72). The growing field of working-class studies, including the work of scholars like Janet Zandy and Laura Hapke and institutions such as the Center for Working-Class Studies (CWCS) at Youngstown University in Ohio, foregrounds the need for historical and theoretical work on the cultures of the American working class. It is important to stress that this call for attention to class does not mean denying the importance of other scholarly and interpretive frameworks such as race, gender, and sexuality. The CWCS home page explains, "while most critics in the field reject the notion that class is a supercategory under which all other identities are subsumed, class is understood as an important connecting element linking the various marginalized groups, all of whom share a position of subordination under capitalism" (CWCS). Although much of the literary scholarship in this field has focused on working-class writers or on representations of workers (see Denning 1998; Hapke 2001; Zandy 2001), I suggest that the study of class in literature can be productively extended to the full range of American literature. This chapter on class in Faulkner's novels is one pathway into a relatively uncultivated field (see Jehlen 1978; Railey 1999; Skinfill 1996), aiming to contribute to an understanding of how class operates in these texts and why such an understanding might be useful to readers of Faulkner.

One of the considerations that arise when approaching class in literature is that literary analysis means dealing with texts, not objective reality. The characters in the text and the communities and worlds they move around in are constructed through words, through perspectives and narration. Close reading, then, is crucial to understanding how the text constructs class identities, and any discussion of class in literature must account for the ways in which the text develops those characters and those worlds, and why. That is, what are the possible reasons why this text is constructing class in these ways? How do these constructions of class serve this text as a whole? This chapter will closely read two of Faulkner's texts, *As I Lay Dying* (1930) and *Absalom, Absalom!* (1936), for their constructions of class in terms of character development, plot, tone, and other literary devices, as well as to exemplify, at least provisionally, why reading with a focus on class is useful to students and scholars of Faulkner.

In addition to closely reading the text itself, though, readers interested in class and literature must also address the question of the relation between the text and the wider culture. Literary historians provide crucial contexts for readers of Faulkner by relating the texts to the times and places of their stories' settings and the times and places in which they were written. But this task becomes more complicated, because culture is not static; it doesn't honor borders of time or place. In Faulkner's work, depending on the specific novel's settings, representations of class need to be read in the context of the nineteenth and twentieth centuries and in terms of Southern literature, history, and culture, as well as that of the US and the Americas. One of the implications of New World studies is that when scholars reject the exceptionalism that has in the past isolated studies of the US South, for example, from other plantation societies, more complicated and interesting connections among the transnational flows of culture, capital, and populations across time and space become visible. Furthermore, as Faulkner studies continue to break out of the boxes of "region," and even "nation," more potential contexts for comparative analysis come into view. For studies of class in Faulkner, attention to geographical scale from the county to the region to the nation to the world can illuminate the ways in which power congeals around the centers of global capitalism and their markets. The relevance of the study of class at each of these scales in the twenty-first century should also be clear, given the current directions of globalization and finance capital expansion (see Aronowitz 2003; Perrucci and Wysong 2003; Seabrook 2002).

Because both these novels reveal flaws in US ideologies of class mobility, albeit in quite different ways and using different textual strategies, this chapter will read the two novels as case studies to demonstrate the relevance of class for Faulkner studies (and conversely that Faulkner is relevant to class studies). *As I Lay Dying* is a relatively small-scale novel, in terms of its geographical range and its time frame, set in the first decades of the twentieth century, in the back roads and small towns of Yoknapatawpha county, highlighting the socio-economic divides between town and country, and especially between so-called white trash and others considered to be the more deserving poor. Looking at class in terms of form, too, is important: each chapter is narrated through the consciousness and voice of one character and the novel's overall comic (or grotesque) tone contributes to the way class is articulated and represented. Class identity is constructed here through the perspectives of the narrators, revealing their own filters and assumptions.

On the other hand, *Absalom, Absalom!* takes place on a wider scale, extending farther over time and space, from around 1807 to 1910, in many locations; the scale of the socio-economic relations is also broader, touching on the American North and South, the US and Haiti, black and white, and poor white trash, middle class, and aristocratic class. The narrative form in *Absalom, Absalom!* is also more intricate, contradictory, and full of conjecture: much of the plot is told in flashback, sometimes in flashbacks of past conversations that were about something still farther in the past, and so on. The multiple layers of narration problematize the notion of truth and emphasize the constructedness of identity and history, from the individual scale of a character's persona and life story to the characterization of regions and nations, such as the South, the US, and Haiti, and of social groups such as planters, slaves, and poor whites.

Yet both novels portray similar processes of class identity construction. Anse Bundren and Thomas Sutpen are both judged by other characters on the basis of their appearance, behavior, and presumed origins. The importance of family ties in defining one's class identity is demonstrated over and over in these texts, as different characters observe Anse and Sutpen and speculate about their group affiliations: family, class, geographic origins. Both men are fathers and heads of families: Anse Bundren is a parody of a patriarch who manipulates and tricks his children to get what he wants, and Thomas Sutpen's failed patriarchy is an allegory for the fall of the South and the impossibility of the American myth of the self-made man. Both men come from rural poor origins and, in the course of the two novels, exemplify in comic and tragic modes, respectively, the contradictions of class in the United States.

Reading Anse

This section examines *As I Lay Dying* in order to demonstrate that reading in terms of class can be a productive critical framework for understanding the novel. I argue that Anse Bundren, the father of the family, is a parody of the myth of the self-made man who achieves the American Dream through hard work and determination. His identity is rigidly defined by most other characters as the lowest of the undeserving rural poor, that is, white trash. Yet he appears clownishly proud of his minuscule advances; the novel makes a grotesque joke of the Bundrens' negative mobility, geographically and socio-economically. This close reading of the novel will show how his class identity is constructed in the text through his own words and deeds and those of other characters, who look down on Anse's poverty as evidence of his character flaws. Seeing Anse as trash gives the other white men a sense of distance from him and thus allows them to see themselves as more upwardly mobile. *As I Lay Dying* uses narration, including first person and more complexly mediated retellings, to construct the class identity of Anse Bundren. The novel also uses important symbols that illustrate his negative mobility: the wagon and the highway (see Leyda 2000).

The construction of Anse Bundren as undeserving white trash in *As I Lay Dying* serves a crucial purpose in the meritocratic class ideology that undergirds the social systems of the South at the time the novel is set, in the 1920s. Anse is portrayed as trash, which allows the other white farmers to see themselves as somehow constitutionally different and more deserving. The white men of Yoknapatawpha may be only marginally better off, but they believe in the meritocracy: that class position is a "reflection of talent and effort" and therefore people who are intelligent and hard-working earn (and deserve) success (Perrucci and Wysong 2003: 285). Poor people, conversely, appear to be "justly placed in the lower ranks because they obviously lack the valued qualities necessary to succeed" (p. 285); for his peers, Anse is clearly a lazy man who doesn't deserve any better than he has.

Although many townsfolk believe Anse is lazy and undeserving, none acknowledges the physical marks of poverty manifested in Anse's body because to do so might destabilize their faith in the meritocracy: if diligence leads to success, then how to explain the disastrous effects of a lifetime of hard work on Anse Bundren? Duane Carr points out how, amid the many casual condemnations of Anse's laziness, only Anse's son Darl mentions his work-related disabilities that are due to a previous bout with heatstroke and bad shoes as a child laborer. Anse's fear of sweating stems from the fact that "as a young man he had been a hard worker who fell deathly ill 'from working in the hot sun,' a reality that gives credence to his otherwise apparently superstitious belief that if he works up a sweat he will die" (Carr 1996: 83; also Rippetoe 2001). And although numerous characters remark upon Anse's custom of working his children as he rests in the shade, only Darl observes that his father's feet are "badly splayed, his toes cramped and bent and warped, with no toenail at all on his little toes, from working so hard in the wet in homemade shoes when he was a boy" (Faulkner 1985: 11). The novel documents how Anse's body is scarred by his life of work, but few in the novel consider physical explanations for his "laziness," seeing him simply as shiftless white trash. It is possible that his disabilities, caused by poverty and overwork, prevent him from working, which makes it more difficult for him to achieve class mobility. Because he doesn't work, his family remains poor. As a result, Anse is constantly borrowing from and imposing on his neighbors.

In his neediness, Anse Bundren is seen as part of a specific group of people, the undeserving poor. Armstid is a Yoknapatawpha farmer, but he has a mule team and apparently more middle-class sensibilities than the Bundrens, who must barter and mortgage for most of their necessities. Distinguishing himself from Anse, Armstid observes: "durn if there aint something about a durn fellow like Anse that seems to make a man have to help him, even when he knows he'll be wanting to kick himself the next minute" (Faulkner 1985: 192). Armstid is talking about a "fellow like Anse" – not just Anse himself, but a group of people like him who need help from Armstid, who will angrily regret it "the next minute." Here Anse is rhetorically lumped together with needy, seemingly humble people, who Armstid believes take advantage of the generosity of others. Explaining a similar representation of the idle poor that recurs throughout English literature, Raymond Williams notes that it is "not only the recurrent and ludicrous part-song of the rich; but the sharper, more savage anxiety of the middle men, the insecure," who have a greater stake in denouncing the poor and defending the lines of class distinction (1973: 44). In *As I Lay Dying*, those most anxious to mark Anse as white trash are those who occupy positions closest to his, socio-economically and geographically – farmers and townsfolk who want to be middle-class and who want to see in the Bundrens' backwardness evidence of their own progress, whether literally progress to town or toward the class status that town represents.

Marking the Bundrens as undeserving trash, though, makes it harder to explain the dogged determination Anse shows as he tries to get Addie's body buried in Jefferson. His stubbornness provokes Samson, a farmer who helps the Bundrens on their journey, to comment on his unswerving attempt to get Addie's body to Jefferson: "I notice how it takes a lazy man, a man that hates moving, to get set on moving once he does get started off, the same as he was set on staying still, like it aint the moving he hates so much as the starting and the stopping" (Faulkner 1985: 114). Although usually seen as lazy, when Anse does "get set on moving" he defies all logic in pursuit of his goal, which is seen as somehow consistent with his laziness. A slave to inertia, Anse at rest remains at rest while Anse in motion remains in motion. While determination is one of the qualities said to enable hard-working Americans to become successful in the myth of the self-made man, in Anse Bundren determination comes across as foolish and stubborn. Although normally determination signals positive traits that can lead to class mobility, characters in *As I Lay Dying* go to great lengths to maintain their image of Anse as lazy trash.

Geography in the white trash identity is also central: town whites must distinguish themselves from rural whites to preserve their own class identity. As Williams demonstrates in *The Country and the City*, the country is represented as the site of backwardness and ignorance at precisely the point in history when national participation in consumer capitalism picks up steam (1973). Although Williams refers to a specifically British context, I find his analysis useful both because it traces the history of the country and city dichotomy in Western culture more generally and because so little has been written about class in American culture. Certainly, as Williams argues, the overdetermined categories of country and city have been invoked since the ancient Greeks to signify not simply geographical difference but also differences in morals, modes of production, and more recently, stages of capitalism. At the time *As I Lay Dying* is set, in the 1920s, rural whites in the New South were only just beginning to participate in consumer capitalism.

Of course, this novel plays the Bundrens as black comedy, and Faulkner insures that readers can understand the townspeople's anxiety by including the dead body as part of the cargo. But in the town characters' descriptions of the family, Faulkner is careful to emphasize not only the outrage of the corpse but the family's origins, "some place out in Yoknapatawpha county" (1985: 203). Because they live on a farm outside the town, the Bundrens' geographical capital declines as the towns grow in size and status. As Carr points out, Faulkner wrote *As I Lay Dying* around the time Southerners realized that the "progress promised by advocates of a New South had not come to pass, that instead the South had acquired industrialization without prosperity, becoming . . . a poverty-stricken replica of the North" (1996: 81). In the context of these economic upheavals, poor rural whites are perceived by striving middle-class whites as outmoded. Anse joins a long line of poor white rural characters in American literature who are perceived by others as "country" and therefore obsolete, primitive, and stupid (see Carr 1996; Cook 1976). Marking the Bundrens as undeserving trash explains their negative mobility in the "land of opportunity" the middle classes need to believe exists.

Simultaneously threatened and reassured by the presence of poor country white trash, the townspeople distance themselves by emphasizing their difference.

The movement of characters from country to city in *As I Lay Dying* accompanies the geographic shift on a national scale from agriculture to industry and from rural to urban spaces: the 1920 census identifies the majority of Americans as city dwellers for the first time. As the balance of the US population shifted from a rural to an urban majority, new relations of space and movement developed in tandem with the changing modes of production that encouraged urbanization. While some Americans were buying cars and making money in growing industrial markets, others were less successful and thus less mobile. Living in town is a form of geographical capital that everyone in the novel can recognize; Jewel thinks that just "because he's a goddamn town fellow" a passerby feels entitled to criticize the Bundrens (Faulkner 1985: 230). The hierarchy is expressed by many of the narrators, including the town druggist Moseley, who relates what another town man tells him about the Bundren wagon, which had just arrived on the main street:

> It was Albert told me about the rest of it. He said the wagon was stopped in front of Grummet's hardware store, with the ladies all scattering up and down the street with handkerchiefs to their noses. . . . They came from some place out in Yoknapatawpha county, trying to get to Jefferson . . . in that ramshackle wagon that Albert said folks were scared would fall all to pieces before they could get it out of town. (p. 203)

The Bundrens are seen as ignorant rural trash, carrying as they do an unembalmed body that has been dead eight days. The grotesque image of the rotting corpse parked on the main street in mid-July isn't complete without the description of the townspeople's horrified reaction.

The passage above, in which Moseley relates Albert's account of the opinion of the whole town, illustrates the role of narrative and perspective in the construction of class in *As I Lay Dying*. Moseley's retelling of the scene comes via another town fellow, Albert, and includes not only the pedestrians' outrage, but also the marshal's argument with Anse trying to get him to leave town quickly. This passage in Moseley's chapter conveys not only his own disapproval but that of the town collectively. Each narrator relies, in this passage, on the evidence of others' actions or opinions to amplify his own. Additionally, the passage describes one of the novel's most important symbols: the Bundrens' wagon. The wagon and its cargo are a source of horror to the townspeople, who make it clear that they are not welcome in town.

The mode of transport reflects the characters and their place in the class hierarchies of town and country, and in the urbanizing nation: the negative mobility evidenced in the Bundrens' dilapidated wagon suggests that "traffic is not only a technique; it is a form of consciousness and a form of social relations" (Williams 1973: 296). Albert reports that the townspeople wanted the Bundren wagon to get out of town as soon as possible, but worried that it would fall apart first. The implication is clear: Moseley, Albert, and more generally "folks" in town recognize in their behavior and in their wagon that the Bundrens are a poor rural family with limited mobility. The grueling incremental progress of the family's wagon exemplifies the profoundly limited opportunities held out by geographical mobility for working people in depressed parts of the country. As Williams points out, "The division and opposition of city and country, industry and agriculture, in their modern forms, are the critical culmination of the division and specialization of labour which, though it did not begin with capitalism, was developed under it to an extraordinary and transforming degree" (1973: 304).

The highway and the ability to use it carry symbolic value in *As I Lay Dying*. For Anse Bundren, the roads represent a tax expenditure that may speed the destruction of his family's subsistence-level farm economy (see also Railey 1999: 91). In the 1920s the Mississippi highway system was in its infancy, and Anse speculates whether such a modernization is worth the tax money: "Durn that road. . . . A-laying there, right up to my door, where every bad luck that comes and goes is bound to find it. . . . it seems hard that a man in his need could be so flouted by a road" (Faulkner 1985: 35, 38). He laments the cost of the road, as the Bundren sons increasingly work as wage laborers rather than exclusively on their farm: "[g]ot to pay for the way [literally the road] for them boys to have to go away to earn it [money]" (p. 37). In his usual hyperbole, Anse attempts to blame Addie's death on the road, since "[s]he was well and hale as ere a woman ever were, except for that road" (p. 37). His resentment of the highway illustrates, on the one hand, the suspicion of change typical of many poor whites during the economic restructuring in the twenties and thirties South. On the other hand, he is right: the road *is* killing his family's way of life, signaling the urbanization and modernization of the agrarian South. To the rural poor in the novel, increased geographical mobility means exposure to consumer goods they can't afford and the growing likelihood of urban migration in search of cash wages (see Willis 1991). Faulkner's death knell for the premodern rural South depicts and problematizes its characters' positions on the highway of modernity.

Moreover, the wagon journey itself signifies mobility only superficially, since the circumnavigation of floods and other calamities that befall the Bundrens ironically marks their inability to reach their destination, a negative mobility rather than progress. The highway is not just to Jefferson via Mottson, but to modernity via consumerism, and the Bundren wagon is barely roadworthy, representing (complete with corpse) the outmoded, bottomed-out agrarian economy of the New South. Driving in circles, mending broken wheels, the Bundrens are proof that just because there is a road doesn't mean everyone can get somewhere. In the high-speed, technologically advanced modern age, the Bundrens are one step above immobile – they can move from one place to another, but only laterally and literally. The class status they are born into and the economy in which they must survive ensure that they will end up, if not where they started out, then somewhere comparable or worse.

The Myth of Mobility

The self-made man is a recurring myth in American literature and culture, perhaps most famous in the form of Horatio Alger's rags-to-riches stories, in which a poor young man who shows initiative, hard work, and ambition achieves success. The "ideology of ascension" has played across movie screens and bestseller lists for generations, providing subject matter for countless stories of upward class mobility with happy endings (Hapke 2001: 62). Sociologists Robert Perrucci and Earl Wysong write that the American Dream has two main tenets:

> First, that everyone can aspire to levels of success that exceed their starting points in life, because where a person starts life is an accident that can be remedied; and second, that there is equality of opportunity to reach one's goals, and that the game has a set of rules that are fair and capable of producing the desired success goals. (2003: 212)

And while this dream persists into the twenty-first century, they argue, it "also serves to legitimate the great inequality in society in wealth, power, and privilege" and "leads to the belief that those who receive high rewards are deserving because they have contributed more in terms of effort and hard work" (p. 212). The liberal idealism of the American Dream and the myth of the self-made man thus implicitly construct a distinction between deserving and undeserving, a distinction that forms one of the foundations of American conceptions of class. Ironically, this distinction between deserving and undeserving can be seen in the ideology of paternalism as well, which is in many ways "fundamentally antithetical to liberalism" (Railey 1999: 7).

In Faulkner's fiction, Kevin Railey identifies a continuous negotiation between the seemingly opposite ideologies of liberalism, outlined above, and those of paternalism, upon which the slave economy was based (1999). Unlike the liberal belief in equal opportunity and individual merit, the paternalistic way of thinking rested on the "natural" and hereditary hierarchies of the family, headed by the powerful but moral patriarch, whose responsibility was to care for those under his authority: his children, his employees, his slaves. There is a static, conservative quality to the paternalistic belief that "some are born to rule, others to obey," and it is clearly compatible with slavery as well as naturalized class divisions (Railey 1999: 7). While I have argued that Anse Bundren in *As I Lay Dying* can be read as a caricature of the self-made man, Railey argues that he embodies a "near-perfect caricature of paternalism – claiming all the authority with absolutely none of the responsibility" (1999: 94). Interestingly, both liberal idealism and paternalism rely on sorting people into two groups: deserving and undeserving. The crucial difference lies in how people are sorted, whether by their lineage, or by their achieved mobility, or more realistically, by some combination of the two. While the Armstid and Mosely chapters in *As I Lay Dying* portray some of the collective nature of that sorting, *Absalom, Absalom!* delves much deeper into the processes of class identity formation and class distinction. The greater complexity of the social hierarchies and relationships in *Absalom, Absalom!* is amplified by greater complexities in narrative form; there are more levels and layers than in *As I Lay Dying*, and they are more intricately woven together.

This section focuses on *Absalom, Absalom!* because its central character Thomas Sutpen's story of class mobility constitutes a critique of the classic American myth of the self-made man; he is "Faulkner's cipher for the mythical Horatio Alger character" (Latham 1998: 455). Sutpen starts out as a poor youth who seeks his fortune abroad through hard work, strength, and determination; he obtains credit from respected members of society, builds a mansion, establishes a plantation, and marries a respected woman. But although these appear to be the requisite steps leading to his happy ending as a member of the paternalistic planter class, Sutpen fails in both spatial and temporal terms. He never fully gains his "place" in the county's planter society because the people never fully accept him: despite his hard work, wealth, and lavish home, he remains an uncouth pretender in their eyes. He also fails to achieve his "design" to create an enduring dynasty that will outlast him, because his obedience to the ideology of white supremacy combines with his ruthless pursuit of wealth to destroy his children.

Absalom, Absalom! is often interpreted as an allegory of the fall of the slave-based Old South, which, Quentin tells Shreve, had "erected its economic edifice not on the rock of stern morality but on the shifting sands of opportunism and moral brigandage," that is, neither the "stern morality" of deserved class mobility nor the nobility of paternalistic noblesse oblige; it can also be read as an allegory of the failure of the American Dream (Faulkner 1986: 209). This chapter argues that class is an integral part of those allegories, located at the formative moment in Sutpen's life. Sutpen's story is constructed through complicated narrations and renarrations, which form not a linear plot but a choppy and incomplete sketch, with hypothetical segments added by various narrators whose own emotional involvement calls into question their reliability. The content of Sutpen's story and the form of the novel itself construct, and expose the constructedness of, class identity as a set of social relations, along with and at times almost inseparable from issues of race. This section first examines Thomas Sutpen's life story as a plot-line that elaborates the formation of his class identity, then turns to a discussion of the novel's layers and levels of narration to examine the ways in which other characters' views of Sutpen construct class identity within the text.

As a 14-year-old boy in Virginia, Thomas Sutpen is turned away from the front door of Pettibone, a rich planter, by a slave who recognizes his class status and tells him to go to the back door. This humiliates the naïve Sutpen, who had grown up in an isolated hill community where in his memory, at least, "the land belonged to anybody and everybody," and where he was unaware of class divisions like those in plantation country in which "the ones who owned the objects not only could look down on the ones that didn't, but could be supported in the down-looking not only by the others who owned objects too but by the very ones that were looked down on that didn't own objects and knew they never would" (Faulkner 1986: 179). But he observes that plantation society is organized according to these differences, internalized by everyone regardless of their positions: the poor know their place or they are told, as he was when he was sent around to the back door. The shock Sutpen receives at the planter's door makes him question his previous assumptions about the world and try to understand the hierarchies he didn't know existed. Though he ultimately fails to realize how completely limited his own mobility really is, Sutpen attempts to make sense of what happened. His process of analyzing this encounter is childish and flawed, and his failure to question the larger framework of class distinction contributes to his downfall.

Pondering the encounter at the door, he realizes that he had explained his class position to himself within what I have described here as a liberal idealist framework, in which everyone's chances are basically equal. Because of what the text repeatedly calls his "innocence," he has believed that even those born less fortunate would have opportunities and he assumed that luckier people would want to help others: "[h]e still thought that that was just a matter of where you were spawned and how; lucky or unlucky; and that the lucky ones would be even slower and lother than the unlucky to take any advantage of it or credit for it" (Faulkner 1986: 183). Sutpen's "design" originates in this trauma at the door, in his initial rebellion against paternalist class privilege and his own positioning within this class identity as undeserving poor (Railey 1999: 115), which he identifies as the root of the problem. In this moment, Sutpen also realizes that white supremacist violence is a distraction for poor whites that does not improve their lot in life.

Until then, Sutpen had never put together all the steps of the process by which poor whites displace their resentment of rich whites onto blacks: he had not fully grasped the way in which class antagonism among poor whites converged with racism. As he considers this, he recalls "a certain flat level silent way his older sisters and the other white women of their kind had of looking at niggers, not with fear or dread but with a kind of speculative antagonism" (Faulkner 1986: 186). Sutpen realizes that "you knew you could hit them" because of the privilege of white supremacy, and he remembers that his father once assaulted "that son of a bitch Pettibone's nigger" in a drunken rage (p. 187). In his father's deed, Sutpen recognizes a pattern of lashing out at the easiest target: he understands that though he could take out his anger on slaves, "you did not want to, because they (the niggers) were not it, not what you wanted to hit" (p. 186).

Although he sees that his class identity means he will face discrimination from rich whites like Pettibone, and house slaves who do as their masters instruct them, he struggles with the question of what to do about it and finally decides to become a rich planter himself. Rejecting individual revenge as doomed to failure and unable to conceive of any political or collective alternative, he places his belief in the American Dream and proceeds to follow the steps that are supposed to lead to success. His eventual failure will demonstrate the impossibility of that dream, but the young Sutpen's indignation at the injustice of class inequality makes him want simply to beat the planter class at their own game: "to combat them you have got to have what they have that made them do what he did. You got to have land and niggers and a fine house to combat them with" (Faulkner 1986: 192). The result of Sutpen's outrage is his decision to become rich. Rather than reject either liberalism's or paternalism's different classifications of deserving and undeserving, he seems to believe that he is simply in the wrong category, a deserving person mistakenly mixed in with the undeserving. From that day forward, he works to join the planter class: he competes with them, attains comparable wealth and power, and finally resembles them in many ways.

Young Sutpen's trauma stems from his sudden recognition of how he appears to others. Specifically, he realizes that the man at the door, "who through no doing of his own happened to have had the felicity of being housebred in Richmond maybe," as Quentin hypothesizes, sees the poor boy as he has been trained to, through the categories of class (Faulkner 1986: 188). The house slave then becomes for Sutpen an inflated, empty "balloon face" that merely obscures a more powerful and extensive social hierarchy that scorns Sutpen and his family because of their class (p. 189). The balloon face here is a racist distraction; it obscures the more powerful view of men like Pettibone the planter who, somewhere behind his slave,

> looked out from whatever invisible place he (the man) happened to be at the moment, at the boy outside the barred door in his patched garments and splayed bare feet, looking through and beyond the boy, he himself seeing his own father and sisters and brothers as the owner, the rich man (not the nigger) must have been seeing them all the time. (pp. 189–90)

Like the individual characters in *As I Lay Dying* who view Anse Bundren as a type, as one of a category of people, the black balloon face both represents and obscures the larger perspective of the dominant society that sees barefoot rural poor people as somehow undeserving of success, comfort, or wealth.

Imagining the social view of poor whites represented and obscured by the black balloon face, Sutpen pictures how the rich man sees the Sutpen family: "as cattle, creatures heavy and without grace, brutely evacuated into a world without hope or purpose for them, who would in turn spawn with brutish and vicious prolixity, populate, double treble and compound, fill space and earth with a race whose future would be a succession of cut-down and patched and made-over garments" (Faulkner 1986: 190). This emphasis on generations of poor whites, who constitute "a race" of miserable, hopeless, and purposeless cattle, clearly informs Sutpen's decision to create a dynasty, as if in defiance of the planter's assumptions. He reasons that wealth and family will earn and hold his place in the aristocracy, although he ultimately fails to produce a male heir to carry on the family name and business. This passage highlights the role of heredity in paternalism and in its justification of slavery and classism, in that the poor whites are seen as an undeserving race, like cattle, whose only inheritance is worn-out clothing (or a worn-out wagon, as in *As I Lay Dying*). Similarly, the supposedly more deserving whites, the sons of planters, inherit their fathers' status in their name, social position, wealth, and property. Rather than repudiate the paternalism that excludes him, Sutpen embraces it and tries to move into the planter class, even though he has recognized at some level that it is almost by definition an inherited status.

This central contradiction in Sutpen's character, his liberalism and recognition of social injustice alongside his "design" to become a Southern slaveholding aristocrat in a hereditary dynasty, eventually leads to his downfall. His failure to break out of this contradiction makes his character's failure an allegorical condemnation of the South, but also of American national ideologies. According to John Matthews, his failure to look "more deeply into the circumstances of his original insult" displays an "oblivious-ness that is American innocence" (2004: 238). The novel's construction of class identity and class hierarchies illustrates the impossibility of class mobility while at the same time showing Sutpen's own failure as partly a result of a faulty interpretation, an incomplete analysis.

Perspective is crucial in *Absalom, Absalom!* and the balloon face passages above illustrate Sutpen's coming to (limited) consciousness about his class identity as he internalizes the planter's perspective. But another way the novel uses perspective is in its layered and collaborative narration; none of the story is told directly by Thomas Sutpen, although some narrators relate his story and attribute quotations to him on the basis of their firsthand memories. The difficulty of reading the novel, which is itself a grand "design" in which the author seems at times to be building on shifting sands, is analo-gous to the difficulty of grasping the complexities and contexts of any complicated story: history, biography, myth, literature. The multiplicity of perspectives and voices in the novel exemplifies in narrative form the social and cultural complexities that the story depicts. At this point, I would like to pull back and examine how some of the narrators emphasize the complexities of class in their tellings of the story. The pas-sages above are narrated in 1909, the novel's "present," by Quentin Compson in his dorm room in Harvard. He is describing the Sutpen story to his roommate Shreve, a Canadian, who comments on the story as a spectator or consumer of entertainment – "the South is fine, isn't it. It's better than the theatre, isn't it. It's better than Ben Hur, isn't it" – and helps fill in gaps in the story by imagining what may have happened: "[m]aybe he had a girl" (Faulkner 1986: 176–7).

But Quentin tells the story to Shreve from memory; it was told to him by Rosa Coldfield, Sutpen's sister-in-law, as well as by his father Mr. Compson, and (through Mr. Compson) his grandfather, General Compson. Furthermore, the story of Sutpen's encounter at the door is recounted, through multiple levels of mediation, from a con-versation that the adult Sutpen had with Quentin's grandfather, and thus is a recon-structed childhood memory told by an adult. The story is told through generations, handed down from father to son, in much the same way that class position itself is often inherited. Moreover, the surreal circumstances under which Sutpen told Compson his story raise further questions about his "innocence": the men are resting during a manhunt, complete with dogs and slaves, to track and capture the architect (of ambigu-ous racial identity) who designed Sutpen's house and was supervising its construction under extreme conditions. The brutal suppression of the architect's right to leave the job site – resembling a hunt for a runaway slave – only underscores Sutpen's narcissistic embrace of paternalistic ideology, with its white supremacist foundations. Clearly, the house represents not only Sutpen's wealth and success, but his desire to build a lasting aristocratic family, a "house" of Sutpen; his failure can be read as the fall of the "house divided" by race, as Sundquist points out (1983). I suggest that his house is divided in more ways than that: certainly it is divided because his "black" son Charles Bon appears, and because of the violence of the confrontation between Bon and his brother Henry (and the Civil War which takes place at the center of the story), but also because Sutpen is divided between his belief in the liberal American Dream and his desire to join the planter-class aristocracy.

The perspective of Shreve, who is neither a Southerner nor even a US citizen, is in itself contradictory; his comments about the South position him as an outsider who can barely comprehend the horrors of slavery and the Civil War, yet at other times he and Quentin seem almost equally invested in the story:

> It was Shreve speaking, though save for the slight difference which the intervening degrees of latitude had inculcated in them . . . , it might have been either of them and was in a sense both: both thinking as one, the voice which happened to be speaking the thought only the thinking become audible, vocal; the two of them creating between them, out of the rag-tag and bob-ends of old tales and talking, people who perhaps had never existed at all anywhere. (Faulkner 1986: 243)

Quentin and Shreve concoct large sections of the story, trying to imagine the motives and feelings of the "shades" in the Sutpen drama, but their narration is itself narrated in ways that make us question all the narrators: "Perhaps Quentin himself had not been listening when Mr. Compson related (recreated?) it that evening at home" (p. 268). The narrator continues in this vein, "perhaps . . . Quentin took that in stride without even hearing it just as Shreve would have, since both he and Shreve believed – and were probably right in this too –" (p. 268). The narrator raises doubts about Quentin's memory but then endorses his grasp of the story after all. When the young men, in their Harvard room, fabricate a whole character, the narrator further encourages us to believe in her, "whom Shreve and Quentin had likewise invented and which was likewise probably true enough" (p. 268).

If the narrator of the chapters quoted above is reliable, then the novel is not simply declaring that truth does not exist or that it is impossible to find. Actually the novel encourages readers to believe that the various narrators, including Quentin and Shreve, are "probably right" about the story they tell, despite our knowledge that they are rec-reating it. This suggests the power of narrative and imagination to make more or less good sense of fragments, to interpret imperfect artifacts and create meanings that are more or less "probably right." In this way, narrative creates material reality, such as the "design" that grew out of Sutpen's analysis. In this way, too, narratives about class create material realities of class. Telling stories, to others and in internal monologues, about a character's class identity constitutes and reinforces that class identity or it questions and analyzes that identity; the perception of a person's class identity often becomes naturalized through narrative in *As I Lay Dying* and in *Absalom, Absalom!* But Sutpen mostly fails in his interpretation of the encounter at the door, as he turns it over in his own mind and re-examines his experiences of class up to that point: he fails to make sense of the ways in which class hierarchies are constructed and fixed in other characters' perceptions of him. He never takes his analysis beyond simple self-interest – I'm being discriminated against because I'm poor, therefore I will get rich – and because he didn't go far enough in his study of how class is constructed, he doesn't realize that he cannot successfully join the planter class (nor does he successfully challenge that class).

Portraying the constructedness of class identity through narrative, particularly the narratives that question the seemingly "natural" distinctions between rich and poor and between black and white, the novel raises a greater question about the possibilities for mobility inherent in the American Dream, the myth of the self-made man, and American exceptionalism. The constructions of class in this novel are not restricted to the social hierarchies and relations of Yoknapatawpha county and the town and country divides that were central to *As I Lay Dying*. Rather, *Absalom, Absalom!* illuminates the ways in which transnational financial networks tie in with regional class systems of planters, slaves, and merchants, by portraying how the "colonial slave trade sustained the South's domestic paternalism" (Matthews 2004: 252). This transnational link helps to clarify how the moral and human rights issues surrounding slavery and white supremacy interlace with white Southern class identities, particularly when, as Matthews points out, the novel's characters "ignore historical truths that they are in a position to admit plainly" (p. 250). Sutpen's limited but significant class mobility is made possible not only by hard work as the myth of the self-made man implies, but by the fact that he was born white and moves to Haiti where he can capitalize on whiteness as a plantation overseer. Moreover, although he becomes wealthy, paternalistic Southerners refuse to respect him as a "natural aristocrat" of the planter class (Railey 1999). In effect enforcing a second line of racial, regional, and national qualifications for membership in their planter class, they see Sutpen as an "underbred" man with "a name which nobody ever heard before," and by implication, not a member of their class, a stranger "who came from nowhere or dared not tell where" (Faulkner 1986: 34, 9, 13).

Maritza Stanchich argues that Sutpen's "unvalorous death and the ensuing destruction of Sutpen's Hundred deposits his supremacy in the trash heap along with the false myths of American 'innocence' and 'freedom'" (1996: 614). *Absalom, Absalom!* exemplifies the complex connections between class divisions, racism, and transnational plantation societies. Sutpen's story moves from his recognition of unjust class hierarchies into a colonial-style narrative in which he capitalizes on his whiteness and his knowledge that "racial hierarchies derive from and depend upon the willful exercise of violence" (Latham 1998: 460; also Matthews 2004). In fact, the only capital Sutpen possesses in Haiti is racial capital, violently enforced: at that point, "he has come to realize that his whiteness means something and that it is all he has to offer" (Railey 1999: 131; also Stanchich 1996: 604). It is this capitulation to racist social mores, repeated in his treatment of his slaves, his architect, his first wife, and his first son, that finally costs Sutpen everything: his children, house, land, and status as "the biggest single landowner and cotton-planter in the county" (Faulkner 1986: 56). Moreover, it is this wider consideration of "the whole history of the new-world plantation that makes Sutpen's career from Haiti to Jefferson entirely legible as a story of colonial crime – Amerindian genocide, slave trade, human chattel, bigamy, rape, incest, the loveless outrage of the land" (Matthews 2004: 256–7). As a critique of the plantation societies of the Americas, the novel is an exposé of "what Faulkner's South shares more broadly with new-world histories and experiences" (Matthews 2004: 239; also Glissant 1999; Handley 2000; Ladd

1994). As Sean Latham demonstrates, the story of Sutpen's rise and fall is simultaneously "a narrative of European colonization" and a "story about the establishment of the American nation itself" (1998: 462), including especially the liberal and paternalist ideas that naturalize and legitimize inequality. Whereas the parody of the self-made man in *As I Lay Dying* portrayed the virtual impossibility of class mobility for a "fellow like" Anse Bundren, *Absalom, Absalom!* shows us in the tragic mode that the United States is a nation built on shifting sands hidden beneath the myth of class mobility.

REFERENCES AND FURTHER READING

Aronowitz, S. (2003). *How Class Works: Power and Social Movement*. New Haven, CT: Yale University Press.

Carr, D. (1996). *A Question of Class: The Redneck Stereotype in Southern Fiction*. Bowling Green: Bowling Green University Popular Press.

Christopher, R. and C. Whitson (1999). Toward a Theory of Working-Class Literature. *NEA Higher Education Thought and Action Journal*, Spring: 71–81.

Cook, S. J. (1976). *From Tobacco Road to Route 66: The Southern Poor White in Fiction*. Chapel Hill, NC: University of North Carolina Press.

CWCS (Center for Working-Class Studies) home page. Working-Class Studies: Why and How? www.as.ysu.edu/~cwcs/Whyhow.html (n.p.)

Denning, M. (1998). *The Cultural Front: The Laboring of American Culture in the Twentieth Century*. New York: Verso.

Faulkner, W. (1986). *Absalom, Absalom!: The Corrected Text*. New York: Vintage. (Original pub. 1936.)

Faulkner, W. (1985). *As I Lay Dying: The Corrected Text*. New York: Vintage. (Original pub. 1930.)

Glissant, E. (1999). *Faulkner, Mississippi*. New York: Farrar, Straus and Giroux.

Handley, G. (2000). *Postslavery Literatures in the Americas: Family Portraits in Black and White*. Charlottesville, VA: University of Virginia Press.

Hapke, L. (2001). *Labor's Text: The Worker in American Fiction*. New Brunswick, NJ: Rutgers University Press.

Jehlen, M. (1978). *Class and Character in Faulkner's South*. New York: Columbia University Press.

Ladd, B. (1994). "The Direction of the Howling": Nationalism and the Color Line in *Absalom, Absalom! American Literature*, 66(3): 525–51.

Latham, S. (1998). Jim Bond's America: Denaturalizing the Logic of Slavery in *Absalom, Absalom! Mississippi Quarterly*, 51(3): 453–63.

Leyda, J. (2000). Reading White Trash: Class, Race, and Mobility in Faulkner and Le Sueur. *Arizona Quarterly*, 56(2): 37–64.

Matthews, J. (2004). Recalling the West Indies: From Yoknapatawpha to Haiti and Back. *American Literary History*, 16(2): 238–62.

Perrucci, R. and E. Wysong (2003). *The New Class Society: Goodbye American Dream?* 2nd edn. Lanham: Rowman and Littlefield.

Railey, K. (1999). *Natural Aristocracy: History, Ideology, and the Production of William Faulkner*. Tuscaloosa: University of Alabama Press.

Rippetoe, R. (2001). Unstained Shirt, Stained Character: Anse Bundren Reread. *Mississippi Quarterly*, 54(3): 313–25.

Seabrook, J. (2002). *The No-Nonsense Guide to Class, Caste, and Hierarchies*. Oxford: New Internationalist.

Skinfill, M. (1996). Reconstructing Class in Faulkner's Late Novels: *The Hamlet* and the Discovery of Capital. *Studies in American Fiction*, 24(2): 151–70.

Stanchich, M. (1996). The Hidden Caribbean "Other" in William Faulkner's *Absalom, Absalom!*: An Ideological Ancestry of U.S. Imperialism. *Mississippi Quarterly*, 49(3): 603–17.

Sundquist, E. (1983). *Faulkner: The House Divided*. Baltimore: Johns Hopkins University Press.

Williams, R. (1973). *The Country and the City*. New York: Oxford University Press.

Willis, S. (1991). *A Primer for Daily Life*. New York: Routledge.

Zandy, J. (ed.) (2001). *What We Hold in Common: An Introduction to Working-Class Studies*. New York: CUNY-Feminist Press.

11

Faulkner's Families

Arthur F. Kinney

Clan rather than class forms the basic unit in Faulkner's world. Pride in family and reverence for ancestors are far more powerful motives in behavior than any involvement with class. . . . It is through [the] breakup of the clans that Faulkner charts the decay of the traditional South. Though the Compsons, Sartorises, and McCaslins, all landowners of prominence, begin roughly on the same social level, their histories from the Civil War serve radically different purposes. Their responses to modern life seem to illustrate the various moral courses that are, or were, open to the South: the chivalric recklessness and self-destruction of the Sartorises, the more extreme and tragic disintegration of the Compsons and, by way of resolution, the heroic expiation for the evil of the past upon which Isaac McCaslin decides. . . . The Yoknapatawpha story is to be read more as a chronicle than as a group of novels [and stories]. It is concerned less with the struggle of the classes than with the rise and fall of the clans, and through its history of the clans it elaborates a moral fable whose source is Southern life. (Howe 1975: 8–9)

Faulkner was obsessed by genealogy. So are all of his characters. More than race, gender, or class, it is the family that defines them, haunts them, and limits them: when young Bayard seeks liberty, it is freedom from the Sartoris family legend that he wants; when Jason Compson is overwhelmed with self-pity, it is because he feels the Compson family has left him with all the responsibility for its future; and when Ike McCaslin chooses to relinquish all of his inheritance, knowledge of his family's past recorded in commissary ledgers prevents him. For Thomas Sutpen, the world is reduced to dynasty. Bloodlines in Faulkner are stronger than land, fortunes, or reputation, stronger than social standing or the lynching rope. When Fonsiba, exiled in Midnight, Arkansas, proudly proclaims "I'm free" (Faulkner 1990b: 268) – echoing the thoughts of Tomey's Turl and Sam Fathers, Uncle Buck and Uncle Buddy, Lucas and Mollie and Butch Beauchamp – we know she is not nor ever can be. Faulkner's rough holograph sketch of the McCaslin–Beauchamp family shows irrevocable entangling alliances (figure 1). The narrative axes of Faulkner's fiction are heritage and legacy. The holograph chronology sketched by Faulkner for *Absalom, Absalom!* (1936) shows his grandest, most agonized, most poetic work to be irredeemably anchored in family genealogy with its incest and miscegenation (figure 2). So does Faulkner's description of characters in

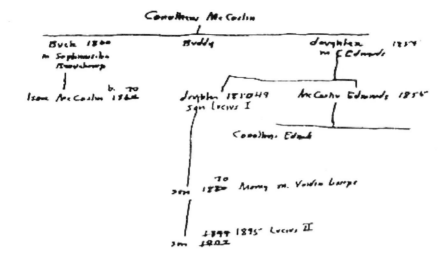

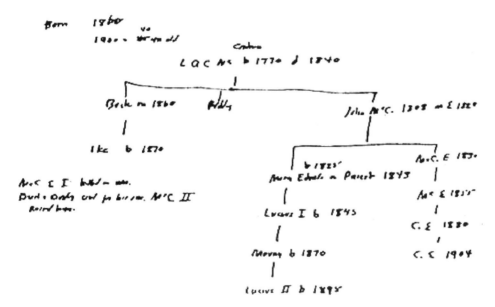

Figure 1 Faulkner's pencil drawing of the McCaslin genealogy. Alderman Library, University of Virginia accession number 6074, item 981f. From *William Faulkner Manuscripts* by William Faulkner. Reprinted with permission of the estate of William Faulkner and Special Collections, University of Virginia Library.

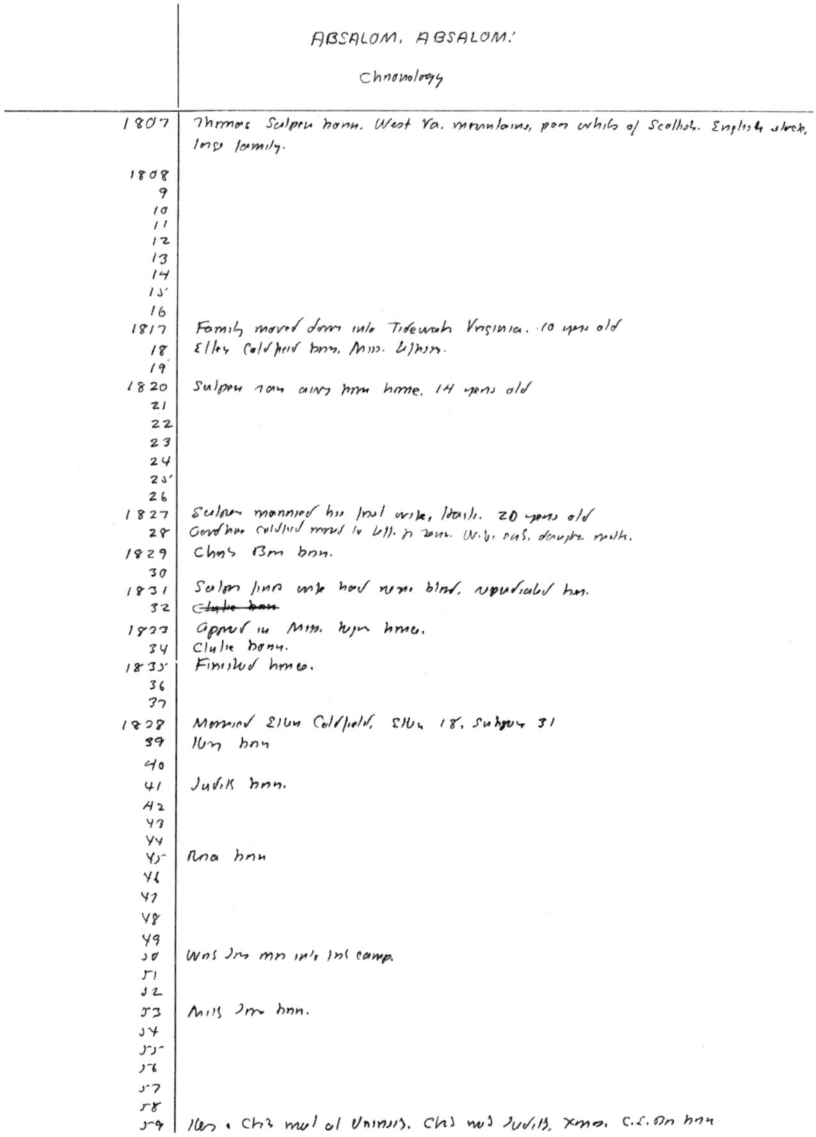

1807	Thomas Sutpen born. West Va. mountains, poor white of Scotch, English stock, large family.
1808	
9	
10	
11	
12	
13	
14	
15	
16	
1817	Family moved down into Tidewater Virginia. 10 years old
18	Ellen Coldfield born, Miss. L)him.
19	
1820	Sutpen ran away from home. 14 years old
21	
22	
23	
24	
25	
26	
1827	Sutpen married his first wife, Haiti. 20 years old
28	Good his children move to Jeff. in 1835. Wife was daughter moth.
1829	Chas Bon born.
30	
1831	Sutpen ran away had new name blind, repudiated her.
32	Clytie ban
1833	Appears in Miss. begins home.
34	Clytie born.
1835	Finished home.
36	
37	
1838	Married Ellen Coldfield, Ellen 18, Sutpen 31
39	Henry born
40	
41	Judith born.
42	
43	
44	
45	Rosa born
46	
47	
48	
49	
50	Was Jim man into Ind camp.
51	
52	
53	Mills Jim born.
54	
55	
56	
57	
58	
59	Hen. Chas met at University. Chas met Judith, Xmas. C.S. on born

Figure 2 Faulkner's chronology for *Absalom, Absalom!* Alderman Library, University of Virginia accession number 6074, item IA:13.h. From *William Faulkner Manuscripts* by William Faulkner. Reprinted with permission of W.W. Norton & Company Inc. and Special Collections, University of Virginia Library.

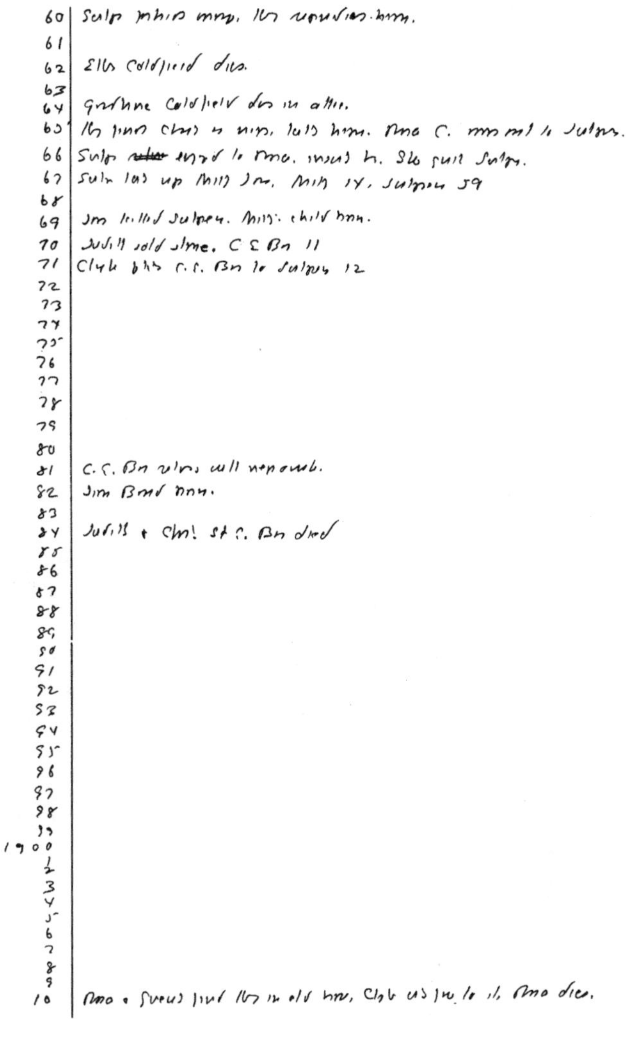

60 | Sulp *illegible*
61 |
62 | Ella Coldfield dies.
63 |
64 | Grandma Coldfield *illegible*
65 | *illegible*
66 | Sulp *illegible*
67 | Sul *illegible*
68 |
69 | Jim killed Sulpen. *illegible* child born.
70 | Judith sold *illegible*. C S Bn 11
71 | Clyk bhs c.c. Bn *illegible* Sulpen 12
72 |
73 |
74 |
75 |
76 |
77 |
78 |
79 |
80 |
81 | C.C. Bn *illegible* will *illegible*.
82 | Jim Bond born.
83 |
84 | Judith + Chs. St C. Bn died
85 |
86 |
87 |
88 |
89 |
90 |
91 |
92 |
93 |
94 |
95 |
96 |
97 |
98 |
99 |
1900 |
1 |
3 |
4 |
5 |
6 |
7 |
8 |
9 |
10 | *illegible*

Figure 2   Continued

Absalom, Absalom! (1990s: 307–9) and *The Sound and the Fury* (Cowley 1946: 737–56). Rupturing or annealing, these too are family matters.

The Sartorises

When Faulkner was asked in Charlottesville, Virginia, on May 23, 1958, where people should begin reading his work, he replied, "Probably to begin with a book called *Sartoris* that has the germ of my apocrypha in it. A lot of the characters are postulated in that book" (1959: 285). Such advice becomes more significant when coupled with a letter Faulkner wrote to Malcolm Cowley in 1945 in which he pointed out that the Sartoris story found its germ in the life of his great-grandfather, the Old Colonel, William Clark Falkner.

> My great-grandfather, whose name I bear [actually the author was William Cuthbert Faulkner] was a considerable figure in his time and provincial milieu. He was prototype of John Sartoris: raised, organized, paid the expenses of and commanded the 2nd Mississippi Infantry, 1861–62, etc. Was a part of Stonewall Jackson's left at 1st Manassas that afternoon; we have a citation in James Longstreet's longhand as his corps commander after 2nd Manassas. He built the first railroad in our county, wrote a few books, made grand European tour of his time, died in a duel and the county raised a marble effigy which still stands in Tippah County. The place of our origin shows on larger maps: a hamlet named Falkner just below Tennessee on his railroad. (1977: 211–12)

In working out his saga of his own Southern heritage through the fictions of Yoknapatawpha, Faulkner based much of *Flags in the Dust*, and of the Sartoris family, on the Falkners. The Young Colonel, John Wesley Thompson Falkner, his grandfather, was fictionalized as Old Bayard; he too was a banker and a student of the War Between the States and even had a wen on his face. According to Faulkner's later relatives, he drew on the daughters of the Old Colonel and the Young Colonel, and perhaps on the tough disciplinarian nature of his own mother Miss Maud, to create Aunt Jenny, and on his brother Dean and himself as models for Young Bayard and Young John Sartoris (Kinney 1985: 23–31). Throughout four generations of the Falkner family, it was the near-mythic stature of the Old Colonel that dominated their family line – the forebear they most admired and against whose accomplishments they continually measured their own. At the age of 14, W. C. Falkner emigrated from his home in Tennessee to that of his uncle in northern Mississippi; a few years later, at the outbreak of the Mexican War, he joined the "Tippah Volunteers" and was elected lieutenant, although he never saw battle. He studied law and entered politics and at the start of the Civil War he organized a volunteer regiment which fought in the first battle of Manassas. After the war, he entered into partnership with Richard Thurmond, a banker and lawyer, and began to build the Ripley, Ship Island, and Kentucky Railroad, completed in 1872. By the mid-1870s, he was one of the most powerful and influential men in Ripley, Mississippi, with a thriving law practice, a large plantation, a grist mill, a cotton mill, and a saw mill. In the late 1880s he extended the railroad southward over Thurmond's protests, defeated him in a race for the state legislature, and the next day was shot by him. But there were other sides to the Old Colonel. After First Manassas, the members of his regiment, the Magnolia Rifles, dismissed him for another leader, and returning to Mississippi, he formed a band of irregulars, the Partisan Rangers. He made a great deal of money by the end of the war, perhaps as a blockade runner. At home during Reconstruction he opposed enfranchising blacks and fought carpetbaggers before his untimely death. In 1993 the historian Joel Williamson visited his marble statue, enclosed in an iron fence in the Ripley Cemetery, before crossing over into the section for the graves of blacks. Less than fifty yards from the Falkner statue he found three other members of the Falkner family, the "shadow family" of the Old Colonel. There were Emmeline and two daughters. A third daughter, Lena, was a servant in the Old Colonel's household and, it is believed, his daughter by Emmeline (Williamson 1993: 64–5; Kinney 1996b: 28).

The full force of such a family history as the basis for the Sartoris clan is largely buried in Faulkner's first book on the Sartorises, *Flags in the Dust*, written by 1929 but published later that year in a shortened version as *Sartoris*. Not until nearly a decade later in *The Unvanquished* (1938) did Faulkner collect stories about Colonel John that showed him sneaking home from the war, escaping the Union army under a ruse, and during Reconstruction stuffing the ballot box to insure a white vote that would eliminate carpetbaggers. And not until the final episode written in 1938, "An Order of Verbena," did he portray the death of Colonel John at the hands of a rival. Not until 1932, in fact, in "There Was a Queen," did he make explicit what had been silently harbored in *Flags in the Dust/Sartoris*: that the black Sartoris cook Elnora Strother was actually Colonel John's mulatto daughter, who had in turn been impregnated by her mother's husband, resulting in the birth of Isom (figure 3).

Instead, *Flags in the Dust/Sartoris* opens with the willed presentation of the grandeur and high-jinks of a lost past. Old man Falls chuckles at Colonel Sartoris's escapade when he escaped the Yankees by telling them that the Sartorises lived down the road, and Colonel John's sister, Virginia Sartoris DuPre, Aunt Jenny, keeps the mythic quality of the past alive: "as she grew older the tale itself grew richer and richer, taking on a mellow splendor like wine" (1994: 14). Although the ancestral story is one of the foolishness of youth, time has converted it to reverie and the family legend takes on the primary colors of a romantic rhetoric. She recalls Colonel John invading a Yankee camp by pretending his army is bigger than it is and frightening off the enemy; she recalls her brother, the Carolina Bayard, and Jeb Stuart sweeping into a Northern camp.

Against the dark and bloody obscurity of the northern Virginia campaigns, Jeb Stuart at thirty and Bayard Sartoris at twenty-three stood briefly like two flaming stars garlanded with Fame's burgeoning laurel and the myrtle and roses of Death, incalculable and sudden as meteors in General Pope's troubled military sky, thrusting upon him like an unwilling garment that notoriety which his skill as a soldier could never have won

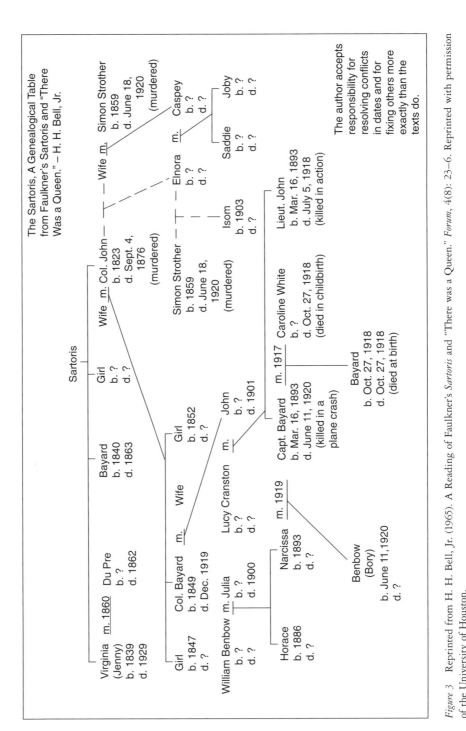

Figure 3 Reprinted from H. H. Bell, Jr. (1965). A Reading of Faulkner's *Sartoris* and "There was a Queen." *Forum*, 4(8): 23–6. Reprinted with permission of the University of Houston.

him. And still in a spirit of pure fun: neither Jeb Stuart nor Bayard Sartoris, as their actions clearly showed, had any political convictions involved at all. (1994:15)

But actually Bayard's gallantry ends when he returns impulsively for anchovies and is ignominiously shot by a cook. Aunt Jenny's chosen legacy of a heroic past does not permit sordid details of defeat, but only gallantry and fun. Her nephew, the Young Colonel, born too late for the War Between the States and too early for World War I, has reveries of his own, as when he visits a trunk of Colonel John's memorabilia in the attic.

> The lock gave at last and he raised the lid. The ghosts fell away and from the chest there rose a thin exhilarating odor of cedar, and something else: a scent dryly and muskily nostalgic, as of old ashes, and his hands, well-shaped but not so large and a shade less capable than his father's, rested for a moment upon a brocade garment. The brocade was richly hushed and the fall of fine Mechlin was dustily yellow, pale and textureless as winter sunlight . . . he laid it aside and lifted out next a rapier. It was a Toledo, a blade delicate and fine as the prolonged stroke of a violin bow, in a velvet sheath. The sheath was elegant and flamboyant and soiled, and the seams had cracked dryly. (1994: 94–5)

Aunt Jenny's veneer of chivalry over childish pranks is underscored by the Young Colonel's treasure chest of tawdry mementoes: the fraying ancestral heritage can only be maintained through myth.

The myth of the Sartoris family as defined by a legendary past which somehow renders victorious a military defeat is exposed in the present generation of twins, John and Bayard, who attempt to emulate their grandfather by enlisting in the RAF during World War I. Their disparate careers would seem determined by their namesakes. John willingly follows the antics of his forebears: when his plane is shot down by German pilots, he passes Bayard and thumbs his nose at him. He is the stuff of Jenny's fancy. But like the Young Colonel Bayard (and unlike the Carolina Bayard), Bayard survives the war, returning home in guilt and remorse. Wherever he turns – his family, his boyhood friends the MacCallums, serene Narcissa Benbow – he is reminded of the foolish heroism of John, nevertheless the stuff of legend. He attempts to exorcise him by burning his belongings, by marrying his girlfriend. But there is no cure for his malaise. He attempts the daring foolishness of a Sartoris by riding a wild stallion, but pulls it to a stop before it can harm children. He races an automobile across the countryside, but always manages, just, to keep it under control. John's fiery death, thumbing his nose, haunts him: was it joy at fulfilling his destiny? Cockiness at beating Bayard at the Sartoris game? An attempt to take Bayard with him? Try as he may to fulfill or escape the Sartoris family legacy, Bayard is caught in a dilemma between foolishness and failure, between a useless death and a useless life. When his grandfather Bayard, the Young Colonel, dies of a heart attack during one of their wild automobile rides, Bayard runs off from the Sartoris home. He seeks solace from his childhood friend Buddy MacCallum, but finds that primitive life in the woods dissatisfying. He visits the home of a poor black family, but finds he does not belong. He wanders ever farther away – to Tampico, Mexico City, San Francisco, Chicago. In a Chicago bar he is offered the job of testing a dangerous plane. For Bayard, such a ride has a purpose, to advance safe aircraft. But he dies in the attempt. Ironically, his attempt to escape the family legacy has only led him to an act that must seem to others to fulfill it.

When Miss Jenny visits Young Bayard's grave she finds it "a shapeless mass of withered flowers" (1994: 426). Next to it, John's has an inscription that is "boastful . . . as though the merry wild spirit of him who had laughed away so much of his heritage of humorless and fustian vainglory, managed somehow even yet to soften the arrogant gesture with which they said farewell" (1994: 426). And then there was the Old Colonel himself:

> He stood on a stone pedestal, in his frock coat and bareheaded, one leg slightly advanced and one hand resting lightly on the stone pylon beside him. His head was lifted a little in that gesture of haughty arrogance which repeated itself generation after generation with a fateful fidelity, his back to the world and his carven eyes gazing out across the valley where his railroad ran and beyond. (1994: 427–8)

For a passing moment, Aunt Jenny seems judgmental. But the keeper of the flame for the Sartoris clan returns home, where once more she sees

> glamorous and old disastrous things. And if they were just glamorous enough, there would be a Sartoris in them, and then they were sure to be disastrous. Pawns. But the Player and the game He plays – who knows? He must have a name for his pawns, though, but perhaps Sartoris is the name of the game itself – a game outmoded and played with pawns shaped too late and to an old dead pattern, and of which the Player Himself is a little wearied. For there is death in the sound of it, and a glamorous fatality, like silver pennons downrushing at sunset, or a dying fall of horns along the road to Roncevaux. (1994: 432–3)

Glory is what the Sartorises yearn for and what destroys them even as their deaths resurrect glory. The saga of the Sartoris family, in many ways paralleling the fate of the Falkners, stops short of hiding the broader implications of the South itself, a society that must continue to find its justification in the glory of a doomed battle that will somehow dispel the reality of defeat.

The Compsons

"I feel sorry for the Compsons," Faulkner commented in 1959 in Charlottesville, long after the first draft of Benjy appeared in "The Kingdom of God" for the *New Orleans Times-Picayune* (April 26, 1925) and three decades after *The Sound and the Fury* (1929). "That was blood which was good and brave once, but has thinned and faded all the way out" (1959: 197). But *The Sound and the Fury*, the chief record of the Compson family, is pointedly and persistently a novel about blood, about bloodlines. Where the genealogy of the Sartorises is often told from the outside by an omniscient narrator, that of the Compsons is more internalized. Quentin cannot rid himself of thinking about "this Compson blood" (1956: 128) and, his family mirrored for him in that of the Blands, a "sort of blood obligation noblesse oblige" (1956: 130), nor can he forget his sister Caddy's promiscuity: "her blood surg[ing] steadily beating and beating against my hand" (1956: 203). Jason ruefully observes that "blood is blood and you can't get around it" (1956: 303). When Caddy leaves her daughter to Jason's care, she reminds her brother, "You'll have to promise to take care of her, too – she's kin to you, your own flesh and blood" (1956: 260). But the sullen and cynical Jason finds her unmanageable: "blood always tells. If you've got blood like that in you, you'll do anything" (1956: 297). He is equally caustic about his younger brother Benjy, whose idiocy for him dismisses any thought of a glorious Compson past: "Blood, I says, governors and generals. It's a damn good thing we never had any kings and presidents; we'd all be down there at Jackson chasing butterflies" (1956: 286). His mother Caroline responds similarly to Quentin IV's disappearance: "It's in the blood" (1956: 374), but she blames the ill fortune of her children and granddaughter on her own unfortunate marriage, talking repeatedly "about how her own flesh and blood rose up to curse her" (1956: 224), and she attempts to save the retarded Benjy from the mental wards of Jackson by changing his name and thinking of him as a Bascomb, not as a Compson at all.

Faulkner seems to have been as preoccupied with the Compsons as they were with themselves. He returned to them in stories like "Lion" and "A Justice" and in novels like *Absalom, Absalom!* and *Go Down, Moses* (1942), and in 1945 he developed a full genealogy of the Compson family line in an "Appendix" entitled "Compson" for Malcolm Cowley's *The Portable Faulkner*. Once it was written he also wrote his editor, Robert N. Linscott, to reprint "Compson" in each new edition of *The Sound and the Fury*, but as an introduction, not as an appendix (1977: 220–1). He opens "Compson" not with the family's direct ancestors but, more telling, with the Indian chief Ikke-motubbe, whose other name, "L'Homme," later corrupted into "Doom," may help to describe the Compsons nevertheless, and, following Ikkemotubbe, President Andrew Jackson. Ikkemotubbe's brief biographical sketch is that of a gambler whose greed finally causes his defeat (in exile), "A dispossessed American King" (1956: 403). Next to the intimidating, exploitative Ikkemotubbe, Andrew Jackson is seen as sentimental, idealistic, and naïve, his innocence the other side of Ikkemotubbe's craftiness. Then follow the Compsons themselves, a gallery of the dispossessed. There are the naïve idealists like Jackson: Quentin Maclachan, or Quentin I, who rebels against the King of England; Charles Stuart, who rebels against the United States; Jason II, or General Compson, who suffers the Confederate Army's defeats at Shiloh and Reseca; Jason III, Mr. Compson, who fails as a father and lawyer; and his son Quentin III, whose despair leads him to suicide during his freshman year at Harvard. There are those who follow Ikkemotubbe, too: Jason I, the Old Governor, who trades a racehorse for the Compson Domain, a square mile of the best land in Jefferson; Jason IV, who extorts money from his niece and sister and steals from his mother; and

Quentin IV, whose rebellion is characterized by disobedience, self-indulgence, and (in a sense) theft. Together they chart the sudden rise and slow decline of an aristocracy weakened by nature as well as by nurture, a family history of sound and fury coming to signify loss.

There are hints of the Faulkner family in the Compsons, however. Mr. Compson is in many ways similar to Faulkner's father Murry, who was thought to be luckless and ineffective; Quentin's moodiness and solitary nature were not unlike Faulkner's; and the spirited Caddy may be drawn from his cousin Sallie Murry Wilkins, with whom the four Faulkner brothers played as children; Dilsey, too, seems an affecting portrayal of the Faulkners' African American servant Caroline Barr. Even so, the Compsons seem drawn even more along the outlines of the Thompson and Chandler families of Oxford, whose combined names seem to suggest *Compson*. The patriarch Jacob Thompson has in common with Jason Compson I his early emigration to Oxford in 1835, his position as a town dignitary, and his interest in politics (he was a member of Congress for Mississippi from 1839 to 1851). Like General Compson, Jason II, Jacob Thompson fought in the battle of Shiloh (as well as the battle of Corinth); and he was, like both Compsons, the most powerful, popular, and successful of the family in northern Mississippi. His home was burned by the Union army during the War Between the States, but his brother William's house was spared, and it occupies the site (on the corner of Buchanan and South 13th Streets) where Faulkner places the Compson house on his map of Yoknapatawpha; William paid $300 for the original property, which belonged then to the parcel of land establishing Oxford as a town. After the war, the iron picket fence surrounding the county courthouse was transferred to William Thompson's house. As a schoolboy, Faulker had to walk past the house each day; it was occupied by his teacher, Anna Thompson, and her sister, Lulu Marie Lucretia Thompson. Some years later, it was the residence of Dr. Thomas Chandler, a physician from Caswell County, Mississippi, who had married Lucretia, William Thompson's eldest daughter. The Chandlers had seven children. One, Thomas Wiley Chandler, jumped to his death from a dormitory at the University of North Carolina where he was a freshman; a second, Luly May, disappeared as a young girl never to return; a third, Wiley, never married, worked in a local hardware store, and died in Oxford; and a fourth, Edwin, had in his thirties, when Faulkner knew him, the mind of a 3-year-old. It was the young Edwin, who had Down's syndrome, in whom Faulkner took a special interest; his niece recalls that he would take his daughter and her to visit the boy every two weeks or so. She remembers that Edwin would sit in the corner cutting various shapes out of paper; at other times, townspeople recalled him running up and down behind the iron fence. Edwin Chandler died by falling into a fire, much as Benjy dies later in *The Mansion* (1959). Whatever Faulkner's sources for the Compson family, however, they were found in families and family relationships.

Faulkner told Jean Stein that the story of the Compson family line nevertheless caused him difficulty. *The Sound and the Fury* "caused me the most grief and anguish, as the mother loves the child who became the thief or murderer more than the one who became the priest" (1957: 130). Even in retrospect, the family seems to have dominated his thinking. When Stein asked him what it was about he replied, "It's a tragedy of two lost women: Caddy and her daughter." When she asked him how the novel first began conceptually, he answered,

> It began with a mental picture. I didn't realize at the time it was symbolical. The picture was of the muddy seat of a little girl's drawers in a pear tree, where she could see through a window where her grandmother's funeral was taking place and report what was happening to her brothers on the ground below. By the time I explained who they were and what they were doing and how her pants got muddy, I realized it would be impossible to get all of it into a short story. . . . And then I realized the symbolism of the soiled pants, and the image was replaced by the one of the fatherless and motherless girl climbing down the rainpipe to escape from the only home she had, where she had never been offered love or affection or understanding. (1957: 130)

The same sense of family that contextualized his initial image permitted the execution of the book as well.

> I had already begun to tell the story through the eyes of the idiot child, since I felt that it would be more effective as told by someone capable only of knowing what happened, but not why. I saw that I had not told the story that time. I tried to tell it again, the same story through the eyes of another brother. That was still not it. I told it for the third time through the eyes of the third brother. That was still not it. I tried to gather the pieces together and fill in the gaps by making myself the spokesman. It was still not complete, not until fifteen years after the book was published, when I wrote as an appendix to another book the final effort to get the story told and off my mind, so that I myself could have some peace from it. (1957: 130–1)

It is the network of family relationships that provides most of the pathways into understanding the import of the Compsons for Faulkner, as if, trying to understand his world and leaving behind his own genealogy in the Sartorises, only another family line would permit him to comprehend it. Leaving one family, he became absorbed in another.

The chronicle of the Compsons combines mother and daughter in their departure from the house where Damuddy's death had been the first loss for them. But in between, the Compson family dynamics dwell on mothers and children – on Mrs. Compson's maternal failings, on the substitute mothers Damuddy, Caddy, and Dilsey – and on the failures of the father. Caddy is requested to act as Benjy's mother by taking him outside on a cold day and is asked at other times not to smother him. Mrs. Compson resolves the problem of bearing the idiot son after Damuddy's death by renaming Maury, named for her brother, as Benjamin, a biblically assigned lost son, and she transfers him to Damuddy's bedroom, separating him from his siblings. As for herself, she too takes to her bed, remaining under the covers with a hot-water bottle.

Her eldest son Quentin feels the loss too: *"If I'd just had a mother so I could say Mother Mother"* (1956: 213); *"If I could say Mother. Mother"* (1956: 117). John Earl Bassett notes that just before his death, Quentin confronts images of both parents, his mother in a complex fantasy and his father in a remembered conversation. He recalls a childhood storybook with a picture of "a dark place into which a single weak ray of light came slanting." The picture, which at some point he "jagged out," obsessed him "until the dungeon was Mother herself she and Father upward into weak light holding hands and us lost somewhere below even them without even a ray of light." The image suggests parental betrayal and withdrawal. In another passage implying a similar dungeon-womb, Quentin is a King replacing his father and wreaking vengeance on his siblings: "I'd break that place open and drag them out and I'd whip them good." Quentin's fantasy, however, is troubled by two other images of his mother – the realistic one of her self-indulgently lying "back in her chair, the camphor handkerchief to her mouth," and the metaphorical one of a masculine woman who "was never a queen or a fairy" but "always a king or a giant or a general." (1982: 413–16)

Quentin counters his sense of isolation and betrayal by fantasies of incest with Caddy, both annealing and controlling family ruptures.

> *I'll tell Father then it'll have to be because you love Father then we'll have to go away amid the pointing and the horror and the clean flame I'll make you say we did I'm stronger than you I'll make you know we did you thought it was them but it was me listen I fooled you all the time it was me you thought I was in the house where that damn honeysuckle.* (1956: 185)

Caddy mocks him by urging such an act, knowing he will not commit incest; his father, too, tells him outright he did not, and could not. Unable to locate a stable family relationship and unable to create a family of his own, Quentin drowns himself.

Things seem no better for the hapless Jason, the third brother, the third narrator of the Compson family story. Repeatedly seeing himself as the family outcast – sent to Sewanee rather than Harvard as Quentin was; required to keep the family solvent after Caddy leaves home – Jason's low self-esteem and self-hatred cause him to lash out at others. Caddy gives him the opportunity when she turns over her daughter to his safe-keeping. Quentin IV's resentment at this coldness only fosters his cold nature; he says of her, "Once a bitch always a bitch, what I say" (1956: 223). Ignored and despised, Jason lives to make a killing in the stock market, showing up his fellow men in Jefferson, the Jews in the stock market, and the Yankees who run it; and when that consistently fails he takes out his deep frustration and anger in controlling and cheating others to get the compensatory upper hand: he determines his own hours at the hardware store; he steals Caddy's gifts of money to Quentin IV; and he chases Caddy's daughter with a kind of salacious glee, perched to find her in acts of rebellion. As for the fourth child, Caddy, she suffers an enforced and humiliating marriage to obscure her pregnancy out of wedlock, a marriage doomed to failure; she feels forced to leave her child as a hostage to Jason; and she disappears only later to turn up again – just possibly – in a faded photograph "ageless and beautiful, cold serene and damned: beside her a handsome lean man of middle-age in the ribbons and tabs of a German staff general" (1956: 415), a betrayal of her nation standing in judgment of her loss of family and of family loyalty, family ties.

Running thin, the bloodline of the Compson family legacy – Benjy, Jason, Caddy, Quentin IV – seems unlikely to reproduce and resurrect the family line. The whole sense of resurrection, as it is preached to a black congregation by the Rev. Shegog, has no effect on Benjy. At the close of the Compson chronicle, he is instead on his routine journey to the family graveyard and taken the wrong way, his broken flower drooping in his hand. "His eyes were empty and blue and serene again as a cornice and façade flowed smoothly once more from left to right: post and tree, window and doorway, and signboard, each in its ordered place" (1956: 401). Where the Sartoris chronicle concluded with the desperate urge to find solace in a mythologizing of the past, the Compson chronicle ends in a kind of existential emptiness, a resignation that the past no longer matters – even carrying a broken flower to the graveyard of the forebears – because the present has made nothing of it.

The Sutpens

Throughout Faulkner's powerful creation of Yoknapatawpha by examining the family lines that constitute it, only once, in tracing ancestors and descendants of Thomas Sutpen, does he study genealogy as dynasty. The formation of the Sutpen–Bon–Coldfield line is marked by crudity, idealism, passion, naïveté, heroism, promise, achievement, grief, sacrifice, and defeat; the family seemed plagued by their will to dominate or their will to survive, pursued by anxiety and shame that seem endemic to the Southern culture they help to construct. The events that signal the stages of Thomas Sutpen's life, for instance – the white boy's humiliating dismissal by a black servant; the slave revolt in Haiti; the permissiveness and promiscuity that mark Creole life in New Orleans; the violent and rapid establishment of a cotton plantation of 100 square miles; the commitment to the Confederacy and later withdrawal from its attempts at reconstruction – all these events and actions not only embody but foster the peculiar characteristics and failings of Sutpen's South: hierarchy, race, class, caste, fratricide, self-destruction. The very attributes that Sutpen swiftly demands to establish his family, and his family line, require a long, irreversible, and unavoidable decline and defeat, for he attempts to redeem his reputation by creating a family that depends on corrupting Southern practices: a racially pure dynasty built on the fortunes of a plantation system that relies on an unnatural possession of the land and the slaves who farm it. To achieve a stature his family did not give him in Tidewater Virginia, Sutpen comes to Yoknapatawpha, where he models his life on the aristocracy around him. But in succeeding within less than a generation in establishing a massive plantation along the rich bottomland of the Tallahatchie, he shames the Compsons, who were never able to establish a plantation, and, further, in succeeding in his fight for the Confederacy, he shames the Sartorises, for they lost Colonel John. He is drawn, then, into finding a quick commercial means to equal their authority by negotiating with the town merchant, Goodhue Coldfield, and making an alliance with Coldfield's daughter Ellen; when, in time, his bigamist past catches up with him, he is left in poor imitation not of the Compsons or Sartorises, but of Coldfield himself, in managing a country cross-roads store.

The Sutpen genealogy stretches one generation fewer than that of either Sartoris or Compson. E. O. Hawkins has drawn the generations from *Absalom, Absalom!*

I.   Thomas Sutpen's father and mother were Scotch-Irish mountaineers. The mother died when Sutpen was 10, and the father returned to the Tidewater area.
II.   Thomas Sutpen (1807–69) married (1) a Haitian woman known later as Eulalia Bon and (2) Ellen Coldfield (1818–62).
III.   Charles Bon (1829–65) was Sutpen's son by Eulalia Bon. Henry (1839–1909) and Judith (1841–84) were Sutpen's children by Ellen Coldfield. Clytemnestra (1834–1909) was fathered by Sutpen on a Negro slave.
IV.   Charles Etienne St. Valery Bon (1859–84) was Charles Bon's son by an octoroon mistress. He married a Negress (1879).
V.   Jim Bond (1882–) was the son of Charles Etienne Bon. He is, ironically, the Sutpen "heir" at the end of the book. (Hawkins 1961: 116–17)

But the sense of Sutpen and his extended family is essentially not one of dispersal but of a singular obsession for a dynasty that contracts and often obliterates difference. According to Quentin and Shreve, Thomas attempts to deny his first marriage to Eulalia Bon because plantations are not established with biracial couples; dynasties are not founded by having mulatto heirs. He needs an acceptable marriage when he moves from Haiti to Yoknapatawpha – and he settles for a middle-class merchant's daughter because she is guaranteed to be purely white. Their two children – Henry and Judith – are thus of pure white blood, an acceptable bloodline in the biracial South of Jefferson, Yoknapatawpha County, Mississippi. But just as for the Sartorises and the Compsons, the present can never escape the past. When white Henry goes off to college, he finds his best friend is Charles Bon, who is, unknown to him, his own mulatto half-brother. Their love for each other seems at some level preordained as the reunion of a family, yet destructive since it is built on the fragile assumption of a shared white racial purity. The situation is compounded when the mulatto Charles, son of Sutpen's first marriage, falls in love with Judith, the white daughter of Sutpen's second marriage.

In such a tight, dynamic family web, incest becomes a natural response, both as fact and as metaphor. While Henry may realize that his love for Judith is incestuous well before he learns his love of Charles is also, Judith's love of Charles is also incestuous. Henry would compound the situation by using Judith's affection for Charles to keep Charles with them. At the same time, Charles's apparent lack of concern for his partner in New Orleans, whom he easily displaces with Judith, only replicates his father's apparently easy dismissal of Eulalia for the more socially desirable, white-blooded Ellen, and, later, even Milly Jones. Sutpen would found his dynasty at any cost to his past and his pride. Such similarities cause the Sutpens, Bons, and Coldfields, both loving and hating each other, to enclose themselves in a constraining, diminishing circle. It is just such a construction that Quentin Compson and his father recognize when, out quail-hunting, they come upon a private cemetery where five graves bring the Sutpen, Bon, and Cold-field family tightly together for eternity: Ellen's tombstone, brought from Italy by Sutpen in 1864; Sutpen's own stone, sent at the same time; Charles's stone, bought by Judith when she has sold her father's store (thus bringing him into Sutpen's design whether he is wanted or not); Charles Etienne Bon's stone, partly paid for by Judith; and Judith's stone, supplied by Rosa (who, once in the family circle, never really leaves it). All this is foreshadowed in the natural and satisfying way Judith nurses the dying Charles Etienne, or in the way Judith, Rosa, and the mulatto Clytie hoeing cotton on Sutpen's plantation appear to any spectator as indistinguishable.

Like the Compson chronicle, the Sutpen chronicle is filtered through subjective perspectives. Quentin Compson's sense of a lack of recognition from his father and his professed love for Caddy may color his understanding of the Sutpen account. Once Quentin identifies with the Sutpen narrative at Shreve McCannon's prompting, "he learns that the genealogical families [of the South] have neither substance nor value," Patricia Tobin notes, and continues,

> In his ruthless rape of the land, Thomas Sutpen is revealed as the prototype of Southern dynasties; and if this seems foreign to the genteel tradition of the aristocrat it is only because Sutpen accomplished in one generation what generally required several genera-tions. Quentin learns the fragility of the father–son relationship, and the tragic absurdity of a racial taboo that makes Henry's four choices – bigamy, incest, fratricide, and misce-genation – all sins against the family. And he learns the threat of incest to be the normal brother–sister relationship. Like Absalom, who kills his brother Amnon for having vio-lated their sister Tamar, Henry is also a fratricide, but his motive for murder is miscege-nation. Incest, he is willing to condone, although he views it as an indication of the rot that is already enveloping the Southern family. In his hypothetical picture of the Sutpens after Bon's marriage to Judith, he imagines them all "together in torment" in a kind of family hell that parallels their damnation in life. (1973–4: 267–8)

At the time he kills Charles Bon, Henry Sutpen does not feel that way: he is acting on the code of family and Southern honor. Yet he must sense a kind of guilt, a deep repulsion, because his next act is flight. Actually, he would not have to fear his father, who would understand and praise his action. Nor need he fear the law that would also prevent miscegenation where possible. The reason Henry flees must be his own stark recognition that in killing Charles Bon he has not only destroyed a man he admires and perhaps loves, but, more horribly, he has fulfilled his father's inhuman design. And, in another way, he is like Rosa "adjunctive or incremental to the design" (1990a: 194); he has begun the destruction of his own white, and his own extended, family. The last shot Henry fired in the Civil War is truly a shot of brother against brother, upholding the narrowness of vision that has already meant defeat for the Confederacy. Barring his brother from the door, as Pettibone once barred Sutpen in the Tidewater, Henry begins the collapse of the Sutpen dynasty as Pettibone once inspired it. Henry's flight, like Charles's courtship of Judith and her acceptance, like Goodhue Coldfield's and Rosa Coldfield's self-incarceration, and like Clytie's final act of arson, freeing the idiot Jim Bond into the larger world uncontrolled, suggests that a Southern family determined to pursue a dream and preserve it at any cost will only destroy itself.

The McCaslins

The genealogical "game" of the Sartorises, the genealogical decline of the Compsons, and the genealogical design of Thomas Sutpen – all genealogical imperatives – lead to genealogical discovery in the ledgers of the McCaslin family commissary in *Go Down, Moses*. The McCaslin family story, writes David Minter, "is primarily the story of what it means to be a descendant and an inheritor," to find there, in "the largest and most complexly entangled of all Yoknapatawpha families," all of Faulkner's abiding and "familiar preoccupations, including such explicitly moral ones as slavery and the land and man's hunger for possession and power" (1980: 186). What distinguishes the McCaslin–Edmonds–Beauchamp family, however, is its persistent recognition of and confrontation with matters of race: what the Sutpens deny in horror, the McCaslins can also grieve. While the complexity and entanglement are not reduced – they are, after all, the very consequences of such events as rape, incest, and miscegenation as buried family matters that must be set free by recognition and acceptance – they are all mani-fest, since nearly every family member is obsessed with the family not simply in terms of genealogy but, more specifically, in terms of racial heritage and composition and their consequent moral obligations and responsibilities. Again and again in the McCaslin family chronicle Ike McCaslin, Cass Edmonds, and Lucas Beauchamp all recall – cannot help but recall – their shared racial lineage.

According to Ike McCaslin, the family tragedy was initiated by its progenitor, his grandfather, Lucius Quintus Carothers McCaslin, who originally purchased the family land and slaves. Ike comes to realize the plantation itself is a "whole edifice intricate and complex and founded upon injustice and erected by ruthless rapacity and carried on even yet with at times downright savagery" (1990b: 285). The primal injustice is the owner-ship of land in violation of man's God-given trusteeship "to hold the earth mutual and intact in the communal anonymity of brotherhood" (1990b: 246). From this derives the greater horror of the ownership of people, which can lead to that final secret of the com-missary ledgers, old Carothers's begetting, without acknowledging, a son upon his own mulatto daughter. Because of this double crime against land and humanity, "the whole South is cursed," Ike thinks, and "descendants alone can – not resist it, not combat it – maybe just endure and outlast it until the curse is lifted" (1990b: 266).

Ike inherits from his grandfather a legacy of guilt and shame; he derives from his father and uncle, Uncle Buck and Uncle Buddy McCaslin, "a little at least of its ame-lioration and restitution" (1990b: 250) in taking Carothers's cynical bequest of 1,000 dollars to his mulatto grandson, Terrel. But Ike is already making excuses for his family line, for Uncle Buck and Uncle Buddy move out of the plantation house, giving it over to their black kin, and triple the legacy for Terrel's three children when Terrel denies the bequest, leaving Ike to pay off his black relatives. Buck never really functions as Ike's father, either; instead, Ike finds paternity in Sam Fathers, who is himself of mixed heritage. Sam's "face and bearing were still those of the Chickasaw chief who had been his father" – a chief, however, who had sold mother and son into slavery, so that sometimes Sam's eyes showed "the mark . . . of bondage" (1990b: 158, 161). The "warriors' and chiefs' blood in him" had been "betrayed through the black blood which his mother gave him" (1990b: 162). The only way Sam could devise not to "be a negro," to resolve the racial tensions figured in his body and perhaps in his surname "Fathers," was to live as a hermit-priest in the big woods where his father was once chief and where he could paternalize young Ike (and at times Cass Edmonds) by teaching him the natural ways of the wilderness. That Sam does not exactly fit the roles of hermit, priest, hunter, or father is suggested by his appearance, "not tall, squat rather, almost sedentary, flabby-looking" (1990b: 160). Despite Sam's counsel to Isaac, the boy never sees him hunt; what Sam does is prepare the wild dog Lion as an instrument to destroy Old Ben, the sacred bear who serves as the image of that very wilderness.

Cass Edmonds, who descends from the distaff side of old Lucius and is 17 years Ike's senior, is also a kind of substitute father for Ike. Cass has no use for Lucius, who is his grandfather, too, likening the heritage he shares with Ike to "the tedious and shabby chronicle of His chosen sprung from Abraham" until "men snarled over the gnawed bones of the old world's worthless evening" (1990b: 246–7). He is more realistic than cynical and can at times even be hopeful, first taking young Isaac to the woods, and later introducing him to the poetry of Keats. Cass has given Terrel's son Lucas Beauchamp and his wife a house and land on the McCaslin plantation which he holds until Ike's majority, but he knows these gifts from him are but "the two threads frail as truth and impalpable as equators yet cablestrong to bind for life them who made the cotton to the land their sweat fell on" (1990b: 286). Ike's surrogate father, Cass is torn between a deep sense of social injustice and social responsibility on the one hand and an analytical intelligence that can only corrode his ideals on the other.

Perhaps because he sees himself potentially mirrored in Cass's dilemma, Ike makes the decision to refuse his inheritance of the McCaslin plantation and legacy, giving Cass "the trusteeship" of his grandfather's black descendants. In this way he can repudiate his grandfather's sins against the land and the African Americans who are enslaved on it, and he can at the same time pay homage to Sam by showing a new respect for natural and as yet unspoiled woods. He will even pay out to Terrel Beauchamp's three children – Lucas, James, and Fonsiba (named for his own mother) – the monetary inheritance left by Lucius and tripled by his father and Uncle Buddy. But his denial of family inheritance is echoed by Fonsiba – who wishes to be free of all McCaslin connections; who will not be bought off – although her blood will never deny her descent from Lucius through his rape of Tomasina (Tomey) and her son Terrel (Tomey's Turl). Ike cannot even locate Jim. But Fonsiba teaches her white cousin Ike nothing, for in his old age he will again offer to buy off the unnamed mulatto mistress of Roth, who, like Fonsiba, refuses. Ike is consequently forced to live with, even if he does not wish to recognize, the Beauchamp side of his family.

Terrel's third child, Lucas, not only accepts his legacy but, at the age of 21, demands it from Ike. He was named for Lucius Quintus Carothers McCaslin, and he both wears the name with pride and possesses it by changing the spelling to *Lucas*. Cass's grandson Roth, in fact, sees a striking resemblance:

> *He's more like old Carothers than all the rest of us put together, including old Carothers. He is both heir and prototype simultaneously of all the geography and climate and biology which sired old Carothers and all the rest of us and our kind, myriad, countless, faceless, even nameless now except himself who fathers himself, intact and complete, contemptuous, as old Carothers must have been, of all blood black white yellow or red, including his own.* (1990b: 114–15)

Like the troubled Ike, Roth errs. Lucas has become the progenitor of the Beauchamp line to be sure, but his attitude is not like old Carothers's (for whom Roth is also named). He is a man of honor and dignity and pride who knows that being the head of a family line calls not for domination but for self-respect. When his white cousin Zack Edmonds takes Lucas's wife Mollie to wet-nurse young Roth, silently citing the privilege of the white race, Lucas feels his own manliness challenged. He demands the return of his wife. Mollie returns but she brings the suckling Roth with her and Zack, whose wife died in giving birth to Roth, remains at home. Outraged when Zack does not come to reclaim his child, thus showing the mutual respect between men which Lucas demands of everyone, especially his own kin, he prepares to kill Zack for dishonoring him. As Lee Jenkins has written,

> Had Edmonds come for the child Lucas would have forgiven him. It is the thing that, as he believes, old Carothers would have wanted him to do. But Edmonds had never tried to demoralize him. He had tried to beat him. "'And you wont never,'" says Lucas, "'not even when I am hanging dead from the limb this time tomorrow with the coal oil still burning, you wont never.'" He continues: "'Because all you got to beat is me,'" Lucas tells him. "'I got to beat old Carothers'" by proving that the masculine imperative is no less potent in him, a black, than it was in Carothers, a white. For Lucas this means an honorable acquitting of and accounting for the self in all situations. (Jenkins 1990: 223)

The duel ends when Lucas's shot misfires. But there is more here merely than manliness and honor, although they are vital. There is also Lucas's behavior in upholding his family, in defending Mollie, and in keeping his family intact. In all these ways, resembling Carothers as he may, he will assert his independence not merely from Carothers but from all the whites who dominate blacks. Lucas speaks for the sanctity and worth of the family, even (and especially) when that family is mulatto.

Lucas's reaction, one of family integrity, not only criticizes Carothers and Zack, but, in the larger sweep of the McCaslin–Edmonds–Beauchamp chronicle, also criticizes Uncle Buck, Uncle Buddy, and Ike. Lucas accepts what is his due of the McCaslin legacy and asks for no more, but he asks for no less either. In *Go Down, Moses* Lucas momentarily falters in old age; he turns from the hard chores of the land to an interest in amassing a fortune by discovering gold on his land or, if that fails, by tricking others into looking for it. His sudden interest in the value of money for its own sake (rather than honest toil) causes him to lapse into the interests of the McCaslins (who would turn family relationships into buy-outs) and the Edmonds (who through Roth would buy out his mulatto mistress, his own cousin, combining incest and miscegenation). This time it is Lucas's wife Mollie who intervenes on behalf of family sanity and sanctity: she asks Roth to get her a divorce and he regrettably accedes to it. The possible dissolution of his marriage is what saves Lucas. He calls off his chance to improve his lot substantially and instead buys Mollie a bag of candy, courting her all over again: "'Here,' he said. 'You ain't got no teeth left but you can still gum it'" (1990b: 125). Lucas's actions are contemporary with the novel and with its other present-day episodes of Rider's lynching and Butch's death in Chicago, both at the hands of angry, bigoted white men, long after the hunt for Tomey's Turl and the bear-hunts, and a short time after Ike's return to the delta as an old man. So juxtaposed, they are Faulkner's way of finding some kind of redemption in genealogy that was missing in the similar confidence tricks of Simon Strother with the Sartorises, that is more helpful than a Jim Bond loosened on the world, and that returns instead to the divine drudgery of Dilsey. It is fitting that *Go Down, Moses* is dedicated to the Faulkner servant Dilsey was modeled on, Caroline Barr, because Caroline was also the model for Mollie – both learn that duty, family responsibility, and self-respect are far more important (and satisfying) than ambition, greed, and self-hatred.

Conclusion

"More perhaps than the chronicler of a mythic corner of Mississippi," Donald K. Kartiganer writes, "Faulkner is the premier American novelist of family." He continues,

> His people, however uniquely and memorably portrayed, invariably trail behind them clouds of familial qualifiers: the grandparents, parents, and siblings whose cumulative identity is the indispensable context of individual character. The bulk of Faulkner's people are not so much single, separate persons as collective enterprises, the products and processes of family dramas apart from which the individual actor is scarcely intelligible. Confronting the single member of the Sartoris, Compson, McCaslin, or Snopes lines, or even of the less amply elaborated lines such as Bundren, Hightower, Sutpen, or Varner, we soon find ourselves addressing family complexes, synchronic and diachronic systems whose individual units take their meanings from their transactions with each other. (Kartiganer 1982: 381)

There are three generations of Snopeses, six generations of Compsons and Sutpens, and seven generations of Sartorises and McCaslins; and the family line is what identifies each member. Cash Bundren's carpentry would make less sense if we did not understand his relationship with Addie. Temple Drake would be less self-centered if she had a father other than the one she has. Hightower's religious zeal is the product of his need to redeem his lineage to himself. Will Varner's defeat comes from Flem Snopes, who learns how to out-Varner him and build a banker's fortune out of a country store. Family identity in Faulkner's Yoknapatawpha makes sense to us as we come to understand his characters more clearly. But the same kind of understanding of family ties is vital to each character's attempt at self-definition of a very *identity*. Indeed, the worst fate in Faulkner's fiction is to be *without* family – to be Joe Christmas. The desperate need for family is seen in Aunt Jenny DuPre trying her best to exonerate and elevate the Sartoris family, or Rosa Coldfield trying just as hard to join the Sutpen dynasty once her own father has deserted her. Those without any possibility of a connection – like Jim Bond and Jim Beauchamp – are lost to the world. When Faulkner answered his questioning audiences in Charlottesville, he clearly had difficulty recalling certain episodes and certain images. But he never had difficulty in recalling the personal relationships of the families he created. Like the South he himself inherited, clan was what made sense of class, race, and gender. Clan is what mattered most.

References and Further Reading

Bassett, J. E. (1982). Family Conflict in *The Sound and the Fury*. In A. F. Kinney (ed.). *Critical Essays on William Faulkner: The Compson Family* (pp. 408–24). Boston: G. K. Hall.

Bell, H. H., Jr. (1965). A Reading of Faulkner's *Sartoris* and "There Was a Queen." *Forum* 4(8): 23–6.

Bleikasten, Andre (1996). Sutpen as Patriarch. In A. F. Kinney (ed.). *Critical Essays on William Faulkner: The Sutpen Family* (pp. 156–61). Boston: G. K. Hall.

Blotner, J. (1991). *Faulkner: A Biography*. One-vol. edn. New York: Random House.

Chabrier, G. (1993). *Faulkner's Families*. New York: Gordian Press.

Cowley, M. (ed.) (1946). *The Portable William Faulkner*. New York: Viking.

Dickerson, M. J. (1982). "The Magician's Wand": Faulkner's Compson Appendix. In A. F. Kinney (ed.). *Critical Essays on William Faulkner: The Compson Family* (pp. 252–67). Boston: G. K. Hall.

Faulkner, W. (1956). *The Sound and the Fury*. New York: Vintage. (Original pub. 1929.)

Faulkner, W. (1957). Interview with Jean Stein vanden Heuvel. In M. Cowley (ed.). *Writers at Work:* The Paris Review *Interviews* (pp. 119–41). New York: Viking Press.

Faulkner, W. (1959). *Faulkner in the University: Class Conferences at the University of Virginia 1957–*

1958 (eds. F. L. Gwynn and J. L. Blotner). Charlottesville, VA: University of Virginia Press.

Faulkner, W. (1977). *Selected Letters of William Faulkner* (ed. J. Blotner). New York: Random House.

Faulkner, W. (1990a). *Absalom! Absalom!* New York: Vintage International. (Original pub. 1936.)

Faulkner, W. (1990b). *Go Down, Moses*. New York: Vintage International. (Original pub. 1942.)

Faulkner, W. (1994). *Flags in the Dust*. New York: Vintage. (Original pub. in shortened version as *Sartoris* 1929.)

Gray, R. (1994). *The Life of William Faulkner*. Oxford: Blackwell.

Hawkins, E. O. (1961). A Handbook of Yoknapatawpha. Unpub. diss. University of Arkansas.

Howe, I. (1975). *William Faulkner: A Critical Study*. 3rd edn, rev. and expanded. Chicago: University of Chicago Press.

Irwin, J. T. (1975). *Doubling and Incest/Repetition and Revenge*. Baltimore: Johns Hopkins University Press.

Jenkins, L. (1981). *Faulkner and Black–White Relations*. New York: Columbia University Press.

Jenkins, L. (1990). Lucas McCaslin. In A. F. Kinney (ed.). *Critical Essays on William Faulkner: The McCaslin Family* (pp. 219–24). Boston: G. K. Hall.

Kartiganer, D. M. (1982). Quentin Compson and Faulkner's Drama of the Generations. In A. F. Kinney (ed.). *Critical Essays on William Faulkner: The Compson Family* (pp. 381–401). Boston: G. K. Hall.

Kinney, A. F. (1978). *Faulkner's Narrative Poetics*. Amherst: University of Massachusetts Press.

Kinney, A. F. (1985). Sartoris. In A. F. Kinney (ed.). *Critical Essays on William Faulkner: The Sartoris Family* (pp. 1–40). Boston: G. K. Hall.

Kinney, A. F. (1996a). Go Down, Moses: *The Miscegenation of Time*. New York: Twayne.

Kinney, A. F. (1996b). Sutpen. In A. F. Kinney (ed.). *Critical Essays on William Faulkner: The Sutpen Family* (pp. 1–46). Boston: G. K. Hall.

Minter, D. (1980). *William Faulkner: His Life and Works*. Baltimore: Johns Hopkins University Press.

Parker, R. D. (1985). *Faulkner and the Novelistic Imagination*. Champaign-Urbana: University of Illinois Press.

Polk, N. (1996). *Children of the Dark House*. Jackson: University Press of Mississippi.

Tobin, P. (1973–4). The Time of Myth and History in *Absalom, Absalom! American Literature*, 45(2): 252–70.

Watson, J. G. (1968). *The Snopes Dilemma: Faulkner's Trilogy*. Coral Gables: University of Miami Press.

Williamson, J. (1993). *William Faulkner and Southern History*. New York: Oxford University Press.

Wittenberg, J. B. (1979). *Faulkner: The Transfiguration of Biography*. Lincoln, NE: University of Nebraska Press.

12

Changing the Subject of Place in Faulkner

Cheryl Lester

Beginning with Malcolm Cowley's post-World War II Viking *Portable Faulkner*, critical readers of Faulkner have had to grapple with Cowley's assertion that Faulkner not only invented a "Mississippi county that was like a mythical kingdom . . . complete and living in all its details," but also that he made "his story of Yoknapatawpha County stand as a parable or legend of all the Deep South" (1965: 2). Readers of Faulkner enter this place – call it a kingdom, county, parable, or legend – as "elaborated, transformed, given convulsive life by [Faulkner's] emotions," yet we bring to it our own memories, traditions, and sources, elaborated and transformed with our own feelings and ideas. We enter a labyrinth of trouble, at a place and point in time that some describe as the lowest point in African American history and life. Inside this labyrinth, where short-sightedness and narrow horizons are the rule, it is easier to lose than to find one's way. We readers have often proven less capable than Faulkner himself of broadening our horizons, and often unconsciously and uncritically restrict our view to the tunnel vision, blind spots, and dead ends whose limits Faulkner sometimes surpassed. Worse yet, we often fail to pick up those threads in Faulkner's writings that do suggest ways outside the labyrinth.

Reflecting on Faulkner's South

In a cogent essay, "From the Benighted South to the Sunbelt: The South in the Twentieth Century," Nancy MacLean reviews an array of competing explanations for what caused the profound transformations of the twentieth-century South. In her view, the single most important factor was the emergence and decline of cotton plantation share-cropping as the primary institution of the South from the end of Reconstruction to World War II. Established after Reconstruction as a way to organize cotton production without slaves, sharecropping was a compromise that allowed tenants and sharecroppers if not economic independence then at least the freedom to live in households as families.

Sharecropping depended, however, on maintaining a large, cheap labor force, which motivated a variety of efforts to keep laborers from improving their opportunities or leaving. Such efforts ranged from the black codes restricting political participation and freedom of mobility, to poor public schooling, to racial terrorism. MacLean argues that, despite the entrenchment of sharecropping in all aspects of Southern life in the early part of the twentieth century, what finally forced the South to change, and to change quite rapidly, were the federal laws concerning agricultural production inaugurated by the Agricultural Adjustment Act of 1933. While she also acknowledges the significance of the African American Civil Rights Movement, MacLean thus gives pre-eminence to political economy. Similarly, she sees migration from the South as a secondary effect of the demise of tenant farming and sharecropping. From the postwar era to the present, she describes the vast differences of a South that is no longer segregated, no longer rural, no longer detached from the national or global economy, and no longer excluded from power at the national level.

During his lifetime, Faulkner experienced both the rise and the fall of cotton plantation sharecropping, along with the intense institutions, practices, and forms of social control that emerged to establish and maintain it, and the abrupt relaxation of those controls as sharecropping lost its hold. Faulkner's writings offer readers a salient and vivid sense of the brutal intensity of social life under Jim Crow, when cotton plantation sharecropping was the dominant political economy as well as the material setting for social life. They also provide a sense of the baffling and disorienting rapidity with which this material setting and the intensity it brought to social relations were dismantled and reconfigured. Yet we cannot simply generalize from Faulkner's vivid yet situated sense of life in Mississippi to understand how all other Jim Crow Southerners felt or experienced these transformations.

Critical Reflections on Place in Faulkner

Critical efforts to resist such generalizations and to revive oppositional aspects of Faulkner's writings have often been abstract, involving metaphysical questions about the ontological status of place and representation; theoretical speculations about the role of representation in the constitution of place; and poststructural refutations of the assumed homogeneity, continuity, and unity of place and history and the assumed unity and universality of the subject. Such critical questioning was aimed at challenging those readings whose assumption of the continuity, homogeneity, or singularity of place in Faulkner foreclosed an analysis and representation of the terrible, unresolved history of slavery and Jim Crow in Mississippi. The purpose of challenging representations of the empirical world in which Faulkner lived and with which his writings engage is not to negate the material history and life of that world, but rather to scrutinize and surpass Faulkner's specific purchase on them. The aim is to encourage more lucid and inclusive explanations of the changing world with which Faulkner's writings grapple and to demonstrate the meaning and significance of these explanations today. As readers of

Faulkner, we circulate beliefs and arguments that have a bearing on enduring struggles in Mississippi for social justice, political representation, and material success. To engage in more informed critical debates about the limits of Faulkner's hold on his world and its diverse peoples, material life, historical formation, geopolitical location, struggles, and possibilities, we need specific, accurate, and salient information about Oxford, Lafayette County, and Mississippi. We also need to critically review Faulkner's purchase on place in the context of the American nationalist, imperialist, and military enterprise; in view of his international experiences during war and peace; and in relation to his increasingly global perspectives on place. Aptly dedicated to the "Global Faulkner," the 2006 Yoknapatawpha and Faulkner Conference was one such initiative to generate and circulate new configurations and more expansive analyses.

In my earliest study on the construction of place in Faulkner (Lester 1987), I articulated three dimensions of the term "topos" to organize my inquiry. I proposed the term in order to describe the way Faulkner is habitually interpreted as well as to characterize the pre-eminent thematic and structural treatment of place in his writing. Thus, I used the term to describe (1) the commonplace assumption guiding Faulkner criticism and popularized by Cowley that a fixed and bounded place, namely Yoknapatawpha County, could suffice to organize and explain the highest achievement of Faulkner's writings; (2) the thematic interconnection and mutual constitution of identity and place; and (3) the structural role of repetition in the emotional orientation that grounds identity in place. I offered three readings to illustrate these different applications of topos to describe the construction of place in Faulkner. First, I offered a critical reading of Malcolm Cowley's *Portable Faulkner* in order to challenge the critical commonplace (topos) that Faulkner's writings can be adequately unified and framed in terms of the chronicle of a fictional place known as Yoknapatawpha County. Second, I examined the short story "Sunset" (1925) and the novel *Sanctuary* (1931) to challenge empirical readings of place in Faulkner by arguing that he explores place not so much as an empirical referent or setting but rather as a kinetic, utopian intention. As a process, impulse, direction, orientation, or aim, place emerges in the context of a migration narrative as the irreducible topos of a quixotic subject moving between an irrecoverable starting point and an unreachable end. Third and finally, I offered a reading of *The Sound and the Fury* (1929) to demonstrate Faulkner's use of repetition (topoi) to propose emotional attachment as the structural link that connects the desiring or quixotic subject to a non-empirical place that is nevertheless grounded in material life.

As a framework for a critical discussion of scholarly analyses of place in Faulkner, John Agnew's model (Cresswell 2004) is perhaps of more use here. A political geographer, Agnew regards place as a meaningful location and offers three basic dimensions for its analysis: location, locale, and sense of place. Citing Agnew's model in his introductory volume on the study of place, Tim Cresswell explains that Agnew treats place as (1) a real or fictive location on earth, (2) a material setting for social relations, or (3) a subjective and emotional attachment. While the concept of location gets at the meaning of place as fixed and stationary, the idea of locale suggests that, whether stationary or in movement, a place serves as the concrete, material setting within which people conduct their social lives. Finally, the concept of a sense of place indicates the fact that places become meaningful through human agency.

As I employ Agnew's analytic categories to organize and examine representative critical writings on place in Faulkner, I introduce other analytic models that suggest directions for further research. The earliest criticism I review, published in 1952 and 1961, reflects perspectives on representation, race, subjectivity, and place that do not reflect current social or critical understanding, but such criticism offers important reminders of the history and the enduring challenges of Faulkner scholarship. They contrast with my own kinetic view of place in Faulkner insofar as they project a unified, static, and linear image of place, precisely at a period (1940–60) when Jim Crow Mississippi and its "discriminatory plural society" were experiencing great and significant change and when Faulkner was struggling to understand and respond to it.[1]

A Disappearing Place

With his article "Is Oxford the Original of Jefferson in William Faulkner's Novels?" which appeared in 1961 in the prominent *Proceedings of the Modern Language Association*, G. T. Buckley challenges the critical commonplace, then seemingly at the center of debate, that Jefferson represents Oxford and that Yoknapatawpha County represents Lafayette County. Still grounding his arguments in the assumption that representation is mimetic and secondary to the empirical world, Buckley makes the point that Faulkner does not faithfully reproduce Oxford or Lafayette County but rather draws upon and combines features from other Mississippi towns and counties as well. Calvin S. Brown refuted Buckley's argument, and *PMLA* published his "Faulkner's Geography and Topography" in the next issue of the journal. As former Mississippi state archaeologist, with degrees in both geology and comparative literature, and as a professor at Ole Miss from 1905 to 1954, Brown had a stake in Faulkner's representation of place, and reprinted his *PMLA* article as an appendix to his 1976 *Glossary of Faulkner's South*. Disagreeing with Buckley's notion that Faulkner's representations were composites of different places, Brown argues that Faulkner's writings make "exact and detailed use of the streets of Oxford and the roads, creeks, and swamps of Lafayette County" (1976: 223). He points out, however, that many of the exact referents that serve as material evidence to support his claims change, erode, or disappear altogether. As he argues, the Oxford and Lafayette County represented in Faulkner reproduce the "geographic reality" and "actual topography" of 1912, when Faulkner was a 15-year-old boy. Since the initial publication of his argument, he notes, "[b]oth the barbershop at the corner of the square and the old jail have gone" (p. 224). Similarly, he adds, "some resemblances have already been obscured by such changes as the rerouting of roads and the building of the Sardis Dam and Reservoir" (p. 226). Gone, he points out, is the memorable church from the fourth section of *The Sound and the Fury* where Frony, Dilsey, Luster, and Benjy hear Reverend Shegog's Easter sermon, the church which formerly stood by the road near the top of the ridge. Already "sacrificed by bulldozers to subdivisions" is the deep ditch from *Light in August* (1932) and *The Town* (1957), with its especially interesting history and local usages (pp. 229–30).

The transformations of place to which Brown draws our attention inadvertently demonstrate the contingencies he wishes to establish as actualities. Moreover, he seems to be focusing more on what is gone than on the significance of their disappearance. What is happening in Oxford and Lafayette County? How can the bulldozing and the creation of subdivisions be connected to the disappearance of the barbershop, the old jail, the black church, and the deep ditch, or to the rerouting of roads and the construction of the Sardis Dam and Reservoir? What do these particular places signify in Faulkner's writings? What are we to make of the racial valence of these locations in the context of the segregated spatial practices of Oxford and Lafayette County? What does their disappearance have to do with the sweeping changes occurring in Mississippi at the time? Which people were affected by these changes and how? How did Faulkner think and feel about these sweeping changes?

Intruder in the Dust (1948) suggests to me that in the postwar era Faulkner was seriously revising his thinking and feelings about racialism, social relations, and spatial practices in Oxford, scrutinizing his privilege, acknowledging his resistance to oppositional action, and exploring strategies for combating racial discrimination by building alliances, marshaling opposition, and employing subterfuge. *Intruder* retrospectively explores the possibilities that might have enabled a privileged white youth in the Jim Crow South to marshal resistance to social wrongs in which he was implicated as a member of the community, but at the same time proposes strategies that the author himself might still have deployed in 1948.

Even a brief glance at Brown's treatment of geography and topography in Faulkner reveals inadvertent and uncritical shifts in the level of analysis that take his argument beyond the investigation of place as a real or fictive location to one that also considers place as a material setting for social relations and as the object of affective attachments. Brown's observations require a closer and deeper interrogation of the uses of location and the treatment of place in Faulkner. In which texts do these references to bygone places appear? What do they mean in those contexts? In *The Sound and the Fury*, for example, familiar markers of location – whether objects, roads, people, or processes – serve as focal points of emotional attachment and security. When they change, are absent, leave, or suddenly reappear, they provoke intense feelings and memories of dramatic action. In Agnew's terms, the reasons for such changes and the emotional reactions that changes provoke require analysis at the level not simply of location but also of locale and sense of place. Brown's desire to establish a mimetic correspondence between the fictive Jefferson and the actual Oxford is poorly served by the unsteady ground of a rapidly changing place. Moreover, these changes served particular interests, exerted multiple effects, and provoked multiple feelings.

In his influential essay "'Paradoxical and Outrageous Discrepancy': Transgression, Auto-Intertextuality, and Faulkner's Yoknapatawpha," Martin Kreiswirth (1996) provides theoretical grounds for more supple and heterogeneous approaches to the examination of place in Faulkner. Kreiswirth's article contributes to scholarly examinations of the discursive process by which Faulkner and his readers have created "Yoknapatawpha, the extensive construct discursively projected" from some of Faulkner's novels and stories (p. 161). Textual and auto-textual analyses of place were part of a theoretical effort to detach the interpretation of place in Faulkner from the mimetic model of representation that governed much of the earliest critical commentaries on place in his work. Recognizing the primary, constitutive role of representation in the material life of place is crucial to the goal of revising and reconstituting the representation and material life of place; historical revision and social reform go hand in hand. In the context of the South, with its history as a discriminatory plural society, the necessity for historical revision is so sweeping as to often escape notice.

Textual criticism has also drawn attention to reading practices that dehistoricize, misrepresent, or misconstrue the construction of place in Faulkner by ignoring or confusing its temporal unfolding or by failing to pay attention to details. A recent analysis along these lines is Thomas L. McHaney's meticulous essay "First is Jefferson: Faulkner Shapes His Domain" (2004), which cautions readers to be accurate when discussing the construction of place in Faulkner's text and shows how the intertextual reading practices provoked by his cross-referenced narratives often obscure significant details. Particularly, McHaney demonstrates that Faulkner treats Jefferson rather than Yoknapatawpha County in most of his early- and mid-career novels and stories. Using concordances of the novels to make his case, McHaney points out that Faulkner began to make liberal reference to Yoknapatawpha County only in the late period of his writing career, under the influence of Cowley's *Portable Faulkner*. With reference to this astonishing yet perfectly understandable sloppiness in our reading practices, which has prompted us to conflate Faulkner's attention to the boundaries and internal work-ings of a town with those of a county, McHaney draws attention to the role of habit, custom, and dominance in the discursive production of meaning. The error of seeing Yoknapatawpha County where the texts treat only Jefferson serves to suggest the broader habits of thinking and feeling that exert a silent impact on the production and reproduction of place. Extreme disparities are required to impede the automatic operation of those familiar pathways of thinking and feeling that generally govern our responses to environment, textual or otherwise. Faulkner's tendency to produce discursive heterogeneity – extreme breaks or disparities in and between his narratives – suggests a strategy for interrupting entrenched thinking and feeling processes like those that supported racial discrimination and segregation in Jim Crow Lafayette County.

A Collapsing Sense of Place

Ward L. Miner, a native Iowan who retired from the English Department at Youngstown State University in 1976, published *The World of William Faulkner* in 1952. Miner examined Oxford, Mississippi and Lafayette County as "actual prototype[s]" of Jefferson and Yoknapatawpha County.[2] In addition to fleshing out the actualities of place by supplying population figures and geographic and geological details, Miner also begins to chronicle the history of Lafayette County and the town of Oxford. Using published and unpublished sources that have become standards, including the 1938 Federal Writers' Project guidebook *Mississippi: A Guide to the Magnolia State*, he also draws liberally from historical narratives that Faulkner produced in the 1950s, for instance, in *Requiem for a Nun* (1951). Miner's study begins as a narrative of location but becomes the narrative of the dissolution of a locale, a place pervaded by "a miasma-like past" that has long ceased to serve as a supportive material setting for particular social relations and institutions (Miner 1959: 13). An outsider, he nonetheless identifies with its privileged white male inhabitants and offers a restrictive and one-sided view of Oxford and Lafayette County. As a consequence of his uncritical identification, Miner's view of Faulkner's world unfortunately narrows and shortens its horizons.

Following what we might call the post-Cowley Faulkner, Miner's chronicle of Oxford and Lafayette County makes liberal use of a sequence of image clusters, rapidly shifting *tableaux vivants* or *mise-en-scènes*. His narrative begins with the Ice Age and the water receding from the alluvial soil to introduce the Mississippi River as the geographic and psychic core of Lafayette County. In a swift transition from the Ice Age to the Civil War, Miner describes a panoply of inhabitants and institutions, beginning with the ancient mound-builders, the Chickasaws, and the Choctaws. From there, he offers representative details to flesh out epochs that appear in *Requiem* as abbreviated chains of referents or clusters of historically evocative nouns and phrases, such as treaties, trading posts, plantations, slaves; Jacksonian democrats, social upstarts, lawyers, credit, flush times, rough justice, depression, Federal Court. He describes changes in the built environment that reflect new pretensions, including the 1848 founding of the university and residences such as Faulkner's Rowan Oak, and material developments that link Oxford to surrounding places, namely the steamboat connections that link Oxford south to Vicksburg, Natchez, and New Orleans, and the stage coach connections between Oxford and Memphis.

As he develops his analysis of Oxford as a material setting for particular configurations of social relations, Miner uncritically reveals the shaping influence of his imagined sense of place. He situates himself alongside and identifies positively with the antebellum prosperity of Oxford when he laments the era when it was a "vital and vigorous" community of around 1,500 and its "leaders were really leaders," individuals whose prominence reached beyond the local community (1959: 46). He contrasts the peak prosperity, boldness, and vigor of white elites in Oxford and Lafayette County before the Civil War with the economic lassitude and spiritual decay of the present: "Like the land, the people in the community have been gullied by a spiritual decay, though covered over with a veneer of respectability. Families once bold and vigorous are now spectators rather than participating actors. What produced this decay? What wasted not only the soil of this county but the minds of these people? Why do all civilizations decay?" (p. 19). Miner's historical narrative of Faulkner's world reproduces the view of some of Faulkner's (elderly, anachronistic, benighted, foolhardy) characters, who regard the upheaval of power that transformed the slaveholding South as the defeat of a bold and vigorous civilization. Miner's observation and understanding are limited by his sympathetic identification with the declining powers and privileges of the white male elites whose fortunes suffered with the collapse of slavery and, more recently, sharecropping. By contrast, Faulkner's view of this decline is more self-critical, informed, and expansive.

Miner confirms his one-sided view of the "decay" of the South and the "tragedy" of Oxford by citing an item from an 1860 Vicksburg newspaper that dwells on the expectation and ambitions of the antebellum Southern gentleman:

> A large plantation and negroes are the *Ultima Thule* of every Southern gentlemen's ambition. For this the lawyer pores over his dusty tomes, the merchant measures his tape, the doctor rolls his pills, the editor drives his quill and the mechanic his plane – all, all who dare aspire at all, look to this as the goal of their ambition. The mind is used, from childhood, to contemplate it, and the first efforts are all lost if the objects in life should be changed. The mind is thus trained from infancy to think of and prepare for the attainment of this end. (quoted in Miner 1959: 35–6)

Citing this description to represent the decline of Oxford and Lafayette County, Miner reproduces the raced, gendered, and class-based viewpoint of the post-Confederate male Southern elite to which Faulkner belonged, yet which he interrogates and criticizes in a parade of characters including Bayard Sartoris, Quentin and Jason Compson, Horace Benbow, and Gavin Stevens. Apparently without irony, Miner poses the following question: "What would you do," he writes, "if you were an ambitious young man in Oxford in the 70's and 80's?" (p. 56) What Miner frames in his study as "the tragedy of Oxford," the disappointment of this dominant and dominating subject, involves an entitled and unreflective sense of place that Faulkner depicts in his earliest writings with some seriousness and melancholy but ultimately with derision as well.

Without Faulkner's ironic self-criticism or his efforts at empathic identification with others, Miner views post-World War II Oxford and Lafayette County from the narrow view of a white elite who suffered a loss of economic and political power, a loss he attributes to soil erosion and the industrialization of the South. His sympathy for the declining fortunes of the white elite of Oxford and the Delta contrasts with his acknowledgment of a new class of corporate elites, who assumed economic and political power with the ongoing collapse of cotton plantation sharecropping in Mississippi and with the consolidation of cotton production as an agribusiness. As Miner notes,

> the representatives of the Delta are the dominant political power in Mississippi. But they are not the Delta-planter aristocracy so well portrayed in William Alexander Percy's *Lanterns on the Levee*; rather they are from the corporations controlling large stretches of fertile Delta valley. . . . Many of the political struggles in the state are to be explained by the clash of interests between the people of the Delta and those on the hills behind (such as in Oxford) who are jealous of the valley prosperity and of the large percentage of Negroes there. (1959: 60)

In 1952, just ten years before Faulkner's life drew to its conclusion, Miner writes about Oxford and Mississippi from an unapologetically homogeneous sense of place, seemingly indifferent to the perspectives of the Afro-Mississippians who made up more than half the population of the state until World War II. In his appendix, Miner's statistics on population also reveal that the black population of Lafayette County decreased as a proportion of the total by 10.1 percentage points from 1910 to 1950, from 9,904 or 45.3 percent of a total population of 21,883 to 8,023 or 35.2 percent of a total population of 22,798. While the black population of the county decreased by nearly 2,000 during this period, the total population of the county increased by nearly 1,000, and the total population of Oxford almost doubled. Miner does not consider the experience of this declining black population or offer any information about black and white population statistics in Oxford during this period. By contrast, Faulkner had already demonstrated in the mid-1930s, for example, with *Absalom! Absalom!* (1936), an imaginative engagement with the irreducibly different experiences of the women and Afro-Mississippians who comprised half the population of Lafayette County in 1860. By 1948, he had undertaken the more serious overhaul of self that unfolds as a retrospective fantasy in *Intruder in the Dust.* Yet these empathic efforts, however limited, appear to have had little impact on Miner's view of Faulkner's world. While Miner's study examines Faulkner's Mississippi not simply as a geographical location but more fundamentally as a material space shaped by politics and economics, his analysis of that locale is narrowly and uncritically aligned with the declining fortunes and disappointed hopes of a fading or residual political and economic elite.

Split Subjects of Place

In his rich 1986 chapter "Out of the South: The Fiction of William Faulkner," Richard Gray rehearses the arguments and some early sources on place in Faulkner. Gray presents an analysis of Faulkner's "spiritual geography," which he views as an effort to understand and respond to the South during a period of critical and rapid change. Particularly attentive to Faulkner's depiction of place as a locale or material setting for prescribed social relations and roles, Gray examines Faulkner's treatment of place as a kind of support structure, a scaffolding for social relations and roles. When place changes, customary social roles and relationships become unsustainable. With reference to multiple characters from Faulkner's repertoire and to aptly chosen passages that depict them, Gray focuses on portraits of characters whose emotional attachment to place is disturbed when they can no longer physically, psychically, or socially fulfill roles they once inhabited or when the roles assigned to them are too confining, oppressive, and life-threatening.

In a 1986 essay on the "racial memory" of Mississippi in Richard Wright and William Faulkner, Thadious M. Davis draws a distinction between the meanings of the past for white versus black Mississippians. Offering a summary review of the history of Mississippi that is quite different from Miner's, Davis reminds readers that the often-cited postbellum longing for the lost opportunities of the antebellum era, when Mississippi was for a short time the fifth wealthiest state in the Union, was felt only by white Mississippians. Black Mississippians, "the real losers" during the postbellum period, had no lost opportunities to lament; in their experience, the state of Mississippi, before and after the Civil War, was "synonymous with degradation and deprivation" (1986: 471). For Davis, the significance of place is not a matter of location or of whether a particular element of the landscape continues to exist or ever actually existed. Instead, she draws our attention to the material life and emotional reality of a population who lived in Jim Crow Oxford and Lafayette County alongside Faulkner, but whose racialized lives situated them in different locations, or differently within the same locations, with subordinate roles in the material settings built and maintained by their labor, with different emotional attachments and senses of place. By insisting on the racial dimension of both experiences and memories of place, and by demonstrating racialized differences in representations of Mississippi in Faulkner versus Wright, Davis offers a concrete argument against mimetic, empiricist, homogeneous interpretations of place. A fact of Oxford and Lafayette County's discriminatory plural society, place in Faulkner cannot be analyzed as singular or unified, but must be understood as multiple and at the very least divided by its racialized regime. Focusing on place as a racialized object of memory and emotional attachment, imaginatively reconstituted and transformed by perspectives, experiences, and observations linked to a racialized structure of dominance, Davis demonstrates that place is constructed not simply of material forms and social hierarchies but also of irreducibly different feelings, struggles, aspirations, disappointments, and attachments.

Change as Thought and Felt

As Tim Cresswell argues in his 1996 volume *In Place/Out of Place: Geography, Ideology, and Transgression*, disturbances have the effect of highlighting the deeply ideological dimension of place and the mutual constitution of location, locale, and sense of place (geography, ideology, and subjectivity). Normative material settings enforce and reinforce appropriate expectations and behaviors for particular subjects in particular locations in order to maintain hierarchical social relations and ideological norms. These social hierarchies and ideological norms are so naturalized that they are difficult to discern without some form of disturbance. To illustrate, Cresswell isolates examples of social transgressions; however, change of any importance creates sufficient disturbance to reveal experiences, relationships, activities, expectations, behaviors, and norms that are otherwise difficult or even impossible to discern. In my view, social action reveals that ideology exerts an impact on place less in terms of a fixed system or structure than as something more like what Raymond Williams describes as a "lived hegemony," "a process," a realized complex of experiences, relationships, and activities, with specific and changing pressures and limits. In practice, that is, hegemony can never be singular. Its internal structures are highly complex, as can readily be seen in any concrete analysis. Moreover (and this is crucial, reminding us of the necessary thrust of the concept), it does not just passively exist as a form of dominance. It has continually to be renewed, recreated, defended, and modified. It is also continually resisted, limited, altered, challenged by pressures not at all its own. (Williams 1977: 112)

As compliant readers, we participate in the renewal, recreation, defense, or modification of place in Faulkner. As oppositional readers, we take part in resisting, limiting, altering, and challenging his construction of place. To this process, we bring different histories, sensitivities, limitations, and desires.

Early novels like *Soldiers' Pay* (1926) and *Flags in the Dust* (published in drastically cut form as part of *Sartoris* in 1929) deploy the departures and returns of servicemen as the source of altered perspectives, expectations, and behaviors that produce disturbances in the enactment of social roles and in the close relationships that depend on them. Novels of the 1930s, such as *Sanctuary, Light in August, Absalom! Absalom!*, and *Wild Palms* (1939), explore confining roles and identities by moving characters in and out of more or less sharply racialized, gendered, and sexualized places. The flow of migration in and out of Faulkner's South created disturbances that made Jim Crow hegemony more visible to him as a realized complex of experiences, relationships, and activities that required continual defense and renewal. The rapid and sweeping change that intensified with World War II influences representations, for example, in *Requiem for a Nun* that present historical change not in terms of human action but rather in terms of sudden structural transformation. The collapse of decrepit structures characterizes human agents as passive and bewildered victims, swept up in rapid changes that strip them of identity, dignity, and purpose and render them superfluous and irrelevant.

Consider, for example, the following discomfiting passage from the prologue "The Jail (Nor Even Yet Quite Relinquish –)" to Act Three of *Requiem*, which condenses the colonial conquest of the Southwest, the upheaval of American Indian life, and the dispossession of American Indians in a kinetic, explosive, and propulsive transformation:

In reality it was as though, instead of putting an inked cross at the foot of a sheet of paper, she had lighted the train of a mine set beneath a dam, a dyke, a barrier already straining, bulging, bellying, not only towering over the land but leaning, looming, imminent with collapse, so that it only required the single light touch of the pen in that brown illiterate hand, and the wagon did not vanish slowly and terrifically from the scene to the terrific sound of its ungreased wheels, but was swept, hurled, flung not only out of Yoknapatawpha County and Mississippi but the United States too, immobile and intact – the wagon, the mules, the rigid shapeless old Indian woman and the nine heads which surrounded her – like a float or a piece of stage property dragged rapidly into the wings across the very backdrop and amid the very bustle of the property-men setting up for the next scene and act before the curtain had even had time to fall;

There was no time; the next act and scene itself clearing its own stage without waiting for property-men; or rather, not even bothering to clear the stage but commencing the new act and scene right in the midst of the phantoms, the fading wraiths of that old time which had been exhausted, used up, to be no more and never return. (Faulkner 1975: 190–1)

This disturbing image of the colonized American Indian subject, ignobly portrayed as brown and illiterate, constructs a portrait of historical change as rapid, sweeping, and irreversible. The collapse of the old locale or structure that "the rigid shapeless old Indian woman" seems to inaugurate with the stroke of a pen is also figured as the culmination of a process over which she had little control. Over time, it seems, other pressures and forces had already been acting to compromise and impinge on the integrity of the old structure, which is figured as "a dam, a dyke, a barrier already straining, bulging, bellying, not only towering over the land but leaning, looming, imminent with collapse." By relinquishing tribal sovereignty over the land, participating in a charade of contractual agreement, the woman relinquishes the social shape, meaning, and vitality she possessed in connection with a particular place. With the disappearance of a material context to support her social place, she loses power and consequence immediately and finds herself relegated to a position of ghostly ineffectuality, swept or hurled into a devitalized junk heap peopled by "the phantoms, the fading wraiths of that old time which had been exhausted, used up, to be no more and never return." The rapid, dramatic, and epochal effects of her last, merely symbolic act were the result not of effective social action but rather of a structural decay so advanced that little or no pressure at all would produce the collapse that was already imminent.

A story from the 1920s that places a black migrant at the center of the action indicates Faulkner's awareness that, beginning with World War I, black Mississippians were gaining historical agency, geographical mobility, and the opportunity to explore new social opportunities. "Sunset" is a brief but significant cautionary tale in *New Orleans Sketches* that treats the fateful migration of an African American farm worker from rural Mississippi to the bustling city of New Orleans. Seeking an imagined homeland in Africa, this tragic figure fails to make a successful transition out of rural Mississippi. His naïve hope of belonging in this imaginary place offers an ironic gloss on the role he occupies as an exploited laborer in the Jim Crow South, where he must struggle for any claim to place. Corresponding to this contradictory position in a material setting, he experiences an ambivalent and even uncanny sense of place, simultaneously alienated from and homesick for the place he flees. Faulkner repeatedly allegorizes this sense in the experiences of characters male and female, black and white, rich and poor, young and old, educated and illiterate.[3]

What are we to make of these repeated allegories of change in terms of hapless victims who suffer uncanny disorientation when their lifelong hopes and dreams are no longer supported by or suited to their environment? Certainly, many Afro-Mississippians experienced the upheaval of Jim Crow, however disorienting, as the fulfillment of their hopes and dreams of escaping life-threatening discrimination, poverty, terrorism, exploitation, degradation, and confinement. A reflective essay by Raymond Williams entitled "Literature and Rural Society" (2001), which protests the uncritical use of literature to draw conclusions about material history, cautions me to regard Faulkner's emphasis on subjects who are powerless or ill-equipped to adapt to change as evidence not of how many, most, or even all people in Jim Crow Mississippi might have thought or felt about change, but rather of how the dominant structure of feeling constructed change as thought and felt.

Faulkner's emphasis on the dialectical or mutually constitutive relationship between subjectivity and place may be rooted in the transformations that characterized Southern life throughout his lifetime and that motivated as many as 29 million people to migrate from the South. Rural depopulation, urbanization, industrialization, war production, consumer capitalism – all contributed to a steady out-migration from the South that lasted for most of the twentieth century. If, as Joseph Urgo argues, Yoknapatawpha County is "only a synecdoche for the writer's larger production of alternatives of self and place and time" (1989: 4), we might still argue that the desire and the need for such alternative production were connected to the repressive social order in which Faulkner was born and raised.

Faulkner's sense of place emerged in the context of the establishment and demise of cotton plantation sharecropping, mass exodus from the South, and modernization, and developed in connection with a close study of the transformations of Oxford and Lafayette County. His situated response to these phenomena was productively disturbed if not altogether shaken by his travels, for example, to the Delta, Memphis, the Gulf, New Orleans, New York, Los Angeles, Europe, Charlottesville, and Japan. Through his writings, he engaged in a process of formulating judgments about his environment that we risk evacuating if we detach altogether from the specifics and the specific trans-formations of place. Perhaps the lone African American voice at a 1979 symposium published as *Sense of Place: Mississippi*, Roy Hudson exhorted his audience to remain alert to "the vestiges of a darker past that still rears its ugly head." "Let those of us who have insight into the realities of the past and the progress of the future," he intoned, "commit ourselves to helping bring about one common view of hope and prosperity for all Mississippians" (1979: 63–4).

Oxford in the Post-Faulkner Era

Readers of Faulkner continue to circulate in and produce meanings about Mississippi, Lafayette County, and Oxford. Many of us have traveled to Oxford as guests to partici-pate in the annual Faulkner and Yoknapatawpha County Conference over the past 33 years. We too have a responsibility to develop insight into the realities of the past and the progress of the future in these places and to commit ourselves to helping bring about hope and prosperity for all their residents. We play a part in the renewal of dominance within what Raymond Williams understood as a lived hegemony, a "realized complex of experiences, relationships, and activities *with specific and changing pressures and limits*" (1977: 112). As readers, we interact with a discursive field that includes such irreducibly different reflections on Oxford as Herman E. Taylor's 1990 memoir *Faulkner's Oxford: Recollections and Reflections*, published in Nashville, Tennessee, by Rutledge Hill Press, and Marilyn M. Thomas-Houston's 2005 ethnographic study *"Stony the Road" to Change: Black Mississippians and the Culture of Social Relations*, published by Cambridge University Press. We need to bring to bear our skills at working with irreducible differences, such as those produced by temporal, chronological, or spatial discontinuities in Faulkner's narratives, with the goal of ameliorating inequalities and discrimination in the material life of these places. We merely reproduce historically entrenched structures in dominance if we do nothing to mediate ongoing and seemingly irreconcilable differences in experience, relationships, activities, and opportunities.

A sixth-generation Mississippian and the descendant of the founder of Taylor, a small town seven miles south of Oxford, Herman E. Taylor's memoir includes an assortment of useful personal photographs of Oxford, especially of antebellum homes, and a particularly informative discussion of roads in Lafayette County. Taylor's triumphalist view of Civil Rights progress in Oxford in the post-Faulkner era merits quoting at length:

Within a quarter of a century after Mr. Billy's death in 1962, the quaint little town of Oxford had undergone many changes and had evolved into a bustling little city. Its population had greatly increased, and its boundaries had been expanded. The industrialization which Mr. Billy had foreseen and detested in 1955 had transpired, and several factories had been established in or near the city.

The Civil Rights Revolution in American had gotten underway shortly after Mr. Billy's death. One of the most important breakthroughs in that revolution occurred on the campus of the University of Mississippi in 1962 as James Meredith, a Negro, was forceably [*sic*] enrolled as a student in that university after a riot was quelled by federal troops. The Civil Rights Act of 1964 brought "Freedom Riders" into Mississippi to encourage Negroes to register and vote. Three of the "Riders" were murdered at Philadelphia, Mississippi, but the right of Negroes to vote was established, and the power of the Negro vote became manifest. By the 1980s Negroes had been elected or appointed to political positions at many levels including sheriffs, mayors, judges, members of the Supreme Court of Mississippi, U.S. Congressmen, and state legislators. Mississippians had elected two Republicans to serve in the U.S. Senate. The Republican Party had become the party of many whites, although Democrats continued to be elected to the U.S. House of Representatives and to state and local offices.

No longer did Negroes live in shanties on unpaved streets and roads near Birney's Branch or in "Freedman Town" or on the outskirts of Oxford. Instead they lived in well-built homes on paved streets. Sometimes they lived in previously all-white neighborhoods. Their children attended the public schools and the university without fear of interference or molestation.

Oxford and Lafayette County, as well as the rest of Mississippi and the entire South, had entered the post-Faulkner Era. (1990: 191–2)

Readers might be forewarned by the author's insensitive use of the term "Negroes" in 1990 that Taylor's memoir might offer a narrow and one-sided view of Oxford and its transformations since Faulkner's death. What was the character of Oxford's growth and whose interests was it serving? Who participated in the riot that occurred when James Meredith sought entrance to Ole' Miss? How did Meredith's actions affect life in Oxford? Have African Americans flourished in Oxford, Lafayette County, Mississippi, and the South, politically, economically, and socially? Has African American life developed evenly in all these places?

Marilyn M. Thomas-Houston's *"Stony the Road" to Change* paints a reluctant picture of Oxford and Lafayette County as "the place the Civil Rights Movement left behind," and seeks to understand why its African American community failed to organize a freedom movement in the Civil Rights era and remains poorly organized and underrepresented to this day. Thomas-Houston describes her observations of race relations in Oxford when she moved there in 1983 as "traumatic," and as the motivation for her personal and academic efforts to not only understand but also to inspire social change in African American life in this region. On the basis of an ethnographic study conducted from 1987 to 1994, she aims at illuminating "the culture of social relations" in this African American community to explain why people with shared identities and experiences behave differently, especially when it comes to social action. She seeks to explain why the way of being black in Oxford was so different from her understanding of being black in the United States in the 1980s and from her understanding of being black in Mississippi, an understanding she derived from reading books like Anne Moody's 1968 autobiography *Coming of Age in Mississippi*, Myrlie Evers's 1967 biography *For Us, the Living*, or June Jordan's 1972 biography *Fannie Lou Hamer*.

From the point of view of Oxford's African American community, which comprised 12 percent of the total population in 1990, Oxford's self-fashioning as a cultural center and retirement community excludes them, devalues and negates their presence, and widens the disparity between rich and poor (Thomas-Houston 2005: 29). While Oxford invests in projects like the University's $2-million baseball stadium, a development outside the city that includes a golf course, new hotels, and a conference center, Oxford's African Americans are earning an average of less than $10,000 per year and more than one in five households lack sufficient means to purchase a vehicle. Economic opportunities for African Americans are bleak in Oxford, where a concerted effort to maintain a quiet and prosperous antebellum appearance have led to a resistance to manufacturing and have restricted employment opportunities for African Americans primarily to low-paying service-oriented jobs (pp. 30–1).

According to Thomas-Houston, the failure of the African American community of Oxford and Lafayette County to assert its presence, and to win sufficient representation to gain the necessary resources to address its needs, contrasts with the pattern of challenging Jim Crow that was typical throughout Mississippi after the 1954 *Brown v. Board of Education* decision. As she explains, the Civil Rights Movement touched Oxford and Lafayette County by way of Meredith, the first African American to be admitted to the University of Mississippi, an institution whose Rebel origins are still commemorated.

Furthermore, the public demonstration at Oxford was not a Civil Rights breakthrough, as Taylor suggests, but rather a demonstration of white resistance to the Civil Rights Movement. Thomas-Houston notes that the African American community in Oxford kept their distance from this conflict, and she looks to the community's institutions, practices, and world-views to explain their reluctance to offer personal or public support to Meredith. As suggested by Cresswell's theoretical argument on transgression and place, Thomas-Houston finds that the presence of federal troops in 1963 only served to increase the awareness and enforcement of racialized space in Oxford and to create contests over previously unregulated spaces (2005: 54–9).

The author looks to the historical development of this community to explain its inability to organize a freedom movement in Oxford to support Meredith in 1963, at the height of Civil Rights activity throughout Mississippi. She also contrasts Oxford's failure to elect an African American to public office until the 1990s with the state of Mississippi's strong record, noted by Taylor, of electing African American officials to public office. Throughout her fieldwork, Thomas-Huston observed continuing pressures aimed at limiting or preventing the African American community from achieving greater public representation, pressures that included both economic reprisals exerted by white employers to "keep Blacks in their place" and political dirty tricks (2005:13 n.13, 95).

Thomas-Houston traces the lack of community organization to the antebellum period. With as much as 44 percent of the population enslaved in the three decades before the Civil War, but only five large plantations with groups of 100–200 slaves each, she calculates that Lafayette County's slave population was spatially distributed over nearly 3,000 households, with an average of only 2.2 slaves per household. Most of the African Americans in this community now were born and raised in the county and have little experience of travel out of state, and many own land near where their ancestors worked as slaves. Beginning with World War I, some members of this community left for Chicago, St. Louis, Omaha, Memphis, Atlanta, Dallas, and Los Angeles. Some of these migrants now send their grandchildren to Oxford and Lafayette County, where the geopolitical landscape disperses the African American community into small groups and militates against the formation of a group identity cohesive enough to support collective social action (2005: 43–52). To indicate the dispersal and splintering of the community, Thomas-Houston notes that there are forty-five African American churches in Lafayette County and that forty of them are scattered across the countryside. Established in this region only after the Civil War, the majority of the churches in the county (sixty-one of which are white) remain segregated. These churches serve as the primary conduit for the exchange of information in a region whose dominant institutions still fail to represent or promote communication within the African American community.

I offer the views of Oxford represented by these irreconcilably different recent publications to provoke us, as readers in the post-Faulkner era, to inform ourselves about the present realities and future opportunities of the people of Oxford, Lafayette County, and Mississippi, and to consider our part in renewing or opposing these realities and opportunities. Tracing the reciprocal meanings of Faulkner and Mississippi, Michael Kreyling asks in "Faulkner in the Twenty-First Century: Boundaries of Meaning, Boundaries of Mississippi," "What Faulkner will we need, what Faulkner will endure, in the twenty-first century?" (2003: 14). Instead of recycling the backward-looking Faulkner of Calvin Brown, who appears to cling to the time and place of his boyhood, we need to assert the Faulkner who – as the changing subject of his place – records his thoughts and feelings and remains lucid or at least truthful amidst the unremitting destabilizations and reconfigurations that assaulted and challenged him.

NOTES

1 I borrow the term "discriminatory plural society" from geographer Mark Lowry II (1971), who glosses it with a useful footnote on social versus cultural pluralism in his informative study of migration in Mississippi from 1940 to 1960.

2 In his rich and wonderfully researched study of the historical roots of Yoknapatawpha County, Don H. Doyle (2001) places Miner's study at the head of the list of works that treat the

relationship between the actual and the apocryphal in Faulkner.

3 Cowley captures the structure of feeling that shapes Faulkner's characters as "well-meaning and even admirable . . . but . . . almost all of them defeated by circumstances and . . . a sense of their own doom." He even cites a passage on the freed refugee slaves from *The Unvanquished* (1938) to describe what all Faulkner's characters are "a little like" (1965: 16–17).

REFERENCES AND FURTHER READING

Brown, C. S. (1961). Faulkner's Geography and Topography. *PMLA*, 77: 652–9.

Brown, C. S. (1976). *A Glossary of Faulkner's South.* New Haven, CT, and London: Yale University Press.

Buckley, G. T. (1961). Is Oxford the Original of Jefferson in William Faulkner's Novels? *PMLA*, 76: 447–54.

Cowley, M. (ed.) (1965). *The Portable Faulkner.* New York: Viking. (Original pub. 1946.)

Cresswell, T. (1996). *In Place/Out of Place: Geography, Ideology, and Transgression.* Minneapolis and London: University of Minnesota Press.

Cresswell, T. (2004). *Place: A Short Introduction.* Oxford: Blackwell.

Davis, T. M. (1986). Wright, Faulkner, and Mississippi as Racial Memory. *Callaloo*, 28: 469–78.

Doyle, D. H. (2001) *Faulkner's County: The Historical Roots of Yoknapatawpha.* Chapel Hill, NC: University of North Carolina Press.

Faulkner, W. (1975). *Requiem for a Nun.* New York: Random House. (Original pub. 1951.)

Glissant, E. (1999). *Faulkner, Mississippi* (trans. B. B. Lewis and T. C. Spear). Chicago: University of Chicago Press.

Gray, R. J. (1986). *Writing the South: Ideas of an American Region.* Cambridge: Cambridge University Press.

Gregory, J. N. (2004). The Southern Diaspora: Twentieth-Century America's Great Migration/s. In M. S. Rodriguez (ed.). *Repositioning North American Migration History: New Directions in Modern Continental Migration, Citizenship, and Community* (pp. 54–97). Rochester, NY: University of Rochester Press.

Hudson, R. (1979). Mississippi: A Native View. In P. W. Prenshaw and J. O. McKee (eds.). *Sense of Place: Mississippi* (pp. 62–4). Jackson: University Press of Mississippi.

Kodat, C. G. (2004). Posting Yoknapatawpha. *Mississippi Quarterly*, 57(4): 593–618.

Kreiswirth, M. (1996). "Paradoxical and Outrageous Discrepancy": Transgression, Auto-Intertextuality, and Faulkner's Yoknapatawpha. In D. M. Kartiganer and A. J. Abadie (eds.). *Faulkner and the Artist: Faulkner and Yoknapatawpha, 1993* (pp. 161–80). Jackson: University Press of Mississippi.

Kreyling, M. (2003). Faulkner in the Twenty-First Century: Boundaries of Meaning, Boundaries of Mississippi. In R. W. Hamblin and A. J. Abadie (eds.). *Faulkner in the Twenty-First Century: Faulkner and Yoknapatawpha, 2000* (pp. 14–30). Jackson: University Press of Mississippi.

Lester, C. (1987). Topoi in Faulkner: The Place of Writing (Yoknapatawpha County). Unpublished dissertation. SUNY Buffalo.

Lowry, M., II. (1971). Population and Race in Mississippi, 1940–1960. *Annals of the Association of American Geographers*, 61(3): 576–88.

MacLean, N. (2000). From the Benighted South to the Sunbelt: The South in the Twentieth Century. In H. Sitkoff (ed.). *Making Sense of the Twentieth Century: Perspectives on Modern America* (pp. 202–26). New York: Oxford University Press.

Meriwether, J. B. (ed.) (2004). *William Faulkner: Essays, Speeches, and Public Letters*. New York: Random House.

McHaney, T. L. (2004). First is Jefferson: Faulkner Shapes His Domain. *Mississippi Quarterly*, 57(4): 511–34.

Miner, W. (1959). *The World of William Faulkner*. New York: Pageant. (Original pub. 1952.)

Prenshaw, P. W. and J. O. McKee (eds.) (1979). *Sense of Place: Mississippi*. Jackson: University Press of Mississippi.

Scarborough, W. K. (1979). From Prosperity to Poverty: Economic Growth and Change to 1900. In P. W. Prenshaw and J. O. McKee (eds.). *Sense of Place: Mississippi* (pp. 153–61). Jackson: University Press of Mississippi.

Spillers, H. J. (2004). Topographical Topics: Faulknerian Space. *Mississippi Quarterly*, 57(4): 535–68.

Taylor, H. (1990). *Faulkner's Oxford: Recollections and Reflections*. Nashville, TN: Rutledge Hill Press.

Thomas-Houston, M. M. (2005). *"Stony the Road" to Change: Black Mississippians and the Culture of Social Relations*. Cambridge: Cambridge University Press.

Urgo, J. (1989). *Faulkner's Apocrypha: "A Fable," "Snopes," and the Spirit of Human Rebellion*. Jackson: University Press of Mississippi.

Williams, R. (1977). *Marxism and Literature*. Oxford: Oxford University Press.

Williams, R. (2001). Literature and Rural Society. In *The Raymond Williams Reader* (ed. J. Higgins) (pp. 109–18). Oxford: Blackwell. (Original pub. 1967.)

13

The State

Ted Atkinson

The timeline of William Faulkner's career as a living fiction writer runs from his first novel, *Soldiers' Pay* (1926), to his last novel, *The Reivers* (1962). If we place that timeline next to one that plots stages of American history, we can see that Faulkner's life as a writer spanned the Roaring Twenties, the Great Depression and consequent rise of the New Deal, World War II, and the onset of the Civil Rights Movement. It ended with Faulkner's death in July 1962, a year and a half into John F. Kennedy's ill-fated presidency. As an American citizen living and writing during this time, Faulkner witnessed the most profound change in the relationship between the individual and the state that the USA has ever known. This signal development in American society influenced and was influenced by the total transformation of liberalism as a guiding social, political, and economic philosophy. For a writer with Faulkner's depth of perception, the transformation of liberalism from its nineteenth-century roots as a philosophy of individual liberty and laissez-faire economics into a twentieth-century agent for collective identity and decisive federal action could not have been missed. Indeed, Faulkner remained attuned to this dynamic process throughout his career, as illustrated by relevant fictional representations and a willingness to speak his political mind that grew exponentially with his rise to prominence. In Faulkner's fiction, we find depictions of nationalism, politics and political figures, and state institutions such as law enforcement and the judicial system that can be read as ideological responses to the debate over reformed liberalism playing out on the American political scene. This complex and sometimes conflicted political dimension of his early fiction serves as a staging ground for the more coherent philosophy of classical liberalism that he professed with impassioned conviction later in his career.

Reformed Liberalism: The Dynamics of Ideological Change

Examining this dimension of Faulkner requires first understanding the revision of liberalism as an ideological and historical process. By the nineteenth century, classical liberalism, as it has been called by many a historian and political scientist, had taken shape in America. Fundamentally, it was perceived as a means for the individual to participate most fully in "life, liberty, and the pursuit of happiness." With the yeoman farmer, the entrepreneur, or the inventor in mind, this philosophy could be professed as a form of self-help capable of inspiring ingenuity, encouraging a vigorous work ethic, and reaping great rewards for those with access to its productive capabilities. Viewed in this way, liberalism was an agent of democracy, freeing individuals from oppressive and restrictive forces and thus enabling them to reach maximum achievement and prosperity. Emerson's all-seeing transparent eyeball, Thoreau's vision of an autonomous and productive harmony between vocation and avocation, and the Whitmanesque persona projected in "Song of Myself" stand as powerful literary testaments to the century's faith in the expansive potential of the individual. With progression from the late nineteenth to the twentieth century, this trend continued, fueling various social, political, and economic developments associated with the advance of modernity – for example, women's suffrage and the rise of the New Woman, the New Negro Movement, and stepped-up urbanization and industrialization under the auspices of the World War I military-industrial complex. The core principles of classical liberalism – individual liberty, property rights, and local control – enabled its rise to the status of dominant ideology in American society. As Raymond Williams explains, a dominant ideology is one that prevails in the service of the status quo, maintaining the existing social order under conditions favorable to those with the greatest influence and power (1977: 121–7).

With the rise of industrialism to its apex in the 1920s, however, classical liberalism was cast in an ironic light, as "robber baron" industrialists took advantage of laissez-faire economic policies and exercised self-help in ways that tarnished the democratic luster of the dominant ideology. With these men wielding considerable power over their workers to amass sizeable personal fortunes, the relatively open door to liberalism's productive capacity seemed to be closing quickly – except to the powerful few. In this climate of industrial excess, the seeds of reform sown under Theodore Roosevelt in the Progressive Era and under the World War I military-industrial complex finally began to sprout. Prominent intellectuals such as John Dewey, Walter Lippmann, Thorstein Veblen, and Charles A. Beard spoke out against unchecked individualism and laissez-faire economics. These thinkers and others laid the conceptual groundwork for a more progressive form of liberalism that stressed communitarian values and central planning as means to alleviate the social ills of capitalist society. After the stock-market crash of 1929 ushered in the Great Depression, conditions were ideal for these theories to be put into practice. As the election of 1932 drew near, Herbert Hoover's insistent reaffirmation of classical liberalism as the best antidote to the hard times grew more woefully out of step with the march of public sentiment. Ultimately, Hoover proved no match for Franklin Delano Roosevelt, with his urgent calls for cooperation and his vow to remember the "forgotten man" while taking decisive action to ease the pain of economic suffering. Hoover's landslide defeat by FDR offered visible proof that the cause of reformed liberalism was now on the rise.

FDR seized on this cause as a way to promote the New Deal, the assortment of policies and programs designed to stem the tide of the Depression. A common refrain among historians is that the New Deal was marked by inconsistency and incoherence, reflecting a tendency on the part of the administration not so much to *act on* as to *react to* the circumstances of the Depression (Brinkley 1998: 17–18; Kennedy 1999: 152–53; Rodgers 1998: 412). This tumultuous activity at the federal level reflected the dynamic condition of liberalism, which was caught in the throes of what Leonard Williams, building on the theories of Antonio Gramsci, calls ideological change. In articulating this concept, Williams notes the tendency among critics to treat ideology as a static force and a dominant ideology as a monolithic one. On the contrary, Williams argues, we must begin from the premise that "ideological change is simply a fact of social and political life" (1991: 4). From this standpoint, a dominant ideology does not speak with one voice but becomes rather a contested space of public discourse in which many voices seek a position of hegemony. During this process, Williams adds, "Ideological traditions similarly face demands both to accommodate novelty and to maintain their identity and thus are simultaneously pluri- and monovocal" (1991: 14). Taking that into account, Williams concludes, the focus should not be on how to break the yoke of a dominant ideology but instead on "how a public philosophy can be transformed" (1991: 39).

Fixed on the New Deal, this critical lens brings into sharp focus an eventful period of transition for American liberalism, characterized by complex negotiations between traditional and progressive forces. The outcome did bring a significantly revised dominant ideology, resulting from a process driven largely by expediency in the service of the status quo. For those harboring deep-seated concerns about capitalism dating back to the emergence of industrialism, hopes for a radically revised social order gave way by the mid-1940s to what Alan Brinkley rightly defines as an "accommodation with capitalism that served in effect to settle many of the most divisive conflicts of the first decades of the century" (1998: 62). This compromise was supported by the belief among many progressives that the New Deal had done enough to address social problems inherent in the capitalist system. In this regard, they set about "defining a role for the state that would . . . permit it to compensate for capitalism's inevitable flaws and omissions without interfering with its internal workings" (Brinkley 1998: 62). Despite the ultimately accommodating nature of the New Deal, it did succeed in harnessing the forces of ideological change to the establishment of the modern welfare state. The transformation of classical liberalism was now for the most part accomplished. This profound development set the stage for a postwar era of activist government. The state was now poised to affect the lives of individuals in the cause of ensuring civil rights and promoting a host of additional social, economic, and political reforms that would reshape the American landscape during the remainder of Faulkner's lifetime and beyond. As this force of ideological change reshaped America, it also exerted considerable influence on Faulkner's literary production and his developing political convictions.

"Once a Bitch, Always a Bitch": Jason Compson Takes on the Capitalist State

For many critics, *The Sound and the Fury* (1929), Faulkner's tragic tale of the Compson family, is his signature novel. Largely on the basis of its experimental form – three interior monologues often unfolding in a stream-of-consciousness followed by a final section told in the third person – Faulkner's fourth novel has been the one cited most often to secure his place among the scions of modernism. The interior form of the novel poses the great temptation to construct a similar critical approach, focused mainly on delving into the minds of the Compson brothers to develop psychological profiles. To do so, however, runs the risk of neglecting the novel's engagement with issues and concerns beyond the pages of the text – in particular, the ways that *The Sound and the Fury* responds ideologically to the formation of the modern capitalist state by exposing the toll it takes on the life and mind of the individual citizen. Philip J. Hanson perceptively notes the regional aspect of this endeavor, suggesting that *The Sound and the Fury* starts a trend in Faulkner's fiction "marked by its anxiety over a traditionalist Southern socio-economic system in the process of disintegrating, a system which had long regarded itself as opposed – and superior – to capitalist marketplace values" (1991–2: 4). This feature of the novel is apparent in all four sections, but it registers with the greatest force through the experiences of Jason, the narrator of the third section.

From the very start of his section, Jason Compson IV emerges as a man who is overburdened and angry, as a result of his new role as head of the family. "Once a bitch, always a bitch," Jason says right away, lashing out at his rebellious niece, Quentin (Faulkner 1984: 305). But the family is not the only target for Jason's anger, nor is it the primary source. Jason's section occurs on April 6, 1928, with the capitalist machine of the Roaring Twenties operating in overdrive and Black Tuesday – October 29, 1929 – just beyond the horizon. From Jason's perspective, the rise of capitalism has shaped the tragic Compson history of material loss and social decline. Once prominent, the Compsons now struggle to survive in a Southern economy transformed by forces unleashed in the post-World War I boom. For Jason, this new economy proves cruelly mystifying, bestowing great wealth on some while foiling each of his attempts to achieve the success he so deeply desires. To put it simply, Jason wants what he cannot have – he feels the intense ambition to succeed that this new consumer culture produces in him but possesses neither the start-up capital nor the good fortune to satisfy himself.

To make matters worse, Jason fancies himself perfectly capable of thriving in the marketplace, if only he had the chance to prove himself. Perhaps this self-assessment is not unfounded, if we take into account his most stellar market prediction. Responding angrily to a delayed market advisory, Jason fires off a bold and strikingly prescient missive: "Market just on point of blowing its head off" (1984: 282). On the whole, however, Jason's critique of capitalism is motivated more by sour grapes than market savvy or moral conviction. Referring to his dead-end job in the feed store, Jason decries his oppressive predicament: "What the hell chance has a man got, tied down in a town like this and to a business like this" (Faulkner 1984: 263). From there, he aims his fury more precisely, spouting impassioned conspiracy theories. In each instance, he fixes on the helplessness of the individual against the determining and indifferent forces that figure the individual as a nameless, faceless source of labor. Accordingly, the hard-working and honest small farmer is but a "whipsaw on the market," a victim of greedy speculators who force him to raise crops for their own benefit. Jason's critique of the speculators grows more pointed as he rages against the market machine: "Well, I reckon those eastern jews have got to live too. But I'll be damned if it hasn't come to a pretty pass when any dam foreigner that cant make a living in the country where God put him, can come to this one and take money right out of America's pockets" (Faulkner 1984: 221). Jason's defense of the "common man" is clearly more qualified than the term might suggest, extending only to those who are "purely American" by the rigid standards of nationalism applied. What emerges here is a tainted form of classical liberalism that preserves the right of the individual to thrive and prosper but defines that individual by xenophobic standards of exclusion. John T. Matthews puts these remarks in the context of a pervasive interwar nativism at work in America, suggesting that *The Sound and the Fury* exposes the basic "logic" of this ideology: "If blood descent determines who belongs to America (and whom America belongs to), then the family gains primacy as the ultimate ground of national identity" (2001: 71).

Indeed, as Jason turns from the national to the familial scene to assert himself, the Compson household is transformed into a site for symbolically staging ideological negotiations under way at the time of the novel's production. As presumptive breadwinner, Jason expresses a begrudging determination to provide for the Compson family that borders on obsession. Accordingly, when facing a state of familial upheaval, he tries to "ensure domestic tranquility," as it were, through a program of central planning aimed at consolidating his power and bringing order to the Compson domain. He then attempts to seize control of the familial economy, working like the proverbial "robber baron" first and foremost for his own financial gain while he professes to serve a greater good. This attempt to pull all the strings is tangibly on display in Jason's check-cashing scheme – a ploy in which he pockets the money sent from his sister, Caddy, to her daughter and then manufactures fake checks for Mrs. Compson to burn ritualistically in mournful recognition of her daughter's supposed defilement. The unscrupulous bilking of Caddy and Quentin recalls Jason's first entrepreneurial endeavor – a childhood venture in which he sold flour from the family barrel for his own profit. Now, with an ironic sense of bravado, he declares himself the only Compson who is "man enough to keep that flour barrel full," ignoring the fact that he has earned this dubious distinction by a process of elimination (Faulkner 1984: 238–9). Over time, the barrel has been changed from a symbol of opportunity to one of obligation, with the line of flour marking Jason's frustration and failure.

True to his male-chauvinist form, Jason figures his lack of freedom, opportunity, and control in terms of his relations with the Compson women. For Jason, Mrs. Compson represents the sense of duty binding him to the apparently lost causes of keeping the family together and bringing about a reversal of fortune. With bitterness and vindictiveness, he repeatedly blames his sister for ruining her engagement with Sydney Herbert Head and thus the promising job prospect arranged for him in a Northern bank as part of an implicit nuptial agreement. When Caddy's daughter, Quentin, is left under Jason's charge, her willfulness makes their relationship mirror his exasperating pursuits in the marketplace. This condition becomes clear to Jason in humiliating fashion when his niece makes off with the stash of money embezzled through his check-cashing scheme. Infuriated, Jason pursues Quentin with an enraged vigor, perceiving her dissidence as further proof of his vulnerability to outside forces. The sheriff's subsequent unwillingness to share Jason's understanding of the incident as theft and Jason's inability to recover the money only add insult to injury, leaving him helpless against the fluid forces of domestic economy now unleashed at him from both familial and national sources. Despite Jason's materialistic tendencies, he measures the toll of Quentin's "theft" in symbolic rather than monetary value. As we learn from the narrator in the fourth section, Jason did not enter his niece and "the arbitrary valuation of the money" as separate items in his memory ledger after the incident. Instead, "together they merely symbolised the job in the bank of which he had been deprived before he ever got it" (1984: 354).

Jason's difficult relations with the Compson women bring home to him, literally and figuratively, the reminder that his reach for the kind of individual fulfillment envisioned by classical liberalism far exceeds his grasp in a new socio-economic order that shapes him as a desiring yet frustrated consumer rather than empowers him to mold himself into an industrious and prosperous individual. In this regard, Jason emerges as the novel's most powerful agent for critiquing the totalizing power of the capitalist state. Through Jason's experiences and state of mind, Faulkner exposes the adverse effects of the market on the subject of capitalism who feels overwhelmed and robbed of individual identity and initiative by the destabilizing and often dehumanizing forces of consumer culture. Faulkner points to these forces as a main source of the anti-democratic, nativist ideology that urgently and fearfully constructs a "pure" America in an attempt to impose order on a socio-economic system in flux. This racially motivated compulsion for order is symbolically staged at the end of the novel when Luster, Benjy's African American caregiver, drives the carriage around the Jefferson town square in a different direction from usual. To silence Benjy's frightened wails, Jason whips Luster with the reins, forcing him to reverse his direction, thus restoring a familiar sense of perception that brings passing landmarks into view with "each in its ordered place" (1984: 371). At the same time that *The Sound and the Fury* highlights the plight of the individual frustrated by the vagaries of the capitalist state, however, it calls into question the antidote of imposing order through the means of central planning. Along these lines, Quentin's challenge to her uncle's authority is instructive. After all, Quentin's rebellion is driven at base by a desire for autonomy — she wants to fashion her own identity and spend her own money as she sees fit, rather than to have those decisions made for her. Quentin's subversive move can thus be read as a strong assertion of individual liberty and property rights at a moment when classical liberalism was under comprehensive reassessment – a process that would gain staggering momentum during the Depression.

(Dis)Order in the Court: The State on Trial in *Sanctuary*

On the basis of Faulkner's own assessments, as well as those of critics, *Sanctuary* (1931) was considered the black sheep of the Faulkner canon for many years. While *The Sound and the Fury* was celebrated as a masterpiece showcasing Faulkner at the height of his creative powers, *Sanctuary* was much maligned as a product of popular culture resulting from the author's desire to turn a quick profit. Faulkner himself promotes this distinction in his introduction to the Modern Library reprint edition of *Sanctuary*, calling the novel a "cheap idea . . . deliberately conceived to make money" and *The Sound and the Fury*, by contrast, the result of a creative exercise done purely "for pleasure" (1965: 176, 177). In the case of *Sanctuary*, Faulkner confesses to surveying the scene of popular culture to chart the most profitable course of action (1965: 177). Citing this element of timeliness, Eric J. Sundquist suggests that *Sanctuary* lays bare the "violent realities . . . of a country poised at a point of passing from the Roaring Twenties to the Great Depression" and then makes the convincing argument that the novel "belongs emphatically to the 'hard boiled' fiction of that period" (1983: 45–6). But Faulkner adds elements of the gangster genre as well, thus fusing two of the most popular forms into one sensationalistic novel enabling him to make his mark, for better or worse, on the national scene. *Sanctuary* was thus aligned with hard-boiled novels such as Dashiell Hammett's *Red Harvest* (1929) and gangster novels such as Francis Edwards Faragoh's *Little Caesar* (1929) and Armitage Trail's *Scarface* (1930) – the last two of which became blockbuster Hollywood movies – in providing shocking entertainment as well as revealing diagnoses of current social ills. With the crash of 1929 ushering in the Great Depression, imperiled law and order, ineffectual government handling of socio-economic distress, and the lack of legitimate means to prosperity were at the forefront of public concern. Consequently, the climate was ideal for the hard-boiled and gangster genres to prosper, transforming into spaces for reflecting and responding to the fears and fantasies of an anxious American public open to renegotiating the terms of social order. Taking cues from these popular forms, Faulkner's *Sanctuary* enters the fray of this vigorous and influential cultural politics, especially in its representation of a justice system in conflict with the unpredictable and destabilizing forces of political corruption, gangster mayhem, and mob rule.

From the first moment Faulkner's gangster Popeye Pumphrey appears, he seems to be cut from the same conflicted mold as the film gangsters who had become so wildly popular with moviegoers – Edward G. Robinson's Rico Bandello in *Little Caesar* (1930) and James Cagney's Tommy Powers in *The Public Enemy* (1931), for example. Like those characters, Popeye is a man of small stature who nevertheless cuts a figure larger than life, commanding respect based on his talent for making money, his reputation for ruthlessness, and his legendary marksmanship. Popeye has so far successfully negotiated the obstacles of the seedy underworld to gain a considerable amount of power and prestige. If we cast aside for the sake of argument the moral and ethical dilemmas posed by Popeye's vocation, he is less a menace to society than a prime example of the sort of individual initiative and fulfillment envisioned by classical liberalism. Andrew Bergman offers a perceptive assessment of this ironic appeal, noting that during the Depression Americans saw in the gangster figure a way of "clinging to past forms of achievement" rooted in individualism. Bergman elaborates: "That only gangsters could make upward mobility believable tells much about how legitimate institutions had failed – but that mobility was still at the core of what Americans held to be the American dream" (1971: 7). While upholding this trend to some extent, Faulkner does make a noticeable departure with his gangster, extending the option of extolling Popeye only so far. Instead of depicting the gangster as tragic hero, as in the gangster films, Faulkner places a distance between Popeye and the reader by revealing early on Popeye's capacity for brutal violence. This turn occurs when the sexually impotent Popeye uses a corncob to rape Temple Drake. Significantly, Faulkner renders the scene with a level of graphic force missing in the popular gangster stories and films, which treat violence not as a function of the individual gangster but as a product of underworld conditions pitting individuals against one another in bloody conflict.

Not surprisingly, the rape scene earned *Sanctuary* its infamous reputation – especially in Faulkner's hometown of Oxford, Mississippi, where citizens dutifully chastised it in public before retiring to their homes to read with prurient fascination. In a prominent 1932 article, Alan R. Thompson drew on the chorus of rebuke from literary critics to observe that Faulkner now appeared in league with "the cult of cruelty" (1932: 477). Once the shock value of the rape scene wears off, however, this charge – one that persisted beyond the confines of immediate critical reception – does not stand up to scrutiny. Rather than rendering the novel anti-social, the rape of Temple does quite the opposite: it establishes *Sanctuary*'s pattern of responding ideologically to issues of social and political relevance. In a typically patriarchal rendering, the rape transforms Temple's body into a symbolic site of conflict between the forces of social upheaval, embodied in Popeye, and those of existing order, embodied in Horace. Horace articulates the foundations of this order explicitly when he offers reassurance to Lee Goodwin, who is set to stand trial on false accusations in the aftermath of the rape and Popeye's subsequent murder of his henchman Tommy: "You've got the law, justice, civilization" (Faulkner 1993: 132). The political struggle and social disruption converging around Goodwin's trial produce a vacuum of power, thus posing questions of textual and contextual relevance: specifically, whether state institutions are viable enough to respond effectively to the demands of a severe crisis and, if so, to what extent they should do so.

In *Sanctuary*, as in contemporary hard-boiled and gangster fiction and film, the bedrocks of law and order come across as ineffectual and inherently prone to bureaucratic inertia and corruption. Bearing out this feature, Horace serves essentially a dual role as detective/attorney, mounting an awkward investigation to track down Temple and Popeye and then staging a misguided courtroom defense appealing to the highest ideals of justice at a time when the community is hastily casting them aside. Both endeavors contribute to a growing sense of dramatic irony, characterized by the fact that Horace seems doomed to failure for not recognizing, as the reader most certainly does, that Goodwin is being tried not in official court but in a court of public opinion driven by the vagaries of mob rule. Horace's opposing counsel in the trial, the district attorney Eustace Graham, presents an even more damning view of the justice system. As his courtroom antics demonstrate, Graham does not share Horace's belief in noble ideals, viewing the trial as a high-profile chance to advance his political career rather than a way for justice to prevail. Rounding out the representation of the ineffectual state is Senator Clarence Snopes, a member of the infamous Yoknapatawpha clan whose members consistently exhibit the basest elements of human nature. Senator Snopes takes belief in individual liberty to an extreme, stating as a matter of fact that "a man aint no more than human, what he does aint nobody's business but his" (1993: 187). The problem, of course, is that such a philosophy is not at all consistent with the values of public service that Snopes has sworn to uphold. True to form, Snopes first tries to use the information he gains about Temple's and Popeye's whereabouts in Memphis for his own political advantage, ignoring completely the value of the information to the ongoing investigation and thus the greater cause of justice. In this instance, Snopes makes good on his earlier promise to Horace: "I aint hidebound in no sense, as you'll find out when you get to know me better" (1993: 206). These representations align Faulkner with the practitioners of hard-boiled and gangster fiction and film. Their emphasis on paralysis and corruption in the state reflected the public mood at the onset of the Depression, as scores of citizens lost faith in traditional legal and political institutions to perform their basic duties – let alone to act decisively in restoring social order and ensuring stability.

Once the trial unfolds and the details of the rape emerge, *Sanctuary*'s critique of an ineffectual justice system shifts gears to register fear of crumbling social order and the resulting danger of mob rule. In another twist on the popular hard-boiled and gangster formulas, Faulkner adds an even greater distance between the reader and the outlaw by recounting the events of the trial and the escalation of mob violence from Horace's point of view. Although this decision moves Popeye to the margins of the narrative, he poses an equally serious threat to the cause of justice and the protection of the existing order. Popeye's disruptive influence renders the trial a parody of the justice system, rather than a model of its faithful execution. Initially unaware of this condition, Horace makes the critical mistake of believing that the agents of the state and the citizens of the community gathered to witness the spectacle share his view of the process. Horace's sense of justice is rooted ideologically in Southern codes of honor that prove hopelessly outmoded – a point made clear by his appeal to a higher power in assuring Ruby that "God may be foolish at times, but at least He's a gentleman" (1993: 280). However, with the unethical practices of Eustace Graham proving so formidable, Horace begins to recognize his gross error of judgment. For Horace, the increasing level of anxiety shapes his perception of the courtroom audience as a mob in formation – a congregation of gullible individuals undergoing fearful transformation into one mass expelling a "collective breath" (1993: 286). The veil of dramatic irony is lifted from Horace when

Temple arrives suddenly to testify. The mockery of Horace's beloved law becomes even more painful to watch, as the corrupt agent of the state, Eustace Graham, invokes and then perverts the Southern code of honor that Horace cherishes. Graham sets out to question Temple by calling to mind for the audience "that most sacred thing in life: womanhood" (1993: 284). Lighting the spark of vigilantism, Graham quotes the doctor who examined Temple and concluded the rape to be "no longer a matter for the hangman, but for a bonfire of gasoline" (1993: 284). When Temple subsequently commits perjury, carrying out the wishes of Popeye and condemning the innocent Goodwin in the process, any hope that Horace's value system might prevail is trampled in the inevitable abandonment of due process and the rush to mob rule that follow. Drawing on Michel Foucault's theory of the Panopticon, a space of control defined by the powers of surveillance employed by state agents and institutions, Jay Watson astutely defines the trial as bringing about a troubling reversal of authority: "Foucault's Panopticon is turned inside-out: the outlaw becomes its silent overseer, while the official representatives of law and the law-abiding are reduced to inmates, the inspected. Popeye has beaten the law at its own game" (1993: 63). Indeed, all that is left in the wake of Temple's shocking and false testimony is for Popeye's unscrupulous gangster ethos to wreak havoc in the streets, with the lynching of Goodwin thus signaling an end to civilization as Horace knows it.

In representing Popeye and the mob as examples of individual and collective extremism, Faulkner responds urgently to the process of ideological change under way in the context of Depression-era political debates about expanded state power. Consequently, *Sanctuary* exhibits a fundamental trait that Dennis Porter assigns to detective fiction when he notes that it "adapts itself easily to the changing objects of popular anxiety" (1981: 127). Along these lines, *Sanctuary* seems every bit as conflicted as American readers and moviegoers who consumed works from the hard-boiled and gangster genres with relish in the early thirties. On one level, the novel expresses frustration with a state apparatus that appears no longer capable of maintaining law and order and thus reflects a growing dissatisfaction with political leadership and state institutions. Through Popeye, however, Faulkner also exposes the dangers of individualism gone awry – a consequence of harsh circumstances transforming entrepreneurial spirit and personal initiative into insatiable greed and brutal violence. Further still, *Sanctuary* registers a high level of anxiety over the prospect of collectivism, figuring it in terms of an unruly and violent mob whose members surrender their individual liberty mindlessly. With the hope of restored order – of tracing "a logical pattern to evil" (1993: 221), as Horace puts it – in peril, Faulkner abruptly fills the vacuum of power with reassuring signs of state authority. The final section of the novel includes not only Popeye's arrest and subsequent public execution but also an exposition designed to give insight into the gangster's psychology, delivering assurances that Popeye's anti-social behavior can be managed. These features suggest in Faulkner the same apprehension felt by civic and religious groups that imagined the gangster craze translating into actual violence and social upheaval. These concerns led to the development of the Hays Office production codes, which grew increasingly more stringent from 1930 to 1934. From the outset, one of the stipulations was that gangsters receive their comeuppance in the end, preferably in a manner upholding received moral precepts and promoting a stable system of justice. Faulkner follows that guideline to a tee in *Sanctuary*, demonstrating a pragmatic confidence in the state to preserve and protect its citizens at a time of great urgency. As these early days of the Depression gave way to the New Deal and the subsequent emergence of the welfare state, however, this confidence would wane, only to be replaced by a chronic mistrust of the state and impassioned defenses of individual liberty that characterized Faulkner's later career.

Case Closed: Mapping Ideological Boundaries in *Intruder in the Dust*

The time between the publication of *Sanctuary* in 1931 and *Intruder in the Dust* in 1948 was eventful, to say the least. The influence of the New Deal proved to be significant in the aftermath of the Depression, putting to rest questions about whether its programs would remain intact. The expanded state power and central planning achieved during the latter half of the thirties enabled the transition to the vast military-industrial complex driving war mobilization and economic recovery. The seeds of social reform planted in the Depression started to sprout at this time as well, with calls for redressing racial inequality growing increasingly more vocal as the Civil Rights Movement drew closer. A movement to pass federal anti-lynching legislation that began in the mid-1930s gained momentum in the late 1940s. After a series of minor executive orders and much political deliberation, President Truman signed an executive order in 1948 forbidding racial discrimination in the military. This landmark decision was complemented by efforts to end segregation in the nation's public schools and institutions of higher learning – a set of related cases that would converge in the 1954 *Brown v. Board of Education* decision by the Supreme Court declaring an end to the longstanding practice of maintaining supposedly "separate but equal" schools divided along racial lines. With these signal developments, a picture emerged in the mid- to late forties of a federal government working actively to remove lines of distinction that had defined social relations for generations. Putting *Intruder in the Dust* in this context offers a compelling historical explanation of Faulkner's emphasis on the protection and transgression of boundaries – a thematic device for conveying the novel's political endorsement of individual liberty and local control as the most effective agents of social reform.

In *Intruder in the Dust*, as in *The Sound and the Fury*, Faulkner establishes the terms of social and political inquiry in the context of familial tragedy. As in *Sanctuary*, the tragedy in *Intruder in the Dust* stems from a shocking murder that poses an imminent threat to the rule of law in Yoknapatawpha. When Crawford Gowrie, a poor white man, murders his prosperous brother Vinson to cover up stealing from him and then pins the murder on Lucas Beauchamp, a poor man of mixed racial ancestry prone to defying social conventions, the false arrest predictably raises the specter of mob rule. The resulting instability works to define Faulkner's fictional locale once again as a site for timely reflection. In this endeavor, he returns to the genre of detective fiction, again drawing on its longstanding tradition of social and political commentary at the same time that he adapts basic conventions to his own ends. The most obvious variation on the standard detective story is the absence of a detective per se, with the role being filled in this case by a set of unlikely cohorts – the teenager Chick Mallison; Aleck Sander, the young son of the Mallisons' housekeeper; and Miss Habersham, an elderly town matriarch. Even more surprising than the diverse composition of this trio is their decision to act on Lucas's directive to Chick to exhume the recently buried body, which is wrongly presumed to be Vinson's. This bit of sleuthing constitutes the novel's most egregious breach of traditional boundaries – a violation not only of the geographical border separating the notoriously rough-and-tumble Beat Four from the rest of Yoknapa-tawpha County but also of the cultural taboos that mark gravesites as sacred spaces. As such, the exhumation is a symbolic act initiating one of the novel's central political themes: that the spirit of the law resides in private citizens who must take it upon themselves to guard it, even if doing so sometimes means defying the letter of the law and circumventing state authority.

Faulkner's use of the coming-of-age narrative to deliver the story from Chick's point of view adds thematic potency, though certainly not formal continuity. As Theresa M. Towner points out, "Faulkner opts . . . to balance the detective story with the *Bildungsroman*, and the tension between the two parallels the conflicting stories of the mystery" (2000: 53; see also Moreland 1997). This admixture of forms yields intriguing political implications, as Chick's foray into the detective business enables him to learn the details of the crime and cover-up and to gain insight into the machinations of law, politics, and social order. Not surprisingly, this construct has led critics to deem Chick Mallison, for better or worse, a literary descendant of Huckleberry Finn – another young boy occupying a social order that forces life's hard lessons to come prematurely (Schmitz 1997; Sundquist 1983: 149). For Chick, as for Huck, most of these lessons pertain to race relations, particularly in terms of the ideology of racial superiority that works to uphold rigid codes of social hierarchy. Chick's initial encounter with Lucas illustrates this feature, establishing their relationship as a mutually constructed ledger that records each interaction between them in units of broader social significance, tracks an ever-shifting set of exchanges, yet defers the prospect of reaching a balance. For Chick, the constant maintenance of this ledger produces a high degree of inner turmoil that drives him to view Lucas as a manifestation of the "white man's burden." The process of maturity is made all the more complicated by the competing influences acting on Chick – the laconic challenges to social conventions staged by Lucas and the verbose political pronouncements delivered by Chick's uncle, Gavin Stevens. With these alternatives delineating the boundaries of Chick's development, his journey toward discovery and knowledge – a staple of the *Bildungsroman* – becomes a contested space for defining the social and political conscience of the novel.

Since the earliest critical reception of *Intruder in the Dust*, Faulkner's depictions of Lucas and Gavin have provoked vigorous scholarly debate. Generally speaking, this exchange has centered on two issues: the extent to which Gavin speaks and acts on behalf of Faulkner and the extent to which Lucas is able to speak and act on his own behalf. On the first count, a longstanding view holds that Gavin is essentially a mouth-piece for Faulkner, delivering a sustained argument for Southern autonomy that renders *Intruder in the Dust* a manifesto against federal intervention on civil rights issues (Wilson 1948; Sundquist 1983: 149). This view has inspired pointed rebuttal, as demonstrated by Noel Polk's alternative interpretation highlighting Gavin's offputting rhetorical style and ultimately fixing on his pipe as a sure sign from Faulkner that the attorney "is largely blowing smoke" (1987: 133). As for the rendering of Lucas, Philip Weinstein makes the compelling case that his lack of voice and agency speaks volumes about the novel's limitations, exposing how it stubbornly reinforces the prerogatives of a dominant white culture inherently subjecting Lucas to confinement while granting freedom of movement, thought, and expression to Chick (1992: 75–81). Challenging this argu-ment, though, Towner submits that Faulkner's depiction of Lucas tests these very limits by imagining the possibility that the white community will respond to Lucas's call for justice (2000: 32). These critical exchanges reflect both the need to make sense of the novel's racial politics and the sense that such an understanding lies in the relationship between Gavin, who speaks more explicitly about current events than any other Faulkner character, and Lucas, whose perceived "intractable" nature provokes Gavin to do so. Indeed, these two figures do seem to embody the forces locked in the contextual politi-cal struggle that the novel engages. However, the key to comprehending the novel's position vis-à-vis this ongoing conflict lies in examining not only what these characters say and do – or are unable to say and do – but also the ideological boundaries that frame their negotiations with each other.

   One reason that Gavin's remarks prove troublesome for critics is because he obvi-ously strikes the pose of the authorial mouthpiece, only to deliver an entrenched message of Southern exceptionalism tinged with racism. Given Faulkner's ardent defense elsewhere of classical liberalism against the forces of progressive reform, Gavin does seem at times to be speaking on behalf of his creator. This mutual political con-viction is vividly on display, for example, in Gavin's statement that Southerners are in the process of "defending not actually our politics or beliefs or even our way of life, but simply our homogeneity from a federal government to which in simple desperation the rest of this country has had to surrender voluntarily more and more of its personal and private liberty in order to continue to afford the United States" (Faulkner 1975: 150). Subsequently, this assertive posturing turns hostile and overtly racist when Gavin con-templates the future of relations with "*Lucas: Sambo*" in the aftermath of a Southern social order upended by renewed federal involvement: "Lucas Beauchamp once the slave of any white man within range of whose notice he happened to come, now tyrant over the whole county's white conscience" (Faulkner 1975: 195). Here Gavin contemplates external pressure transforming the "white man's burden" from a force of obligation to one of oppression, with the terms of future negotiations duly reconfigured. But these outside influences, for the time being, remain just that: outside. The socially symbolic negotiations between Gavin and Lucas in the latter half of the novel, witnessed always by the young Chick, unfold in a narrative form that closes off the novel to conceptions of race relations incompatible with the ideological imperatives of the white power structure. Under these circumstances, it becomes abundantly clear that Gavin will deal with Lucas himself. Significantly, he sets about doing so "with all deliberate speed," to borrow the paradoxical phrase from the *Brown* decision. Assuming narrative dominance, Gavin delivers an extended monologue that performs the traditional task in detective fiction of exposing the details of the crime to signal restored social order. Moreover, his remarks include digressive attacks on federal encroachment and the numbing effects of consumerism that reveal a political agenda at work. When Lucas finally arrives to settle up with Gavin, their dealing sends the unmistakable symbolic message that their "business," as Gavin puts it, is between them (Faulkner 1975: 240). Lucas's request for a receipt, which leaves the novel open-ended, suggests that the negotiation will continue and that Gavin will remain engaged out of obligation. The ideological boundaries exposed here indicate that the path to greater understanding forged for Chick – and, by extension, for the reader – is actually a process of socialization and political persuasion. The crux of the argument defines the pursuit of authentic racial equality as a matter for individual conscience and local autonomy rather than for intruders looking to kick up some dust.

Yoknapatawpha, USA: Faulkner's Political Property

In an addendum to *Absalom, Absalom!* (1936), Faulkner stakes an unequivocal claim to one of the most valuable pieces of property in American culture. He does so in the form of a hand-sketched map of Yoknapatawpha County – rendered by the author himself – that bears the inscription: "William Faulkner, Sole Owner & Proprietor." Several years later, Faulkner reinforces the claim in one of his most often-cited interviews. Reflecting on the experience of writing *Sartoris* (1929), the first of his Yoknapatawpha novels, Faulkner describes the simple yet groundbreaking finding that "my own little postage stamp of native soil was worth writing about." He credits this breakthrough with leading him to discover that "by sublimating the actual into the apocryphal I would have complete liberty to use whatever talent I might have to its absolute top. It opened up a gold mine of other peoples, so I created a cosmos of my own" (1965: 255). Both statements reflect Faulkner's trademark flair for playful self-aggrandizement, but they also suggest striking parallels between intellectual property and private property, defining his fiction as a site where creative, personal, and political interests converge. As such, Faulkner's Yoknapatawpha is heavily influenced by the forces of ideological change working to forge the modern American welfare state under the increasingly assertive and accepted auspices of planned society. Seeking a level of autonomy and control not possible in the "actual," Faulkner turns to the "apocryphal" to plan his "cosmos" through a process of sublimation resistant to but also reliant on the close ties between fiction and social reality that his claims to ownership implicitly acknowledge. As an artistic and political space, Yoknapatawpha County stands as a bold and sustained alternative to the sort of oppressive state apparatus that Faulkner increasingly came to perceive as a threat to American individual liberty – from both domestic and foreign sources. When Faulkner arrived on the public stage, he most certainly came by way of Yoknapatawpha, developing in the process a staunch belief in the fundamental tenets of classical liberalism and a strong determination to defend them at every turn. In this context, Faulkner's fictional property is both an artistic enterprise and an agent of political idealism, performing much the same function that Faulkner assigns to the American Dream when he defines it as "a sanctuary on the earth for individual man: a condition in which he could be free not only of the old established closed-corporation hierarchies of arbitrary power which had oppressed him as a mass, but free of that mass into which the hierarchies of church and state had compressed and held him individually thrilled and individually impotent" (1965: 62).

Acknowledgment

An expanded version of this chapter's sections on *The Sound and the Fury* and *Sanctuary* appeared in my *Faulkner and the Great Depression: Aesthetics, Ideology, and Cultural Politics* (Athens, GA: University of Georgia Press, 2005).

References and Further Reading

Atkinson, T. (2005). *Faulkner and the Great Depression: Aesthetics, Ideology, and Cultural Politics.* Athens, GA: University of Georgia Press.

Bergman, A. (1971). *We're in the Money: Depression America and Its Films.* New York: Harper and Row.

Blotner, J. (1974). *Faulkner: A Biography.* 2 vols. New York: Random House.

Blotner, J. (1984). *Faulkner: A Biography.* One-vol. edn. New York: Random House.

Brinkley, A. (1998). *Liberalism and Its Discontents.* Cambridge, MA: Harvard University Press.

Faulkner, W. (1965). *Essays, Speeches, and Public Letters* (ed. J. B. Meriwether). New York: Modern Library.

Faulkner, W. (1975). *Intruder in the Dust.* New York: Vintage International. (Original pub. 1948.)

Faulkner, W. (1984). *The Sound and the Fury.* New York: Vintage. (Original pub. 1929.)

Faulkner, W. (1993). *Sanctuary: The Corrected Text* (ed. N. Polk). New York: Vintage International. (Original pub. 1931.)

Hanson, P. J. (1991–2). The Logic of Anti-Capitalism in *The Sound and the Fury. Faulkner Journal*, 7: 3–27.

Kennedy, D. M. (1999). *Freedom from Fear: The American People in Depression and War, 1929–1945.* New York: Oxford University Press.

Matthews, J. T. (2001). Whose America?: Faulkner, Modernism, and National Identity. In J. R. Urgo and A. J. Abadie (eds.). *Faulkner and America: Faulkner and Yoknaptawpha, 1998* (pp. 70–92). Jackson: University Press of Mississippi.

Meriwether, J. B. and M. Millgate (eds.) (1968). *Lion in the Garden: Interviews with William Faulkner, 1926–1962.* New York: Random House.

Moreland, R. C. (1997). Contextualizing Faulkner's *Intruder in the Dust*: Sherlock Holmes, Chick Mallison, Decolonization, and Change. *Faulkner Journal*, 12: 57–68.

Polk, N. (1987). Man in the Middle: Faulkner and the Southern White Moderates. In D. Fowler and A. J. Abadie (eds.). *Faulkner and Race: Faulkner and Yoknaptawpha, 1986* (pp. 130–51). Jackson: University Press of Mississippi.

Porter, D. (1981). *The Pursuit of Crime: Art and Ideology in Detective Fiction.* New Haven, CT: Yale University Press.

Rodgers, D. T. (1998). *Atlantic Crossings: Social Politics in a Progressive Era*. Cambridge, MA: Harvard University Press.

Schmitz, N. (1997). Faulkner and the Post-Confederate. In D. M. Kartiganer and A. J. Abadie (eds.). *Faulkner in Cultural Context: Faulkner and Yoknapatawpha, 1995* (pp. 241–62). Jackson: University Press of Mississippi.

Sundquist, E. J. (1983). *Faulkner: The House Divided*. Baltimore: Johns Hopkins University Press.

Thompson, A. R. (1932). The Cult of Cruelty. *Bookman*, 74: 477–87.

Towner, T. M. (2000). *Faulkner on the Color Line: The Later Novels*. Jackson: University Press of Mississippi.

Watson, J. (1993). *Forensic Fictions: The Lawyer Figure in Faulkner*. Athens, GA: University of Georgia Press.

Weinstein, P. (1992). *Faulkner's Subject: A Cosmos No One Owns*. New York: Cambridge University Press.

Williams, L. (1991). *American Liberalism and Ideological Change*. Dekalb: Northern Illinois University Press.

Williams, R. (1977). *Marxism and Literature*. Oxford: Oxford University Press.

Wilson, E. (1948). William Faulkner's Reply to the Civil Rights Program. *New Yorker*, October 23: 106–13.

14

Violence in Faulkner's Major Novels

Lothar Hönnighausen

Whether violence is "due to genetic formation" or "socially learned" (Kum-Walks 1995: 4), it seems inherent in human behavior and plays a central role in cultural life. Therefore, it comes as no surprise that such a keen observer of *Homo sapiens* as William Faulkner explored it in many of his works. In fact, violence and its ramifications seem to have occupied him so much that they warrant a rereading of his oeuvre in terms of this topic.

In literary studies, biological concepts of violence, relating it to "high levels of the androgenic hormone testosterone," are usually less useful than psychological and sociological categories such as "personal" and "community violence" (Kum-Walks 1995: 3) or "structural violence," the latter enabling us to assess how "economic and political structures place constraints on the human potential" (De Rivera 2003: 582). However, to recognize that Temple Drake in *Sanctuary* "exhibits the classic signs of a victim of sexual assault and rape, a dislocation from her body, self-accusation, emotional ties with her captor" (Eddy 1999: 23), or to identify McEachern's beating of his foster son Joe Christmas in *Light in August* as family violence and the violence of sheriff Butch in *The Reivers* as misuse of "violence in social control" (De Rivera 2003: 579), are only first steps toward a better understanding of Faulkner and those of his novels that most critics regard as major works. What matters in literature is not violence per se, but the writer's modes of rendering it.

Psychoanalytic and Sociological Imagery of Violence: *The Sound and the Fury* (1929)

The very title of *The Sound and the Fury*, taken from Shakespeare's *Macbeth* ("[Life's a tale] told by an idiot, full of sound and fury / Signifying nothing" [V.v. 26–8]), signals violence. Already in a key scene in the opening Benjy section, Caddy fights Jason, who has sadistically cut up Benjy's dolls, and the repetition of the words "fighting" and "fought" appear as a local leitmotif (Faulkner 1954: 79). There is more fighting in the Quentin section, although Quentin Compson is not a violent person. Nevertheless, he is the attacker in fights with Dalton Ames and Gerald Bland (p. 207). In both cases, he takes on idealistic roles, but in both cases he is no match for his opponent. In the attempted fight with Caddie's lover, Dalton Ames, he rather pointlessly tries to defend his sister's honor, assuming the posture of a Western hero ("I'll give you until sundown to leave town" [p. 198]). In the fight with Gerald Bland, Quentin is not only driven by his fascination with his sister but provoked by Bland's arrogant and cynical treatment of women (Bleikasten 1976; Bockting 1995).

The source of Quentin's idealism, of his infantile refusal to accept reality and of his fatal insistence on replacing it with a dream of virginity, is evoked in a psychoanalytic dream sequence. It shows him suffering from his mother's neglect (Weinstein 1989) and disconcerted by his father's ironic nihilism. Through very original psychoanalytic imagery Faulkner reveals how Quentin imagines Caddy breaking open their dungeon and whipping their indifferent parents, in a dramatic outburst of violence:

> When I was little there was a picture in one of our books, a dark place into which a single weak ray of light came slanting upon two faces lifted out of the shadow. *You know what I'd do if I were a King?* she never was a queen or a fairy she was always a king or a giant or a general *I'd break that place open and drag them out and I'd whip them good.* (Faulkner 1954: 215)

In contrast to Quentin's real or imagined scenes of violence, erupting only when psychic pressure overwhelms him, Jason's violence manifests itself as a permanent aggressiveness in the social sphere. His dominant impulse being violent resentment, he voices a whole host of contemporary prejudices from anti-Semitism and racism to chauvinism and misogyny: "'I have nothing against jews as an individual,' I says. 'It's just the race'" (p. 237); "Let these damn trifling niggers starve for a couple of years" (p. 237); "any damn foreigner, can come to this one" (p. 239); "Always keep [women] guessing. If you cant think of any way to surprise them, give them a bust in the jaw" (p. 240).

Faulkner masterfully dramatizes Jason's violence in his mad and frustrating pursuit of his niece Quentin, who has "robbed" him of the money that Caddy has sent him for Quentin and that he had been keeping as his own. The sheriff suspects as much, and therefore, to Jason's chagrin ("his sense of injury and impotence feeding upon its own sound, so that after a time he forgot his haste in the violent cumulation of his self justification and his outrage" [1954: 378]), proves less than helpful. Faulkner captures the intensity of Jason's mad rage by depicting him both as actually attacking a showman (whom he groundlessly suspects of being in league with Quentin's lover) and as imagining himself attacking people: "He thought of how he'd find a church at last and take a team and of the owner coming out, shouting at him and of himself striking the man down" (p. 381). Jason's imagined violence peaks in his grotesque vision of deposing the Almighty: "Dragging Omnipotence down from His throne" (p. 382).

At the end of the novel, we experience a final outburst of Jason's violence, revealing again the sociological nature of his characterization. Luster, driving the wagon as it approaches the town square, has forced the old mare Queenie to turn left instead of right, thereby upsetting her and making Benjy "bellow" (1954: 400). Jason, feeling acutely the family shame of having retarded Benjy Compson roar in the town square, savagely beats Queenie, Luster, and Ben and swings the horse to the right of the monument. When Queenie's feet begin to "clop-clop steadily" again, Benjy immediately stops roaring. By his violent intervention, Jason has restored "order" (p. 401), but he has broken the stalk of the flower in Benjy's hand.

Faulkner's Most Violent Novel: *Sanctuary* (1931)

Sanctuary is the only Faulkner novel in which violence has been recognized as a central theme by most critics, with feminist critics paying special attention to Temple Drake's rape (Werlock 1990; Toombs 1995; Eddy 1999). In addition to the several instances of rape that Temple Drake suffers at the hands of the sexually handicapped gangster Popeye, using a corncob and later his underling, Red, as sexual prostheses, there is also Lee Goodwin's homosexual rape before he is burned by the lynching mob. Popeye shoots Tommy and is also responsible for Red's shooting. While Lee Goodwin is in jail, we are given a gruesome account of how an African American murderer "slashed [his wife's] throat with a razor so that, her whole head tossing further and further backward from the bloody regurgitation of her bubbling throat, she ran out the cabin door and for six or seven steps up the quiet moonlit lane" (Faulkner 1993: 114). This murderer's execution is only mentioned in passing ("hung on a Saturday without pomp, buried without circumstance" [p. 131]), but we get a detailed description at the end of the novel of Popeye's execution and his inhuman aloofness.

It is intriguing to see that, apart from the razor murder, all violence revolves around Temple Drake (Bleikasten 1990: 235). Goodwin and the gangsters get into a fight over her (Faulkner 1993: 65, 72), and her presence is the focus of tensions and violence between Lee Goodwin and Ruby (p. 95). In her revelatory scene with Horace Benbow, she transforms her rape trauma – through psychoanalytic imagery – into a sadistic vision of an "iron belt in a museum" with "long sharp spikes," and says "I'd jab it all the way through him and I'd think about the blood running on me" (pp. 217–18). In a second novelistic development, in Horace's imagination, Temple's confessions fuse with his own guilt complex about his stepdaughter Little Belle, evoking in turn a male dream image of Temple's rape: "like a figure lifted down from a crucifix. She was bound naked on her back on a flat car moving at speed through a black tunnel, the blackness streaming in rigid threads overhead, a roar of iron wheels in her ears" (p. 223).

The choice of Horace Benbow, a sophisticated and morbid member of the Jefferson upper class, as the figure of reflection is another of Faulkner's means of deepening the nightmare of violence into a vision of disgust and evil. In view of "the evil, the injustice, the tears" (1993: 221) of the cynical trial, in which Goodwin is found guilty because of Temple Drake's false testimony and self-righteous Narcissa Benbow's intrigue with the ambitious district attorney, lawyer Benbow may well feel the need of an all-encompassing act of cleansing. But he is not the man to win justice for his client or stem the tide of corruption. While the district attorney perorates in lofty tones about "that most sacred thing in life: womanhood" (p. 284), the lynch mob is getting the gasoline cans ready. The violence in *Sanctuary* is the correlative of the failure of the upper class, of the Stevens, the Benbows, the Drakes – and the Falkners of Oxford.

Violence and Protestant Culture: *Light in August* (1932)

Light in August, the novel following *Sanctuary*, is hardly less violent, especially because of the violence Joe Christmas enacts, provokes, and eventually suffers (Pitavy 1982; Millgate 1987). But the character reflecting most deeply on violence as an essential trait of Southern culture is Rev. Gail Hightower, deducing as much from his own painful experience as from a Protestant inability or unwillingness to accept and integrate "pleasure, ecstasy," and "catastrophe" (Faulkner 1972b: 347). Instead of preaching sermons he has kept rehearsing his grandfather's military exploits in the Civil War, so that eventually his congregation ousts him (pp. 56–63). The same Southern obsession with the past makes him neglect his wife, who dies a violent death in Memphis (p. 61). Moreover, when he refuses to leave the town, he becomes himself the victim of violence, suffering a severe beating at the hands of the Ku Klux Klan (p. 66). No wonder that the organ strains appear to him "as if the freed voices themselves were assuming the shapes and attitudes of crucifixions, ecstatic, solemn, and profound" and as "demanding in sonorous tones death as though death were the boon, like all Protestant music" (p. 347). In regard to the religious roots of racial violence, we should note how Joanna Burden takes up the old pro-slavery argument derived from Genesis 9: 25 ("Cursed be Canaan [Cham]; a servant of servants shall he be unto his brethren"), although she follows it up with her own abolitionist rereading (p. 240).

The fatal repercussions of the ideology of racial violence are demonstrated by Joe's grandfather, Doc Hines, a religious madman persecuting him his whole life. In the case of the man-hunt led by the would-be Nazi Percy Grimm (1972b: 425) and the crowd in Mottstown, getting ready to lynch Christmas (p. 337), the religious excuses for violence are supplemented by right-wing political motives ("a belief that the white race is superior to any and all other races and that the American is superior to all other white races" [p. 426]). In his novel of 1932, Faulkner, like Sinclair Lewis in *It Can't Happen Here* (1935), was reading the signs of the time and seeing National-Socialist or Fascist tendencies not only in Germany and Italy but also in the US (Brinkmeyer 1993; Williamson 1993).

In presenting the genesis of Joe Christmas's violence, Faulkner worked with great care. Particularly revealing in terms of Joe's murder of Joanna Burden are the episodes showing his ill-fated attempts to come to understand the female body and his evolving misogyny. The depersonalized and hasty experience of sex with the black girl, "smelling the woman, smelling the negro all at once; enclosed by the womanshenegro and the haste, driven" (1972b:147), has a claustrophobic effect on Joe which Faulkner, compounding Joe's sexual and racial fears, captures in the daring neologism "womanshenegro" (p. 147). The scene ends not with sexual fulfillment but with an outburst of sadistic and desperate violence: "He kicked her hard, kicking into and through a choked wail of surprise and fear" (p. 147). Between this scene and Joe's encounter with Bobbie, Faulkner has interpolated two scenes which, in contrast to the realistic accounts of Joe's affairs with Bobbie and with Joanna Burden, emblematize through atavistic action and surrealist imagery complex masculine feelings of anxiety and loathing vis-à-vis the feminine: "He shot a sheep. Then he knelt, his hands in the yet warm blood of the dying beast" (p. 174); and "In the notseeing and the hardknowing as though in a cave he seemed to see a diminishing row of suavely shaped urns in moonlight, blanched. And not one was perfect. Each one was cracked and from each crack there issued something liquid, deathcolored and foul" (pp. 177–8).

While Joe's sexual experience with the anonymous black girl has the indefinite contours of puberty and myth, the encounter with the waitress and prostitute Bobbie is more personalized, although violence also overshadows this episode. "He struck her, without warning, feeling her flesh" (1972b: 186). After the ballroom scene, in which McEachern attacks her ("Away, Jezebel! Away, harlot!" [p. 191]) and Joe knocks him down with a chair, Bobbie leaves Joe in the hands of her boss Max and his thugs. Their violence is that of Memphis criminals who professionally beat up or kill people. In contrast, Joe's apparent killing of his adoptive father McEachern has an emancipatory character which Faulkner heightens by endowing his hero in the ensuing nocturnal ride with a Faustian, indeed demonic, aura: "The youth upon its back rode lightly, balanced lightly, leaning well forward, exulting perhaps at that moment as Faustus had" (p. 194).

We first learn of Joe's central act of violence, Joanna Burden's near beheading, through the countryman's grisly, crude account of his discovery of her body. But this shock is necessary to fully prepare us for the violence characterizing both their love and their parting. In this regard, the photographic realism and even the brutal black humor of the countryman's moralizing seem fitting:

> Her head had been cut pretty near off; a lady with the beginning of gray hair. . . . she was laying on her side, facing one way, and her head was turned clean around like she was looking behind her. And he said how if she could just have done that when she was alive, she might not have been doing it now. (1972b: 85)

As a consequence of Faulkner's innovative structuring of the novel, Joanna's gruesome icon hovers over the several episodes of Joe's prehistory, interpolated between the discovery of Joanna's murdered body (pp. 83–5) and the telling of their tragic love story (pp. 215–70). It is important to note that this love story is presented from Joe's perspective and that Joanna is very much Joe's male construct. Further, their encounters appear as male rape fantasies and, in a way, as homoerotic rape fantasies: "It was as if he struggled physically with another man" (pp. 221–2).

Eventually, Joe feels he must destroy the white woman who makes it impossible for him to continue his life as a split personality. When he enters her room with the deadly razor, she is waiting for him with an "old style, single action, cap-and-ball revolver" (1972b: 267). There is no hatred, but the sober realization that the end has come. When Grimm later kills and castrates Joe with a butcher knife, "he looked up at them with peaceful and unfathomable and unbearable eyes" (p. 439), and thanks to Faulkner's mannerist imagery, Joe's miserable death becomes an apotheosis: "the pent black blood seemed to rush like a released breath. It seemed to rush out of his pale body like the rush of sparks from a rising rocket; upon that black blast the man seemed to rise soaring into their memories forever and ever" (pp. 439–40).

Violence of Content and Violence of Expression: *Absalom, Absalom!* (1936)

In examining the treatment of violence in *Absalom, Absalom!*, "violence of content" refers to characters such as Thomas Sutpen, Rosa Coldfield, and Charles Etienne Bon and to events and acts such as the Civil War, the final conflagration of the Sutpen mansion, and above all, Henry Sutpen's murder of his half-brother Bon and Wash Jones's killing of Sutpen. "Violence of expression" is needed as a complementary term to refer to violence that manifests itself in the novel only through the several narrators and their stylistically very diverse retellings.

In the great opening of the novel, the two narrators, Rosa and Quentin, co-produce a Sutpen that has already some of the mythic violence with which Rosa later provides him so amply. However, as a consequence of the narrative situation – Rosa speaks as if Quentin is unfamiliar with Sutpen – Sutpen's violence remains rather subdued. Quentin sees Sutpen, the pioneer and founding figure of Southern plantation culture, emerge from Rosa's narration with operatic pizzazz, but also with a tinge of irony. The indications of Sutpen's violence ("thunderclap," "abrupt," "demon," "sulphur-reek," "wild niggers, like beasts" [Faulkner 1972a: 8]) are counterbalanced by narrative irony ("faint sulphur reek still in hair, clothes and beard" [p. 8]) and by parodic imagery ("a scene peaceful and decorous as a schoolprize water color" [p. 8]). Moreover, Sutpen is presented from a distance as in an allegorical or historical painting of "The Peaceful Conquest," as an equestrian statue imitating the pose and gesture of a Roman emperor or Renaissance condottiere ("Immobile, bearded and hand palm-lifted the horseman sat" [p. 8]). However, after we have been entertained for a time with this painterly and sculptural vision of Sutpen, Quentin imagines a sudden dynamization of the picture and, as in a movie, we witness an outburst of creative energy: "Quentin seemed to watch them overrun suddenly the square miles of tranquil and astonished earth and drag house and formal gardens violently out of the soundless Nothing" (pp. 8–9). A bit later

Rosa's phrasing is echoed in Quentin's ironic retelling of Sutpen's arrival and his creation of a plantation: "*It seems that this demon – his name was Sutpen – (Colonel Sutpen) – Colonel Sutpen. Who came out of nowhere and without warning upon the land with a band of strange niggers and built a plantation – (Tore violently a plantation, Miss Rosa Coldfield says) – tore violently*" (p. 9). Whether Sutpen "*dragged violently*" or "*tore violently*" his plantation "out of the soundless Nothing," he appears, in this passage, at the beginning of the novel, as a demiurge and in the romantic light of a foundation myth. *Violence* is here a concomitant of *creativity*, of the beginning of a new culture.

The greatness of *Absalom, Absalom!* lies partly in the way, throughout the novel, that this image comes to be dismantled and to be replaced by revisionist interpretations of what plantation culture really entailed. A powerful instrument in this process is Faulkner's disillusioned rewriting of one of the favorite Southern myths, that of the Civil War. In contrast to Margaret Mitchell's *Gone With the Wind*, also published in 1936, with its copious and grandiose pictures of the war, Faulkner's *Absalom, Absalom!* offers only snippets of it. However, these small particles of description, intensified through imagery like that of rape in the following example, reveal what the violence of the war and its disastrous end did to the Southern psyche: "the ultimate degradation to which war brings the spirit, the soul – into the likeness of that man who abuses from very despair and pity the beloved wife or mistress who in his absence has been raped" (1972a: 157).

No less important in Faulkner's analysis of Southern culture than his critical assessment of the Civil War are his probings of racial violence:

> You knew that you could hit them, he told Grandfather, and they would not hit back or even resist. But you did not want to, because they (the niggers) were not it, not what you wanted to hit; that you knew when you hit them you would just be hitting a child's toy balloon with a face painted on it, a face slick and smooth and distended and about to burst into laughing. (1972a: 230)

Through the overall rhetorical pattern ("*You* knew that *you* could. . . . But *you*"), the word repetition à la Hemingway ("hit"), and the image of a "child's toy balloon," Faulkner communicates Sutpen's frustrating awareness that personal violence against blacks, although possible, is a doubtful palliative for the hurt pride of whites of his class. Sutpen decides that the only way to escape the humiliations of poor whites is to become a plantation owner oneself, which will involve its own kind of violence (p. 246).

Quentin's Grandfather, retelling and soberly interpreting his friend Sutpen's Haiti adventure, serves as counterpoint to its excitements and Conradian ambience. While the luscious prose mirrors the wealth, danger, and brutality of the exotic world, the narrative stance provides a moral dimension in which violence appears as the concomitant and consequence of colonial exploitation: "A spot of earth which might have been created and set aside by Heaven itself, Grandfather said, as a theater for violence and injustice and bloodshed and all the satanic lusts of human greed and cruelty" (1972a: 250).

In contrast to the exoticized violence of the Haiti episode, Sutpen's violent second attempt to establish a plantation dynasty – despite the disastrous end of the Civil War and Henry's fratricide – has a desperate quality. Rosa Coldfield identifies Sutpen's mental violence in this final phase as "that cold alert fury of the gambler who knows that he may lose anyway" (1972a: 160). Her alliterative prose bordering on blank verse tends toward an all-encompassing metaphoricity, as when she expresses Sutpen's futile hopes through a kind of *metaphysical* shadow imagery. "He was a walking shadow. He was the light-blinded bat-like image of his own torment cast by the fierce demoniac lantern" (p. 171).

Corresponding with Rosa Coldfield's rhetorical violence is the book's structural violence, manifesting itself in a series of carefully arranged confrontation scenes. Particularly noteworthy in this regard are the several clashes between Rosa Coldfield and Clytie; the psychologically involved, incestuous scenes between the Sutpen siblings Henry, Judith, and Charles Bon (Irwin 1975); Henry's quarrel with his father (Faulkner 1972a: 99), and the fatal scene in which Sutpen – acting the biblical part of David – acknowledges and reinstalls Henry, but not his half-caste son Bon, as his Absalom: "Henry, Sutpen says – My son" (p. 353).

In terms of a psychoanalytical reading of violence, Henry's confrontations with his half-brother Bon (as imagined by Quentin and Shreve) constitute the thematic center of the novel. Particularly memorable is their encounter after the key scene between Sutpen and Henry. Their brotherly and homoerotic affection remains strong, but Bon is envious and bitter. As Bon will not desist from marrying Judith and Henry will not allow this, Bon offers Henry his pistol, "holding his pistol by the barrel, the butt extended toward Henry" (1972a: 357). However, at this stage, the act of violence remains only potential because Henry, overcome by his love, rejects Bon's self-sacrifice: "You are my brother" (p. 357). But Bon fails to respond in kind, answering challengingly: "No I'm not. I'm the nigger that's going to sleep with your sister. Unless you stop me, Henry" (p. 358). At this point, the painful tension of the scene, resulting from Henry's conflicting love of his half-brother Bon and of his sister Judith, escalates: "*Suddenly Henry grasps the pistol, jerks it free of Bon's hand stands so, the pistol in his hand, panting and panting*" (p. 358). The narrative irony of this scenic violence lies in the fact that the novel has already reported the murder in chapter 4 that is here in chapter 8 only being prepared and explained.

Because of the profound analogies and affinities between Quentin and Henry as lovers of their sister and problematic Southerners, we witness the most important act of violence in the novel, the fratricide, from Quentin's viewpoint: "It seemed to Quentin that he could actually see them, facing one another at the gate. . . . the two faces calm, the voices not even raised: *Dont you pass the shadow of this post, this branch, Charles; and I am going to pass it, Henry*" (1972a: 133). Faulkner renders the scene quite realistically, but he emphasizes its importance by envisioning it as a piece of sculpture ("as if cast by some spartan and even niggard hand from bronze" [p. 133]). The scene is liminal in a symbolical as well as physical sense. Henry, the white Sutpen son, denies his black half-brother and rival Bon access to the plantation as well as to Judith, the sister they both desire. The scene, in addition to being informed by the specific Southern theme of race, has also far-reaching archetypal implications, suggesting the motives of "the hostile brothers" as well as that of the "incestuous siblings" (Irwin 1975). However, the shooting death resolving the tension and ending this scene of high drama is not presented with the pathos one would expect. Instead, Wash Jones informs Rosa Coldfield of her nephew's murderous deed by bawling from his saddleless mule in the quiet street before her house: "Air you Rosie Coldfield? Then you better come on out yon. Henry has done shot that durn French feller. Kilt him dead as beef" (Faulkner 1972a: 133). The image ("dead as beef") brings the chapter and Sutpen's grand design of a plantation dynasty to a brutal and banal end.

Bon's death is arguably caused by Henry's incestuous desire as much as by Sutpen's (and his society's) adherence to his racist code and his lack of fatherly feelings. Sutpen's own death is the consequence of having mortally offended Wash Jones by abusing and then discarding his granddaughter when she failed to bear Sutpen a plantation heir. That Wash Jones kills Sutpen, whom he had elevated into a paternalistic icon ("on his black stallion, galloping about the plantation [. . . such that] for that moment Wash's heart would be quiet and proud" [p. 282]), means the end of his illusion that the self-made plantation aristocrat would ensure the superiority of poor whites over blacks. It also means the spurious, but historic alliance of poor whites and whites in power (Reed 1986).

The circumstances and murderous weapons of both violent deaths reflect the social status of the combatants. Henry confronts Bon on horseback and shoots him with his military pistol, whereas Wash Jones, like the rebellious farmers in the peasants' war of Luther's time, uses a rusty scythe, with Sutpen in vain defending himself with his horsewhip and appealing to his status: "Stand back. Dont you touch me, Wash" – "I'm going to tech you, Kernel" (Faulkner 1972a: 185). Finally, the two violent deaths in *Absalom, Absalom!* have different dramatic weight: Bon's death decides the fate of Sutpen's grand design and is thus structurally the most important event, while Sutpen's death only confirms his utter failure.

Violence in the World of the Rednecks: *The Hamlet* (1940)

As a consequence of Faulkner's increasingly ironic world-view, violence in *The Hamlet* does not have the radically evil quality pervading, for example, *Sanctuary*. Further, the roots of violence in *The Hamlet* are, above all, socio-economic, not as psychological in the Freudian sense as in *The Sound and the Fury* or *Light in August*. This becomes apparent in the scene in which Ratliff, the sewing-machine merchant, observes Ab Snopes plowing with two mules he knows as Varner's. He reflects with bitter irony that Will Varner owns not only the mules, but – as a consequence of the exploitative sharecropping system – also the man working with them (Kirwan 1951). The description of Ab Snopes's "needless violence" and "senseless savageness" (Faulkner 1956: 48) in handling the mules reveals the tragic potential of this humorous novel and shows how much the modernist of *The Sound and the Fury* (Moreland 1990) has become the engagé author of the "hungry thirties." This is confirmed by the novel's most dramatic act of violence, Mink Snopes's murder of the yeoman farmer, Jack Houston, which also has socio-economic causes. The quarrel has arisen because Mink Snopes, one of Varner's sharecropping tenant farmers, with the sly parasitism of the indigent, lets a young heifer of his graze with Houston's cattle in the erroneous hope that Houston will not notice or mind.

What distinguishes the murder-scene in *The Hamlet* from comparable ones in ordinary crime fiction is the fact that Faulkner presents it first from Houston's and then from Mink's viewpoint, exploring two different mental responses to the same event. In Houston's case, he seeks to render the peculiar activity of perception and imagination in the moments before death. The language he creates for this purpose is so pliable that it can accommodate metaphorizing self-observation ("watching the ravelled and shattered ends of sentience and will projecting into the gap" [1956: 217]) and vivid allegorization ("saw the pain blast like lightning across the gap") as well as direct speech, first to himself ("Wait, wait, he said. Just go slow first") and then, irritated and arrogant, to Mink ("couldn't you even borrow two shells, you fumbling ragged –").

The beginning of chapter 2 of this section is no less impressive. The narrator, assuming Mink's perspective, opens the passage with dramatic word repetitions: "That shot was too loud. It was not only too loud for any shot, it was too loud for any sound, louder than any sound needed to be" (1956: 218). Then, employing cognitive, moral, and legal concepts, he extends the frame of reference and prepares for Mink's final heroization ("It was as though the very capacity of space and echo for reproducing noise were leagued against him too in the vindication of his rights and the liquidation of his injuries" [p. 218]).

Like Mink Snopes, Labove, law student and schoolteacher in Frenchman's Bend, comes from a hillbilly family of poor dirt farmers, but his violence and its cultural context are of an altogether different kind (Kirwan 1951; Reed 1986). "He says he wants to be Governor" (1956: 105). In fact, Labove represents the growing social and political ambitions of poor whites. He gets into trouble when he attacks his student Eula Varner, with whom he is madly in (some kind of) love, "as if she had a football or as if he had the ball and she stood between him and the final white line which he hated and must reach" (p. 121). Eula is neither shocked nor afraid, but, being a semi-mythic embodiment of female power as well as a schoolgirl, "she managed to free one of her arms, the elbow coming up hard under his chin," and "her other hand struck him a full-armed blow in the face" (p. 121). The grotesque melee is important in illustrating how the element of violence plays a major role in Faulkner's treatment of gender relations: "'That's it,' he said. 'Fight it. Fight it. That's what it is: a man and a woman fighting each other. The hating. To kill, only to do it in such a way that the other will have to know forever afterward he or she is dead'" (p. 121). The furious wrestling of Labove and Eula – what in the humorous context of *The Hamlet* appears as "a priapic hulla-balloo" (p. 121) – is caused by a peculiarly Manichaean, ascetic, and self-destructive quality accompanying sexuality in the particular American culture in which Labove has grown up and which Faulkner was among the first to explore: "He continued to hack in almost an orgasm of joy at the dangling nerves and tendons of the gangrened member" (p. 120). That Labove's is not merely a personal psychological problem, but one arising from the puritan culture of the American South – Faulkner himself speaks of "the light precarious balance, the actual overlapping, of Protestant religious and sexual excitement" (p. 128) – is confirmed by the peculiar, hateful attraction between Mink Snopes and his wife ("It's like drink. It's like dope to me" [p. 221]; "Because when they come to hang you, I'm going to be where I can see it" [p. 220]).

What makes *The Hamlet* so much more important a book than a previous generation of critics, identifying Faulkner chiefly as the modernist master of *The Sound and the Fury* and *Absalom, Absalom!*, seem to have realized is its immense scope. Besides this last scene of family violence in the depressed rural South of the thirties (Jehlen 1976), it comprises the cosmic violence of the imagery in the "Ike Snopes and the Cow" episode, as well as the "purposeless violence" of Flem Snopes's Texan ponies (Faulkner 1956: 286) and Mink's eerie fight with Houston's hound.

Obviously, violence in *The Hamlet*, a watershed in Faulkner's oeuvre, plays a less prominent role and functions differently than in his previous fiction, notably in *Sanctuary* or *Light in August*. The crash on a wooden bridge "just wide enough for a single vehicle" (1956: 303) between one of the ponies and Tull's mule wagon is one of several examples in which Faulkner uses violence as a constituent of a comic genre scene. He gives grotesque features to the horse that suddenly interrupts the sleepy journey of Tull and his folks as well as to its victims: the horse behaves "like a mad squirrel" that moves "as if it intended to climb into the wagon," flings Tull backward "among the overturned chairs and exposed stockings and undergarments of his women" (p. 304), and gallops off again "while the five women shrieked about Tull's unconscious body" (p. 304). The punch line is Eck Snopes's: "Which way'd he go?" he said (p. 304).

Equally funny is the scene in which Will Varner and his wife respond to the fact that their daughter Eula is pregnant. We experience this scene, potentially one of family violence, as a comic genre painting. The narrator has an eye for authentic regional color and humorously tells us that Mrs. Varner's main concern is that Jody with his yelling and Eula with getting pregnant have disturbed her afternoon nap ("in a loose old wrapper and the lace boudoir cap in which she took her afternoon naps" [1956: 141]) and that she is fetching a stick of stove wood to fix both of them. With Will Varner's sardonic remark ("'All right,' Varner said. 'Go and get it'" [p.142]) and the grotesque image of her being "sucked violently out" the door, the scene comes to an effective close: "She went out; she seemed to have been sucked violently out of the door by her own irate affrontment" (p. 142).

The Violence of the Plantation System: *Go Down, Moses* (1942)

This new coexistence of violence and humor also characterizes *Go Down, Moses* (1942). Before the sexual violence and racial guilt of the founding father are revealed, we are amused by the tall-tale humor of "Was." Inversely, a flashback in the tragicomic story of Lucas Beauchamp's treasure hunt and divorce problem ("The Fire and the Hearth") presents the dramatic confrontation between Lucas and his white relative Zack Edmonds. In this violent scene ("I dont need no razor. My nekkid hands will do. Now get the pistol under your pillow"[Faulkner 1973: 53]), Lucas demands that his wife Molly return to him. For Lucas, the conflict between himself and his white relative is complicated by the guilty past, the founding father's sexual abuse of his slaves: Old Lucius Quintus Carothers McCaslin had raped not only his slave Eunice but also his and her daughter Tomasina, whose son Turl is Lucas's father (Sundquist 1983).

In "Pantaloon in Black," the violence of the black sawmill worker Rider – in killing both the white night watchman Birdsong and, eventually, himself – arises from his grief and derailment ("Ah'm snakebit. Ah kin pass wid anything" [1973: 153]) at his wife's death. When he discovers Birdsong's second pair of dice and the night watchman tries to draw his pistol, Rider's reaction is fast and deadly. "In the second before the half-drawn pistol exploded he actually struck at the white man's throat not with the blade but with a sweeping blow of his fist, following through in the same motion so that not even the first jet of blood touched his hand or arm" (pp. 153–4).

In contrast to the burlesque character of the opening tale "Was" and the tragic dignity of "Pantaloon in Black," the concluding title story, "Go Down, Moses," is a humorous account of the humane and comic attempt of county attorney Gavin Stevens and local newspaper editor Wilmot to keep the criminal past of Butch Beauchamp from his grandmother Mollie Beauchamp and to see to it that his body, arriving by train from Chicago, is buried with dignity. The humor of the story "works" only against the background of past violence – Butch's portrait before his execution in Chicago.

While stories like "Go Down, Moses" or "Pantaloon in Black" focus on particular cases of violence in race relations, "The Bear" treats the complex historical and moral context of plantation culture from which such particular acts arise. It comes as a shock to the young kinsmen Ike and Cass when they finally figure out what the cryptic entries in the plantation ledgers of their family mean. From Ike's Manichaean standpoint the whole land is cursed (1973: 298), because the violence of slavery corrupts everything:

> The whole plantation in its mazed and intricate entirety – the land, the fields and what they represented in terms of cotton ginned and sold, the men and women whom they fed and clothed . . . the machinery and mules . . . that whole edifice intricate and complex and founded upon injustice and erected by ruthless rapacity and carried on even yet with at times downright savagery not only to the human beings but the valuable animals too. (p. 298)

Humor and Violence: *The Reivers* (1962)

Most critics duly acknowledge the humor in Faulkner's last novel, *The Reivers* (1962), while they tend to ignore its violence. However, since violence is plentiful in the book and essential to its specific humor, we ought to assess how it functions and how violence and humor in their interaction affect the reader. In fact, the hero and narrator, Lucius Priest, starts his reminiscence with the account of a quarrel among the drivers at his father's livery stable leading to a shooting incident. Boon Hogganbeck, the part-Chickasaw factotum of the firm, is incensed at the unreliability and snottiness of Ludus, a black driver, and, pursuing him into the square, fires five shots at him. This bare account of the action leaves no doubt about its violence but fails to do justice to the attraction and achievement of the story. What the reader enjoys is watching humor interfere with the impact of violent action.

That we should also expect a sophisticated initiation story becomes clear from the reflections of the hero on his tutor and on himself. "He was six feet four inches tall and weighed two hundred pounds and had the mentality of a child; . . . any moment now I would outgrow him" (Faulkner 1962: 19). The narrator's ironic discourse on virtue (p. 52), with parodic allusions to Faustus (p. 60) and to a pact with Satan (p. 66), confirms that morality – tempered by humor – is a major issue of the book. In the course of the Memphis adventure, Lucius is subjected to a complex initiation experience in which he loses his innocence and is subjected to a shattering experience of evil. Its representative is Otis, a boy of Lucius's age, but a Mephistophelean and grotesque figure. Lucius characterizes him through two major leitmotifs: "He was not even as big as me but there was something wrong with him" (p. 106), and "But Otis looked like two or three years ago he had already reached where you wont be until next year, and since then he had been going backward" (p. 141). Contrasting with Otis's age and his strangely stunted and wizened appearance (p. 157) is his "worldly wisdom" and his experience, especially with regard to making money through voyeuristic sex and the exploitation of women like Lucius's idol, Corrie.

In a strange night-time episode, in which Lucius has to share "a mattress made up into a bed" (1962: 153) with Otis ("with the moon-shaped window lying across mine and Otis's legs" [p. 154]), he feels not only that something is wrong with Otis, but also that "suddenly there was something wrong with me too" (p. 154). This is the situation in which he is exposed to Otis's reflections on sex as a commercial proposition, which the latter presents with cynical detachment and in the tone of a jaded professional.

To express his shock and disgust at Otis's sinister initiation, Lucius, the narrator, employs images of violence: "Because you should be prepared for experience, knowledge, knowing: not bludgeoned unaware in the dark as by a highwayman or footpad" (1962: 155). He emphasizes that his first reaction was still the regression of a child ("I wanted my mother" [p. 155]) and stresses his inability to mentally and psychologically cope with the experience that Otis, the "*demon-child*" (p. 157), forces on him: "I had nowhere to put it, no receptacle, pigeonhole prepared yet to accept it without pain and lacerations" (p. 155). The consequence of Lucius's frustration is his sudden outbreak of violence, its intensity suggesting that it proceeds from shock and the denial of the evil world that Otis represents: "Standing now, I was hitting him, so much to his surprise (mine too) that I had had to stoop and take hold of him and jerk him up within reach . . . not just to hurt him but destroy him" (p. 157).

In contrast to Lucius's open violence, Otis's is insidious: "Only then did I see the blade of the pocketknife in his fist . . . I never felt the blade at all; when I flung the knife away and hit him again, the blood on his face I thought was his" (1962: 157–8). Sensitive readers will associate Lucius's wound with his psychic injury, a tragic but inevitable concomitant of the maturing process. However, in the context of the narrative, it is celebrated as a badge of honor won in Lucius's chivalrous fight on Miss Corrie's behalf. In his idealistic admiration of her, Lucius seems a descendant of Gavin Stevens. The relationship of an 11-year-old boy and a prostitute who reforms because he believes in her is one of those impossible topics that only somebody like the late Faulkner could dare to tackle. How he manages to do this can be seen from the following passage, in which Miss Corrie thanks her "champion." For one thing, the phrasing is deceptively simple and direct, but what makes Miss Corrie's moral resolve aesthetically effective is the insertion into the idealistic context of her comic reference to the realities of her past life: "I've had people – drunks – fighting over me, but you're the first one ever fought for me. I aint used to it, you see. That's why I dont know what to do about it" (pp. 159–60).

One of the reasons why *The Reivers* is among Faulkner's underestimated books, is that most critics have not paid much attention either to Lucius's exposure to the specifically sexual kind of evil that Otis represents, or to the way Lucius's chivalrous violence is related to the violent abuse of legal power. As demonstrated by Sheriff Butch's treatment of African Americans, but also of the white prostitute, Miss Corrie, political violence in *The Reivers* is largely, but not exclusively, racial violence. The narrator registers not only Sheriff Butch's threatening and arrogant behavior vis-à-vis adult African Americans like Uncle Parshham and Ned, whom he addresses as "boys," but also their angry reaction, including Uncle Parsham's ironic double entendre: "'We all knows you here, Mr. Butch,' Uncle Parsham said with no inflection whatever" (1962: 172), and Ned's courageous answer to the constable: "'There's somewhere you stops.' The constable became completely motionless" (p. 243).

In addition to these direct confrontations, *The Reivers* explores the psychological aspect of political violence. Ned's ironic explanation of Sheriff Butch's abuse of his legal power as the result of a deferred childhood dream ("that pistol, that likely all the time he was a little boy, he wanted to tote" [1962: 185]) is a brilliant example of this. The subtle humor in this passage arises from the contrast between the folksy language and the level of its analytic sophistication. Similarly, in revealing the psychological ramifications of political violence, Faulkner employs the voice of the young Lucius because through that voice he can more naïvely, and more movingly, express how, in his frustrating powerlessness, Lucius transformed his hatred against his oppressor into hatred of himself and his friends. "Hating all of us for being the poor frail victims of being alive, having to be alive" (p. 174). Overtaxed by the situation, Lucius first gives in to a regression, but then acknowledges there is no turning back and shows that he is indeed growing up and will learn to cope with political violence. "Because I couldn't [turn back] now. It was too late. Maybe yesterday, while I was still a child, but not now. I knew too much, had seen too much. I was a child no longer now" (p. 175).

Whether we think of Lucius Priest's fierce attack on Otis or of Quentin Compson's fights against Dalton Ames and Gerald Bland, these acts of violence help Faulkner reveal the complex psychology of puberty. Often the psychological aspects of violence interrelate with sociological or racial factors, as can be seen in novels as diverse as *Light in August, Absalom, Absalom!*, and *Go Down, Moses.* Throughout his career Faulkner remains fascinated both by individual cases and by recurring patterns of racial or class violence, and by historical and contemporary manifestations of family and mob violence. While in the novels from 1929 to 1936 violence manifests itself primarily in tragic contexts, this changes with *The Hamlet* (1940) and several of the following novels that are inspired by his ironic world-view. Faulkner's sense of the ineradicability of violence remains, but in the Snopes trilogy, as in *Go Down, Moses* and *The Reivers,* he foregrounds the interplay of violence and humor. What seems to attract him most throughout his career is to closely observe and capture in new narrative structures and innovative language precise pictures of the violence he has seen or imagined. Even in *Sanctuary,* however, violence does not proceed from mere sensationalism, but serves to embody a very complex threat of evil. Similarly, the painfully precise description of Joanna's murdered body in *Light in August* or of Rider's deadly use of his razor in "Pantaloon in Black" fulfill particular thematic functions. The scope of Faulkner's explorations of violence is as wide as his novelistic world. Only by readjusting our perspective for each of his major novels, can we hope to do justice to his infinite variety.

References and Further Reading

Bleikasten, A. (1976). *Faulkner's Most Splendid Failure: Faulkner's* The Sound and the Fury. Bloomington and London: Indiana University Press.

Bleikasten, A. (1990). *The Ink of Melancholy: Faulkner's Novels from* The Sound and the Fury. Bloomington and Indianapolis: Indiana University Press.

Blotner, J. (1974). *Faulkner: A Biography.* 2 vols. London: Chatto and Windus.

Blotner, J. (1984). *Faulkner: A Biography.* One-vol. edn. New York: Random House.

Bockting, I. (1995). *Character and Personality in the Novels of William Faulkner: A Study in Psychostylistics.* Lanham and New York: University Press of America.

Brinkmeyer, R. H., Jr. (1993). Fascism, the Democratic Revival, and the Southern Writer. In L. Hönnighausen and V. G. Lerda (eds.). *Rewriting the South: History and Fiction* (pp. 244–50). Tübingen: Franke.

Eddy, C. (1999). The Policing and Proliferation of Desire: Gender and the Homosocial in Faulkner's *Sanctuary. Faulkner Journal* 14: 21–39.

Faulkner, W. (1954). *The Sound and the Fury.* New York: Random House/Vintage. (Original pub. 1929.)

Faulkner, W. (1956). *The Hamlet.* New York: Random House/Vintage. (Original pub. 1940.)

Faulkner, W. (1962). *The Reivers.* New York: Random House/Vintage.

Faulkner, W. (1972a). *Absalom, Absalom!* New York: Random House/Vintage. (Original pub. 1936.)

Faulkner, W. (1972b). *Light in August.* New York: Random House/Vintage. (Original pub. 1932.)

Faulkner, W. (1973). *Go Down, Moses.* New York: Random House/Vintage. (Original pub. 1942.)

Faulkner, W. (1981). *Sanctuary: The Original Text* (ed. with afterword and notes by N. Polk). New York: Random House. (Original pub. 1931.)

Faulkner, W. (1985). *Novels 1930–1935* (eds. J. Blotner and N. Polk). New York: Library of America.

Faulkner, W. (1990). *Novels 1936–1940* (eds. J. Blotner and N. Polk). New York: Library of America.

Faulkner, W. (1993). *Sanctuary.* New York: Random House/Vintage International. (Original pub. 1931.)

Faulkner, W. (1994). *Novels 1942–1954* (eds. J. Blotner and N. Polk). New York: Library of America.

Faulkner, W. (1999). *Novels 1957–1962* (eds. J. Blotner and N. Polk). New York: Library of America.

Geen, R. G. (1994). Violence. In V. S. Ramachandran (ed.). *Encyclopedia of Human Behavior.* Vol. 4 (pp. 459–67). San Diego: Academic Press.

Gray, R. (1994). *The Life of William Faulkner: A Critical Biography.* Oxford and Cambridge, MA: Blackwell.

Hönnighausen, L. (1997). *Faulkner: Masks and Metaphors.* Jackson: University Press of Mississippi.

Irwin, J. T. (1975). *Doubling and Incest/Repetition and Revenge.* Baltimore: Johns Hopkins University Press.

Jehlen, M. (1976). *Class and Character in Faulkner's South.* New York: Columbia University Press.

Kirwan, A. C. (1951). *Revolt of the Rednecks: Mississippi Politics, 1876–1925.* Lexington: University Press of Kentucky.

Kum-Walks, D. A. (1995). Are We Trained to Be Violent? A Look at Gender-Bias and Violent Images in Popular Culture through Selected Theories of Violence. In W. Wright and S. Kaplan (eds.). *The Image of Violence in Literature, the Media, and Society* (pp. 2–10). Pueblo, CO: Society for the Interdisciplinary Study of Social Imagery, University of Southern Colorado.

Materassi, M. (2004). *Faulkner, Ancora.* Bari: Palomar Athenaeum.

Millgate, M. (1987). *New Essays on Light in August.* Cambridge: Cambridge University Press.

Moreland, R. C. (1990). *Faulkner and Modernism: Rereading and Rewriting.* Madison: University of Wisconsin Press.

Pitavy, F. (ed.) (1982). *William Faulkner's* Light in August: *A Critical Casebook.* New York and London: Garland.

Reed, J. S. (1986). *Southern Folk, Plain and Fancy: Native White Social Types.* Athens: University of Georgia Press.

De Rivera, J. (2003). Aggression, Violence, Evil and Peace. In I. B. Weiner (ed.). *Handbook of Psychology.* Vol. 5 (pp. 569–98). Hoboken, NJ: John Wiley.

Sundquist, E. (1983). *Faulkner: The House Divided.* Baltimore: Johns Hopkins University Press.

Toombs, V. M. (1995). Deconstructing Violence Against Women: William Faulkner's *Sanctuary* and Alice Walker's *Possessing the Secret of Joy.* In W. Wright and S. Kaplan (eds.). *The Image of Violence in Literature, the Media, and Society* (pp. 212–17). Pueblo, CO: Society for the Interdisciplinary Study of Social Imagery, University of Southern Colorado.

Weinstein, P. M. (1989). "If I Could Say Mother": Constructing the Unsayable about Faulknerian Maternity. In L. Hönnighausen (ed.). *Faulkner's Discourse* (pp. 3–15). Tübingen: Niemeyer.

Werlock, A. (1990). Victims Unvanquished: Temple Drake and Women Characters in William Faulkner's Novels. In K. A. Ackley (ed.). *Women and Violence in Literature: An Essay Collection* (pp. 3–49). New York and London: Garland.

Williamson, J. (1993). *William Faulkner and Southern History.* New York and Oxford: Oxford University Press.

Zacharasiewicz, W. (ed.) (1993). *Faulkner, His Contemporaries and His Posterity.* Tübingen: Francke.

Zender, K. (1989). *The Crossing of the Ways: William Faulkner, the South, and the Modern World.* New Brunswick, NJ: Rutgers University Press.

15

An Impossible Resignation: William Faulkner's Post-Colonial Imagination

Sean Latham

When *Absalom, Absalom!* appeared in 1936, William Faulkner's readers were greeted with something unexpected: a handsome fold-out page in the novel's endpapers containing a map of the fictional Yoknapatawpha County. Printed in red and black ink, it carefully delineates in Faulkner's small, neat handwriting the location of key spaces for the novel, ranging from the "Fishing Camp where Wash Jones killed Sutpen, later bought and restored by Major Cassius de Spain" to "Miss Rosa Coldfield's" house (Faulkner 1936: n.p.). Far more than a decorative appendix to the novel, this document constructs a visual synthesis of Faulkner's earlier fictions. Sartoris's railroad dominates the space as do the tiny squares identifying the homes and landmarks vital to *Light in August* (1932), *The Sound and the Fury* (1929), and *As I Lay Dying* (1930). Indeed, the spaces most powerfully charged with meaning in the fictional world of *Absalom, Absalom!* – Kentucky, Haiti, and New Orleans – are missing entirely, as if Faulkner were somehow trying to constrain the vast and terrifying reach of the novel within the imaginative lands bound by the Yoknapatawpha and Tallahatchie rivers. This cartographic passion would seize Faulkner again a decade later when he prepared a second map for the *Viking Portable Faulkner* (1946), an edited collection of works that, unlike *Absalom, Absalom!*, is much more narrowly focused on Jefferson and Yoknapatawpha. Faulkner produced the first of these two maps in an attempt to preserve the integrity of his fictional world – including its stubborn resistance to readerly orientation. While working steadily on the manuscript of *Absalom, Absalom!*, he had a sense that he was reaching the very apex of his imaginative powers, but Harrison Smith, his editor at Random House, worried about the potential incoherence of the narrative and began to send a string of requests for revision (see Blotner 1974: 937). Seeking to short-circuit such concerns, Faulkner decided to create an appendix to the text containing capsule biographies of the major characters, a brief timeline, and the map itself. Neither a summary nor a part of the diegesis, it is an odd, idiosyncratic document that testifies to the intensity of Faulkner's imaginative capabilities while sustaining a vital strand of realism threaded through the novel's narrative experiments.

More than just an attempt to ward off editorial intervention, however, this map and its 1946 counterpart frame the boundaries of a vital constellation of texts in which Faulkner begins to grapple with the interlinked issues of space, ownership, and identity. In the decade spanned by creation of the two maps, Faulkner begins what will prove to be a transformative engagement with the aftermath not of the Civil War, but of the original colonization of the Americas. Quentin Compson, at the end of *Absalom, Absalom!*, cries out to his Canadian roommate Shreve in the cold Massachusetts night that he does not hate the South (Faulkner 1990a: 303). The sheer gothic horror of Thomas Sutpen's tireless pursuit of a white male heir drives the young student to a despair that nevertheless cannot be translated into disavowal. Unable to escape the past yet incapable of squaring the ideology of the Southern gentleman with the horrors and contradictions of slavery, Quentin finds himself at a subjective impasse arguably more damning than that which precipitates his suicide in *The Sound and the Fury*. The final unraveling of the Sutpen family genealogy brings *Absalom, Absalom!* to an ambiguous close, the novel, its characters, and its readers all still haunted by the incomprehensible wail of Jim Bond that encodes what I have elsewhere called an "inarticulate . . . record of the shared violence that inhabits Euro-American modernity" (Latham 1998: 463). Both this novel and Faulkner's own larger project reach a vital impasse in Quentin's refusal to disavow the South whose painful narrative ends in this ideological and psychic disaggregation. Faulkner scholars have, by and large, seen only tragedy in the *agon* of a South that can be neither renounced nor embraced, neither destroyed nor redeemed. It is populated by figures like Charles Bon, Quentin Compson, Joe Christmas, and Rider, all of whom are killed precisely because they are torn asunder by this tragic contradiction and ensnared in "*the maelstrom of unbearable reality*" (Faulkner 1990a: 186). The only consolation these texts appear to offer are those Faulkner himself describes in a 1941 letter to Warren Beck: "I have been writing all the time about honor, truth, pity, consideration, the capacity to endure well grief and misfortune and injustice and then endure again, in terms of individuals who observed and adhered to them not for reward but for virtue's sake" (cited in Blotner 1974: 1081). In what Philip Weinstein compellingly calls "a cosmos no one owns," all that remains is either the deluded suicide of a character like Quentin or the mute endurance of the black characters (Weinstein 1992: 2).

Faulkner's potent sense of tragedy cannot be disputed, but this chapter will argue that the tools of post-colonial theory and criticism, while not perfectly adapted to the task, nevertheless offer a fundamentally new optic for viewing the *agon* of the American South. More narrowly, they allow us to see Faulkner's work – particularly in the period stretching from roughly the completion of *Absalom, Absalom!* to the publication of the *Portable Faulkner* – from a perspective skewed not by tragedy but by a liberating impulse to escape the anguish of a South turned hopelessly inward on itself. This new optic, which emerges with startling clarity in *Go Down, Moses*, is no longer focused so obsessively on the trauma of the white, Southern male, but instead attempts to take the measure of what Edward Said, in *Culture and Imperialism*, calls "overlapping territories" (Said 1994: 3). It is no accident, I shall argue, that Faulkner not once but twice provides a map of Yoknapatawpha County in this period, as he too becomes fascinated by what

Said identifies as the distinctly post-colonial attempt "to rechart and then occupy the place in imperial cultural forms reserved for subordination, to occupy it self-consciously, fighting for it on the very same territory once ruled by a consciousness that assumed the subordination of a designated inferior Other" (Said 1994: 210). Drawing explicitly on a cartographic metaphor, Said offers here a model for negotiating the contradictions that novels like *The Sound and the Fury* and *Light in August* imagine only as tragedy. As Faulkner turned his attention both to the narratives of black characters like Lucas Beauchamp and to the more profound questions of ownership, inheritance, and disavowal in *Go Down, Moses*, he begins to map and remap the same space from a series of different perspectives. This essentially cartographic endeavor extends throughout his fiction and into the appendices, creating not the nihilism of a cosmos no one owns, but the rich multiplicity of a cosmos too diversely owned. Ultimately, this vision of plenitude proves too daunting for Faulkner, the complex palimpsests of even his own Yoknapatawpha County threatening to overwhelm its coherence. Post-colonial theory helps us to peel back much of the racism and sexism that encrust Faulkner's work and to perceive beneath them an alternative and potentially productive map of "overlapping territories" that can be disowned.

Empty Space

Faulkner's cartographic impulse is everywhere evident in his fiction's fascination with space, which rarely functions conventionally as mere backdrop or landscape. Land – its acquisition, maintenance, and loss – pervades the major novels, but it is striking how rarely this land is actually described, how little of it is surveyed by a narrative consciousness. Consider, for example, the opening paragraphs of E. M. Forster's *A Passage to India*, another novel fascinated by questions of land and ownership:

> Except for the Marabar Caves – and they are twenty miles off – the city of Chandrapore presents nothing extraordinary. Edged rather than washed by the river Ganges, it trails for a couple of miles along the bank, scarcely distinguishable from the rubbish it deposits so freely. There are no bathing-steps on the river front, as the Ganges happens not to be holy here; indeed, there is no river front, and bazaars shut out the wide and shifting panorama of the stream. (Forster 1924: 3)

Though the novel will eventually turn around the threat of the incomprehensible as it echoes through the Marabar caves, the narrative nevertheless retains a measured confidence in its ability to map, survey, and describe the landscape of India with perfect competence. The same narrative confidence in the fixity of space even in the midst of epistemological and psychic crisis is evident in Conrad's *Heart of Darkness* (1898–9) (where the river grants Marlow a stable point of reference amidst the radical alterity of Africa) as well as Kipling's *Kim* (1901). The boy protagonist of the latter faces a moment of radical subjective dissolution at the novel's climax: "'I am Kim. I am Kim. And what is Kim?' His soul repeated it again and again" (Kipling 2002: 234). His sense of self is restored, however, precisely by the power of space to provide some sense of rootedness and orientation. He begins to cry and then

> with an almost audible click he felt the wheels of his being lock up anew on the world without. Things that rode meaningless on the eyeball an instant before slid into proper proportion. Roads were meant to be walked upon, houses to be lived in, cattle to be driven, fields to be tilled, and men and women to be talked to. They were all real and true – solidly planted upon the feet – perfectly comprehensible – clay of his clay, neither more nor less. (Kipling 2002: 234)

That click is precisely the grid of the imperial gaze snapping the world into focus, warding off the psychic crisis here as it does in Conrad and Forster, by providing Kim with a stable relationship to the land made once more fixed, objective, and thus comprehensible.

Much of Faulkner's work, however, lacks just this sense of cartographic stability as the texts themselves consistently emphasize the failure of maps, the impropriety of ownership, and the instability of the land itself. *The Sound and the Fury* proves so resistant to its readers, in part, because the fiction refuses to provide the kind of organizing gaze that can suture the self to the fixity of the land. The opening pages of the text, so different from those we find in British imperial novels, do not position us in any kind of immediately meaningful relationship to the land. The measured confidence of Forster and Conrad is lacking, and the gap is filled instead by the damaged consciousness of Benjy Compson as he and Luster walk along the fence bounding a golf course built on the land which once sustained his family's wealth and prominence:

> Through the fence, between the curling flower spaces, I could see them hitting. They were coming toward where the flag was and I went along the fence. Luster was hunting in the grass by the flower tree. They took the flag out, and they were hitting. Then they put the flag back and they went to the table, and he hit and the other hit. Then they went on, and I went along the fence. (Faulkner 1990b: 3).

The stream-of-consciousness narrative structurally limits the organizing power of the kind of spatial gaze employed by Forster and Kipling, and as a consequence critics have attended more carefully to the dislocations of time rather than space. When Benjy catches his clothes on a nail, for example, temporal disorientation results: "*Caddy uncaught me and we crawled through. Uncle Maury said to not let anybody see us, so we better stoop over, Caddy said. Stoop over, Benjy. Like this, see. We stooped over and crossed the garden, where the flowers rasped and rattled against us. The ground was hard. We climbed the fence, where the pigs were grunting and snuffing*" (Faulkner 1990b: 4). This transition from the present to the past jars our expectations and as these shifts multiply in the chapter we find ourselves tossed continually between the past and the present, clinging to any narrative markers we can grasp in order to make what narratologists call "discourse time" and "story time" align with one another (see Genette 1980: 33). "The past," Jean-Paul Sartre argues in his analysis of *The Sound and the Fury*, "takes on a sort of super-reality; its contours are hard and clear, unchangeable. The present, nameless and fleeting, is helpless before it" (Sartre 1966: 89). Such temporal instability has become a recognizable element of the high-modernist literary practice inflected by Bergsonian philosophy and what Anthony Giddens calls the "emptying of time" in transnational modernity (Giddens 1990:18).

Our reading of both this novel and Faulkner's larger project has powerfully been shaped by this sense of temporal instability that leads always and insistently to majestic tragedy. There is more at work in *The Sound and the Fury*, however, than the disorder of psychic time, for space too is out of joint in this passage. Indeed, we can learn to read temporally across the italics; recognizing that the presence of Caddy and Uncle Maury locates the action in 1898 and following other clues eventually allow us to assemble a reasonable sense of linear, temporal coherence. The spaces, however, cannot be so easily coordinated with one another – and it is precisely this instability of place that finally proves so troubling to Benjy. All events are simultaneously available to him and thus they cannot be disaggregated into a linear structure that would allow him either to record or to recover from Caddy's absence. As a consequence, he lives an entirely spatial existence yet is unable to map this space, to provide any kind of grid that might allow us to navigate it successfully. Giddens contends that the emptying of time he associates with modernity is linked to the simultaneous "emptying of space," a process which he attributes to the loss of subjective mappings and their replacement by objective grids of measurement that do not imagine a localized or interested point of view. "The 'discovery' of 'remote' regions of the world," he continues, was precisely the origin of this fundamental reorganization of space: "The progressive charting of the globe that led to the creation of universal maps, in which perspective played little part in the representation of geographical position and form, established space as 'independent' of any particular place or region" (Giddens 1990: 19). Such independence of perspective produces and sustains the imperial gaze and it is precisely this organized sense of space that unravels in Benjy's chapter. Narratively ensnared within his consciousness, we are unable to locate ourselves in any kind of objective relationship to the land. Instead, we must negotiate a marred psychic landscape organized around nails jutting from fences, a Confederate statue, and other subjective points of reference.

Again, this challenge to imperial cartographies constitutes a vital part of what Said calls the post-colonial attempt "to rechart and then occupy" spaces that have been appropriated by imperial regimes. The objectivity of the gaze, in other words, must be challenged, and what Giddens calls the emptiness of space must be repopulated with alternative symbolic and phenomenological geographies that emphasize their rootedness in a historically contingent place or consciousness. As Bill Ashcroft and his collaborators argue in *The Empire Writes Back*, this spatial and experiential disjunction constitutes an essential element of post-colonial literatures, which often strive to "negotiate a gap between 'worlds,' a gap in which the simultaneous processes of abrogation and appropriation continually strive to define and determine their practice" (Ashcroft et al.

1989: 38). Faulkner's work plunges into this abyss in *The Sound and the Fury*, but can find there only tragedy, loss, failure, and damage. Post-colonial literature, on the other hand, seeks actively to recover from this gap an alternative sense of space, one which can find a way to repopulate the objective cartographies generated by the imperial gaze with living, habitable subjective spaces. As Anne McClintock argues, this is a difficult task, one always on the brink of failure if only because it must, of necessity, accommodate itself to the realities of imperial practice. "Even the term 'post-colonial,'" she argues, "is haunted by the very figure of linear 'development' that it sets out to dismantle. Metaphorically, the term 'post-colonialism' marks history as a series of stages along an epochal road from the 'pre-colonial' to the 'colonial,' to the 'post-colonial' – an unbidden, if disavowed commitment to linear time and the idea of 'development'" (McClintock 1992: 85). So too is the post-colonial project haunted by the problem of a space that has been multiply written, crossed and recrossed by so many different and often competing cartographies that even the concept of a native origin finds itself haunted by imperial ideologies of aboriginal primitivism. The problem is not, as Giddens suggests, that space is emptied, but that there are no longer any coordinates for mapping it definitively, no grid of organization or control that can discipline the disparate measures of subjective and objective maps.

In *The Sound and the Fury*, Faulkner discovers the destabilizing plentitude of space – its ability to become overpopulated with meanings that do not cohere around a single, unifying gaze. This may, in fact, be one of the most vital contributions of this early work to the larger narrative experiments in stream-of-consciousness that were underway in the novels of Proust, Joyce, and Woolf. Each of these writers also plunges us into profoundly subjective experiences of time, exploring the famous Bergsonian *durée* in which the present expands and contracts to accommodate memory, fantasy, and physical sensation. In Benjy's shattered consciousness, however, this temporal subjectivization becomes spatial as the Compson acre at the heart of Jefferson also expands and contracts to include a golf course, a pasture, and a tree holding a little girl with muddy drawers. Woolf and Joyce never manage to produce a similar effect, never grasp that the instability of time is matched by the uncertainty of space. As Mrs. Dalloway strolls down Bond Street we become aware of the many different reactions to the airplane flying overhead, but all the characters still see and experience the same street, the same object circling in the sky. Similarly, *Ulysses* presents a bewildering array of styles, but as Joyce himself suggested, it attends so carefully to the details of space that if Dublin were destroyed, the novel could be used to rebuild it brick by brick. Faulkner, however, generates in *The Sound and the Fury* a stream-of-consciousness capable of disrupting space as well as time, opening up a gap between the objective measurements of the imperial gaze and the subjective experience of an inhabited place that cannot be rendered along the lines of latitude and longitude. This realization, lodged though it is in this novel in a tragically shattered consciousness, marks the beginning of what will become for Faulkner a particular fascination with the problem of space that will remain largely quiescent until he appends his first map of Yoknapatawpha County to the first edition of *Absalom, Absalom!*

Map Making

In one of his short fictions, Jorge Luis Borges imagines a map of such grand scale and intricate precision that it swells to cover the very territory it attempts to describe, effectively overwriting the land itself. This oft-referenced story concludes with the map's destruction, as it is left to wither and waste over time, revealing once more the space it attempted to cover (Borges 1988). When Faulkner constructs his first map of Yoknapatawpha in 1936, it shares something of the grandiosity of the document that Borges imagines. While Jefferson is based loosely on Faulkner's native Oxford, the city and the county are essentially fictional constructs, grafted imaginatively onto the real space of Mississippi. Bounded on the north by the Tallahatchie River and on the south by the Yoknapatawpha River, this first map is remarkably exact in its description of a place that does not exist. The map is cut into almost perfect quarters by the roads running into and out of Jefferson, each clearly drawn with sharp, ruled edges. The page is bisected by the equally straight line of the railroad tracks, while two other roads run arrow-straight to the Sutpen's plantation in the northwest and McCallum's in the northeast. Small lines indicating "Pine Hills" are scattered across the page, adding to the sense of precision. Some traces of the act of colonization which first carved this space from Indian lands remain, particularly in the names of the rivers which trace the map's extreme boundaries. These appear to set Jefferson off from a more hostile territory, an effect heightened by the clustering of Indian names near the northern border, largely removed from the little squares describing the sites of vital interest to the white inhabitants of the county. The words "Chicksaw Grant" also appear in neat, block letters, providing a faint yet palpable trace of the county's past.

This first map is typically small in current editions of the novel, reduced to fit on the pages of the widely used Vintage paperbacks. The original document, however, was considerably larger, folding out from the endpapers and distinguished as well by the use of red ink. The map's caption names the city, county, and state while also providing a census which divides the population strictly into two groups: "Population, Whites, 6298; Negroes, 9313." If the map fails adequately to erase the county's increasingly distant imperial past, the caption does so more effectively by neglecting to count at all a native population which is neither white nor black. The grandiose effect of the document – its large size, its measured exactness, and its fanciful census – is capped by the final line of the caption in which the author claims possession of the entire imaginative space: "WILLIAM FAULKNER, Sole Owner & Proprietor." This is just the kind of map Thomas Sutpen or Carothers McCaslin might have drawn when they arrived in the county, for it requires an imagination able "to believe the land was his to hold and bequeath" (Faulkner 1990b: 244). The precisely drawn lines marking the roads, the intricate detail, and even the acknowledgment of another past in the Indian names he retains single this map out as a particularly imperial act of cartographic exuberance.

Even that redundant phrase, "Owner & Proprietor," though worn smooth by its colloquial usage, nevertheless encodes a distinctly imperial fantasy and an acknowledgment of an older past tied directly to European expansion that even Faulkner himself likely did not grasp. The term "proprietor," according to the *OED*, is etymologically rooted in the word "proper" (from the Latin *proprius*), and is a corruption of "proprietary" which refers explicitly to the "owner of any one of certain N. American colonies, which were granted by the Crown to particular persons." It conveys, in other words, not simply ownership acquired through a legally obtained purchase, but the bestowal of a specific imperial grant directly from the royal dominions. To be both owner and proprietor is to signal a particular kind of genealogical claim to the land, one which extends to the moment of its very creation as private property. Though Faulkner was likely unaware of this archaic sense of the term, it nevertheless reveals the almost entirely effaced colonial legacy even of the fictional Yoknapatawpha County. Like that original royal decree which could, through the fictional act of naming, declare a particular part of the American continent to be the state of Mississippi, so Faulkner too invokes this same nominative power in the construction of his own imaginative map. Here, of course, the power to create such a space does not devolve through the explicit violence of colonization, but through the imaginative leap necessary to overwrite the land with the town of Jefferson and the events of his novels partakes of the same imperial impulse.

David Spurr argues in *The Rhetoric of Empire* that the "very process by which one culture subordinates another begins in the act of naming and leaving unnamed, of marking on an unknown territory the lines of division and uniformity, of boundary and continuity" (Spurr 1993: 4). His rhetorical study of imperial practices suggests that one task of post-colonial theory is to recover the arbitrary process of this act of geographical and ideological cartography. As Walter Benjamin writes, we must learn "to brush history against the grain" by realizing that "there is no document of civilization which is not at the same time a document of barbarism" (Benjamin 1968: 256, 257). Throughout his work, Faulkner proves an able chronicler of barbarism, ruthlessly exposing in the lives of characters like Clytie, Joe Christmas, and Lucas Beauchamp the rapacity of a white supremacism that cloaked its extraordinary violence in the rhetoric of gentility and heroism. The *agon* of these revelations, however, is consistently stabilized by the land itself, by the fixity of a South that Quentin can still refuse to renounce at the end of *Absalom, Absalom!* Even Faulkner himself – first in his purchase of Rowan Oak and later in his acquisition of Greenfield Farm – seems to share this passion for the possession of land. Its stability and endurance as a guarantor of identity pervade both Faulkner's life and work, even as he attempts somehow to separate it from the violent history of slavery and colonization which brought it into existence.

This impulse to record the violence of Southern history while still preserving a potentially redemptive connection to the land enacts the same struggle between abrogation and appropriation that Ashcroft et al. argue is a constitutive element of postcolonial writing. In the novels stretching from *The Sound and the Fury* through *Absalom, Absalom!* this struggle produces with brutal consistency the tragedy of an irresolvable conflict. Unable either to renounce or to embrace the South, formed within its crucible of violence and unable to escape the scorching fires set alight by the Civil War, Faulkner's protagonists spiral endlessly toward death, suicide, and tragedy. It is possible, of course, to see in such tragedies the budding of a post-colonial consciousness, albeit one that remains entirely contemplative so that, as Ramón Saldívar argues, the most that can be achieved is "not verification and inviolate reconstructions of self-consciousness but overt exposures of the limitations of disillusioned subjectivity" (Saldívar 1995: 119). That is, the post-colonial promise of these texts emerges precisely in the irresolvable contradiction of the decentered subject which must learn to inhabit a world that can never be rendered as a full totality. The publication of *Go Down, Moses* in 1942 can be fit into this same theoretical trajectory, with Ike McCaslin's renunciation of his inheritance – his status as owner and proprietor – transformed into yet another iteration of this devastating logic. Like Quentin Compson at the end of *Absalom, Absalom!*, he strives to renounce the violence of slavery even as he struggles to form some more enduring connection to the land. The polarization of Ike's place in the text – schizophrenically located between the small rented room in town and the utopian hunting camp in the pine forest – appears to transform Quentin's subjective *agon* into a powerfully spatialized expression of the two irreconcilable sites of Southern identity. As Linda Wagner-Martin argues, however, "Issac McCaslin, often read as the protagonist of *Go Down, Moses*, is not another Quentin Compson" (Wagner-Martin 1996: 5). "By 1942," she continues, "Faulkner had stopped romanticizing his inheritance of southern history, tradition, legend, and myth," and had instead begun producing what she calls "a shameful and shaming story, rather than a prideful one" (1996: 10). Thadious Davis, in *Games of Property*, notes a similar emphasis on shame rather than tragedy in *Go Down, Moses*, arguing that Faulkner begins to interrogate "the strong belief in the right to property as a base right and constructs his characters, both black and white, around the right to property and use and abuses of property within a patriarchal society and family and within a slaveholding economy" (Davis 2003: 35). This shift in attention toward the contradictions of ownership, propriety, and space generates a moment of post-colonial possibility that extends beyond the mere *agon* of an individual consciousness. Here Faulkner engages in the process of recharting and reclamation that Edward Said describes, beginning a process that will culminate in the subtle but profound reinscription of his own map of Yoknapatawpha County.

Go Down, Moses

When Isaac McCaslin first sees Lion, the dog that will eventually kill the bear that rampages through the hunting stories of *Go Down, Moses*, he thinks to himself that "it was the beginning of the end of something, he didn't know what except that he would not grieve" (Faulkner 1990b: 216–17). A sense of ending, in fact, pervades this entire novel, and this sensation is compounded by the fact that it has generally come to be considered the last of Faulkner's greatest works, completed just as he begins a disastrous surrender to alcoholism. Unlike the earlier novels, the seemingly disparate collection of stories gathered in this text do not drive relentlessly toward the same sense of high tragedy. Indeed, the work is so crossed by various stories that the tight narrative structure tragedy requires simply does not precipitate from the mix, leaving both the book and its readers suspended in a fictional history that ranges over roughly a century and a half. Articulating the concerns of a wide array of critics, John Pilkington argues in *The Heart of Yoknapatawpha* that *Go Down, Moses* is, in fact, little more than a collection of poorly integrated short fictions: "The connection between the stories dealing with the relations between whites and Negroes on the one hand and the romance of the wilderness on the other never seems either logical or compelling. Regardless of the beauty and brilliance of both halves, Faulkner's failure to relate them convincingly becomes a crucial hurdle for readers" (Pilkington 1981: 245). Rider's suicidal grief, the struggles of both the white and black descendents of Carothers McCaslin, and the odd final piece describing Gavin Stevens's attempt to bring Samuel (Butch) Beauchamp home cannot, Pilkington concludes, be synthesized into a novel.

Rather than attempting to intervene directly in the long-running debate about the coherence of this text, however, I want to suggest that this structural dissonance is precisely the point of *Go Down, Moses*. The work, in fact, creates a deliberate series of narrative aporias and failed endings around which, paradoxically, the stories can be usefully constellated. This is, in the words of Ike McCaslin, "the beginning of the end of something," but it is an end that the book itself never reaches. Indeed, the novel struggles precisely with the problem of how to live without an ending, of how to forge some kind of life without the comforting arc of a narrative structure deliberately established to produce meaning, coherence, and stability. Much the same could be said of a good number of modernist texts, of course, but the structural incoherence of *Go Down, Moses* – its impossible renunciation of an ending – is generated not through narrative experimentation, but through a self-conscious confrontation with the emptiness and thus the incoherence of space itself. As he does in naming himself "owner and proprietor" of Yoknapatawpha County, Faulkner deliberately invokes the discourse of legal property and ownership, placing it alongside both a more aboriginal fantasy of the land (embodied most potently in Sam Fathers) and the radical sense of dispossession and exile experienced by black characters like Lucas Beauchamp, Rider, and Butch Beauchamp. The contradictions between these distinct narratives of spatial relationships do not move to a moment of either heroic reconciliation or tragic failure; instead they reveal the way in which the land – so consistently constructed throughout the book as the vital ground of individual identity – is crossed and recrossed by different histories, meanings, experiences, and inhabitants.

The raw power of exploitation and settlement, which transforms native lands into the state of Mississippi and the Chickasaw land grant into Southern plantations, haunts Ike McCaslin throughout the text and generates much of the work's lyric potency. Unlike his grandfather, he cannot see the land simply as property to be taken and held, cannot ground his own sense of identity in the violent appropriation by "him who saw the opportunity and took it, bought the land, took the land, got the land no matter how, held it to bequeath, no matter how, out of the old grant, the first patent, when it was a wilderness of wild beasts and wilder men, and cleared it, translated it into something to bequeath to his children" (Faulkner 1990b: 245). Carothers McCaslin's heirs

– both black and white – struggle throughout *Go Down, Moses* with this legacy of alienation from a land they can never fully possess. "The title of every single piece of property in the United States," Joseph William Sanger notes in *Continuing Conquest*, "can be traced to a system of violence" (cited in Davis 2003: 176). The various narratives of *Go Down, Moses* are shot through with the consciousness of such violence and the guilt, shame, and confusion it generates. The sections of the text focusing on the Beauchamps and the McCaslins, in fact, gyrate between the attempt to renounce this imperial inheritance on the one hand and the desire to naturalize it on the other. Uncle Buck and Uncle Buddy, the first white heirs to the plantation, give the grandiose plantation house to the slaves and move into a pioneer-like cabin, producing a male heir only in the accident of a poker game. Buddy's son, Ike, goes one step beyond even this, renouncing his inheritance of the land and the house in its entirety. These acts of denial are matched by the aristocratic fantasies of blood and descent that haunt both the white Edmonds to whom the property passes after Ike refuses it and the black Lucas Beauchamp, Carothers's grandson. The anxieties generated by a space that can never be fully owned, in other words, are displaced onto a more familiar Faulknerian matrix of familial relationships. As Lucas and Zack engage in a murderous contest of wills over the former's wife, each obscures the anxieties and contradictions of property with the language of blood and inheritance. Lucas, in particular, attributes his own suicidal courage in confronting the white man to his paternal inheritance: "You knowed I wasn't afraid, because you knowed I was a McCaslin too and a man-made one. And you never thought that, because I am a McCaslin too, I wouldn't" (Faulkner 1990b: 52). Roth Edmonds, Zack's son, will later rely on this same fantasy of paternity, attributing Lucas's autonomy as well as his own felt impotence to "the impenetrable face with its definite strain of white blood, the same blood which ran in his own veins, which had not only come to the negro through male descent while it had come to him through a woman, but had reached the negro a generation sooner" (Faulkner 1990b: 68–9). The Edmonds's sense of illegitimacy and the subsequent alienation and hostility which this produces appears to derive from the fantasy of paternal supremacy, drawing on the same ideological reservoir from which Lucas himself generates his own deeply conflicted sense of self.

The problem of blood, however, which drives so many of Faulkner's fictions, becomes in *Go Down, Moses* a site of transference, onto which the deeper problems of land and propriety can be displaced. Lucas himself, in the midst of his excruciating struggle with Zack, glimpses this underlying problem of alienation from the land: "You thought I'd do it quick, quicker than Isaac since it aint any land I would give up. I aint got any fine big McCaslin farm to give up. All I got to give up is McCaslin blood that rightfully aint even mine" (Faulkner 1990b: 55–6). Lucas, of course, actually possesses a sizeable bank account – his share of the legacy McCaslin left his father. One of the mysteries of "The Fire and the Hearth," in fact, is why Lucas runs his still and why he goes to such great lengths to acquire the metal detector without having to pay a single dime of his own money. The solution to this lies precisely in his profoundly felt alienation from the land as a source of both identity and history. When he discovers the coins that will lead to his extravagant treasure hunt, he suddenly enters into a new relationship with the land, one that promises to forge a potent and stabilizing bond between himself and the space of the plantation where he was a slave. The money is first found in "a squat, flat-topped almost symmetrical mound rising without reason from the floor-like flatness of the valley. The white people called it an Indian mound" (Faulkner 1990b: 37). This aboriginal site becomes for Lucas the site of subjective authentication, offering him a means symbolically to stake his own empowering (and enriching) claim to a land that precedes the act of colonization. A navel-like space bearing much of the same symbolic resonance as the woods which enfold Ike McCaslin, the mound escapes the organization of the plantation system and the enslavement that produced Lucas's own punishing sense of exile. The money Lucas, a wealthy man, holds in the bank is still the profit of slavery, the abstract rendering of his own violent sub-jugation. As such, it may offer him the comforts of wealth, but it leaves unresolved the same problem which haunts Rider in "Pantaloon in Black": the inability to return home, to activate some sense of relationship to the land and space of Yoknapatawpha County that is not steeped in blood, violence, and slavery. Rider, having watched his own attempt to recuperate this same space destroyed by the death of his wife, is left to wander in a drunken and enraged stupor:

> When he put his hand on the gate it seemed to him suddenly that there was nothing beyond it. The house had never been his anyway, but now even the planks and shingles, the hearth and stove and bed, were all a part of the memory of somebody else, so that he stopped in the half-open gate and said aloud, as though he had gone to sleep in one place and then waked suddenly to find himself in another: "What's Ah doin hyar."
> (Faulkner 1990b: 135)

As the descendents of slaves, Rider and Lucas share this alienating sense of having awakened in a strange place, which generates for the former a suicidal grief and for the latter the contradictory mystifications of blood and the ultimately ridiculous pursuit of some more primal connection to the land.

Lucas's own lingering consciousness of the land as a potential site of authority as well as his own contradictory relation to it are shared by the other male McCaslin descen-dents as well. Buck and Buddy, in moving out of the plantation house, generate from themselves a sense of internal exile as they too attempt to escape from the tyranny of a house under whose shadow they nevertheless continue to live. Isaac McCaslin seeks an even more radical solution to the problem of his deeply felt homelessness, attempting like Lucas (his contemporary) to establish an aboriginal relationship to the land. He, in fact, struggles to transform radically the spatial logic of Yoknapatawpha County, orienting himself not around its plantation houses and (later) Confederate monuments, but around the traditions and experiences of a native population impossibly condensed into the hybrid figure of Sam Fathers. Seemingly orphaned for most of the novel, Ike sees in Sam an alternative paternity that leads not to the violence of old Carothers, but to a close connection to the land, one in which he could be "consecrated and absolved . . . from weakness and regret" (Faulkner 1990b: 175). The absolution Ike seeks leads explicitly to a refusal of the imperial conception of space as a marked and bounded entity which can be surveyed and controlled from a single, objective point. Attempting to see the bear whose death he will eventually witness, Ike wanders deep into the woods without his gun before realizing that "he was still tainted" and had to relinquish his watch and his compass as well (Faulkner 1990b: 199). This deeply resonant moment in the novel activates simultaneously the primitivist fantasy of the woods and the profound sense of alienation that the imperial rationalization of space and time generates.

Though Ike, after surrendering himself to the now "dimensionless" woods, does indeed gain a vision of the bear, the renunciation symbolized by the loss of the watch and the compass finally proves a failure, for it does not generate the aboriginal relationship to the land he desires. He eventually must leave the forest, and when he crosses that boundary into the organized space of farmhouse, fields, and towns, he returns as well to the fact of his own violent inheritance. Later, of course, he will attempt to renounce the McCaslin property just as he renounced the watch and the compass, telling his cousin that God had "created man to be His overseer on earth and to hold suzerainty over the earth and the animals on it in His name, not to hold for himself and descendents inviolable title forever, generation after generation, to the oblongs and squares of the earth, but to hold the earth mutual and intact in the communal anonymity of brotherhood" (Faulkner 1990b: 246). By this point, Ike's pursuit of an authentic origin, a sense of space in which his identity can be firmly rooted, has extended beyond even the native populations of the Americas (they too were "already cursed" and "already tainted") to the mythic expulsion from Eden itself (Faulkner 1990b: 248). Though cast as part of an essentially providential narrative, this section of "The Bear" actually reveals the profound emptiness of space itself – its ability as land, property, and symbol to be multiply mapped and crossed from an array of contradictory and often mutually competing perspectives. Ike wants to find some meaning in the imperial act itself, in the original voyage from Europe's "corrupt and worthless twilight," but finally discovers only that "we have never been free" (Faulkner 1990b: 248, 282). That is, there is no aboriginal relationship to the land, no organization of space that can finally guarantee proprietorship as anything other than an arbitrary act of violence.

Ike's renunciation, which brings "The Bear" to something of a climax, is destined to fail, for even though he rejects his ownership of the land, he remains bound by the ledgers, "the frail iron thread strong as truth and impervious as evil and longer than life itself and reaching beyond record and patrimony to join him with the lusts and passions, the hopes and dreams and griefs of bones whose names while still fleshed and capable even old Carothers' grandfather had never heard" (Faulkner 1990b: 285–6). History cannot be renounced, nor can the organization of the land as property and proprietary, leaving Ike caught in a familiar post-colonial conundrum: the paradoxical attempt to build an identity based on a past of violation, alienation, and dispossession. The enormity of Ike's failure becomes apparent in the work's penultimate story, "Delta Autumn." No longer offering even a respite from the legacy of the ledgers, much less a site of potential regeneration, the woods become instead a site where Roth's assignation with a black woman repeats the acts of miscegenation and incest that Ike had sought to elude. The woman who comes to seek Roth embodies the very force of history itself – a history that stuns the old man into a vision of profound despair. "No wonder," he thinks, "the ruined woods I used to know don't cry out for retribution! . . . The people who have destroyed it will accomplish its revenge" (Faulkner 1990b: 347). He sees a future of radical racial indeterminacy, in which *"Chinese and African and Aryan and Jew, all breed and spawn together until no man has time to say which one is which nor cares"* (Faulkner 1990b: 347). What Ike sees here is the final rupture of any kind of aboriginal or redemptive relationship between a people and the land. The mystical promise Sam Fathers once embodied now recedes before the logic encoded in the ledgers – the logic of ownership and propriety, undergirded by a final reification of the land as a commodity, organized by "usury and mortgage and bankruptcy and measureless wealth" (Faulkner 1990b: 347). What Ike fails to recognize, however, is that there is no prior and proper relationship to the land to be recovered and that the sense of homelessness he experiences in fact constitutes him as a post-colonial subject.

Go Down, Moses, more than any other work by Faulkner, captures the ambiguities of space and the final failure of any attempt to forge an aboriginal relationship to the land. It also marks the moment when Faulkner himself recognizes that his proprietorship of Yoknapatawpha County is constrained by the ideologies of race and ownership that he can recognize but never fully renounce. Critics have long been puzzled by the text's final story, which, though it bears the same title as the larger volume, seems to touch only marginally on the history of the McCaslin plantation and the problems of land and ownership. At the center of the chapter is Butch Beauchamp, Lucas's grandson, who is executed for murder in Chicago as Gavin Stevens struggles to raise money in Jefferson to bring his body home. Like "Pantaloon in Black," this too is a story about grief, and just as the sheriff in the earlier work fails to understand Rider's refusal to be jailed, so too Stevens fails to understand why Lucas's grandmother insists that Roth Edmonds has "sold my Benjamin . . . to Pharaoh" (Faulkner 1990b: 362). In this story, however, we are not allowed narrative access to either of the black characters, leaving us, like Stevens, to puzzle out their motives and their often cryptic reactions to Butch's homecoming. Indeed, Stevens's final response to the grandmother's request that the story of Butch's death be printed in a newspaper she cannot read should be treated with precisely the same kind of suspicion that underwrites the sheriff's account of Rider's death. *"It doesn't matter to her how,* Stevens thinks, *[s]ince it had to be and she couldn't stop it, and now that it's all over and done and finished, she doesn't care how he died. She just wanted him home, but she wanted him to come home right"* (Faulkner 1990b: 365). In a novel that has reiterated consistently the impossibility of home as a redemptive or originary space, Stevens's interpretation of this event reveals little more than his own deep entanglement in an ideology of property that is capable of imagining the violently appropriated spaces of Mississippi as anything like a home. Furthermore, Faulkner's own refusal to narrate Butch's experience suggests that the author too recognizes here his inability to articulate the voice of diasporic black identity. Butch's motivations as well as his grandmother's cryptic allegations against Roth grow out of their collective alienation from the space of Jefferson and Yoknapatawpha County. They cannot, in effect, be recorded on the map whose "Sole Owner & Proprietor" is William Faulkner, belonging instead to an alternative space of exile and violence that must be mapped and recorded elsewhere. In closing *Go Down, Moses* with this story, Faulkner reveals essentially the fictional nature of his own relationship to space, emphasizing the fact that all maps are merely provisional attempts to organize a space that is always already crossed by other cartographies, other lines of limitation and demarcation.

This essentially post-colonial process of recharting what Said calls "overlapping territories" is nowhere more visible than in the remarkable revision of the map of Yoknapatawpha County that appears in the *Portable Faulkner* in 1946. The carefully drawn lines of the earlier map here give way to more improvisational squiggles denoting roads that wander through the territory rather than decisively crossing it. More significant than this, however, is the inclusion of a good deal more detail about the explicitly colonial history of the county. The town of Jefferson includes not only a label indicating Compson's Mile, but a brief appended description of it as well: "for which Jason I swapped Ikkemotubbe a race horse & the last fragment of which Jason IV sold in order to become free." Similarly, the area's original inhabitants appear in the first map only as the after-image of the "Chicksaw Grant" legend in the upper-left quadrant, whereas the later document includes the caption: "Where by 1820 his people had learned to call it 'The Plantation' just like the white men did" (Faulkner 1946). This short addition, in particular, reveals just how provisional this new map has become; rather than a definitive description of the county, in other words, it now acknowledges explicitly that this same territory had once born other names and other landmarks. Even more remarkable than this acknowledgment of an alternative cartography, however, is the way in which Faulkner assigns the titles of particular books and stories to different sites on the map. Indeed, these labels, written in block capital letters, stand out more clearly than anything else and indicate a new set of coordinates around which Yoknapatawpha County has been organized. The upper-left portion of the map, for example, now not only includes the "Chicksaw Grant" and "Sutpen's Hundred," but also adds the titles ABSALOM, ABSALOM!, THE BEAR, A JUSTICE and RED LEAVES. While these terms do indicate where the primary action of each work is roughly located, they more tellingly emphasize the fact that the entire county is itself a fictional invention, one marked not by the boundaries of particular rivers but by the pages of individual texts. In other words, Faulkner appears to realize that, like all maps, this one too is historically contingent, merely one way of organizing the land that now explicitly acknowledges the instability of space as the intersection of a series of "overlapping territories." Even the caption, which earlier named Faulkner as "Sole Owner & Proprietor," now notes that the territory has been "Surveyed & mapped for this volume by WILLIAM FAULKNER." This subtle yet significant change bears within it the same insights gleaned from *Go Down, Moses*: that the land is shaped powerfully by ideologies of ownership, property rights, and exile. As a consequence there can be no single map capable of containing the entire territory, only multiple and competing fictions that will always fail to provide the ground for an aboriginal identity and will consistently undermine the foundational concept of home. This is a space that can be neither fully owned nor fully renounced, leaving Faulkner and his characters locked in a distinctly post-colonial paradox. Facing a past that can be neither abrogated nor appropriated, they must instead attempt to carve out a survivable fiction, to tie themselves to the shifting spaces they might survey but which they can never own.

Treating William Faulkner as a post-colonial writer, as I have done in this chapter, carries with it an array of risks and contradictions. As a relatively wealthy white male who owned a farm and plantation house himself, the concerns of his fiction seem far removed from the movement toward human liberation typically associated with the post-colonial project. Furthermore, the optimistic trajectory I have outlined here, which follows through the major works a line of thinking that culminates in a recognition of the essential instability of space, home, and identity, would seem to disintegrate in the later novels. These works, as Thadious Davis argues, include "the ridiculing of women" and "the dismissal of blacks from all but the most visually benign texts" (Davis 2003: 251). These objections are indeed legitimate, yet they fail to acknowledge the possibility that Faulkner simply could not, in the end, generate the kind of narrative necessary to fill the gap opened by his own startling revelation. Facing not Weinstein's "cosmos no one owns," but a map of Yoknapatawpha County over which even he could no longer assert full ownership, Faulkner instead generated the only survey available to him, one inevitably shaped by the optics of sexism and the stubborn ideology of race. As a 1938 photograph perhaps inadvertently reveals, Faulkner had come to see that his own near mythic role-playing, far from a unique aberration, constituted the very essence of an always already homeless and displaced subjectivity. The picture shows Faulkner, his family, and his servants dressed in what can only be described as "imperial drag," with the author himself attired self-consciously as an English lord and his guests variably fitted out in English clothing or the costumes of various colonized peoples (see Davis 2003: 186). Like Sophonsiba Beauchamp, who assures everyone that her plantation ("Warwick") in *Go Down, Moses* descends directly from a royal British family, so too Faulkner in this photograph appears to stage explicitly a myth of blood, land, and ownership only to reveal its final absurdity. Though perhaps unable to articulate a solution to the *agon* of land, space, and history, Faulkner at least proves able to recognize the limits of his own cartographic imagination and glimpse through the tatters of the imperial map the alternative, shifting, and overlapping territories which his more explicitly post-colonial heirs would learn to narrate.

REFERENCES AND FURTHER READING

Ashcroft, B., G. Griffiths, and H. Tiffin (1989). *The Empire Writes Back: Theory and Practice in Post-Colonial Literatures*. London: Routledge.

Benjamin, W. (1968). *Illuminations* (trans. H. Zohn). New York: Schocken.

Blotner, J. (1974). *Faulkner: A Biography*. Vol. 2. New York: Random House.

Borges, J. L. (1988). On Exactitude in Science. In *Jorge Luis Borges: Collected Fictions* (trans. A. Hurley) (p. 325). New York: Penguin.

Conrad, J. (1988). *Heart of Darkness*. New York: Norton.

Davis, T. (1995). Reading Faulkner's Compson Appendix: Writing History from the Margins. In D. M. Kartiganer and A. J. Abadie (eds.). *Faulkner and Ideology* (pp. 238–44). Jackson: University Press of Mississippi.

Davis, T. (2003). *Games of Property: Law, Race, Gender, and Faulkner's* Go Down, Moses. Durham, NC: Duke University Press.

Faulkner, W. (1936). *Absalom, Absalom!* New York: Random House.

Faulkner, W. (1946). *The Portable Faulkner* (ed. M. Cowley). New York: Viking.

Faulkner, W. (1990a). *Absalom, Absalom!* New York: Vintage. (Original pub. 1936.)

Faulkner, W. (1990b). *Go Down, Moses*. New York: Vintage. (Original pub. 1942.)

Faulkner, W. (1990c). *The Sound and the Fury*. New York: Vintage. (Original pub. 1929.)

Forster, E. M. (1924). *A Passage to India*. New York: Harcourt.

Genette, G. (1980). *Narrative Discourse: An Essay in Method* (trans. J. E. Lewin). Ithaca, NY: Cornell University Press.

Giddens, A. (1990). *The Consequences of Modernity*. Stanford, CA: Stanford University Press.

Kipling, R. (2002). *Kim*. New York: Norton.

Latham, S. (1998). Jim Bond's America. *Mississippi Quarterly*, 51: 453–63.

McClintock, A. (1992). The Angel of Progress: Pitfalls of the Term "Post-Colonialism." *Social Text*, 31/32: 84–98.

Pilkington, J. (1981). *The Heart of Yoknapatawpha*. Jackson: University Press of Mississippi.

Said, E. (1994). *Culture and Imperialism*. New York: Vintage.

Saldívar, R. (1995). Looking for a Master Plan: Faulkner, Paredes, and the Colonial and Postcolonial Subject. In P. Weinstein (ed.). *The Cambridge Companion to William Faulkner* (pp. 96–120). Cambridge: Cambridge University Press.

Sartre, J.-P. (1966). On *The Sound and the Fury*: Time in the Work of Faulkner. In R. P. Warren (ed.). *Faulkner: A Collection of Critical Essays* (pp. 87–93). Englewood Cliffs, NJ: Prentice Hall.

Spurr, D. (1993). *The Rhetoric of Empire: Colonial Discourse in Journalism, Travel Writing, and Imperial Administration*. Durham, NC: Duke University Press.

Wagner-Martin, L. (1996). Introduction. In L. Wagner-Martin (ed.). *New Essays on* Go Down, Moses (pp. 1–20). Cambridge: Cambridge University Press.

Weinstein, P. (1992). *Faulkner's Subject: A Cosmos No One Owns*. Cambridge: Cambridge University Press.

Religion: Desire and Ideology

Leigh Anne Duck

Each time I teach one of Faulkner's novels, at least one student will ask, with evident discomfort, "Was he a Christian?" Such students seem to have internalized the old interpretive dictums against inferring meaning from the author's biography, or perhaps they consider it impolite to discuss the writer's religious beliefs. But they ask nonetheless, because Faulkner's novels raise religious questions with particular insistence, and with remarkably deft references – through structure, trope, and plot – to biblical scripture and scholarship (Meeter 1991). Hence, though resolution of the author's spiritual stance may be impossible – and though a reductive answer to this question would be unhelpful – readers understandably wonder what to make of the multiple contradictions that inform Faulkner's theological allusions. Hardly devout, nor are they simply parodic; rather, they raise surprising tensions. One might wonder, for example, why Faulkner narrates a family's dissolution in *The Sound and the Fury* (1929) through calendrical references to Holy Week, a season theologically associated with hope and regeneration, or why the title character's beliefs in *Requiem for a Nun* (1951) lead her to kill an infant.

Faulkner was famously equivocal concerning the influence of religion on his work, explaining that "the Christian legend" was an inescapable part of "his background" and also averring that he believed in humanity's religious aspirations (Gwynn and Blotner 1959: 86; Meriwether and Millgate 1968: 100). Interestingly, critical commentary on his work has tended to align itself with these two quite different approaches to religion, focusing on how Faulkner's fictions critique a historically embedded Southern Protestantism or how they commend a broader – Christian, Western, or universal – spiritual impulse. This chapter essays a middle path, observing how Faulkner explored the often idiosyncratic interactions between the Southern religious context and individuals' spiritual perceptions. Probing religious ideology at its most intimate level of influence, Faulkner shared the project Pericles Lewis attributes to European and US modernism more generally: his works not only criticize "apparently outmoded institutions of formal religious belief" but also suggest an "underlying spiritualism" (2004: 672, 670–7). Influenced by early twentieth-century intellectual currents suggesting that people are drawn toward encompassing systems of faith and ritual, Faulkner's novels explore the fate of that impulse in a society shaped by rigid racial hierarchies.

Examining *Light in August* (1932), a novel that vividly demonstrates Faulkner's lasting concern with the stultifying effects – both social and psychological – of fixed ideologies, I argue that it presents the absolute devotion to a divine authority as both a model and a vector for support of a white supremacist status quo. In other words, characters' familiarity with the religious imperative of unquestioning submission reduces their ability to question social and political norms, while many of the novel's dogmatists explicitly insist on racial difference and hierarchy. Simultaneously, however, in exploring how thoroughly individuals succumb to religious dogmas, the novel posits their desire for a meaningful and fulfilling system of belief. Rather than suggesting that religion must necessarily frustrate that hope, Faulkner initially attributes the possibility for a more beneficial and communal spiritual life to the African American church. As demonstrated in *The Sound and the Fury* and *Requiem for a Nun*, this representational strategy creates a tension in Faulkner's work of which he may have become more aware as his career progressed.

Rigid Attachments/Ineffable Longings

Critics have often noted the damaging effects of Southern Protestantism in the social worlds of Faulkner's novels. As more recent scholarship observes, interpretation of Faulkner's work was long dominated by the perspective of the Southern Agrarians, who sought to promote the cohesive power of Southern communities (Duvall 1990: 6–18). But while such approaches generally sought to obscure the oppression manifest in these locales, even the most influential of such celebrants, Cleanth Brooks, recognized Faulkner as "a Protestant anticlerical, fascinated and also infuriated by some of the more violently repressive features of the religion that dominates his part of the country" (1963: 62). Contemporary scholars argue that Faulkner's critique was more inclusive, exploring how various institutions and ideologies within the South – among them, churches and Christian theology – converged to support racial segregation.

Thus, though critics examining the representation of religion in *Light in August* long focused on the parallels between the life of Christ and that of the novel's Christmas (see, for a well-developed example, Kartiganer 1979: 37–68), this text has recently proven a fertile source for scholarship analyzing how Faulkner situates religion among a nexus of racially oppressive belief systems. Tim Caron describes how white Southern theologians historically mobilized the biblical story of Noah's son Ham, who was cursed by his father, to support white supremacy; as *Light in August* "intertextually summons elements of the white South's religiosity . . . through allusion, parody, silent quotation, and appropriation," then, it displays the insidious effects of racist doctrine and hermeneutics (2000: 53, 53–81). Charles Reagan Wilson argues that this novel also "explores the pathology of the Southern civil religion," a "body of institutions, myths, values, and rituals" that amounted to "a cult of ancestor worship" (1991: 32–3). Seeking to preserve not only the memories but also the social standards and hierarchies of the past, this movement was inherently conservative, arising amid and vitally supporting the segregationist efforts that led to the spread of "Jim Crow" laws during the 1890s (Wilson 1980).

Light in August is unique in Faulkner's oeuvre in that it explicitly pairs Civil War memorialization with religious belief and doctrine. Characters in much of his work are fixated, in a more secular way, on the Southern past: in *Sartoris* (1929), for example, the spirit of a man killed in that war, "freed . . . of time and flesh," becomes "far more palpable than the two old men" that remember him, as they are "cemented . . . to a dead period" (Faulkner 1951: 1). *Absalom, Absalom!* (1936) extends that dynamic more broadly: Quentin Compson presents his fictional world as "the deep South dead since 1865 and peopled with garrulous outraged baffled ghosts . . . looking with stubborn recalcitrance backward" (Faulkner 1990a: 4, 7). Though *Light in August*'s Gail Hightower was born after the Civil War, his "memories" are similarly hallucinatory and even gothic: every evening, he witnesses the cavalry galloping toward the scene of his grandfather's death. Though these visions constitute, in his mind, all he knows "of life," they also deprive him of vigor in the present (1990b: 60). But because this character imaginatively links his memorialization of the past to religious faith, he mistakes his fixation for vocation, attending seminary with the belief that "God must call me to Jefferson because my life died there, was shot from the saddle of a galloping horse in a Jefferson street one night twenty years before it was ever born" (p. 478).

Though Hightower's conviction is sincere, his conflation of "the church . . . all that it ramified and evoked" with his idiosyncratic memorial project turns out to be as damaging as hypocrisy could be. On the one hand, it contributes to the corruption of the church hierarchy, as his wife's campaign to achieve Hightower's desired end is based in "demagoguery, . . . abasement [and] small lying" (1990b: 482). On the other, it alienates his parishioners from their church, ultimately eliciting a spiteful response: unable to understand why Hightower "couldn't get religion and that galloping cavalry and his dead grandfather shot from the galloping horse untangled from each other," the congregation suspects that "he did not care about the people" and begins to judge him and his unhappy wife, eventually ostracizing them both (pp. 62, 61, 66, 69). Though Hightower suffers loss, hostility, and physical abuse, he ultimately determines that he was, at least in part, culpable: in attempting to use this institution to achieve commemorative comfort rather than to help others find "truth" and "peace," he has helped to destroy the "Church," creating of it an institution of "adjuration, threat, and doom" (p. 487).

Furthermore, though appalled by racial violence, he concludes by the end of his life that, because of his literal worship of the past, he has been complicit in it. Picturing others with whom, because of his temporal dislocation, he has been unable fully to interact, he sees one "inextricable composite," which gradually resolves itself into the two faces of Joe Christmas, the man so recently castrated and killed in Hightower's own kitchen, and Percy Grimm, the perpetrator of this lynching (1990b: 487–92). Listening to Christmas's grandmother, Hightower has already identified with the image of him as a helpless child; he now identifies Grimm, too, as a "boy," at which point an "ultimate dammed flood within him breaks and rushes away," and he imagines "all heaven, filled with the lost and unheeded crying of all the children who ever lived, wailing still like lost children" (p. 492). Believing that he has failed to offer needed direction to the "children" around him, he is too deeply distressed to pray even at what appears to be the moment of his death.

Like Hightower's repetitive and consuming Confederate memorialization, the white supremacist theology described by Caron is also associated in this work with remarkable fixity, an attribute reflected further in the characters' bodies and actions. The text vigorously – and harshly – insists on Hightower's stagnation, describing his torso as "shapeless, almost monstrous, with a soft and sedentary obesity" (Faulkner 1990b: 89). Other characters, with more aggressive theologies, are marked by similarly unvarying embodiments: though their philosophies are internally inconsistent, their actions are adamant. Doc Hines, who lives off the charity of African American women, is repetitive in syntax and unyielding in delivery as he denounces "bitchery" and preaches white supremacy in a "harsh, dead voice" (pp. 127, 341, 343). Calvin Burden forges a theology of his father's New England Unitarian "bleak and bloodless logic," the Catholic "mysticism" he learns in California, and the Methodist "immediate hellfire and tangible brimstone" he picks up, apparently, in the Midwest, but this combination of religious strands yields neither beneficence nor respect for the possibility that others might want similar freedom in their spiritual development. On the contrary, Burden hates both "black folks" and "slaver[s]" and repeatedly attempts "to beat the loving God into" his four children with a "hard hand" (pp. 3, 247). The dogmatic theology of these men thus supports the South's governing white supremacy in form – as it urges against critical or even rational thought – and in content.

In each of these cases, theological rigidity is associated with psychopathology. Hines and Calvin are explicitly described as "mad" and "fanatical" (1990b: 127, 147). The origin of Hightower's fascination is narrated more thoroughly and situated in childhood experience: the only child of uncommunicative parents, whom he considers "phantoms," Hightower is overwhelmed when he discovers one day the dark blue patch on his father's Confederate uniform (pp. 468–9, 474). Unable to deal with the contradictory emotions causing his heart-stopping anxiety and "intestinal fits," he cannot simply ask whether "his father had killed the man from whose blue coat the patch came" (pp. 469–70). Instead, he displaces his "horrified triumph and sick joy" onto his late grandfather, a man quite different from his father: he asks the family servant, "Tell again about grandpa. How many Yankees did he kill?" This strategy helps him to survive a difficult childhood episode, and, perhaps because his strange theological focus constitutes a post-traumatic adaptation, Hightower's perspective often provides the novel an opportunity to contemplate spiritual possibilities. But while Hightower's fixation does not produce the single-minded bigotry seen in Faulkner's other dogmatists, it still, as we have seen, consumes his life.

Despite the inflexibility of its religious characters, however, the novel repeatedly points to the potential for multiplicity in religious faith, as its imagery suggests surprising theological juxtapositions. As Virginia Hlavsa argues, *Light in August* richly demonstrates how Faulkner was influenced by earlier modernists' use of diverse mythologies to structure their work: though this novel, in plot, diction, and narrative form, appears to be modeled on the gospel of John, it reads these biblical images and structures through Sir James Frazer's *The Golden Bough* (original publication 1890) (Hlavsa 1985: 27–43). This anthropological volume, noted for its influence on modernist aesthetics, was devoted to elucidating the "varied circumstances [and] variety of institutions" through which "the human mind has elaborated its first crude philosophy of life" (Frazer 1922: 2). And though Frazer's discourse seems committed to certain distinctions – particularly that accorded to "barbarous" peoples – his method, as Christopher Herbert demonstrates, yields an inevitably countervailing tendency: each "cultural form seems never to attain definitive statement in any ritual, however vivid and extravagant, but to improvise itself anew again and again, in one society after another, perpetually unsatisfied" (1995: 149). (In an interview, Faulkner expressed such a view of religion quite explicitly: "Man isn't universal. In different places he conceives of God differently, and these ways vary in time and space" [Meriwether and Millgate 1968: 71].) This mobility and multiplicity suffuse the imagery of *Light in August*, in which varied targets for and images of worship permeate the landscape. Mule-drawn wagons – emblems of the motion so cherished by Lena Grove – are described as "avatars," the Protestant Hightower displays the "attitude . . . of an eastern idol," McEachern on horseback constitutes a kind of "juggernaut," and "countrymen in overalls," gathered in town, have "almost the air of monks in a cloister" (Faulkner 1990b: 7, 90, 203, 416).

But while this multiplicity undercuts monolithic understandings of God, the novel also insists on their prevalence among the citizenry, even among individuals who do not habitually embrace religiosity. Though such characters as Lucas Burch/Joe Brown and Percy Grimm are largely mute on theological subjects, they are, at their moments of greatest strain, described as if they are contending with a deity – as if the imaginative structure through which they understand their lives has exceeded the boundaries of their consciousness to influence the narrative itself. Hence the novel introduces an "Opponent" who impedes Burch's "just" receipt of the reward for capturing Christmas as well as a "Player" who aids Grimm's pursuit of Christmas (1990b: 438, 462). The novel reveals numerous ways in which these characters are deluded, and their idiosyncratic conceptions of a deity defend their aggrandized self-concepts. But the fact that they have recourse to religious ideas for this purpose suggests just how pervasive and dangerous the structures of belief, exemplified by Hines and Burden, may be.

For though Percy's brutality does not originate in a religious ideology, his self-image as the servant of an interventionist god both fortifies his mission and, apparently, draws others to join him. Percy seems never fully to have understood his motives in chasing Christmas: he imagines himself to be preserving legal order, though he is ultimately more concerned with racial hierarchies and sexual behavior. But he understands the emergence of his most violent and hate-mongering tendencies as the moment of his incorporation into a divine plan, and this conviction gives him unusual energy and stamina. Others join his chase as zealously as if they had been assimilated into a practice ordained by the sun, which suddenly appears to be "upon them, of them: its shameless savageness" (1990b: 463). Though Percy is previously, as Brooks argued, "cut off from the community" and distinct in his motives and his mission, his singularity does not render him anomalous: rather, his zeal and violence merge seamlessly with religious patterns apparent throughout the novel, such that others follow him with the same unthinking verve that he exhibits (Brooks 1963: 61). In this way, the novel suggests that the danger of those who preach unyielding and hostile theologies may not be simply that others might believe them, but rather that this form of religiosity becomes more readily accessible to others experiencing violent impulses.

This menace is compounded by the fact that, following prominent strands of early twentieth-century thought, Faulkner depicts the desire for violence as endemic to social life. Influenced by *The Golden Bough* not only in its representations of multiplicity but also in its focus on sacrifice, *Light in August* further reflects tenets of psychoanalytic theory, which suggests that religious groups' efforts to promote affiliation and ethical behavior result in an overflow of violence. In *Civilization and Its Discontents*, Freud held that "people are . . . creatures among whose instinctual endowments is to be reckoned a powerful share of aggressiveness," and though "it is always possible to bind together a considerable number of people in love," such communality can only be guaranteed if "there are other people left over to receive the manifestations of their aggressiveness" (1962: 58, 61). In *Light in August*, as in Freud's account, this desire to wreak "vengeance" does not emerge from religious belief itself, but rather from the myriad disappointments of social life, which is shaped, the novel argues, by economic competition and deception as well as sexual frustration (Faulkner 1990b: 289–90). This state of dissatisfaction leads people to seek release in acts or beliefs that enable one to cede individual responsibility and cognition in following a leader or a group (Freud 1962: 21–2, 31–2).

Hence the novel suggests that Protestantism – the most prominent religion in Yoknapatawpha, as in the South more generally – responds to desires for an absolute system of values and a condoned outlet for frustration in volatile ways. This argument becomes clear in the parallels between the novel's description of the crowd that gathers after Joanna Burden's death and Joe Hightower's contemplation, from a distance, of a subsequent church service. So deeply influenced by the liturgical rhythms that once "governed and ordered" his life that they remain in "his subconscious" 25 years later, Hightower listens expectantly for the music of the Sunday evening meeting (1990b: 366). Following the "stern and formal fury" of the morning rite, this ceremony, in Hightower's mind, best exemplifies "that peace which is the promise and the end of the Church," as the worshippers, "purge[d]" of the painful emotions that attend their daily lives, experience "the cool soft blowing of faith and hope" (p. 367). But in depicting the earlier crowd, the narrative, similarly considering the mundane frustrations that shape individual lives, warns, "Peace is not that often" (p. 289). Rather than believing Joanna Burden's dead body and burning home to be "affirmations of an attained bourne beyond the hurt and harm of man," these watchers prefer to create and focus on a villain, enabling them to turn the event into "an emotional barbecue, a Roman holiday almost." This suggestion that groups long to witness the sacrifice of others is echoed by Hightower's observations, as he argues that Southern Protestants are unable to "bear" pleasurable emotions, "escap[ing]" them through "violence" (pp. 367–8). The church not only fails to quell this tendency but even encourages it by increasing its adherents' anxiety: its ethical requirements, as Freud argued, are "impossible to fulfill" (Freud 1962: 90). Accordingly, Hightower notes that Protestant music "has a quality stern and implacable . . . demanding in sonorous tones death as though death were the boon," and though its singers "accept" and even "praise" this message, they also harbor feelings of "revenge." Thus he concludes that Protestantism leads its adherents "*to crucifixion of themselves and one another*," a violent urge that, in this novel, is deflected onto Joe Christmas (Faulkner 1990b: 367, 368).

The novel demonstrates, then, that desires for ritual sacrifice are particularly dangerous in a society where African Americans are denied the political authority that would enable them effectively to counter white supremacist violence. Though the novel does not present the white church as the dominant source of local racial hatred (Doc Hines is depicted as an overtly eccentric theologian), it suggests that, in encouraging adherents to find all meaning and authority in the words of a deity, this institution suppresses faculties – such as empathy or critical self-analysis – that might enable its members to question racial oppression. Accordingly, expecting the nearby congregation to participate in lynching Christmas, Hightower believes that "they will do it gladly . . . since to pity him would be to admit self-doubt and to hope for and need pity themselves" (1990b: 368). Protestant theology is dangerous not only because it has incorporated, in some instances, overtly racist strands, but also because it encourages unquestioning devotion to accepted values.

Because it so prohibits doubt, however, religion maintains a profound influence on not just social behavior but even the very self-concept of its residents, such that those individuals whose desires might lead them to challenge oppressive beliefs lack the psychological ability to do so. Growing up amid families where religion not only dictates values but also provides an encompassing understanding of one's role in the world, both Joanna Burden and Joe Christmas are ultimately ready to rebel, but unable to revise: vigorously resisting the faiths in which they were initially inculcated, they are unable to forge a more habitable perspective on life. Joanna Burden – Calvin's granddaughter – is a child when her father leads her to believe that she is "cursed" to struggle against a suffocating racial hierarchy that she must nonetheless accept and perpetuate; she absorbs this paradoxical message along with a traumatizing image of divinely ordained mass infanticide (1990b: 252–3). Though she sits and writes "tranquilly" as long as her strange theological mission is unchallenged, she is reduced to a "spiritual skeleton" when her faith wavers, an event described as a conflict between implacable forces – "the abject fury of the New England glacier exposed suddenly to the fire of the New England biblical hell" (pp. 256, 258). In her absolute inability to negotiate the values she has learned, Burden resembles her lover Christmas, who, early in life, defies his adoptive father's violent attempts to school him in the Presbyterian catechism with the same upright and physically "rigid abnegation of all compromise" exemplified by the man who beats him (p. 148).

Their religious upbringing, in sum, has left these characters unable to imagine questioning their understandings of either God or their own identities. Of course, Christmas's difficulties – compulsive violence and an inability to forge either meaningful relationships or an inhabitable sense of self – are not only or even primarily theological: uncertain of his racial background and raised amid intense white supremacist hatred, Christmas places himself on the margins of his society and seems driven relentlessly to explore the tensions of such social positions. Still, the novel suggests that this question of his racial identity is so perpetually troubling because Christmas cannot imagine any agency in its resolution: though his biological parents are inaccessible and his body unreadable, he believes that his position in society must be socially mandated, and he can only struggle to discover or evade it. His religious training provides a model for this structure of belief, in which an aspect of one's existence that might seem to be determined in the realm of personal connections (one's parentage, one's relationship with God) is instead constructed through discrete and unassailable social codes that are read by others. Hence, for example, his adoptive father can say, "Now there is nothing for it but I must misdoubt my own eyes or else believe that at last you are beginning to accept what the Lord has seen fit to allot you" (1990b: 18).

By presenting their spiritual quandaries in this way, the novel explores a vital tension in white Southern Protestantism, in which its ideals of spiritual development have been contained in and controlled by institutions often unamenable to individual variation. Though most discussions of *Light in August* focus on the Calvinism to which the novel overtly refers, Wilson notes that, in the South, this strand of Protestantism converged so powerfully with Evangelicalism that even denominations believing in predestination shared the belief that individuals must seek and experience God's grace in direct and personal ways (1991: 25–6). This theology would seem to privilege unpredictable and transformative moments, and thus also to encourage proliferating forms of spirituality. But characters in Faulkner's world lack any models for how to fulfill such a goal. Though this theological paradox is hardly narrated, it appears prominently when Christmas has a psychological crisis, feeling so bereft of agency that he cannot imagine controlling even his impending actions. During this moment of acute loss, his memories are suddenly returned to him with surprising fullness, as he imagines

> voices, murmurs, whispers: of trees, darkness, earth; people: his own voice; other voices of names and times and places – which he had been conscious of all his life without knowing it, which were his life, thinking *God perhaps and me not knowing that too* He could see it like a printed sentence, fullborn and already dead *God loves me too* like the faded and weathered letters on a last year's billboard *God loves me too*. (1990b: 105)

Even as he spontaneously apprehends a mode of existence in which his sensory perceptions, transcending chronological time, signal an encompassing spiritual connection – simultaneously "his life" and *"God"* – this revelatory sensation is displaced by an image of religious propaganda. Printed for all to see, and insisting on God's intimate and targeted love, this hegemonic religious language is nonetheless "dead" – spiritually significant for no one.

Crucially, though this scene depicts a character noted for his "religious hatred," and though it occurs in a novel that poses a multi-leveled critique of Southern Protestantism, it nonetheless suggests a moment of profound spiritual loss and disappointment (1990b: 184). The potency and source of Christmas's feelings are indicated by the fact that, immediately afterwards, he goes to sleep in the barn, desiring to be close to and "smell" horses: though he imagines them to constitute a mere antidote to "women," it seems relevant, given his previous reflections, that his adoptive father once accused him of "believ[ing] that a stable floor, the stamping place of beasts, is the proper place for the word of God" (pp. 109, 149). Following a model established in his relationship with McEachern, Christmas perhaps unconsciously seeks to create a kind of personal (if, in his elder's terms, heretical) religious space from which he can defy those asserting themselves as theological authorities. Such intrusion is, after all, the source of his rage and perceived helplessness: Joanna Burden has begun "praying over" him, a purported form of spiritual succor that actually constitutes an injunction for him to accept a defined racial position and a role in her own religious mission (p. 105). Though her project elicits multiple forms of resistance prominent in Christmas's life – toward women and African American identity, particularly – it also reinforces one apparent source of his religious alienation, for he cannot identify with any of the segregated congregations in his social world.

Though other conflicts have received greater attention in critical analysis of the novel, identifying Christmas's frustration over the spiritual absence in his life as an additional – and intricately linked – factor in his psychological impasse helps to explain his later violent and utterly unprovoked attack on an African American revival service. The novel repeatedly suggests that Christmas tends to lash out whenever he finds himself, voluntarily or not, violating the prohibitions that he has perhaps unwittingly absorbed: accordingly, though his attack on this congregation could suggest an effort at violent differentiation, it may also reflect resentment or even longing. Christmas often suggests that to identify oneself as African American would be merely to accept the status of "Negro" amid Southern apartheid, a form of social relegation he imagines as a "black tide creeping up his legs, moving from his feet upward as death moves"; still, in assuming that this identity formation attaches marginalized persons to itself, he also attributes to it an extraordinary form of intimacy, such that "not only voices but moving bodies . . . must become fluid" (1990b: 339, 114). Christmas's life, of course, is painfully lacking in meaningful relationships, and the fact that he targets a specifically religious gathering for his vitriol, in which he curses God and assaults the preacher and deacons, could suggest envy of the qualities he attributes to this group – not only communal sharing but also, perhaps, a spiritual life more beneficial than that to which he has been exposed. For while Christmas may not share his author's theological biases, he here singles out for attack an institution associated in *The Sound and the Fury* with precisely the sort of sustaining beliefs lacking in his life.

Read in this way, the representation of Christmas would indicate that, in a society shaped by broad and strictly enforced racial segregation, individuals may project traits perceived to be absent on their side of "the color line" – a division the text nonetheless challenges – onto those from whom they are separated. In keeping with this possibility, Thadious Davis has attributed this tendency to the author himself, arguing that Faulkner uses "the black world, as he perceives it from the outside, in order to characterize the weaknesses or, more rarely, the strengths of the white world and its inhabitants" (1983: 70). This seems particularly true in his representations of religion: generally unable to credit the white churches he held culpable of oppression with beneficial spiritual effects, Faulkner nonetheless associates such prospects with the South's African American churches. As Davis argues of *The Sound and the Fury*, this bifurcation allows for greater theological balance in the fiction, rescuing it from "nihilism" and "stasis" (1983: 107). But this use of racial segregation as a fundamental aesthetic principle also creates representational problems. To encode such a distinction is to support both theological and racial barriers, an irreducible tension in Faulkner's work.

Religion, Race, and Representation

Were it not for its final section – largely focused on an African American character, Dilsey, and centrally featuring the Easter service at her church – *The Sound and the Fury* would be an unequivocally nihilistic novel. The perspectives of Quentin and Jason – two white characters who narrate much of the book (Benjy lacks theological, though perhaps not spiritual, awareness) – use religious imagery for distinctly ironic purposes: Quentin, channeling his father, imagines "that Christ was not crucified: he was worn away by a minute clicking of little wheels," and his brother justifies his lack of concern for Benjy with the assertion, "God looks after his kind" (1990c: 77, 236). But such theological assessments are sharply contrasted with Dilsey's values, as well as those expressed in the sermon of the African American church. Though the Compsons' internal monologues share an inability to look upon and comprehend loss, the Reverend Shegog insists that he "sees" the Crucifixion, particularly the suffering of Mary, and that only recognition of others' suffering and sacrifice can sustain one "when de long, cold years rolls away" (pp. 296–7, 295). Meanwhile, Dilsey emerges as the single character affiliated with the family who is able to comprehend its past and to act in its present: abused and devalued by the Compsons, she is nonetheless the only figure in the novel who can attend to its events without succumbing to bitterness, despair, or indifference. But while Dilsey's family and faith are presented as models through which the Compsons could "sav[e] themselves," the novel, as Davis argues, also suggests that the substance of Dilsey's life is "inaccessible to the whites" (1983: 92).

Indeed, racial representation is central to the depiction of Shegog's sermon, leading Walter Benn Michaels to argue that this scene epitomizes Faulkner's commitment to an essentialist form of "racial identity" (1995: 109). Though Shegog initially sounds "like a white man," his voice later becomes "as different as day and dark from his former tone, with a sad, timbrous quality like an alto horn," and then, as his speech develops, "his intonation, his pronunciation, became negroid" (Faulkner 1990c: 294–5). Further, the preacher's physical form is vigorously denigrated through racist imagery; he is described as "insignificant looking" and "undersized" with "a wizened black face like a small, aged monkey" (p. 293). As Davis argues, the repeated derision of Shegog's appearance detracts from the scene (1983: 115). It also undoubtedly contributes to critics' dismissal of Shegog's message (Sykes 1989: 27–9).

But because Shegog's performance is so closely tied, through both textual and extra-textual suggestion, to Faulkner's own artistic project, it seems possible to read this preacher, in Michael North's useful term, as a "private double" for the author – one enabling Faulkner to occupy a belief system toward which he may be skeptical while simultaneously distancing himself through stereotypical racist representation (North 1992: 57). Shegog is, after all, a verbal "virtuos[o]" who appears physically and spiritually "consumed" by his efforts to create a venue in which his congregation's "hearts were speaking to one another in chanting measures beyond the need for words" – a transformation that occurs, incidentally, before his shift in dialect (Faulkner 1990c: 293, 294; see also Matthews 1982: 108–10 and Watson 2000: 5–8). An author who described his fictions as the product of arduous labor, Faulkner had been rejected from army pilot training because of his small size, suggesting the physical as well as vocational resemblance of these figures (Meriwether and Millgate 1968: 71–2; Blotner 1974: 196). Further, Shegog shares his name with the home Faulkner aspired to buy and restore (Blotner 1974: 651–61). Thus it seems possible that, in his crude, stereotyped mask, Shegog serves as an idealized, if not comprehensive, figure for the author, one notable for the beauty, effectiveness, and wisdom of his language even as he models a faith rare in Faulkner's oeuvre. While the style of Faulkner's representation insists on an essential racial difference, then, that representation simultaneously functions to undercut such ideas. But the effect of disguise, of course, is to mute this more counter-hegemonic reading, such that this stereotypical and devout African American character might appear thoroughly differentiated from an overtly complex and apparently cynical white author.

Given his apparent use of this racialized mask in *The Sound and the Fury*, it is interesting that, 22 years later, Faulkner published a novel that similarly teams a stereotyped black woman of unqualified faith with a complicated and skeptical white woman. (Notably, Karl Zender argues that this later work encodes "meditation[s]" on Faulkner's shifting views concerning both art and religion [1987: 273, 285].) In the dramatic scenes of *Requiem for a Nun*, the central protagonist is a white woman so resistant to representation that the novel's characters can hardly agree on her name – variously Temple Drake and Mrs. Gowan Stevens, which are said to designate very different people. She also lacks any religious certainty, questioning whether "there is [a heaven] and somebody waiting in it to forgive me" and lacking recourse to any belief system that would enable her to live in her current realm – to endure "tomorrow and tomorrow" (Faulkner 1975: 242–3). Nancy Mannigoe, in contrast, is represented through the repeated assertion of a particularly demeaning stereotype – "nigger dope-fiend whore" – but is so confident of her "salvation" that she claims not even to need "hope" (p. 234). Despite denigrating Nancy ceaselessly and, further, despite the fact that Nancy has killed Temple's baby, Temple feels close to Nancy, her "confidante" and "sister . . . in sin"; she also describes Nancy as her confessor, a function she explicitly analogizes to the Catholic sacrament, and directs her theological questions to Nancy (p. 137). In sum, Temple flaunts both her scorn of and her similarity to Nancy, much as Faulkner both lampoons and elevates Shegog; further, Nancy serves as Temple's only conduit for contemplating religious faith. But while this pairing replicates so many of the relations displayed by the more uneven juxtaposition of Faulkner and his character, these later figures are crafted in ways that begin to historicize the dynamic of displacement and desire apparent in *The Sound and the Fury*.

In many ways, for example, Faulkner's representation of Nancy's spirituality is essentializing. Unquestioning even as her belief leads her to a horrible act – the killing of Temple's baby girl in an effort to preserve the family for the older boy – Nancy's relationship to religion is notable in other ways as well. When the judge requests her plea at her trial and when he announces his verdict, she addresses her response to the "Lord," rather than to the court (1975: 45, 172). Rejecting the protocols of this legal institution, she has little more respect for dominant theological tenets: her conception of Christianity is so jarring to Temple that she asks Nancy not to "blaspheme" (p. 235). Compounding Nancy's alienation from organizations, her speech, which articulates her willingness to "get low for Jesus" and effectively speaks on behalf of God, further suggests an unmediated relationship with the deity (pp. 234, 238). As Zender notes, associations of African Americans with such extraordinary "authenticity" were "common" among white US intellectuals at this time; based, to some extent, on the exclusion of African Americans from dominant institutions and "the relatively high prevalence of illiteracy among blacks in the premodern South," the suggestion of African Americans' "pure being" – an ontological distinction – nonetheless implied an innate incommensurability between their mode of existence and that of whites (Zender 1987: 283, 295n10).

But as it exoticizes Nancy's faith, the text also situates it in significant social and historical contexts. Nancy's mode of address in the courtroom is largely irrelevant, as the judge dismisses even her plea of "guilty": hence Richard Moreland describes this as a moment when, by appealing to a "higher authority," Nancy disrupts a Southern courtroom in which African Americans, notoriously, would have no standing (Faulkner 1975: 172; Moreland 1990: 210). The content of Nancy's faith is also said to be shaped by her particular experiences of physical abuse, poverty, and marginalization: Temple sardonically asks, "Who am I to challenge the language you talk about Him in, when He Himself certainly cant challenge it, since that's the only language He arranged for you to learn?" (Faulkner 1975: 235). Rather than unequivocally attributing to the African American character a particularly profound form of spirituality, as we saw in *The Sound and the Fury*, *Requiem* raises the question of how Nancy's expressions and conceptions of religion might be shaped by a context of social oppression.

Similarly, though Temple seems more overtly complex than Nancy – in Noel Polk's terms, much more so than "Nancy can ever understand" – Temple's struggles to produce some sense of continuity in her life and to achieve "love" and "forgiveness" explicitly emerge from the sort of traumatic past and social marginalization that isolate Nancy in her adamant faith (Polk 1981: 62; Faulkner 1975: 134). Having been kidnapped, raped, and ensconced in a brothel, and, adapting to this situation, passionately "lov[ing]" one of her abusers, Temple feels that she has irrevocably violated the norms of her social position "in the high proud annals of our sovereign state"; unable, however, to "quit" her prohibited desires, she hires Nancy, a former prostitute, "to talk to" (Faulkner 1975: 128, 105). Each of these women clearly longs for a productive life: Temple testifies to her own struggles, and Nancy's violent act seems motivated by her desire to secure one child a stable home, a goal apparently shaped by a past in which her unborn child was beaten to death while still in her body. These women's similarly painful histories and desperate longings undercut the possibility that they can be essentially differentiated by race.

But the economic corollaries of race in the South do affect their relationship, as Temple literally uses Nancy to maintain her own psychological health. As the circumstances of her labor force Nancy to "just keep quiet and listen" while Temple pours out her problematic yearnings and memories – for Nancy's reputation is such that she cannot easily find work – Temple is, in her own words, provided the kind of catharsis that, were it available globally, "there wouldn't even be any war" (1975: 137). But this panacea to violence would depend, as she notes, on "the world [being] populated with a kind of creature half of which were dumb, couldn't do anything but listen, couldn't even escape from having to listen to the other half" – a meditation implying her belief that the imbalance in their relationship contributed to Nancy's horrific act (p. 137). Able to describe her frustrations but unchallenged in her beliefs, the cynical Temple prepares to flee the structures of her life; forced to listen without responding, Nancy cultivates a religious faith that seems largely inhumane. Though they come together at the end of the novel to discuss their religious differences – the matter of the dead child having been forgiven and accepted – they are unable to forge any shared understanding.

In these ways, *Requiem* suggests that Faulkner had, by 1951, achieved a greater critical purchase on the idea of racially bifurcated spiritual experience than he manifested in *The Sound and the Fury*. Where this idea enabled him, in the earlier novel, to associate sustaining faith with African American Protestantism while portraying white Southerners' spiritual lives with great cynicism, the later work questions whether the corrosive effects of oppression and marginalization can be overcome by even the most devout of persons, regardless of racial identification. Though Nancy alone bears the burden in this novel of describing some sense of connection with a deity, this "nun" suffers from her lack of support and care, and her beliefs seem to beg for interrogation. Still, the white characters who turn to her for spiritual insight display an even greater sense of inner desolation. Persuasively tracing both the structure and the allusions of this novel, Noel Polk argues that it criticizes the corruption of Christianity into a dogma that denies humanity the "freedom" offered by Christ (particularly as understood in Dostoyevsky's *The Brothers Karamazov*) (Polk 1981: 158–9, 215–22). But *Requiem* further links this distortion, I would argue, to social constraints, which serve both to render questioning dangerous – as those who engage in such activities may be ostracized – and, concomitantly, to preclude active exchange and exploration among those who do seek new or revised spiritual understandings. Here, as in *Light in August*, such social restrictions are not embedded in theology: it is racial exploitation, after all, that limits Nancy's opportunities for livelihood and education, and class-related gender norms that so marginalize Temple's sexuality. But through these social and ideological structures, these women are so profoundly isolated that even when they come together – for Nancy to earn money and Temple to feel companionship – they are unable to communicate. And it is in their essential solitude that their apparent spiritual crises – though not recognized as such – fester.

In tracing these shifts between an earlier and a later novel, I do not mean to imply that Faulkner, by the end of his career, overcame his stereotypical views of race or his uncertainties about religion, neither of which is remotely the case. I have sought, rather, to demonstrate that his explorations of each issue generated creative tensions in his work – not only in and of themselves, but also, importantly, in their interaction. Reflecting on how racial identification and division shape Southerners' religious lives and exploring how spiritual yearnings affect both individual psychology and broad social dynamics, Faulkner found in the consideration of religious themes a dynamic way of understanding how individuals experience and negotiate racial segregation. For him, religious systems of belief exist not alongside but in vital reciprocity with others, many of which produce violence and oppression. Accordingly, there is still much to be learned concerning how ideas about religion inflect Faulkner's exploration of gendered identities and sexuality, or how the theological themes in *Go Down, Moses* (1942) and *A Fable* (1954) interact with – neither supplant nor merely mask – Faulkner's participation in broader modernist investigations of historiography and politics.

In this respect, scholarship on Faulkner's approach to religion reflects broader trends in Americanist literary criticism. For many decades, studies of this topic, even when imbued with acute psychological or historical awareness, tended to examine Faulkner's fiction in relation to the grand narratives with which religions are more typically associated (Irwin 1975; Sykes 1989). This history helps to explain why the study of religion in literature is so often posed against scholarship focused on power and social division: there has been little overlap, in either chronology or methodology, between these two aspects of literary analysis (Franchot 1995). As this impasse appears to be clearing, we are left with a warning, from a scholar who championed critical attention to spirituality, that theoretically informed and culturally oriented investigations of religion in literature tend, in effect, to evacuate the category of the spiritual, as the experiences and longings that might properly belong to it get translated into other vocabularies (Franchot 1995: 834–6, 839–41). But if we remain attuned to that danger, I suspect that, by examining how aspects of religiosity interact with other cultural and psychological forms in Faulkner's work, we may discover insights into spiritual life that may earlier have seemed too fragmented and variable to attribute to a writer who seemed himself to constitute "the divine icon of a literary religion" (Kreyling 1991: 153). Acutely aware of the difficulties of spiritual questioning in a society that seeks to assimilate its denizens to restrictive norms, this "Faulkner" – more seeker than icon – may prove for that reason particularly relevant to our contemporary cultural moment.

References and Further Reading

Blotner, J. (1974). *Faulkner: A Biography*. London: Chatto and Windus.

Brooks, C. (1963). *William Faulkner: The Yoknapatawpha Country*. New Haven, CT: Yale University Press.

Caron, T. P. (2000). *Struggles Over the Word: Race and Religion in O'Connor, Faulkner, Hurston, and Wright*. Macon: Mercer University Press.

Davis, T. M. (1983). *Faulkner's "Negro": Art and the Southern Context*. Baton Rouge: Louisiana State University Press.

Duvall, J. N. (1990). *Faulkner's Marginal Couple: Invisible, Outlaw, and Unspeakable Communities*. Austin, TX: University of Texas Press.

Faulkner, W. (1951). *Sartoris*. New York: Harcourt Brace. (Original pub. 1929.)

Faulkner, W. (1975). *Requiem for a Nun*. New York: Vintage. (Original pub. 1951.)

Faulkner, W. (1990a). *Absalom, Absalom!* New York: Vintage. (Original pub. 1936.)

Faulkner, W. (1990b). *Light in August*. New York: Vintage. (Original pub. 1932.)

Faulkner, W. (1990c). *The Sound and the Fury*. New York: Vintage. (Original pub. 1929.)

Franchot, J. (1995). Invisible Domain: Religion and American Literary Studies. *American Literature*, 67(4): 833–42.

Frazer, J. G. (1922). *The Golden Bough: A Study in Magic and Religion*. Abridged edn. New York: Collier. (Original pub. 1890.)

Freud, S. (1962). *Civilization and Its Discontents* (trans. J. Strachey). New York: Norton. (Original pub. 1963.)

Gwynn, F. L. and J. Blotner (eds.) (1959). *Faulkner in the University: Class Conferences at the University of Virginia, 1957–1958*. New York: Vintage.

Herbert, C. (1995). Frazer, Einstein, and Free Play. In E. Barkan and R. Bush (eds.). *Prehistories of the Future: The Primitivist Project and the Culture of Modernism* (pp. 133–58). Stanford, CA: Stanford University Press.

Hlavsa, V. V. (1985). The Mirror, the Lamp, and the Bed: Faulkner and the Modernists. *American Literature*, 57(1): 23–43.

Irwin, J. T. (1975). *Doubling and Incest/Repetition and Revenge: A Speculative Reading of Faulkner*. Baltimore: Johns Hopkins University Press.

Kartiganer, D. M. (1979). *The Fragile Thread: The Meaning of Form in Faulkner's Novels*. Amherst: University of Massachusetts Press.

Kreyling, M. (1991). The Divine Mr. F. *American Literary History*, 3(1): 153–61.

Lewis, P. (2004). Churchgoing in the Modern Novel. *Modernism/Modernity*, 11(4): 669–94.

Matthews, J. T. (1982). *The Play of Faulkner's Language*. Ithaca, NY: Cornell University Press.

Meeter, G. (1991). Quentin as Redactor: Biblical Analogy in Faulkner's *Absalom, Absalom!* In D. Fowler and A. J. Abadie (eds.). *Faulkner and Religion: Faulkner and Yoknapatawpha, 1989* (pp. 103–26). Jackson: University of Mississippi Press.

Meriwether, J. B. and M. Millgate (eds.) (1968). *Lion in the Garden: Interviews with William Faulkner, 1926–1962*. New York: Random House.

Michaels, W. B. (1995). *Our America: Nativism, Modernism, and Pluralism*. Durham, NC: Duke University Press.

Moreland, R. (1990). *Faulkner and Modernism: Rereading and Rewriting*. Madison: University of Wisconsin Press.

North, M. (1992). The Dialect in/of Modernism: Pound and Eliot's Racial Masquerade. *American Literary History*, 4(1): 56–76.

Polk, N. (1981). *Faulkner's Requiem for a Nun: A Critical Study*. Bloomington: Indiana University Press.

Sykes, J. (1989). *The Romance of Innocence and the Myth of History: Faulkner's Religious Critique of Southern Culture*. Macon: Mercer University Press.

Watson, J. G. (2000). *William Faulkner: Self-Presentation and Performance*. Austin, TX: University of Texas Press.

Wilson, C. R. (1980). Religion of the Lost Cause: Ritual and Organization of the Southern Civil Religion, 1865–1920. *Journal of Southern History*, 46(2): 213–38.

Wilson, C. R. (1991). William Faulkner and the Southern Religious Culture. In D. Fowler and A. J. Abadie (eds.). *Faulkner and Religion: Faulkner and Yoknapatawpha, 1989* (pp. 21–43). Jackson: University of Mississippi Press.

Zender, K. (1987). *Requiem for a Nun* and the Uses of the Imagination. In D. Fowler and A. J. Abadie (eds.). *Faulkner and Race: Faulkner and Yoknapatawpha, 1986* (pp. 272–96). Jackson: University of Mississippi Press.

17

Cinematic Fascination in
Light in August

Peter Lurie

[T]he image exerts the attraction of the void, and of death in its falsity.

Maurice Blanchot, *The Writing of the Disaster*

From his earliest appearance in *Light in August* (1932), Joe Christmas makes a particular impression. On the day he begins work, Byron Bunch and the other men at the planer shed notice something odd about Joe, a paradoxical quality to his appearance that both holds their collective scrutiny and functions as a warning of attendant danger. The source of this interest derives in part from the contradictory aspect of Joe's appearance, a paradox that at first seems to have to do with his economic status: "He looked like a tramp, yet not like a tramp either" (Faulkner 1985: 421), the narrator indicates. Yet as we soon learn, the indeterminate quality that defines Joe for the other men also has to do with perceptions of his race, a fact that becomes clear after they learn his name. As the foreman asks one of them, "'Did you ever hear of a white man named Christmas?'" (p. 422). Faulkner then indicates how quickly the danger inherent in this character's provocative name and his racial identity suggests itself.

> It seemed to [Byron] that none of them had looked especially at the stranger until they heard his name. But as soon as they heard it, it was as though there was something in the sound of it that was trying to tell them what to expect; that he carried with him his own unmistakable warning, like a flower its scent or a rattlesnake its rattle. They just thought that he was a foreigner, and . . . they watched him for the rest of that Friday. (p. 422)

This passage reveals not only the fact that, upon hearing of Joe's name, the men at the planer shed become that much more curious about him. What is also clear is the particularly visual form that interest acquires. As the men learn more about who Christmas is, they also become involved in watching him.

This quality of visually arresting the gaze of others had in fact begun even before Christmas's naming. Joe's appearance at the shed is marked by an oddly specular nature, as the men working there notice him first and begin watching him because of his own activity of surveying them. The chapter that introduces Joe to the novel (and to Jefferson) begins by emphasizing these acts of looking. "Byron Bunch knows this: It was one Friday morning three years ago. And the group of men at work in the planer shed looked up, and saw the stranger there, watching them. They did not know how long he had been there" (1985: 421). The activity of silent looking marks Joe's encounter with the men throughout this opening scene. Soon after Joe appears, the narrator indicates that "The others had not stopped work, yet there was not a man in the shed who was not again watching the stranger in his soiled city clothes" (p. 422), an action that only continues as Joe begins work. "The newcomer turned without a word. The others watched him go down to the sawdust pile and vanish and reappear with a shovel and go to work" (p. 422).

Significantly, this quality defines Joe throughout the novel. From this moment in the book's narration and, ultimately, through his premature and violent death, Christmas is defined by the activity of his being looked at by others – as well as by an aggressiveness behind such acts of looking. When, as a young man, he returns to the diner he'd been to with McEachern, Joe finds himself the object of a series of belligerent looks.

> He entered the screen door, clumsily, stumbling a little. The blonde woman behind the cigar case . . . watched him. At the far end of the counter the group of men with their tilted hats and their cigarettes . . . watched him. . . . He went to the counter, clutching the dime. He believed that all the men had stopped talking to watch him. (1985: 529–30)

We see this activity of watching elsewhere. Doc Hines's fanatical observing of Joe occurs insistently in the narration of his grandson's early life at the orphanage. " 'You've been watching him, too,' " says the dietician to Hines (p. 492), after she discovers Joe in her closet. " 'Sitting here in this very chair, watching him. You never sit here except when the children are outdoors. But as soon as they come out, you bring this chair here to the door and sit in it where you can watch them' " (p. 493). Later, Joe himself muses on the reason for his supposed "difference" from the children: *That is why I am different from the others: because he is watching me all the time*" (p. 501). On the night before Christmas is killed, Percy Grimm and other members of Mottstown's vigilante force commit themselves to an ongoing search for and visual monitoring of Joe and of the town's community (pp. 736–7), an aggressive, even violent form of watching that leads to Christmas's murder. The antagonism behind such looking is in fact implied at the novel's start, when the foreman at the planer shed indicates that "We ought to run [Joe] through the planer" in order to "take that look off his face" (p. 421). Above all, we will see, there is the unique force of Joe's image upon the final moment of his life, a climactic scene in the novel and in the community that makes use of the particularly compelling, once again specular quality of Joe's and others' acts of looking.

The fact of Joe's being looked at and watched so insistently suggests something unique about his position in Jefferson and in the novel. In his capacity to provoke curiosity, as well as a vague apprehension, Joe exerts an influence on other characters that may usefully be described as *fascination*. As a theoretical model, fascination has interested both film critics and Faulknerians. Michel Gresset's idiosyncratic reading, *Fascination: Faulkner's Fiction 1919–1936* (1989), is organized around variations on what he describes as the fascinated gaze in Yoknapatawpha. Gresset traces a sustained and distanced observation in all of Faulkner's novels, an oneiric blending of inner and outer perception by characters and, by extension, readers that grants his fiction its mesmerizing hold. Oliver Harris offers a useful explication of fascination in a discussion of film noir (2003), one that, as we will see, has particular relevance for considering Joe. For such critics, fascination connotes a quality of opacity or of mystery, a power that an image holds that relies on it being seen but, importantly, also on the dynamic nature of visual perception. What determines fascination is its reflexive quality, a projective sense of meaning conferred upon the object by the person seeing but that seems to inhere in the image itself. One of the most abstract but also most sustained accounts of fascination comes from the French philosopher Maurice Blanchot. Blanchot is interested in the peculiar vagaries of looking, the ways in which vision often occludes as well as clarifies what is seen. He also suggests how the conceptual category of fascination relates to film. Evoking the spectatorial pleasure of the cinema, Blanchot declares, "fascination is passion for the image" (1982: 32), a passion that has prompted varied theoretical accounts of film viewing (Kracauer 1997: 158; Heath 1981: 87; Mulvey 1992: *passim*; Wallace 2003: 88). Given its aptness to a consideration of Joe's position, one that is both textual and historical, an account of fascination helps understand what constitutes the visual and, I suggest, cinematic character of Faulkner's novel. More importantly, the role of vision and of watching Joe Christmas will reveal an aspect of *Light in August*'s deep historical significance, its oblique commentary on the legacy of violence in the Jim Crow South evident in fascination's "deathly" preoccupation with the image.

Light in August appeared at a precipitous moment of both social and cultural history. Following a range of developments in the South including Jim Crow laws and the Great Migration, as well as a burgeoning and national popular culture, Faulkner's depiction of Joe points up ways of thinking about African Americans that had become widespread by the time this novel appeared. After Reconstruction and in the first decades of the twentieth century, newly freed African Americans left the South in a massive, "internal" migration, one that lasted several years and was to have a profound impact on demographics nationally and on race relations in Northern cities. Those Southern blacks who remained were subject to adverse laws surrounding enfranchisement, labor, and segregation that were designed by Southern states to maintain African Americans' oppression and economic marginalization. The period of the turn of the twentieth century also saw the rise of the South's terrorist and vigilante police force, the violent and extra-legal legions of the Ku Klux Klan. The Klan's origins lay in the Reconstruction era, but its membership grew to its highest numbers in the 1910s and 1920s. Contemporaneously with these developments – and in one singular case, contributing to them – the early twentieth century also saw the rise of a new, truly mass form of culture. Newspapers, illustrated magazines, and above all the cinema appeared for the first time in this era or developed technical and commercial means of disseminating a broad-based, national product. The late 1800s saw the rise of the "dime novel," for example, and after 1900 magazines and book publishers began printing on cheap, more easily manufactured wood-pulp paper (hence the name "pulps" for the novels and stories they sold). The same period also saw the first exhibition of motion pictures with the Lumière Brothers' *actualités* in 1895. Already by the 1910s, movies became not only a sensational novelty but a widespread, mainstream form of entertainment.

By 1915, those developments crystallized in the production of one of the most influential films ever made. Released that year, D. W. Griffith's *The Birth of a Nation* enjoyed enormous notoriety. The first epic-length feature, it became one of the most successful movies ever produced, and it was rereleased in 1930 – two years before Faulkner published *Light in August* and in the midst of his developing thoughts about depictions of race and history in his native region. Joseph Blotner reports that Faulkner received a copy of the novel on which the movie was based, Thomas Dixon's bestseller *The Clansman* (1905), when he was a young student at school (Blotner 1984: 20). He was 18, and still impressionable, when the film of Dixon's novel was originally released. His older brother Murry reported that, like most Americans, Faulkner was an inveterate moviegoer in the early days of the medium (Falkner 1967: 49–51). Given Faulkner's interest in ways of representing the South and, particularly, depictions of its history, it seems inevitable that he would have seen Griffith's widely heralded film in one if not both of its incarnations.

At the heart of Griffith's movie (and, as we have intimated, of Faulkner's novel) is a violence toward African Americans. In the case of *Birth of a Nation*, that impulse grew out of responses in the South to black freedom during Reconstruction and in the period that followed it. The movie's dramatic conclusion shows a righteous legion of Ku Klux Klansmen riding to the rescue of an imperiled white family and suppressing a black assault on their home. This episode follows an earlier scene in the film in which the Klan is born of a perceived need to avenge the attack in the South on whites (and in particular, on white women) by former slaves who, the film suggests, had been emboldened by Northern agitators. In its original form, *Birth of a Nation* included a lynching scene that depicted an African American victim of Klan violence being castrated, a detail that Griffith later cut because of concerns about its impact on Northern audiences. Notwithstanding this edit, the film's release has also been connected to the rise of activity by the Ku Klux Klan in the years that followed it and, in the South, the incidence of actual lynchings.

Key to the success of Griffith's film was the spectacle of menace. Audiences responded to *Birth* in part because of its ability to inspire their worst fears about African Americans, including mass black uprisings, African American political power, organized violence, and, above all, interracial sexuality. What was also instrumental to the movie's success, however, was Griffith's facility in handling the viewer's gaze, his ability to manipulate the cinematic image in the service of telling a certain kind of story. Much has been made of Griffith's formal innovations with this picture and others, developments in narrative cinema that earned him the label "the father of film." Although he had been a successful director before *Birth*, with his epic Griffith linked stylistic and technical modes he'd used before to a story that exploited deeply felt worries about African Americans. The image of the former slave, Gus, for instance, framed by a fence whose boundary he "transgresses" in sexual pursuit of a young white woman (Fabe 2004: 11–12), or the shots of a white family under attack by marauding blacks cross-cut with the "heroic" arrival of the Ku Klux Klan, made *Birth* a new and, for many viewers, a particularly compelling experience. Simply put, nothing like it had ever been seen before. Although critics like Clyde Taylor have pointed to the problematic connection between Griffith's reactionary politics and innovative aesthetics (Taylor 1996: 16–19), Griffith's primarily white audiences were awestruck by the overwhelming power of the film medium as Griffith wielded it. In addition to its novel mode of manipulating the activity of looking, the movie's notoriety contributed to its stunning success (it was strenuously protested by the newly formed National Association for the Advancement of Colored People [NAACP]), and to the fact that more people saw it than any film in history before.

Although *Birth*'s appearance marked a watershed in American cultural history, it also expressed what, for Griffith and other Southern whites, was a disastrous moment in American social life. That "disaster" was the extended establishing of emancipation and race equality. The events the film depicts amounted for Griffith to a personal and regional trauma, one that left deep scars on the South's psyche and caused the suspicion and fear that have marked certain white encounters with African Americans ever since. It is this dread, I suggest, that conditions characters' responses to Joe Christmas (the impression that his presence evokes a "warning"). Like the apprehensive gaze of characters who encounter Joe, viewers of Griffith's film were both alarmed by the images it offered and fascinated by the spectacle of blackness and its supposed threat.

Key to understanding the fascination Christmas holds and, thus, his affinity with film (as well as with Griffith's movie) is the role in both of vision. In explaining fascination, Blanchot begins by describing the comforting safety associated with acts of looking. "Seeing presupposes distance," he writes, "decisiveness which separates, the power to stay out of contact" (1982: 32). Such distance, however, does not prevent a particular encounter taking place. As Blanchot puts it,

> But what happens when what you see, although at a distance, seems to touch you with a gripping contact, when the manner of seeing is a kind of touch, when seeing is *contact* at a distance? What happens when what is seen imposes itself upon the gaze, as if the gaze were seized, put in touch with the appearance? (p. 32)

As we have seen, Joe seems precisely to "seize" the gaze of those he meets. From his first scenes in the novel Christmas offers an example of "[w]hat happens when what is seen imposes itself upon the gaze." As Blanchot elaborates on his notion of fascination, he offers other ways of considering Christmas's position. I mean to define that position both socio-historically and within the novel's narrative. But in addition, and in a way that is closer to both Blanchot's philosophy and Faulkner's characterization, that position is defined conceptually. That is, the fascination Christmas provokes and the "contact" he offers the gaze of onlookers is filled with assumptions they make about him. Joe compels the men's gaze partly because of his appearance ("He looked like a tramp, yet not like a tramp either"). Yet Faulkner's novel also reveals the degree to which the people in Jefferson assert themselves into the act of scrutinizing him. When Christmas makes his appearance, the men at the planer shed look at him – as do Doc Hines or Percy Grimm in their more pointed acts of monitoring or surveillance. What they *see*, however, is not the way Christmas appears. Faulkner is at pains throughout the novel to point to Joe's blanched, "parchment colored" appearance (Faulkner 1985: 30, 112, 115). Despite Christmas's light complexion, however, such characters – and indeed, the whole Jefferson community, including Hightower, Sheriff Watt Kennedy, and Joanna Burden – persist in considering Joe black. Provoking the men's resentful gazes at the shed, and especially the fanatical and murderous gazes of Hines and Grimm, Christmas acts as the embodiment for their racist anger. Looking at Joe, characters see something more than his appearance; they see something they carry in them.

In *The Writing of the Disaster*, Blanchot provides ways of understanding the nature of that "something." In a celebrated revising of the Narcissus myth, Blanchot suggests what is fascinating about both Joe Christmas and *Birth of a Nation* as well as the role in considering both of Southern history's "disaster." As Blanchot reads the myth, Narcissus falls in love not with himself or even with his own image. Rather, he falls in love with the image per se. "Narcissus, bending over the spring, does not recognize himself in the fluid image that the water sends back to him. It is thus not himself . . . that he loves . . . Narcissus falls 'in love' with the image because the image as such . . . is attractive" (Blanchot 1986: 125). Cinema offers a clear example of the attraction of "the image as such." Yet it is the image's separation from life, the fact that it is not a living and mortal presence, that renders it (and the fascination it compels) so deathly. As Blanchot puts it in a statement that furnishes my chapter's epigraph, "[E]very image . . . is attractive: the image exerts the attraction of the void, and of death in its falsity" (p. 125). The "falsity" of the image is our belief in its possessing something other than its inertness. Michael Newman explains Blanchot's idea, suggesting that "What Narcissus sees, without recognizing it, is 'the nonliving, eternal part,' namely that in him which is death" (Newman 1996: 153). The non-living or eternal part of the self is precisely the self's non-being, understood by Blanchot as the death that is immanent in everyone and figured, in Joe Christmas, by the "warning" he offers to the men at the planer shed. I suggest that this warning is specifically the deathly attraction of the void, that void of the (narcissistic) self that is fascinated by the image and one that, throughout *Light in August*, Christmas's presence reveals.

This is the same fascination that Griffith's film exploited and that, as another singular example suggests, draws special force from the experience of cinema. In "Film Noir Fascination: Outside History, but Historically So," Oliver Harris (2003) offers an account of filmic fascination that specifies its uniquely historical character. Fascination is a crucial category for understanding the experience of film viewing for Harris, for at its center is an irreducible historical knowledge that registers precisely in its seeming ahistorical nature. As a category of film experience, fascination has generally possessed a negative valence. In the view of theorists who are critical of film viewing, such as Theodor Adorno and Fredric Jameson, fascination describes the passive, uncritical state in which viewers accept the images they see as overwhelmingly "real" – despite their ideologically or politically questionable nature. Such an account of film experience renders it pernicious, as it reduces the viewer to a spectator without the capacity to resist, much less respond thoughtfully to a film's political content or its powerful aesthetic form. This is the aspect of film viewing to which figures like Adorno and Jameson have objected so strenuously in works like Adorno and Horkheimer's "The Culture Industry" and Jameson's "Reification and Utopia in Mass Culture" and "Magical Realism in Film." Such works assert that when confronted by the film spectacle, critical thought and resistance are not the primary conditions of our experience. Rather, viewers become enmeshed in an experience that is equal parts aesthetic, sensory, and imaginative (Adorno and Horkhiemer 1988: 126–7; Jameson 1982: 22, 25; see also Kracauer 1997: 158). Presented with the sensuous images on the screen, viewers are also encouraged to project onto those images their own fantasies, prejudice, longing, or fear. It is this aspect of *Birth of a Nation* that struck a chord with viewers. And it is this phenomenological aspect to cinema – and to fascination – that makes it so captivating. Inserting ourselves into what we see, we are bound by a narcissistic but also uncanny and uncomfortable experience of looking at an aspect of ourselves that we did not know we possessed.

While of course not a film, and thus not an example of cinematic fascination as Harris and others have defined it, *Light in August* nevertheless posits a fascinated gaze at its center that may be said to evoke a historical dimension. This gaze involves the forceful and curious regard that Christmas prompts in other characters and that seems to define their impressions of him throughout the book. The final example of this impression occurs at Christmas's death, a scene that is particularly unsettling because of what may be described as Joe's suicide. In his essay on fascination, Harris (2003) offers an account of a signature and similar moment in Robert Siodmak's *The Killers* (1946). Because the moment in question relies on a series of looks that, like those that attend Joe's death, follow from but may also be said to participate in an act of killing, Harris's discussion has profound implications for understanding the cinematic – but also powerfully historical – character of fascination in Faulkner's novel.

The sequence Harris refers to is the drawn-out event of Swede's murder. Following Nick Adams's warning that two menacing-looking men are on their way to his boarding-house room, Swede (played by Burt Lancaster) decides not to try escaping their threat. Lying on his bed for the next several minutes of the film, he appears to have given up hope as he awaits the gunmen. Building an interminable tension, Siodmak constructs the scene of Swede's impending death – and his intolerable passivity as he sits, motionless, waiting for it to occur – as a series of shots that meaningfully incorporate the viewer's experience of watching the scene. Of course, one of the most disturbing aspects of this sequence is the simple fact that throughout it, Swede accepts his impending death so willingly. The look he demonstrates suggests a look into the "void" of fascination because it contemplates the genuine void of his non-being, the "nothingness" that Swede seems to accept in a gesture that amounts to suicide.

As Harris describes it, however, the field/reverse field (the technique of showing a character looking off screen, followed by a shot of what they see) reveals to the viewer another disquieting absence: their own, as the object of Swede's gaze remains, throughout his seemingly interminable looking, empty. We know that he looks upon the scene of his coming death (the door to his room, through which the killers will pass) in a manner that is almost longing. Yet included in that suicidal regard is another, even more haunting element. Harris refers to the fact that the object of Swede's intense looking becomes a kind of mirror – but one that, curiously, is empty of any reflection.

> Staring at Swede, we see ourselves looking. Staring at the door, we *are* Swede; the door also takes the place of a mirror, and to our horror, the mirror is *empty*. Siodmak takes one function of the shot/reverse-shot system – to remind us of ourselves – and renders it uncanny, as the blank space of the door not only reflects our disavowed presence as spectators but simultaneously screens our own existential absence. (2003: 10)

The scene's particular disquiet inheres in the fact that Swede waits and gazes so fully, so abjectly, on what will become the moment of his own death. And yet, what also endows the sequence with such force is our complicity in Swede's abject gaze. "Sutured" into Swede's position by way of the field/reverse field pattern, we also partake of a manner of gazing upon (our own) death, figured in the empty space of the doorframe. (On the concept of suture in film, see Heath 1981; Oudart 1977–8; Dayan 1974.)

The absence in Swede's look is at the heart of Harris's reading of this scene – and indeed, of the entire film. He seizes on it because such a lack at the heart of filmic fascination, the passive, uncomprehending gaze of the credulous spectator, is what film in general, and a genre like film noir in particular, both relies on and needs to disavow. In another example Harris offers, fascination operates as the projected look of the "*homme fasciné*" (2003: 8), a male subject who fixates on an erotically charged object of equal parts desire and dread. The fascinating object of many films noir is, of course the femme fatale, a figure possessed of the ability to lure men and their gazes not so much because of her own qualities but because of what men attribute to her. The aspect of desire to which Harris refers, and that defines many noir narratives for viewers, relates to the overwhelming "attractiveness" of both the film image and the image of the woman – an attraction that merges when encountering the figure of the femme fatale. Such films reveal how fascination threatens to draw us into a vortex of projected desire in which we lose our bearings in the material world of physical (and social and psychic) reality through an overidentification, Narcissus-like, with the cinematic image. (On viewers' powerful identification with the screen image, see Doane 1987: 1–4.) In other words, fascination draws us closer to an encounter with loss – specifically the loss of self and of death. The example of Swede is paradigmatic of cinematic fascination, pointing up what is forceful and even threatening about such an aspect of film viewing. Transfixed by the image of longing, but looking upon an absence, Swede shows us something about the nature of that looking; specifically, its basis in an emptiness or lack. Swede's gaze upon dying feels interminable – as will Christmas's at his own death – because it countenances something not regularly associated with vision: absence, a *failure* of sight, and both a literal and a figurative dying.

It is important to point out that this account of filmic fascination stands in stark opposition to aspects of cinema we have already encountered. We have noted the stunning success of *Birth of a Nation*, a film I contend bears a close relation to *Light in August* because of its reliance on the fascinating quality of the (racialized) image. Yet significantly for my argument, this aspect of fascination is not how Griffith himself understood his film. With *Birth*, Griffith purported to offer a *fullness* of vision – of understanding and a "knowledge" of Southern history – and thus a corresponding fullness of the viewing self. He did so by maintaining, not that his film's depiction of its events was fictionalized, but that the story *Birth* told was irrevocably "true." Part 2 of the movie begins with the intertitle, "This is an historical presentation of the Civil War and Reconstruction and is not meant to reflect on any race or people of today." Although the public events on which the film is based are, in fact, historical, Griffith weaves into them the fictionalized story of two families – the Northern Stonemans and the Southern Camerons – and their conjoining through friendship, sacrifice, marriage, and war. He also used historical events as the backdrop for the story in Piedmont, South Carolina, of the rise of the White Knights of Christ and to make stereotypical claims about African Americans – a presentation that, contrary to his claims, reflects quite vividly on Griffith's race biases. He used this highly sentimental melodrama to suggest that the rise of the Ku Klux Klan in the South was a necessary development, one that responded to the threat of black violence and sexuality to innocent white families. In purporting to offer a view of history as "actually . . . what happened," Griffith not only claimed to offer audiences a fullness of historical knowledge; he imagined that *The Birth of a Nation* could assert the ultimate power and "truth" of the cinema. As he put it in 1915, "The time will come, and in less than ten years . . . when the children of the public schools will be taught practically everything by moving pictures. Certainly they will never be obliged to read history again . . . There will be no opinions expressed. [Viewers] will merely be present at the making of history" (quoted in Lang 1994: 4). Watching *Birth of a Nation*, Griffith avers, would be analogous to being present at various historical events and watching them unfold.

Griffith's faith in his film's capacity to reproduce history was based on his commitment to what he claimed was a scrupulous formal realism. Several elements of *Birth* support his idea that he was reproducing the material facts of the scenarios and events the film depicted. He patterned certain scenes after photographs of particular locations, such as the South Carolina state legislature, and used historical facsimiles in recreating famous moments like the signing of the treaty at Appomattox. In pursuing such realism, Griffith sought to offer something other than the fascinating image; he believed he was reproducing genuine historical fact. ("[Viewers] will merely be present at the making of history.") Such a notion of his film's historicity, however, is of course illusory. For rather than provide viewers with an accurate, true account of the past, *Birth* (no less than *The Killers* or other examples of film) relies on a version of fascination. I say this not only because the image of Southern history that Griffith offers is far from historically accurate. Much of the film indeed falsifies the history it purports to tell, including several scenes in the South Carolina legislature that portray the first integrated state Congress. There, for instance, Griffith depicts a completely African American House of Representatives whose members engage in stereotypical behavior such as eating chicken (while debating), sitting with their feet up on their desks, and passing a motion that requires all members of the Congress to wear shoes. Griffith also invents a piece of legislation in this scene when he shows the Congress pass a law that requires whites to salute blacks on the street.

More importantly than these historical inaccuracies – but in fact, of a piece with them – what *Birth* offers is not realism but a deathly fascination with the image. One way of establishing the particularly phantasmatic quality of Griffith's film is through his use of blackface. Michael Rogin and others have pointed to the incongruity of blackface in a film that Griffith otherwise prided himself had several aspects of realism (Rogin 1996: 14; Taylor 1996: 23). Griffith's depictions of blackness in the film, for which he was credited for his "egalitarian" casting, relied on non-actor African Americans to play the roles of contented slaves on the Cameron plantation or political novices at the South Carolina state house. Yet in the film's two principal black roles, Thaddeus Stevens's protégé Silas Lynch and the former slave Gus, Griffith cast white actors in blackface. What the images of Henry Long and George Seigmann in blackface amount to is a patently *un*realistic representation of race. Rather than fidelity to historical reality and the presence of African Americans in the South (and in the film), the roles of Gus and Lynch attest to Griffith's abhorrence of interracial contact. He could not cast an African American in a role that involved touching and attempting to rape a female character who is white – as Gus and the "mulatto" Lynch both do. With these roles, Griffith falls back on a convention that mocks the realist capacity of the film medium. In the several scenes involving Silas and Gus, Griffith requires viewers to suspend disbelief, prompting what might well be called their fascinated response. Rather than realism or "history," in such cases he offers the fascinating, deathly attraction of the (cinematic) image. Asking his audience to accept images of whites in blackface – or even to be suitably scandalized by them – Griffith depended on an uncritical audience, one that would be in thrall to the fully imagined and phantasmatic image he presented to them of a menacing, licentious blackness.

It is this quality of the racialized gaze (mesmerized, fascinated) that Faulkner takes up with several characters' response to Joe. Beginning with his first appearance in the book, Christmas prompts the "credulous" but also suspicious and tendentious gaze of others. True to Byron's predictions, Joe's name and people's reactions to him lead to profound problems of identity and acceptance that, over and over again, follow from skewed perceptions of his race. Even Joe himself appears caught in a contemplation of his image that Faulkner relates to problems of his self-perception. Joe's difficulties with identity hardly need elaborating; nor do their origin in the vexed sense he possesses of his appearance and racial identity. We may say that such uncertainty contributes to Joe's wariness in nearly any social context, such as his work at the planer shed, his visit to the diner, or the extended series of encounters he has in his years wandering, events that the reader does not witness but that we learn lead to repeated confrontations and Joe's frequent bouts of violence. At certain moments that we do see, this confusion manifests itself in his awareness of not only other people's regard of him, but the environment's. On the day on which he will murder Joanna Burden, Joe sits alone in the forest, seeing himself observed by an enveloping, not altogether benign force. "It seemed to him as he sat there the yellow day contemplated him drowsily, like a prone and somnolent cat . . . his whole being suspended . . . in quiet and sunny space" (Faulkner 1985: 481). "His whole being suspended" is an apt way to describe Joe's tragic life generally. It also provides a useful way to understand other characters' habit of watching him, holding him arrested within the gaze, like a photographic or cinematic still image. Intriguingly, one moment of Christmas's self-regard elsewhere in the book – and the deathly stillness it suggests – even relates to the technology of photography, the mechanical reproduction of images on which film depends. Standing in a roadside field one night, Joe is revealed by the lights of an oncoming car in which "[h]e watched his body grow white out of the darkness like a kodak print emerging from the liquid" (p. 478). Like other descriptions of Joe's pale complexion, this moment gives the lie to accounts of him as African American. As such, it reveals the extent to which others' perception of Joe, or even his self-perception, is conditioned by pre-existing attitudes about race. It also says much about the role played in these attitudes by the image. Faulkner's reference here to the processing of photographic development does more than insert a technical, chemical element to Joe's self-awareness and an anomaly to the natural environment of the rural South. In addition to emphasizing the alienation Joe feels throughout his life, such a moment also evokes the phantasmatic, fascinating quality of the (cinematic) gaze, exerted here by Christmas on himself in a fashion similar to that we've seen exercised throughout the novel by others.

Yet it is at his death that the fascinating qualities I associate with Joe Christmas and with film culminate. After he's been shot and then castrated, Joe gazes at his attackers with a look that is hard to understand. Lying prostrate, fatally wounded, and bleeding, Joe looks at them "peacefully," we are told, returning the gaze they extend to him as he is dying. The effect of Joe's look back though is uniquely *un*-peaceful, even otherworldly, and it possesses a force that has unsettled countless readers and proven elusive to many efforts to analyze it.

> But the man on the floor had not moved. He just lay there, with his eyes open and empty of everything save consciousness, and with something, a shadow, about his mouth. For a long moment he looked up at them with peaceful and unfathomable and unbearable eyes. (Faulkner 1985: 742)

The arresting quality of Joe's dying look is lodged in the string of adjectives Faulkner uses in describing it. Critics have lingered over this moment for years, held by its compelling nature much as are the characters in the scene (Slatoff 1972: 180; Kartiganer 1979: 48; Pitavy 1974: 77; Gresset 1989: 210; Porter 1981: 252). There is yet something important about this moment, however, part of which is suggested by its capacity to hold the critical as well as imaginative gaze. In Joe's "peaceful and unfathomable and unbearable eyes" lingers a quality that Blanchot and Harris attribute to the fascinated gaze. The peacefulness of Joe's look is what is perhaps most unsettling about it, sharing as it does the unfathomable, unknowable qualities of his expression. What I suggest is unbearable about Joe's regard, however, is what it says, not about him, but about the men who look upon the death they are witnessing.

For there is a quality to Joe's expression and his look that reveals much about the men who surround him when he's dying. In addition to the preternatural calm of Joe's gaze is the fact that what his look includes or "holds" may be these men's own death. As with Harris's account of Swede and the viewer's reflective encounter of his look, when Percy Grimm and the other men linger over Joe's death, they also see themselves looking. More damning still, more troubling (to them), is the specific content of their look. What Grimm and the other men see is their own abyss, their deathly fascination with race and the murderous, blind hate that seizes them and that is conditioned by a racist dread. Confronted with the object of that hate, but simultaneously with a gaze that is neutral and unceasing and that flatly mirrors their own, the men lose their comfortable visual separation from Joe and become implicated in an encounter at his death that demands their recognition of their own hauntedness.

Joe's passivity, at the moment of his death no less than during events that lead up to it, resembles the fascinated gaze that defines cinema and that is suggested both by Faulkner's novel and by particularly self-conscious films. Swede in *The Killers* is not a racialized Other in the manner that Christmas is. In his unsettling "welcoming" of his death, however, Swede performs in a way that helps us understand a similar attitude in and gesture by Joe. Faulkner's narrator describes how, on the day after Joe is killed, the townspeople speculate on his death.

> [W]hat the town wondered at was not so much how Christmas had escaped but why when free, he had taken refuge in the place which he did, where he must have known he would be certainly run to earth, and why when that occurred he neither surrendered nor resisted. It was as though he had set out and made his plans to passively commit suicide. (1985: 727)

Both Swede and Christmas appear to will, or at the least, to welcome their own death, a position that results in both the novel's and the film's demonstration of a fascinated gaze. However self-willed it is, though, Joe's death possesses qualities of attraction for the onlookers, a way of holding their gaze that we have seen Joe prompt in his encounters with characters generally and that possesses a reflexive dimension. It is this quality that makes Faulkner's display of fascination so penetrating and, especially for those "seized" by Christmas's gaze at his death, so enduring. As the narrator says of the men who witness his final expression,

> They are not to lose it, in whatever peaceful valleys, beside whatever placid and reassur-ing streams of old age, in the mirroring faces of whatever children they will contemplate old disasters and newer hopes. It will be there, musing, quiet, steadfast, not fading and not particularly threatful, but of itself serene, of itself alone triumphant. (1985: 743)

Joe returns the men's fascinated gaze in a manner that leads to their seeing themselves mirrored in it not only as they look down on him and on his "empty" eyes. When Faulkner indicates that Joe's face will "be there" in the faces of these men's children in the future, he suggests that Joe's haunting look at his death will continue to be reflected at them for years or even generations to come.

Christmas's gaze —or more properly, what it reflects – quite clearly has the property of fascination in its suicidal dimension. Looking at Christmas, Percy Grimm and the other men see an emptiness, an absence. That cipher returns to them as a ghostly reminder of the "existential absence" attendant on Grimm's and the South's racist regard of blackness, their unconscious dread of their own complicity in slavery and racial violence and the moral lack such a history reveals (a history suggested by Faulkner's reference to "old disasters"). Harris's remarks about the film spectator's experience of Swede's death resonate with what I suggest is a dimension of Christmas's. "Our acute discomfort as spectators of Swede's last moments is unsurprising, caught as we are in the look *at* and *of* the camera: forced to internalize both looks, we find our curiosity to see returned to us as both sadistic and masochistic complicity" (2003: 10). Reading Christmas's death scene, as well as scenes throughout the book, we recognize how char-acters are caught in the look *at* and *of* Joe. We also see the violence that is complicit in such looking. Percy Grimm and Southerners like him clearly possess a sadistic impulse to punish African Americans, even men like Joe who are thought to be of mixed-race identity and are mistakenly perceived as black. Viewed through the perspective of a kind of cinematic spectacle, one that partakes of the fascination with the racial Other that we have seen demonstrated by *Birth*, the exchange of looks attending Joe's death may acquire another kind of meaning. As an example of cinematic fascination, this moment in the book points up structures of looking and of perceiving that are products of the historical race conflicts of the South and that contributed to both the conception and the reception of Griffith's film – the fact that it persuaded so many viewers, Northern as well as Southern, of its racist vision. (See Rogin 1994: 253 for the role of immigration in the movie's Northern reception.) It also suggests a source for those conflicts and the fascinated gaze in an unresolved masochistic tension within those who wield it.

This account of Joe's death may return us to both his arrival on the scene of the novel and the problematic nature of Griffith's film. The spectator's fascinated gaze at *Birth of a Nation* mirrors the deathly fascination of social subjects like Grimm and other Southerners for whom race was an object of equal parts allure, dread, and a projective self-loathing. This aspect of fascination is also, then, a dimension of Christmas's onlookers that Faulkner sought to stress: a contemplation of their own "existential absence," a masochistic, even suicidal impulse manifest in their collective gaze, one that will haunt them with the same paradoxical quality that Joe's first appearance possesses. We have noted earlier the way in which Joe's arrival in the novel signals a kind of warning. This impression, oriented toward an expectation of violence and punishment, finds its culmination in the scene of Joe's castration and death. Yet what this outcome also reveals is the full measure of Christmas's first appearance and its "warning." As the several gazes attending his death reveal, Christmas's arrival in Jefferson serves to warn those who meet him about the threat he poses not only to himself, but also to their own sense of identity, social position, or being.

That threat arises from the specifically historical dimension of Christmas's death: its connection to or even culmination of the trauma of Southern history that his presence evinces. As indicated earlier, Joe Christmas arrives on the scene of the novel as well as in the scenario of Southern social reality at a particular point in history. I have been at pains to point out the traumatic quality of that history, the line that runs from Jim Crow laws and violence toward African Americans back to earlier events like the Civil War and slavery. This history is lodged, however obscurely, in the "meaning" of Joe Christmas, a meaning found, for other characters, in his appearance and his image.

As several writers have suggested, such historical meaning is difficult to plumb. Theorists such as Walter Benjamin, Blanchot, and others point to the traumatic quality of history generally and to the fact that, because of its painful effects, history's real nature cannot be readily assimilated into narrative. In this context, Benjamin's concept of history's ephemera and fragmentary "traces" are helpful. As he asserts, "To articulate the past historically does not mean to recognize it 'the way it really was.' It means to seize hold of a memory as it flashes up at a moment of danger" (1968: 255). According to Benjamin, what is most genuinely "historical" about historical events is their incommensurability with representation or exegesis. (See also Silverman 1992: 53–60.) Blanchot views history and its representation similarly. In describing the disaster, which functions for him like historical trauma, he writes, "The disaster . . . is the time when . . . in place of men comes the infinite calm (the effervescence) which does not embody itself or make itself intelligible" (1986: 40). Declaring that "Blanchot's philosophy is fundamentally nocturnal," Harris extends the idea of history's unintelligibility; like fascination, that is, history in Blanchot's thinking remains a presence and an effect that cannot be measured or "seen." As Harris says of fascination's force, "[I]t pursues knowledge that lies behind the truth of the visible and beyond narrative telling, a knowledge that is a kind of nothingness, a negativity, death itself" (2003: 6).

In its "negative" aspect, its uncritical, haunted, and rapt quietude, fascination can be seen to offer a productive resistance to the false accounts of the past offered by historicism. Joe's silence during much of *Light in August*, but especially and unnervingly at his death, like Swede's in *The Killers*, forces questions far more than it hopes to answer. Above all, what moments such as Swede's and Joe's death compel us to ask is: why are these men so willing to die? What in their circumstances or social world has made living so intolerable? Fascination appears, for Faulkner as for Siodmak, when a situation or a narrative exists that defies ready explanation. Faulkner's Joe Christmas dies because of a conception of race on the part of individuals like Grimm or Doc Hines, as well as the broader community of Jefferson, that cannot possibly be explained rationally. Nor can it effectively be narrated. Rather, Joe's death and life show the endless, affective, and irrational hold that his presence and appearance exert on those who meet him. Within the vast narrative of the novel, its seemingly inexhaustible reach and its willingness to continually start its story over, the fascination Joe exerts points up the limits of Faulkner's ability to convey fully or explain discursively other characters' reactions to him. It is this cipher-like quality to Joe Christmas, and his incommensurability not only with Jefferson's understandings of race but with realist conceptions of character, that critics have noted (Kartiganer 1979: 37–48). In the fact of that genuine problem of representation and of the dark world of the novel, Faulkner offers a variation on Blanchot's "nocturnal," fascinated gaze.

In Joe Christmas, *Light in August* offers a singular example of fascination and its relationship to narrating history. The power of fascination, however, holds particular interest when the historical narrative in question is a film. What Faulkner's novel allows us to see in closing is how different an approach to fascination occurs in the case of historical cinema and, in particular, in the case of an early and influential film. Griffith's cinematic practice in *Birth* opposes utterly the notion of historical trauma being inherently illegible or "invisible." Rather, Griffith believed that his film and the history it treats were defined by a radical *visibility*, a full bearing-forth and re-presenting of the historical past. Tracing the black presence in America from its origins in slavery, Griffith's film opens with a statement that indicates the course he believed American history to have taken. Referring to the rift that produced the Civil War but that also, as subsequent events in the movie suggest, created a role for the Ku Klux Klan (and for Griffith's film) to fulfill, the movie's first intertitle reads, "The bringing of the African to America planted the first seed of disunion." Following this we see a shot of a pilgrim blessing an arriving slave. It is this "disunion" – and not the South's vigorous effort to prolong it – that Griffith saw as the cause of the Civil War, the wounds from which he imagined his film would heal. At the end, in a split screen with the film's final shot of a white Northerner and his Southern beloved is an image of Christ and the City of God – a suggestion of the sanctified peace the country would enjoy following the act of closing its (racial) ranks and containing the black threat it faced from within. This is the image of the new "nation," united in its racism and violent suppression of African Americans, that Griffith saw his film inspiring.

The South offers a unique example of the problematic nature of history and its representation precisely because of the deep trauma that particular periods of Southern history inflicted. The most traumatic series of events for the American South throughout the period of the late nineteenth to the early twentieth centuries, as for the country generally, culminated in Griffith's wildly popular film that treated these same events directly. In addition to the broader events of slavery, the Civil War, Reconstruction, and the rise of the Ku Klux Klan, *Birth* includes traumatic events such as the burning of

Atlanta, Lincoln's assassination, Gus's lynching, and the violent death of Flora Cameron, who throws herself off a cliff to avoid her would-be black rapist. *Birth* was also, as we noted, the first epic film to be widely distributed. Before it, audiences had been seeing film entertainment for nearly twenty years. But with this three-hour feature, Griffith ushered in the serious drama and the wedding of film to a particular *kind* of historicity. *Birth* claimed to narrate the traumas of history in a manner that was objective and "true." Yet as we have seen, such a notion of history as knowable is belied by the true nature of history and by film's own temporal operations. This is the case both on the level of the specific, discrete moment – the fascinating image – and on that of the invisible but palpable presence in film of an ongoing, fluid temporality (Deleuze 1989).

Unlike historical narratives of the South such as *Birth of a Nation* that seek to present viewers with a hermeneutic view of history – explicable and contained within a particular view – *Light in August* insists upon what is *un*narratable, outside "objective" or clear representation. "Outside history, but historically so," the subtitle of Harris's article and a reference to Blanchot, describes that aspect of fascination that marks the look of a traumatized subject. Joe's uncanny regard at his death acquires its inassimilable quality, its "unhistorical" aspect, precisely because it registers the trauma of racial experience in the South so fully. That Faulkner even provides a willfully false commentator on Joe's death in the person of Gavin Stevens, who appears in the novel with the ostensible purpose of "explaining" Joe's behavior leading up to his death (1985: 730–1), suggests Faulkner's awareness of the limitations of such an ordered, controlling narrative. Joe's look upon dying is the most authentically historical moment in the novel – and arguably in all of Faulkner's fiction, an expression of suffering and trauma that Joe experiences personally but that transcends his own particular life to encompass, in its awful, "unfathomable" "peace," the historical trauma of the South generally. Unlike *Birth*, which situates its (historical) events within a strict causality and a commensurately linear narrative, Joe's death remains stubbornly outside any such effort to understand fully or to know its meaning. It is in this traumatized aspect that *Light in August* seeks to negotiate the Southern history it treats. And in permitting it to remain traumatized, "unhistorical," *fascinating*, Faulkner allows a way to distinguish his novel from narratives of the South, like *Birth of a Nation*, that present this history so falsely.

REFERENCES AND FURTHER READING

Adorno, T. W. and M. Horkheimer (1988). The Culture Industry: Enlightenment as Mass Deception. In *Dialectic of Enlightenment* (trans. J. Cumming). New York: Continuum (pp. 120–67). (Original pub. 1944.)

Benjamin, W. (1968). Theses on the Philosophy of History. In *Illuminations* (ed. H. Arendt, trans. H. Zohn) (pp. 253–64). New York: Shocken Books.

Blanchot, M. (1982). *The Space of Literature* (trans. A. Smock). Lincoln, NE: University of Nebraska Press. (Original pub. 1955.)

Blanchot, M. (1986). *The Writing of the Disaster* (trans. A. Smock). Lincoln, NE: University of Nebraska Press. (Original pub. 1980.)

Blotner, J. (1984). *William Faulkner: A Biography.* One-vol. edn. New York: Random House.

Dayan, D. (1974). The Tudor Code of Classical Cinema. *Film Quarterly*, 28(1): 22–31.

Deleuze, G. (1989). *Cinema 2: The Time-Image* (trans. H. Tomlinson and R. Galeta). Minneapolis: University of Minnesota Press. (Original pub. 1985.)

Doane, M. A. (1987). *The Desire to Desire: The Woman's Film of the 1940s*. Bloomington: Indiana University Press.

Doane, M. A. (1991). *Femmes Fatales*. New York and London: Routledge.

Fabe, M. (2004). *Closely Watched Films: An Introduction to the Art of Narrative Film Technique*. Berkeley: University of California Press.

Falkner, M. (1967). *The Falkners of Mississippi: A Memoir*. Baton Rouge: Louisiana State University Press.

Faulkner, W. (1985). *Light in August*. In *William Faulkner: Novels 1930–1935*. New York: Library of America. (Original pub. 1932.)

Gresset, M. (1989). *Fascination: Faulkner's Fiction, 1919–1936* (trans. T. West). Durham, NC: Duke University Press. (Original pub. 1982.)

Griffith, D. W. (1971). The Future of the Two-Dollar Movie. In F. Silva (ed.). *Focus on* The Birth of a Nation (pp. 99–102). Englewood Cliffs, NJ: Prentice Hall.

Harris, O. (2003). Film Noir Fascination: Outside History, but Historically So. *Cinema Journal*, 43(1): 3–24.

Heath, S. (1981) On Screen, in Frame: Film and Ideology. In *Questions of Cinema* (pp. 1–18). Bloomington: Indiana University Press.

Jameson, F. (1982). *Signatures of the Visible*. New York and London: Routledge.

Kartiganer, D. M. (1979). *The Fragile Thread: The Meaning of Form in Faulkner's Novels*. Amherst: University of Massachusetts Press.

Kracauer, S. (1997). *Theory of Film: The Redemption of Physical Reality*. Princeton, NJ: Princeton University Press. (Original pub. 1960.)

Lang, R. (1994). *The Birth of a Nation*: History, Ideology, Narrative Form. In R. Lang (ed.). *The Birth of a Nation: D. W. Griffith, Director*

(pp. 3–24). New Brunswick, NJ: Rutgers University Press.

Mulvey, L. (1992). Visual Pleasure and Narrative Cinema. In G. Mast, M. Cohen, and L. Braudy (eds.). *Film Theory and Criticism: Introductory Readings*. 4th edn (pp. 746–57). New York and Oxford: Oxford University Press.

Newman, M. (1996). The Trace of Trauma: Blindness, Testimony, and the Gaze in Blanchot and Derrida. In C. B. Gill (ed.). *Maurice Blanchot: The Demand of Writing* (pp. 153–73). London and New York: Routledge.

Oudart, J. P. (1977–8). Cinema and Suture. *Screen*, 18(1): 35–47.

Pitavy, F. (1974). *Faulkner's* Light in August (trans. G. E. Cook). Bloomington: Indiana University Press.

Porter, C. (1981). *Seeing and Being: The Plight of the Participant Observer in Emerson, James, Adams, and Faulkner*. Middletown, CT: Wesleyan University Press.

Rogin, M. (1994). "The Sword Became a Flashing Vision": D. W. Griffith's *The Birth of a Nation*. In R. Lang (ed.). *The Birth of a Nation: D. W. Griffith, Director* (pp. 250–93). New Brunswick, NJ: Rutgers University Press.

Rogin, M. (1996). *Blackface, White Noise: Jewish Immigrants in the Hollywood Melting Pot*. Berkeley: University of California Press.

Silverman, K. (1992). *Male Subjectivity at the Margins*. New York: Routledge.

Slatoff, W. (1972). *Quest for Failure: A Study of William Faulkner*. Westport, CT: Greenwood Press.

Sobchack, V. (1992). *The Address of the Eye: A Phenomenology of Film Experience*. Princeton, NJ: Princeton University Press.

Taylor, C. (1996). The Re-Birth of the Aesthetic in Cinema. In D. Bernard (ed.). *The Birth of Whiteness and the Emergence of U.S. Cinema* (pp. 15–37). New Brunswick, NJ: Rutgers University Press.

Wallace, M. F. (2003). The Good Lynching and *The Birth of a Nation*: Discourses and Aesthetics of Jim Crow. *Cinema Journal*, 43(1): 85–104.

18

Faulkner's Brazen Yoke: Pop Art, Modernism, and the Myth of the Great Divide

Vincent Allan King

Because it is himself that the Southerner is writing about, not about his environment: who has, figuratively speaking, taken the artist in him in one hand and his milieu in the other and thrust the one into the other like a clawing and spitting cat into a croker sack.

William Faulkner, Introduction to *The Sound and the Fury*, 1933

Like and unlike together / In the same brazen yoke.

Horace, *Odes* i.33

Having waste ground enough, / Shall we desire to raze the sanctuary, / And pitch our evils there?

Shakespeare, *Measure for Measure*

Critics have long recognized the importance of William Faulkner's participation in the popular culture industry. This participation includes selling the film rights to many of his novels, working as a screenwriter in Hollywood, and producing scores of short stories for popular magazines such as *Cosmopolitan* and the *Saturday Evening Post*. More recently, scholars have begun to explore how a variety of popular arts – including film, cartoons, detective stories, and other popular genres – influenced Faulkner's fiction. Unfortunately, critics have largely ignored how their own attitudes toward popular culture have shaped the way we read Faulkner's oeuvre. In other words, while it is important to document the many connections between Faulkner and both the business and the artifacts of popular culture, it is just as important to consider how shifting perceptions about the aesthetic and moral value of popular culture have shaped the reception of his canon.

The best place to begin such a history is with the irascible Leslie Fiedler. Fiedler, of course, was an early champion of both popular art and postmodern literature. Moreover, it was his growing appreciation of popular art and his growing disdain for the modernist art novel that shaped his reaction to Faulkner's fiction. In two famous essays, "William Faulkner, Highbrows' Lowbrow" (1950) and "Pop Goes the Faulkner: In Quest of Sanctuary" (1990), Fiedler embarked on a characteristically herculean task: to metamorphose Faulkner from a high modernist working in the art novel tradition into a sentimental entertainer who was committed to writing for a popular audience. Fiedler defines popular fiction as short stories and "novels which please the many who prefer their reading pleasure unmediated and unexamined, like *Gone with the Wind*, rather than those, like James Joyce's *Ulysses*, which provide opportunities for classroom exegesis and analysis to the few who get their kicks out of such second-hand responses to literature" (Fiedler 1990: 75).

As this rather pointed passage makes clear, Fiedler's project falls just short of a literary jihad, and his mission is to save Faulkner from the diabolical clutches of high art and return him to the familial embrace of popular culture. Irritated that his first essay had not brought about the desired effect, he complains in the second that his initial essay

> seems to have made almost no impression on the Faulkner critical establishment; which is, I suppose, why I am moved once more to try and make clear the sense in which Faulkner's "pop" stories (and by the same token, his "pop" novel, *Sanctuary*) represent not works of the left hand, irrelevant or peripheral, but the essence, the very center of his achievement. (1990: 77)

Despite Fiedler's best efforts, few critics today would willingly exchange *The Sound and the Fury, As I Lay Dying, Light in August, Absalom, Absalom!*, and *The Hamlet* for Faulkner's short fiction and *Sanctuary*.

Even so, Fiedler's advocacy of a popular Faulkner – one who, as Fiedler insists, has more in common with Dickens and Twain than Proust, Mann, and Joyce – has had a considerable impact on Faulkner studies (Fiedler 1990: 77). The major benefit of Fiedler's influence is that it is no longer possible to think of Faulkner as a modernist deity disinterestedly paring his fingernails above the heads of the equally disinterested masses. Now we can juxtapose that tired portrait with a portrait of Faulkner the professional writer, a writer who was not alienated from the masses but who wrote with them in mind. While we have wisely abandoned Fiedler's effort to replace the modernist Faulkner with the popular Faulkner, we find ourselves at the beginning of the twenty-first century with two apparently irreconcilable Faulkners. Lacking the critical imagination to place the modernist Faulkner and the popular Faulkner in one "brazen yoke," we are left with a schizophrenic Faulkner or, more accurately, a slew of schizophrenic Faulkners (Horace 1997: 87).

A few examples will help me illustrate this point. In *Heart in Conflict*, Michael Grimwood argues that Faulkner was torn between his allegiance to his pastoral roots and his artistic ambitions. This "divided imagination" (Grimwood 1987: 84) led to a series of "discontinuities in Faulkner – between his crass and his artistic intentions, between urban and rural identities, between 'low' and 'high' audiences, between himself and his own writing" (Grimwood 1987: 195). In *The Making of a Modernist*, Daniel J. Singal describes a Faulkner torn between "two divergent approaches to selfhood – the Victorian urge toward unity and stability . . . and the Modernist drive for multiplicity and change" (Singal 1997: 15). In *Faulkner's Questioning Narratives*, David Minter also speaks of Faulkner's "divided impulses," arguing that "Faulkner's imagination was, in one of its aspects 'conservative' and that it was in another 'radical'" (Minter 2004: 20, 56). And in *The Novel Art*, Mark McGurl insists that Faulkner's canon may be split neatly down the middle between works written for lowbrow readers and works written for highbrow readers (McGurl 2001: 147–8).

While these studies have much to recommend them, they, like Faulkner scholarship in general, leave us where Fiedler left us: unable to reconcile the works of the right hand with the works of the left hand. If Faulkner studies are to advance beyond this tiresome stalemate, we must put these two Faulkners and their separate canons in the same croker sack. In short, we must blur the distinction between Faulkner the modernist and Faulkner the purveyor of pulp fictions. The best way to do this, I believe, is to question the two assumptions upon which this distinction rests: the assumption that there is a natural antipathy between modernism and popular culture and the assumption that Faulkner's works fall neatly into either a modernist or a popular canon.

Since the idea that there is a "great divide between modern art and mass culture" (Huyssen 1986: 59) has become accepted wisdom, I'd like to begin by recalling that this distinction is simply a product of the more general distinction between fine and popular art. And while we may assume that these categories have a long and venerable history, they are not only relatively recent inventions but also ones that have clearly outlived their original purpose. In *The Invention of Art*, Larry Shiner summarizes the historical development of the split between fine and popular art:

> in the eighteenth century a fateful division occurred in the traditional concept of art. After two thousand years of signifying any human activity performed with skill and grace, the concept of art was split apart, generating the new category fine arts (poetry, painting, sculpture, architecture, music) as opposed to crafts and popular arts (shoe-making, embroidery, storytelling, popular songs, etc.). (Shiner 2001: 5)

By the beginning of the nineteenth century this distinction culminated in what I, with a nod of appreciation to Richard Rorty, will call the divinization of art. Shiner observes that

> Whereas the eighteenth century split the older idea of art into fine art versus craft, the nineteenth century transformed fine art itself into a reified "Art," an independent and privileged realm of spirit, truth, and creativity. Similarly, the concept of the artist, which had been definitively separated from that of the artisan in the eighteenth century, was now sanctified as one of humanity's highest spiritual callings. (2001: 187)

In this newly created Church of Art, the masterpieces of the various canons serve as a haven or sanctuary for the reader. Shiner quotes the German philosopher Karl Philipp

Moritz: "As the beautiful object draws our attention completely to itself, it makes us forget ourselves for a while so that we seem to lose ourselves in it" (2001: 145). Seen from another perspective, however, this sanctuary serves not just as a refuge from the self but also as a citadel from whose lofty height one may gain perspective on all things human. This elevated perspective allows us to escape the vagaries of time and history and to discern the timeless, the universal. So whether one turned to the fine arts to escape the world or to render it transparent, their function was the same: to enable the participant to transcend what Hawthorne called "the muddy tide of human activity" (quoted in Wilson 1994: 446).

The original purpose behind the divinization of the fine arts was not primarily to marginalize the popular arts, which, after all, were protected by the fact that they were intertwined with everyday life. Instead, the purpose was to protect the arts which, to paraphrase Huyssen, had become uncoupled from the church and the state and, thus, vulnerable to charges of frivolity or, worse, immorality (Huyssen 1986: 17). The best way to insulate these vulnerable arts from these charges was to divinize them, to bathe them in a quasi-religious aura that made it easy to claim that they produced effects which were congruent – if not synonymous – with the teachings of the church and the aims of the state.

At the same time, however, the divinization of the fine arts also created a series of insidious binary oppositions, pitting high art versus low art, sensitive intellectuals versus the brutish masses, approved genres and mediums versus pernicious mediums and genres. Furthermore, this conception tended to reduce critics to sanctimonious prigs whose primary task was to preserve these oppositions, to keep the sanctuary of art from being defiled by the temporal, the sensual, and the monetary.

Shiner makes precisely this point when he notes that Kant "begins his *Observations on the Feeling of the Beautiful and Sublime* with a contrast between those of grosser appetites who look at things in terms of money or sex and persons 'of noble sensitivity' who are concerned with 'finer feeling' " (Shiner 2001: 97). This distinction between writing to express finer feelings and writing to make money became an important if facile way of separating high art from low. As Shiner explains, "Attracted to the world of art by its spiritual aura, hero worship, and rhetoric of freedom, the aspiring artist in the nineteenth century found a ready-made discourse of 'spirit versus money' to explain lack of success." "Given such a climate," he continues,

> it is no wonder that George Sand would remember her decision to become a writer in just those terms: "To be an artist! Yes, I wanted to be one, not only to escape from the material jail, where property large or small, imprisons us in a circle of odious little preoccupations, but to isolate myself from the control of opinion . . . to live away from the prejudices of the world." (2001: 201)

For Sand, the conception of fine art is liberating, providing a sanctuary situated well above the pressures of bourgeois life. Yet as we have already seen, post-World War II critics such as Fiedler chafed at this divinization of the fine arts.

Fiedler's most famous criticism of the fine arts can be found in his highly influential essay "Cross the Border – Close the Gap." There he contends that "The notion of one art for the 'cultured,' i.e., the favored few in any given society . . . and another subart for the 'uncultured,' i.e., an excluded majority as deficient in Gutenberg skills as they are untutored in 'taste,' in fact represents the last survival in mass industrial societies . . . of an invidious distinction proper only to a class-structured community" (Fiedler 1971a: 478). Fiedler concedes that he had once condescended to popular literature, but he serves notice that he has renounced "the Modernist canon of subtle and difficult works" for "the kind of books which no one has ever congratulated himself on being able to read: books which join together all possible audiences, children and adults, women and men, the sophisticated and the naïve" (Fiedler 1971b: 403–4). This conversion was prompted, he says, by the fact that he had become "more and more uncomfortably aware that the cult based on the appreciation of works available only to a few has proved not only repressive in a political sense, but even more damaging in a psychological one" (1971b: 404).

Fiedler illustrates just how difficult it is to break the habit of divinizing the arts. While he claims "to cross the border which once separated High Art from Pop," he still essentializes both categories (Fiedler 1971b: 404). Modernist art, Fiedler claims, is both elitist and politically and psychologically damaging. Popular art, on the other hand, appeals – somehow – to all possible readers. It should now be clear, however, that the terms "high" and "popular" art say almost nothing about the works to which they supposedly refer. Instead, these terms are an attempt to validate a preference for one type of art over another by insisting that works of art have an essence, by claiming, for instance, that some works always produce positive effects (such as joining together all possible audiences and providing an unmediated reading experience) and that some works always produce negative consequences (such as causing political and psychological damage).

The divide between modernism and mass culture, then, is a divide created by critics such as Greenberg and Adorno who elevate modernist works at the expense of popular works, and by critics such as the late Susan Sontag who elevate popular and/or postmodernist works at the expense of modernist works. Fiedler helps us see this point by recounting his conversion from the first type of critic to the second. But what changed after his conversion wasn't the *essence* of either modernist or popular art but Fiedler's mind. Yet instead of arguing that a change in his values had resulted in a change in his literary taste, he justified his change of taste by claiming that the consumption of popular art would somehow produce those values in consumers and, conversely, that the consumption of modernist art would necessarily endanger those values.

In the preceding paragraphs I have argued that the distinction between high and popular art – as well as the broader distinction between the fine arts and the crafts – is less necessary and less descriptive than it is often taken to be. Not only is it a relatively recent distinction, but it is one that has outlived its original purpose. While this distinction once protected especially vulnerable arts by providing them with an aura of religious value, our age is sufficiently secular and the existence of those arts is sufficiently secure for this protective shield to be safely abandoned. This doesn't mean that we may no longer want or need to justify the cultural significance of art, but simply that we won't have to do so by divinizing or essentializing it. Furthermore, I have shown that such strategies are unfortunate because to divinize one type of art is to exclude others a priori. And only the clumsiest of critics would dismiss a work of art on the basis of its genre or medium. Finally, while we might like to think that certain works of art can make us good, that would mean that other works, inferior works, can make us bad. Simply put, essentializing works of art attributes too much power to art objects and too little power or responsibility to human beings.

Although Fiedler and others are guilty of perpetuating the myth of the two Faulkners, Faulkner himself encouraged this myth in a series of unfortunate private and public statements. One of the clearest expressions of Faulkner's commitment to the distinction between fine and popular art is his famous acceptance speech for the Nobel Prize. In this speech, which is reminiscent of the quotations from Kant and Sand cited earlier, Faulkner identifies two very different kinds of literature. The first is written not for "glory" or for "profit" "but to create out of the materials of the human spirit something which did not exist before" (Faulkner 2004a: 119). Such works, Faulkner proclaims, examine "the problems of the human heart in conflict with itself" (2004a: 119). The human heart is a fitting subject, of course, because within it we find "the old universal truths lacking which any story is ephemeral and doomed" (2004a: 120).

The second type of literature, which we may associate with popular art, is produced by the artist who "writes not of love but of lust," who "writes not of the heart but of the glands" (2004a: 120). In this familiar speech, Faulkner divinizes the fine arts. Like a magician pulling a rabbit out of his hat, he constructs the Sanctuary of Art before our very eyes, claiming that the writer's "voice" "can be one of the props or pillars" of humanity (2004a: 120). Faulkner is also idealizing himself, making the case that his "life's work" had nothing to do with profit or the glands (2004a: 119). Having constructed his temple, he is now enshrining himself within it.

What makes Faulkner's hubris easier to forgive is that he often made the opposite argument. The most obvious example is the Modern Library edition of *Sanctuary* (1931), where he claimed that the novel "was deliberately conceived to make money" (Faulkner 2004b: 176). He reinforces the notion that it was a work of the left hand by declaring that by rewriting *Sanctuary* he was "trying to make out of it something which would not shame" the works of his right hand, namely *"The Sound and the Fury* and *As I Lay Dying* too much" (2004b: 178). Despite the fact that Faulkner claims to have "made a fair job" of his revision of *Sanctuary*, the clear implication is that *Sanctuary* is an example of popular rather than high art (2004b: 178). And Faulkner's well-documented derogatory comments about writing for Hollywood and for popular magazines place his screenplays and short fiction in the same category. The fact that critics see a divided Faulkner and a divided canon must be blamed at least partly on Faulkner himself.

But his suggestion that his oeuvre divides neatly into a modernist canon on the one hand and a popular canon on the other hinges on two dubious assertions. The first is that the works in Faulkner's popular canon are inferior because they are written from the glands rather than the heart, which is to say that they are more violent, more sexually explicit and sadistic. This assertion simply doesn't hold. While the works in Faulkner's modernist canon are wrapped in a fog of Southern mythos which may blunt the force of the violence and sex within them, those books are every bit as full of "grotesqueries," to borrow a word from Alfred Kazin, as the books in the other canon (Kazin 1995: 461).

The second assertion is that the works in Faulkner's popular canon are inferior because they were written merely (or mostly) to make money. Nevertheless, many of the works in his popular canon are now celebrated for their aesthetic excellence. Faulkner shares screenwriting credit on two important American films (*The Big Sleep* [1946] and *To Have and To Have Not* [1945]) and is generally credited with writing a handful of classic short stories. More significantly, if we accept David Minter's assertion that Faulkner's "greatest work is to be found among the nine novels written between 1929 and 1942" – *The Sound and the Fury* (1929), *As I Lay Dying* (1930), *Sanctuary*, *Light in August* (1932), *Absalom, Absalom!* (1936), *The Unvanquished* (1938), *If I Forget Thee, Jerusalem* (published as *The Wild Palms*, 1939), *The Hamlet* (1940), *Go Down Moses* (1942) – then five of these novels may be attributed to the popular Faulkner (Minter 2004: 1). *The Hamlet*, *Go Down Moses*, and *The Unvanquished* were all constructed from previously published short stories (Minter 2004: 1). And of Faulkner's three popular novels, novels which sold well when they were published and were regarded as either sensational or topical, both *Sanctuary* and *If I Forget Thee, Jerusalem* appear on Minter's honor roll. For my part, I wouldn't be surprised if Faulkner's other popular novel, *Intruder in the Dust* (1948), eventually finds a home among these esteemed works.

If the distinctions between Faulkner's modernist canon and his popular canon are so easily blurred, then why did he make them? One answer is that Faulkner wasn't a particularly astute – or original – literary critic. When he thought and spoke about fiction, he generally turned to the vocabulary provided by his culture. Furthermore, Faulkner's identification of a high and a low canon must have been emotionally satisfying, for it allowed him to channel two related anxieties. The first was the anxiety that his art was – as all art always is – intertwined with financial interests. While Faulkner could not deny being caught in George Sand's material jail, dividing his canon in two allowed him to say, yes, *these* works are contaminated by the profit motive, but *these* works, *these* works are pure. To gain admittance to the Sanctuary of Art, Faulkner had to send part of himself – the part that had glands, the part that thought about money – to the sty.

The second anxiety was more serious. If Faulkner had defiled the Temple of Art by writing for money, then surely he had further defiled it by filling it with images of grotesque violence and depravity. In other words, while Faulkner chafed at the idea that he would be remembered as the corncob man, what he feared even more was the prospect that he *was* the corncob man, that he, like Harry Wilbourne in *If I Forget Thee, Jerusalem*, was a pulp fictionist, a sensationalist, who, even in his best work, presented images that corrupted those who looked upon them. In *Sanctuary*, Horace Benbow gives voice to this fear. Horace says to Aunt Jenny, "Dammit, say what you want to, but there's a corruption about even looking upon evil, even by accident; you cannot haggle, traffic, with putrefaction" (Faulkner 1993: 129). Postulating two canons – one prompted by glandular and financial desires and the other prompted by a search for universal truths – allowed Faulkner to exile his worse angel (the corncob man) to the ruined House of Popular Entertainments while his better self ascended, reader in tow, to the Temple of Art.

I am suggesting, of course, that Faulkner's literary theorizing was as secretly self-serving as Fiedler's. Fortunately, Faulkner's best thinking about fiction, just like his best thinking about race and class, was done in his novels rather than in his private and public statements. More specifically, in *Sanctuary* and *If I Forget Thee, Jerusalem*, Faulkner examines and eventually rejects Horace's claim that images of evil – the kinds of images that novels, especially popular novels, regularly traffic in – necessarily corrupt those who view them. Since I have discussed *If I Forget Thee, Jerusalem* at some length in an earlier article (King 1998), I would like to devote most of my attention to *Sanctuary*, where Faulkner documents the dangers of divinizing art and brazenly suggests that we must pitch our evils in our most sacred places.

It is clear from the opening scene of the novel that *Sanctuary* is largely a meditation on the nature and function of images. Popeye Vitelli, a bootlegger who is keeping an eye out for interlopers, accosts Horace Benbow, who is getting a drink of water from a small spring. After a brief conversation, they do something remarkable: they stare at each other in silence for two hours. Then, without commenting on their bizarre pastoral contest, they resume their conversation as Popeye escorts Horace back to the Old Frenchman Place, the home of Lee Goodwin and the headquarters for his moonshining operation. This is easily the most incredible scene in the entire novel and, indeed, in Faulkner's oeuvre. To put it as baldly as possible, it is inconceivable that these two strangers, that any two human beings, would gaze at each other across a small stream for two hours, much less do so in total silence. As far as I can tell, in the many years since the novel's publication, not one critic has accounted for the absurdity of this strange staring match.

Nevertheless, this contest has important consequences, for the sheer outrageousness of this scene suspends the suspension of disbelief. And this disbelief effectively wrenches the scene out of the novel, leaving the reader with what Stanley Greenspan and Stuart Shanker call a freestanding image, a multisensory mental picture (Greenspan and Shanker 2004: 27). As they explain in *The First Idea: How Symbols, Language, and Intelligence Evolved from Our Primitive Ancestors to Modern Humans*, generating a freestanding image is the first step toward creating a symbol. But "to create a meaningful symbol" a freestanding image must first "be invested with emotion" (Greenspan and Shanker 2004: 25). An example borrowed from Greenspan and Shanker will make this clearer. Initially a newborn child merely *perceives* its mother. Eventually, however, the child will develop a freestanding image or mental picture of its mother. This image may then be called to mind at will. The child begins by investing this mental image with a handful of relatively simple emotions. As the years go by, though, the child will invest this image with additional and more complex emotions. Thus, "A freestanding perception that becomes an internal symbol continues to define itself throughout life" (Greenspan and Shankar 2004: 27).

By making the staring match between Horace and Popeye absurdly long, Faulkner maximizes the likelihood that this scene will be lodged in the reader's imagination as a freestanding image. At the same time, he deliberately makes it difficult for the reader to invest this image scene with emotion, to turn it into a meaningful symbol. This point is best made by noting that in the 1929 version of *Sanctuary* this scene appears in chapter 2. "In the original text," Peter Lurie explains, it's clear "why Horace is at the spring, as well as his state of mind upon arriving there" (Lurie 2004: 28). Yet by placing this scene at the very beginning of the 1931 edition, Faulkner not only obscures Horace's state of mind but also makes it unclear whether the reader's sympathies should lie with Horace or Popeye. As Lurie observes, "in the revision we do not immediately know that Horace is the book's antagonist," in part because the reader initially apprehends this scene from Popeye's perspective (2004: 28).

If the job of the novelist is to present readers with arresting images that they can easily turn into symbols, then why does Faulkner go to the trouble of creating such a vivid image and then delay our ability to give it meaning? The answer, I believe, is that this exercise allows Faulkner to demonstrate how meaning is made. More specifically, it allows him to show that while artists create images, it is *readers* who invest them with meaning. Thus, this opening scene is something of a test. Faulkner, echoing Popeye, seems to be deliberately taunting the reader. Popeye asks Horace, "Do you read books?" (Faulkner 1993: 5). Faulkner seems to be asking, do you know the difference between my job and yours? Do you know that you make meaning? What kind of meaning will you make out of this scene, this novel?

One way for readers to invest this scene with meaning – and to answer Faulkner's challenge – is to use the details of the scene to characterize its two antagonists. In *Vision's Immanence: Faulkner, Film, and the Popular Imagination*, Lurie argues that in this contest between Horace and Popeye "we see Faulkner's effort to allegorize the two main strands of thirties cultural production – modernism and mass art – as figured in the characters Horace Benbow and Popeye" (Lurie 2004: 9). Horace's connection to high art seems clear. Dubbed "the Professor" by Popeye, Horace is a university-educated lawyer, bears the name of the Roman poet, and reads highbrow classics such as *Madame Bovary*, whereas Popeye's name evokes a newly popular comic-strip character. Moreover, Horace uses his affection for books – and his assumption that Popeye doesn't share this affection – to establish a sharp distinction between them. When Popeye asks Horace to identify the book in his hand, Horace replies haughtily, "Just a book. The kind that people read. Some people do" (Faulkner 1993: 5). Horace assumes that Popeye is unfamiliar with the unidentified highbrow tome he carries in his coat pocket.

Furthermore, Horace seems to regard Popeye's ignorance as a sign of his own moral superiority. Since Horace believes that images have essences – that good images make us good and that bad images make us bad – he also believes that people who read the right books, books full of ennobling images and sentiments, are superior to people such as Popeye who do not read at all or who read the "wrong" books. This point is made even more forcefully when Horace notes that Popeye "smells like that black stuff that ran out of Bovary's mouth and down her bridal veil when they raised her head" (Faulkner 1993: 7). Although Bovary committed suicide by drinking arsenic, she actually begins her long slide toward death when she decides to emulate the heroines of popular romances. By connecting Popeye to the arsenic that runs out of Bovary's mouth, Horace identifies Popeye as the poisonous paragon of pop culture.

Since Horace is a more sympathetic character than Popeye, the reader may feel compelled to accept Horace's insistence that the divide between modernism and mass art is both aesthetic and moral. It quickly becomes clear, however, that Horace's divinization of fine art (and demonization of popular art) is problematic, for it leads him to believe that virtue is a matter of fleeing evil, of finding a sanctuary where he can insulate himself from the images that might corrupt him. One of the images that bedevils Horace in *Sanctuary* is that of his stepdaughter Little Belle, for whom he has more than paternal affection. To escape the pernicious effects of her image, Horace, like his namesake, leaves the corruption of the city and seeks physical and spiritual refreshment in a pastoral landscape where the images are more felicitous. But if we are tempted to think of the stream from which Benbow drinks at the beginning of the novel as a potential source of poetic inspiration, then this Hippocrene spring has been polluted. Popeye not only spits into this stream, but its waters are an integral part of the moonshining operation that Lee Goodwin runs nearby out of the Old Frenchman Place. This chthonic Hippocrene, then, has lost its special properties. Its waters do not inspire or provide clarity as much as they intoxicate and obscure.

So instead of finding a Sabine farm where he can regain his moral equilibrium, Horace finds the Temple of Art in disarray, defiled by the profit motive and, very shortly, by violence, notably Popeye's murder of Tommy and his rape of the aptly named Temple Drake. The activities that take place within the Old Frenchman Place – whose name evokes Faulkner's French literary masters Flaubert and Balzac – suggest that art cannot be separated from either the operation of the glands or economic concerns. Faulkner emphasizes the connection between art and the muddy tide of human activity by noting that "the people of the neighborhood had been pulling" the Old Frenchman Place "down piecemeal for firewood for fifty years" (Faulkner 1993: 8). The Temple of Art, it seems, is not a classical temple that stands – as Gail Hightower imagines his life – "complete and inviolable" but a house of horrors constructed out of pulpwood (Faulkner 1972: 453). Like Hightower, Horace would like to slip into "a classic and serene vase, where the spirit could be born anew and sheltered from the harsh gale of living and die so, peacefully, with only the far sound of the circumvented wind" (1972: 453). But just as religion fails to provide such a sanctuary for Hightower, art fails to provide such an abode for Horace.

In fact, Horace finds the "pervasiveness of evil" so upsetting that he begins to think that death might offer him the sanctuary he seeks (Cohen 2002: 379). Near the end of the novel, after Temple describes what happened to her at the Old Frenchman Place, Horace thinks,

Better for her if she were dead tonight. . . . For me, too. He thought of her, Popeye, the woman, the child, Goodwin, all put into a single chamber, bare, lethal, immediate and profound: a single blotting instant between the indignation and surprise. And I too; thinking how that were the only solution. Removed, cauterized out of the old and tragic flank of the world. And I, too, now that we're all isolated, thinking of a gentle dark wind blowing in the long corridors of sleep; of lying beneath a low cozy roof under the long sound of the rain: the evil, the injustice, the tears. (Faulkner 1993: 221)

Much like Faulkner the literary theorist, Horace longs to escape the sty of human sin, and if art will not help him transcend a world rife with evil and injustice and tears, then a cozy grave might just provide the sanctuary he desires.

Even if we ultimately reject Horace's divinization of fine art, there is still a great deal of textual evidence which suggests that Horace and Popeye are polar opposites separated by an artistic divide that cannot be bridged. For example, as Popeye escorts Horace to the Old Frenchman Place, he wants to avoid a shortcut that would force him to wade through a "jungle" of trees that looks "like a lake of ink" (Faulkner 1993: 7, 8). On one level, Popeye's fear of this dense landscape may simply be read as a city slicker's fear of the woods. But as the novel's representative of pop culture, Popeye's fear is best read as a fear of the dense literary terrain associated with the masterpieces of modernism. Popeye, it seems, finds fine art as threatening as Horace does popular art. Popeye's fear of drowning in highbrow literary works may explain why he prefers watching to reading. The opening refrain of the novel is "Popeye watched," "Popeye watched," which connects him to the most popular of the popular arts: cinema (1993: 3). Indeed, much about Popeye seems designed to make us think of film. Popeye watches Horace from a "screen" of bushes (1993: 3), and Horace first becomes aware of Popeye when he spies the bootlegger's image in the stream. Since Popeye's speech, dress, and behavior echo familiar images "from pulp fiction and film," the nature of this first encounter seems more than appropriate (Lurie 2004: 27). Even the two-hour duration of this pastoral contest suggests a cinematic spectacle. Popeye is also a kind of director figure, arranging love scenes between Temple and Red and throwing a violent (and deadly) tantrum when they deviate from his script.

Just as Popeye expects his actors to stick to their script, so he is devoted to the script provided to him by popular culture. It is no surprise, then, that he "had that vicious depthless quality of stamped tin" (Faulkner 1993: 4). Pressed from the mill of popular culture, Popeye is more machine than man. This is why "His face had a queer, bloodless color, as though seen by electric light" (1993: 4), his eyes are "two knobs of soft black rubber," his hands and face are "doll-like" (1993: 4; 5), and his "tight suit and stiff hat" are "all angles, like a modernist lampstand" (1993: 7). Popeye "is a manufactured, commercial product" (Lurie 2004: 27), the living embodiment of a work of art in the age of mechanical reproduction.

This idea that the conflict between Horace and Popeye symbolizes the conflict between high and popular art also appears to be supported by Thomas McHaney's assertion (1992) that *Sanctuary*'s opening scene is borrowed from the opening pages of

James Frazer's *The Golden Bough*. There the priest-king of Diana's sanctuary anxiously waits to be attacked by those who aspire to his office and who can only claim it by taking his life, just as he attained his position by murdering his predecessor. If we apply Frazer's template to the contest between Horace and Popeye, Popeye would appear to be the high priest of mass entertainments who carefully eyes a potential rival, Horace, who, we might imagine, hopes to return the Temple of Art to its classical glory.

In many ways, then, *Sanctuary* invites readers to regard Horace and Popeye as antagonists representing irreconcilable artistic traditions. Consequently, we may be inclined to agree with Lurie that "The interpenetration of high and low modes of literary production . . . reveals Faulkner's divided and contradictory approaches to the novel" (Lurie 2004: 56)."Viewed thus," he continues, "it suggests the contradictions in Faulkner's position writing in the thirties, circumstances that confronted Faulkner and other writers in the modern period and that manifest themselves in the novel's uniquely divided style" (2004: 56).

But a closer examination of the novel's opening scene, especially as it relates to the rest of the novel, forces us to reconsider Lurie's assessment. As has often been noted, Horace and Popeye may also be seen as reflections of each other. For example, when Horace lifts his face from the spring in which he once saw only "the broken and myriad reflection of his own drinking," he now sees "the shattered reflection of Popeye's straw hat" interspersed among the reflections of his face (Faulkner 1993: 4). Horace and Popeye also "reflect" each other when they squat on opposite sides of the spring, each man transfixed by the sight of the other. They mirror each other too in their behavior. While Popeye threatens Horace with his gun, Horace, as we have already seen, assaults Popeye with his caustic condescension. More significantly, Horace shares Popeye's proclivity for following social and cultural scripts. Even though his marriage is loveless, and his defense of Goodwin has revealed the deep corruption of local culture, he returns to his wife and his stepdaughter, submitting, once again, to the familial and social script that virtually reduces him to the shrimp he associates with that marital role.

Horace's acquiescence helps explain why Popeye, when he is arrested for a murder that he did not commit, refuses legal counsel and effectively sentences himself to death. He does so because he, too, is following a conventional script: one that insists that the villain is always caught and that evildoers are always punished. Furthermore, like Lee Goodwin, and both the Tall Convict and Harry Wilbourne in *If I Forget Thee, Jerusalem*, Popeye sees jail as a sanctuary, a place where he can circumvent "the hurricane of human passions" (Brown 1991: 174). And, like Horace, Popeye knows that death, in the form of his execution by the state of Alabama, is the only sanctuary which can truly protect him from life.

It is hardly new to say that Horace and Popeye are mirror images of each other; it bears emphasizing, however, that by blurring the distinction between them Faulkner is simultaneously blurring the distinction between fine and popular art. As the embodiment of fine art, Horace should be a paragon of virtue. As it turns out, though, he bears an uncanny resemblance to the vile Popeye. Both are grotesqueries. Similarly, both fine and popular art can legitimately be accused of trafficking in images of grotesque violence. For example, if we are creating lists of abominations – the kind of lists that Faulkner's early critics were fond of compiling – then the violence decried in the films of Quentin Tarantino falls well short of the violence in the Old Testament or the *Iliad* or the *Purgatorio*. The Temple of Art, Faulkner seems to be telling us, is best seen not as a sanctuary but as a screen upon which we project, among other things, our grosser appetites.

And even if there were images or art works which could somehow inculcate noble virtues just by being consumed, there would still be complications. First, one would have to identify those works, keeping in mind, of course, that any mistake might be morally fatal. Second, even if such works existed and could be identified, *Sanctuary* makes a convincing case that even well-born, high-minded, and well-read individuals cannot hope to escape images of grotesque violence, for they are a staple not only of popular and fine art but, most importantly, of life itself. No matter how we might insulate ourselves from life's grotesqueries, in the end we cannot avoid them all. What we can do is learn how to read the images of evil that we cannot escape.

As it turns out, Faulkner constructs the opening scene of *Sanctuary* in a way that might teach us precisely that lesson. First, he presents readers with an image which, initially at least, frustrates our attempt to invest it with meaning. Second, he encourages us to misread this scene by structuring it as a stand-off between competing types of men and art. Third, he then encourages us to reinterpret this scene, to see the affinities between these men as well as between fine and popular art. The result of this process is that the reader learns firsthand that images and symbols have little power in and of themselves to fix their meaning. In other words, since images have no essence that determines their meanings, their power depends on the power we give them. And after an image has been turned into a symbol, we are free to change that symbol's power by investing it with new meanings. One cannot be ennobled or corrupted by merely looking at an image, just as one cannot be ennobled or corrupted by merely reading this or that book. However, the meaning that an individual or community gives to an image or a novel (or, for that matter, any artifact) may be a sign of the individual's or community's virtue or corruption. That is not to say that we can't or shouldn't hold artists responsible for the images that they create; it is only to say that, in the end, and by necessity, consumers are responsible for what they do with the images they consume.

In addition, by inviting the reader to engage with this freestanding image, Faulkner encourages the reader to forsake the fatal passivity which characterizes Horace and Popeye. Both men largely submit themselves to the images foisted upon them. Popeye is content to play out the role of the gangster shaped by the brute forces of his childhood. Horace temporarily fights his role as town shrimp, but he eventually settles into that role as readily as Popeye does his prison cell. Ironically, it is this willingness to be inscribed by others that, in turn, allows them to think of others as blank slates upon which they can inscribe their fantasies. Popeye inscribes his fantasies on Temple, and Horace, at least in his imagination, does much the same to Little Belle. To put it in slightly different terms, just as they are willing to be sacrificed to the scripts that are imposed upon them, they are willing – either literally or imaginatively – to impose their scripts on others. What they won't do is create a script for themselves. They fail to accept their own autonomy. To forego one's autonomy, Richard Rorty writes, is "to execute a previously prepared program, to write, at most, elegant variations on previously written poems" (Rorty 1989: 28). Despite their very real differences, Horace and Popeye may be said to belong to the same cult of cruelty. Both submit to the scripts handed to them by society and, to different extents, they also try to impose their private scripts on others.

Unlike the novel's opening scene, the final scene in the Luxemburg Gardens seems all too transparent. Like the statues that surround her, Temple is a doomed queen, transfixed by her own image as she adjusts her make-up in a compact. If she chanced to look into the nearby fountain, she might recognize herself as the spitting image of Horace and Popeye. On the one hand, she is unable to take responsibility for her autonomy. She travels with her father, who orchestrates her movements almost as closely as Popeye once did. And the fact that Temple is apparently indifferent to the cultural landscape suggests that she is a long way from rewriting the script that has been thrust upon her and that she has all too readily embraced. She is also indifferent to other human beings, for it is her false testimony that has led to the conviction and death of Lee Goodwin. All Temple has to offer is a yawn, a gesture which perfectly emphasizes her gross indifference to those around her. But the reader hardly needs this final scene to see the similarities between Temple and her male counterparts. As a result, the conclusion initially seems anti-climactic.

This scene takes on new life, however, when we realize that it mirrors the pastoral staring contest that opens the novel. To emphasize this point, Faulkner even includes a small body of water (in the form of a fountain and pool). This time, though, Faulkner asks the reader not to judge a contest but to become one of the contestants. He plops the reader in front of Temple Drake, lets us stare at her for two minutes, and then asks, in effect, how will you respond to the image of this young woman? As we consider this question, we can't help but remember how Faulkner encouraged us to misread the opening scene, to regard Horace and Popeye as vastly different kinds of men representing equally distinct types of art. With this lesson in mind, and unwilling to make the same mistake twice, we begin to *consider* the idea that there may be important similarities between Temple and ourselves.

We are free to conclude, of course, that there *isn't* a meaningful connection to be made. We may stare at Temple as dumbly as Horace and Popeye stare at each other in the opening scene. But to see Temple in this way is to content ourselves with seeing *her* evil, to believe that it bears no relation to us and, thus, to slip into the sanctuary of false superiority. Just as Faulkner the literary theorist hoped to enter the Temple of Art by exiling the corncob man to the House of Popular Entertainments, readers may choose to elevate themselves by demonizing Temple. In many ways, this is an attractive option. By denying our relation to her, we can unyoke ourselves from evil, and once we are free of that terrible burden, we can ascend to moral and aesthetic sanctuaries far above the tragic flank of the world. Yet as we saw earlier in the passage from Karl Philipp Moritz, the consequence of excluding evil from our vision and focusing merely on beautiful objects is that we forget or lose ourselves. And to see life in this way is to exchange our humanity for "a life of serene vegetation," a life in which we stare mutely at the world with the "serene and stupid impregnability of heroic statuary" (Faulkner 1993: 107).

If, on the other hand, we forego a complacent serenity and give Temple Drake the scrutiny that she deserves, then we are likely to see one final grotesquerie. What Faulkner wants us to see, I believe, is that we are to Temple as Horace was to Popeye: a lesser version of the same evil. On some lesser level, Temple's crimes are our crimes, for we all swim in the same muddy tide of human activity. Yet by recognizing that good and evil are ineluctably intertwined, we activate our humanity. It is the image of our own moral culpability that moves us to re-evaluate and rewrite the old scripts, that allows us to raze the sanctuaries where, in a genuine cult of cruelty, we sacrifice autonomy for a spurious security.

Faulkner's interest in placing modernism and mass art in one brazen yoke is practical as well as moral. After all, his fiction blends modernist techniques and aspirations with the subjects and violence and sexual frankness associated with pulp fiction. Yet as I noted at the beginning of this chapter, critics have balked at placing like and unlike in the same yoke. Indeed, each of the three major periods of Faulkner criticism has been shaped by the tension between those who wish to characterize Faulkner as working in the art novel tradition and those who insist that he is a purveyor of pop – or, less appreciatively, pulp – fiction. In the first period of Faulkner scholarship, from the publication of *Soldiers' Pay* in 1926 to the publication of *A Rose for Emily and Other Stories* in 1945, Faulkner had yet to become America's moral modernist. Despite the fact that he received laudatory reviews from some of the country's most astute critics, he was generally seen not as an artist who wrote from or appealed to the finer feelings but one who, to paraphrase both Fiedler and Kant, appealed to those deficient in Gutenberg skills and untutored in taste. Faulkner's early critics – both those who admired and those who deplored his fiction – understood that the violence in his work was not limited to one or two novels but was more or less a uniform presence in *all* of his fictions. Moreover, this pervasive violence suggested to early critics that Faulkner was writing not in the art novel tradition but in a popular art tradition, a tradition that included pulp novels and Hollywood films and that specialized in gratuitous acts of brutality. This attitude is evident in Alfred Kazin's complaint that Faulkner's novels were marred by his "inability to choose between Dostoevsky and Hollywood Boulevard" (Kazin 1995: 462).

The second era of Faulkner criticism began with the publication of Malcolm Cowley's *The Portable Faulkner* in 1946. As Frederick Crews points out, the idea that Cowley's *The Portable Faulkner* changed Faulkner's reputation overnight is something of a myth. More accurately, Cowley's volume may be seen as the tipping point in which those voices who had been identifying Faulkner as an artist, as America's greatest modernist, finally began to overwhelm the voices of those who recognized the pulp fictionist, the short story writer, the Hollywood hack. We can begin the third era in 1990 with the publication of Fiedler's "Pop Goes the Faulkner" in *Faulkner and Popular Culture*.

The publication of these two works marks another tipping point. The Faulkner critical establishment had, at long last, officially recognized the importance of Fiedler's popular Faulkner. No longer an object of derision, this Faulkner was perfectly suited to postmodern critical approaches and more egalitarian conceptions of art. Yet just as Cowley was unable to bury the pop Faulkner, Fiedler was unable to bury the modernist Faulkner, leaving critics and readers transfixed by the sight of two apparently irreconcilable portraits of the artist.

My hope is that this chapter, which builds upon the work of scholars such as Joseph Urgo, John Matthews, and Tom Dardis, will confirm the advent of a fourth era, an era in which we can stop thinking of modernism and popular art as irreconcilable forces and, thus, can exchange the slew of schizophrenic Faulkners for more complex portraits of the artist. In this era scholars will emphasize "not the dualistic nature of popular and modernist art, but their mutual identity and constitution" (Lurie 2004: 30).

References and Further Reading

Brown, C. B. (1991). *Wieland* and *Memoirs of Carwin the Biloquist* (ed. J. Fliegelman). New York: Penguin. (Original pub. 1798.)

Cohen, P. (2002). *Madame Bovary* and *Flags in the Dust*: Flaubert's Influence on Faulkner. In L. Wagner-Martin (ed.). *William Faulkner: Six Decades of Criticism* (pp. 377–96). East Lansing: Michigan State University Press. (Original pub. 2000.)

Crews, F. (1991). The Strange Fate of William Faulkner. *New York Review of Books*, 38(5): 47–52.

Faulkner, W. (1972). *Light in August*. New York: Vintage. (Original pub. 1932.)

Faulkner, W. (1993). *Sanctuary*. New York: Vintage. (Original pub. 1931.)

Faulkner, W. (2004a). Address upon Receiving the Nobel Prize for Literature. In J. B. Meriwether (ed.). *Essays, Speeches and Public Letters* (pp. 119–21). New York: Modern Library. (Original pub. 1950.)

Faulkner, W. (2004b). Introduction to the Modern Library Edition of *Sanctuary*. In J. B. Meriwether (ed.). *Essays, Speeches and Public Letters* (pp. 176–8). New York: Modern Library. (Original pub. 1932.)

Fiedler, L. (1971a). "Cross the Border – Close the Gap." In *The Collected Essays of Leslie Fiedler* (vol. II, pp. 461–85). New York: Stein and Day.

Fiedler, L. (1971b). Introduction to "Cross the Border – Close the Gap." In *The Collected Essays*

of *Leslie Fiedler* (vol. II, pp. 403–5). New York: Stein and Day.

Fiedler, L. (1971c). William Faulkner, Highbrows' Lowbrow. In *The Collected Essays of Leslie Fiedler* (vol. I, pp. 331–8). New York: Stein and Day. (Original pub. 1950.)

Fiedler, L. (1990). Pop Goes the Faulkner: In Quest of *Sanctuary*. In D. Fowler and A. J. Abadie (eds.). *Faulkner and Popular Culture: Faulkner and Yoknapatawpha, 1998* (pp. 75–92). Jackson: University of Mississippi Press.

Greenspan, S. I. and S. G. Shanker (2004). *The First Idea: How Symbols, Language, and Intelligence Evolved from Our Primitive Ancestors to Modern Humans*. Cambridge, MA: Da Capo Press.

Grimwood, M. (1987). *Heart in Conflict: Faulkner's Struggles with Vocation*. Athens: University of Georgia Press.

Horace (1997). *The Odes of Horace* (trans. D. Ferry). New York: Farrar, Straus and Giroux.

Huyssen, A. (1986). *After the Great Divide: Modernism, Mass Culture, Postmodernism*. Bloomington and Indianapolis: Indiana University Press.

Kazin, A. (1995). *On Native Grounds: An Interpretation of Modern American Prose Literature*. New York: Harcourt Brace. (Original pub. 1942.)

King, V. (1998). The Wages of Pulp: The Use and Abuse of Fiction in William Faulkner's *The Wild Palms. Mississippi Quarterly*, 51(3): 503–25.

Lurie, P. (2004). *Vision's Immanence: Faulkner, Film, and the Popular Imagination*. Baltimore: Johns Hopkins University Press.

McGurl, M. (2001). *The Novel Art: Elevations of American Fiction after Henry James*. Princeton, NJ: Princeton University Press.

McHaney, T. (1992). *Sanctuary* and Frazer's Slain Kings. In J. D. Canfield (ed.). *Twentieth Century Interpretations of* Sanctuary (pp. 79–92). Englewood Cliffs, NJ: Prentice Hall.

Minter, D. (2004). *Faulkner's Questioning Narratives: Fiction of his Major Phase, 1929–42*. Urbana and Chicago: University of Illinois Press. (Original pub. 2001.)

Parini, J. (2004). *One Matchless Time: A Life of William Faulkner*. New York: Harper Collins.

Rorty, R. (1989). *Contingency, Irony, and Solidarity*. New York: Cambridge University Press.

Shiner, L. (2001). *The Invention of Art: A Cultural History*. Chicago: University of Chicago Press.

Singal, D. J. (1997). *William Faulkner: The Making of a Modernist*. Chapel Hill, NC: University of North Carolina Press.

Wilson, A. J. (1994). The Corruption in Looking: William Faulkner's *Sanctuary* as a Detective Novel. *Mississippi Quarterly*, 47 (3): 441–60.

PART III
Genres and Forms

19

Faulkner's Genre Experiments

Thomas L. McHaney

William Faulkner served a long apprenticeship in the writing of poetry and explored several other genres of literary and graphic arts expression before and after settling upon the form of the modernist novel as his true métier. The Mississippi writer's poetry, despite its flaws and failures, reflects his wide reading in Romantic, symbolist, and modernist verse and is an early sign of an unwavering desire for a career in art. He undertook repeated revision of individual lyrics, gathering poems into several coherent book-length sequences. His graphic art begins as cartoons for high-school publications but, like his poetry, increases in sophistication as he encounters popular and fine art styles (Faulkner 1962; Hönnighausen 1987: 13–77). These interests come together in some of the hand-made books he produced for friends in the early 1920s, before poetry and graphic art proved to be a false path and he gave them up. Nonetheless, poetry and drawing represent essential experience for his career as novelist. They were media in which he experimented with the language and design of the past as well as the present and performed representations of himself as artist and lover, parodist and satirist, storyteller and psychologist, trying to find his identity and voice, as well as his subject. At the same time, he represented himself more familiarly to family and friends in the prose of self-conscious correspondence, skeins of letters that his mother proudly retained. And, finally, he engaged in a series of prose exercises in the fictive that preceded his highly successful assault upon long prose fiction beginning in 1925.

More specifically, from 1918 to 1925 Faulkner experimented with imitative fin de siècle and imagist poetry and book illustration, including satiric and erotic cartoons. For friends, he assembled several collections of his poems, some of them illustrated (*The Lilacs, Vision in Spring, Helen: A Courtship, Mississippi Poems*). For publication he submitted, but could not publish, another collection, "Orpheus and Other Poems." With the financial backing of his friend and mentor Phil Stone of Oxford, he published *The Marble Faun* (1924), a collection of mildly erotic verses that cohere by virtue of their issuing from the consciousness of the title figure, a stone representation of the half-human Greek satyr or Roman faun. During this period of apprenticeship, Faulkner also wrote and illustrated an experimental drama, *The Marionettes* (1920), and a mock-medieval romance, *Mayday* (1926). He wrote book reviews and literary essays for University of Mississippi student publications, and in New Orleans in 1925 he wrote more than two dozen lyrical prose sketches and short-short stories, mostly about street life in the French Quarter, and collaborated with Sherwood Anderson in an exchange of tall tales intended for a book, all while composing his first novel at a prodigious rate of daily work.

Some of this early experimental writing is vaguely echoed in commercial genre forms Faulkner would return to later: that is, his writing for motion pictures and the short stories he composed for the popular magazine market. But much influence from this wide-ranging apprenticeship shows up in his novels, strangely transformed, including his poetic prose, his construction by using sequential or overlapping scenes, not to mention themes, characters, anecdotes, and incidents. Later, for both commercial and more serious purposes, Faulkner would experiment with additional genres: detective fiction (*Knight's Gambit*, *Intruder in the Dust*), historical narrative and closet drama (*Requiem for a Nun*), film treatments and film scripts (see Kawin 1977), and, on a more or less one-time basis, "travel" writing for *Holiday Magazine* and sports reporting about hockey and the Kentucky Derby (see Faulkner 2004a). Before and after the fame purchased by his Nobel Prize, he would add to his body of private correspondence several sequences of public letters for local and regional newspapers, and, beginning with the reluctantly delivered acceptance speech for the Nobel Prize award ceremony in 1950, he prepared public speeches for a variety of local, regional, national, and international occasions. Beginning in the 1930s, and invariably under the urging of his publisher or an editor, he penned introductions to his own work, not all of them printed in his lifetime. Few modernist writers have to their credit so much serious endeavor in so many genres.

To speak of Faulkner's experiments in genres involves two meanings of the word *experiment*. Faulkner is now regarded as an "experimental" writer, a not uncommon trait among modernists who responded to the spirit of the times expressed in Ezra Pound's dictum "Make it new." Whether they heard Pound or not, this generation could not miss the acclaim and notoriety provoked by the radical transformations in common arts made by Picasso, Stravinsky, Virginia Woolf, T. S. Eliot, James Joyce, for these and many other artists and thinkers of the new were featured prominently in both the non-commercial and the widely distributed popular high-brow magazines of their day, from the *Little Review* and the *Dial* to the *Egoist* and *Vanity Fair*. Faulkner's true reputation as experimental derives primarily from his contributions to this context of the "new," thanks to the striking structural and verbal innovations of *The Sound and the Fury*, *As I Lay Dying*, *Sanctuary*, *Light in August*, *Absalom, Absalom!*, *Go Down, Moses*, and *The Wild Palms*, to name the most obvious examples from among his 19 novels. From *Soldiers' Pay* (1926) to *The Reivers* (1962), however, he avoided the narrative strategies predominant in the popular novel. His unwillingness to settle for a predictable form earned the praise and often the envy of other novel writers. He was "poetically the most accurate man alive," according to Eudora Welty (1954), "the Picasso of literature," according to French novelist Claude Simon (McHaney 1980), and in Robert Penn Warren's summation at a time when Faulkner's career was at its lowest point financially and critically, the Mississippi genius was "the most challenging single task in contemporary American literature for criticism to undertake. . . . a novelist who, in mass of work, in scope of material, in range of effect, in reportorial accuracy and symbolic subtlety, in philosophical weight can be put beside the masters of our own past literature" (Warren 1951: 100). Such judgment by his peers, which might be multiplied dozens of times from an international list of writers that includes many Nobel Prize winners, is good enough reason to take a serious look at Faulkner's work in genres other than the novel. Several examples originate in the period before he turned to the novel. They are experiments largely in the sense that they are apprentice work by a writer who had not yet found his true calling or his writing voice. They are experiments also in that most often they represent imitation of other writers, the trying on of other writers' subjects and styles. They lack the transforming genius that characterizes Faulkner's long prose fictions, which may reflect borrowing too, but almost invariably as something absorbed and meditated on, not plagiarism, pastiche, paraphrase, or parody. And if I may extend the definition of experiment slightly, Faulkner's genre experiments may be seen to include any kind of writing he did outside the bounds of the two kinds of fiction – novels and short stories – that became his professional stock in trade.

In a sense, Faulkner's first recorded experiment in writing is actually a personal letter to his mother written in 1912 shortly before his fifteenth birthday. His parents are away from Oxford, and Faulkner and his brother Jack are staying at the "Big House" with his paternal grandparents, also in Oxford. This letter begins "Dear Miss Lady"– in quotation marks to call attention to its reference to the realm of romantic courtesy – and ends *Yure erfexxionnite sun*, the dialect glossed underneath within the author's parentheses as "(Your affectionate son)" (Watson 1992: 39–40). As he would do later, the young author typographically marks a feature of his work, in this instance to acknowledge deliberate borrowing from another genre, the epistolary frontier humor that he and his mother had shared reading and that he would later imitate. Within the body of the letter, between his courteous greeting and the frontier burlesque closure, are a domestic anecdote and a bloody adventure tale, a blend of genres that will characterize a good deal of his mature fiction. Faulkner's subsequent extant letters, published so far in two volumes (Blotner 1978; Watson 1992), confirm that he could use the medium in many ways: self-invention, manipulation, humor. Several letters become sources of his later fiction, and the letter is a genre that he employs far more frequently than poetry as an element of his novels. James G. Watson, editor of Faulkner's letters to his parents, also has written two critical studies that trace the variety of Faulkner's experimentation in letter writing and the potential meaning such expression has for the writer's career (Watson 1987, 2000). Poetry, however, was young Faulkner's first serious literary passion.

Faulkner must have experimented with the composition of poetry earlier, but in the summer of 1914, he first came under the tutelage of Phil Stone of Oxford, at 21 just a little more than four years Faulkner's senior, and home from New Haven where he had completed a second baccalaureate degree at Yale to complement one already earned at the University of Mississippi (Blotner 1984: 45). Stone was a brilliant classicist and a student of modern languages with a deep interest in modern literature. In the words of his biographer Susan Snell, Phil became "tutor, librarian, and purveyor of books during Faulkner's initiation into modern letters" (Snell 1992: 2). By his own account, Stone subscribed to *Poetry: A Magazine of Verse*, and he would direct Faulkner's attention to that remarkable journal and later to other important little magazines – the *Dial*, the *Double Dealer*, the *New Republic* (where Faulkner would publish his first poem), the *Egoist*. The June 1915 issue of *Poetry* that Stone would later show Faulkner contained T. S. Eliot's "The Love Song of J. Alfred Prufrock," a poem Faulkner would blatantly imitate in a 1921 gift book (Blotner 1984: 97). Stone and his little magazines also directed Faulkner's attention to Swinburne, A. E. Housman, the French symbolists, Yeats, Joyce, Sherwood Anderson, Conrad Aiken, and others who became literary influences. In 1915 Stone acquired Amy Lowell's *Some Imagist Poets* and studied it so hard he had to have it rebound (Snell 1992: 72, 78–9). When Stone and Faulkner spent hours walking the woods near Oxford, Stone regaled Faulkner with classics in their original tongue, and Faulkner sometimes carried a tiny leather-bound copy of A. E. Housman's *A Shropshire Lad*, no bigger than a shirt pocket. The authors Stone thrust upon Faulkner emerge repeatedly in the young writer's attempts to find himself in poetry. Reflecting Stone's classicism and their Arcadian saunterings, Faulkner's first published poem concerns a faun and borrows its title from one of the symbolists, Stéphane Mallarmé.

That poem appeared on August 6, 1919, in a prestigious American magazine, the *New Republic*, to which Stone subscribed. Faulkner's "L'Apres-Midi d'un Faune" is very different from Mallarmé's poem. In an Arcadian setting, the speaker follows an elusive female figure "through the singing trees / Her streaming clouded hair and face / and lascivious dreaming knees / Like gleaming water" (Faulkner 1962: 39) Faulkner's Arcadia might well represent "The Grove" on the campus of the University of Mississippi, where a hopeful suitor pursues a short-skirted coed. That, at least, may have been the reaction on the Ole Miss campus to its opening lines when Faulkner later published the poem in the student newspaper, the *Mississippian*. It is one of many pieces, in poetry and prose, that Faulkner wrote about the allure and danger of the feminine in terms of nymphs and water. Several of his poetic personae would, like the speaker in this poem, follow such a figure and drown (*Mayday*, *The Sound and the Fury*) or nearly drown ("Nympholepsy," *Mosquitoes*, *The Wild Palms*). An early prose sketch by Faulkner, "And Now What's to Do," glosses the plot and magnifies the danger: "Nothing to Girls. . . . Soft things. Secretive, but like traps. . . . No. Quicksand" (1973: 401). Another poem of the post-World War I era, published in the Ole Miss student newspaper in 1920, continues the image: in "Naiad's Song," the nymphs call "Come ye sorrowful and keep / tryst with us here in wedded sleep, / The silent noon lies over us / And shaken ripples cover us, / Our arms are soft as is the stream" (Faulkner 1962: 55).

These were common preoccupations in the poems of Faulkner's youth, though not the only preoccupations. Judith Sensibar, who has compiled an invaluable bibliographical guide to the poems that lists 120 published and 34 unpublished poems plus 14 poem sequences, argues convincingly, however, that this image of drowning or envelopment was deeply important for Faulkner in many ways. In his poetry it is expressed as a cry, she explains, while in his fiction it acquires a plot (1988: 221).

One of the poetry sequences that Sensibar catalogues is Faulkner's first commercially published book. Its title, *The Marble Faun* (1924), links it to his first published poem. The book was financed with $400 from Phil Stone through the Four Seas Company in Boston, a legitimate publisher that had introduced Amy Lowell, Gertrude Stein, and the imagist poets, among others, but required a subsidy payment from its writers. *The Marble Faun* was not the young writer's first idea for a sequence – he had previously assembled *The Lilacs* (1920) and *Vision in Spring* (1921), and in 1923 he had submitted to Four Seas a volume titled "Orpheus and Other Poems" that does not survive in manuscript. *The Lilacs* is a slight hand-lettered and hand-bound volume of old work presented to Phil Stone. *Vision in Spring,* a gift to Estelle Oldham Franklin, his former sweetheart and future wife, is much more ambitious, though that is its flaw; as his biographer Joseph Blotner writes: he "well could have subtitled the collection *Homage to T. S. Eliot*" (1984: 96). Many poems in the sequence look back to Phil Stone's June 1915 issue of *Poetry: A Magazine of Verse* and rather more than echo Eliot's "Prufrock." One poem is titled "Love Song" and begins with "Shall I walk, then, through a corridor of profundities / Carefully erect (I am taller than I look)" (1984b: 55).

The Marble Faun poems, however, are less obviously imitative, though epigonic, more like fellow Mississippian William Alexander Percy than anything new. They do, however, speak more to a reading public than to a local friend or simply a love interest. The persona here is identified as a faun, but not a living one: a "marble bound" statue in a summer garden where nymphs cavort among the trees and around the fountain. The enchanted "speaker" (who should be mute) is doubly removed from the sexuality of life around him – a sentient garden ornament in stone representing a creature that is half animal and half human. If Faulkner did not, as he and Stone claimed, know Nathaniel Hawthorne's novel by the same title, he intuited the common feelings of the melancholy artist that Hawthorne himself often dramatized: a youth unfit by virtue of sensitivity and introspection for life and romance.

Thanks to Judith Sensibar, our knowledge of the canon of Faulkner's poems is much enlarged and their importance is much clearer. Her critical writing about the poems also appears to validate attention to a conjunction between Faulkner's letter writing and his poetry. In her epilogue to *The Origins of Faulkner's Art*, Sensibar cites a 1925 letter that Faulkner wrote from Paris to his mother crowing about a piece of new prose: "such a beautiful thing," he claimed, "that I am about to bust – 2000 words about the Luxembourg Gardens and death. It has a thin thread of plot, about a young woman, and it is poetry though written in prose form" (1984: 221). The moment expressed in this letter, Sensibar observes, connects images in the unsuccessful poems to images that will appear in the successful fiction, and so at this turn to prose in Faulkner's life the setting is, in Sensibar's words, "as it was in the beginning: a formal garden, love, death, and a maiden." But instead of a "lyric cry," she writes, Faulkner has turned to prose and a plot, "a new beginning" (p. 221).

Faulkner's letter to his mother reporting his triumphant prose is as self-consciously literary in style as the 1912 "Dear Miss Lady" letter to her previously quoted and discussed. The 1925 letter is chatty, also summing up Faulkner's recent acute observations of culture, art, daily life in Paris, and World War I's terrible effects on "poor France, so beautiful and unhappy, and so cheerful." It sports a closure perhaps meant to assure his mother that her 28-year-old unemployed son is growing more confident: "My beard is coming along fine. Makes me look sort of distinguished, like someone you'd care to know," he writes, and he draws a picture beneath to show her. He looks like a faun (Blotner 1978: 17–18).

The "garden, woman, water, death" images that Sensibar identifies as recurring often in Faulkner's poetry and fiction also figure not merely in the narratives but in the illustrations for the two most beautiful hand-made books that Faulkner created in the 1920s: *The Marionettes* (1920), a dream play, and *Mayday* (1926), a mock-medieval tale that owes a little to James Branch Cabell's then-sensational novel *Jurgen* (1920) and a great deal to Faulkner's poetry. Several of Faulkner's genre experiments are involved in these two works: the dream play *The Marionettes* suggests knowledge of European experimental drama, the illustrations of Aubrey Beardsley, and many other sources or parallels that are summarized by Noel Polk in his introduction to a facsimile edition of the play (Faulkner 1977a). Without the illustration and artful hand-lettering, *The Marionettes* would not be very appealing, since nothing really happens in the play. But the nine illustrations present Faulkner's theme of garden, water, woman, death – all for a rejected suitor who sleeps drunkenly and dreams what passes for dramatic action in the piece. The illustrations convey Faulkner's themes in elegant visual shorthand: tableaus of silhouetted characters in erotically rendered gardens, where blatant curving poplars and open circle moons loom over a bare-breasted Marietta posing between two peacocks, a naked nymph fountain statue, and the sad Pierrot, almost bodiless in his capacious clown suit.

Mayday, a hand-lettered prose piece, has fewer illustrations, but the tailpiece shows three mysterious figures – Hunger and Pain who flank the Lord of Sleep brooding over the tomb of the lovesick and much-rejected knight, Sir Galwyn ap Arthgyl, whom the nymphs finally have drowned. The "Persons" – that is, dramatis personae – page of *The Marionettes* shows a kneeling Pierrot and a turned-away Marietta flanked by two towering and faceless figures identified as Grey and Lilac. Both works employ visual symbolism – as well as symbolist prose – to place the characters between extremes: pain and hunger, dawn and dusk; and both stories play out in the context of garden, woman, water, death, the images Sensibar draws from the poems. Images in these two illustrated works strangely unpack images, relationships, and events in *The Sound and the Fury*, *Sanctuary*, and other Faulkner novels, including *Mosquitoes*, *As I Lay Dying*, and *The Wild Palms*. Hand-made books, of course, like the publication of poems in prestigious "little" magazines, would not provide Faulkner with a living or a reputation, though at the time he worked in these media he did not need a living, "thanks to my father's unfailing kindness which supplied me with bread at need despite the outrage to his principles at having been of a bum progenitive" (Faulkner 1932: v).

As with these key images elaborated in hand-lettered texts and striking pen-and-ink illustrations, Faulkner did not give up his interest in the pure products of his pen – in 1936 he would draw and hand-letter the first maps of Yoknapatawpha County using red and black ink. The map is reproduced as a facsimile foldout in the 1936 limited edition of *Absalom, Absalom!* and now again in the trade hardback of the 1986 "corrected edition" prepared by Noel Polk. Other printings of the novel contain a reduced reproduction of the map, which Faulkner drew again, with important revisions, for Malcolm Cowley's *The Portable Faulkner* (1946), though the map is redrawn in a style unlike Faulkner's and much reduced for publication in first and subsequent printings and editions of the *Portable*. During his Hollywood love affair with Meta Carpenter, he drew erotic cartoons for her (Blotner 1984: 369), though not with the patience and skill he exercised in the 1920s or later when he drew the Yoknapatawpha maps.

Faulkner's many hand-made books are reflected in a lifelong interest in the forms of his published works, though he had little power to affect their production. He had novel ideas about publishing – for example, the hope that he could more effectively present the levels of time in Benjy's chapter of *The Sound and the Fury* by using not the binary shift from roman to italic type but colored inks – suggesting the color language he had used for the figures in *The Marionettes* (lilac and grey) and *Mayday* (red and green). When he received the chance, he welcomed illustration in his novels (*The Unvanquished* and *Big Woods*) and suggested revision in a drawing used as frontispiece depicting the Bear and its hunters in *Big Woods*. As for the poetry, to repeat Eudora Welty's judgment, he wrote prose as if he were "poetically, the most accurate man alive" (Welty 1954).

Most of Faulkner's early poems reflect homage to poets he admired, whether French, British, or American: Mallarmé, Verlaine, Villon, Swinburne, Housman, Aiken, Eliot, and others. This, as the prolific writer of poems, novels, and stories George Garrett has observed, is a normal course for the beginning writer (Garrett 1957). Faulkner pretended to be many different things all through his life, and in a sense he was pretending to be a poet and an "artist" during these early years, but not in vain. The regard for language, for image, for patiently getting the look and feel of things right, was doubtless what he had in him that poetry and drawing helped to bring out.

It is possible, though the evidence is scant, that he attempted more prose during the apprenticeship to poetry than has survived. He published a short story, "Landing in Luck," in the *Mississippian* as early as November 1919 (Faulkner 1962: 42–50). This is the same period when he published there the imitative poems often derided and parodied by Ole Miss students. The reason that he published no more fiction may be that the student newspaper had little room for short stories and perhaps had published that first story because of its relationship to the just-completed world war.

As short fiction "Landing in Luck" has the flaws of a beginner: not a story but an elaborated anecdote. The beginning creative writer's response to such a criticism is usually, "But it really happened!" and Faulkner might have said the same thing, but, since the story is about a young aviator taking his first solo flight, we are pretty sure it did not happen, since Cadet Faulkner never got out of ground school during his training period with the Royal Air Force in Toronto (Blotner 1984: 67). Similar judgment can be applied to many of the sketches and "short-short" stories he would publish in venues in New Orleans when he went there in 1925 after the appearance of *The Marble Faun*. Again, Faulkner had the mixed fortune to come under the scrutiny of an older mentor. The mentor in this case was not a recent Yale graduate but a mature published author, Sherwood Anderson, someone Faulkner doubtless first read in Phil Stone's copies of the *Dial*. As a fiction writer, Anderson was at the peak of his fame in 1925 when Faulkner met him. The older writer had similarly, though less intimately, advised and encouraged Ernest Hemingway, whose spare style closely resembled Anderson's, with some important variations.

How Faulkner came to Sherwood Anderson's attention in New Orleans in 1925 is a story of experiment itself. In 1921, Faulkner interrupted his casual career as "Count No 'Count," the non-enrolled Ole Miss poet, and traveled to New York City with the avowed purpose of enrolling in art school (Blotner 1984: 203–5). Phil Stone had solicited notice of young Faulkner from one of Oxford's and Mississippi's currently most successful *littérateurs*: poet, playwright, classicist, teacher, and drama reviewer Stark Young, who frequently visited Oxford to see his father from about the time Stone discovered Billy Falkner. In 1921, Young was teaching at Amherst but already well established in the New York literary scene, and Faulkner put up very briefly in Young's small New York apartment when he arrived in the city. There he met Elizabeth Prall, Young's landlady, and she offered Faulkner a few days of part-time work during the 1921 pre-Christmas shopping season in the Doubleday bookstore that she managed in Saks Fifth Avenue. What happened that fall in New York would be magnified over the years, with "Miss Elizabeth" and Young both claiming their early recognition of Faulkner's genius. Prall's remarks about the bookstore period also made it seem to some commentators on Faulkner that he held a long tenure as well-read book clerk in New York City, but the experiment in sales was quite brief and Faulkner never took art lessons, hurrying home to his family before Christmas and then reluctantly accepting the now-famous post office job at the University of Mississippi, where his father was in the business office and the family lived on campus.

As the bookstore job is too frequently regarded as lodestone experience for Faulkner of some duration, the post office job is frequently regarded, despite the simple evidence, as a despised and brief interlude in Faulkner's life. In actuality, it lasted for three years and was the source of leisure for Faulkner to indulge in most of the experiments so far discussed. It's true that the postmaster experiment might have been a fatal step away from poetry, art, and fiction – a real job, as it in fact was, and as dispiriting as Hawthorne's time in the Salem Custom House. But Faulkner's gift for productive idleness turned the experience into a three-year postgraduate program in reading, all the while writing and polishing his poems (McHaney 1986). This was an illusory relief for the Falkner family, whose son still lived in their home across from the Ole Miss Grove but now drew a salary. Faulkner, however, turned his postmastership into a literary sinecure, and he could do so because his staff handled much of the work. He was manager and accountant. He gave the term "keeping the books" new meaning, holding on to patrons' literary mail to read their magazines before putting them into mailboxes, and borrowing books, perhaps from patrons without their knowledge but certainly from friends, faculty, and the nearby university library.

Immediately upon assuming the position he began, interestingly enough, to imitate Stark Young, with whom he had just stayed briefly in New York, by reviewing the dramatic writing of Edna St. Vincent Millay and Eugene O'Neill and placing an essay titled "American Drama: Inhibitions" (1962: 93–7) in the student newspaper. This was another of the many experiments in genres for which he had leisure and venues on the Ole Miss campus. It is important to remember that this campus job, unlike the bookstore interlude in New York in 1921, lasted a very long time, 36 months, and we can peruse a list of book orders Phil Stone made just in 1922, the first year, from the Brick Row bookshop in New Haven: Aiken, Cather, Ferber, Fitzgerald, Doolittle, Masters, Melville, Mencken, Swinburne, William Carlos Williams, Elinor Wylie, Henry Adams, and several classical writers. Stone may have ordered as many books in other years, but the surviving record has gaps; we do know he sent for Joyce's *Ulysses* in 1926 (Blotner 1964: 123–7; McHaney 1965–6: 48).

In addition to the drama criticism, poems, a prose sketch, and several drawings in student publications in 1922, by the end of the academic year at Ole Miss Faulkner had placed a poem in the *Double Dealer*, the new literary magazine published in New Orleans. In 1923, Faulkner's attention appears to have focused on revising his poetry for publication in a collection for which he began negotiation with the Four Seas Company in Boston, and possibly working on short stories written a year or so earlier that he was unable to place in the commercial or literary magazine market (Collins 1963: 18–23).

Faulkner and Stone, both now fully employed, still had weekends and vacations to travel to Memphis, New Orleans, and a few Delta hotspots high on the lusty bachelor Stone's list of venues for gambling and other pleasures. Whatever Stone did, Faulkner mainly watched, listened, and absorbed material. Stone, who subscribed to the *Double Dealer*, found out that Sherwood Anderson had married the bookstore manager Elizabeth Prall and moved to New Orleans. He grabbed Faulkner and took him down to renew acquaintances, call on the *Double Dealer* crowd, and meet Anderson. Anderson was away, but Miss Elizabeth was charmed by the two very different Mississippi boys, one flamboyant and brilliant and the other shy and brilliant, both gallant, and she invited Faulkner to come back. Whereby Faulkner, again with Stone's encouragement, made plans to sojourn in New Orleans on his way to finding a freighter that would take him to Europe, a trip they supposed would somehow lead to the kind of fame other American literary exiles were achieving while abroad. This would require another genre experiment of the sort that Stone had helped Faulkner with before.

Stone was more than sympathetic to Faulkner's penchant for exaggeration, role-playing, and outright biographical falsehood. Among Faulkner's experiments must be counted Stone and Faulkner's 1918 creation of spurious biography and documents to grease the younger man's enrollment in the Canadian training program of the Royal Air Force: a phony recommendation letter written by Stone above the name of a non-existent British clergyman, an equally fictitious British citizenship for Faulkner's mother, and the addition of the "u" in Faulkner's name to make it seem as British as the clipped accent he was developing in New Haven. Now they hoaxed Faulkner out of the post office with a similar plot of forged documents and falsified events (Crane 1989). Faulkner lost the post office job and headed for New Orleans, where he quickly entered the *Double Dealer* circle and was befriended by Anderson. While it was not Anderson who turned Faulkner from a writer of poems to a writer of prose, from on the spot Faulkner does give Anderson credit for giving him the secret of how novel writing is done. As Faulkner explained it in another key letter to his mother, "What really happens, you know, never makes a good yarn. You have got to get an impulse from somewhere and then embroider it. . . . I am now giving away the secrets of our profession, so be sure not to divulge them" (Watson 1992: 194–5). As someone who had always embroidered on his own life, Faulkner must have felt that he had received a license to continue not only with his own life but with all the lives about which he possessed knowledge. Within a week or so he reports to his mother "My novel is going splendidly. I put in almost 8 hours a day on it" (1992: 195), and thereafter he reports his phenomenal progress, often more than weekly, commenting that "Both Sherwood and Elizabeth say it is a good one" (1992: 203).

At this point, the novel he wanted to call "Mayday" is an experiment, too, and the experimental writer Sherwood Anderson, he reports to his mother, said "he wishes he had thought of it first" (1992: 203). As exercises, however, Faulkner also wrote street scenes and sketches for the *Double Dealer*, combining them, as he had the poems, into sequences, one called "Mirrors of Chartres Street" and another that bore the title "Sinbad in New Orleans" (Faulkner 1977b).

The novel was finished the second week of May, little more than a month after he had begun it, retitled "Soldiers' Pay," and in July he finally boarded a freighter for Europe. His New Orleans friend William Spratling, a teacher of architectural drafting and an artist whose "hand was shaped to a brush" as Faulkner's was not, was his traveling companion. Spratling recalls that on the trip Faulkner threw piles of manuscript overboard. Though the author of *The Marble Faun* and *Soldiers' Pay* hoped to support himself in Europe by sending more sketches to the New Orleans newspaper and the *Double Dealer*, his sketch writing, like his painting and his poetry, was apparently over too.

Now he was William Faulkner the novelist, and in Europe, though he would write a few poems and sketches, mainly he worked on projects in the genre of the novel. Later, because of his attempts to hit the lucrative market for short fiction in popular American magazines, Faulkner would undergo a rigorous period of self-education to master the short story form. The short story career became almost as remarkable as his career in long fiction, despite the constraints writing for popular magazines put upon plot structures, psychological depth, or frankness. But it would take Faulkner another five years – and the publication of his first four novels, *Soldiers' Pay* through *The Sound and the Fury* – before he got a check for a short story. The break came with "A Rose for Emily," now his most anthologized and written-about short story. It appeared in a forgotten magazine called *Forum*, and he was paid only $50, but in the same year, 1930, he broke into print in many better-paying magazines.

Commercial short stories first and then later the much-disliked writing for Hollywood studios would become his main means of support through the 1930s, just beyond the end of which, in 1942, he became almost completely dependent upon Hollywood. This lasted until he sold movie rights to *Intruder in the Dust* (1948) for $50,000.

Faulkner's experiments in the short story have been covered brilliantly by the Norwegian scholar Hans Skei, who observes that "of the six short stories or sketches that he wrote before the New Orleans burst of activity in 1925, only the first one ['Landing in Luck'] does not relate to an experience that might just as well have been turned into a poem." And, Skei goes on, "Even his many drawings from this period . . . have a quality of allusiveness, mystery, and poetry," as does the 1920 experiment in drama, *Marionettes*, which "belongs to a world of fantasy and imagination" (1999: 17). The same can be said of the hand-made book containing the allegorical tale *Mayday* and his strange and experimental children's story *The Wishing Tree* (1928), presented as a gift to several different children of friends over the years.

As Skei observes, the short story career begins to take off with the experimental prose in New Orleans in 1925 and reaches an apogee of production and high quality between 1930 and 1938. Faulkner's *Collected Stories* (1951) contains 42 stories, a few of them still to be regarded as "experimental" prose, including the consciously placed final story, "Carcassonne," more an artistic *cri de coeur* than a standard short story; and thus, to repeat Judith Sensibar's interpretation of what happens in his shift from poetry to prose fiction, in "Carcassonne," Faulkner's vision was still "expressed as a cry . . . while in his fiction it acquires a plot" (1984: 221).

Even more than his letters and his poetry, his short stories repeatedly find their way into his novels, sometimes with an economy of production whereby the author discovers sufficient threads between stories to revise and link them into novel-length narratives. The seven Civil War and Reconstruction stories that make up *The Unvanquished* and, more complexly, the seven-chapter *Go Down, Moses* are examples. Unlike the pre- and post-Civil War pieces about the Sartoris family that were published in magazines almost as a serial, *Go Down, Moses*, though in seven parts, is a reimagination of, and meditation upon, a considerable amount of material that Faulkner previously used for commercial stories in some of the most lucrative markets in America. Faulkner insisted to his publisher that these books were novels, since novels earned an advance and collections of short stories did not, but other writers accept the form as experimental, a hybrid that is neither collection of stories nor novel (Mann 1989).

As a popular medium, the short story usually depends upon action, which Faulkner learned to express like almost no one else, and it does not provide much, if any, room for exploring psychology, society, or morality. These are the things that Faulkner engaged with so powerfully in his novels. As Robert Penn Warren wrote,

> If respect for the human is the central fact of Faulkner's work, what makes that fact significant is that he realizes and dramatizes the difficulty of respecting the human.

> Everything is against it, the savage egotism, the blank appetite, stupidity and arrogance, even virtues sometimes, the misreading of our history and tradition, our education, our twisted loyalties. That is the great drama. (Warren 1958: 79)

Such complex drama is hard to reduce to a dozen pages. Writing short stories in financial desperation, however, ironically may have spurred Faulkner's invention of characters, themes, issues, and events that could serve a higher fictional purpose when he could take the time to manifest his respect for the human.

The Snopes stories are a good example. They originated in tale-swapping with Phil Stone as caricatures of poor white sharecroppers – the naming alone goes far beyond its Dickensian inspiration into such travesties as Wallstreet Panic, Montgomery Ward, Watkin's Products, and I. O. Snopes. Even before he brings off *The Hamlet* (1940), however, the long story "Barn Burning" interrogates the humanity of both Ab and Colonel Sartoris Snopes, and the final volume of the trilogy, *The Mansion* (1959), constructs an apotheosis for Mink.

The Snopes stories bear some relationship to the writing game Faulkner played with Sherwood Anderson in New Orleans, a contest in composing the tall tales about Al Jackson and his family already mentioned. Anderson lived in the Pontalba Building, which had a view of Jackson Square, where the large equestrian statue of General Andrew Jackson stood. Faulkner lived down a side street right beside the cathedral. Inspired by their playful speculations on why the statue's boots were so large, and stealing from an episode in Owen Wister's novel *The Virginian* (1903) about frog ranching in California, they invent the luckless Jackson family of swamp-based sheepherders. For Faulkner, this was an easy and delightful imitation of literature he had known since childhood, when his mother had read to him from the family copy of *Sut Lovingood's Yarns Spun by a Nat'ral Born'd Durn Fool* (1867) by George Washington Harris, as well as Mark Twain and other writers of the frontier humor tradition. For Anderson, Faulkner's contributions were one of many signs that things were too easy for his protégé; Faulkner had so much talent, Anderson once told him, "You can do it too easy, in too many different ways. If you're not careful, you'll never write anything" (Faulkner 2004b: 7).

Happily, Anderson was wrong, and even the tall tale would reappear in various forms throughout Faulkner's career, most vividly as humor in *The Hamlet*, where a horse-swap goes wild because a devilish trader is not above attaching an inner tube valve to the underside of a skinny horse and blowing it up. In *Go Down, Moses*, the tradition is used both for humor and to evoke what one writer of the tradition, Thomas Bangs Thorpe, referred to in one of his titles as "the mysteries of the backwoods." In his final novel, *The Reivers*, Faulkner makes the adventures of Boon Hogganbeck, a rude giant, Ned McCaslin, a black sorcerer, and Lucius Priest, a knight errant, approach the magic realism that is an unselfconscious trademark of many frontier tall tales (McHaney 1986). Marginally related are the ghost tales that Faulkner used to tell on occasion at his Oxford home, Rowan Oak, when young people were there for parties with his daughter or his niece Dean, and these are recounted by Dean Faulkner Wells (Faulkner 1980a).

Detective stories, one of the most popular forms of short fiction, are something that Faulkner wrote apparently first simply because they represented a commercial submarket of the short story genre. Like the comic story or the action story or the romantic story or the sentimental war story popular with magazine audiences, the detective story is a form Faulkner apparently sat down to learn, literally, for the report is that he often entered his friend Mack Reed's Oxford drugstore and sat on the floor by the magazine stand to read current publications (Reed 1965: 182–3). He parodies the practice of this pulp genre and also "true confessions" in *The Wild Palms* (and takes a quick stab at the motion picture industry as well). In *The Wild Palms* (which in 1990 was published in the Library of America edition and in a Vintage paperback under Faulkner's original title, *If I Forget Thee, Jerusalem*), the protagonist of the river story, "Old Man," is sentenced to prison because he gets his plan, and equipment, to rob a train from reading the *"Detectives' Gazette."* Harry Wilbourne, protagonist of "Wild Palms," the novel's contrapuntal plot, is a long-time virgin runaway lover who seems to know nothing about women, but he attempts to write stories of "female sex troubles" for the pulp confession market (Faulkner 1990: 22, 115). Since Faulkner wrote for two of the media he pillories in *The Wild Palms* (movies and detective fiction), it is tempting to suspect that in some hour of financial desperation he at least considered submitting a "moronic fable" that began, like one of Harry Wilbourne's, "I had the body and desires of a woman yet in knowledge and experience of the world I was but a child" (p. 103).

Faulkner seemed no happier about plunging into the detective genre than he was about slaving for movie studios, though in April of 1943 he writes his stepdaughter about "making a splendid collection of 25¢ paper-back whodunits to bring home from California" and recommends work by Dorothy Sayers, Agatha Christie, and Rex Stout, but suggests, perhaps considering his audience, that Ngaio Marsh may be "too arty" (Blotner 1978: 170). As screenwriter, Faulkner worked on Raymond Chandler's *The Big Sleep* (1946) in 1944 and 1945 (Kawin 1977: 113–21), and he liked the company of fellow Southerner Dashiell Hammett, author of *The Maltese Falcon* and other classics of the genre (Blotner 1984: 293).

Not long after this stint of work on the script of a detective story, however, Faulkner received notice that he had won second prize in the *Ellery Queen Mystery Magazine* annual contest for "An Error in Chemistry," one of his Gavin Stevens detective stories collected in *Knight's Gambit* (1949). The prize was a trumped-up way to pay Faulkner, as a distinguished writer, a little extra, but he still received very little, and his response upon getting the check reflects his feeling about prostituting himself in the popular short story market: "Thank you for the Ellery Queen check. What a commentary. In France, I am the father of a literary movement. In Europe I am considered the best modern American and among the first of all writers. In America, I eke out a hack's motion picture wages by winning second place in a manufactured mystery story contest" (Blotner 1978: 218).

Another genre in which Faulkner developed a mixed but interesting history is the essay introducing a work of one's own. In 1954, in an introduction for *The Faulkner Reader*, an anthology of his work issued by his regular publisher, Random House, his three-page foreword begins by speaking of how he received his "early education" in his grandfather Falkner's "moderate though reasonably diffuse and catholic library." There, he says, he read a novel by Henryk Sienkiewicz (author of *Quo Vadis* and a Nobel Prize winner himself). The Polish author had an introduction, Faulkner recalled, that "went something like this: This book was written at the expense of considerable effort, to uplift men's hearts, and I thought: *What a nice thing to have thought to say*" (Faulkner 1954: vii). Faulkner then uses the anecdote to explain that, ideally, this is why writers write, to "uplift men's hearts," because if a writer "can engender this excitement," he "himself partakes of the immortality which he has engendered" (1954: ix). Thus it is, Faulkner generously declares, "the same for all of us: for the ones who are trying to be artists, the ones who are trying to write simple entertainment, the ones who write to shock, and the ones who are simply escaping themselves and their own private anguishes" (1954: viii–ix). Each of these types reflects a place on the literary ladder where Faulkner had worked, or at least stumbled. The much-misunderstood introduction to the 1932 Modern Library edition of his *succès de scandale Sanctuary* (first published in 1931), rates authorship similarly, although with tongue some way in cheek: "This book was written three years ago," he wrote in 1932. "To me it is a cheap idea, because it was deliberately conceived to make money" (2004a: 176*).* Failing to make money with his first four serious novels, he explains, and having magazine editors routinely reject his stories, "I took a little time out, and speculated what a person in Mississippi would believe to be current trends, chose what I thought was the right answer and invented the most horrific tale I could imagine and wrote it in about three weeks" (2004a: 177).

The *Sanctuary* introduction is both imitation and parody, as well as exaggeration. First, he parodies the tough-guy school of detective writers, and he parodies Ernest Hemingway's parodic asides between the chapters of *The Torrents of Spring* (McHaney 1975: 19). Most of the claims of humility or shame regarding the book must be taken as tongue-in-cheek. Two drafts of introductions he wrote the following year, 1933, for a projected limited edition printing of *The Sound and the Fury* are very different. Both are moving and perceptive accounts of Faulkner's frustrations over rejections, his pride concerning his achievement as a writer, and his amazement and surprise regarding the experience of writing *The Sound and the Fury.* That novel flowed from his pen effortlessly, he wrote, because a door had closed between himself and all publishers' addresses, so that he could say to himself, "Now I can write. Now I can just write" (2004a: 293). The edition, which would have used colored ink to identify the different time levels of the Benjy section, was never published. However, in 1946, when one of the drafts was found in the Random House files and he was asked if he would like to have it used now to introduce the text, possibly the Modern Library edition that contains both *The Sound and the Fury* and *As I Lay Dying* (1946), he replied,

> Bless you for finding that introduction and sending it back to me. Random House paid me for it and I remember writing one, but I had forgotten what smug false sentimental windy shit it was. I will return the money for it, I would be willing to return double the amount for the chance of getting it out of danger and destroyed. (Blotner 1978: 235)

The purple passages in both of the draft introductions, which now appear in the new edition of *Essays, Speeches and Public Letters* (2004a) as well as in the Norton Critical Edition of *The Sound and the Fury,* nonetheless make startling observations about the novel's symbolic images – the branch in which the Compson children play is the "dark stream of time," Caddy's muddy drawers presage her fate in the family, Dilsey is the gaunt chimney towering over the fallen house of Compson. Faulkner's reaction against these unfinished pieces may reflect that such unpacking of his own symbols did not match the country squire persona he was beginning to assume in his relations with the world. This is ironic, because only a year before, in 1945, he had restored his grasp of his subject and his literary life by completing a long piece to accompany the publication of *The Portable Faulkner.* Of course, he had done it his own way and thereby turned the genre of the introduction on its ear. Malcolm Cowley had asked for an introduction to provide context for the stories and novel excerpts contained in the *Portable.* The essay Faulkner produced, "Appendix Compson 1699–1945," is not precisely an essay and definitely not an introduction. It was so clearly *not* an introduction that when the "Appendix" to *The Portable Faulkner* became a strangely authorized "fifth" chapter of *The Sound and the Fury,* and that novel, in return, became paired with *As I Lay Dying* in a 1946 Modern Library edition, Faulkner drafted an introduction to explain the presence of the "appendix." It, too, like the draft introductions for the Compson novel, was published in the writer's lifetime. Later, the Appendix would appear, oddly, as a prelude to the four incomparable sections of *The Sound and the* Fury. Regarded as experiments, these rejected and transfigured introductions record bizarre adventures in a little-studied genre.

Before Faulkner embraced the country squire/gentleman farmer public performance, perhaps as a result of Cowley's discovering to him that Yoknapatawpha was his great gift to world literature (see McHaney 2005), he endured years in the persona of the Hollywood hack, the down-and-out writer of great but lost reputation who succumbs to the blandishments of America's west coast Babylon. The Coen brothers film *Barton Fink* pushes this image to the extreme, but Faulkner pushed it pretty far himself. It is a story that is indeed complicated, and whether or not it has a Hollywood happy ending is up for discussion.

Work in Hollywood was a dire necessity for Faulkner, but it ate up much of his time and energy when he was at the peak of his writing prowess and imaginative drive. Starting just after his remarkable run of four extraordinary novels – *The Sound and the Fury* (1929), *As I Lay Dying* (1930), *Sanctuary* (1931), and *Light in August* (1932) – which themselves followed three apprentice works, *Soldiers' Pay* (1926), *Mosquitoes* (1927), and *Sartoris* (1929), the flight to Hollywood coincided with his father's death (1932) and the mounting economic depression that affected the sale of many commodities in the entertainment industries, of which publishing was one, though not the movies, which operated like penny candy machines, making lots of small profits from lots of outlets nationwide. Yet the Hollywood years demonstrate how dogged Faulkner could be even under extreme duress. He accepted his fate as the economic engine and paterfamilias of an increasingly large and expensive clan, but he never relinquished his ambitions as a serious artist.

Faulkner's fierce defense of time to write novels during these years is extraordinary, both punishing and productive. After the short break starting in 1932, when his father died, and culminating in 1934 when his youngest brother was killed while flying the airplane Faulkner used movie profits to give him, he actually embarked on another run of six extraordinarily innovative novels: *Pylon* (1935), *Absalom, Absalom!* (1936), *The Unvanquished* (1938), *The Wild Palms* (1939), *The Hamlet* (1940), and *Go Down, Moses* (1942) – all while bound to Hollywood and playing the short story market whenever he could. Unlike many writers in his position, he did not drink himself out of a job, or a life, though he certainly drank; and although his final employer, Jack Warner, bragged that he had the best writer in America for peanuts, Faulkner's salaries from Hollywood work were dizzyingly high when contrasted with the economy of Mississippi.

Whatever the financial gain from Hollywood, the artistic dividends have been seen by many of Faulkner's interpreters as nil. And it is true that Faulkner's screenplay writing is mostly forgettable on its own terms – much like the poetry or the hand-made books. Yet those who have studied the Hollywood writing – one of Faulkner's major and longest-lasting experiments in genres outside the novel – find that his fiction shows many signs of being positively affected by film writing. Though overall the experience was distasteful, Faulkner appears to have regarded some of his Hollywood projects, or concepts for such projects, positively. Bruce Kawin in *Faulkner and Film* (1977), and Louis Daniel Brodsky and Robert Hamblin in their volumes reprinting screenplay materials for *Battle Cry*, *Country Lawyer*, and *The DeGaulle Story*, do a good job of discussing the serious import of Faulkner's work for the screen and, in Brodsky and Hamblin's volumes, the resonances of film work in the later fiction (Faulkner 1984a, 1985).

This makes sense. Writing for film is not exactly authorship, so many other voices get involved – directors, actors, producers, craftspeople, and sometimes gauntlets of screenwriters who may handle a single script. But Faulkner's experiments in drafting treatments and shooting scripts did more than demonstrate his work ethic, and they put him in touch with a great many very intelligent, well-read, creative people at a time when many in Hollywood were politically engaged and actually called on to produce propaganda to fight both the Depression and later World War II, a legacy from Hollywood, Brodsky and Hamblin argue, Faulkner took up in *A Fable* (1954) and elsewhere (Faulkner 1985: lv).

Faulkner made one mid-career foray into so-called legitimate drama, a genre no more truly suited to his talents than film writing. This foray is double-edged. It begins with a promise he made to a pretty Ole Miss coed, Ruth Ford, to write a play for her. And so when, after the Nobel Prize, he makes good on a novelistic project he had advertised to his publisher under the title *Requiem for a Nun* years before, he also refashions the novel genre to honor his promise to Ms Ford, now a promising actress. In *Requiem* (1951), he combines one of his best skills, bardic narrative of Southern cultural history, with one of his weakest to juxtapose three acts of dramatic dialogue in counterpoint to the historical passages. The drama intends to tell the second, or later, story of Temple Drake from *Sanctuary*. Such was new Nobel Prize winner Faulkner's fame that Albert

Camus would adapt the "drama" – considerably– for the French stage before Ruth Ford and her husband, the actor Zachary Scott, could mount an American production on the New York stage. It is interesting to note that the excessively expositional nature of the Temple Drake portions of *Requiem for a Nun*, especially the play version produced in America in 1959, come at a time when Faulkner is in an expositional mode himself. As he settles into his fame, not taking it lightly and making those speeches and writing those public letters mentioned already, he also finished *A Fable*, the novel that took over a decade to conclude, carries on with the Snopes trilogy he had promised (which had been waiting since 1940 for its second volume), and fulfilling proposals for novels summarized to his editors or agent much earlier, writing first *Intruder in the Dust* (1948) and then *Requiem for a Nun*. In a sense, *Intruder* is burdened with some exposition, as talkative lawyer Gavin Stevens tries badly to explain the South and Southern racial violence. *Requiem* depends upon what happened to Temple Drake in *Sanctuary*, so that must be brought on stage, and here we have the garrulous Gavin Stevens again. The 1957 second volume of the Snopes trilogy, titled *The Town*, is itself very much burdened with exposition, and yes, it too features Gavin Stevens, perhaps not a coincidence. In a sense, it is as if Faulkner were still writing appendices to his earlier and more successful novels, as he had done for Cowley's *Portable Faulkner*.

The sense of an ending that these post-1945 projects reflect may have come to the writer not only because he slipped past the age of 50 in 1947, but because he was very much concerned during these years with the Cold War. As he said in his 1950 Nobel Prize acceptance speech, "Our tragedy today is a general and universal physical fear so long sustained by now that we can even bear it. There are no longer problems of the spirit. There is only the question: When will I be blown up?" (2004a: 118).

Because he was concerned about America's reputation in countries that were, or could be, pawns in the contest with the Soviet Union, he began to speak out on important issues. One of these was right in his face – the racial issue in the South. This would bring Faulkner strongly into the public arena through letters published in his regional newspaper, the *Memphis Commercial Appeal,* the paper of record, more or less, for the Mid-South. Possibly he sent letters to the major Mississippi paper, the *Jackson Daily News*, too, though that race-baiting sheet constantly editorialized against him. And he might have sent letters to the Pulitzer Prize-winning *Delta Democrat Times* in Greenville, where the editor, Hodding Carter, was an acquaintance, a future Pulitzer Prize winner, and, incidentally, the publisher of an episode of the long in-progress *A Fable*, a limited edition pamphlet titled *Notes on a Horse Thief* (1951).

Faulkner also wrote his hometown paper, the *Oxford Eagle*, on a variety of personal or local issues. The *Eagle* published his lament for a family dog run down by a cowardly motorist and Faulkner wrote his support for the paper's editorializing about historic preservation in Oxford. In 1950, the *Eagle* refused his request to publish an advertisement taking sides against local ministers in a campaign to outlaw the local-option sale of beer in Oxford. Mississippi then still was a dry state, but local governments could ratify exceptions for beer sales. Denied an advertisement that attacked church ministers, Faulkner had a broadside handbill printed and distributed it throughout the city

(2004a: 207–8). "To the Voters of Oxford" wryly countered the arguments of the local clergymen, who had issued in the newspaper a statement opposing the legalization of beer, starting with their observation that "Beer was voted out in 1944 because of its obnoxiousness." Faulkner's response is "Beer was voted out in 1944 because too many voters who drank beer or didn't object to other people drinking it, were absent in Europe and Asia defending Oxford where voters who preferred home to war could vote on beer in 1944" (2004a: 207).

He wrote the *New York Times* against the red-scare expulsion from the United States of the Metropolitan of the Russian Orthodox Church and about an airliner that crashed at New York's Idlewild Airport because, in Faulkner's view, the pilot was forced to rely on technology instead of seat-of-the-pants instinct. He wrote *Time Magazine* to defend Ernest Hemingway from the critics, noting that they were people who "didn't write" Hemingway's best works and thus had nothing to stand on when they savaged *Across the River and Into the Trees* (2004a: 210). His most significant public letters, however, are the ones that touch the brewing racial discontent in America and especially the reactive white violence that accompanied it in his native state. The same subject is one theme of many of his public speeches, although he also delivered two commencement addresses for his daughter's graduations – from high school and from Pine Manor Junior College – and talks to literary clubs at the University of Virginia during his tenure as visiting writer there in 1957–8.

In the 1952 talk he gave to the Delta Council – an economic development organiza- tion concerned with agriculture and business in the Mississippi Delta region – Faulkner focused on the theme of responsibility (2004a: 126–34), a theme he had addressed both comically and seriously in *Requiem for a Nun*. In one of the historical narratives of that unusual text, he writes the secret history of the naming of the Yoknapatawpha County "capital," its county seat, Jefferson. It is not the great Virginian, it turns out, who inspired the town's name. The naming was instead a bribe to a Federal mail rider named Thomas Jefferson Pettigrew, from whom the town borrows the lock on a Federal mailbag that is immediately stolen, along with the door it was intended to secure, by some escaping Natchez Trace bandits the townspeople had captured. Not wanting to take responsibility for the mishap, the little unincorporated backwoods village where this occurs refuses to raise the $15 that is the lock's cost. Instead, they promise to name the town for the mail rider if he will just report the lock as stolen, which he does. But naming the town means incorporating it, and this starts a government that in what seems like no time spirals into a state system of government with a capital building in Jackson that has a golden dome and laws that cannot distinguish between motives and results. So, because the town has not taken responsibility, the world is forever 15 dollars short, and, as retribution, American civilization suffers under the mechanical rule of institutions that become their own reason for being. Surely Faulkner was looking back on Nazi Germany and directly at the Soviet Union, but just as sharply at home, where he had deplored the effects of New Deal farm and public works projects.

As Robert Penn Warren noted, Faulkner saw abstraction as one of the great enemies of humankind, along with irresponsible power, although, he also argued, "There are, in one way, no villains in his work, except those who deny the human bond" (1958: 78). Poetry and letters, with which this discussion of Faulkner's genre experiment began, are genres that speak to and from "the human bond." Faulkner's early poetry, unfortunately, dealt largely in abstractions or clichéd personifications of abstractions. His letters, however, did not, and when he turned to the prose of fiction, especially to long prose fiction where he could lay out a world, a cosmos of his own, he achieved what Warren says about him. Without that apprenticeship, perhaps he would not have had the good long practice with abstractions that he turned to flesh and blood, place and time, present and past event.

If that is so, Faulkner served a useful apprenticeship as an experimenter with genres other than the one that was his true fate. Making personal books explicitly for his friends is another demonstration, and so is the act of a shy and reticent private citizen who mounts a podium to speak about the need to give up cultural fear and to rebuke injustice. Faulkner spoke in the Nobel Prize address of abstractions – the "old verities of the human heart in conflict with itself" – and this phrase, and the litany of qualities he appends to it – courage, honor, hope, pride, compassion, pity, sacrifice – may sound like cliché. But Faulkner frequently put his life on the line, literally, to perform a verity or two, and he repeatedly created characters and situations that tested themselves against the world with similar performances.

Perhaps, then, it is better to say that in his speeches he reached out. In response to a question about J. D. Salinger's *The Catcher in the Rye* Faulkner not only made one of his rare admissions of reading his contemporaries, he spoke movingly about the plight of the novel's narrator, Holden Caulfield. Holden's tragedy, Faulkner told an audience at the University of Virginia in 1958, "was that when he attempted to enter the human race, there was no human race there" (Gwynn and Blotner 1959: 244). Unlike Holden, Faulkner never stopped trying to find the human race, even when he couldn't select the right genre for his vision or when circumstances forced him to adopt a genre alien or inadequate to that vision. He accepted and built upon the fact that he was himself that most interesting of experimental genres, a human being, a work in progress.

REFERENCES AND FURTHER READING

Anderson, S. (1953). *Letters of Sherwood Anderson* (ed. H. Mumford Jones and W. B. Rideout). Boston: Little, Brown.

Blotner, J. (1964). *William Faulkner's Library: A Catalogue.* Charlottesville, VA: University of Virginia Press.

Blotner, J. (ed.) (1978). *Selected Letters of William Faulkner.* New York: Random House.

Blotner, J. (1984). *Faulkner: A Life.* One-vol. edn. New York: Random House.

Collins, C. (1963). Faulkner at the University of Mississippi. In W. Faulkner. *Early Prose and Poetry* (ed. C. Collins) (pp. 3–33). London: Jonathan Cape.

Crane, J. St. C. (1989). Case No. 133733-C: The Inspector's Letter to Postmaster William Faulkner. *Mississippi Quarterly*, 42: 229–45.

Fant, J. L. and R. P. Ashley (eds.) (1984). *Faulkner at West Point.* New York: Random House.

Faulkner, W. (1924). *The Marble Faun.* Boston: Four Seas.

Faulkner, W. (1932). Introduction. In *Sanctuary* (pp. v–viii). New York: Modern Library.

Faulkner, W. (1954). Foreword. In *The Faulkner Reader* (pp. vii–x). New York: Random House.

Faulkner, W. (1962). *Early Prose and Poetry* (ed. C. Collins). Boston: Little, Brown. (Written 1916–25.)

Faulkner, W. (1967). *The Wishing Tree*. New York: Random House. (Written 1928.)

Faulkner, W. (1973). And Now What's To Do. *Mississippi Quarterly*, 26: 399–402. (Written c. 1925–7.)

Faulkner, W. (1977a). *The Marionettes* (ed. N. Polk). Charlottesville, VA: Bibliographical Society of the University of Virginia. (Written 1920.)

Faulkner, W. (1977b). Sinbad in New Orleans: Early Short Fiction by WF – An Annotated Edition (ed. L. H. Cox). PhD diss. University of South Carolina. (Written 1925.)

Faulkner, W. (1980a). *The Ghosts of Rowan Oak: William Faulkner's Ghost Stories for Children* (recounted D. F. Wells). Jackson: University Press of Mississippi.

Faulkner, W. (1980b). *Mayday* (ed. Carvel Collins). Typeset edn with representative illustrations. South Bend, IN: University of Notre Dame Press. (Written 1926.)

Faulkner, W. (1984a). *The DeGaulle Story* (eds. L. D. Brodsky and R. W. Hamblin). In *Faulkner: A Comprehensive Guide to the Brodsky Collection. Vol. III*. Jackson: University Press of Mississippi. (Written 1942.)

Faulkner, W. (1984b). *Vision in Spring* (ed. J. Sensibar). Austin, TX: University of Texas Press. (Written 1921.)

Faulkner, W. (1985). *Battle Cry* (eds. L. D. Brodsky and R. W. Hamblin). In *Faulkner: A Comprehensive Guide to the Brodsky Collection. Vol. IV*. Jackson: University Press of Mississippi. (Written 1943.)

Faulkner, W. (1990). *If I Forget Thee, Jerusalem* [*The Wild Palms*]. New York: Vintage International. (Original pub. 1939.)

Faulkner, W. (2002). *New Orleans Sketches* (ed. C. Collins). Rpt. edn. Jackson: University Press of Mississippi. (Written 1925.)

Faulkner, W. (2004a). *Essays, Speeches and Public Letters* (ed. J. B. Meriwether). Updated edn. New York: Modern Library.

Faulkner, W. (2004b). Sherwood Anderson: An Appreciation. In *Essays, Speeches and Public Letters* (ed. J. B. Meriwether) (pp. 3–10). Updated edn.

New York: Modern Library. (Original pub. 1953.)

Garrett, G. (1957). An Examination of the Poetry of William Faulkner. *Princeton University Library Chronicle*, 18: 124–35.

Gwynn, F. L. and J. Blotner (eds.) (1959). *Faulkner in the University: Class Conferences at the University of Virginia, 1957–1958*. Charlottesville, VA: University Press of Virginia.

Hönnighausen, L. (1987). *William Faulkner: The Art of Stylization in His Early Graphic and Literary Work*. Cambridge: Cambridge University Press.

Kawin, B. (1977). *Faulkner and Film*. New York: Frederick Ungar.

Mann, S. G. (1989). *The Short Story Cycle: A Genre Companion and Reference Guide*. New York: Greenwood.

McHaney, T. L. (1965–6). Review *William Faulkner's Library: A Catalogue*. *Mississippi Quarterly*, 19: 44–8.

McHaney, T. L. (1973). Sanctuary and Frazer's Slain Kings. *Mississippi Quarterly*, 24: 223–45.

McHaney, T. L. (1975). *Faulkner's* The Wild Palms: *A Study*. Jackson: University Press of Mississippi.

McHaney, T. L. (1980). Watching for the Dixie Limited: Faulkner's Impact on the Creative Writer. In D. Fowler and A. Abadie (eds.). *Fifty Years of Yoknapatawpha: Faulkner and Yoknapatawpha 1979* (pp. 226–47). Jackson: University Press of Mississippi,.

McHaney, T. L. (1986). What Faulkner Learned from the Tall Tale. In D. Fowler and A. Abadie (eds.). *Faulkner and Humor: Faulkner and Yoknapatawpha 1984* (pp. 110–35). Jackson: University Press of Mississippi.

McHaney, T. L. (1999). Untapped Faulkner: What Faulkner Read at the P. O. In D. M. Kartiganer and A. Abadie (eds.). *Faulkner at 100: Retrospect and Prospect* (pp. 180–7). Jackson: University Press of Mississippi.

McHaney, T. L. (2000). Faulkner's Birth into Fiction. In A. Bleikasten, M. Gresset, N. Moulinoux, and F. Pitavy (eds.). *Etudes Faulkneriennes II: Naissances de Faulkner* (pp. 29–33). Rennes: Presses Universitaires de Rennes.

McHaney, T. L. (2005). First is Jefferson: Faulkner Shapes His Domain. *Mississippi Quarterly*, 57: 511–34.

Prall, E. (1969). *Miss Elizabeth: A Memoir* (by E. [Prall] Anderson and G. R. Kelly). Boston: Little, Brown.

Reed, W. McN. (1965). Four Decades of Friendship. In J. W. Webb and A. W. Green (eds.). *William Faulkner of Oxford* (pp. 180–8). Baton Rouge: Louisiana State University Press.

Sensibar, J. L. (1984). *The Origins of Faulkner's Art.* Austin, TX: University of Texas Press.

Sensibar, J. L. (1988). *Faulkner's Poetry: A Bibliographic Guide to Texts and Criticism.* Ann Arbor: UMI Research Press.

Skei, H. (1999). *Reading Faulkner's Best Short Stories.* Columbia: University of South Carolina Press.

Snell, S. (1992). *Phil Stone of Oxford: A Vicarious Life.* Rpt. edn. Athens, GA: University of Georgia Press.

Warren, R. P. (1951). William Faulkner. In F. J. Hoffman and O. W. Vickery (eds.). *William Faulkner: Two Decades of Criticism* (pp. 82–101). East Lansing: Michigan State University Press. (Rpt. of Warren's review of Malcolm Cowley's *The Portable Faulkner* in *New Republic*, August 12 and 26, 1946.)

Warren, R. P. (1958). William Faulkner. In *Selected Essays* (pp. 59–79). New York: Random House.

Warren, R. P. (1966). Introduction. In R. P. Warren (ed.). *Faulkner: A Collection of Critical Essays* (pp. 1–33). Englewood Cliffs, NJ: Prentice Hall.

Watson, J. G. (1987). *William Faulkner: Letters and Fictions.* Austin, TX: University of Texas Press.

Watson, J. G. (ed.) (1992). *Thinking of Home: William Faulkner's Letters to His Mother and Father, 1918–1925.* New York: Norton.

Watson, J. G. (2000). *William Faulkner: Self-Presentation and Performance.* Austin, TX: University of Texas Press.

Wells, D. F. (1980). *The Ghosts of Rowan Oak.* Oxford: Yoknapatawpha Press.

[Welty, E.] (1954). Place and Time: The Southern Writer's Inheritance. *Times Literary Supplement*, September 17: xlviii. (Pub. anonymously.)

Young, S. (1938). New Year's Craw. *New Republic*, 12: 283–4.

20

"Make It New": Faulkner and Modernism

Philip Weinstein

Faulkner and modernism: the topic has been exhaustively treated, yet remains inexhaustible.[1] I make my way through this many-faceted field of thought and practice by concentrating on two related inquiries. The first, focused on influence, identifies some modernist precursors without whose work it is difficult to imagine Faulkner becoming Faulkner. The second compares Faulkner's practice with that of his most compelling peers, such that a sense for the larger powers and limits of modernist fiction becomes more salient.

"Make it new!" Pound famously urged his modernist peers, suggesting that the first task is to reflect on what they took to be "old." At the onset of the twentieth century, a number of Western European artists took nineteenth-century cultural/aesthetic procedures to be "old." First to be written off was early nineteenth-century Romantic poetry – with its trust in visionary moments, its investment in natural rather than urban values, its Wordsworthian speaker/narrator positioned as one who confessed home truths in accents others could immediately recognize. Unmediated vision, repudiated city, confessional voice: these stances struck the modernists as naïve, retrograde, egotistical – at odds with the linguistic constructedness of art, the dynamic and inhuman city from which art arose, the inevitable bias that comes with personal utterance. No less dubious (for Anglo-American modernists) were later nineteenth-century literary developments in England – Tennyson replacing Wordsworth, and the Victorian novelists (Dickens, the Brontës, George Eliot) replacing Scott and Austen. The city tends to be either absent or present as a "heavy" in the Victorian imaginary; pre-Raphaelite and Ruskinian urges to return to past values preclude the Poundian urge to make it new. A Romantic commitment to seeing and saying the unvarnished truth holds sway in the major realist writers who come after the Romantics: reform of the individual heart remains the century's deepest liberal dream.

The four modernist precursors who make Faulkner possible do not share this dream. Conrad and Freud probe, instead, a heart of impenetrable darkness. Eliot and Joyce delineate a cultural landscape resistant to reform, operating on premises not only alien to aspiration, but already at work within individuals and dislocating their most intimate patterns of thought and feeling. The self, for these writers, figures less as society's liberating other than as the local and embodied site of its stubborn contradictions. However Faulkner differs from such precursors, he takes from them a beleaguered human being at the center of the social canvas. That beleaguered figure is modernist.

Conradian impressionism – its insistence on representing the world according to the limited perspective of individuals inhabiting it rather than the objective stance of an all-seeing narrator – underwrites a revolution in Western novelistic procedures. Gone is the linear, logically unfolding text authorized by a disinterested and unsituated speaker. Drawing on Jamesian experimentation with limited centers of consciousness, Conrad produces a fiction of unauthorized "takes" upon the world: Jim's and Marlow's in *Lord Jim* (1900) and *Heart of Darkness* (1898–9), an entire range of figures in *Nostromo* (1904). Conrad's fiction enters the perspectival jungle of uncertainty – producing mutually incompatible narratives in which conflicting individuals pursue inarticulable goals as they move through a field of others' opaque intentions. Marlow making his way to Kurtz deep in the Congo, Marlow grasping bits and pieces of Jim's tantalizing drama (a drama with Jim as its central but mystified player) – these narrative *données* produce a new figure–ground model. Rather than the familiar ground of coherent social thought and behavior, against which the individual figure shows itself for what it is (as, for example, in George Eliot's way of positioning Dorothea and Lydgate within the knowable community of *Middlemarch*), Conrad follows his figures into landscapes that neither know them nor share their conventional assumptions. Convention itself – the "coming together" of notions about the world – shatters: cultural crisis emerges as Conrad's central (dis)organizing insight.

Everyone speaks in Conrad, no one speaks authorized truth. Jim mutters, Marlow stammers, individual utterance reaches toward but never masters the scene in which it finds itself. "Do you see the story? Do you see anything?" Marlow implores his friends on the *Nellie*, knowing that their conventions – models of shared understanding – have little purchase on his materials, and that he must put yet further pressure on his own language if he is somehow to get protected Englishmen to grasp the exposure of other men lost (to themselves) in black Africa (Conrad 1988: 30). This alienated writer who reached English by way, first, of Polish, then of French – who wrote an elegant English but never spoke it without mangling it – reveals a pathos of articulation foreign to, subversive of, Victorian confidence. Fiction emerges, in the practice of Conrad, as a constitutively enigmatic unfolding. When Henry James praised Conrad as "absolutely alone as a votary of the way to do a thing that shall make it undergo most doing," he identified Conrad's modernist investment in the "ungivenness" that attends all partial acts of understanding and that mandates such rigorous "doing" (James 1964: 131).

Conradian skepticism is everywhere in Faulkner. At the level of phrase or event, Conrad's ship infamously "firing into a continent" (Conrad 1988: 17) reappears in *Absalom, Absalom!* (1936), where the young Sutpen and his boss "fired at no enemy but at the Haitian night itself" (Faulkner 1990a: 209). More structurally, *Nostromo's* intricate deployment of partial narratives – Decoud's, Giorgio's, Gould's, Emilia's, Nostromo's, Monygham's, Mitchell's, among others – re-emerges in *Absalom*'s multi-layered weave of Mr. Compson's, Rosa's, Quentin's, and Shreve's partial narratives. Each narrative is grounded in its own subjective necessity, each fails to master a scene of cultural crisis transcending individual grasp. It comes together, in Conrad as in Faulkner after him, as a composite weave requiring unprecedented readerly attention just to keep track of the different strands. Although Faulkner fondly described his fictional world as "a cosmos of my own," the Conradian paradigm is more instructive: these are composite weaves that no one can own. If in Conrad a plausible motive for such designed non-mastery is the foreignness of the writer (such alienation functioning as the key to Conrad's untethered intelligence), in Faulkner the motive might well be the reverse. Conrad taught him how to write narratives – without owning them. Or, put more diagnostically, how to "tell the South" outside the parochial perspective of the white master. Faulkner can become Faulkner only – thanks to Conrad – by learning to write narratives in which he absents himself, becomes not-Faulkner.

Unlike Conrad, Freud taught Faulkner little about how to produce fiction. But Freud supervened upon Faulkner's conceptual world more powerfully, perhaps, by authoring a number of its shaping presuppositions. "Memory believes before knowing remembers," Faulkner writes of the grown-up Joe Christmas's relation to his own infancy; the phrasing is hard to imagine before Freud (Faulkner 1985a: 487). Conscious memory, in Faulkner as in Proust, is an affair of the will and the defenses; it bites its owner only skin-deep, and neither writer accords it much respect. Unconscious memory is another story: it "believes" outside the purview of its owner's consciousness, biting deeper, shaping behavior inexorably because unknowingly. Everything Joe Christmas cannot remember from his past remembers him. The literal violence of a stepfather seeking to beat prayer into him joins with the figurative violence of that same stepfather seeking to inculcate the Calvinist catechism into his very marrow. Both violences reappear, unremembered and unknown, in the rage fueling his murder of Joanna Burden. "She ought not to started praying over me" (1985a: 481), Joe thinks as he makes his way toward her door. Outside that door, minutes from an as yet uncommitted murder, "he believed with calm paradox that he was the volitionless servant of the fatality in which he believed that he did not believe. He was saying to himself *I had to do it* already in the past tense; *I had to do it*" (1985a: 605). Thanks to Faulkner's grasp of both Freudian condensation and the unceasing life of traumatic events, he luminously accesses Christmas's deformed and deforming motives. The earlier McEachern inhabits the present Burden and helps mandate her execution; the repudiated Calvinist theology speaks unknowingly in an act at once already done and not yet executed.

Freudian thought operates no less in Faulkner's attention to the reverberation of formative childhood experiences. When Dickens and George Eliot insist that Agnes replace Dora, as Ladislaw replaces Casaubon, they testify to Victorian belief in progress. Matters (and minds) can improve in time. But when *The Sound and the Fury* (1929) shows "sister" replaying Quentin's sister Caddy (in the theater of Quentin's mind), as Jason's niece Quentin replays his sister Caddy (in the theater of Jason's mind), Faulkner is testifying not to progress but to – indeed, his supreme effect – repercussion. Now is suddenly seen as – has never escaped from – then. *"Maybe happen is never once,"* Quentin muses in *Absalom, Absalom!* (1990a: 216). What could be more Freudian than this conviction that the roles our later experience deploys are but reconfigurations of roles enacted first in infancy and childhood? Freudian time goes underground rather than passing; Freudian space is both "out there" and "in here." Each of Faulkner's modernist masterpieces espouses this non-realist sense of space and time as the haunted frames in which we re-enact ourselves over and over again.

Freudian thought may appear most powerfully, however, not in Faulknerian charac-ter psychology or the prominence of repercussion, but rather in his emphasis upon return to the past itself. In Faulkner as in Freud: any direction forward requires strenu-ous movement backward. It is not only that what matters most has already happened, but that we are not yet in possession of what has already happened. Was it the Civil War (ended over 30 years before his birth) that catalyzed Faulkner's conviction that the past shapes the present in primordial ways beyond mapping? Or was it, as a more diffuse effect of that war, his dawning awareness that his culture's decapitated ante-bellum ideology (mis)shaped irremediably that same culture's way of lurching into the future? No one has put it better than Sartre: "Faulkner's vision of the world can be compared to that of a man sitting in an open car and looking backwards. At every moment, formless shadows, flickerings . . . rise up on either side of him, and only afterwards . . . do they become trees and men and cars" (1994: 267). If Sartre's claim foregrounds an existentialist focus on the moment, it no less intimates Freudian pre-history's deforming mark on present history. What predates us is stronger and more stubborn than we are. "I am older at twenty than a lot of people who have died," Quentin darkly muses at the end of *Absalom* (1990a: 301). Still alive, he carries the dead with him (within him) – a burden they have mercifully escaped.

T. S. Eliot's poetry shapes Faulknerian modernism in ways related to both Conrad's fiction and Freud's psychoanalytic theory. Indeed, Eliot's morbidity is as indebted as Faulkner's melancholy is to Conradian skepticism. "Mistah Kurtz – he dead" – the black native's stark utterance near the end of *Heart of Darkness* (1988: 69) – functions as epi-graph to "The Hollow Men." In Eliot's poetry one begins with death – "In my end is my beginning" (*Four Quartets* [1944]) – and the death in question is a death unfinished, endlessly happening. Eliot's capacity to evoke unforgettably the death that weighs on life in the years following the Great War marks the language of all his modernist peers. Prufock conceptually floating in an ether of weightless fantasies – "like a patient ether-ised upon a table" – foreshadows Rosa Coldfield *clinging yet to the dream as the patient clings to the last thin unbearable ecstatic instant of agony* (1990a: 116). In both cases there is no question of waking to a progressive future. The best that can be hoped for is the surcease that comes, as with Prufrock, when "human voices wake us, and we drown."

Eliot showed Faulkner not only how to articulate contemporary despair, but how to counterpoint it against the language of an older dispensation of grace. The ways in which *The Waste Land* (1922) brilliantly juxtaposes vulgar phrases against poetic and religious fragments – its refusal of Victorian linguistic decorum – arguably reappear in *The Sound and the Fury*'s equally indecorous juxtapositions of high and low. Consider the centrifugal scattershot of Quentin's mindscape:

> *I have committed incest I said Father it was I it was not Dalton Ames* And when he put Dalton Ames. Dalton Ames. Dalton Ames. When he put the pistol in my hand I didn't. That's why I didn't. He would be there and she would and I would. Dalton Ames. Dalton Ames. Dalton Ames. If we could have just done something so dreadful and Father said That's sad too people cannot do anything that dreadful they cannot do anything very dreadful at all they cannot even remember tomorrow what seemed dreadful today and I said, You can shirk all things and he said, Ah can you. And I will look down and see my murmuring bones and the deep water like wind, like a roof of wind, and after a long time they cannot distinguish even bones upon the lonely and inviolate sand. Until on the day when He says Rise only the flat-iron would come floating up. It's not when you realise that nothing can help you – religion, pride, anything – it's when you realise that you dont need any aid. Dalton Ames. Dalton Ames. Dalton Ames. If I could have been his mother lying with open body lifted laughing, holding his father with my hand refraining, seeing, watching him die before he lived. *One minute she was standing in the door.* (1994: 51)

If you combine Eliot's yoking of heterogeneous phrases with Freud's anatomy of the roiled neurotic mind, you get something like Quentin's vertiginous mangling of syntax, reference, and setting: a fantastic declaration to Father, a stuttering and fixated memory of Dalton Ames, a reverie of his own coming extinction, a vision of the Second Coming that will nevertheless leave his remains undisturbed, a fantasy of Dalton Ames being unconceived just before being conceived, a glimpse of Caddy in motion at her wedding with Herbert Head: this prose outrages all continuities of time, place, or coherent subjectivity. It is as though Faulkner absorbed *The Waste Land*'s refusal of an organizing subjective voice and went Eliot one further: the creation of a voice (Quentin here, but Benjy before and Jason after) that would, in the (il)logic of its sequential deployment on the page, resemble no prior voice in Western fiction. Make it new indeed.

Finally, none of these effects might have come into being without the exemplary influence of Joyce's *Ulysses* (1922). There is no exaggerating the imaginative release that Joycean stream-of-consciousness prompted in Faulkner. Not only would we have neither *The Sound and the Fury* nor *As I Lay Dying* (1930) without *Ulysses*, but perhaps more subtly, we might not have Faulkner's subsequent (and sustained) irreverence toward traditional narrative forms, thanks to Joyce's unmatched subverting of conventions. Not that Faulkner's Quentin or Jason or Darl resembles Joyce's Stephen or Bloom. As Franco Moretti (1996) has demonstrated, Joycean stream-of-consciousness is devoted to the quotidian – anti-epiphanic, non-sublime – in ways foreign to all subsequent modernist deployment of it. Return for a moment to the citation above and the point becomes clear. Faulkner uses stream-of-consciousness to articulate the wracked nerves of Quentin's careening interiority – not his dailiness but his suicidal con-fusing of experiences, memories, fears, and desires: too intense to sustain for long. (June 2, 1910, the day of his monologue, is his death-day.) Faulkner draws on this technique to render the unspeakable, white-hot core of his characters' inner being.

As with Eliot, the effects Joyce most makes available to Faulkner are steeped in Freudian assumptions. It is not for nothing that stream-of-consciousness so resembles Freudian free association: both are deliberate techniques for evading psychic censorship. Both evoke a form of utterance that might elude the defenses and subterfuge imposed by the conscious mind, seeking instead to hone in on what lies *beneath*. As early as 1888, Nietzsche had declared that "we are not rid of God because we still have faith in grammar" (1954: 483). Subject, verb, object – the first acting through the second upon the third – what is this sacred trio but a microcosm of individual agency, dedicated to the efficacy of the ego? Joycean stream-of-consciousness undresses realist propriety, repudiates its subject, verb, object model in order to register, instead, the assault of experience – remembered, encountered, imagined – upon the receptive mind. The traffic between inner and outer thus articulated answers to no shaping "I" but, rather, bespeaks a receptive and responsive "me." Prior to "I" and its filtered projects, "me" is unselectively exposed to what registers as prior and coming toward it. "*Something is going to happen to me*" (Faulkner 1985a: 486), Faulkner writes of Joe Christmas's thought process as he walks toward Joanna Burden's house. Not "I am going to do X" but "X is going to happen to me." No awareness of the murder he is about to commit (and that was already thought of in the past tense, as already done), but rather subject motion without agency, an approaching act that may leave *her* beheaded, but which consciousness records as happening to *him*.

Such procedures take us not to the realist ethos of agency and the reformable heart but to the modernist pathos of a Heideggerian subject thrown into the world – in it before he knows he is, beleaguered from the outset. As Rilke writes, "There are no classes in life for beginners. It is always the most difficult that is asked of one right away" (1949: 80). Modernist texts are difficult in just these ways – opening obscurely, refusing tutelary hand-holding, seeking to honor the distinction between life's radical unpreparedness (no one goes through it twice) and fiction's cozy conventionality. To frustrated readers, such techniques may seem perversely alienating, but their rationale lies deeper. It is nothing less than an attempt, as Kafka put it, to reach and thaw the frozen sea within the reader, to expose – beneath all domesticating habit – the deeper outrageousness of our lives in space and time.

Faulkner as a cluster of modernist assumptions and procedures made possible by the thought and practice of Conrad, Freud, Eliot, and Joyce: that has been the focus of the first part of this chapter. But it would be misleading to suggest that modernism is therefore all of a piece, partaking of this pattern. I turn now to comparative analysis of Faulkner and some of his most compelling peers, focusing as much on difference as likeness. Modernism speaks in several different voices, Faulkner's but one among many.

Proust's work predates Faulkner's, looming over it as monumental precursor and revealing counterpoint. More intimately than any other modernist writer, Proust shares with Faulkner an alertness to time's deforming power. For both of them, the present moment is radically unbound; one is a player, but never a master, in that moment. Proust's stance toward temporal non-mastery is as innovative as Faulkner's. He makes the present moment unamenable to subjective mapping; the protagonist of his more-than-3,000-page novel never manages to coordinate his present experiences, never matures in time. To avert the incoherence that might follow from an incapacity to read oneself in present time, Proust deploys a brilliantly dualistic narrative strategy. On the one hand, there are others, actively immersed in the present, unaware of their own motives. On the other hand, there is Marcel/the narrator: an entity at once single and double, the child and the adult, the former locatable in present experience, the latter freed from it. Marcel/the narrator is granted, unlike all others in *la Recherche*, a life in two times – then and now – with the narrator able to see, in retrospect, what was all a blur as it actually happened to Marcel. A life in two times, yes, but two times that cannot be bound into the unified, continuous temporality that is normative in nineteenth-century realism.

To see how this dualism works – others caught up and displayed in the opaque present, Marcel/the narrator seeing past their blindness and delivering insight – let us consider the familiar cameo of Mlle Vinteuil and her lesbian friend, eavesdropped upon, by Marcel, some years after M. Vinteuil's death.[2] The scene is memorable. Divided beyond healing between daughterly modesty ("a shy and suppliant maiden") and lesbian desire ("a rough and swaggering trooper"), Mlle Vinteuil engages in an elaborate ritual of inauthentic moves. Prior to her lover's entry into the house, she places her father's photograph on a nearby table, so that when their embrace commences, it will be readily at hand – though not apparently by her doing. As for the embrace, she hungers for it, and is ashamed to want it, in equal measure; her gestures are consistently false.

Pretending to close the shutters, she answers her friend's retort with "But it's too tiresome! People will see us," followed by "When I say 'see us,' I mean, of course, see us reading. It's so tiresome to think that whatever trivial little thing you do someone may be overlooking you" (1981: I, 176). Her lover replies "And what if they are?" in a practiced (and anticipated) cynical tone, but still the embrace is withheld: "Mlle Vinteuil's . . . sensitive and scrupulous heart was ignorant of the words that ought to flow spontaneously from her lips to match the scene for which her eager senses clamored" (1981: I, 176). After reciting another rehearsed phrase, the friend suddenly kisses Mlle Vinteuil on the breast, the two women chase each other about the room "squealing like a pair of amorous fowls" (1981: I, 177), and – the moment now arrived – Mlle Vinteuil points to the portrait of her father, saying "I can't think of who can have put it there" (1981: I, 177). Overhearing this, Marcel remembers how, in visits made to her father long ago, M. Vinteuil had similarly excused the "inexplicable" presence of his sheets of music, a move allowing him to receive – without seeming to seek – his guests' admiration for his work. The scene gathers intensity: "This photograph was evidently in regular use for ritual profanations, for the friend replied in words which were clearly a liturgical response: 'Let him stay there. . . . D'you think he'd start whining . . . if he saw you now with the window open, the ugly old monkey?'" At which point she ritually threatens to spit on the photograph, is disingenuously rebuffed by Mlle. Vinteuil, then carries out her threat/promise. The love-making commences; the window and shutters are finally closed.

"Someone may be overlooking," Mlle Vinteuil complains. Rarely was a scene more populated with unseen and invisible overlookers. (How many of *la Recherche*'s memorable vignettes would we have to give up if scenes of eavesdropping were removed?) Overlooking, Marcel describes a ritual of pure bad faith, centered on a young woman hopelessly riven by, unaware of, conflicting motives. It takes the overlooker, Marcel, to tell us what is at stake:

> Sadists of Mlle Vinteuil's sort are creatures so purely sentimental . . . that even sensual pleasure appears to them as something bad . . . And when they allow themselves for a moment to enjoy it they endeavor to impersonate . . . the wicked, and to make their partners do likewise, in order to gain the momentary illusion of having escaped beyond the control of their own gentle and scrupulous natures into the inhuman world of pleasure. (1981: I, 179)

Not wicked, she tries to appear wicked; not spontaneous, she recites a long-rehearsed script of rising desire. Though seeking to escape (by humiliating) her father, her repetition of his gesture with the sheet of music places him all the more authoritatively in the scene. Marcel emphasizes her mannerisms, facial features, and blue eyes as so many heirlooms announcing the spectral presence of the father she would elude.

Indeed, the scene is so narrated that two males (the dead M. Vinteuil and the concealed Marcel) provide shaping lenses for understanding the behavior of two females (Mlle Vinteuil and her friend), both rendered as objects under scrutiny, lost to their own motives. A lesbian escape ("into the inhuman world of pleasure") is pre-empted by the narrator's installation of an Oedipal narrative. The scene centers, therefore, on unaccommodated remembering, failed forgetting. Ritual predominates in the form of their rehearsed script of desire, as a result of Marcel's relentless recall of what Mlle Vinteuil herself repeats without recognizing. He cues us in to what we henceforth register as a scene of dysfunction and distress, almost of traumatic repetitions.

Finally, if this portrait of Mlle Vinteuil attends to just a few all-revealing moments of her behavior, its own genesis *as* a portrait requires a much greater passage of time. Its analytic coherence is unobtainable without this sustained incubation period. The vignette begins by announcing that it is from an "impression which I received at Montjouvain, some years later, an impression which at the time remained obscure to me, that there arose, long afterwards, the notion I was to form of sadism" (1981: I, 173). *She* is the victim of a momentary experience that *he* has had untold time to ponder, digest, and master. The vignette reveals its logic, thanks to his temporal privilege: "And yet I have since reflected . . ." (1981: I, 178), Marcel thinks, recognizing (over time) that, even in blaspheming her father's memory, Mlle Vinteuil evinces, however obscurely, her kindred "goodness of heart" (1981: I, 178). A more pervasive narrative logic is here embedded. Like all embodied characters in this text, Mlle Vinteuil must take on the accusative form, if her onlooker, Marcel, is to assume his proper nominative (better would be "pronominal") form. She must be object to his subject. More, it is precisely scenes like this one that establish Marcel's authority *as* subject. His knowing requires an unnarrated temporal continuum, exactly as her unknowing must be situated within a narrated, revelatory moment. *In* the moment, he is no wiser than she is.

I have described Proustean practice enough to establish his modernist treatment of the present as a temporal space unamenable to mastery, and thus a space resistant to realist insistence on coming to know. (The narrator can – in time – map Mlle Vinteuil's present moment, but Mlle Vinteuil herself, blind to her own motives, cannot.) We see, thus, the indispensable role of the Proustean narrator: he who – unplaced in present space and time, disembodied and plotless – develops the negatives this text luxuriantly strews onto its pages, develops them *later.* Faulkner, by contrast, will have none of Proust's privileging dualism. His modernist masterpieces display no interest in anyone becoming smarter, later, than anyone else about the engulfment of experience in time. *Later* has no purchase in modernist Faulkner; his experimental texts are immersed in the unbound time of now. None of his early, innovative novels enacts this temporal stance more shockingly than *Sanctuary* (1931):

> She felt herself flying through the air, carrying a numbing shock upon her shoulder and a picture of two men peering from the fringe of cane at the roadside. She scrambled to her feet, her head reverted, and saw them step into the road . . . Still running her bones turned to water and she fell flat on her face, still running. (1985b: 205)

> She could hear silence in a thick rustling as he moved toward her through it, thrusting it aside, and she began to say Something is going to happen to me. She was saying it to the old man with the yellow clots for eyes. "Something is happening to me!" she screamed at him, sitting in his chair in the sunlight. . . . "I told you it was!" she screamed, voiding the words like hot silent bubbles into the bright silence about them until he turned his head and the two phlegm-clots above her where she lay tossing on the rough, sunny boards. "I told you! I told you all the time!" (1985b: 250)

Although two people are in that car, Faulkner's text accesses only the female body flying through the air. The prose represents her as gravitationally unhinged, her mind so shocked as to lose its connection with her own body. Relentlessly, she is being temporally and spatially discoordinated: unable to control her movement, unable to guess what comes next. In the second passage, she appears unable to think as well. The rape "abrupts" into Faulkner's prose as a "something" long dreaded, "all along," whose impact on her she can acknowledge only by sidestepping it, hurling it at Pap. Faulkner inserts Temple into a spatial/temporal frame so unrecognizable – so destructive of all that she has known – that her fragile coherence uncoheres. The text dilates on the pieces in disarray, the body out of mental/moral harness, the speech in confusion or halted altogether.

Throughout the novel, Temple is undergoing rape. Jerked, gripped, lifted, entered, she ceases to be an intentional ego moving in purposive time, unified under the name of Temple Drake. Rather than an organ for speaking, her mouth reduces to matter, opening and closing soundlessly, leaving a half-masticated piece of sandwich unswallowed on her tongue. Like Benjy wailing incoherently, like Rider unable to swallow the food or drink he stuffs into his mouth, Temple literally loses control of body and mind.

Unable to move from Popeye, Temple moves anyway – Faulkner records unforgettably the second-by-second moves one makes when one cannot move – but it avails her nothing. In these terrifying moments, Temple emerges as what can happen to her body – a poor bare forked animal, undone in a moment (a sequence of discontinuous moments) of trauma. Joe Christmas's "Something is going to happen to me" explodes here with unstoppable consequences. The novel is wholly undidactic.

Both modernist writers, it is clear, refuse realism's confidence in the capacity of individuals to bind present experience into meaning. But the unmastered Proustean present is available for replay, later. Time that has been lost can – thanks to fortuitous coincidences and painful labor devoted to developing the negatives contained in them – be regained. By contrast, Faulkner accesses his "sanctuary" only in the form of a promise suddenly broken, a coherence inexplicably shattered. His focal characters are all beginners for whom no life classes exist; what is asked of them at the beginning is not only difficult but annihilating.

I turn now, in more abbreviated manner, to three other modernist writers – Woolf, Hemingway, and Mann – before exploring a final pairing, Faulkner and Kafka.

Woolf's fictional world refuses the violence that so often brings Faulkner to his memorable effects. Her crises are quieter; their ways of calling into question patriarchal convention do not leap into view as Caddy's loss of virginity, or Bon's drop of black blood, throws into relief the gender and racial norms of Faulkner's patriarchal South. Woolf's modernist model was avowedly Proust (she never, to my knowledge, spoke of Faulkner). In Proust she seems to have found both a lyrical attention to impressions and a vivid sense of the comedy of subjectivity (its stubborn, shaping biases). Marcel's impressionistic meanderings along the Swann and Méséglise ways find their place in Woolf as Clarissa Dalloway's and Mrs. Ramsay's perception-filled journeys from home to city or village and back again. Likewise, the round of conflicting meanings attaching to Swann on his evening visit to Marcel's family in Combray (meanings that differ according to the grandfather in search of gossip, the great-aunts seeking obliquely to thank Swann for a gift, the mother wishing to console him for his sacrificial marriage in the service of his daughter, the child Marcel seeing in Swann the incarnate motive of his missed goodnight kiss): this simultaneity of subjective motives recurs, in Woolfian fashion, in the cluster of differential experiences of a handful of participants seated round the Ramsays' dinner table and partaking of *boeuf en daube*.

Perhaps it is crisis, though, that lets us most tellingly relate Woolf to Faulkner. "Quieter," I called the crises in her work, and one needs to press on the representation of Septimus (in *Mrs Dalloway* [1925]) to make it yield its quotient of social distress. Woolf "speaks" the fleeting and manic thoughts roiling inside Septimus's unhinged mind in ways quite unlike Quentin's stream-of-consciousness anguish. Yet both figures register as seismographs of their culture's ills. Septimus embodies England's class inequality, going to the Continent to fight a war for an England whose culture he mistakenly idealizes as Shakespearean. No less, he rubs up against its insistent gender polarity, in his doomed affection for a superior officer (Evans). He returns home shell-shocked, incapable of feeling, and is made to suffer the legitimized aggression of London doctors with their intrusive therapies. In Septimus's suicide Woolf limns the deforming force of institutionalized norms of sickness and health, class and gender — much of which one might miss in an inattentive reading. But there is no way of missing Quentin's malady, for Faulkner's novel obsessively plumbs Quentin's distress for 65 uninterrupted pages. Deploying narrative procedures that burrow deeper and deeper into Quentin's pathless mindscape, Faulkner harrows his reader, indeed risks his reader's abandoning the book. By contrast, Woolf interweaves Septimus's dysfunctional malaise with Clarissa's sensuous receptivity, aligning the doomed figure with a cluster of surviving ones — like them in essential ways, unlike them in fatal ways. One finishes both novels far from Victorian renewal or reform, but the Woolfian tone is accepting, in some ways even celebratory, whereas the Faulknerian tone is tragic. No reader, emerging from the whirlpool of Quentin's consciousness, can envisage Compson (not to speak of Southern) reality as anything but intolerably damaging. If Septimus is a problem society would do well to address, Quentin is a wrenching disaster Southern society cannot confront without recognizing its own indictment.

Hemingway and Faulkner: much ink has been spilled comparing these two towering American modernists, and I shall be brief. Each recognized the other, early on, as his main competitor for the top spot. Hemingway's reputation waxed in the 1920s and 1930s; Faulkner's waxed during the 20 years following World War II. By the early sixties both were dead, and the deconstructive decades that followed have chiseled away at the posture of hero-worshiping either of them. Rather than continue that line of inquiry, let us unpack Faulkner's own distinction between his work and Hemingway's. Faulkner claimed, notoriously, that Thomas Wolfe was the supreme novelist of their generation, because Wolfe sought to put "the whole history of the human heart on the head of the pin" (1964: 144). Wolfe failed at this, of course, but the failure was noble precisely because inevitable. It followed, then, that Faulkner's own striving for all-plumbing sentences and structures never before attempted in narrative fiction earned him second place, behind Wolfe. The point to note is not the strategic motives fueling this criterion which, dropping Wolfe out of the equation, puts Faulkner above Hemingway. Rather, one could wish the criterion *were* simply strategic, for Faulkner's fiction risks perdition (even as Wolfe's fell into perdition) by striving to realize such a program. Writing so as to put all of human history on the head of a pin produces not *Absalom, Absalom!*, but *A Fable* (1954) — the largest, most ungainly novel he ever wrote.

Whatever else one might say of *A Fable*, it is a book Hemingway could never have written. Hemingway's devotion to form as control of material invariably reveals its masculine underpinnings: a prose in which more is always meant than is said, in which pain is understated, though omnipresent, a prose drawn to stoic, wound-riddled figures like Jake Barnes, Frederic Henry, and — as a sort of epitome — the old man of the sea. To produce such stark effects Hemingway resembles Racine more than Shakespeare: less vocabulary rather than more, tighter conventions rather than looser ones. Poundian horror at confessional voice, Hulmean disgust at emotional display — these modernist imperatives find their fruition in Hemingway. Every dimension of the modernist aesthetic premised on less as more finds itself championed in Hemingway's universe, where the aim is, so to speak, to take away each support that can be taken away, while the human center yet stands. If one places next to these taciturn Hemingway males, stripped of illusion, reduced to minimal and stylized voice, Faulkner's Benjy and Quentin Compson, his Joe Christmas, one sees Faulkner moving in another direction. That direction is Wolfian interior expressiveness, freed from Wolfian flabbiness: a prose in which the pain of outrage attains something like pure articulation – shows itself to be at once personal and impersonal, the pain of an entire culture's misdoings, coming to rest upon individual shoulders, as in Benjy's wailing: "It might have been all time and injustice and sorrow become vocal for an instant by a conjunction of planets" (Faulkner 1994: 179).

Mann is perhaps the major modernist prose writer most temperamentally and procedurally different from Faulkner. Mann moves unerringly into portentous fictional forms. His *Buddenbrooks*, *The Magic Mountain*, and *Dr Faustus*, each in its own way, seem to gather and distill previous cultural paradigms of the widest import. *Buddenbrooks* (1900) takes the nineteenth-century, three-generational family novel into a Freudian thicket of opaque motives that spells the end of extroverted, naturalist narrative. *The Magic Mountain* (1925) rehearses, in virtually symphonic fashion, the range of Western voices and concerns – focused through Settembrini (Enlightenment reason) and Naptha (nineteenth-century irrationalism) – that confront the thinking mind in the wake of World War I. *Dr Faustus* (1949) redeploys the Faust legend to explore the powers of darkness summoned creatively in Nietzsche, unleashed demonically by Hitler. Mann is so richly endowed, as a man of European letters, that he can convert into modes of fictional inquiry the crises besetting the twentieth-century West. Put otherwise, Mann is capable of pondering, more directly than any of his peers, the meanings of Western culture, given the cataclysmic violence of 1914–18 and 1939–45.

As a legatee of the Civil War, a would-be pilot in the Great War, and a concerned patriot during World War II, Faulkner would have dearly liked to emulate Mann's role as the voice of the West in distress. Luckily, his own gifts, as well as the modernist examples that spoke most to him, pointed elsewhere, inward. Trauma rather than speech-making, the imploded local family rather than the menaced West, the treatment of race in a post-slavery South: these are the concerns that fuel his supreme fictions from *The Sound and the Fury* through *Go Down, Moses* (1942). Only his failed *Mosquitoes* (1927) contains the talkiness – the speech-making, the topical – that distinguishes Mann's great work: until, that is, *A Fable*, which seeks, at its peril, the biggest take imaginable on the future of the West. At its peril, I claim, because the brilliance of *A Fable* remains strangely parochial, lodged in its Southern-soaked vignettes so ill-suited to epic deployment. Is it too much to say that Faulkner is regional in his very bones, and that he reaches the universal (justly celebrated by Malraux and Sartre) by leaping directly from the South to the world, bypassing, so to speak, the West that is in between?

Although no one would call Kafka "regional," his work is as undesigned as Faulkner's for the delivery of universal statements about the modern world. At the opposite extreme from Mann, Kafka mines an inner territory suggestively akin to Faulkner's:

collapse of the nuclear family, fixation on arrested, "abrupted" individuals. He is drawn, as though magnetically, to man-as-accused. Here is Joseph K. being called:

> But it was no congregation the priest was addressing, the words were unambiguous and inescapable, he was calling out: "Joseph K.!" K. paused and stared at the ground before him. For the moment he was still free, he could continue on his way and vanish . . . It would simply indicate that he had not understood the call, or that he had understood it and did not care. But if he were to turn round he would be caught, for that would amount to an admission that he had understood it very well, that he was really the person addressed, and that he was ready to obey. (1968: 209)

For K. to answer this call – to say "here I am" – is to assent to his own annihilation.[3] He has been called by a power to which no institutional name can be attached, called to self-immolation. Although this deeper call might understandably replace the corrupt and surface one of the Bank, the meaning of its depth remains inscrutable. The cited passage is saturated in the language of understanding, of distinguishing between surfaces and depths, calls and codes. Deep down, though, K. remains (like the call made upon him) uninterpretable. So far as we can tell, the Yes of his assent seems to be, however final, unknowing.

As critics have noted, K.'s words and gestures are, from the beginning, irreducible to a single set of intentions:

> "I'd better get Frau Grubach –" said K., as if wrenching himself away from the two men (though they were standing at quite a distance from him) and making as if to go out. (1968: 3)

> K. was surprised, at least he was surprised considering the warders' point of view, that they had sent him to his room and left him alone there, where he had abundant opportunities to take his life. Though at the same time he also asked himself, looking at it from his own point of view, what possible ground he could have to do so. (1968: 9)

> "It must be a black coat," they said. Thereupon K. flung the coat on the floor and said – he did not himself know in what sense he meant the words – "But this isn't the capital charge yet." (1968: 9)

As if: the Kafka text recurrently cites K.'s gestures toward "another scene" of significance, even as he remains scrupulously blank as to their portent. These gestures are never clarified. As if to go out – but not really: half of Kafka's critics fall into the trap (identified by Walter Benjamin [1968]) of filling in the "really", and saying why. But we cannot know why, even as we cannot ignore the telltale gesture inviting us to figure out why. In like manner, one could unify that second passage by arguing that K. is (atypically) imagining the case against him held by others though not by himself. Yes, possibly, but the sequence seems to intimate something more, by its way of opening with "K. was surprised" and then going (in a sort of bad-faith explanatory way) to a mitigating, later-supplied logic of others' point of view. He *does* think his own suicide, exactly as he wonders why he should think his suicide. The third passage is perhaps the most confusing, for it puts us in the presence of a verbal event inconceivable in realism: a strong claim, followed by denial of responsibility for it. No literature of project can afford this scandal of a claim simultaneously asserted and emptied. The scandal is less at the level of logic than at that of subject-coherence: how can we engage a figure who claims but does not know why he claims? The assertion remains, but *who* is it coming from?

Sequence in Kafka enacts a temporality foreign to project-resolution. The consequences that arrive have nothing to do with the "I" of "I can." Figures of lack, each of his protagonists is brought upon the scene to reveal, in endlessly differing ways, what cannot be done. If realism invokes arrest so as to deepen the stakes of release and arrival, Kafkan modernism invokes the fantasy of arrival in order to deepen the stakes of arrest. We realize, at a certain point of our reading, that we're not going to get anywhere; or, that where we are is *where we are.* The point of Kafka's arrests seems not to be their resolution; nothing in his world gets better in time. Rather than plot, then, in which a subject encounters obstacles and comes to terms with them – a sequence that treats time as a medium for the becoming of selfhood – Kafkan narrative produces something else. Rather than develop, it repeats (but not in the realist form that allows recognition the second time around). Rather than deliver an arrival in time, it delivers doublings in space. Let us call this an obscurely diagnostic fiction about *trouble.* Let us say that its project is to deliver the drama of being un-can-ed.

Hardly Faulknerian, these parabolic scenes of arrest and undoing, yet perhaps – on further scrutiny – not so far from Faulkner after all. The ordeal of being "un-can-ed" is, after all, central to his fiction. As with Kafka, a focus on interiority does not deny the presence of outer forces (mis)shaping the drama of the subject. It took Adorno to show how Kafka's representational contortions enact – rather than ignore – unmastered social pressures deforming the urban subject.[4] In like manner, the Faulkner text is compelling insofar as it articulates the modernist pathos of radiating damage rather than the realist ethos of gathered resolution. It has little interest in the canniness of "I can."[5] Quentin's last words in *Absalom, Absalom!* conclude the book only by *not* resolving its plot, and this because Quentin – like his author – is inescapably in and out of a scene he must but cannot master and hence judge. For the act of judgment, at its core, assuages an anxiety of our being in time itself, an anxiety about knowing what others in the world outside us mean: finally, now, once and for all. By contrast, Faulknerian style stages the hemorrhaging of pre-judgment in the unanticipated and uncontrollable moment: it stages unknowing as an assault upon the known. Faulkner's modernist style – his restless syntax and discontinuous sequences – registers time's disorienting power, not time mastered into non-contradictory significance and offered up for judgment. Faulkner's style lets him – and his fiction – not know and not judge, lets the fiction set up, by way of gathering juxtapositions and differed/deferred information, emergent patterns of dysfunction whose repercussions and permutations he sees – and lets us see – but does not pretend to see beyond. Such seeing achieves something perhaps finer than the judgment based on knowledge: it turns into structural resource the blindness inherent in *all* present moments of seeing. Faulkner's greatest fiction articulates the caughtness of human judgment in time itself – rather than the fantasy of outwitting time that fuels judgment in its dismissive phase.

Becoming not-Faulkner, I suggested near the beginning of this chapter, is an enabling capacity for absenting oneself from the scene of narration – something that Conrad's practice may have taught the burgeoning younger writer. I conclude by seeing the emptying out of personal identity as, at the same time, the pathos of Faulknerian character – a pathos embodied in his most resonant figure, Quentin Compson. Although the Quentin of *Absalom* has been granted syntactic coherence, he nevertheless emerges in that later novel – in a more intricate way – as, yet again, a figure of stalemate. Pondering, in the mid-1930s, the wrecked Quentin of *The Sound and the Fury*, Faulkner seems to have grasped that his very depletedness, on the plot-model of realism, would permit a different kind of serviceability. Quentin is 100 percent dead, plot-extinguished: what role can he play *now*?

Of the many ghosts resurrected in *Absalom*, the most resonant is Quentin himself. Resurrected, not transformed: this is the same Quentin – still headed for his suicide, unresolved, plotless – but now available (suggestively like K.) for the modernist task of diagnostic insight. Quentin's own story over – no longer an I – Faulkner makes him serve as an endlessly passive and available (read: open to assault and accusation) me: "not a being, an entity, he was a commonwealth" (1990a: 9). Executed like Joseph K. (but before the narrative even begins), Quentin is/is not Rosa's nephew, Sutpen's offspring, Bon and Henry's spectral third brother, Judith's doomed fraternal lover. Being a mere Compson (sufficient to drive him to suicide in the earlier novel) is not confusing enough, in this most identificatory of Faulkner's novels. The opening pages' rhetoric inaugurates the uncontrollable con-fusing of poor Quentin's I/here/now into a miasmal mass, immeasurable and contaminating, made up of him and Rosa and the Sutpens, of here (Jefferson) and the Caribbean and New Orleans, of now (1909) and 1865 and 1860 and 1833. Quentin descends into his inescapable cultural history ("I am older at twenty than a lot of people who have died" [1990a: 301]) and his foreclosed cultural future. If, as Will Varner puts it in *The Hamlet* (1940), "breathing is a sight-draft dated yesterday" (1990b: 1019), Quentin's was first cashed in *The Sound and the Fury*, and is being cashed again in *Absalom, Absalom!* Othered on such a scale, he thus reveals that the "maelstrom of unbearable reality" (1990a: 124) bears, not on the doings of one Quentin Compson, but on the crucifixion, at once deserved and undeserved, of the American South. The only individual appropriate for this task is one already terminally othered. The only text that can articulate this crucifixion in all its post-individual, post-realist pathos and complexity is a modernist one.

NOTES

1   Two landmark studies of Faulkner and modernism are John Irwin (1975) and John T. Matthews (1982). For later commentary, see Richard C. Moreland (1990) and André

Bleikasten (1990). Both my *Faulkner's Subject* (1992) and my *Cambridge Companion to William Faulkner* (1995) focus recurrently on Faulkner's insertion into a modernist schema of assumptions and procedures. See also Daniel J. Singal (1997).

2   As my study of modernism (2005) centers on Proust, Kafka, and Faulkner, my commentary here on Proust, and later on Kafka, draws on arguments worked out more extensively in that study.

3   The dynamic of Kafkan interpellation echoes – by way of the absurd – the well-known Althusserian argument for "interpellation" as the identity-bestowing activity of ideological state apparatuses. Within Althusser's model, attainment of individual subjectivity just is the process of heeding voluntarily an ideological call to participate in a combination of beliefs, rituals, and practices. It is the empowering entry into group-bestowed, group-shared iden-tity. In Kafka, by contrast, K.'s heeding the priest's call is tantamount to the erasure of his institutional identity, prior to the erasure of his life itself.

4   See Adorno's brilliant 1967 essay on Kafka in *Prisms* (1983).

5   To put this more accurately, there is, in Faulkner's earlier masterpieces centered on outrage, little interest in canniness. But the Snopes trilogy (conceived in the 1920s but written only from the late 1930s forward) revolves around the machinations of a figure of supreme canniness, Flem Snopes. I think it is fair to say that, for Faulkner the modernist, canniness is a secondary stance (though never negligible: see Jason in *The Sound and the Fury* and Cash in *As I Lay Dying*).

REFERENCES AND FURTHER READING

Adorno, T. W. (1983). Notes on Kafka. In *Prisms* (trans. S. Weber and S. Weber) (pp. 243–71). Cambridge, MA: MIT Press. (Original pub. 1967.)

Benjamin, W. (1968). *Illuminations* (ed. H. Arendt, trans. H. Zohn). New York: Harcourt, Brace, and World.

Bleikasten, A. (1990). *The Ink of Melancholy*. Bloomington: University of Indiana Press.

Conrad, J. (1988). *Heart of Darkness* (ed. R. Kimbrough). 3rd edn. New York: Norton.

Faulkner, W. (1964). *Faulkner in the University* (eds. F. L. Gwynn and J. L. Blotner). New York: Vintage.

Faulkner, W. (1985a). *Light in August*. In *William Faulkner: Novels, 1930–1935*. New York: Library of America. (Original pub. 1932.)

Faulkner, W. (1985b). *Sanctuary*. In *William Faulkner: Novels, 1930–1935*. New York: Library of America. (Original pub. 1931.)

Faulkner, W. (1990a). *Absalom, Absalom!* In *William Faulkner: Novels, 1936–1940*. New York: Library of America. (Original pub. 1936.)

Faulkner, W. (1990b). *The Hamlet*. In *William Faulkner: Novels, 1936–1940*. New York: Library of America. (Original pub. 1940.)

Faulkner, W. (1994). *The Sound and the Fury* (ed. David Minter). 2nd edn. New York: Norton. (Original pub. 1929.)

Irwin, J. (1975). *Doubling and Incest/Repetition and Revenge*. Baltimore: Johns Hopkins University Press.

James, H. (1964). The New Novel. In M. Shapira (ed.). *Selected Literary Criticism: Henry James* (pp. 311–42). New York: McGraw-Hill.

Kafka, F. (1968). *The Trial* (trans. W. Muir and E. Muir). New York: Schocken. (Original pub. 1937.)

Matthews, J. T. (1982). *The Play of Faulkner's Language*. Ithaca, NY: Cornell University Press.

Moreland, R. C. (1990). *Faulkner and Modernism: Rereading and Rewriting*. Madison: University of Wisconsin Press.

Moretti, F. (1996). *The Modern Epic: The World-System from Goethe to García Márquez*. New York: Verso.

Nietzsche, F. (1954). *Twilight of the Idols*. In W. Kaufmann (ed. and trans.). *The Portable Nietzsche* (pp. 463–563). New York: Viking.

Proust, M. (1981). *Remembrance of Things Past* (trans. C. K. Scott Moncrieff and T. Kilmartin). 3 vols. New York: Random House. (Original pub. 1913–30.)

Rilke, R. M. (1949). *The Notebooks of Malte Laurids Brigge* (trans. M. D. H. Norton). New York: Norton. (Original pub. 1910.)

Sartre, J.-P. (1994). On *The Sound and the Fury.* In
  D. Minter (ed.). *William Faulkner,* The Sound
  and the Fury*: An Authoritative Text* (pp. 265–72).
  2nd edn. New York: Norton.

Singal, D. J. (1997). *William Faulkner: The Making
  of a Modernist.* Chapel Hill, NC: University of
  North Carolina Press.

Weinstein, P. M. (1992). *Faulkner's Subject: A Cosmos
  No One Owns.* New York: Cambridge University
  Press.

Weinstein, P. M. (ed.) (1995). *Cambridge Companion
  to William Faulkner.* New York: Cambridge University Press.

Weinstein, P. M. (2005). *Unknowing: The Work of
  Modernist Fiction.* Ithaca, NY: Cornell University
  Press.

21

Faulkner's Versions of Pastoral, Gothic, and the Sublime

Susan V. Donaldson

Even though William Faulkner experimented with a bewildering variety of modes and genres ranging from detective fiction to cubist narrative throughout his long career, he generally resorted to the vocabulary of the romantic sublime when he talked about the ideals that shaped his ideas of art and his role as an artist. From the earliest days of his career, art for him evoked a struggle for vision so ambitious in its reach that it was ultimately defined by its unattainability and failure, its sublimity, as it were; and it was in terms of the grandeur of that failure that he measured the worth of his own writing when he pronounced *The Sound and the Fury* (1929) "the most splendid failure" – and the accomplishments of his fellow writers. Thomas Wolfe, he remarked in one interview after another, was the writer he admired the most precisely because his writing aimed the highest and failed the most spectacularly.

When Faulkner's first reviewers and critics talked about his work, though, it was more often than not in terms of its modern gothicism, drawing on a long tradition of encounters with otherness and terror, or its pastoralism, situating the agrarian South in opposition to urban modernity. Many of his earliest reviewers, like Henry Seidel Canby and Henry Nash Smith, were inclined to regard Faulkner as the founder of "The School of Cruelty" and Southern gothicism, defined by its penchant, in Smith's words, for "hatred, passion and frustration" (quoted in Inge 1995: 58, 49). Those who championed his writing early on, alternatively, like George Marion O'Donnell, tended to see Faulkner as a prominent ally in the Southern Agrarian campaign against industrialism and urbanism, the opening volley of which was provided by the 1930 publication *I'll Take My Stand: The South and the Agrarian Tradition*.

Since he first began receiving public notice for his fiction, in fact, Faulkner has often been hailed and condemned as the founding father, oddly enough, of both Southern pastoralism and Southern gothicism in modern literature. It is another matter altogether, though, to explain with any clarity just what it means to have originated those two central modes, not just because of furious debates and disagreements over what pastoralism and gothicism constitute in his oeuvre but because of his own unending reinventions and interrogations of those modes, from *The Marble Faun* (1924) to *The Mansion* (1959), the final volume in the Snopes trilogy (1959). Two of his most eminent commentators, Cleanth Brooks and Lewis P. Simpson, sharply disagreed on just how to characterize Faulkner's relation to the Western tradition of pastoral. In his landmark 1963 study *William Faulkner: The Yoknapatawpha Country*, Brooks implicitly defined the fiction of Yoknapatawpha as pastoral in form and content, critical of urbanism and commercialism in the twentieth century and rooted in "the standpoint of a provincial and traditional culture" (1963: 2). Simpson (1975) in contrast declared that Faulkner's work was strongly antipastoral – resistant to the notion of retreating to a green world safe from the exigencies and pressures of historical change. More recently Faulknerians like Eric Sundquist (1984) and gothic specialists like David Jarraway (1998) have applauded Faulkner's use of the gothic – a term largely derogatory in its application to Faulkner's fiction in the 1930s and 1940s – to evoke something of the complexity of Southern and American history and representations of race in particular.

Faulkner for his part began his career as a pastoral poet immersed in the imagery and language of nineteenth-century Romantic, symbolist, and Decadent poetry, but over the years his evocations of pastoral green worlds and retreats underwent interrogation and transmutations into something like their "dark twin," his own term from his second novel *Mosquitoes* (1927) – that is, into gothic quests for truth and identity amid ambiguous shadows, ruins, and social and familial upheaval. So too did his evocations of the sublime and the unrepresentable, which would continue to define the far limits of his powers of imagination and invention throughout his career but which began to shift, with the writing of *Sanctuary* (1931) and in particular *Light in August* (1932), from an early obsessive preoccupation with gender, femininity, and eros to race and boundaries between whiteness and blackness. Nowhere would those shifts from pastoral to gothic and from the erotic sublime to something like a racial sublime be more pronounced or more startling than in his seventh novel, *Light in August*, a work that has often frustrated the best efforts of Faulkner's readers and critics and that has been pronounced at various times both pastoral comedy and gothic nightmare.

Faulkner himself seems to have been intensely aware very early on in his career of critical assessments of his work as both pastoral and gothic, and he even brings fairly explicit attention to that dual characterization of his public persona, as both pastoralist and gothicist, in drafts of a highly revealing introductory essay he wrote – roughly in the same period he was writing *Light in August* – for a 1933 edition of *The Sound and the Fury* that never came about. James Meriwether speculates in a headnote prefacing one of the drafts of that essay that it was written sometime between October 1932 and the fall of 1934 – not too long after Faulkner had made a widely heralded appearance at a 1931 Southern Writers Festival in Charlottesville, Virginia, where he attracted considerable attention as the author of *The Sound and the Fury*, *As I Lay Dying* (1930), and *Sanctuary* – and as a drinker of formidable capacity. Attendance at that conference, in fact, might well have spurred Faulkner's thinking for that essay, for Southern Agrarian Allen Tate and his wife Caroline Gordon were prominent attendees as well, vocal proponents of a self-conscious Southern literary regionalism rooted in agrarianism. In later remarks on the festival, both Tate and Gordon assumed that the author of *The Sound and the Fury* was in complete agreement with their notions of Southern traditionalism and pastoral critiques of Northern urbanism and industrialism, but in the aborted introductory essay for *The Sound and the Fury* Faulkner sounded like anything but a Southern Agrarian ally – although the draft did bear interesting parallels here and there to Tate's own highly ambivalent and emotionally charged relationship with Southern literary traditions. In the opening of one of the essay's drafts, Faulkner flatly declared, "Art is no part of southern life," and then went on to speculate that if art was to achieve visibility in the region, it had to "become a ceremony, a spectacle: something between a gypsy encampment and a church bazaar given by a handful of alien mummers who must waste themselves in protest and active self-defense" (quoted in Meriwether 1973: 411). In that endeavor, he added, only two options seemed to be open to the Southern writer:

> We seem to try in the simply furious breathing (or writing) span of the individual to draw a savage indictment of the contemporary scene or to escape from it into a make-believe region of swords and magnolias and mockingbirds which perhaps never existed anywhere. Both of the courses are rooted in sentiment; perhaps the ones who write savagely and bitterly of the incest in clayfloored cabins are the most sentimental.

He himself, Faulkner observed, had tried both: "I have tried to escape and I have tried to indict. After five years I look back at *The Sound and the Fury* and see that that was the turning point: in this book I did both at one time" (quoted in Meriwether 1973: 412).

In many respects Faulkner was writing as much about the novel that was preoccupying him in this period – *Light in August* – as he was about *The Sound and the Fury*. Perhaps even more explicitly than *The Sound and the Fury*, *Light in August* weighs and considers both escape and indictment, pastoral retreats and gothic journeys, as it also ponders the dangers and attractions of obsessive, transporting visions of an all-but-unrepresentable past. Written and revised over the second part of 1931 and completed in February 1932, *Light in August* underwent significant shifts and changes, as Regina K. Fadiman notes in her 1975 study of the novel's revisions. Faulkner himself commented on those revisions in language suggesting a growing self-consciousness about the tools of his trade and his own reading during the time when he attended the 1931 Southern writers' festival. He wrote his seventh novel, he said in yet another version of the aborted *Sound and the Fury* introduction, without that sense of ecstasy marking the composition of the earlier novel – and with something of that sense of constraint he evoked to describe the two options of escape and indictment available to the Southern writer:

> I was deliberately choosing among possibilities and probabilities of behavior and weighing and measuring each choice by the scale of the Jameses and Conrads and Balzacs. I knew that I had read too much, that I had reached that stage which all young writers must pass through, in which he believes that he has learned too much about his trade. (quoted in Meriwether 1972: 709)

In a novel often described as the work inaugurating the writer's evolving social critique of his region and culture, Faulkner was looking inward as much as outward – at those two options of pastoralism and gothicism he saw restraining the reach and vision of Southern writers, just as he also contemplated the shape and reach of those unattainable visions that provided the motivation for so much of his art.

That *Light in August* did indeed prompt unusual "weighing and measuring" of such central features of his art can be discerned in the novel's complicated history of writing and revision. Faulkner himself tended to remember the novel as beginning with an image strongly pastoral in import. In one of the drafts for the abortive introductory essay, Faulkner claimed that he began *Light in August* "knowing no more about it than a young woman, pregnant walking along a strange country road" (quoted in Meriwether 1972: 709). When he spoke about the novel in interviews, he often referred to the title, with its evocation of a special kind of light in late summer first commented upon casually by his wife in conversation. Tellingly enough, though, both his biographer Joseph Blotner and Regina K. Fadiman insist that the novel actually began with three pages focusing on the minister Gail Hightower sitting in his study at twilight and awaiting his recurring vision of galloping horses and cavalrymen amid a chaos of shooting and shouting (Fadiman 1975: 31). Hightower and his obsessive, half-articulated visions, in fact, dominated the early stages of the manuscript, which was initially titled "Dark House," and it was only later that Lena Grove's sunnier presence emerged in passages commentators have almost invariably described as pastoral and comic. In the late stages of the manuscript's composition, Fadiman argues, the history of the elusive, racially ambiguous drifter Joe Christmas makes its appearance and draws the narrative back into a shadowy and gothic past and farther away from the pastoral present associated with Lena Grove. By the novel's end, with the lynching of Joe Christmas and the birth of Lena's baby, Hightower has resurfaced, and his obsessive, unintelligible visions of his grandfather's Civil War feats have transmuted into a new, half-formed glimpse of two merging, symbiotic faces, that of the dead Joe Christmas and his lyncher Percy Grimm. What emerges from these pronounced narrative shifts – from Hightower's visions to Lena Grove's pastoral presence to Joe Christmas's quest for identity amid shadows and settings nothing if not gothic – is something very like a weighing and measuring of elusive and seemingly unattainable visions amid stories alternately pastoral and gothic in mood and intensity. It is no wonder, then, that a host of critics have commented on the novel's difficulty and the fragmented character of its narrative, juxtaposing multiple stories, multiple endings, and ultimately multiple interpretations, ranging from the comic to the tragic.

Indeed, the novel itself appears to comment upon its own difficulty and on the elusiveness of its vision in the last chapter on Gail Hightower, who contemplates both the events of violence that have unfolded before him, culminating in Joe Christmas's death, and the elusiveness, mutability, and ultimate futility of his visions. Initially evoking half-formed notions of chivalric glamour and martial glory, his visions finally emerge as composite pictures of the wife and the townspeople he has failed as husband and as minister, of Christmas and Grimm, both separate and bound to one another, and finally once again of "the wild bugles and the clashing sabres and the dying thunder of hooves" (1990b: 493). Hightower's own story ends with that final vision – still chaotic and unformed, still out of reach and unarticulated – as Hightower himself fears that he is dying. More than any other image in Faulkner's work, those last passages of Hightower's elusive and finally unattainable visions underscore the vast ambition of Faulkner's art – its straining toward transcendence and transport – and his acute awareness of its ultimate elusiveness and potential self-destructiveness.

Locked in his visions, as evoked by his very name, Hightower suggests both the lure of beckoning transcendent visions and the ultimate impossibility of attaining them, and in this respect the very imagery and language hearken back to a story probably written in 1925, as speculated by Cleanth Brooks, but published in 1931: "Carcassonne," a slight tale that nevertheless articulates the ambitious reach of the aspiring artist's emerging vision of art. It is a story often described as crucial in Faulkner's development as an artist self-conscious about the materials and aims of his art, and, accordingly, it serves as a touchstone of sorts for deciphering those brief moments of vision and transport marking a good deal of Faulkner's art. In that brief, formless, but highly revealing tale, a nameless, would-be poet reduced to a garret owned by the Standard Oil Company in an unidentified, vaguely Central American city welcomes his seclusion to ponder artistic ambitions so vast that they defy articulation. Sequestered in a dialogue of sorts with his own skeleton, after the fashion of A. E. Housman's "The Immortal Part" (Brooks 1978: 61), the would-be poet finds solace in half-formed visions of transport and transcendence:

> *I want to perform something bold and tragical and austere* he repeated, shaping the soundless words in the pattering silence *me on a buckskin pony with eyes like blue electricity and a mane like tangled fire, galloping up the hill and right off into the high heaven of the world* Still galloping, the horse soars outward; still galloping, it thunders up the long blue hill of heaven, its tossing mane in golden swirls like fire. Steed and rider thunder on, thunder punily diminishing: a dying star upon the immensity of darkness and of silence with which, steadfast, fading, deepbreasted and grave of flank, muses the dark and tragic figure of the Earth, his mother. (*Collected Stories* 1950: 899–900)

The vision itself, though, never materializes, and the story ends with these words of both ambition and unfulfilled yearning, simultaneously underscoring the reach of the nameless poet's imagination and the sense of paralysis and futility created by that straining of his imagination.

What is most noteworthy about this ebbing moment of transport, half-achieved and half-failed, is the striking use it makes of the language and central concerns of the sublime as articulated by a long line of commentators. Originating with a classical, first-century text, *On the Sublime* (*Peri hupsous*), by the Roman writer Longinus, who counseled the attractions of transport in writing, the sublime was expounded upon by a host of eighteenth-century writers seeking an alternative to mimetic art and finding possibilities in representations of supernatural beings evoking, in Joseph Addison's words, "a pleasing kind of Horrour in the Mind of the Reader" (quoted in Clery 2002: 27). The possibilities of the sublime were to be explored most fully by Edmund Burke in his 1757 tract *A Philosophical Enquiry into the Origin of Our Ideas of the Sublime and Beautiful*, which championed strong emotions of transport, partaking of delight and fear, as an antidote to the familiar and the everyday.

Primary among the attractions of that sublime moment, as later commentators have argued, were both its elusiveness and its utter strangeness or otherness. From the perspective of Thomas Weiskel in *The Romantic Sublime*, that momentary sense of transport could be measured by the sheer impossibility of representing or articulating it, in a word, by its unattainability. The intensity of the moment and its vaunted transcendence, Weiskel argues, underscored the bare limits of the human imagination, and faced with those limitations, he concludes, "We are 'admonished' and placed in an attitude of respect as we feel our incapacity of attaining that 'other world'" (1976: 44). More recently feminist and postmodern theorists have brought attention to the sublime as a fleeting encounter with otherness, "a radical alterity," Barbara Claire Freeman suggests in *The Feminine Sublime*, "that remains unassimilable to representation. A confrontation of this sort, she adds, "marks the very limits of the representable, for it entails the question of symbolizing an event that we cannot represent not only because it was never fully present, but because it presents the subject with an unrecuperable excess of excess" (1995: 11). The sublime in her argument, accordingly, foregrounds certain key issues – "the construction and destruction of borders (be they aesthetic, political, or psychic), the permutations of identity formation and deformation, and the question of how such limits may or may not be represented" (p. 6).

In this respect, Freeman sounds a good deal like postmodernist theorist Jean-François Lyotard, who considers himself a long-term student of Immanuel Kant's Analytic of the Sublime in *Critique of Judgement* and thus defines the sublime in terms of the imagination's far limits. In the presence of something immense or excessive, Lyotard suggests in a highly influential essay, "The Sublime and the Avant-Garde," the imagination "fails to provide a representation corresponding to this Idea." The result, he says, is the surfacing of "a pain, a kind of cleavage within the subject between what can be conceived and what can be imagined or presented." He adds, though, that such pain

> in turn engenders a pleasure, in fact, a double pleasure: the impotence of the imagination attests *a contrario* to an imagination striving to figure even that which cannot be figured, and that imagination thus aims to harmonize its object with that of reason – and that furthermore the inadequacy of the images is a negative sign of the immense power of ideas. (1991: 98)

That pain and pleasure posed by Lyotard evokes to an eerie degree the anguished ecstasy marking the visions of that nameless artist in "Carcassonne," but it also suggests something of apprentice Faulkner's earliest engagement with alterity and the unrepresentable through the motif of nympholepsy, portraying the clumsy pursuit of an elusive nymph by a mortal male, that Faulkner had inherited from his intensive reading in

Romantic poetry, particularly that of Keats and the early Yeats, and in early modernist texts, most notably Conrad Aiken's poetry and James Branch Cabell's 1919 novel *Jurgen*. Cleanth Brooks aptly referred to this motif as Faulkner's version of the erotic sublime, and a good deal of his early prose and poetry, especially in the gift books he wrote for the women he courted, from Helen Baird to his future wife Estelle Oldham Franklin, are shaped by fruitless quests for unattainable, alluring women who defy every possible attempt at mere representation (Brooks 1978: 45). Providing a striking companion piece to "Carcassonne" and its misty visions of transport is a very early story, "Nympholepsy," probably written in 1925, which portrays a weary farmhand heading home who feels a sudden surge of fear and disorientation as he falls into a stream and then briefly encounters "death like a woman shining and drowned and waiting" (*Uncollected Stories* 1981: 335). The farmhand gives chase to the nymph-like figure, who disappears into the twilight and leaves him mourning her absence in bewildered pain.

Something of that motif – the unattainable woman defying the best efforts of her pursuer to capture her even within the tenuous bonds of representation – would appear again and again in Faulkner's apprentice work: in *Mayday* (1926), for example, the gift book he dedicated to Helen Baird that follows the ultimately fruitless quest of a knight for an unattainable lady, a quest that ends with the knight's choice of death over acceptance of his failures and loss. Hints of the erotic sublime – a fleeing femme fatale forever out of reach – can be detected in works as early as his 1920 symbolist play *The Marionettes*, which features the clownish alter ego of Pierrot, inert and impotent, defeated by his best efforts to capture his ideal of woman who appears to him in many forms from demonic temptress to virgin (see in general Sensibar 1984). Ultimately, though, Faulkner would explore the erotic sublime most fully in *The Sound and the Fury*, in which each of the three Compson brothers, as well as the third person narrator in the last section, strains to catch sight of and capture their ever-absent sister Caddy, whose character eludes the narrative nets cast by each of the novel's four sections.

From *The Marionettes* to *The Sound and the Fury*, in fact, the motif of nympholepsy largely shapes Faulkner's evocations of the sublime, as Faulkner himself sought to define a role for himself as artist that could also serve to draw and reinforce the lines between femininity and masculinity in an era of increasingly fluid boundaries between gender roles and identities. In pursuit of his own elusive ideal, he turned to the guidance of past poets, to the Romantic poetry of the past that was often couched in the vocabulary of pastoral, of green gardens of simplicity and containment populated with nymphs and fauns and presided over by Pan – part of the legacy that he had inherited as an avid reader of Keats, A. E. Housman, early Yeats, Oscar Wilde, Baudelaire, Verlaine, Mallarmé, and James Branch Cabell, whose own medieval fantasies of fanciful quests and eventual disillusionment left their mark on the whole of Faulkner's career. Indeed, Faulkner's earliest publications – "L'Apres-Midi d'un Faune," appearing in the *New Republic* in 1919, and his first book, *The Marble Faun* – bore explicit witness to his nearly obsessive engagement with pastoral, with its wistful evocations of green retreats from a complex and bewildering present and its melancholy mood of longing for a Golden Age of innocence.

Pastoral itself has often been linked with loss and absence – of earlier, simpler times and of innocence – by a host of commentators from Erwin Panofsky (1982) to Raymond Williams (1973). "This idea that the world has been a better place and that men have degenerated is remarkably widespread, and a regular feature of pastoral poetry," Frank Kermode observes in *English Pastoral Poetry* (1984: 14). He notes as well that pastoral usually appears as a predominant literary mode at a particular historical moment, when cities are emerging and consciousness of the contrast presented by those cities to rural life is still pronounced (1984: 15). Renato Poggioli in turn identifies the origins of pastoral in the configuration of desire: "The psychological root of the pastoral is a double longing after innocence and happiness, to be recovered not through conversion or regeneration, but merely through a retreat" (1975: 147).

That Faulkner himself returned to pastoral again and again in his apprentice years says a good deal about his attraction to moments of stasis and containment and his affinity for its mood of loss and yearning. This was, after all, an aspiring poet whose sad, questing knight Sir Galwyn in the gift book *Mayday* is told that life is but "a ceaseless fretting to gain shadows to which there is no substance" (1980: 71). But that insistent engagement with the vocabulary of pastoral – with fauns and nymphs of a lost past intruding even into his early fiction, like *Soldiers' Pay* (1926) and *Mosquitoes* – also reveals something very like incarceration within that mode and mood – a sense of confinement to which many of those early works bring attention. Faulkner's first published book, *The Marble Faun*, is replete with references to incarceration and impotence, as the marble statue ponders his stillness and muteness in the midst of passing years in an ever-changing garden. So too do so many of the early artist figures in Faulkner's work, from the inert and impotent Pierrot in *The Marionettes*, to Horace Benbow and Quentin Compson in *Flags in the Dust* (1973; published as *Sartoris*, 1929), *Sanctuary*, and *The Sound and the Fury*, ponder their sense of imprisonment within the figurative gardens of their own lofty dreams and even loftier language. Horace meditates obsessively upon the glass vases he blows and refers to alternately with his sister's name and with the language of pastoral lifted from Keats's "Ode to a Grecian Urn," and Quentin in turn retreats to his fragmented memories of lost childhood and faint images of his sister Caddy forever slipping out of sight. For these later versions of marble fauns, elusive nymphs evoking something of the erotic sublime remain forever out of reach, and pastoral itself suggests nothing so much as an illusionary escape into a past all too ready to lend itself to the stillness and slow time praised by one of Faulkner's favorite poems, Keats's "Ode to a Grecian Urn." If pastoral sometimes by Faulkner's lights appeared to offer too easy and sequestered a retreat from the passage of time and from history, as he pointedly suggests in his draft introductions to *The Sound and the Fury*, it also seemed to offer scant protection at best against the forces of change and even at times to hint of hidden histories and nightmares repressed in the interest of maintaining the smooth facade of green retreats.

In both *The Sound and the Fury* and *Sanctuary* pastoral often threatens to turn into its opposite, an exposed arena of conflict and fluid identities ravaged by time and change and more often than not finding its aptest emblem in houses haunted by their own histories – the shabby hulk of the Compson manor, nearly empty of furniture but echoing with past and present misery, and the ruin of the Old Frenchman place in *Sanctuary*, now populated by petty criminals and bootleggers. The far limits of the unrepresentable, in turn, become both unsettling and frightening as the erotic sublime in *Sanctuary* blurs into something like its dark underside – a fleeting and sinister confrontation with female sexuality as disruptive, fluid, and ultimately ego-dissolving, rendering boundaries between subject and object, masculinity and femininity, all but non-existent.

Whereas the absent Caddy Compson evokes the erotic sublime in *The Sound and the Fury* as the narrative's missing center, *Sanctuary* shifts the far boundaries of its representational strategies to Temple Drake's rape, the story of which attorney Horace Benbow seeks and eventually hears but which is never related directly to the reader. Never fully represented in the narrative itself, the rape is detectable only in its aftermath, in the wake of the destruction it wreaks upon multiple lives, in fleeting glimpses of Temple's newly voracious sexuality, and in the momentary sense of dissolution Benbow experiences after he hears Temple's account and feels his sense of self blurring with hers as he relives the rape himself. That moment in turn foreshadows the dissolution of everything in which Horace believes – justice, redemption, romantic love, white masculine chivalry – as *Sanctuary*'s nightmarish vision of contemporary life reveals itself in the gangster underworld of Memphis and the backwoods of Mississippi, in Miss Reba's brothel, in Clarence Snopes's political machinations, and above all in Temple Drake's brief appropriation and expression of her own sexuality. It is as though that vision of the fleeing nymph, propelling so much of Faulkner's fiction in this period, darkens and transmutes into something very like a crisis of meaning erasing all boundaries between self and otherness, containment and dissolution, femininity and masculinity, and, not incidentally, whiteness and blackness. Time and again Temple's plunge into the Memphis underworld and into the darker corners of her own sexuality takes on the contours of black female sexuality – in the pronounced contrast set up between her and the statuesque, inviolable whiteness of Narcissa Benbow, in Popeye's repeated associations with blackness, and in the unsettling way *Sanctuary* as a whole threatens to metamorphose from a tale of white gangsters to the age-old scenario of race, rape, and lynching.

It is small wonder, then, that for a good many commentators *Sanctuary* is perceived as the founding text of modern Southern gothicism, setting its story as it does first in the ruins of the Old Frenchman place and later in the shadowy corners of Miss Reba's brothel in Memphis. To an unsettling degree, the novel displays many of the features of gothic narratives dating back to the publication of Horace Walpole's *The Castle of Otranto* in 1764 and Ann Radcliffe's *The Mysteries of Udolpho* in 1794 – claustrophobic settings of ruins or dark, ambiguous houses, uncanny secrets to be discovered, anxieties over what those secrets will reveal, and above all, the repressed histories and phantoms unleashed by those secrets. The secret lying at the heart of Faulkner's novel, the secret that attorney Horace Benbow tries to seek out, is the destabilizing, destructive force of female sexuality, so distant from the ideal of white Southern womanhood associated with Horace's sister Narcissa that it evokes nothing so much as white fears of repressed blackness, dissolving carefully constructed categories of class, race, and gender as Horace's very sense of self is dissolved in his confrontation with the story of Temple's rape. *Sanctuary* is, in many respects, a novel haunted by blackness – with Temple's implicit association with black sexuality, with those odd, repeated, ambiguous references to the very pale Popeye's "blackness," and to the scenario of avenged white womanhood and lynching violence with which the novel concludes.

The turn toward blackness in *Sanctuary* signaled in Faulkner a move away from the erotic sublime – although the figure of Eula Varner in the Snopes trilogy would often evoke dim, parodic reflections of nympholepsy – toward something like a racial sublime in the novels of the 1930s and 1940s that would take race and African Americans as a primary narrative concern. For the more that Faulkner began to explore the legacy of race in American culture in the novels to come – in *Absalom, Absalom!* (1936), *Go Down, Moses* (1942), and *Intruder in the Dust* (1948), but most of all *Light in August* – the more elusive and indecipherable African Americans would appear in his fiction, fleeing the novels' narrative grasp even as the dimly perceived wood nymph had slipped beyond the reach of the yearning farmhand in that early story "Nympholepsy." In the case of Joe Christmas, the ambiguous drifter finally labeled by the white community of Jefferson as a black rapist-murderer, the narrative pursues his shadowy presence back into his childhood and youth and into the present of his flight through the countryside, with nearly as much frustration and failure to locate and define him as experienced by his relentless white pursuers. Although Christmas's section of the novel, according to Fadiman, is the last part to be written, it is by far the longest and most detailed of the novel's fragmentary and disconnected narratives, and Christmas remains from first to last a phantom haunting the pages of *Light in August* and the collective imagination of its white characters, never fully coming into direct sight, forever slipping into competing narratives, speculation, and scenarios, finally appearing to his white pursuers in the very end as nothing so much as the abject, in the sense meant by Julia Kristeva in *Powers of Horror*: "a massive and sudden emergence of uncanniness, which, familiar as it might have been in an opaque and forgotten life, now harries me as radically separate, loathsome. Not me, Not that. But not nothing either. A 'something' that I do not recognize as a thing" (1982: 2).

To a startling degree, Kristeva's description of the abject evokes a good deal of the horror and the uncanniness – the sublime, if you will – that attends Joe Christmas's final appearance in the novel, in the castration-lynching he undergoes at the hands of his white supremacist pursuer Percy Grimm. For what the passage describes is not so much the mutilation and death itself as its impact upon Grimm's white followers, one that defies articulation but nonetheless promises to haunt their memories in the years to come. Joe – for those pursuers something very like the abject – evokes as powerful a confrontation with alterity as can be found in Faulkner's fiction, one that simultaneously posits his utter otherness as well as his capacity – captured in the blood that virtually explodes from his body – to dissolve all boundaries between the hunted and the hunters, object and audience, femininity and masculinity, and especially blackness and whiteness.

Replete with all the horror and dissolution of meaning accompanying the sublime, Joe's death, drenched in the obsessive language and imagery of race and racism, underscores as well Faulkner's turn in *Light in August* away from pastoral to the language and imagery of American gothicism, which had already by the mid-nineteenth century claimed slavery and race as the repressed otherness of American history. In texts as diverse as *The Narrative of Arthur Gordon Pym* (1836) and *Uncle Tom's Cabin* (1852), literary precursors like Edgar Allan Poe and Harriet Beecher Stowe had resorted to the imagery and narrative motifs of the gothic – secrets, phantoms, entrapment, sudden eruptions of the uncanny – to address the growing crisis of slavery and the underlying instability of racial hierarchies in the nineteenth century. So closely had gothic literature become linked with race, blackness, and slavery by the end of the century that Leslie Fiedler felt compelled to declare in his classic study *Love and Death in the American Novel* "that the proper subject for American gothic is the black man" (1966: 297). More recent commentators on gothicism in general and American gothic, like Eric Savoy and Anne Williams, have argued that gothicism, with its preoccupation with secrets exposed to light and with contested versions of the past, reveals deep anxieties and fears about our most basic forms of social and symbolic organization, about the otherness that has been repressed and repudiated in order to establish our systems of order and normalcy (Savoy 2002: 168; Williams 1995: 70–1).

Light in August, in fact, is a text that reverberates with precisely those anxieties, detectable nowhere as much as in the very narrative form of the novel, which splinters into multiple stories, moods, modes, perspectives, and even rumors and whispers after the seemingly impervious pastoral opening of a very pregnant Lena Grove striding through the countryside looking for her seducer. Even in the opening passages, that countryside, with its abandoned saw mills and machinery, ravaged timber, isolated general stores, and rundown farmhouses, evokes nothing so much as pastoral ruined by the ravages of time, change, and exploitation, all potent reminders of Mississippi's economic devastation in the earliest and darkest days of the Great Depression. Indeed, whatever pastoral note is initially struck by the opening of *Light in August* is not long sustained, as André Bleikasten (1990) among others has pointed out, as Lena's story gives way first to that of Byron Bunch and his confidante Gail Hightower, and finally to that of Joe Christmas himself, whose narrative presence and shadowy history erupt from under the preceding narrative fragments like a phantom suddenly released by the shattering of the novel's pastoral opening.

What Christmas's history ultimately reveals is the underlying instability of the sunny world through which Lena strolls, and of its gender, class, and racial categories defining the make-up of the community. An outsider from the beginning, Joe eludes those categorizations as easily as he slips in and out of the shadows and corners of the town, of its white and its black neighborhoods. So too does his history emerge as something like the story that is never told by the white inhabitants of Jefferson who so avidly exchange the gossip and rumors of his whereabouts during his final flight through the countryside. A good many commentators, following the lead of Cleanth Brooks's pivotal reading of the novel as a conflict between community and outsiders, have pronounced Joe

Christmas's story as a narrative aberration of sorts, one brought to an end by his death and by the restoration of Lena's story and the mood of pastoral accompanying her acceptance and incorporation into the white community. Such readings, though, fostered in part by Brooks's famous emphasis on the importance of community and tradition in the novel, ignore the ways that Christmas's presence and shadowy history disrupt and destabilize pastoral in *Light in August*, ultimately revealing the bankruptcy of a mode that Faulkner rightly saw as part of his crippling inheritance as a Southern writer – and one from which he would increasingly come to distance himself and his work. For whatever mood of pastoral is suggested by Lena Grove's initial presence is complicated and rendered highly ambiguous by the novel's subtle but insistent reminders of the industrialization of the Mississippi countryside in those brief glimpses of destroyed timber, abandoned machinery, and, perhaps more to the point, the hard labor undergirding life in the countryside. In ways that anticipate Raymond Williams's critique of pastoral and its repression of economic underpinnings in *The Country and the City* (1973), *Light in August* portrays not the sort of idealized farmwork that the Southern Agrarians depicted in *I'll Take My Stand* as a virtuous and worthwhile alternative to Northern industrial capitalism, but the hard physical labor of shoveling sawdust and lifting logs in lumber mills, of plowing new furrows behind swaybacked mules, of predawn feeding of farm animals, of hard bargaining for farm equipment, and of endless wagonloads of commodities transported to far-distant town markets.

Above all, it is labor that is implicitly linked with blackness, as the narrative of *Light in August* progresses from Lena Grove to Gail Hightower to Joe Christmas. In *As I Lay Dying* Faulkner had undertaken a similar project of disrupting pastoral associations and images by presenting the story of the poor white backwoods Bundrens through imagery and expectations largely associated with journalistic exposures of the US South in the 1920s – the kind of newspaper stories of hookworm, unregulated sexuality, and economic shiftlessness that built a lasting stereotype of the region as benighted and backward. But in *Light in August*, a work that represents Faulkner's first full engagement with race and blackness, the labor underlying and defining the countryside through which Lena Grove walks subtly shifts from that of white lumber hands and farmers to the kind of bottom-rail labor undertaken by Joe Christmas as he is introduced into the narrative – a man whose mysterious appearance at the saw mill in Jefferson hints at other worlds and lives "behind the veil, the screen of his negro's job at the mill" (1990b: 36).

The world of blackness and labor, however much it unsettles and eventually dissipates vestiges of pastoral, never fully comes into sight in *Light in August* but is manifested in brief, shadowy glimpses – of blacks questioned and harassed by white legal authorities in search of Joanna Burden's murderer, and emerging fleetingly to report and complain of Joe Christmas's sudden, disruptive appearances. There are swift glimpses as well of "parchmentcolored" Joe Christmas himself, who is revealed more as he is perceived and categorized by others than he is seen directly. From start to finish, he frustrates the best efforts of the other characters to read and categorize him, from the planing mill laborers alongside whom he works to Joanna Burden, who uses both sexuality and money to force him into the identity of "Negro." Just so does he ultimately elude the narrative itself, however much he feels blackness slowly engulfing him toward the end of his flight through the countryside. Even in the end, bleeding to death before his white tormentors, he seemingly eludes every effort to see, grasp, and comprehend who and what he is. The white district attorney Gavin Stevens may afterwards sum up what for him captures the full meaning of who and what Joe Christmas is – a man supposedly driven by the conflicting demands of both white and black blood – but Stevens's brief narration is presented like something of a hastily conceived afterthought, a rationalizing bid at finally capturing and containing what Joe Christmas is that is no more successful, ultimately, than the novel itself or, for that matter, the final lynching scene. In his death scene Joe once more eludes his pursuers, who will remember, the narrative tells us, not who and what he is and was but the horror – and the sublimity – that his death and his ultimate unrepresentability inspire.

A markedly similar elusiveness would cloak a good many of Faulkner's black characters to come – Charles Bon, Jim Bond, and Lucas Beauchamp, to name a few – and they, like the shards and broken bottles ornamenting black graves at the beginning of "Pantaloon in Black," often described as the "anomalous" story in *Go Down, Moses*, would appear possessed "of a profound meaning and fatal to touch, which no white man could have read" (1990a: 132). Time and time again, Faulkner's narratives and white characters would ponder the indecipherable surfaces of those characters and their ready ability to slip outside the boundaries of white gazes and to foil the best efforts of whites to capture them within the confines of representation, whether in the story-telling efforts of Mr. Compson, Quentin Compson, and Shreve McCannon in *Absalom, Absalom!*, or in Ike McCaslin's frustrated efforts to extend recognition of sorts to his black cousins in his attempt to rectify and redeem the consequences and reach of his grandfather's legacy in *Go Down, Moses*.

Nowhere, though, would the racial sublime that haunted Faulkner's efforts to explore the legacy of slavery, race, and segregation be more powerfully evoked than in *Light in August* – in the death of Joe Christmas, the horror of which would remain in his pursuers' memories but would forever frustrate any effort to decipher, categorize, and finally contain him. The very form of the novel – its shattering into multiple shards of stories and abruptly shifting from pastoral into gothic – testified to the limits of what Faulkner saw as his literary legacy of escape and indictment, pastoral and gothicism, but above all to the limits of his own powers of imagination and representation, constrained ultimately by the even more confining legacy of race.

REFERENCES AND FURTHER READING

Bleikastan, A. (1990). *The Ink of Melancholy: Faulkner's Novels from* The Sound and the Fury *to* Light in August. Bloomington: Indiana University Press.

Brooks, C. (1963). *William Faulkner: The Yoknapatawpha Country.* New Haven, CT.: Yale University Press.

Brooks, C. (1978). *William Faulkner: Toward Yoknapatawpha and Beyond.* New Haven, CT: Yale University Press.

Clery, E. J. (2002). The Genesis of "Gothic" Fiction. In J. E. Hogle (ed.). *The Cambridge Companion to Gothic Fiction* (pp. 21–40). New York: Cambridge University Press.

Fadiman, R. K. (1975). *Faulkner's* Light in August: *A Description and Interpretation of the Revisions.* Charlottesville, VA: Bibliographical Society of the University of Virginia/University Press of Virginia.

Faulkner, W. (1950). *Collected Stories of William Faulkner.* New York: Random.

Faulkner, W. (1965). *The Marble Faun and A Green Bough.* New York: Random. (*The Marble Faun* original pub. 1924.)

Faulkner, W. (1980). *Mayday* (ed. C. Collins). South Bend, IN: University of Notre Dame Press. (Written 1926.)

Faulkner, W. (1981). *Uncollected Stories of William Faulkner* (ed. J. Blotner). New York: Vintage.

Faulkner, W. (1990a). *Go Down, Moses and Other Stories.* New York: Vintage International. (Original pub. 1942.)

Faulkner, W. (1990b). *Light in August: The Corrected Text.* New York: Vintage International. (Original pub. 1932.)

Faulkner, W. (1990c). *The Sound and the Fury: The Corrected Text.* New York: Vintage International. (Original pub. 1929.)

Faulkner, W. (1993). *Sanctuary: The Corrected Text.* New York: Vintage International. (Original pub. 1931.)

Fiedler, L. A. (1966). *Love and Death in the American Novel.* Rev. edn. New York: Stein and Day.

Freeman, B. C. (1995). *The Feminine Sublime: Gender and Excess in Women's Fiction.* Berkeley: University of California Press.

Hogle, J. (ed.) (2002). *The Cambridge Companion to Gothic Fiction.* New York: Cambridge University Press.

Inge, M. T. (ed.) (1995). *William Faulkner: The Contemporary Reviews.* New York: Cambridge University Press.

Jarraway, D. R. (1998). The Gothic Import of Faulkner's "Black Son" in *Light in August.* In R. K. Martin and E. Savoy (eds.). *American Gothic: New Interventions in a National Narrative* (pp. 57–74). Iowa City: University of Iowa Press.

Kermode, F. (ed.) (1984). *English Pastoral Poetry, from the Beginnings to Marvell.* Freeport, NY: Books for Libraries Press.

Kristeva, J. (1982). *Powers of Horror: An Essay on Abjection* (trans. L. S. Roudiez). New York: Columbia University Press. (Original pub. 1980.)

Lyotard, J.-F. (1991). The Sublime and the Avant-Garde. In *The Inhuman: Reflections on Time* (trans. G. Bennington and R. Bowlby) (pp. 89–107). Stanford, CA: Stanford University Press. (Original pub. 1988.)

Martin, R. K. and E. Savoy (eds.) (1998). *American Gothic: New Interventions in a National Narrative.* Iowa City: University of Iowa Press.

Meriwether, J. B. (ed.) (1972). An Introduction for *The Sound and the Fury, William Faulkner. Southern Review,* NS 8: 705–10.

Meriwether, J. B. (ed.) (1973). An Introduction to *The Sound and the Fury. Mississippi Quarterly,* 26: 410–15.

Panofsky, E. (1982). *Meaning in the Visual Arts.* Chicago: University of Chicago Press.

Poggioli, R. (1975). *The Oaten Flute: Essays on Pastoral Poetry and the Pastoral Ideal.* Cambridge, MA: Harvard University Press.

Savoy, E. (2002). The Rise of American Gothic. In J. E. Hogle (ed.). *The Cambridge Companion to Gothic Fiction* (pp. 169–88). New York: Cambridge University Press.

Sensibar, J. (1984). *The Origins of Faulkner's Art.* Austin, TX: University of Texas Press.

Simpson, L. P. (1975). Faulkner and the Southern Symbolism of Pastoral. *Mississippi Quarterly,* 28: 401–16.

Sundquist, E. J. (1984). *Faulkner: The House Divided.* Baltimore: Johns Hopkins University Press.

Weiskel, T. (1976). *The Romantic Sublime: Studies in the Structure and Psychology of Transcendence.* Baltimore: Johns Hopkins University Press.

Williams, A. (1995). *Art of Darkness: A Poetics of Gothic.* Chicago: University of Chicago Press.

Williams, R. (1973). *The Country and the City.* New York: Oxford University Press.

22

Faulkner, Trauma, and the Uses of Crime Fiction

Greg Forter

Faulkner's relationship to crime fiction, like his attitude toward genre writing more generally, was at once complex and highly ambivalent. He seems to have shared the intuition of many high modernists that genre fiction represented a capitulation to market demands that truncated human expression, and his greatest novels can in this sense be read as resolutely anti-generic. But to leave it at this is to risk obscuring a more complicated relationship to the problem of genre and, in particular, to the genre of crime fiction. Faulkner's library contained at his death a surprising number of detective and mystery stories, including books by John Dickson Carr, Dashiell Hammett, Rex Stout, and Dorothy Sayers (Gidley 1973: 97). That these titles represented more than a casual interest on the author's part – an escape from the rigors of his own creative process, as one friend put it (Gidley 1973: 120, note 1) – is evident in the use Faulkner made of precisely those elements of detective fiction least congenial to creative original- ity. The author of such modernist monuments as *The Sound and the Fury* (1929), *As I Lay Dying* (1930), *Light in August* (1932), and *Absalom, Absalom!* (1936) published as well a relatively straightforward detective novel (*Intruder in the Dust* [1948]), a collection of mystery stories (*Knight's Gambit* [1949]), and a novel he himself considered, or pro- fessed to consider, a potboiler in the genre of crime (*Sanctuary* [1931]). He took second place in the *Ellery Queen Mystery Magazine* short story contest of 1946 (see chapter 19, "Faulkner's Genre Experiments"), and worked on the film version of Raymond Chandler's *The Big Sleep* (1946), for which he received credit as chief screenwriter.

Perhaps most interestingly, as critics have noted with increasing frequency since the mid-1970s, even many of the most idiosyncratic and "Faulknerian" of Faulkner's novels contain a kernel of generic substance out of which all else appears to unfold. *Light in August* has at its center the mystery of Joanna Burden's murder, which turns out to be inseparable from the secret of Joe Christmas's birth (i.e., of his racial identity). In *Absalom, Absalom!*, the proliferating narrators and, especially, the figures of Quentin and Shreve function in part as historical sleuths who comb through meager documen- tary evidence while projecting themselves into the problem of why Henry Sutpen shot

Charles Bon at the gates of Sutpen's Hundred, and how this murder follows from the South's historical crimes (Holman 1971). There is even a case to be made for seeing *The Sound and the Fury* in a similar light: John Cawelti (1991) proposes, for example, that the multiple narratives of this novel record Faulkner's (unsuccessful) efforts to explicate the mystery inhering in the image he often cited as the book's genesis. Each successive section, on this view, is a narrative investigation of the girl in a tree with muddy drawers, who peers through the window at her grandmother's funeral as her brothers look on helplessly from below.

There are of course important differences in these books' relation to their generic materials. In what follows, I plot these differences at three points along a continuum. At one extreme are the books in which Faulkner most fully subordinates his characteristic thematic and formal concerns to the conventions of the detective story: *Knight's Gambit* and *Intruder in the Dust*. The conservative impulses of the mystery genre – the impulses that tend *formally* toward neat resolutions and easy accessibility, and *thematically* toward the affirmation of the social order's dominant values – enable Faulkner in these books to enact some of his culture's most disturbing fantasies about gender, race, and the project of epistemological mastery. At the heart of each text's project is thus the assertion of clear, ascertainable differences between a good "us" and a threatening "them," and a purification of the social order through a purging of those who transgress against it. (See Auden's 1948 account of the work performed by detective fiction [Auden 1980] and Cawelti's 1976 revision of that account.)

Light in August and *Absalom, Absalom!* stand at the opposite end of this spectrum. In these novels, the conventions of crime writing are assimilated and practically dissolved in the formidable idiosyncrasy of Faulkner's imaginative vision. The tension between authorial invention and generic formula is weighted heavily toward inventiveness. Much of what is compelling in these books, however, resides precisely *within* this tension: in the play between the moral and epistemological clarity promised by the generic "kernel" of detective fiction and the relentless subversion of that promise in the kernel's narrative elaboration. That subversion is partly what makes *Light in August* and *Absalom* more politically promising than Faulkner's conventional "crime" texts: they complicate the gestures of othering so central to the genre's misogyny and racism, insisting upon the radical elusiveness of any firm borders between self and "object," black and white, masculine and feminine. At the same time, the books in this category evince a tendency toward political pessimism and paralysis; the subversion of formulaic, dualistic categories gives rise in practice to a deep despair, since without those categories, the world appears to be knowable for Faulkner only by way of traumatic shocks that cripple his characters' capacity for meaningful or autonomous action.

The third place on the continuum is occupied only by the remarkable *Sanctuary*. This dark, disturbing, and inscrutable experiment is unique in the Faulkner canon. It resembles the more straightforward of his crime texts in the depth of its adherence to generic conventions, but those conventions are in this case less those of the *detective* story than those of the psychological suspense story or *roman noir* (Hilfer calls it, confusingly to my mind, the "crime novel"). This is a genre concerned above all with the seamy, insurmountably destructive underworld that such books figure as the hidden truth of our daytime social world; its focus is on the psychology of criminals and the existential significance of violent crime, rather than on the solution of a mystery. In Faulkner's case, this focus appears to have resonated so fully with his own preoccupations that his experiment in the genre practically eliminates the tension between inventiveness and generic formulae. *Sanctuary*, in other words, resides at the still center of the continuum I have described; in it, the competing strains of invention and formula paradoxically cancel and intensify each other. The novel thus resembles *Absalom* and *Light in August* in its subversion of dominant social categories, but this subversion takes place by way of an almost total *identification with* the formal conventions and thematic commitments of the *roman noir*, rather than through an incorporation that preserves generic conventions in order to demonstrate one's distance from them.

Faulkner's "Straight" Crime Texts

Intruder in the Dust is in many respects the most formulaic of Faulkner's crime writings. Its basic shape derives from the scenario of a wrongly accused man, a scenario common to mystery stories of both the traditional and the *noir* kind. Here, the man is Lucas Beauchamp; he is arrested and charged with murder after being discovered holding a gun beside the murdered Vinson Gowrie. His incarceration and imminent trial produce both mystery and suspense: we're encouraged from early on to believe that Lucas is in fact innocent, so the questions commanding our attention become: if Lucas is not the killer, then who is? And will that killer be caught in time to prevent an innocent man from being punished? *Intruder* concludes, conventionally enough, by resolving this mystery and relieving the suspense generated by the race against time. The law's representatives catch the killer before the allotted time has run out; Lucas is then exonerated and released; and Faulkner's "detective" explains for the reader what happened at the scene of the crime and why.

This pattern's affinity with traditional detective fiction is accentuated by the relationship between two of the book's central characters, the young Chick Mallison and his uncle Gavin Stevens. Stevens is here, as elsewhere in Faulkner's fiction, a county attorney who functions as a detective (i.e., he investigates crimes); Chick's awe-filled admiration for Stevens's investigative wisdom makes the nephew a kind of Watson to his uncle's Sherlock Holmes. Readers, in turn, are asked to identify, through Chick and thus in mediated fashion, with the uncle's capacity for masterful solution – a scenario that enables us at once to marvel at the sleuth's capacities (through Chick's eyes, they often seem impressively beyond us) and to partake of those capacities as they engage in the ritual expunging of a threat to social order.

Even a text that adheres as closely to genre fiction as this one, however, contains recognizably "Faulknerian" elements. The detective plot is in this case fused to an exploration of racial preconceptions in matters of justice in the New South. Lucas Beauchamp is a black man; more, he is a proud and munificent black man who refuses the forms of obsequiousness that pass for "respect" in the white community. Such a portrayal enables Faulkner to turn the town's unquestioning assumption of Lucas's guilt into a commentary on the racial prejudice that criminalizes black behavior prior to any actual transgression – especially for those black Americans who decline to occupy the place assigned to them by whites. The seriousness of Faulkner's inquiry in this direction is signaled by the fact that even Stevens begins by assuming Lucas's guilt; the novel has him do so, in part, to dethrone him from the position of mastery and endow Chick and his (black) friend Alek, who do some of the more serious sleuthing, with a kind of subaltern investigative authority that exposes the inadequacies of Southern law. This shift has the further effect of questioning the social order's most sympathetic representative (Stevens), as if to insist that the problem of racism is systemic rather than idiosyncratic and personal. Solving the mystery then becomes a gesture that "corrects" the law's initial misperceptions, relocating the violence projected onto black men back where it belongs: in the minds and deeds of white men, one of whom turns out to have committed the crime.

And yet these complexities are, in the end, sacrificed to the generic exigencies of the detective story. A novel that starts by criticizing white racism, and does so by undermining the dichotomy between a "good" white South and its black transgressors, ends by reasserting this dichotomy with a disturbing and racist vengeance (see on this point Gidley 1973: 118–19). This happens first through a remarkable and thematically unmotivated speech that Stevens delivers toward the middle of the book:

> Only a few of us know that only from homogeneity comes anything of a people or for a people of durable and lasting value – the literature, the art, the science, that minimum of government and police which is the meaning of freedom and liberty. . . .
>
> That's why we must resist the North: not just to preserve ourselves nor even the two of us [i.e., blacks and whites] as one to remain one nation because that will be the inescapable by-product of what we will preserve . . . : the postulate that Sambo is a human being living in a free country and hence must be free. That's what we are really defending: the privilege of setting him free ourselves: which we will have to do for the reason that nobody else can since going on a century ago now the North tried it and have been admitting for seventy-five years now that they failed. . . .
>
> And as for Lucas Beauchamp, Sambo, he's a homogeneous man too, except for that part of him which is trying to escape into not even the best of the white race but the second best. (Faulkner 1991: 151–2)

Stevens here embraces a kind of ontology of difference – a view of the world as composed of homogeneous and totally distinct racial groups – in a way that *need* not, perhaps, have racist consequences, but in this case does. Lucas becomes a stereotypical "Sambo," his freedom something the white South alone can grant him. The proof of the latter is that Reconstruction was a catastrophe caused by Northern interference. Any further meddling of that kind can only make racial tensions worse, on Stevens's view. This is, in short, the ideology of paternalism and racial essentialism. The novel's final chapters suggest that this ideology is not just Stevens's but Faulkner's as well. As Mark Gidley argues (1973: 118), they *show* us Lucas as a Sambo-buffoon who has only himself to blame for his troubles, since he "*got himself* into the position where *they had had to believe he had murdered a white man*" (Faulkner 1991: 231; my emphasis). *Intruder*'s racial critique is thus contained by a generic formula that re-enthrones Stevens as a figure of the law whose activity ultimately enforces – rather than challenging – conventional socio-racial (and sectional) divisions.

A dynamic similar to this one but operating primarily in the area of gender informs the other text in this category, *Knight's Gambit*. In that volume's title tale, as John T. Irwin has persuasively shown (2002), the narrative devices of detective fiction serve as mechanisms through which Faulkner elaborates a pattern basic to much of his fiction. That pattern concerns a rivalry between two men, sometimes over the love of a woman, in which the "healthy" outcome is that the older man helps the younger submit to paternal authority by sublimating his rivalrous anger into identification with the older man's mastery, receiving in recompense the promise of male prerogatives (including possession of a woman) in the future.

This is of course an Oedipal pattern in the classically Freudian sense. Irwin shows how "Knight's Gambit" develops two versions of the structure that mirror each other with a difference. On one hand, there is (again) the relationship between Gavin Stevens and Chick Mallison. Here, the potentially lethal violence of the Oedipal relation has been productively contained. Stevens facilitates his nephew's maturation by offering a form of rivalry that Faulkner figures through the game of chess: a competition that is both symbolic (rather than literal) and symbolically winnable by either party, and that can therefore serve as a metaphor for the possibility of the boy's successful accession to manhood.

The second version of this pattern is more volatile and socially threatening. At the tale's opening, Chick and Stevens's game of chess is interrupted by the entrance of Max Harriss and his sister, children of the wealthy widow Melisandre Backus Harriss. Max demands that Stevens "do something" about Captain Sebastian Gualdres, an Argentinean man who had been courting the sister, but then switched his affections to Max's mother under circumstances that suggest he's a fortune-hunter. Irwin demonstrates that the relationship between Max and Gualdres is a perverse reflection of Chick's with Stevens. The violence sublimated by the uncle and nephew remains quite literal and lethal in this case; Harriss and Gualdres compete with each other not in the displaced form of chess-matches, but by riding and fencing against each other and testing each other's romantic prowess. Furthermore, in these competitions, the older man seeks the younger's devastation rather than his identificatory submission. Max's sister puts it this way: "It [the hostility between them] wasn't even because of Mother. It was because Sebastian always beat him. At everything" (1978: 181–2).

Max's challenge to Stevens is then in part a request for a "father" who can beneficently contain this murderous rivalry between him and the Captain. At another level, however, the challenge is Oedipal in the broader, more social sense: Max pointedly asks Stevens if he isn't "the Law here"; he indicates that, if Stevens doesn't uphold that law by banishing the usurper-father, he (Max) will take matters upon himself and dispose of Gualdres through violence. The story's opening in this sense sets up a crisis in the masculine order. It raises the question of whether the story's representative of the law is adequate to his patriarchal role, especially whether he can successfully deploy the authority necessary for keeping the community's women safe *from* alien outsiders on one hand, and *for* the (white) men inside the community on the other.

Stevens's role as detective is thus inseparable from his role as Oedipalizing father. The problem in detection he faces is how to ascertain Max's plan and so prevent his murdering the usurper-father. Success in this area will lead, in turn, to an amicable – a pacific – solution to Harriss's Oedipal rivalry, and so ensure that the rule of law and patriarchal transmission remain essentially intact. These gestures are finally affirmed and extended by Faulkner's grafting a third Oedipal structure onto those that Irwin identifies. "Knight's Gambit" ends not just with Harriss submitting to the law by agreeing to enter the army; nor does it conclude merely with Gualdres marrying Max's sister and renouncing his claim to the widow's property. It ends in addition with Gavin himself becoming betrothed to Melisandre Harris, who turns out to be a woman he had loved and lost many years ago. The triumph of detection issues, in this sense, in the detective's vanquishing of a rival suitor and taking for himself the woman who has been the unnamed prize of that unnamed contest from the story's inception.

That these Oedipal complexities mark a rich and distinctly Faulknerian manipulation of the detective form seems to me indisputable. And yet here, too, the genre's tendency toward moral clarity and the affirmation of order infects the materials that Faulkner brings to bear. "Knight's Gambit" fails, for example, to question the *value* of Oedipalization (a failure that Irwin's analysis abets); it grants in advance that the success of this process is purely beneficent, that boys *can* and *should* become adults by identifying with a figure of patriarchal authority. It further implies that the business of living is in essence an affair between men, in which women figure as tokens or prizes who lack any autonomous selves worth mentioning. Such positions mark a retreat from the ferocious critique of Oedipal gender in, say, *Absalom, Absalom!* – a book in which the romantic triangle of Judith, Henry, and Bon is shown to be extraordinarily fluid (each character occupies both male and female positions in it), fundamentally perverse (Henry desires Bon as much as he identifies with him), and essentially pathogenic (any resolution of the conflict seems guaranteed to produce disaster). Viewed in this light, the Oedipal triumphalism of "Knight's Gambit" is a symptom of how the detective fiction formula at once required and thereby enabled Faulkner to resolve psychological, moral, and epistemological ambivalences that his most ambitious works keep open.

Light in August and *Absalom, Absalom!*

A passage toward the beginning of *The Wild Palms* (1939) can help us see the place of crime fiction in Faulkner's great works of the 1930s. "Once," Faulkner writes,

> there were two convicts. One of them was about twenty-five . . . with . . . pale, china-colored outraged eyes – an outrage directed not at the men who had foiled his crime,

not even at the lawyers and judges who had sent him here, but at the writers, the un-corporeal names attached to the stories, the paper novels – the Diamond Dicks and Jesse Jameses and such – whom he believed had led him into his present predicament through their own ignorance and gullibility regarding the medium in which they dealt and took money for. . . .

. . . [H]e had saved the paper-backs for two years, reading and rereading them, memo-rising them, comparing and weighing story and method against story and method, taking the good from each and discarding the dross as his working plan emerged. . . . And then when the day came, he did not even have a chance to go through the coaches and collect the watches and the rings . . . because he had been captured as soon as he entered the express car where the safe and the gold would be. . . . So now from time to time . . . he cursed in a harsh steady unrepetitive stream, not at the living men who had put him where he was but at what he did not even know were pen-names, did not even know were not actual men but merely the designations of shades who had written about shades. (1966: 23–5)

The humor of this passage hinges in part on the distance between the convict's confu-sion of life and art, on one hand, and the reader/narrator's appreciation, on the other, of the distinction between these two realms. The convict appears to us funny because he is fooled by words in a way we would not be. More trenchant is the passage's point about its own imaginative designs, however. Faulkner clearly means to imply that the powerfully "realistic" ambitions of crime stories are *in themselves* ontologically seductive, that crime texts lend themselves to being read as unambiguous transcriptions of the real and prescriptions for successful action. *This* text, in contrast – *The Wild Palms* – will complicate the relation of language to world in a way that thwarts such naïve under-standings. The passage in this sense ironizes the generic conventions it describes, highlighting the distance between its procedures and the formulae that *Intruder* and *Knight's Gambit* will assume less critically.

This kind of ironic incorporation of the popular is, of course, a defining feature of high modernist literature. Its purpose is to highlight the difference between authentic expression and its commodified debasement, and a line of influence can be traced in this context from Flaubert's treatment of his heroine's addiction to sentimental fiction in *Madame Bovary* (1857) to Eliot's ironic assimilation in *The Waste Land* (1922) of what the poem disparages as cultural waste matter. It is perhaps unsurprising to find that Faulkner, too, employs this method. More striking is the extent to which the novels in which he most fully does so retain a kind of parasitic ambivalence toward the crime materials they ironize. *Light in August* and *Absalom, Absalom!* at once poke fun at the conventions of detective fiction, subvert those conventions in order to expose their epistemological and ideological limitations, *and* remain structurally dependent upon the very conventions they ironize.

We can start to see this complex relation by turning to a scene in *Light in August* that echoes with a difference the one in *Wild Palms* from which I have quoted. The scene takes place the morning of the day on which Joe Christmas will murder Joanna Burden, the woman with whom he has been carrying on a clandestine affair. Joe leaves his cabin carrying "a magazine of that type whose covers bear either pictures of young women in underclothes or pictures of men in the act of shooting one another with pistols" (1990b: 110). After buying a breakfast of "crackers and potted meat," he sits in the ditch by a spring to read and eat:

> [H]e began now upon the second one [story], reading the magazine straight through as though it were a novel. Now and then he would look up from the page, chewing, into the sunshot leaves which arched the ditch. "Maybe I have already done it," he thought. "Maybe it is no longer now waiting to be done." . . . Then he read again. . . . [N]ow and then he would seem to linger upon one page. . . . He would not move, apparently arrested and held immobile by a single word which had perhaps not yet impacted, his whole being suspended by the single trivial combination of letters in quiet and sunny space, so that hanging motionless and without physical weight he seemed to watch the slow flowing of time beneath him. . . .
>
> . . . He read now like a man walking along a street might count the cracks in the pavement, to the last and final page, the last and final word. Then he rose and struck a match to the magazine and prodded it patiently until it was consumed. (pp. 111–12)

Like the passage from *Wild Palms*, this one concerns the overly predictable, formulaic character of mass-market crime stories – stories whose content goes without saying since they appear in magazines with women in underwear or men holding pistols on their covers. Like that passage, this one links the fictional crimes consumed by Faulkner's character to the plot in which the character finds himself ensnared: the convict reads crime stories in preparation for his own transgressive undertakings; Joe Christmas thinks, while reading the magazine, that "Maybe [he has] already done it," that perhaps he has already killed Joanna rather than merely thought about it.

The differences between the two passages are equally telling, however. *Light in August* is less broad in tone, less concerned than *Wild Palms* to score points at the expense of either Joe Christmas or the fiction he reads. If it plays on the meaning of "consumption" by having Joe "chew" his breakfast as he devours the magazine – if it stresses the ephemerality of this kind of reading by way of the fire that literally "consume[s]" the magazine once Joe has finished it – the passage equally emphasizes those moments at which Joe's attention resists such mindless intake: moments when "his whole being [is] suspended by the single trivial combination of letters in quiet and sunny space, so that hanging motionless and without physical weight he seemed to watch the slow flowing of time beneath him." Nor does Faulkner suggest a directly *causal* relationship between crime fiction and the murder Joe is contemplating. Christmas's barely articulated, undefined "plot" and the plots of the stories he reads exist side by side (so to speak) rather than following logically from one another. His contemplated crime may in some sense correspond to those about which he reads, but this is less because he models his actions on his reading than because *Faulkner* has drawn on crime fiction in imagining Joe's predicament: because the novel (not its characters) deliberately deploys the conventions of crime. In doing so, *Light in August* relinquishes a portion of that superiority over crime stories and crime stories' readers that *Wild Palms* so brazenly flaunts.

This is not to suggest that the book adopts crime conventions uncritically. Its irony is merely subtler and less all-encompassing, more fused to a sense of the crime story's fruitfulness once it is subject to creative adaptation. The first and most important of these adaptations concerns the way that *Light in August* places the crime story in the service of a deep *historical* inquiry into the psychology of racism and racial identity. (The historical scope distinguishes both this book and *Absalom* from the straight crime texts in the previous category.) In Faulkner's hands, that inquiry demands the elaboration of an ever-deeper personal past for each of the main characters. This elaboration reveals, in turn, how the characters' apparently "personal" stories cannot be told independently – are, indeed, inextricably intertwined, regardless of whether the characters know each other – precisely inasmuch as all are implicated in the social history and legacy of slavery, the bloodshed of Civil War, and the violent suppression of Reconstruction. The mystery pursued by the novel in this sense leads it "through" Joanna's murder and to the enigma of Joe's racial identity. The surest sign that this inquiry will resist not just the unambivalent irony of *The Wild Palms* but also the resolutionary certainties of *Intruder* is Faulkner's refusal of even the most basic forms of clarity with regard to these two questions.

Who, for example, kills Joanna Burden? I have chosen so far to speak as if Joe does, and the novel certainly authorizes such a reading. It devotes entire chapters to elaborating the dynamic of his affair with Joanna. The depth of its inquiry in this direction encourages us to think that the impasse created by the racial and gendered scripts these characters have internalized leads to Joe's increasing despair and finally to his murdering Joanna. But any reasonably attentive analysis must reckon with the fact that the narrative eye closes – the textual consciousness blacks out – at the climactic moment in the murder scene. One moment Joe is in Joanna's bedroom, the razor that will kill her not even in his hand, watching as she fires a pistol at him; the next he is "Standing in the middle of the road," waving down a car with that same pistol (1990b: 283). In between – nothing, an empty narrative space. The sheer willfulness of this exclusion in a novel as expansively inclusive as this one requires that we take the exclusion seriously as a narrative fact with a dignity of its own (see Duvall 1987).

To do so is to begin to suspect that the murder scene taunts us with the threat of solution at the mere mid-point of the novel, only then to withdraw that solution into a zone of almost pure ambiguity. We *cannot* know who killed Joanna for the simple reason that Faulkner does not tell us. He seems, indeed, to delight in introducing details that keep the secret inviolate. The person first suspected of the murder is not Joe Christmas but his roommate Joe Brown (a.k.a. Lucas Burch), whom a witness finds in Joanna's house as it burns the following morning. Brown is a coward and a consummate scoundrel, abandoner of the woman he has made pregnant, who openly admits that he wants Christmas caught so he (Brown) can get the reward. And yet it is he and he alone who claims to "know" that Joe Christmas did it. Neither the third person narrator nor any more reliable character ever corroborates his story. The evidence against Joe thus remains either psychologically circumstantial (based on the dynamic of his relationship with Joanna) or highly unreliable (based on Brown's accusation).

Furthermore, Brown offers as his clinching piece of evidence the assertion that Christmas is "part nigger." "Go on," he says. "Accuse me. . . . Accuse the white man and let the nigger go free. Accuse the white man and let the nigger run." To which, astonishingly, the sheriff replies: "I believe you are telling the truth at last. You go on with Buck, now, and get a good night's sleep" (1990b: 97, 99). The credulousness of this statement is astonishing because almost nothing in the novel is murkier than the "fact" of Joe Christmas's black blood. Everything turns on it, yet nothing proves it. The story of his blackness appears to be born in the lunatic mind of his grandfather Hines, whose religious misogyny and racism lead him to "know" that the man his daughter sleeps with is a "nigger," not a Mexican. ("Bitchery and abomination! Bitchery and abomination!" (p. 370): this is about what his evidence amounts to.) More than thirty years later, Hines's wife will tell Gail Hightower that her husband's suspicions were confirmed by the owner of the circus where the daughter's seducer (Joe's father) worked – but again, this is hearsay, based on no evidence, and clearly shaped by the force of memory and the culture's dominant narratives about race.

The book's major characters manage little more than this kind of retrospective, circular reasoning: Joe is black because he behaves like a black man, and the proof that he behaves like a black man is the murder for which his blackness convicts him ("I always knew there was something funny about that fellow," a deputy remarks after Brown divulges the "secret" [1990b: 99]). The characters seize on this "fact" of blackness as the simple solution to the straightforward mystery of who killed Joanna Burden and why. Faulkner, in contrast, insists that race is itself the mystery, the enigma. Joe behaves "like a black man" because he has come to believe that he is one, and the question then becomes, how did this belief come to pass, and what are the concrete effects of holding it?

In response to these questions, *Light in August* offers perhaps the most stunning account in our literature of how and to what effect "blackness" gets internalized. It does so through a passage in which Joe *ingests* then seeks to *vomit* a substance that identifies him with blackness and femininity. Christmas is then five years old and living in an orphanage. He has slipped into the bedroom of the institution's dietician, a woman Faulkner describes as "young, a little fullbodied, smooth, pink-and-white." Joe goes to her room in order to eat in "worm"-like dollops the sweet, "pinkcolored" toothpaste that she keeps by the washstand. He has been doing this surreptitiously "for almost a year." But today the dietician returns to the room while he is still there. She brings with her "a young interne" with whom she is having an affair. Joe withdraws behind "a cloth curtain which screen[s] off one corner of the room." He "squat[s] among the soft womansmelling garments and shoes," listening as the intern coerces the woman into having sex with him. Transfixed and immobilized, he continues smearing the toothpaste into his mouth and eating it, until at last "it refuse[s] to go down":

> At once the paste which he had already swallowed lifted inside him, trying to get back out, into the air where it was cool. It was no longer sweet. In the rife, pinkwomansmell-ing obscurity behind the curtain he squatted, pink-foamed, listening to his insides,

waiting . . . for what was about to happen to him. Then it happened. He said to himself with complete and passive surrender: "Well, here I am." (1990b: 121–2)

"Well, here I am" . . . and then he vomits. But who is "I" and where is "here"? An identity announced by throwing up is a strangely elusive identity, since vomit is at once "me" and "not-me," at once a substance assimilated to self and one that the self has violently rejected. Faulkner invents this scene, in other words, as an allegory for how identity is formed through a primitive dialectic of assimilation and expulsion: Joe incorporates the feminine pinkness, the sticky, blobby, shapeless matter whose color links it to the dietician. Faulkner accentuates this link by saying that when Joe first "discovered the toothpaste in her room he had gone directly there [to the washstand] . . . as if he already knew that she would possess something of that nature" (p. 120). The toothpaste is in this sense a kind of inevitable expression of the feminine. The meanings internalized when Joe eats that paste are then given content by the sexual character of the scene he overhears. To "be" the woman is here to be a passive, subordinated, penetrable object, unable to resist the force of a masculine agent of penetration. When Joe throws up, the act expresses a disgusted refusal of these combined meanings; his vomit says "I am not this," "I refuse to be this," "I *will not* be this," but this brutely physical marking of limits is predicated on a prior recognition that the thing he refuses to be has already taken up residence inside him.

The account does not stop here, however. Faulkner concludes it with the woman dragging Joe "out of his vomit" and hissing: "You little rat! . . . Spying on me! You little nigger bastard!" (1990b: 122). The point of this exclamation is to extend the dynamic of assimilation/repudiation into the realm of race. Faulkner is suggesting that in social hierarchies organized around *both* race and gender, black masculinity is often internalized as an impossible contradiction. The very meaning of being a black man is in part "feminization," since black men are disempowered and rendered vulnerable in ways that the culture codes as "castration." (This does not of course preclude the construction of black men as enviably virile; sexual prowess does not map smoothly onto social power.) By having Joe called "nigger" to his face for the first time at the end of this passage, then, Faulkner insists that his sense of blackness results from the internalization of social meanings rather than being the natural expression of a purely putative "black blood."

To seek to solve the mystery of Joe's blood is thus to miss the point entirely. Faulkner makes his paternity uncertain ("nigger *bastard*" is key) precisely in order to insist upon the impurity and internal conflictedness of identity. He makes it equally possible for Joe to be thought of as black as to be seen as white. He makes it hard for him to resist constructing his identity around the forms of abjected otherness imbibed in this scene, even as Joe also identifies with whiteness and conventional manhood. Christmas will spend a lifetime trying to repudiate this racio-sexual "impurity," but it remains stubbornly lodged at the very heart of his self-understanding. It's this internal ambiguity that the characters deny when they treat his racial identity as a fact to be discovered and used as evidence to explain the mystery of Joanna's murder.

It would be possible to show that *Absalom, Absalom!* offers a similar subversion of the will-to-know elicited by the detective conventions it employs. The book is in part a historical murder mystery that refuses objective verification of its most persuasive hypotheses. It encourages us to believe that the best solution to the mystery of why Henry Sutpen killed Bon, his sister's betrothed, is the one offered by Quentin and Shreve: that Charles is "the nigger that's going to sleep with your [Henry's] sister. Unless you stop me, Henry" (1990a: 286). The terms for preferring this solution, however, have less to do with its susceptibility to objective verification than with a plausibility that hinges upon the motivations for telling the story. Quentin and Shreve's version is most plausible because most comprehensive; its comprehensiveness, in turn, follows from the fact that they exhibit both compassion for the characters whose motives they're trying to interpret and an intersubjective openness to each other's imaginative designs. Their account in this sense contrasts markedly with the less persuasive efforts of Rosa Coldfield and Quentin's father: Rosa's hatred for Sutpen distorts her version of the past with a desire to revenge herself narratively upon him; Mr. Compson distorts his version with a narrative insistence upon the inevitability of the disasters he recounts.

Still, it is Mr. Compson who articulates the novel's view of why historical detection cannot and should not issue in tidy, objectively verifiable truths:

> It's just incredible. It just does not explain. Or perhaps that's it: they don't explain and we are not supposed to know. We have a few old mouth-to-mouth tales; we exhume from old trunks and boxes and drawers letters without salutation or signature, in which men and women who once lived and breathed are now merely initials or nicknames. . . . [The dead] are there, yet something is missing; they are like a chemical formula exhumed along with the letters from that forgotten chest. . . . [Y]ou bring them together in the proportions called for, but nothing happens; you re-read, tedious and intent, poring, making sure that you have forgotten nothing, made no miscalculation; you bring them together again and again nothing happens: just the words, the symbols, the shapes themselves, shadows inscrutable and serene, against that turgid background of a horrible and bloody mischancing of human affairs. (1990a: 80)

In short, the interpreter of historical mysteries must at once strive toward total solution and bow before what remains inscrutable, unknowable, uninterpretable in the traces of human activity bequeathed over time from one generation to the next. Faulkner's own text enacts this duality through the legendary difficulty of its style – a difficulty that exceeds even that of *Light in August*, and one that invites interpretive untangling while nonetheless rendering the mystery of its meaning far from fully resolvable.

There is a further way to think about *Absalom* in the context of detective fiction. The novel exploits in highly idiosyncratic fashion what John Cawelti calls "the detective story's double plot" (Cawelti 1991). He means by this something fairly straightforward: that in a conventional detective story, the key event (i.e., the crime) takes place once in the actual happening, then a second time in its gradual reconstruction and retelling by the detective. Or, to put this another way, the main action of the detective story is in some sense the repetition in narrative of a "plot" that precedes the story we are reading.

This repetition functions as a correction of all the false hypotheses generated along the way. It can therefore be judged on the basis of its fidelity to an initial, unrepresented event, as well as on the basis of its highlighting the mistaken character of the reconstructions offered to that point. (See Todorov 1977 for another version of this distinction.)

Faulkner's originality lies in his transposition of this double plot into an internal space (i.e., the mind) which nonetheless opens out onto problems of how historical forces shape and constrain human subjectivity. He suggests that subjectivity *is itself* structured by a kind of "double plot": something external happens to us, an event intrudes upon consciousness in an incipiently traumatic way, and yet this event remains unrecognized as such, unknown and therefore unassimilated to our self-understanding. It then requires a second, retroactivating event to bring this knowledge into consciousness, where it is now experienced, for the first time, *as* the trauma that it was in the first place. (This is indeed the temporality of trauma as described by Freud [1989].) The detective story's double plot is in this way both condensed and folded inward. Faulkner effects this transformation in order to make the following points: that any conventional, external mystery has as its secret subject the actors who did the deed or were its victims; that this requires a displacement of emphasis from the question "whodunit?" to the question, "why?"; that central to *this* mystery is the problem of how psychic motivations are also always social motives; and that these latter are installed through the incursion on the psyche of external, socio-historical meanings, which mark us even before we know either *what* those meanings are or *that* we have internalized them.

Two instances of this dynamic are worth discussing in detail. The first and most striking concerns Thomas Sutpen, the self-made Southern planter whose dynastic ambitions lie behind the mystery of Bon's murder. (Quentin and Shreve speculate that Henry, who is Sutpen's son, kills Bon after Sutpen tells him of Bon's black blood, since it's he – Sutpen – whose dream of a dynasty will be spoiled by admitting racial otherness into the family.) In chapter 7, Faulkner proposes that Sutpen's ambitions have their origin in an "affront" he suffers as an adolescent boy. Born and raised in the wild, unsettled mountains of Virginia, he has remained brutally unsocialized and, accordingly, "innocent" of the sins attendant upon the intertwined systems of private property, slavery, and the subjugation of women. But then the family moves down into the Tidewater area of Virginia. After a couple of years, Sutpen is sent one day by his father to deliver a message at one of the local plantations. A black house-slave opens the door and, before Sutpen can say what he has come to say, rebuffs him for using the front entrance, instructing him to go around back and telling him never to make the mistake again.

What happens next is this:

> before the monkey nigger who came to the door had finished saying what he did, he
> [Sutpen] seemed to kind of dissolve and a part of him turn and run back through the
> two years they had lived there like when you pass through a room fast and look at all
> the objects in it and you turn and go back through the room again and look at all the
> objects from the other side and you find out you had never seen them before, rushing

back through those two years and seeing a dozen things that had happened and he hadn't
even seen them before. . . . [He saw] his own father and sisters and brothers as the owner,
the rich man (not the nigger) must have been seeing them all the time – as cattle, creatures heavy and without grace, brutely evacuated into a world without hope or purpose
for them, who would in turn spawn with brutish and vicious prolixity . . . a race whose
future would be a succession of cut-down and patched and made-over garments bought
on exorbitant credit because they were white people, from stores where niggers were given
the garments free. (1990a: 186–90)

The brilliance of this passage lies in the way it models as a psychic event the interpretive doubling back to which Cawelti calls attention. The act of interpretation is dele-
gated to a character rather than the reader, and the "mystery" is not an external event
but a psychic experience. It cannot therefore be a mystery in quite the conventional
sense; it cannot be a matter of Sutpen's not possessing the requisite knowledge. It is,
rather, a matter of his knowing yet not knowing: he has *looked at* the metaphorical
"objects in the room" but has done so without really "see[ing]" them. They have made
a sensory impression on him that has for a time lain dormant, resisting its translation
into conscious, meaningful experience. The reason for this appears to be that Sutpen
does not yet possess a sufficiently direct experiential base through which to process and
render his initial impressions significant.

It is, therefore, only through the second event – through Sutpen's affront at the hands
of the plantation owner, for which the slave serves merely as medium – that the humiliating content of his initial impressions becomes both *conscious* and retrospectively *significant*. This second event in some deep sense "retrodetermines" the initial one. It takes
impressions of inferiority and feelings of incipient shame that might never have crystallized – might never have become inferiority and humiliation at all – and through an
act of historical contingency gives them a significatory content that constitutes the core
of Sutpen's subsequent sense of self. Faulkner in this way seeks to suggest that the self
is formed through the traumatic incursion of ascribed identities that shape us before
we even know we have been subject to them, identities internalized as unsolved and,
indeed, unrecognized mysteries whose latent and determinative significance is only
retrospectively unveiled.

The significance in question is of course social rather than narrowly personal. What
Sutpen discovers as he meditates on this scene is the entire system of social hierarchies,
privileges, and deprivations entailed in the slave system, including his own position
within it – namely, that as a poor white he does not even figure in the system, is in
some sense (on Faulkner's view) less socially significant and more existentially impoverished than even a slave. And yet the power of the novel derives from its insistence
that these social meanings are *also* psychic ones: Sutpen responds to his affront by
engaging in what the book codes as an Oedipal rivalry with the plantation owner; he
conceives a "design" that requires he "beat" the man by surpassing him, by replicating
yet bettering his position in the social hierarchy, rather than by seeking (for example)
to smash the hierarchy itself. This socially induced Oedipal rivalry is for Faulkner the

very mechanism of slavery's social reproduction. From it issues everything most toxic in the novel: the brutal coercion of unpaid labor and concomitant exploitation of the land; the instrumentalization of women as merely "adjunctive to the forwarding of Sutpen's] design" (1990a: 211) (or not, as the case may be); the repudiation of a son on the basis of his black blood (since filial blackness would render Sutpen's Oedipal victory a sham); and the degradation of poor whites like Wash Jones, who serves as the post-bellum repetition of Sutpen's initial condition. To approach the novel's mystery is to trace the "double plot" by which these catastrophes are perpetuated by being internalized in the form of psychic traumata, the retroactivated shock of which then leads to their compulsive and social repetition.

The second version of this process is in fact a commentary upon it. Toward the middle of *Absalom*, in one of the extensive sections narrated by Quentin and Shreve, Quentin thinks:

> *Maybe nothing ever happens once and is finished. Maybe happen is never once but like ripples maybe on water after the pebble sinks, the ripples moving on, spreading, the pool attached by a narrow umbilical water-cord to the next pool which the first pool feeds, has fed, did feed, let this second pool contain a different temperature of water, a different molecularity of having seen, felt, remembered, reflect in a different tone the infinite unchanging sky, it doesn't matter: that pebble's watery echo whose fall it did not even see moves across its surface too at the original ripple-space, to the old ineradicable rhythm. . . . (1990a: 210)*

The passage offers a kind of allegory of the double emplotment traced so far. It suggests that events or historical "happenings" are by their nature traumatic. Before they occur, the waters of the self are smooth, undisturbed, still. There is then a splash; a pebble breaks the water's surface. The sudden, punctual character of this rupture suggests the traumatic incursion of historical forces on the self's composure. More than this, the passage insists that the disturbance never "happens once and is finished." It produces "ripples" that radiate outward in concentric circles or ringlets, reverberating beyond their initial occurrence in time and location in space.

At the level of individual psyches, this process offers a variant of the doubling back in the previous passage: a given psychic event does not "happen once," but is quite literally constituted through its recursive repercussions. More generally, however, the passage proposes that history is itself a trauma that never ceases to happen; it suggests that historical events are disturbances that travel outward to affect even those who were neither geographically nor temporally present when the stone first disturbed the waters of consciousness. Faulkner emphasizes this latter fact by imagining a second "pool" that is at once radically distinct from the first one – with its own "molecularity of having seen, felt, remembered" – and nonetheless marked by the "watery echo" of the pebble's "fall" as it moves irresistibly "across its surface."

The similarities between this model of history and that in the previous passage are striking. Both emphasize the fundamental opacity of historical events – their status as mysterious shocks that befall us "too soon" and so require recursive attention and retrospective interpretation. Both propose that, because of this first fact, even the successful historical detective will not be spared the devastating effects of the processes he or she unveils. The second passage can even be read as a philosophical justification for this proposition. If history indeed happens in the way this passage describes, then the fact that Sutpen's interpretive unveiling of his prior humiliation leads him to affirm the system that humiliated him becomes as inevitable as a pool of water rippling at the drop of a stone: he is the passive recipient of a shock that he can repeat and transmit but never alter. The fact that *Quentin* is equally traumatized follows from this view as well. The current generation experiences the past as a concussive force that it *cannot* have felt directly. Precisely because of Quentin's belatedness – precisely because he is, metaphorically, that second "pool" of water that did not experience the "splash" of slavery and Civil War – he can only know those events as "ripples" whose cause will evade all efforts at recall. No amount of investigative insight will be sufficient to "work through" the kind of disequilibrium inherited in this fashion.

It is from here a very short step to seeing historical experience itself as intrinsically destructive. Faulkner's language suggests, for example, that by virtue of existing in historical time Quentin is not a "self" at all. He is instead "an empty hall echoing with sonorous defeated names; he was not a being, an entity, but a commonwealth. He was a barracks filled with stubborn back-looking ghosts still recovering, even forty-three years afterward, from the fever which had cured the disease" (1990a: 7). Here, the novel's subversion of the historian/detective's will-to-know leads it to posit the transmission of history as a form of catastrophic self-dispossession. Because history happens to us "too soon" to be assimilated – because all knowledge is the retrospective interpretation of a mystery that has always already befallen us – the present self is little more than an empty corridor inhabited by ghosts it can neither comprehend nor exorcise, and toward which its ambivalence is sufficiently profound to issue in suicide ("I dont hate [the South]! I dont! I don't!" [p. 303]). Slavery and racism may be bad, on this view, but by the time one possesses the knowledge necessary to making this observation, she or he has internalized wholesale the social system condemned by this judgment. The result is a suicidal self-loathing that leaves the system itself intact. The world as it is becomes an expression of "the old ineradicable rhythm" of history, inflicting itself on a consciousness that never stops deepening and extending the very wounds against which it rails.

Sanctuary

Some of *Sanctuary*'s differences from this pattern will be apparent to anyone familiar with the novel. The book is less historically ambitious than these others, less concerned with the kind of collective past that figures so centrally in *Absalom* and *Light in August*. Except for explorations of the gangster Popeye's personal past and of Horace Bembow's erotically charged history with his mother, sister, and stepdaughter, *Sanctuary*'s plot remains firmly rooted in the present. More particularly, it focuses on the meaning and effects of the three central crimes in that present: the murder of the halfwit Tommy; the corn-cob rape of Temple Drake, along with her subsequent abduction; and the lynching of Lee Goodwin after Temple's lie convicts him of the crimes against her. This focus on present crimes would seem to place *Sanctuary* closer to *Knight's Gambit* and *Intruder* than to Faulkner's other crime-related works. The similarity is confirmed by the presence in *Sanctuary* of a detective figure – Horace Bembow solves the book's crimes and defends Goodwin in court – who appears to promise at least some of the genre's conventional satisfactions.

Yet even a cursory reading will show that, at a second level, *Sanctuary* is closer in spirit to *Absalom, Absalom!* and *Light in August*. Nothing could be further from its aims than the meting out of conventional justice or the celebration of society's rituals for purifying itself of "evil." Far more extensively than even *Light in August*, it exposes the impurity of all identities and the consequent impossibility of separating a good "us" from a bad "them" that transgress against our rules. Like both *Light* and *Absalom*, moreover, *Sanctuary* breaks crime fiction's epistemological promise by insisting on what Faulkner calls here the "corruption . . . in looking" (1993: 129) – a corruption attendant on the bodily sense (vision) upon which all detection depends.

Sanctuary draws on the resources of the *roman noir* in order to explore this corruption. As indicated earlier, this is a subspecies of crime fiction that explores the contamination of the official social world by its perverse underside (the "underworld"). Its aim is often to implicate the detective in an "evil" he believes to be something separate and external to himself. What gives *Sanctuary* its extraordinary power is that it makes this critique coextensive with a thwarting of efforts at visual mastery while embedding both within the texture of its form. The novel employs an almost willfully "objective" style that contrasts starkly with the stream-of-consciousness elaborations in *Absalom, Absalom!* (It also contrasts with the originally unpublished, significantly more "modernist" version of *Sanctuary*[Polk 1981].) But this apparently objective style is designed to lure us into believing we can master the world as detectives would – with a vision that knows the difference between itself and the objects external to it – only to spill us into those objects and thwart the project of visual mastery. *Sanctuary*, in short, asks us to gaze upon evil in order to shatter the visual distance that conventionally allows us to know the difference between that evil and ourselves.

We can start to see this process in action by turning to the novel's opening sentences. "From beyond the screen of bushes which surrounded the spring, Popeye watched the man drinking. A faint path led from the road to the spring. Popeye watched the man . . . emerge from the path and kneel to drink from the spring" (1993: 3). This scene is staged as a visual transaction in which the novel's main gangster (Popeye) peers unseen at its protagonist (Horace). The visual transaction is in its turn extended by a third person style that invites the reader to engage in a kind of "metavision": we "watch" Popeye watching Horace, and do so from a position of apparently objective distance and visual clarity. But the scene is significantly more disturbing than this description implies. The reason for this lies not just in the ominous inequality the passage inscribes – one man watching another clearly implies the vulnerability of the second – but also in the way the action itself is almost literally impossible to focus. The first sentence asks us to look at Horace already drinking from the spring; the third sentence then *moves back in time*, tracing his movement as he emerges from the path and prepares to drink (see Toles 1982). Such a procedure makes it hard to know where or when the novel begins. It cannot suffice to choose one image and grant it a definitive chronological priority. For the first effect of this abrupt inversion is to ask us to see both moments at once: to hold the past instant "within" the present, in a manner expressive of a time so distressed as to wreck the ordered heterogeneity of sequence. Horace emerges from the path to drink water *while he is already drinking* from the spring. Temporal order in this way bleeds off in a present simultaneously captured and missed. The novel implicates our optical apprehension in a time that is, on the one hand, accelerated in the virtual concurrency of its images, and on the other, elongated into a practically undifferentiated and eternally monotonous "now."

Even more striking than this visual derangement is that *Sanctuary* links it, within the representation, to a problematics of oral expulsion. There are two central components to this link. First is the fact that in this opening Popeye repeatedly *spits into* the spring from which Horace drinks. Second, Horace's drinking is accompanied by a species of narcissistic gazing, but one that precisely fails to recover an adequate image of self. "In the spring the drinking man leaned his face to the broken and myriad reflection of his own drinking. When he rose up he saw among them the shattered reflection of Popeye's straw hat, though he had heard no sound . . ." (1993: 4). The passage is organized as a specular scene that disturbs the objective function of vision by putting the self in the externally visible place where the object should be. I mean by this that, when Horace looks out at the world before him, he discovers less an external object than a surface that appears to reflect his own image. The scene then proceeds to expose an alienation at the heart of this self-reflection. It supplants the reflected "self" with an other (Popeye), in order to propose that selfhood is grounded in visual identifications that take one away from "oneself." But beyond both of these – and this is most crucial – the passage insists that this specular drama *cannot even enable the self to find a coherence-in-self-alienation*. For when the alien image "is" Horace, it has already been torn into pieces ("broken reflection"). And what comes then to take its place is less a human figure at all than an anti-figural dispersion of matter that's incapable of reflecting back to him even the most fleeting or transient sense of coherence.

Popeye's spit turns out to be both substance and cause of the disturbance I am describing. By emphasizing that he spits into the very "mirror" that Horace confronts, the novel links the disturbance of vision to a confrontation between sight and oral expulsion. It shows how the latter ruins the former by returning the gazing self to a moment in which self and object are mired together in a presubjective, anti-visual, fluid-yet-fragmented materiality. We might even read this process back into the novel's opening sentences. It is as if Faulkner were suggesting the *cause* of the opening's optical opacity. It's as if he were telling us that the novel frustrates our visual movements toward its world as a way of recalling us to the condition that the novel's "detective" discovers in his encounter with Popeye. *Sanctuary*'s narrative mode is in this sense best described as visually ruinous. It solicits our gestures of ocular mastery through a kind of feigned, hard-boiled "objectivity" – but then blurs the visual clarity of its world through a process that *Sanctuary* links, in turn, to the eruption of oral expulsion in the visible. The effect of this is to insist upon the primal implication of self in its objects, of the observer in the "evil" that the novel will ask us to see – and so to resist any moral formulations that rely upon a commitment to the sanctity of the self's borders.

There is a competing tendency in the novel that asserts the self's sanctity with a misogynist vengeance. That tendency centers on the character of Temple – the Southern debutante whom Popeye kidnaps and rapes. In the wake of this ordeal, Faulkner tries to make her into the source of the book's evil. He does this in part by turning her from a victim into a voracious nymphomaniac and a woman who perjures herself in order to enforce a tidy solution to her story – a solution that most easily reintegrates her into her family while protecting it from scandal. More than this, however, the denigration of Temple takes place through the recoding *as feminine* of the being-in-the-other that the book has previously imagined as an ungendered condition. Faulkner performs this recoding by switching the metaphor from oral expulsion to menstrual blood – a fluid men experience as external, alien, and bad, at once visibly apprehensible and non-essential to their selves.

To demonstrate this argument in detail would take a good deal of space (see Forter 2000: 85–125). I want instead to close by looking at a moment where this gesture fails. The moment takes place when Horace returns from visiting Temple in the brothel. The visit has profoundly shaken him. Not only has he heard there, for the first time, the story of Temple's rape, but he has also found that the events have unleashed in her a depravity which seems to prove she wanted it all along. Contemplating this, Horace drinks a cup of coffee at the train station that "lays in a hot ball on his stomach" (1993: 221). "Three hours later, when he [gets] off [the train] at Jefferson, it [is] still there, unassimilated" (p. 221). He then returns home to muse despondently over his encounter with Temple while looking at a picture of his stepdaughter:

> [Suddenly] he knew what that sensation in his stomach meant. He put the photograph down hurriedly and went to the bathroom. He opened the door running and fumbled for the light. But he had not time to find it and he gave over and plunged forward and struck the lavatory and leaned upon his braced arms while the shucks set up a terrific uproar beneath her thighs. Lying with her head lifted slightly . . . she watched something black and furious go roaring out of her pale body. She was bound naked on her back on a flat car moving at speed through a black tunnel. . . . Far beneath her she could hear the faint, furious uproar of the shucks. (pp. 221–3)

This passage charts with a disturbing difference the gesture of oral repudiation that we observed in *Light in August*. It again describes the encounter with femininity as the imbibing of something alien and "bad." To hear Temple's story is, implicitly, to internalize the inassimilable "ball" that Horace has in his stomach, and which he then throws up in an effort to assert the difference between a "good" (masculine) inside and a "bad" (feminine) outside. But where Joe Christmas's act of ejection at least provisionally succeeds, here the expulsion is accompanied by visual fantasies that indicate the depth of its failure. The pronominal shift within the third sentence indicates the breakdown: "*he* had not time to find [the light] and *he* gave over and . . . struck the lavatory and leaned upon *his* braced arms while the shucks set up a terrific uproar beneath *her* thighs." The "her" is clearly meant to be Temple, who spends the night just prior to her rape on a mattress filled with corn shucks. And the remainder of the fantasy indicates the extent to which Horace is unable to distinguish himself from the woman who represents "evil" to him.

The coffee that pours out of him is thus doubled by the "something black [that goes] roaring out of her pale body." Horace in this way *becomes* the thing he denies by spitting up. He vomits the "evil" imbibed from Temple only to imagine her spewing forth a substance akin to his own. This correlation of male mouth and female orifice signals a kind of identificatory confusion, a blurring of psychic meanings and borders, precisely at the moment when Horace is attempting to reassert those borders. Nor is it accidental that Faulkner encodes this breakdown in a resolutely visual fantasy. It is as if he were highlighting the irredeemable contamination by vomit of the sense upon which successful detection depends. The effort to see the world, and so to master its (feminine) evil as an external, non-intrusive fact, is thwarted by the internalization of feminine evil — an internalization that vomiting fails to undo, since it is accompanied by hallucinations in which the male self has become indistinguishable from the female object-to-be-mastered.

Such a portrayal reflects a collapse of the detecting function more devastating than that suggested by André Malraux's influential comment: "*Sanctuary* is the intrusion of Greek tragedy into the detective story" (Malraux 1966: 274). The novel remains completely unleavened by even those forms of tragic "enlightenment" conventionally found in Greek drama. The darkness of its vision should not, however, blind us to its value. *Sanctuary*'s greatest strength lies in its insistence that male readers participate in these identificatory collapses — not, perhaps, as something pleasurable, but as the necessarily disintegrative experience of a masculinity beginning to avow what it habitually expels, hates — and calls woman.

REFERENCES AND FURTHER READING

Auden, W. H. (1980). The Guilty Vicarage. In R. W. Winks (ed.). *Detective Fiction: A Collection of Critical Essays* (pp. 15–24). Englewood Cliffs, NJ: Prentice Hall. (Original pub. 1948.)

Cawelti, J. G. (1976). *Adventure, Mystery, and Romance: Formula Stories as Art and Popular Culture*. Chicago: University of Chicago Press.

Cawelti, J. G. (1991). Faulkner and the Detective Story's Double Plot. *Clues: A Journal of Detection*, 12(2): 1–15.

Duvall, J. N. (1987). Murder and Communities: Ideology in and around *Light in August*. *Novel: A Forum on Fiction*, 20(2): 101–22.

Faulkner, W. (1966). *The Wild Palms*. New York: Vintage. (Original pub. 1939.)

Faulkner, W. (1978). *Knight's Gambit*. New York: Vintage. (Original pub. 1949.)

Faulkner, W. (1990a). *Absalom, Absalom!* New York, Vintage International. (Original pub. 1936.)

Faulkner, W. (1990b). *Light in August*. New York: Vintage International. (Original pub. 1932.)

Faulkner, W. (1991). *Intruder in the Dust*. New York: Vintage International. (Original pub. 1948.)

Faulkner, W. (1993). *Sanctuary*. New York: Vintage International. (Original pub. 1931.)

Forter, G. (2000). *Murdering Masculinities: Fantasies of Gender and Violence in the American Crime Novel*. New York: New York University Press.

Freud, S. (1989). *Beyond the Pleasure Principle* (trans. and ed. J. Strachey). New York: Norton. (Original pub. 1920.)

Gidley, M. (1973). Elements of the Detective Story in William Faulkner's Fiction. *Journal of Popular Culture*, 7: 97–128.

Hilfer, T. (1990). *The Crime Novel: A Deviant Genre*. Austin, TX: University of Texas Press.

Holman, C. H. (1971). *Absalom, Absalom!*: The Historian as Detective. *Sewanee Review*, 79: 542–53.

Irwin, J. T. (2002). *Knight's Gambit*: Poe, Faulkner, and the Tradition of the Detective Story. In L. Wagner-Martin (ed.). *William Faulkner: Six Decades of Criticism* (pp. 355–75). East Lansing: Michigan State University Press. (Original pub. 1990.)

Malraux, A. (1966). A Preface for Faulkner's *Sanctuary*. In R. P. Warren (ed.). *Faulkner: A Collection of Essays* (pp. 272–4). Englewood Cliffs, NJ: Prentice Hall. (Original pub. 1933.)

Polk, N. (ed.) (1981). *Sanctuary: The Original Text*. New York: Random House.

Polk, N. (2003). Faulkner and Crime Fiction. *Philological Review*, 29(1): 1–26.

Todorov, T. (1977). The Typology of Detective Fiction. In R. Howard (trans.). *The Poetics of Prose* (pp. 42–52). Oxford: Blackwell.

Toles, G. (1982). The Space Between: A Study of Faulkner's *Sanctuary*. In J. D. Canfield (ed.). *Twentieth-Century Interpretations of* Sanctuary: *A Collection of Critical Essays* (pp. 120–8). Englewood Cliffs, NJ: Prentice Hall.

Wilson, A. J. (1994). The Corruption in Looking: William Faulkner's *Sanctuary* as a Detective Novel. *Mississippi Quarterly*, 47(3): 441–60.

23
William Faulkner's Short Stories

Hans H. Skei

William Faulkner often complained that short story writing took time and energy away from work on his novels, yet there is little doubt that he regarded the short story highly, ranking it second only to poetry. At times he thought of himself as a failed poet, and perhaps also as a failed short story writer, but he also saw that the novel offered opportunities for the reuse of short stories, slightly revised and integrated in longer narratives. This practice could result in "episodic" or loosely joined novels, but brief episodes and anecdotes also added strength to his novels. Faulkner may not have thought in terms of novel-length units, so many of his novels seem to have originated in an episode or a central image, often first written as a short story, which might in some cases later be abandoned for the longer form. This does not mean that Faulkner was not primarily a novelist, yet his achievement in the short story genre is one of the most impressive in American literature of the twentieth century. His short stories are in some cases so closely related to his novels that a study of how stories function when they are integrated in novels such as *The Hamlet* (1940) is perhaps even more revealing than to see how he revised a series of related stories to create what some critics call a short story cycle, but which reads surprisingly like a well-made novel (e.g. *The Unvanquished* [1938]).

In Faulkner's literary practice – a more revealing commentary on his literary ambitions than comments he gave late in his career – the novel was always the preferred genre, and he felt that he wasted time for novel writing when he had to write short stories for money. Many of his short stories would probably not have been written were it not for the market and the money. On the other hand, he might have written more "literary" stories of high merit had he not had the novelistic tendency to sacrifice stories, anecdotes, fragments, and drafts and subsume them in longer narratives that were published as novels. Faulkner had an almost intuitive understanding of the novel's capacity to include all sorts of narrative units, its ability to integrate and transform and combine episodes and incidents into the larger framework of its dialogic structure. Yet one should not exaggerate the novelistic tendency in Faulkner's short fiction. Most of his short stories do not in any significant way relate to or depend on his novels; they are autonomous and independent short stories in their own right. Yet so many of his stories are so closely interlinked with novels that any study of his short fiction must include a discussion of his use and reuse of material in short story cycles and novels. In some cases there is even a close relationship between "non-episodic" novels and short stories (Millgate 1997), not only because Faulkner felt free to include previously published stories in a novel, but also because he discovered in and through his writing of a story what would become the central imagery and tragic theme of great novels such as *The Sound and the Fury* (1929) and *Absalom, Absalom!* (1936).

Faulkner's best short stories are outstanding. "Barn Burning," "Red Leaves" and "That Evening Sun" are masterpieces in the genre. Yet his short story writing is uneven; most stories are merely competent, and a few are downright bad. Despite the uneven quality of the over 100 stories he wrote, there are more than enough of them to secure him a place as a major writer in the genre. Faulkner's lifelong interest, as he once stated in a discussion at the University of Virginia, was "primarily in people, in man in conflict with himself, with his fellow man, or with his time and place, his environment" (Gwynn and Blotner 1959: 19). To render man in his ageless struggle and by arresting motion for a moment, Faulkner developed his own storytelling techniques, of which the use of frozen tableaux is but one among the many and varied approaches he uses to get a story told. He was not always successful, but in most cases he managed to keep the precarious balance between content and presentation. He was always willing and even eager to revise stories or rewrite them completely, or rethink the whole narrative structure if a story were to be reused in a new context. Forty years of relentless struggle with elusive words not only gave us the novelist of genius, but also led to the creation of one of the most impressive bodies of short fiction in American literature.

In many of his novels Faulkner was innovative and experimental, whereas his contribution to the short story form is less significant. Malcolm Cowley was surely wrong when he claimed that Faulkner was not primarily a novelist, but may be closer to a fair judgment when he also claimed that Faulkner was "perhaps most consistently at his best in his short stories" (Cowley 1946: 18). Compared to his great novels the short stories may appear less impressive; compared to most other short story writers, though, Faulkner is a major practitioner of the form. He referred to Chekhov and the good stories he wrote, and one should not overlook Sherwood Anderson's decisive influence on the young man who struggled to become a writer. Anderson's *Winesburg, Ohio* (1919) must be deemed crucial in helping Faulkner discover his "region" and find his material. This short story cycle most certainly also inspired Faulkner to join stories together in cycles that, through substantial revision, really became novels. Faulkner's stories also rely on his familiarity with Southwestern humor and with the oral storytelling tradition in the South, and the stories are almost invariably about people from his own region, although we may encounter characters with no Southern connection in stories set outside of his fictional kingdom of Yoknapatawpha. Faulkner's stories did not achieve fame and set a standard like the stories of Hemingway, and in the early 1930s when he published short stories most frequently, his short stories mattered little compared to those by Hemingway and Scott Fitzgerald. Great Southern short story writers Eudora Welty and

Flannery O'Connor published much of their work when Faulkner was still active, and he most certainly was an inspiration for them if not a direct influence. Faulkner's short story achievement has little by little got the credit it deserves, even if this may well be seen as a by-product of an enormous output of scholarship primarily devoted to his novels.

A good many of Faulkner's short stories may be regarded as a concentration of material better suited for novels. But condensation and concentration are important characteristics of the short story, and Faulkner's material was abundantly rich. The immense array of strange local characters, hunting stories, the Southern legacy of a lost cause, slavery, and aristocratic families all seemed to require the longer form. Thus stories might grow into novels, or related stories might be combined into unified works of greater length; but short stories could also remain self-contained and independent, even when they gained support from other stories and novels in the larger framework of the Yoknapatawpha fiction.

In his short fiction Faulkner writes about the country and his village, about the South, and about the people living there. This includes the Indians who originally owned the land, the blacks who slave on it, and the poor whites who barely eke out a living, as well as the well-to-do businessmen and plantation owners. Race is one of his subjects; war is another; and love and sex may well be said to be a third, although often linked with violence and even brutal death. In a more general sense, and in accordance with the author's reiterated statements, his short stories deal with love, compassion, pride, pity, and sacrifice. They do this successfully because they are rooted in a certain time and place, and thus the historical dimension must be taken into consideration. Broadly speaking the stories are placed in three major periods: (1) the remote past, which includes the early days of the Indian tribes, the Civil War, and the undisturbed and apparently changeless rural parts of Yoknapatawpha; (2) the recent past – World War I and the years immediately following it; and (3) the immediate past – Yoknapatawpha and the world beyond it in the 1920s, 1930s, and 1940s.

Early Sketches and Stories: The New Orleans period

Faulkner published a brief prose sketch called "Landing in Luck" in the *Mississippian*, the university's student paper, on November 26, 1919. It draws on Faulkner's experience during aviation training in Toronto in 1918 and tells about a young cadet's first solo flight. It displays some technical skill and has some interest as the author's first sketch about flyers and flying.

The second prose sketch to be published, "The Hill" (*Mississippian*, 1922), has been hailed by critics as Faulkner's most important early short story. It shows an author in complete control of his limited material and foreshadows many narrative techniques and themes in Faulkner's later fiction. A nameless figure climbs a hill after a day of hard work and remains immobile there, till he slowly descends again. Through a detailed description of the view from the hilltop the story gives a succinct picture of man in his struggles and dreams.

In the early 1920s Faulkner also wrote a few intricate and overworked stories ("Moonlight," "Love," "Adolescence") whose only interest is that they foreshadow his later use of local backgrounds and exploit themes he would return to some years later. He also wrote an expanded version of "The Hill," with dreams of a more sexual nature than in the first text – "Nympholepsy." These stories were first published in the 1960s and 1970s. Accordingly, Faulkner's only moderate and limited success with short fictional texts before 1930 was with the sketches he wrote in New Orleans in 1925. These sketches, influenced by Sherwood Anderson and Faulkner's close contact with the literary bohemia of New Orleans at that time, gave Faulkner useful practical experience in the handling of narrative and the presentation of character. The sketches are uneven, and we see the hand of the uncertain apprentice in them. Faulkner seems to be most interested in character, and he presents his characters from shifting perspectives, often through a character-narrator. Most of the sketches he published in 1925 appeared in the Sunday magazine section of the *New Orleans Times-Picayune*. A number of completed sketches that survived in typescript were not published till the 1970s.

Few of the New Orleans sketches are extended narratives, although "The Liar" and "Yo Ho and Two Bottles of Rum" may be considered short stories. The former is rooted in the backwoods country of Yoknapatawpha; the latter has an international setting and cast of characters. The texts point to two distinctly different types of stories that Faulkner would write in the near future.

Faulkner's experimentation in the New Orleans period seldom went further than an imitation of Joseph Conrad and Sherwood Anderson, but the variety of narrative methods anticipates the technical brilliance of *The Sound and the Fury*. These sketches may be said to emphasize the individual's alienation from a natural world but also his search for communal ties, participation, and sharing.

In 1926 Faulkner's first novel, *Soldiers' Pay*, was published, and the author was pursuing a number of writing ideas in many directions – poetry, short stories, and novels. Most of the short story attempts from these years were later revised and appeared in print only after 1930. One story that found its final form in 1926 was *Mayday*, an allegorical tale about Sir Galwyn, who travels through life accompanied by the shadowy figures of Hunger and Pain and who finally finds peace in death by water. The hand-lettered, illustrated, and beautifully bound booklet that Faulkner put together in 1926 was not meant for publication, however, and was not published until 1976. Probably the best and certainly the most ambitious story written in this period of Faulkner's career, "Father Abraham" (probably written late 1926) is the germ of the Snopes trilogy and Faulkner's first attempt with material that he would return to over and over again in the years ahead, till, in 1940, he brought the many loose ends together in *The Hamlet*. "Father Abraham" shows that the basic outline of the whole trilogy was there at a very early point, since Flem's position as a Jefferson banker is described briefly before the story moves backwards to its central concern: the auction of the spotted horses.

There is no straight or continuous line of development or growth in Faulkner's short fiction from the 1920s. If we find signs of talent and promises of a great future career in these writings, this is so because we always construct the early career in retrospect. The promises we find in the early career are only there because Faulkner later kept them, and in the field of short story writing he would reach mastery almost as abruptly and inexplicably as he did in his novels. It is perhaps not surprising, but it is revealing, that Faulkner wrote a high number of his very best stories during the same years of intensive work that produced *The Sound and the Fury*, *As I Lay Dying* (1930), *Sanctuary* (1931), and *Light in August* (1932).

Short Story Writing For a Living: Faulkner's First Short Story Collection

Faulkner painted a bleak picture of the world as a wasteland in many of the stories that were originally written in 1926 and 1927. These stories demonstrate the outrage of a potential believer, and the criticism of a stifling social life is harsh. Faulkner's narrators lament the loss of traditional values and criticize the materialistic, ephemeral values that replace them. When Faulkner had finished the typescript of *The Sound and the Fury* (in October 1928), he began his first sustained effort to market his short stories. The record of his endeavors is a short story sending schedule that he kept, as well as his correspondence with editors and agents. On January 20, 1930, he could record his first sale to a national magazine: *Forum* had bought "A Rose for Emily" (published in April 1930), and this obviously encouraged him to continue his short story writing for the profitable American magazine market of the 1930s. From the time of the acceptance of "A Rose for Emily" till he began work on *Light in August* in August 1931, Faulkner submitted more than 20 different stories to various magazines and made more than 70 submissions and resubmissions during this period. This productivity and the acceptance of stories by the better-paying magazines enabled Faulkner to buy Rowan Oak in April, 1930; the family moved there in June. But this in its turn led to a chronic shortage of money, and in May, 1932, Faulkner had to leave for Hollywood, to find a steady income. His short story writing then came to a sudden halt, and only for brief intervals later in his career would he concentrate on short story writing, never with more than moderate success.

The more than 40 short stories that Faulkner wrote in the late 1920s and early 1930s are his most autonomous and "pure" short stories. With a few exceptions they do not stand in any close relationship to his novels, and only a few were reused in novels. Some of the stories had different titles in their original versions, and some were so much revised as to become virtually new stories before they were published. Some stories, obviously, never saw publication. Twenty-one new stories seem to have been written in 1930. In 1931 five new stories were sent out and three more stories, never submitted to magazines, appeared in his first short story collection, *These 13*. Only two stories can be dated to 1932.

A number of recurrent patterns can be found in the stories from this period. Characters are exposed to untenable situations, if they simply do not want to adjust to a changing world. The implied author – or the text as a whole – always seems to sympathize with the losers and the loners who fight losing battles against a non-permissive society. Progress is shown as a threat against human values, and man's misuse of man for selfish ends is part of a recurrent motif in most of the stories from the major years, as is man's destruction of nature, understood as physical nature as well as the natural qualities in man. Faulkner did not always think highly of individual man, but his belief in mankind seems to have grown stronger over the years. And among the basic qualities which are required for man to live peacefully in an ordered and civilized society we find the capacity for endurance, love, compassion, and sharing to which the stories always return.

Faulkner's narrative method varies much in the short stories from this period. He had no privileged approach, but used all conceivable strategies in order to get a story told. He maneuvers first and third person with great ease, so that the distance from characters and events becomes more of a question of attitude and language than of technical skill, although the narrator (especially when we have a personal narrator, perhaps even a child narrator) always commands our attention and interest. Faulkner's use of the first person plural narrator, representing a community conscience or consensus, is typical for the many stories located in Jefferson, where the social control is very rigid. The village stories differ considerably from those placed in the countryside, not least because of the stronger group pressure and the role expectations in the small town.

During the spring of 1931 Faulkner put together his first short story collection. He then had some 40 stories from which to choose. One can only guess his motives for selecting the 13 stories he included in the book, but the resulting volume presents a rather coherent and convincing picture of the world as wasteland filled with dust and dreams, hopes and frustrations, stasis and death.

In the first of the three sections of *These 13* we find four stories from World War I. In the second section Faulkner grouped together six stories from village and country in Yoknapatawpha, and here we find a number of his very best stories: "Red Leaves," "A Rose for Emily," "That Evening Sun," and "Dry September." The final section includes three stories about Americans abroad and present experiences far removed from Yoknapatawpha. Faulkner took great care in structuring this collection to achieve a greater unity than the individual stories would seem to provide.

"Victory" opens the collection. With its wide scope and long time span, it deals with World War I and its aftermath. A God-fearing young Scot, Alec Gray, is one of the many losers in the years of unemployment after the war. He has risen to the officer class through bravery, but his downfall after the war is as rapid as his rise. The generalizations in the other World War I stories, about the sad and undeserved fate of the soldiers who served their countries, are made concrete in the description of Gray's destiny. "Victory" is in some respects Faulkner's most successful World War I story, not the least because it is a long story and shows a development over time. The other World War I stories combine to give an almost painful image of loss and decay, and of the futility and waste of war. Rather vague "lost generation" sentiments slip into these stories. The pilots and soldiers who survived the war are all dead now, because they have adjusted to a quiet, bourgeois life. The dreams of bravery and glory could only be realized by dying a hero's death. But the terrors of war, depicted in other stories, show what kind of reality the soldiers' complaints must be viewed against. The final impression of these stories is one of darkness and despair.

"Red Leaves" is placed first in the second section of the collection. It is a story about the Indians of Yoknapatawpha County, and is one of Faulkner's best. It is structured around a burial ritual, which holds that the body servant of the dead Indian chief must die because tradition requires it. The black servant runs away, however, and must be hunted down before the corpse of the chief starts decomposing. "Red Leaves" is followed by "A Rose for Emily," Faulkner's most widely read, criticized, and anthologized short story. It begins with the announcement of the death of Miss Emily Grierson, who has lived so long she has become an anachronism. A "we" narrator recounts Emily's life of loneliness and poverty because her father drove away her suitors and little was left for her when he died. Critics have found in "A Rose for Emily" a description of a whole society that lived with a dead but unburied past, and much energy has been expended in attempts to establish the chronology of events in the story. "A Rose for Emily" is not Faulkner's best story, but it may well be regarded as the central one in his short story career.

Quentin Compson is the unreliable narrator of the second Indian story in *These 13*, "A Justice." He is an innocent child and does not grasp what his story is really about. But this story, which shows a development over a long period, establishes important links between time past and time present in Yoknapatawpha.

"A Justice" is followed by "Hair," the weakest story in the collection. Quentin takes over the narration again in the next story, "That Evening Sun," and the tragedy inherent in the story is seldom surpassed in Faulkner's short fiction. One of the most inexhaustible of Faulkner's short stories, and a favorite among critics, "That Evening Sun" tells about the black servant Nancy and her irrational fear of being killed by her husband, Jesus. The white Compson household is juxtaposed with Nancy and her world, and Quentin tells the story some 15 years after the events took place. By implication, "That Evening Sun" becomes a story about race but also the general human plight: despair, guilt, and lack of love.

"Dry September," another of Faulkner's best stories, is classical in its tragic intensity and described as a ritualistic acting out of the scapegoat pattern to achieve redemption. The story is a superb example of how the description of landscape and climate can be used to set and amplify tone. After many rainless days the men in town are restless, and Minnie Cooper, barren and dry in her empty life, initiates the action when she accuses a black man of rape.

The final group of stories is enigmatic. The three stories are experimental departures from the rest of the volume. "Mistral" may foreshadow narrative techniques Faulkner would use later on, whereas "Divorce in Naples," with its grim humor and rich use of similes and metaphors in pure, lyrical passages, reminds us of Faulkner as a failed poet. "Carcassonne" is perhaps the most abstract of Faulkner's stories, with a protagonist who endures all sufferings because he has a dream of performing something, of negating death's ultimate effect, which is to make one lie still. "Carcassonne" also reflects Faulkner's preoccupation with the agony and fear an artist has to face in order to create.

Doctor Martino and Other Stories: Miscellaneous Stories

After 1932 Faulkner's writing of short stories declined drastically. But he already had more than enough stories for a new volume, *Doctor Martino and Other Stories* (1934), which has no internal organization, and the stories of which accordingly do not form any discernible pattern.

There is a clear shift from the preoccupation with war, wilderness, and townspeople in *These 13* to a focus on sex, death, and loss in *Doctor Martino*. The title story presents a love triangle of a peculiar kind, and usurpation and manipulation for private ends create an emotional parasitism. Even if all the stories in *Doctor Martino* are competent, only "Wash," "A Mountain Victory," and "The Hound" show Faulkner at his best. "Wash" is a forceful narrative of almost apocalyptic horror, reused by Faulkner in *Absalom, Absalom!* (1936). "A Mountain Victory" is set in the years after the Civil War, like "Wash." Here one sees the tragic development of a conflict that arises suddenly and inevitably from what should have been a normal encounter between strangers. The movement toward disaster is implacable, and brutal death comes at the end. A deeply felt humanity pervades this story, which should not be considered just another tale about the Civil War and its effects on people.

Doctor Martino includes a couple of stories set in "the village" area of Yoknapatawpha, and we also find stories of love and death, of stunt flying and wing walking, as well as full-fledged World War I stories. "Turn About" differs from earlier such stories in being set in England and in its depiction of an unusual brand of courage. The volume also includes stories that were later reused for totally different purposes: "The Hound" was reused in *The Hamlet*, although it was not originally a Snopes story. "Smoke" is Faulkner's first story of detection, but it is decidedly one of the weakest of his mystery stories, although it was later allowed to open his 1949 collection of detective stories, *Knight's Gambit*.

The final three stories in *Doctor Martino* are all strange, so-called "Beyond" stories: tales of the supernatural or the fantastic. The story titled "Beyond" was the only one of these that found periodical publication; "Black Music" and "The Leg" are the other two.

A number of stories from the 1930s were later revised and integrated in the first Snopes volume, *The Hamlet*. Faulkner maintained that this book was "incepted as a novel. When I began it, it produced Spotted Horses, went no further. About two years later suddenly I had THE HOUND, then JAMSHYD'S COURTYARD" (Cowley 1966: 196). As we have seen, "Father Abraham" was Faulkner's first and very early attempt at the Snopes material, and some of the other stories may indeed have been written because "Spotted Horses," published in 1931, was praised by editors and because Faulkner here created a character (Suratt, later Ratliff) he wanted to use again. "The Hound" was not a Snopes story, and had to be considerably revised to become an integrated and very central part of "The Long Summer" section in *The Hamlet*. The same is true for "Fool About a Horse" (published in 1936), which was changed to become a Snopes story, without really being integrated fully into the novel. "Lizards in Jamshyd's

Courtyard" was originally a Snopes story and easily found its place in *The Hamlet*. The intricate relationship between short stories and their use in this novel that some critics have called episodic or loosely connected exemplifies the flexibility both of the novel as a form and of Faulkner's creative genius. He reused previously published stories, but he also wrote a new novel in which the stories were given new functions.

A number of autonomous stories from this period were later collected in *Collected Stories* (1950). Two Snopes stories in this collection – "Centaur in Brass" and "Mule in the Yard" – were even reused later in the second Snopes volume, *The Town* (1957). Some stories from these years had their first book appearance in *Uncollected Stories* (1979). This is true for "Thrift," published in the *Saturday Evening Post* in 1930, a humorous World War I story about a proverbial Scotsman who makes a profit from his participation in somebody else's war. This was the first Faulkner story in the *Post* and hence a first encounter with this writer for thousands of readers, yet he seems to have consigned this story to oblivion. His third Indian story, "Lo!" (1934), went into *Collected Stories*, however, as did another story in the humorous vein, "A Bear Hunt," from the same year. And when Faulkner finally sat down and "pulled together" his Snopes material for *The Hamlet* in 1938, it yielded "Barn Burning," published in 1939. Many critics and readers hold this to be Faulkner's best short story. It was originally written as the opening chapter of *The Hamlet*, but excised from the typescript; only scattered minor fragments of the story can be found in the book. "Barn Burning" draws its interest, quality, and aura of deep personal suffering from its relationship with *The Hamlet*, which is a marvelous novel about the Snopeses' incursion into Yoknapatawpha and about how myths are created. Yet it is also a superb story in its own right. Faulkner was capable of fusing so many elements in this story because of his lasting interest in the Snopeses and because of the longer work in progress.

With a few exceptions Faulkner's best short stories, and many of his good stories, were written in the early 1930s. More than before or after, they are short stories in their own right: conceived, executed, and published as such. Only in a few instances can they be seen as by-products of Faulkner's novels. The richness and diversity of themes and techniques were never to be surpassed in the years to come.

The stories Faulkner wrote from 1933 until his last attempt to write short stories for a living in 1942 fall, roughly, into four major categories: miscellaneous stories, some reused in novels, others collected in *Collected Stories*, and others not collected till the publication of *Uncollected Stories*. These stories have been presented above. The second category comprises stories that were later considerably revised and used in *The Unvanquished*, and the stories for *Go Down, Moses* (1942) form a third group. Finally, there are the detective stories collected in *Knight's Gambit*, most of which were written before 1940.

Short Story Cycles or Novels?

In 1934 Faulkner also wrote the first six stories in *The Unvanquished* series, and in December 1935 the first germ of *Go Down, Moses* was seen in the short story "Lion." In

1939, 1940, and 1941 Faulkner wrote most of the short stories he later revised for use in *Go Down, Moses,* and he also wrote four Gavin Stevens detective stories in this period. During some hectic months from spring to autumn 1934, the first six "Bayard-Ringo" stories were written: "Ambuscade," "Retreat," "Raid," "The Unvanquished" (later titled "Riposte in Tertio"), "Vendée," and "Skirmish at Sartoris" (the Drusilla story). A seventh story, "An Odor of Verbena," was written in order to complete and finish the book, but Faulkner also made unsuccessful attempts to sell it as a short story. For *The Unvanquished* Faulkner had to revise the stories, some of them substantially. He felt that he sacrificed more important work by writing his romanticized tales about heroic Southern action during the Civil War, but when he undertook the work of revising and transforming the stories into a unified book, more of his genuine concerns were included. In his revision work Faulkner carefully brought the thematic content of the earliest stories in line with the serious direction of the later stories, adding a more mature narrator who could give a more clearly retrospective view of the incidents and cruelties of war. The issue of race became more significant, and Faulkner proved that he could make a unified book out of short fiction he had described as trash. *The Unvanquished* is certainly not a mere collection of short stories, but the question is whether it should be called a short story cycle or a novel. Critical consensus seems to be that the book undoubtedly is a novel, but its genesis indicates that if any of Faulkner's books should benefit from an understanding of it as a cycle of stories (or a short story composite), it would be *The Unvanquished.*

Forrest L. Ingram claimed that he discovered a new literary genre, the short story cycle, in his 1971 book *Representative Short Story Cycles of the Twentieth Century.* Ingram discusses the balance that must be sought between the individuality of each story and the demands of the larger unit, and points to patterns of recurrence and of development, which operate concurrently. *The Unvanquished* is for him a superb example of a short story cycle. His essentialist definitions become rather rigid and normative, and if unifying elements are found everywhere, the book in question might as well be called a novel. The search for unity, and the concept of unity as having numerous unifying factors, seem to have been basic also to Susan Garland Mann in her *The Short Story Cycle: A Genre Companion and Reference Guide* from 1989, whereas later theories have tried to be more relational, more open to the great possibilities of variety and renewal that the form offers. Robert Luscher states that a short story sequence – he prefers this term because the reader's experience of these books is sequential – "should be viewed, not as failed novels, but as unique hybrids that combine two distinct reading pleasures: the patterned closure of individual stories and the discovery of larger unifying strategies that transcend the apparent gaps between stories" (Luscher 1989: 150). He also lists a number of simple textual strategies – a title, preface, an epigraph, or framing stories – and "more organic unities such as common narrators, characters, images, locale, and themes" (1989: 150). Rolf Lundén in his 1999 study, *The United Stories of America,* insists on the open nature of the short story composite, so that the inherent tension between discontinuity and fragmentation on the one hand and the totalizing demands of the larger book on the other informs his reading. The search for unifying elements has made critics overlook contradictions, lacunae, silences and all the narrative strategies of disruption, which in Lundén's view are basic to the form (Lundén 1999). There is little doubt that an awareness of the inherent tension between fragmentation and continuity will enrich our readings of *The Unvanquished* as well as of *Go Down, Moses*, and if we expect from the novel great unity and continuity, the "new genre" may be of help in our analysis since it makes us aware of contending forces in a narrative.

The stories for *Go Down, Moses* were all written over a relatively short span of time, with almost no other short story activity intervening. One may thus say that this continuous process resembles the writing of a novel, and it is commonplace today that *Go Down, Moses* is a novel and not a collection of short stories, although, by some editorial mistake, it was originally published as *Go Down, Moses and Other Stories*. Yet some critics still insist that *Go Down, Moses* must be regarded not only as a loosely connected novel, but as a short story cycle (Lundén 1999: 137–45). And the reason for this is one short story or one book chapter, "Pantaloon in Black," which at first sight seems to have little if anything to do with the rest of the book. Also, what comes before this story might be considered one continuous long story, and what follows after "Pantaloon in Black" may be seen as another and very different long story. Thus "Pantaloon in Black" would function as a transitional story, linking together the two major parts of the book – the story of Lucas Beauchamp and the story of Isaac McCaslin. Faulkner revised the short stories that went into *Go Down, Moses* considerably, and he could obviously have added unifying elements that would have integrated the "fringe story" "Pantaloon in Black" better. He did not, and *Go Down, Moses* is a greater challenge – and a better case – for theorists of the short story cycle than *The Unvanquished*. Individual stories that went into the book – "Pantaloon in Black" and "Delta Autumn" – are among Faulkner's best, as is of course "The Bear," which does not have a short story version comparable to the book chapter.

Go Down, Moses is one of Faulkner's most convincing artistic creations, a unified volume with tremendous emotional impact, far greater than that of any of the individual stories, though it is possible to discuss them independently. "Was" is the opening section of *Go Down, Moses*, while three more stories in extensively revised form make up the second section, "The Fire and the Hearth." It focuses on the scheming and cheating Lucas Beauchamp, and may appear at first to be a light, comic collection of anecdotes. Lucas and his wife, Molly, appear as stereotyped blacks, but little by little people as well as tone are modified and softened. The central symbol of the fire burning on the hearth is strengthened, and Faulkner barely avoids melancholy and pathos in the description of the old woman's plight. Molly becomes the embodiment of all the virtues cherished in her society.

"Pantaloon in Black" then intervenes between what may be regarded as the two main parts of the book, and in the second part ("The Old People," "The Bear," and "Delta Autumn") Isaac (Ike) becomes the central character. "The Old People" to an unusual degree provides links with the past of Yoknapatawpha and with other stories. The book chapter gives much space to the formative years in Ike's development, to explain where he got his knowledge of "the old people" and his deep respect for the untamed wilderness. Sam Fathers, an Indian of mixed ancestry, has been Ike's substitute father and mentor. Ike's renunciation of his inheritance later in life and most of his subsequent behavior may be considered as acts of sacrifice and expiation, but they may also be viewed as acts of weakness and escape.

Most of the elements in the believable fictional character Isaac McCaslin are found in "The Bear." The book version is often anthologized, frequently without the long fourth part (a practice begun by Malcolm Cowley in his *Portable Faulkner* [1946]). "The Bear" is one of the great hunting stories in world literature and one of the truly great stories in Faulkner's career.

Ike's three-part saga ends with "Delta Autumn," set in a wilderness that is slowly being destroyed by civilization. "Delta Autumn" is a moving and penetrating story. Human beings in conflict with nature and with themselves are presented in a web of ideas and thoughts about race, history, morality, and love.

The story "Go Down, Moses" tells about Molly Beauchamp's struggle to get her dead grandson back home to be buried where he belongs. It opens onto a larger world beyond the plantation, beyond Yoknapatawpha, and is thus a fitting conclusion to *Go Down, Moses*, whether seen as a novel or as a cycle of stories.

Late Stories: *Knight's Gambit, Collected Stories*

In "Smoke," written circa 1930, Faulkner created Gavin Stevens, a lawyer and detective with resources that could be put to use in the investigation of mysteries within the borders of Yoknapatawpha County. The second whodunit, "Monk," was not written till 1937. In this story Gavin is only in the background, uncovering the truth about the deception of Monk by a fellow convict in prison. Gavin functions much more prominently as a detective in "Hand Upon the Waters" (1939), perhaps because he shares so much with the story's central character, Louis Grenier (Lonnie Grinnup). Gavin and Lonnie are the only surviving offspring of the three original founding fathers of the county. Young Chick Mallison works with his Uncle Gavin in solving some crimes, and in "Tomorrow" (1940) the ingenious detection leads to insights into human nature that teach Chick a moral lesson. "An Error in Chemistry," written in 1940, was published in the June, 1946, issue of *Ellery Queen's Mystery Magazine*, having won second prize in a competition. The last of Faulkner's detective stories, "Knight's Gambit," was written in 1942. Unable to sell the story, Faulkner expanded it into a novella with the same title, to make his collection of detective fiction large enough for publication in book form in 1949. The short, early version has never been published.

Knight's Gambit is closer in form to *The Unvanquished* and *Go Down, Moses* than to ordinary short story collections, because it has a central figure and central themes: detection, justice, and the relation between outsiders and the community. Yet it remains a collection of stories, for which Faulkner simply collected his detective stories in the chronology of their periodical publication.

In 1942 Faulkner made a short but concentrated attempt at short story writing, with only moderate success, and near the end of that decade he started planning for publication of his collected stories, which finally resulted in two very different volumes: *Knight's Gambit* and *Collected Stories*. The short version of "Knight's Gambit" was the first work in Faulkner's 1942 outburst of short story activity. He hoped to earn enough money on the sales of these stories to stay home from Hollywood. Two are emotional stories written in dramatic times of war. In "Two Soldiers" a 9-year-old boy narrates a patriotic story about loyalty and endurance. In "Shall Not Perish," a sequel to "Two Soldiers," the young narrator tells about receiving a message concerning his brother Pete's death and about the family's reaction. Another soldier, the son of wealthy parents, has also been killed in the war, and in the course of the narrative the boy slowly seems to grasp that he is part of a larger community and that if you love your country you may also die for it. In "Shingles for the Lord" we meet members of the same stricken family again in a humorous, almost incredibly funny story. "My Grandmother Millard and General Bedford Forrest and the Battle of Harrykin Creek" – closely related to central elements in *The Unvanquished* – and "A Courtship" are also very funny stories, the latter about courtship and a competition between a white man and an Indian. Faulkner's attempt to write and sell short stories for a living failed drastically in 1942, and the stories he produced are not among his best.

With *Collected Stories* in 1950, Faulkner further consolidated his reputation in the world of letters. The Nobel Prize for Literature in 1949, received by Faulkner in Stockholm in December 1950, was the ultimate proof of his success and achievement. *Collected Stories* is, of course, Faulkner's major short story collection, a milestone marking the culmination of a long and varied short story career and including almost all of his previously published stories that do not stand in close relationship to his novels. He had suggested this new collection as early as 1939, but serious discussion did not begin till 1948. According to lists that Faulkner made, he planned to include only previously uncollected short stories, including the Gavin Stevens stories, in the new book. The decision to leave out the detective stories and publish a separate volume of them changed his plan, and it was decided to publish a volume of previously collected and uncollected stories. Faulkner intended the volume to be comprehensive, but it is not. Yet it may be said to include the 42 stories Faulkner wanted to represent his achievement as a short story writer. Even though the book contains most of his independent short stories, it does not include all such stories, and most of the stories not collected here also deserve attention.

Twenty-five of the 42 stories had been collected before in *These 13* and *Doctor Martino*, while the other 17 had not been collected before. Some of them date back to 1930, and most of them were written before 1940. Planning his collection, Faulkner wrote to Malcolm Cowley on November 1, 1948, that "even to a collection of short stories, form, integration, is as important as to a novel – an entity of its own, single, set for one pitch, contrapuntal in integration, toward one end, one finale"(Cowley 1966: 115–16). He organized *Collected Stories* with such principles in mind, although the criteria for arrangement are often difficult to determine.

Collected Stories was reviewed widely, and the reviewers stressed the practicality and usefulness of the volume as an introduction to Faulkner's rich fictional world. *Collected Stories* thus marked another important step forward in the general acknowledgment of his total achievement. Many reviewers stated or implied that recognition of Faulkner as the leading American novelist of his generation would soon come, and they did this on the basis of the richness of his short stories. *Collected Stories* received the National Book Award for the most distinguished book of fiction by an American author published in 1950.

After the publication of *Collected Stories* Faulkner published few stories of importance. Those that were written relate in significant ways to his longer fictions, such as *Requiem for a Nun* (1951), *A Fable* (1954), *The Town*, and *The Mansion* (1959). The last short fiction to be published in his lifetime, "Hell Creek Crossing" (1962), is hardly a short story in its own right, but rather an excerpt from *The Reivers* of the same year. In addition to these stories with their close relationship to novels, two independent short stories were written and published. "Race at Morning" (1955) is Faulkner's most successful story from his later years. It is also his last hunting story, a tribute to the wilderness. A slightly revised version of this story was incorporated into a book of hunting stories, *Big Woods* (1955). The second independent short story is "Mr. Acarius" (written circa 1953, not published till 1965), a story about alcohol abuse and personal conflicts.

Summing Up

Faulkner's short stories were his most marketable merchandise, the product he could sell at the highest price in the American magazine and book market in the 1930s and 1940s. His many attempts to sit down and write stories for the best-paying magazines demonstrate the confidence of a storyteller who knew his worth. What he despaired about was his failure to sell enough stories to concentrate on his writing and nothing else. Many letters and public statements show that Faulkner regarded the short story as a literary form very highly, although he rather often complied with editors' suggestions to cut and revise a story. In a few cases he accepted revisions to suit the taste of the popular market, but he also rewrote whole stories because he felt that they needed revision and improvement. This he did for artistic reasons, to get the story right, as he often said. Faulkner became more and more of a novelist as he grew older, and in the latter half of his career the short narratives he wrote and published as short fictional pieces very often were the result of early and tentative work on what would finally become a novel. It is too simple to say that Faulkner wrote short stories for money, because he also wrote novels to make a living. All in all it is fair to say that despite his willingness to comply with editors' wishes, he revised and rewrote his stories not to suit the needs of a market, but in order to satisfy himself and his own artistic demands. It is at any rate difficult to generalize about Faulkner's practice in the writing, selling, and reuse of short stories, because his practice is by no means consistent, and each short story seems to be a separate or individual case.

Faulkner's stories do not only deal with the old verities of the human heart, of which he spoke so often. Yet he may have thought that the episodes and incidents he recorded were part of some basic, unchanging way of being alive in the world. The old verities often become virtues, perhaps something we have lost in the modern world. Accordingly, Faulkner may come closest to a persuasive and convincing portrayal of these verities in stories about the illiterate and poor people of Yoknapatawpha, who seem somehow to live their lives as if they were living under ancient laws where myths are still believed in and where destiny cannot be chosen or changed. This is only part of the world in Faulkner's short stories, however, and all in all change must be one of the key terms in a description of his achievement as a writer, and then, of course, time inevitably becomes a central concern. The conflicts of the human heart may well be ageless and eternal, yet Faulkner's stories show that man must change with an ever-changing world, and that adjustment to new situations is required, despite the pain it causes. In sum, his short stories record the minimal and almost invisible changes in different social groups and succeed in making them reflect the passing of a way of life and of an era. His was the rich heritage of a heroic past, a sense of history which included defeat and defiance, a strong sense of belonging to a stable, well-ordered albeit somewhat rigid community. What he had inherited could not be changed quickly, but he saw the changes, and he became the chronicler of them, also in his short fiction.

REFERENCES AND FURTHER READING

Carothers, J. B. (1985). *William Faulkner's Short Stories*. Ann Arbor: UMI Research Press.

Cowley, M. (1946). Introduction. In *The Viking Portable Faulkner* (pp. vii–xxxvii). New York: Viking Press.

Cowley, M. (1966). *The Faulkner–Cowley File: Letters and Memories 1944–1962*. New York: Viking Press.

Creighton, J. V. (1977). *William Faulkner's Craft of Revision: The Snopes Trilogy, "The Unvanquished" and "Go Down, Moses."* Detroit: Wayne State University Press.

Ferguson, J. (1991). *Faulkner's Short Fiction*. Knoxville: University of Tennessee Press.

Gwynn, F. L. and J. Blotner (1959). *Faulkner in the University: Class Conferences at the University of Virginia 1957–1958*. Charlottesville, VA: University Press of Virginia.

Harrington, E. and A. J. Abadie (1990). *Faulkner and the Short Story: Faulkner and Yoknapatawpha, 1990*. Jackson: University Press of Mississippi.

Holmes, E. M. (1966). *Faulkner's Twice-Told Tales: His Re-Use of His Material*. The Hague: Mouton.

Ingram, F. L. (1971). *Representative Short Story Cycles of the Twentieth Century: Studies in a Literary Genre*. The Hague and Paris: Mouton.

Jones, D. B. (1994). *A Reader's Guide to the Short Stories of William Faulkner*. New York: G. K. Hall.

Kinney, A. F. (1980). Faulkner's Narrative Poetics and *Collected Stories*. *Faulkner Studies*, 1: 58–79.

Lundén, R. (1999). *The United Stories of America: Studies in the Short Story Composite*. Amsterdam: Rodopi.

Luscher, R. (1989). The Short Story Sequence: An Open Book. In S. Lohafer and J. E. Clarey (eds.). *Short Story Theory at a Crossroads* (pp. 148–67). Baton Rouge: Louisiana State University Press.

Mann, S. G. (1989). *The Short Story Cycle: A Genre Companion and Reference Guide*. New York: Greenwood Press.

Millgate, M. (1971). *The Achievement of William Faulkner*. New York: Vintage.

Millgate, M. (1997). Was Malcolm Cowley Right? The Short Stories in Faulkner's Non-episodic Novels. In H. Skei (ed.). *William Faulkner's Short*

Fiction: An International Symposium (pp. 164–72). Oslo: Solum.

Skei, H. H. (1981). *William Faulkner: The Short Story Career*. Oslo: Universitetsforlaget.

Skei, H. H. (1985). *William Faulkner: The Novelist as Short Story Writer*. Oslo: Universitetsforlaget.

Skei, H. H. (ed.) (1997). *William Faulkner's Short Fiction: An International Symposium*. Oslo: Solum.

Skei, H. H. (1999). *Reading Faulkner's Best Short Stories*. Columbia, SC: University of South Carolina Press.

24

Faulkner's Non-Fiction

Noel Polk

One relatively slim volume contains all of Faulkner's formal non-fiction prose – *Essays, Speeches and Public Letters*, edited by James B. Meriwether, was published by Random House in 1966; in 2004 Meriwether corrected a few errors and added to this volume the non-fiction material from Carvel Collins's 1962 *William Faulkner: Early Prose and Poetry* and several other items that have become available since 1966. Faulkner critics have understandably spent more time mining these essays for what they might tell us about his life and his fiction, assuming them to be directly related to his fiction, than in examining them on their own merits. No one would claim that his is a substantial body of non-fiction prose, either in its quantity or in its quality, and certainly not by comparison with his fiction; but it is a very interesting body of writing and some of it is outstanding. Most of his early criticism and occasional pieces tell us something about his youthful attempts to find his own niche in contemporary literature, and a good deal of it is well worth reading for its own sake.

It is important to keep the distinctions between the fiction and non-fiction active at all times, though Faulkner readers and critics have usually failed to do so, especially with regard to his writings on race and on his late fiction. These we continue to read through the filter of a relatively few public speeches he made after he became a Nobel laureate – the Nobel Prize acceptance speech and two commencement addresses in particular have been mined for signs of hope from the old tragedian (his daughter Jill was present at all three occasions) – whose rituals called for, demanded, declarations of optimism and hope for the future, though his other writings of the first lustrum of the fifties clearly indicate that he was deeply depressed and drinking heavily: he was personally hardly optimistic about much of anything. That is, we should not take Faulkner's non-fiction as any sort of guide to his fiction, but rather as emerging out of a more discursive and public part of his character and interests. If he did not quite write them with his left hand, they certainly did not exact from him the sort of energy and intelligence that went into his fiction. Especially in the fifties, his non-fiction seems to have been generated by a desire to be responsible in his duties as citizen, friend, father.

For my purposes here I will treat only the materials in *Essays, Speeches and Public Letters* (2004). Though to be sure letters and interviews are non-fiction prose, they emerge from different impulses and needs. Meriwether groups Faulkner's non-fiction prose into several categories according to genre and he prints them in chronological order within each category. I will, however, discuss them briefly according to themes, hoping only, in this small space, to touch some high points.

Race

The most-often-discussed of his essays are those several pieces of the fifties in which he weighed in on the single most important social issue of the twentieth century, race. His prominence as a "Southern" writer, as a "modern" writer, and as a writer about race in his fiction seem to have forced him out of his modernist ivory tower. In 1956 he published three major statements on the racial situation: "Letter to a Northern Editor" (published in *Life*); "On Fear: Deep South in Labor: Mississippi" (published in *Harper's*), and "A Letter to the Leaders of the Negro Race" (published in *Ebony*), as well as numerous letters to the editors of the *New York Times*, the Memphis *Commercial Appeal*, and the *Oxford Eagle*. The three formal essays argue the complementary necessities for whites to give up their intransigence in racial matters and for blacks to be patient. "Go slow now," he wrote to a black readership:

> Stop now for a time, a moment. You have the power now; you can afford to withhold for a moment the use of it as a force. You have done a good job, you have jolted your opponent off-balance and he is now vulnerable. But stop there for a moment; dont give him the advantage of a chance to cloud the issue by that purely automatic sympathy for the underdog simply because he is under. . . . You have shown the Southerner what you can do and what you will do if necessary; give him a space in which to get his breath and assimilate that knowledge. (pp. 107–8)

Understandably, modern readers – and contemporary black ones – chafe at his suggestion that blacks should "go slow," since that is essentially what whites had been telling blacks for decades, and modern readers can only imagine how that advice fell on contemporary black ears. Yet there is no real reason to doubt Faulkner's sincerity in advising that course or to doubt that he felt that it was good, pragmatic advice, offered not at all to give whites a chance to retrench, but to give them a chance to deal just as pragmatically with the alterations to the social order that he saw as inevitable. He never overestimated whites' capacity to act in their own best interests in his fiction.

His arguments for racial justice are to a certain extent a multi-layered response to the Cold War, which had just begun to lay its hand upon the Western world's throat in particularly vicious and unsettling ways, and Faulkner seems to have been seriously concerned. He did not, of course, believe that there were Communists under every bed, and did not approve of Joseph McCarthy's scandalous proceedings; but he did believe that Communism's monolithism was a threat to America's and the world's valuation of individual freedom, and that America, the South in particular, could not hold its claim to individual freedom as long as so many of its citizens were in economic and political bondage. In a series of concentric circles, his thinking is: Southern blacks and whites, for all our differences, have more in common with each other than we have with Northerners; Southerners and Northerners have more in common with each other, as Americans, than we have with foreigners, especially Communists. We in the South can and must fix our own problems or we will invite the North to invade as it had done a century before to presume to fix them for us; likewise, Americans North and South must unite to keep the Soviet menace at a respectable and safe distance. America's survival demands that Southern blacks slow down and Southern whites, in effect, speed up, so that we as Americans could fend off Communism's advance together, because separated we would all be vulnerable to an enemy that did not care whether we are black or white, Northern or Southern.

While insisting that whites must give up their intransigence, he also argued that blacks must "earn" equality. In this, at best, he follows Booker T. Washington's admonitions at the turn of the century that blacks should prepare themselves for equality through humility and education and should not expect to be accepted as equals until they earned the right to equality; at worst, Faulkner insists, especially in "A Letter to the Leaders of the Negro Race" (originally published as "If I Were a Negro"), that blacks must add personal cleanliness to their list of social amenities, along with a sense of responsibility, rectitude, and reliability, before whites will accept them. At first cleanliness is part of his plan for blacks to pursue a course of non-violent confrontation, part of a uniform black children must wear:

> If I were a Negro in America today . . . I would advise the leaders of my race . . . to send every day to the white school to which he was entitled by his ability and capacity to go, a student of my race, fresh and cleanly dressed, courteous, without threat or violence, to seek admission; when he was refused I would forget about him as an individual, but tomorrow I would send another one, still fresh and clean and courteous, to be refused in his turn, until at last the white man himself must recognise that there will be no peace for him until he himself has solved the dilemma. (p. 109)

But soon cleanliness becomes a sort of theme which he hammers home in the last three paragraphs of the essay:

> But always, let us practise cleanliness and decency and courtesy and dignity in our contacts with [whites]. . . . But above all I would say this to the leaders of our race: . . . "We must learn that our inalienable right to equality, to freedom and liberty and the pursuit of happiness, means exactly what our founding fathers meant by it: the right to *opportunity* to be free and equal, provided one is worthy of it, will work to gain it and then work to keep it. And not only the right to that opportunity, but the willingness and the capacity to accept the responsibility of that opportunity – the responsibilities of physical cleanliness and moral rectitude, of a conscience capable of choosing between right and wrong

and a will capable of obeying it, of reliability toward other men, the pride of independence of charity or relief." (pp. 111–12)

Such sentiments make us uneasy today, since of course Faulkner makes no parallel requirement that the whites who are finally to permit blacks access to equality always be clean and responsible and moral themselves. It is clear from his fiction that he didn't believe that all whites were clean and upright or absolve them from the need to be. Even so, and from whatever reservations Faulkner seems to have had about blacks socially, it seems proper to assume that at least in his arguments for equal opportunity he believed that his was an absolutely pragmatic political position, if not a social one; he must have believed sincerely that the giant hurdles that blacks must face were not just legal ones, but the complicated social ones, and that whites, clean or dirty, would be the arbiters of their fate and would expect at least a minimum of hygiene of people who would be their social and political equals. But it is a curious sort of hectoring, as if being unclean in any sense of the word rendered blacks, or anybody else, ineligible for freedom.

Books and Writers: Art

Faulkner never developed anything resembling a systematic aesthetic, never showed much interest in such, until in the fifties, when he was often interviewed in situations in which he answered questions about his art and art in general. His responses were anything but formal, and seemed to center on a fairly limited number of comments that, in the interviews especially, became almost rote as he responded over and over to variations on the same questions, both general and specific, about his work. He frequently invoked, often without citing it specifically, Keats's "Ode on a Grecian Urn," from which he derived his general comment that art, like the figures on the urn, freezes life so that when readers come to it again it becomes life, motion, again. Usually when asked about a scene or a character in one of his works he was likely to say something very general, like, "Well, that just seemed to me the best way to do that." In more formal statements, for example in "Upon Receiving the Nobel Prize for Literature" in 1950 and in his "Foreword" to *The Faulkner Reader* in 1954, he imputed to art a high moral, almost therapeutic purpose, to help mankind "endure" and "prevail": "To uplift man's heart; the same for all of us: for the ones who are trying to be artists, the ones who write to shock, and the ones who are simply escaping themselves and their own private anguishes" (p. 181).

Early and late, however, he commented on numerous fashionable individual authors and works. Early on, his comments bear all the seriousness of the very young: he reviewed works by Joseph Hergesheimer, Edna St. Vincent Millay, Eugene O'Neill, William Alexander Percy, and others in terms often brash if not quite smart-alecky; above all, he was very modern, and a good deal of his commentary, perhaps not surprisingly, centered on language. Later commentary tends to come in response to invitations to write something and is often less about literature than about himself, and for his own purposes. He doubtless agreed, for example, to review and say nice things about Hemingway's *The Old Man and the Sea* (1952) as partial expiation for his highly publicized and misunderstood comment to a University of Mississippi class that Hemingway had no courage. And in "A Note on Sherwood Anderson" (1953) he was clearly making late amends for his own unintentional faux pas in the twenties when he and William Spratling produced *Sherwood Anderson and Other Famous Creoles* (1926). Faulkner's introduction to that volume was a gentle, even warm, caricature of Anderson's "primer-like" (p. 6) style. It was not even close to the vicious parody of Anderson's style that Hemingway had used in *The Torrents of Spring* (1926), but it hurt Anderson's feelings nevertheless and caused a rift between them.

"A Note on Sherwood Anderson" is perhaps the best and most sustained of Faulkner's comments on writing and art; it is a lovely tribute to Anderson, but it also reveals a good deal about Faulkner's own artistic sources and aims – again, not in formal commentary, but in what we can extrapolate from what he says about Anderson. In this piece Faulkner warmly recounts his relationship with Anderson in New Orleans in the twenties, Anderson's role in getting Faulkner's first novel published and, more, teaching him that his "little patch up there in Mississippi where you started from" (p. 8) was worth writing about. We don't have to believe that Anderson actually said these words (they could easily be Faulkner's own words, attributed to Anderson); it is easy enough to understand that Faulkner could have learned this truth simply from Anderson's example. He suggests that neither he nor Hemingway "could have touched, ridiculed, his work itself. But we had made his style look ridiculous," and that was what hurt Anderson's feelings to the extent that by the time when his subject had dried up, by the time he "had reached the point where he should have stopped writing, he had to defend that style at all costs because he too must have known by then in his heart that there was nothing else left" (p. 6). What Faulkner learned from Anderson that Hemingway perhaps never did was that "style" as a thing in itself was not very useful to a writer, that style was a function of the needs of an individual book.

Technology and the Modern World

In his fiction and in most of his comments about the contemporary world, Faulkner was ever a proponent of the need to accept change as a vital sign of life: once it stops, it dies, he so famously said, in one form or another, on many occasions. But in his life as a citizen, he seems to have been leery of change for change's sake, as when he writes commending the editor of the *Oxford Eagle* for an editorial that argued to preserve the Lafayette County Courthouse (1947). Faulkner believes, though, that the Courthouse will "go the way of the old Cumberland church": it might be tougher than Yankees, but it isn't "tougher than the ringing of a cash register bell." He regrets this change: "They call this progress. But they don't say where it's going; also, there are some of us who would like the chance to say whether or not we want the ride" (p. 203). Not long after this letter, though, he wrote and printed his infamous "Beer Broadside" (1950), in which he argued for a change in the law that would allow beer to be sold in Oxford by refuting some facts that some local clergy had put forward in their campaign against the change. In a follow-up letter to the editor, he responded to the town's various commentary on the broadside: "I notice that your paper has listed me among the proponents of legal beer. I resent that. I am every inch as much an enemy of liberty and enlightenment and progress as any voting or drinking dry either in Oxford" (pp. 208–9), it began.

He was also suspicious of technology, at least in so far as it threatened to make human beings more and more dependent on it and less and less dependent on themselves, as he argues in a letter to the *New York Times* (1954) concerning an airliner that had crashed at Idlewild Airport in New York, apparently because the plane's instruments went out of order just before the pilot committed the plane to an instrument landing, after three previous failed attempts to land. The pilot, "along with his unaware passengers, was victim not even of the failed instruments but victim of that mystical, unquestioning, almost religious awe and veneration in which our culture has trained us to hold gadgets – any gadget, if it is only complex enough and cryptic enough and costs enough" (p. 213).

Travel

Faulkner is at his best in two essays that respond to his travels. In "A Guest's Impression of New England" (1954), he reports an automobile trip with his friend Malcolm Cowley through the New England countryside, during which Cowley teaches him that even in asking directions from New Englanders one must ask very precise questions because New Englanders, laconic and stoic, will answer only the questions they are asked: the question "where is" a certain place must be followed by another: "Can we get there going in this direction?" The encounter leads Faulkner into a brief discursus on the New England character, which believes "that there is no valid reason why life should be soft and docile and amenable, that to be individual and private is the thing and that the man who cannot cope with any environment anywhere had better not clutter the earth to begin with" (p. 46).

"Impressions of Japan" was originally published as a press release by the United States Embassy in Tokyo in 1955, and presumably written for such publication, though it was collected in *Faulkner at Nagano* in 1956. "Impressions" is an elegant and deeply felt paean to the country he visited for several weeks in 1955, a collocation of observations and experiences he had during the visit. Clearly Japan made a powerful impression on him, bringing him into contact with an otherness different from any other otherness he had ever experienced. He genuinely respected the order, the humility, the clothes, the complicated and meaningful simplicity of their rituals, and their worship and their living, and their language:

It is visible and audible, spoken and written too: a communication between man and man because humans speak it; you hear and see them. But to this one western ear and eye it means nothing because it resembles nothing which that western eye remembers; there is nothing to measure it against, nothing for memory and habit to say, "Why, this looks like the word for house or home or happiness;" not even just cryptic but acrostic too, as though the splashed symbols of the characters held not mere communication but something urgent and important beyond just information, promising toward some ultimate wisdom or knowledge containing the secret of man's salvation. But then no more, because there is nothing for western memory to measure it against: so not the mind to listen but only the ear to hear that chirrup and skitter of syllables like the cries of birds in the mouths of children, like music in the mouths of women and young girls. (pp. 76–7)

And their kindness: "So kind the people that with three words the guest can go anywhere and live: Gohan: Sake: Arrigato . . ." (p. 81).

In "To the Youth of Japan," written for and published as a pamphlet by the US Information Service (1955), Faulkner draws some parallels between Japan's defeat and occupation after World War II and the South's defeat and occupation in the Civil War and Reconstruction to hold out to Japanese young people the hope of a future, a future largely driven, as he offers it, by art. Here he is on grounds familiar to those who have read his other statements on art: "That art is the strongest and most durable force man has invented or discovered with which to record the history of his invincible durability and courage beneath disaster, and to postulate the validity of his hope" (p. 83).

Sports

Faulkner is also at his best in two essays that he wrote on commission from *Sports Illustrated*, which asked him to cover the 1955 Kentucky Derby, assuming correctly that he would know something about horses, and an ice hockey match, assuming, again correctly, that he wouldn't know anything about ice hockey: he produced two splendid pieces. In the latter, "An Innocent at Rinkside" (1955), Faulkner makes his "innocence" a filter through which he views the considerable action on the ice. He notes at first how the ice looks "tired" even though it had been put down only moments before the match, and then the match turns into an incomprehensible blur of motion, speed:

> To the innocent, who had never seen it before, it seemed discorded and inconsequent, bizarre and paradoxical like the frantic darting of the weightless bugs which run on the surface of stagnant pools. Then it would break, coalesce through a kind of kaleidoscopic whirl like a child's toy, into a pattern, a design almost beautiful, as if an inspired choreographer had drilled a willing and patient and hard-working troupe of dancers – a pattern, design which was trying to tell him something, say something to him urgent and important and true in that second before, already bulging with the motion and the speed, it began to disintegrate and dissolve.

Then he learns to follow the puck and the game begins to make some sense: "individual players would emerge. They would not emerge like the sweating barehanded behemoths from the troglodyte mass of football, but instead as fluid and fast and effortless as rapier-thrusts or lightning." He, the innocent, likes the game because of the "excitement of speed and grace, with the puck for catalyst, to give it reason, meaning" (pp. 48–9). He closes the essay with a wry, almost acerbic, observation about the playing of the national anthem at the beginning of such ceremonies that brings the essay into line with his other comments about the waning of Americans' sense of personal responsibility:

> What are we afraid of? Is it our national character of which we are so in doubt, so fearful that it might not hold up in the clutch, that we not only dare not open a professional athletic contest or a beauty-pageant or a real-estate auction, but we must even use a Chamber of Commerce race for Miss Sewage Disposal . . . to remind us that liberty gained without honor and sacrifice and held without constant vigilance and undiminished honor and complete willingness to sacrifice again at need, was not worth having to begin with? (p. 51)

"Kentucky: May: Saturday" (1955) is a small historical epic which sets the modern derby in the context of the bluegrass that Daniel Boone saw and allows Faulkner another opportunity to remind his new readers of "our duties and responsibilities as citizens if we wished to continue as a nation" (p. 53). It too is an epic of speed and power as Faulkner, with a reporter's pass touring down on the track among the horses and riders, including Eddie Arcaro and Earl Sande, responds viscerally to the place and the moment, recurring to themes of his fiction when he maintains that the horse, though "economically obsolete," nevertheless supplies to man "something deep and profound in his emotional nature and need," as does the betting; but it of course is not just betting:

> It is much deeper than that. It is a sublimation, a transference: man, with his admiration for speed and strength, physical power far beyond what he himself is capable of, projects his own desire for physical supremacy, victory, onto the agent – the baseball or football team, the prize fighter. Only the horse race is more universal because the brutality of the prize fight is absent, as well as the attenuation of football or baseball – the long time needed for the orgasm of victory to occur, where in the horse race it is a matter of minutes, never over two or three, repeated six or eight or ten times in one afternoon. (p. 58)

Mississippi

In a series of letters to the *Oxford Eagle* over the years, Faulkner argued, sometimes gently, sometimes acerbically, sometimes humorously with his home town over such issues as race, beer, and the squirrels in Bailey's Woods. None of these letters is more affecting than "His Name Was Pete" (1946), a eulogy to the Faulkner family dog that was killed by a driver who hit him and didn't stop to see if he could be saved.

Faulkner's most elaborate foray into autobiography is the magnificent "Mississippi," a *sui generis* essay-story that combines fiction and non-fiction to allow Faulkner to explore north Mississippi's history and his own life and antecedents as they merge. The world of "Mississippi" is a seamless combination of the real Mississippi and Faulkner's created one: Snopeses appear along with historical Mississippians; incidents from his own life appear alongside and inextricable from those of Mississippi history: his life, his fiction, and his Mississippi are never very far apart. His citizen protagonist is not a professional writer but a man who lives in circumstances similar to Faulkner's, but in Jefferson, not in Oxford. Faulkner nominates him differently – the boy, the young man, the middle-aged – as he ages and becomes more and more aware of the racial injustices that drive Mississippi's politics and economics, and of the ignorance and insularity which more often than not marked Mississippi's attitude toward his work as a writer, though of course he never mentions that work. Faulkner moves toward conclusion with a list of things he hates about Mississippi: that insularity and ignorance, that violent racism, the intolerance and the injustice: the lynchings, the poor schools, the hovels, Mississippi a condition in which blacks "could worship the white man's God but not in the white man's church; pay taxes in the white man's courthouse but couldn't vote in it or for it" (p. 37); and hating the bigotry that "could send to Washington some of the senators and congressmen we sent there and which could erect in a town no bigger than Jefferson five separate denominations of churches but set aside not one square foot of ground where children could play and old people could sit and watch them" (p. 38).

It is a serious list of Mississippi's faults. But he counters this list in closing with a powerful paean to Mammy Caroline Barr, the freed slave of the Faulkner family who elected to stay with the family after Emancipation. He makes her death and burial an occasion for reflecting, yet again, on the nature of black–white relations in Mississippi and makes of Mammy Callie a paradigm for himself and others to emulate, to learn how to love even that which has oppressed you: "Loving all of it," he concludes, "even while he had to hate some of it because he knows now that you dont love because: you love despite; not for the virtues, but despite the faults" (pp. 42–3). His "Funeral Sermon for Mammy Caroline Barr" (1940), published in the Memphis *Commercial Appeal*, extols the virtues he recalls in "Mississippi."

Like his other comment on race, Faulkner's description of his relationship with Mammy Callie has its problematic side. Some recent commentary has rightly suggested that Faulkner's treatment of Ms Barr is patronizing and proprietorial. At least to the extent that as he describes her funeral he seems to have excluded her own family from the arrangements, there could be some truth to the charge. More disturbingly, perhaps, in "Mississippi" he may assume some things about her "loyalty and devotion" to the Faulkner family that may or may not have been true, since he understandably makes no attempt to give her voice to her own thoughts about her white family. What he sees as love and fidelity, she might indeed have had, or thought she had, no option but to give, or to pretend to give. In his fiction he might well have accounted somehow for her point of view, or at least problematized or compromised the attitude of the white protagonist in ways that allowed for her to see the world differently.

Even so, whatever shortcomings we may attribute to his writings on race, it is clear that they emerge from what his own fiction had taught him about racial injustice in Mississippi and the rest of the South and from his desire, as the public figure his fiction had made him, to do something about it, to be a responsible citizen rather than the high modernist author he had been for three decades, writing about but not really otherwise seriously engaged in or with his own world. If his writings on race do not satisfy a post-Civil Rights Movement liberal thinker, they were nevertheless courageous for their time and he took many risks, including that of the contumely of his family and friends, for arguing so openly against the status quo. He was by no means an integrationist, but did understand that the constitution and the laws of the land worked against blacks and that it was immoral for them to pay taxes and not be eligible to vote, among other things. For him, it was an issue of simple fairness. I know of only two or three white people of his generation in Mississippi who spoke more openly than he did, and no one who in his books spoke more eloquently or more profoundly about race in America.

REFERENCES AND FURTHER READING

Faulkner, W. (1978). *Selected Letters of William Faulkner* (ed. J. Blotner). New York: Random-Vintage.

Faulkner, W. (2004). *Essays, Speeches and Public Letters* (ed. J. B. Meriwether). New York: Modern Library.

Hamblin, R. (1996). Homo Agonistes, or, William Faulkner as Sportswriter. *Aethlon*, 13: 13–22.

McMillen, N. R. and N. Polk (1992). Faulkner on Lynching. *Faulkner Journal*, 8: 3–14.

Peavy, C. D. (1971). *Go Slow Now: Faulkner and the Race Question*. Eugene, OR: University of Oregon Books.

Towner, T. (2000). Race and the Nobel Prize Winner. In *Faulkner on the Color Line: The Later Novels* (pp. 119–44). Jackson: University Press of Mississippi.

25

Faulkner's Texts

Noel Polk

Faulkner left an astonishing trove of his papers, literally thousands of pages of holograph, typescript, tear-sheets, and galley proof. Together with their counterpart texts published in magazines and books, these papers constitute a very detailed record of the processes by which he created his fictional world – the false starts, the second thoughts, the positioning and re- and re-repositioning of passages ranging in length from one or two lines to two or more chapters, by which he gained the juxtapositions and connections he wanted his fictional structures to have. In many cases, the papers provide materials for reconstructing previous "versions" of a work and for following a work's development from inception to published book and even beyond. They constitute an unusually rich record of his working life and are a resource for access to his life and works that we have only begun to understand.

He left complete holographs of every novel from *The Sound and the Fury* (1929) through about three-quarters the way through *The Hamlet* (1940), at which time he seems to have begun composing at the typewriter, perhaps because his handwriting was getting too difficult for even him to read. There are fragmentary and/or preliminary holographs for the first three novels and for most of the short stories. Very few titles – and those minor – are not preserved in any pre-publication form. Most are preserved in the actual typescript setting copies, the typescripts that editors marked and the compositors used to set the texts from; these documents preserve a good deal of the interaction between author and editor during the editorial intervention in those texts as they passed from pre-publication documents to published texts, and so make it fairly easy to trace the source of changes in certain passages, phrases, and words in the movement from Faulkner's hand- and typewritten texts to published novels. Typescripts for the first three novels are preliminary drafts which Faulkner subjected to considerable revision before submitting them for publication; the typescript for *The Sound and the Fury* is a carbon copy apparently identical to the setting copy, but among the *Sound and the Fury* typescript pages are just over 40 ribbon typescript pages of the Quentin section that were copy-edited by an editor at Smith and Haas before Faulkner revised them;

the *Sound and the Fury* carbon typescript also bears numerous holograph changes in Faulkner's hand, some of which made it into the published book, many of which didn't. Most of the typescripts bear evidence of such post-typing second thoughts.

Faulkner's preservation of these papers was purposeful, not the predilection of a pack rat; it was more nearly an obeisance to the work that he had done, a manifestation of pride in what he had accomplished by himself. In fact, he seemed uninterested in a work once he had finished his part in the creation: he was for the most part an indifferent proofreader, mostly responding to editorial queries but almost certainly never rereading a novel in proof stage, and certainly never after a novel was published, not even, for example, rereading *The Hamlet* in the mid-fifties when rereading it might have helped him avoid some discrepancies in the writing of *The Town* (1957) and *The Mansion* (1959), its siblings in the Snopes trilogy. He preserved the papers, then, as a sort of act of piety toward what he himself had done as an individual and was much less interested in the editorial and mechanical – the collaborative – parts of production. He even hand-bound certain early texts, such as the carbon typescript of *The Sound and the Fury*.

These papers and certain of Faulkner's letters allow us to speculate about his methods of composition. Typically, it would seem, through *The Hamlet*, Faulkner composed in ink on special bond paper, ruled across the top and down the left side, to create margins wide enough to allow him room to revise, which he did liberally. These manuscripts are beautiful to behold, almost themselves objets d'art, the lines so straight across the page that one can only suspect that he held a ruled page under the sheet he was writing on as a guide. Nearly all manuscript pages show evidence of the care and determination with which he composed: they all bear traces of heavy revision, of individual words and phrases crossed out and substitutions interlined or following in the same line; of sentences and phrases and paragraphs moved from one position on a page to another or added in the left margin; and of whole pages, chapters, and even longer sections shuffled about as – especially in *Sanctuary* (1931), say, many of whose pages record, in the upper left corner, as many as 25 or so different page numbers – he struggled to get the novel's various fragmented narratives juxtaposed into the montage that he wanted. All of these changes in one way or another show Faulkner at work and frequently give insight into or pose serious questions about interpretations of problematic passages in the finished works: in the Benjy section of *The Sound and the Fury*, for example, occurs the well-known passage in which during the preliminaries to Caddy's wedding Quentin kicks T. P. repeatedly. In the manuscript Faulkner originally wrote that it was *Father* who kicked T. P. – Father at least until he had finished writing the passage, though there's no real way to determine how long after, when he looked back at the passage, he inked through all appearances of "Father" and carefully interlined "Quentin" above.

Many of the holograph pages also bear lines, from a couple to several, scissored from previous pages and pasted on – many times, it would appear, when it would have been simpler, easier, for him to have recopied the passage from the earlier typescript. These pasted-on passages affirm the existence of previous holograph pages which do not survive, pages which he disposed of after superseding them; doubtless there were many such discarded pages preliminary to the final holograph document which he preserved so carefully. That is, clearly the preserved holographs suggest not that he wrote the manuscript versions straight through, and then typed them for the printer, but that he kept each work in a constant state of revision, a regular state of preliminariness until he got it the way he wanted it.

The typescripts of the works after *The Hamlet*, and especially those of the 1950s, record that preliminariness almost with a vengeance. Up through the fifties, Faulkner carefully prepared very clean ribbon typescripts to send to the editor and printer. Beginning with *Requiem for a Nun* (1951), however, the setting copies are themselves composite typescripts, final versions of individual chapters and passages assembled and pages renumbered, older and revised versions of those passages simply deleted in ink or grease pencil: doubtless this is the kind of text he earlier assembled before typing from it a clean final copy to send to the printer. In his later years, he simply bypassed this final typing, allowing the typesetter, in essence, to do that for him. As noted, for the most part he composed at the typewriter on the later novels (though he also used a pen for those times when the going was difficult or when he didn't have access to a typewriter), but for some reason he didn't dispose of the hundreds of pages of preliminary material. He saved paper assiduously, typing on versos of rejected pages from the current work and from previous novels. Among the *A Fable* (1954) papers are sometimes several retyped versions, almost identical, of the same passages, as though there were something ritualistic about these passages or perhaps retyping them was his way of warming up, getting his creative juices flowing again for another stint of composing. We have no way of knowing what part these extant papers represent out of the total number of pages he used in writing the works of the fifties, or whether the evidence they provide offers any insight into his working methods of the career up to 1940. I can only guess that they do.

That is, it has to be almost certain that he discarded many more pages than he preserved, and it seems to me that he worked like this during the twenties and thirties. Probably he did not write *The Sound and the Fury* completely in hand and then type it. He composed with pen in hand as his preferred way of striking new ground: writing, revising, adding, discarding, replacing, until he was tired or had simply run out of juice, then stopped and went to the typewriter to do the relatively mindless job of typing a clear copy of what he had just written by hand. Or perhaps he saved typing that new holograph material for the next stint of composition, used the typing as a way of getting back to where he was when he had stopped composing. In either case, it is almost certain that with typescript, he started the process all over: he revised as he typed, then went through page after page of typescript with his pen, revising and discarding and then retyping in an almost infinite loop, until he got the text the way he wanted it to be.

Most of the time in the twenties and thirties he seems to have finished a novel before sending it to his editor, though letters suggest that he sent *Absalom, Absalom!* (1936) and *Pylon* (1935) chapter by chapter as he finished them, working under a great deal of pressure. There is some evidence that he saw copy-edited proof of some but not of all the works. In the fifties, his preferred method of dealing with his editors was to finish a novel (or nearly), send it to his editor at Random House, Saxe Commins and then Albert Erskine, and give them three or four weeks to read and think about it. Then he would go to New York and sit in an editorial office where he and the editor would work through the editor's queries and suggestions. Sometimes he would retype passages there, delete and add material in ink or, more likely, in grease pencil. Depending on the addition made, it is often difficult, impossible, to tell who, Faulkner or editor, made which additions or deletions. Faulkner's handwriting is distinctive, but not always so if the mark is a punctuation mark or a simple word or a deletion of a word, a phrase, or a paragraph. Nor does the color of the grease pencil always help prove whether author or editor made a change; and even if it did, it is of course not possible to recover the discussion (if any) of a given change or to know who suggested it.

Faulkner, as noted, was an indifferent reader of galley proofs. So far as the evidence shows, he never read them word for word, but rather contented himself with responding to editorial queries and only occasionally repairing problems which editorial intervention had caused. He did not, for example, argue more than perfunctorily with the serious deletions that editors had made on the *Absalom, Absalom!* typescript, but when reading the *Pylon* proofs he painstakingly changed back to dashes the ellipses that the editor had told the compositor to use.

The new, "Corrected" texts that have been published by Random House, the Library of America, and Vintage International are texts based on these original documents, which by and large contain Faulkner's "intentions" in most major and minor matters. To the extent that any document or set of documents can contain a single definitive form of a text, Faulkner's papers do just that. But recent editorial and critical discourse, focusing on the problematics of "intentionality," have forced a reconsideration of the term and of its implications for understanding any text. Indeed, "intentionality" at one level – the level assumed by so many scholars who were trained as New Critics – is an intensely romantic notion of the heroic author which assumes that any author is in complete control of a work from its inception, that an overarching "intention" informs the work's progress from beginning to end and indeed controls the work. To be sure, New Criticism warned us all against the intentional fallacy, but only the most fundamental of New Critics are, post-theory, still naïve enough to accept intentionality in its rawest form, especially since common sense and the evidence of Faulkner's and others' manuscripts argue that because literature gets written one word at a time, "intentionality" necessarily becomes something dynamic and provisional, is not subject to some sort of creative telos controlling from beginning to end: invention rather than intention might better describe the word-by-word operation of writing. And besides, no sense of "intention" has dealt properly with the varieties of extra-authorial interventions in the mechanical processes of writing, typing, typesetting, and proofreading, interventions ranging from editorial rewriting, even reconceiving of a work to simpler matters like typographical and compositorial error.

In producing the new texts, variously called "Corrected" or "New, Corrected" texts, published since 1984, I have worked with all this range of manuscripts and typescripts to produce texts in the new format that are as close as possible to Faulkner's typescript intentions at the time of his original release to his editors, as far as that intention can be determined. Waiving for a moment the larger question of those intentions, I should say first that what I have tried to do in preparing the new texts is not at all to "edit" them, but rather, to use James B. Meriwether's term of years ago, to "de-edit" them; that is, to free them as completely as possible of the editorial – and other – interventions that prevented their original published forms from reproducing the texts that Faulkner had given to his editors. Such interventions range from simple corrections of obvious mistakes – spelling errors, obvious grammar problems, and the spelling of names of historical figures – to more complicated and problematic interventions, as when Ben Wasson reduced *Flags in the Dust* by about a third to produce *Sartoris* (1929), and as when a team of editors simply butchered *Absalom, Absalom!*, by deleting difficult passages they didn't understand, by repunctuating complicated sentence structures, shortening long paragraphs, and supplying identifying names where Faulkner had deliberately used personal pronouns whose antecedents were not clear; and, finally, by changing Faulkner's title *If I Forget Thee, Jerusalem* to *The Wild Palms* (1939) over his strong protest – perhaps his most, his only, significant challenge to the editorial prerogative.

There are clear dangers in such "corrections." For example, what constitutes a mistake in Faulkner's typescripts? And even if you can identify a "mistake," should you correct it? In texts as complicated as *The Sound and the Fury* and *As I Lay Dying* (1930), is it always possible to determine with certainty whether a sentence that ends without a full stop constitutes an error or whether the period's absence represents Faulkner's deliberate attempt to illustrate something about a character's thoughts or even about texts, textuality, that the period would forefend – a problem of closure? An interrupted thought that ellipses or a dash might also have represented? We can check such instances against the parallel texts in the holograph manuscripts of these novels, but we cannot be sure that Faulkner did not revise between holograph and typescript: both manuscripts show plenty of evidence that he revised right up until the last possible moment. More serious "mistakes" are those that occur when historical fact differs from fictional fact or when Faulkner's memory is at play. In the first "Old Man" section of *If I Forget Thee, Jerusalem*, for example, Faulkner has a newspaper headline declare that "President Hoover" had come to the area of the 1927 Mississippi River flood to assess the damage, but Hoover was not president in 1927: he came to the devastated areas as Calvin Coolidge's secretary of commerce. It hardly seems likely that a contemporary newspaper would have made a mistake like that, so it seems clear that Faulkner, writing the novel more than 10 years later, had a lapse of memory. That made it relatively easy to correct "President Hoover" to "Secretary Hoover," as the editors of the 1939 first edition had failed to do, though it might not have been so easy to correct, for example, if a character had named "President Hoover" as the man coming to survey the damage.

It is fair, perhaps even necessary, to question whether anybody should be re-editing texts that Faulkner himself had approved, and many, to be sure, have asked this question. An answer may be as prickly as the question itself. Part of the answer lies in the discussion, above, about Faulkner's general attitude toward his books as products of collaboration with the mechanical processes of publication. As noted, he didn't usually care much for his published books, and was an indifferent proofreader who involved himself minimally, especially in the books of the thirties, in proofreading. By the time he got galleys of one novel, he was usually already engaged with another book and didn't take the time he might have. For another very important thing, Faulkner's books were not making his publishers a lot of money, and he simply didn't have much clout with them. Thus he was virtually powerless, as one gathers from Blotner's biography (1984), even to negotiate very much with editorial decisions. So that to claim that the first editions of his novels are texts that he "approved," even tacitly, is not to understand completely his relationships with his editors and his profession: he "approved" them largely, first, because he didn't have the financial power with the publisher to disapprove of and prevent their changes and, second, because he was already busy on the next book. His financial clout with the publisher changed considerably with the publication of the bestselling *Intruder in the Dust* in 1948 and with the Nobel Prize in December 1950: so did his editorial clout. Typically, as I've noted above, he did in fact collaborate more and more directly with his editors Saxe Commins and Albert Erskine. Even so, throughout the "correcting" of the texts, it has been my primary desire to let Faulkner stand for himself in so far as that is recoverable from the typescripts, to restore warts – if any – as well as honeysuckle, under the assumption that what he wrote was nearly always what he intended.

References and Further Reading

Blotner, J. (1984). *Faulkner: A Biography*. One-vol. edn. New York: Random House.

Creighton, J. V. (1977). *William Faulkner's Craft of Revision: The Snopes Trilogy,* The Unvanquished, *and* Go Down, Moses. Detroit: Wayne State University Press.

Gregory, E. (1973). Faulkner's Typescripts of *The Town*. *Mississippi Quarterly*, 26: 361–86.

Langford, G. (1972). *Faulkner's Revision of* Sanctuary: *A Collation of the Unrevised Galleys and the Published Book*. Austin, TX, and London: University of Texas Press.

Linnemann, A. E. C. and P. Cohen. (2004). Textual Criticism. In C. A. Peek and R. W. Hamblin (eds.). *A Companion to Faulkner Studies* (pp. 279–306). Westport, CT: Greenwood Press.

Meriwether, J. B. (1961). *The Literary Career of William Faulkner: A Bibliographical Study*. Princeton, NJ: Princeton University Press.

Meriwether, J. B. (1982). The Books of William Faulkner: A Revised Guide for Students and Scholars. *Mississippi Quarterly*, 35: 265–81.

Polk, N. (1972). The Manuscript of *Absalom, Absalom! Mississippi Quarterly*, 25: 359–67.

Polk, N. (1975). The Textual History of Faulkner's *Requiem for a Nun*. *Proof*, 4: 109–28.

Polk, N. (1981). Afterword. In W. Faulkner. *Sanctuary: The Original Text*. New York: Random House.

Polk, N. (1987). Some Notes on Reading Faulkner's Hand. In T. L. McHaney (ed.). *William Faulkner's Manuscripts I:* Elmer *and "A Portrait of Elmer": The Typescripts, Manuscripts, and Miscellaneous Pages* (pp. xiii–xxiii). New York and London: Garland.

Polk, N. (1996). Where the Comma Goes: Editing William Faulkner. In *Children of the Dark House:*

Text and Context in Faulkner (pp. 3–21). Jackson: University Press of Mississippi.

See also the bibliographical notes under (1) "Abbreviations for Texts to be Cited in *The Faulkner Journal*" in the final pages of each issue of the *Faulkner Journal*, (2) the "Notes on the Text" sections of the various Library of America volumes of Faulkner's novels, and (3) the introductions to the individual volumes of William Faulkner Manuscripts (44 vols., New York: Garland, 1986).

The largest collection of Faulkner's papers are those of his personal collection, which he deposited at the Alderman Library of the University of Virginia. Other important collections are at the Ransom Center Library at the University of Texas, the Berg Collection at the New York Public Library, the Wisdom Collection at Tulane University, and the University of Mississippi Library.

PART IV
Sample Readings

"By It I Would Stand or Fall": Life and Death in *As I Lay Dying*

Donald M. Kartiganer

As I Lay Dying (1930) is a novel about making a journey in order to fulfill a promise, combining private need with family duty, lyric meditation with narrative action – conceived by a writer who has reached a moment in his career when these conflicting drives have become the terms of his own personal and professional situation. The novel, in other words, is self-reflexive in the most basic, even literal sense: the fictional characters and action mirror the writer's drama of composition, an art of tragic/comic compromise whose rewards and costs we are still learning to measure.

When Faulkner and the former Estelle Oldham Franklin returned to Oxford from their honeymoon in Pascagoula in the late summer of 1929, he was probably aware that not only his life but his writing would be taking new directions. As his letter that spring to his publisher Hal Smith, asking for a loan of $500, clearly indicates, he had entered the marriage with very mixed feelings: "I am going to be married. Both want to and have to. . . . For my honor and the sanity – I believe life – of a woman. . . . It's a situation which I engendered and permitted to ripen which has become unbearable, and I am tired of running from devilment I bring about" (Blotner 1984: 240). The "running from devilment I bring about," like the reference to "bastard" children elsewhere in the letter, is likely that degree of posturing that Faulkner rarely avoided even in his most serious communications – part of the mask he never wholly dropped – yet there is no reason to doubt the conflict of desire and skepticism he felt toward marriage to Estelle. The honeymoon itself, climaxed by an apparent attempt by Estelle to drown herself in the Gulf, hardly allayed the misgivings both of them had about a relationship that had begun in childhood but was now being renewed only after her 12-year marriage to Cornell Franklin had ended.

During that summer Faulkner also read the galley proofs of *The Sound and the Fury* (1929). This too must have inspired a mixture of exhilaration and realistic reassessment. Although on the verge of publishing his fourth novel, it was difficult for Faulkner to feel optimistic about the task of reconciling the responsibilities of married life (which included two children by Estelle's first marriage) with the responsibilities of a writer.

In terms of sales his situation was hardly promising. The reception of his most recently published novel, *Sartoris*, in January 1929, a radically cut version of *Flags in the Dust*, was discouraging. His attempt that spring, with marriage to Estelle looming, to write a novel that would sell had proved abortive when Smith deemed the original *Sanctuary* (1931) too sensational for publication. Moreover, Alfred Harcourt, the publisher of *Sartoris*, had expressed doubt about the salability of *The Sound and the Fury*, and did not object when Smith took it with him when he formed the firm of Cape and Smith. However impressed Faulkner may have been by the novel to which he later insisted "the shabby term Art not only can but must be applied" (Faulkner 1994: 226), he must have realized that whatever he wrote in the future would have to be of a far different character.

In subsequent essays, interviews, and classroom discussions Faulkner often paired the genesis and writing process of *The Sound and the Fury* and *As I Lay Dying*. In the spring of 1928, nearly 31 years old, he was living with his parents in the former Delta Psy chapter house on the University of Mississippi campus, where his family had moved not long after his father was appointed assistant secretary at the university in 1918. He may have been thinking of that arrangement when he later acknowledged "my father's unfailing kindness which supplied me with bread at need despite the outrage to his principles at having been of a bum progenitive" (Faulkner 1932: v). His bedroom was in a two-story, round tower with a conical roof, attached to the building. It was there, over a six-month period in a kind of self-imposed incarceration, that Faulkner wrote *The Sound and the Fury*: "When I began it I had no plan at all. I wasn't even writing a book. I was thinking of books, publication, only in the reverse, in saying to myself, I wont have to worry about publishers liking or not liking this at all" (Faulkner 1994: 227). The lack of preconception provided an excitement he would say he never experienced again, "that ecstasy, that eager and joyous faith and anticipation of surprise which the yet unmarred sheet beneath my hand held inviolate and unfailing, waiting for release" (p. 226). Applying to the novel his highest accolade, he referred to it as "the most gallant, the most magnificent failure" of his career (Faulkner 1959: 61).

In the fall of 1929 Faulkner and Estelle were living in the first-floor rental of Elma Meek's house on University Avenue, their first home as a married couple. He began working the night shift at the University of Mississippi Power Plant – 6:00 p.m. to 6:00 a.m. – acting as supervisor to two African American men who did the work of getting coal into the boiler. Improvising a table out of a wheelbarrow in the coal bunker and working between 12 midnight and 4:00 a.m., when the need for heat at the university declined, all the while listening to the methodical hum of a dynamo on the other side of the wall, Faulkner wrote *As I Lay Dying*.

The descriptive terms for this novel were "deliberate" and *"tour de force"* – the latter always implying for Faulkner success of a lesser nature: long on virtuosity but a bit short on profundity, not to mention gallantry and magnificence. "I took this family," he said, "and subjected them to the two greatest catastrophes which man can suffer – flood and fire, that's all. That was simple *tour de force*. That was written in six weeks without changing a word because I knew from the first where that was going" (Faulkner 1959: 87). The immediate inspiration, the setting, the emotional state – all are changed. The married man, needing to earn a living, leaves home at 5:30 p.m. He walks the mile to his power plant work place, carrying his manuscript and already writing sentences in his head (and probably passing, unacknowledged, acquaintances on the street). He performs whatever his supervisory role requires, and around midnight sits down to his wheelbarrow as the dynamo whirrs in the next room. There is no mention in retrospect of ecstasy or joyous faith, and apparently no surprise, as he begins writing on October 25 and completes the manuscript on December 11. Presumably he doesn't bring his typewriter to the power plant, and finishes the typescript at home January 12, 1930. To be sure, some words are changed, but manuscript and typescript confirm Faulkner's later claim that, of all his novels, *As I Lay Dying* required the least rewriting (Faulkner 1959: 121).

What I find particularly striking here is how the circumstances of writing, as well as how Faulkner chose to describe those circumstances, permeate the written, invest the narrowness, the elemental quality of the fictional experience, becoming its strategy and its theme. In place at the outset, waiting upon the imminent death of Addie Bundren, is the journey to Jefferson: a fixed line of narrative dictated by a woman's request made almost 30 years earlier. Fulfilling that request is her hill-country farming family, each member of which – except one, *always* except one – is reduced to a private obsession as powerful as the promise, yet inseparable from it. However delayed the progress, circuitous the route, or compromised the motive, the Bundrens are always on the way to Jefferson. "I give her my promise," Anse Bundren says repeatedly, "Her mind is set on it" (Faulkner 1990: 115).

The constraints of the act of writing and the novel they produce are reflected as well in the absence of much that had already become distinctive in Faulkner's work, published and unpublished – as if time and circumstance were also forcing him to abandon certain concerns he had once considered an essential part of his chosen fictional locale. One of these is race, which would always be a standard omission in his fiction about country people in the southeastern quarter of what in this novel he named Yoknapatawpha County. In a number of respects Faulkner modeled the area on his own Lafayette County, the southeast sector of which indeed had a sparse black population, unlike the northern and western sectors of richer soil and larger plantations, where the great majority of black tenant farmers was employed (see Aiken 1977: 4–5). Black representation in *As I Lay Dying* consists of one nameless figure, a man living on the outskirts of Jefferson who says, as the wagon with the nine-day-rotting body of Addie Bundren rolls by, "'Great God . . . what they got in that wagon?" (Faulkner 1990: 229). By the time Jewel Bundren turns to respond to the insult, he is already abreast of a white man.

Another omission is memory, and here the difference between *As I Lay Dying* and other Frenchman's Bend fiction is notable. To be sure, unlike the Sartorises and Compsons, unlike, that is, the descendants of the white planter aristocracy, the people of Frenchman's Bend do not have a multi-generational past to deal with, no proud forebears they are prepared to honor or attempt to equal. In "Father Abraham," the novel

Faulkner probably began in 1926 and left unfinished until *The Hamlet* (1940), the local population recalls neither the name nor the nationality of the former great planter of the area; every outlander is simply a "frenchman" (Faulkner 1984: 14). They value his large abandoned holdings only for the wood of the house they can burn for fuel and the rumor of buried gold they dream of digging up. In *As I Lay Dying*, however, Faulkner reduces the significance of memory still further. There is one "memory" beyond the lives of the current Bundrens, and it is neither a person nor an incident but a single utterance recalled only by Addie: "I could just remember how my father used to say that the reason for living was to get ready to stay dead a long time" (1990: 169). This is memory not as ignorance of the past or pragmatic use of it, but as outright dismissal: the past as merely the necessary route to the single experience that endures.

A more significant and more surprising omission from the novel is the economic factor. In "Father Abraham" it is central and revolves around Will Varner, who holds iron-clad, if outwardly benign, control over the largely tenant farmer citizenry: "Uncle Billy Varner is the big man of the Frenchman's Bend neighborhood. Beat supervisor, politician, farmer, usurer, present owner of the dead Frenchman's homestead and the legend. . . . [H]e looks like a Methodist elder, and is; and a milder mannered man never foreclosed a mortgage or carried a voting precinct" (Faulkner 1984: 16). Subsequently, in *The Hamlet* Faulkner builds on the spotted horses episode of "Father Abraham," bringing to full maturity the rise of the Snopeses as the ultimate logic of an economic code that operates with free-market brutality in a cultural climate of affability – trade as what Ratliff affectionately refers to as "the science and pastime of skullduggery," protected by a policy of laissez-faire summed up in Frenchman's Bend as "'it aint none of our business'" (Faulkner 1991: 91, 79).

In *As I Lay Dying* Faulkner registers the difficult life of the small farmer, but he leaves out most of the dehumanizing and inequitable practices he describes at great length elsewhere. To begin with, Anse Bundren is not a tenant but a landowner, which puts him in a category of less than 30 percent of the farm population of 1930 Mississippi (Federal Writers' Project 1988: 101). His neighbor Vernon Tull is also a landowner and has paid off his mortgage (Faulkner 1990: 142). Anse's reputation when he meets Addie is that of a man with a "new house" and "a good farm," a man "forehanded" with "a good honest name" (p. 171). The Bundrens are obviously not well off; their clothes are patched, the men are thin, Addie's coffin is made at home rather than purchased, Anse has genuine health problems as well as possibly spurious ones. But there is every indication that they make and sell a crop and feed themselves. The supper of greens they eat the night Addie dies, and about which the 300-lb Peabody complains, is not their typical fare. Both the Bundrens and the Tulls speak of the hardship of their lives compared with those of town folks, and prior to harvest their supply of cash is limited. Vardaman is especially conscious of what he believes town boys can have and the costliness of staples they cannot raise on the farm, like flour and sugar and coffee (p. 66; see Luce 1990: 37) But the Bundrens manage, especially if we compare them with the

Armstids of "Father Abraham" and Mink Snopes in *The Hamlet*. It is also clear that some of the Bundrens' frugality – waiting until the last minute before calling the doctor, using cement on Cash's leg because "'We done bought the cement, now' pa says" (Faulkner 1990: 207) – are as much owing to Anse's pettiness as to genuine poverty. (The three dollars Darl and Jewel will earn for hauling lumber are obviously useful but not a necessity for the trip to Jefferson. The money is never mentioned afterwards. The three-day delay that ensues is owing to the broken wagon wheel.)

Of major importance, as Sylvia Jenkins Cook pointed out years ago, "No class of oppressors or exploiters exists in the book" (Cook 1976: 45). Will Varner is mentioned in *As I Lay Dying* only in his role as veterinarian, called in to tend Cash's broken leg in Peabody's absence. The Bundrens are not tenants of Varner, paying a percentage of their crop and always running the risk of ending a season in debt owing to compulsory, high-priced purchases at a company store. Nor is there any reference, as in *The Hamlet*, to the kind of implicit intimidation Varner wields as the owner of store, cotton gin, grist mill, and blacksmith shop: "it was considered, to put it mildly, bad luck for a man of the neighborhood to do his trading or gin his cotton or grind his meal or shoe his stock anywhere else" (Faulkner 1991: 6).

Cook comments on the longstanding custom among Anse's neighbors and friends of helping him out: "In a world where charity like this exists, the question of pervasive poverty is made irrelevant" (1976: 46). This is a very different world from the French-man's Bend of "Father Abraham" and *The Hamlet*, where economic hardship drives men like Henry Armstid mad and Mink Snopes to murder. Above all, there is the simple fact that the great "catastrophes" of flood and fire that the Bundrens endure on the journey to Jefferson have nothing to do with their poverty but with the chance of weather and the exceptional character in the novel, Darl Bundren.

The stream-of-consciousness technique of *As I Lay Dying* also has a leaner look than its predecessor in the modern mode, *The Sound and the Fury*. Much shorter in length, the references and allusions, the twists of memory easier to follow, the interior mono-logues of *As I Lay Dying* may reflect what Faulkner considers the less complex movement of mind of country people, as opposed to townspeople, especially of the planter aristoc-racy. More important, however, they are keyed directly to the narrative action. Each monologue, with the significant exception of Addie's (expressed at no identifiable time) and the two monologues surrounding hers by Cora Tull and Whitfield, follows the previous one in terms of the temporal progress of the action. Whether immediately after or hours later, the monologues serve the family project, the journey, even as the individual characters do, despite the private obsessions that surface primarily in the monologues themselves.

What all this amounts to is our need to recognize that *As I Lay Dying* is a novel that strips away much of what normally goes into Faulkner's characterization of human experience, whether in the town or the country. It strips away as well a characteristic exuberance of expression present even in the darkest of his novels. The product of what he consistently described – and to a large extent his biography confirms – as a contained and controlled writing experience, answering to the new demands of marriage and family, *As I Lay Dying* descends toward some instinctual base circumscribed by the "dying" that dominates the novel. Addie Bundren is the ostensible "I" of the title, but her father's sentence she is always responding to seeks to expand that dying into the solitary goal of life: "the reason for living was to get ready to stay dead a long time" (1990: 169).

As I Lay Dying exhibits an almost inhuman reduction of character to the barest urges of desire and destination, reflecting a level of reality unique in Faulkner's fiction. The prominence of Addie's father's flat insistence that our lives are no more than preparation for death, whatever the form our "readiness" may take, draws the novel into consideration of the hypothesis Freud raises in *Beyond the Pleasure Principle*: "that *'the aim of all life is death'* " (Freud 1961a: 32). The death to which life drives, according to Freud and more than likely according to Addie's father, is not the higher, heavenly existence of Christian belief, but an original inanimacy, a stasis beneath being from which we have been disturbed by external stimuli.[1]

In *Beyond the Pleasure Principle*, Freud revises the dualism he always insists on as the core of psychic life by replacing the conflict between ego instincts and sexual instincts with the conflict between life and death (Freud 1961a: 47): the forces of Eros and Thanatos. Eros is the instinct "towards change and development . . . towards progress and the production of new forms" (1961a: 30–1). It moves outward to an external object of love, to family, to community, aiming "to establish ever greater unities and to preserve them thus – in short, to bind together" (1969: 5). Ideally it is the "instinct toward perfection at work in human beings, which has brought them to their present high level of intellectual achievement and ethical sublimation" (1961a: 36). Eros is countered by the drive to destruction, "to undo connections and so to destroy things" (1969: 5), ultimately to fulfill the basic human need to replace all psychic disturbance with former psychic calm by returning to "the quiescence of the inorganic world" (1961a: 56). As for "living," it is nothing but the process of our return to inanimacy, what Freud calls the "detour," "the circuitous path . . . to death, faithfully kept to by the conservative instincts" that constitutes "the picture of the phenomena of life" (1961a: 33). Those phenomena are in fact determined by the urge to die, to restore "an earlier state of things" (1961a: 31).

Beyond the Pleasure Principle provides us with an illuminating perspective on this moment in Faulkner's life and career and the novel that ensues from it, as he explores the elemental matters of life and death and the emerging question of which is primary, which the source most his own. What life, now radically altered by marriage, would be his and how would it affect his work? What would he write that would be of and for that life, and yet still speak with the power of the inviolable privacy that might reflect the death that was always with him? For the first time in his published work Faulkner places country people at the center of a fiction, as if, in the manner of Wordsworth, he sees in them the opportunity to describe the most fundamental human condition. He assigns them what is for him an uncharacteristically straightforward, if lugubrious task: transporting a dead body from Frenchman's Bend to Jefferson. For the Bundrens there will be no plot that "doesn't get anywhere and has a thousand loose ends," as Faulkner's publisher claimed about *Flags in the Dust* (Blotner 1984: 204–5), and might well have repeated about *The Sound and the Fury*. Like Faulkner, beginning a writer's life as a married man, the Bundrens have a job to do and the novel tells the story of how they get it done. But what are the compromises required to complete it, the conflicts of personal and familial loyalties? How do purpose and detour relate to each other? Is it a journey of life or death the Bundrens carry out, life or death that this novel sings?

The implications Freud draws from the possibility of a death instinct "beyond the pleasure principle" are the implications Faulkner explores in *As I Lay Dying*. He widens the net of "detours" until it enfolds virtually all the action and motive of the text, so that life and death engage each other in a reciprocity impossible to sort out into separate categories. The Bundrens are living as dying, dying as living, each drive engendering, distorting, depending on the other. If this is Eros as the paradigmatic narrative quest, it is also Eros as a long and torturous burial of the dead.

Addie Bundren is the one who enacts that reciprocal relationship with the greatest awareness, treading the paths of life and death with a deliberate and brazen simultaneity. Father, she insists, may have been right in his grim pronouncement, but "he couldn't have known he was right" (Faulkner 1990: 173), in fact "he could not have known what he meant himself" (p. 175). Her intention is to replace her father's vision with one that "knows" it is right and what it "means" to be right. As a result she becomes the central figure of compromise in a novel of compromises, one feature of which is the terrible price they exact.

Addie's life is partly a series of joinings, the creation of "greater unities" in defiance of her father, and partly the subversion of such joinings in defiance of her husband Anse. She instigates the journey, sets in motion a purpose to be achieved, but she also undermines that journey, transforming it into detour. She effects a doing that "goes along the earth" but that also has the quality of words going "straight up in a thin line, quick and harmless" (1990: 173). Her dual motives constitute the reciprocity that is a way of living with and through dying.

For Addie, Eros is the means of containing death by exploiting its very destructiveness. Freud argues that the two instincts rarely if ever appear in isolation from each other. Given his theory that the inherent masochism of the death instinct can be turned outward as sadism, as aggression, the death instinct "could be pressed into the service of Eros, in that the organism was destroying some other thing . . . instead of destroying its own self" (Freud 1961b: 66). Addie expands this concept by demonstrating how that aggression can serve Eros by moving toward greater unities. This is not merely the aggressive component of sexuality, but a violence that enables her to free herself, at least temporarily, from the isolation, the privacy that partakes of the original inanimacy itself. Observing her pupils, "each with his and her secret and selfish thought, and blood strange to each other blood and strange to mine," Addie thinks, "I would hate my father for having ever planted me" (Faulkner 1990: 169–70). Her retaliation against the death wish, ironically, is to make connection through corporal punishment: "only through the blows of the switch could my blood and their blood flow as one stream" (p. 172). Versions of this violence characterize all her attempts at binding together. She "takes" Anse as a husband, she experiences childbirth as "aloneness . . . violated and then made whole again by the violation," but now a wholeness that includes the child, Cash: "time, Anse, love, what you will, outside the circle" (p. 172). She discharges the "duty to the alive, to the terrible blood" (p. 174) through adultery with the minister Whitfield, violating marriage, sanctifying sin. Finally, Addie balances accounts, "cleaning up the house afterwards" (p. 176), by coercing sexual engagement and the pains of childbirth into matrimonial duty: Eros in its service to Addie's sense of domestic equity.

For her vengeance on Anse, however, she turns her aggression against Eros itself, or rather the form of it he represents for her. She assigns him the task of transporting her dead body to Jefferson for burial. The rationale of her revenge as a required burial journey has puzzled readers because it seems empty of any logical basis. At the time of the request, following the birth of Addie's second son, Darl, Anse ignores the choice of burial site, thinking only that Addie expects to die as a result of the birth itself: " 'Nonsense,' Anse said; 'You and me aint nigh done chapping yet, with just two' " (1990: 173). Neither he nor the rest of the family ever asks Addie or even speculates on why she wants to be buried in Jefferson.[2]

Angry at finding herself pregnant with Darl, Addie claims she has been

> tricked by words older than Anse or love, and that the same word had tricked Anse too, and that my revenge would be that he would never know I was taking revenge. And when Darl was born I asked Anse to promise to take me back to Jefferson when I died, because I knew that father had been right, even when he couldn't have known he was right any more than I could have known I was wrong. (1990: 172–3)

That there exists a relationship of any kind between revenge and journey is complicated by the "And when" that joins them, rather than the "And so" that would indicate a cause-and-effect logic (see Parker 1985: 24–5). Even more perplexing, assuming that "And when" establishes a sufficient if not conclusive link, is the question of how the journey would constitute a revenge at all. Granted, Anse does not like to move much – he has not been to Jefferson in 12 years – other people make the journey regularly and uneventfully; it is probably no more than a two-day ride (40 miles) by mule and wagon.[3] That Addie has anticipated by so many years the three-day delay while Darl and Jewel are away hauling wood or the river-raising rain is, of course, inconceivable.

"My revenge would be that he would never know I was taking revenge." The revenge of the journey is that Anse Bundren should not know its reason. That *is* its reason, and no other one is ever stated by Addie. The journey is Addie's decreed "detour," exemplifying death's darkest ramification, the truth "older than Anse or love," what living amounts to if it only serves to consume the path to dying. The burial ritual is wholly incidental: a long march grave-ward whose primary burden is the corpse of its meaning. That Anse Bundren, whose central commitment in life has been to emulate the stationariness of a tree or a stand of corn, should be forced to set forth on an 80-mile detour is the heart of Addie's vengeance: a quest emptied of any goal other than its secret emptiness. It is the appropriate journey for the man Addie designates as "a significant shape profoundly without life like an empty door frame" (1990: 173).

Addie calls for the journey when Cash and Darl are infants, but by the time she is ready to die, the loyalty and private needs of all the Bundrens come into play. The effect of this is to complicate immeasurably the ironies already present. All of the Bundrens but Darl, as if following Addie's lead, also transform the burial journey into detour, in the sense that each of them has an ulterior motive in going to Jefferson, as Faulkner makes patently clear. In their case the "detour" traverses the identical path of those ulterior motives. Moreover, given the fact that Addie's alleged purpose is the absence of purpose, the ulteriority of motive of the rest of the Bundrens is actually at variance with nothing. Even Anse has his own reason for going to Jefferson, quite apart from the "reason" of Addie's that is beyond him.

The sources of the Bundrens' motives lie in the images that each of them but Darl takes hold of. These images represent initially the devotion of the Bundrens to Addie, but they also contain the seeds of their release from her, their turning away from her toward self-serving interests. Cash's coffin, Jewel's horse, Dewey Dell's fetus, Vardaman's fish, Anse's teeth – they incorporate Addie, and thus keep her alive (and themselves still joined to her) in the specific forms of devotion each entails. Cash's meticulous labor on the coffin that will house her, Jewel's violent love/hate possessiveness of the horse that, as Darl surmises, is his "mother," Dewey Dell's duplication of her in impending motherhood, Vardaman's belief in her transformation into a fish, Anse's recollection of their sexual relations – these all represent Addie's continuing presence for them, at times achieving a symbolic intensity close to incarnation.

These same images, however, also refer to personal desires that lead the Bundrens away from Addie toward Jefferson and the continuation of life. The coffin embodies not only Addie but Cash's vocation of carpentry, contiguous with the tools he brings on the trip so as to begin work afterwards on Tull's barn. The horse is the prize of Jewel's private night-time labor that he plans to ride into town, accompanying yet significantly separate from the rest of the mourning family. For Dewey Dell, the fetus is the focus of the grief she has no time to expend on Addie, and that she hopes to abort, breaking the connection of motherhood. Vardaman gradually turns his attention from the fish that keeps changing forms and locations to other, more mundane shifts in identity: the buzzards that disappear at night, the toy tracks that flash in and out of sight as the train runs over them in the store window (1990: 66). Anse adapts desire to his need for a new wife. Sentenced by Addie, as she was by her father, to a death journey, the family carries out resistance through the dynamic of devotion and release, answering to life and death forces on the same journey, detour and purpose fueling each other in inseparable reciprocity (see Kartiganer 1990 for a fuller discussion of these images in terms of metaphor and metonymy, the vertical and the horizontal, farm and journey).

Purposeful action exploiting the burial journey has the sound of life facing down death's claim on it, but there remains the accumulation of loss and suffering, the awful damage that journey inflicts. Except for Anse, the personal desires of the Bundrens

come to naught, and the costs of the attempts are incredibly high. Cash, his leg rebro-
ken, swelling black through its sleeve of cement, will not be repairing Tull's barn or
anything else for some time. Jewel loses his horse in Anse's trade for a new team of
mules, then returns to the family to suffer severe burns on his body while saving the
coffin from the fire in Gillespie's barn. Dewey Dell is not only unsuccessful at aborting
the baby, but she has to pay for it by submitting to the violation of sex with the
ruthless McGowan. Vardaman finds in the buzzards, the destruction of Gillespie's barn,
the fact that bananas once eaten are gone (1990: 66), and in the toy train new manifestations of the mutability that has traumatized him: "Where do they stay at night,
Darl?" (p. 210); "The barn is still red. It used to be redder than this. Then it went
swirling, making the stars run backward without falling. It hurt my heart like the
train did" (p. 225).

Beyond the individual losses and suffering there is the whole enormous nine-day
ordeal. Close to home are generous but skeptical neighbors who cannot penetrate the
collective privacy of this family, whose actions no one fully understands. Then there is
the threshold event, the nightmare river crossing, when, like the debris skimming along
the surface, the Bundrens find themselves "rootless, severed from the earth, spectral
above a scene of immense yet circumscribed desolation" (1990: 142). Finally, in the
towns of Mottson and Jefferson they pass into increasingly less sympathetic surroundings, as onlookers grow more distant, contemptuous, always ready to invoke the law,
confirmed in their sense of country people as virtually of another species.

But what of Anse? Alone among the Bundrens, he suffers no loss, either physically
or psychically, and in addition to keeping his "promise" acquires all he has sought: new
teeth, a new wife. His "image" – "God's will be done. . . . Now I can get them teeth"
(1990: 52) – contains in its possible memory of sexual desire less of a commitment to
Addie than to the sexual potency he wishes to implement again. He is able to transfer
that desire to another partner with the least amount of conflict and the largest amount
of equivalent satisfaction. The two references to "Mrs Bundren" by Cash (pp. 235, 236)
before Anse marries her may be Faulkner's slip, Cash's foresight, or the possibility that
she is a relative by marriage (hence Anse's foreknowledge of her existence), but it also
suggests that "Mrs Bundren" is for Anse less a specific woman than a title, a position
to be filled by anyone ready to take the job. Anse transforms the death march of his
wife of 30 or more years into a one-size-fits-all prothalamion.

We might gather from this that Addie's revenge has been a godsend for Anse
Bundren, a reversal of irony at her expense, but I believe this completely misses the
point. Addie has Anse right, and his actions on the journey are perfectly typical of what
she expects from him. The difference between Anse and the other Bundrens, especially
Addie, is that for him there is no true reciprocity of the primary instincts at work.
Anse's Eros is contrived altogether of words; it is desire unmixed with death. There is
no aggression, no violence from "below" – self-destruction turned to the intruding world
– from which powerful attachment, obsession might come forth. Anse's erotic movements outward betray only the speciousness of words "quick and harmless" (1990: 173),

words that "don't ever fit even what they are trying to say at" (p. 171). They do not own the power of the Bundrens' impassioned bondage (necessarily smacking of the absurdity of obsession) to their images of desire, or of Addie's adultery torn from sin "to shape and coerce the terrible blood to the forlorn echo of the dead word high in the air" (p. 175). In short, as a "pure" Eros, Anse lacks the power Eros borrows from its foe in order to create its own costly significance. He lives the life of detour beyond even Freud's hypothesis, a detour that has cut itself entirely loose from origin, not unconsciously dying but living, as it were, aloft, "straight up in a thin line," wholly in words like "sin and love and fear . . . just sounds that people . . . have for what they never had" (pp. 173–4). It is as if Anse has reached a level of sublimation absent of the transferred energy to give it significance even as detour: Eros attenuated to non-existence.

If there is a figure opposite Anse in the novel, it is not Addie and the Bundrens who follow her example into the reciprocities of life and death, but Darl Bundren, who belongs entirely to the sphere of death. His remarkable powers of vision are the gift of a virtual inanimacy-in-life from which he looks out on the world. He has no part of Eros: no desires, no images, no obsessive attachments – no palpable substitute for Addie to threaten him with too deep a devotion, or for him to transform into the cunning displacement that will urge him to Jefferson.

Addie denies him at conception – "Then I found that I had Darl. At first I would not believe it. Then I believed that I would kill Anse" (1990: 172) – and at his birth she devises the revenge of the promise that she be buried in Jefferson. Unlike her other children, there is no erotic dimension in his creation: not, as with Cash, the "answer" to the discovery that "living was terrible" (p. 171); not, as with Jewel, the adultery that is "the duty to the alive"; not even, as with Dewey Dell and Vardaman, the obligation to clean one's house, conceiving children as payments on a debt: "now he had three children that are his and not mine" (p. 176).

Having nothing of Eros, Darl has no neurotic need to exploit his inherent masochism in aggressive pursuits. He functions out of a perfect detachment that is the source of his exactingly objective vision that registers the world as it is, divested of desire. His narrative description of the death of Addie and the immediate responses of the Bundrens to it has the power of a passion based not on empathy but on its absence, on an indiscriminate wonder that spreads evenly among the outraged mourners: from the daughter keening across the lifeless body to the husband fumbling helplessly over the wrinkled quilt he cannot smooth over.

What Darl sees or miraculously infers is magnificent to read but in the family or society within which he exists it is not to be borne. He does not act with the violence of Addie Bundren challenging death, but he is the supreme agent of violation in the novel. He invades the people around him, not for sex but for secrets, that private, interior world, the residue of inanimacy that survives in life not as an intimation of immortality but of the death we all harbor, seek to protect and to delay. It is the inviolable self, hidden even from the family, that Darl, like Hawthorne's diabolical inquisitors, enters as through an open door. He knows the secret of Dewey Dell's pregnancy, that Jewel is not Anse's son, perhaps even that the entire journey is Addie's fabricated detour.

The vision is monstrous because it lacks even the intelligibility of malice. We wonder whether Darl is aware that he wounds in his probing questions: "I said to Dewey Dell: 'You want her to die so you can get to town: is that it?'" (1990: 39–40); "Your mother was a horse, but who was your father, Jewel?" (p. 212). While at Armstid's house, as Anse provides the details of his trade with Snopes for the mules, Darl suddenly realizes that Anse has used Cash's money as part of the deal, and says, in front of Armstid and the family, "So that's what you were doing in Cash's clothes last night" (p. 190). The public exposure of his father's theft is not a matter of filial aggression or fraternal support. Armstid observes, "He said it just like he was reading it outen the paper. Like he never give a durn himself one way or the other."

Occasionally he is permitted awareness of his own condition, although here Faulkner is careful to see to it that the sense of pathos is ours, not Darl's. In the well-known passage in which his preparation to "empty" himself for sleep becomes an attempt to establish his own identity, Darl retains the marginality of the detached observer. He confines himself to question and negation: "And before you are emptied for sleep, what are you. And when you are emptied for sleep, you are not. And when you are filled with sleep, you never were" (1990: 80). The same principle of negation applies to his exploration of definition through ownership: "the load [of wood] that is no longer theirs that felled and sawed it nor yet theirs that bought it and which is not ours either, lie on our wagon though it does." Darl uses what is for him the ignorance of Jewel – who "knows he is, because he does not know that he does not know whether he is or not" – as the contrast of a blind erotic assurance. The substantiality Darl achieves, his "is"ness, turns out to depend on Addie's existence, which depends on Jewel's ("who does not know"), which refers back to Darl's original ability to "empty myself for sleep in a strange room," which culminates in the condition of non-being: "filled with sleep, you never were." Thus: I think I am not, therefore I am.

In circular meditations such as these as well as his precise representation of events, of the inevitable "deceit" of erotic attachments that even Addie Bundren finds herself having to practice (1990: 130–1), Darl exposes the fraudulence of detour. Ultimately, the Bundrens must expel him, lest the dying whose ubiquity he manifests become the reality that consumes all. When Darl burns down Gillespie's barn, he is not only trying to burn up Jewel's contribution to the journey, he is trying to separate life and death, render death as the only reality and Eros as an illusion pretending to bring together words and deeds, the dream of greater achievement and the drive toward death.

Darl's destruction of the barn is the climax of his vision and his distance from what the other Bundrens regard as reality. Setting fire to the barn is his only significant action in the novel, and yet the act seems designed less to end what for him is an absolutely meaningless journey than to provide occasion for his lyrical description of it. Although Darl uses figurative language throughout the novel, in his account of the burning barn and the rescue of the animals and coffin, his expression rises to poetic heights as well as to an extreme remoteness from the tenor of the description, an event that a farmer must regard as catastrophic. While some of the figures are apt enough, most convey not merely metaphysical strain, but a kind of irrelevance: Mack's freckles "like english peas on a plate"; the frightened cow's "tail erect and rigid as a broom nailed upright to the end of her spine"; the burning hay "like a portiere of flaming beads." Most remarkable, of course, are the figures from classical and modern art: "two figures in a Greek frieze," "the conical facade," the coffin "like a cubistic bug," and finally the allusion to theater, "the dissolving proscenium of the doorway" (1990: 220–1).

Nowhere in the description is there the slightest sense that the monologue is coming from the man who started the fire. On the contrary, the language has an autonomy to it, as if independent of the practical disaster it so brilliantly describes, as if emphasizing that all of it – the fire, the frantic effort at rescue, the journey, the very language used to register all of this momentous struggle – it is all aimless but for the original death that draws it forward, is nothing but metaphor "isolated out of all reality by the red glare" (1990: 221). Significantly, at the end of his monologue, at the peak moment of his aestheticization of detour, Darl registers the victory of Jewel. Jewel saves the coffin, "riding upon it, clinging to it," having transferred his displacement of the horse back to Addie. Perhaps compelled by the remorseless honesty of the poet or by an undeniable awareness of the power of detour, however ghostly it may appear to him, Darl acknowledges Jewel as a god "enclosed in a thin numbus of fire," the fire burning "crimson-edged holes that bloom like flowers in his undershirt" (p. 222).

To return to the issues I raised at the beginning of this chapter, in arranging the expulsion of Darl Bundren from the novel, Faulkner is describing the expulsion of a certain kind of artistry from his work, as he moved from *The Sound and the Fury* to *As I Lay Dying*. His respect, even affection for Darl, in his extratextual comments, is clear enough: "Who can say how much of the good poetry in the world has come out of madness, and who can say just how much of super-perceptivity the – a mad person might not have? . . . That maybe the madman does see more than the sane man" (Faulkner 1959: 113). "Madness," however, and all that it might imply for Faulkner were not what he was about in the fall of 1929. If he were going to remain a writer, he had to write: expeditiously, professionally, if possible profitably – and if not profitably then in a way that provided opportunity to earn money by other means, either by writing short stories (which he always considered, even at his best in this genre, "boiling the pot") or, as in October, 1929, by taking a job that, ostensibly, had nothing whatsoever to do with writing.

There is more to the shift marked by *As I Lay Dying*, however, than the speed with which it was written and published. He turned to the life of country people, free from the kinds of historical obsessions and race-related complexities inherent to the Southern culture Faulkner knew best, and free from what many would consider the major issue concerning country people: their economic plight. His purpose was to confront issues that marriage and family had thrust upon him. How does one negotiate the conflict of family obligation and personal desire? Of a privacy that seems to reach back and down into an "abject nakedness we bring here with us" (1990: 46) and a world of engagement encroaching constantly on that privacy, compelling a different kind of responsibility? Perhaps inspired by Freud's stark delineation of life and death as antagonistic instincts, Faulkner found in the journey of the Bundrens life and death forces in an inextricable interdependence that might suggest, if one knew how to read it, the possibility of achievement.

Only by their individual, private commitments can the Bundrens muster the strength and resilience that enable them to complete the journey that, as it turns out, is not the primary purpose of any of them. Among the ironies of this novel whose compromises are constantly folding back on themselves is the fact that the "getting ready to stay dead," the empty request, is subservient to most of the action and motive in the text and yet it is the force that compels everything into motion. The novel delivers itself over to a reciprocity comparable to that of Freud's text, whose own efforts to establish priority among instincts are constantly deferred. Is life the elaborate detour of an urge to die, an enormous displacement of a quest for silence? Or is death only the illuminating background of life that, as Emily Dickinson writes, sets it significant? Where does "mastery" lie: in the death that darkens all or in the "circuitous paths to death," the abundant evidence that "the organism wishes to die only in its own fashion" (Freud 1961a: 33)?

Darl, like Anse, rejects, or perhaps better to say, is incapable of, the dynamic. But he is the one to be expelled. He is the source of "good poetry," perhaps sees "more than the sane man," but he speaks out of a death vision that is closer to the spirit of *Flags in the Dust* and *The Sound and the Fury* than to that of *As I Lay Dying*. The Lost Cause ethic, the backward look, control both novels, however different the textual tone. In *Flags* there is the unmistakable insistence on beauty in the "ghosts of glamorous and old disastrous things" (Faulkner 1974: 432). In *The Sound and the Fury*, a far richer work of course, there is the great death-infested lyricism of Quentin Compson, dismayed at the loss of a past he represents in his failures to duplicate it, as well as in sexual fantasies he has no interest in fulfilling. While both novels are clearly aware, especially the second one, of the hopelessness of their infatuation with the past, neither one offers a feasible alternative.

In *As I Lay Dying* the death drive of Darl Bundren is contested powerfully by the rest of his family. For all his hold on Faulkner – he is given the largest number of monologues and with only a few exceptions the most memorable – he is expelled in the name of erotic quests: the Bundrens' to complete their mission, however compromised by ulterior motives, to get to Jefferson, to get the body into the ground, no matter its condition or scandalous treatment; Faulkner's to complete the novel, to build what Cash praises as a "tight chicken coop" rather than a court house, "shoddy" or "built well" (1990: 234), methodically pushing it out on swing-shift power-plant breaks, the novel of compromise itself compromised by the contract he and Estelle had entered into June 20, 1929.

Of the Bundrens Faulkner said that, confronted with a difficult "fate," they "pretty well coped with theirs" (1968: 254). Of his marriage he told a friend in Pascagoula,

"Tom, they don't think we're gonna stick, but it is gonna stick" (Blotner 1984: 243). Of *As I Lay Dying* he wrote, "I sent it to Smith and wrote him that by it I would stand or fall" (Faulkner 1932: vii).

NOTES

1 Faulkner claimed on more than one occasion that he never read Freud, although he certainly was familiar with some who had. The first English translation of Freud's 1920 text by C. J. M. Hubback was published in London in 1922 and in the United States in 1924 by Boni and Liveright. In 1925 Boni and Liveright became the publisher of Sherwood Anderson, with whom Faulkner spent a good deal of time in New Orleans that same year, and of Faulkner's first two novels: *Soldiers' Pay* (1926) and *Mosquitoes* (1927).

2 By way of explanation for Addie's anger at discovering she is pregnant, critics have suggested the violation of the wholeness she shares with Cash as well as the limits of her autonomy that

this pregnancy signifies. See Pierce (1980: 299–300).

3 Cora Tull claims that the distance from the Bundrens' farm to Jefferson is 40 miles (Faulkner 1990: 22), whereas Faulkner consistently said in interviews that it was 20 (see Faulkner 1959: 112, for example). Tull's statement that it is a two-to-three-day trip by mule and wagon supports the longer distance. According to Hinkle and McCoy, "a wagon drawn by mules can go slightly less than twenty miles a day" (1995: 96). Luce argues that the entire geography of *As I Lay Dying* differs considerably from the Frenchman's Bend of the later novels (1990: 77–8).

REFERENCES AND FURTHER READING

Aiken, C. S. (1977). Faulkner's Yoknapatawpha County: Geographical Fact into Fiction. *Geographical Review*, 67: 1–21.

Blotner, J. (1984). *Faulkner: A Biography*. One-vol. edn. New York: Random House.

Cook, S. J. (1976). *From Tobacco Road to Route 66: The Southern Poor White in Fiction*. Chapel Hill, NC: University of North Carolina Press.

Faulkner, W. (1932). Introduction. In *Sanctuary* (pp. v–viii). New York: Random House.

Faulkner, W. (1959). *Faulkner in the University: Class Conferences at the University of Virginia, 1957–1958* (eds. F. L. Gwynn and J. L. Blotner). Charlottesville, VA: University of Virginia Press.

Faulkner, W. (1968). *Lion in the Garden: Interviews with William Faulkner 1926–1962* (eds. J. B. Meriwether and M. Millgate). New York: Random House.

Faulkner, W. (1974). *Flags in the Dust*. New York: Vintage. (Original pub. 1973.)

Faulkner, W. (1984). *Father Abraham* (ed. J. B.

Meriwether). New York: Modern Library and Random House. (Original pub. 1983.)

Faulkner, W. (1990). *As I Lay Dying: The Corrected Text*. New York: Vintage International and Random House. (Original pub. 1930.)

Faulkner, W. (1991). *The Hamlet: The Corrected Text*. New York: Vintage International. (Original pub. 1940.)

Faulkner, W. (1994). An Introduction for *The Sound and the Fury*. In D. Minter (ed.). *The Sound and the Fury* (pp. 225–8). New York: Norton. (Original pub. 1972.)

Federal Writers' Project of the Works Progress Administration (1988). *Mississippi: The WPA Guide to the Magnolia State*. Jackson: University Press of Mississippi. (Original pub. 1938.)

Freud, S. (1961a). *Beyond the Pleasure Principle* (trans. J. Strachey). New York: Norton. (Original pub. 1920.)

Freud, S. (1961b). *Civilization and its Discontents* (trans. J. Strachey). New York: Norton. (Original pub. 1930.)

Freud, S. (1969). *An Outline of Psycho-Analysis* (trans. J. Strachey). New York: Norton. (Original pub. 1940.)

Hinkle, J. C. and R. McCoy (1995). *Reading Faulkner: The Unvanquished*. Jackson: University Press of Mississippi.

Kartiganer, D. M. (1990). The Farm and the Journey: Ways of Mourning and Meaning in *As I Lay Dying*. *Mississippi Quarterly*, 43: 281–303.

Luce, D. C. (1990). *William Faulkner: Annotations to the Novels: As I Lay Dying*. New York: Garland.

Parker, R. D. (1985). *Faulkner and the Novelistic Imagination*. Urbana: University of Illinois Press.

Pierce, C. (1980). Being, Knowing, and Saying in the "Addie" Section of Faulkner's *As I Lay Dying*. *Twentieth-Century Literature*, 26: 294–305.

27

Faulkner and the Southern Arts of Mystification in *Absalom, Absalom!*

John Carlos Rowe

Faulkner is often praised as a Southern writer who drew upon the region's rich traditions of storytelling, just as he is admired for his powerful indictment of the moral corruption that resulted from slavery and fueled the economic failures and social inequities of the New South. Storytelling and the sins of slavery are usually treated as separate and distinct legacies, the former representing all that is good about the region and the latter containing its evil. I will argue in this chapter that Faulkner recognized the perverse complicity of his own imaginative talents and a storytelling tradition in the South that was deeply involved in the rationalization of the many different fantasies on which slavery and Southern racism relied. Faulkner's obsessive fascination with Southern storytelling as crucial to regional culture is evident in all of his writings, but *Absalom, Absalom!* (1936) displays in the greatest detail his personal struggle to draw upon that culture while distinguishing his own narrative from its inherent immorality.

The issue is an old one facing imaginative writers. Faulkner's predecessor, Mark Twain, struggles to distinguish his work from the "lies" eloquently and skillfully told by the rich, powerful, and corrupt (see Rowe 2005). Joseph Conrad's Marlow infamously declares his hatred of "a lie," even as the reader knows him to be a pathological liar, leaving Conrad's own status as the author of *Heart of Darkness* (1898–9) in considerable doubt. Whom do we trust when the narrator of the story betrays an immoral unreliability? Is the "author" lurking somewhere in the blank places of the text, impossibly *between* the words, giving us hints of the truth? Although this problem has attracted many scholars, the ethical status of unreliable narration remains a troublesome one for readers of all competencies and thus an attractive option for writers precisely because such unreliability poses the fundamental question of literary authority: how do we know when to trust an absent author dealing in ostensibly fictive situations?

In Faulkner, such unreliability is usually integral to a culture built upon systematic deception and the constant labor of maintaining fragile social illusions of honor and respectability. In his *Narrative of the Life of Frederick Douglass*, Douglass describes in vivid detail the deceptiveness of the slave-master, Covey, who is called "the Snake" by the other slaves. Douglass and his fellow workers know how slavery is maintained by trickery, even though they do not have the obvious means to overturn the system of laws and everyday practices through which such illusory power is maintained (Douglass 1982: 103).[1] In the longer history of the South covered by Faulkner's Yoknapatawpha narratives, the symbolic system of racial, gender, and class discriminations has developed into an even more elaborate order of "fables," often told and retold by individuals from all segments of that society as a means of internalizing and thus giving reality to its lies. "Unreliable narration," then, is much more than merely a technical device for Douglass and Faulkner, but an integral part of a deluded society. Yet if this is the moral situation of the South for both authors, then why can't they simply tell the truth?

In a certain sense, of course, such truth-telling is precisely what we identify as the task of great literature, but how a literary work accomplishes this work by way of imagined forms – character, plot, setting, and style – remains another one of the enduring problems for literary theorists. One compelling answer is that the literary text's obsessive interest in its own formal and communicative means can be used to mimic and sometimes expose the broader social modes of producing accepted meanings. The otherwise self-indulgent "metaliterariness" or "self-consciousness" of a literary text can thus be turned into a representation of the symbolic machinery of the culture that prompted it. Just how the internal commentary on literary possibility is transformed into an effective political critique, even potential *reform*, of social discourse and behavior is a more complicated question that can only be addressed in individual cases.

Absalom, Absalom! is one of the best possible test cases for how narrative unreliability and literary self-consciousness might serve the political and moral criticism of social reality. The novel is narrated formally by Rosa Coldfield, Quentin Compson's father, and Quentin Compson in parts that overlap and often offer different versions of the Sutpen family's history. Each of these narrators, of course, relies on numerous other sources and on auditors like Quentin, who listens to "Miss Coldfield's" and his father's versions, and Quentin's Canadian classmate at Harvard, Shrevlin McCannon, whose questions and comments end up forming parts of the narrative. The purpose of this multiple narration is ostensibly realistic: to imitate the diverse ways in which we apprehend historical events, especially those involving scandal distorted by repression and prone to different versions. The traditional assumption has been that such realism renders the psychological complexity of scandalous events in ways far more truthful than any historical chronicle, and that the different narrations allow responsibility for the repressed past to be shared by the community.[2]

The repressed, scandalous event cannot be overcome simply by uttering it, in part because its very repression makes literal statement impossible. As every reader of the novel is aware, the "secret" past of the Sutpen family has many different versions: Thomas Sutpen disavowed his son, Charles Bon, who is African (Haitian) American; Thomas Sutpen's son, Henry Sutpen, murdered his half-brother, Charles Bon; Charles Bon and Judith Sutpen, half-brother and half-sister, were incestuous lovers; and so on (there are still other versions). Each family "scandal" in Faulkner's South derives from the deeper sin of slavery, which for Faulkner has an even more profound source:

ownership. So what is the *real* scandal to be "revealed" in the course of the novel: miscegenation, incest, murder, suicide, slavery, ownership? For Faulkner, they are all part of the same cultural narrative, linked parts that surface in the course of ordinary people attempting to account for extraordinary events.

For Faulkner, then, the novel is distinctly different from the repressive mechanisms of the chronicle. Every student of Faulkner's classic "The Bear," at least the long version that includes section 4, knows the dramatic events of the narrative revolve around Ike McCaslin's reading of his Uncle Buck and Uncle Buddy's account ledgers in the Commissary of their plantation. Interpreting bare facts as a novelist would, Ike uncovers the history of systematic miscegenation – the rape of African-American slave women by white masters – on which his family's wealth, power, and kinship relations are based. The Christ-like Ike, by turns transcendentally good and divinely foolish, is certainly an alter-ego for Faulkner, even though the author never quite makes clear what personal qualities Ike possesses that allow him to read the moral truth of the otherwise commodified accounts in those ledgers. Ike and Faulkner are above all *good* readers, in which "good" means both skilled and ethical.

In "The Bear," Faulkner sets those ledgers, which commodify human beings, against the "stories" through which people achieve their identities and social relations. The contrast is not so clear in the earlier *Absalom*, in which storytelling is not inherently good or liberatory. Faulkner knows how cultural work shapes the social fabric in which slavery and ownership are integral to its design. Rosa Coldfield and Mr. Compson tell their versions of Thomas Sutpen's tragic family history to distance themselves from what the Sutpens represent: ambitious nouveaux riches, social climbers, and iconoclasts who violate social propriety. Storytelling is for both Quentin's father and "Miss Coldfield" cathartic in the worst sense: a purgation of all they find objectionable in Thomas Sutpen and his family. In telling the story of the Sutpens, however, they cover up their own complicity in that tragedy and yet allow us to see their responsibility for it. That *difference* is what distinguishes Faulkner (and his moral characters, like Ike McCaslin) from the mystification of the Old South, its rationalization of plantation life and the slavocracy, and its insistent projection of evil onto other social forces, usually coming from outside the South: Sutpen's Haiti, the carpetbagger's North, even Shreve McCannon's Canada, one major destination for the Underground Railroad.

Rosa Coldfield tells her story to Quentin because she thinks he might

> enter the literary profession as so many Southern gentlemen and gentlewomen too are doing now and maybe some day you will remember this and write about it. You will get married then I expect and perhaps your wife will want a new gown or a new chair for the house and you can write this and submit it to the magazines. (Faulkner 1964: 9–10).)

Quentin thinks, *"Only she dont mean that, . . . It's because she wants it told"* (p. 10). Quentin doesn't specify what Rosa "dont mean," but he's probably referring to her suggestion of a profit-motive, because Rosa elsewhere does imagine that Quentin might bear his

Southern legacy, wherever he might live, by taking over the storytelling responsibilities for his family. The "literary profession" is indeed proper work for "Southern gentlemen and gentlewomen too," Rosa believes, because it contributes to the veneer of respectable culture that covers the ugly history of the white South. Quentin thinks that Rosa herself might well have told publicly the Sutpens' story, because

> if she had merely wanted it told, written and even printed, she would not have needed to call in anybody – a woman who even in his (Quentin's) father's youth had already established herself as the town's and the county's poetess laureate by issuing to the stern and meager subscription list of the county newspaper poems, ode, eulogy and epitaph, out of some bitter and implacable reserve of undefeat. (p. 11)

Faulkner satirizes women authors, especially those like Rosa who write occasional poetry for the local newspapers, but he also has in mind his own pretensions to authorship. Anxious to distinguish his authority from Rosa's and yet well aware of how deeply indebted he is to this Southern legacy of storytelling, Faulkner struggles through *Absalom, Absalom!* to find a proper literary ethics.

In mocking Rosa's dilettantism, Faulkner recalls Mark Twain's notorious parodies of Julia A. Moore's maudlin verse and thus indulges a familiar, if tiresome, sexism.[3] Yet in the context of the novel his trivialization of Rosa as "poetess laureate" repeats Thomas Sutpen's more devastating "insult" of her. What causes Rosa to break her engagement to Thomas Sutpen is his proposal "that they breed together for test and sample and if it was a boy they would marry" (1964: 177). Just as Toni Morrison's Sethe is infuriated by schoolteacher's treatment of his slaves as livestock, so Rosa is horrified to be reminded that Sutpen considers women primarily means of reproduction.[4] When Sutpen comes to town in search of a wife, "the women merely said . . . that he had now come to . . . find a wife exactly as he would have gone to the Memphis market to buy livestock or slaves" (p. 42). Unlike the Compsons and DeSpains, Sutpen makes no effort to disguise his treatment of women (or slaves). In defending his marriage to the Octoroon wife who gives birth to their son (Charles Etienne de Saint Velery Bon), Charles Bon lectures Henry Sutpen on the close relationship between the courtesans of New Orleans and the Southern belle:

> No: not whores. Not even courtesans – creatures taken at childhood, culled, and chosen and raised more carefully than any white girl, any nun, than any blooded mare even, . . . For a price, of course, but a price offered and accepted or declined through a system more formal than any that white girls are sold under since they are more valuable as commodities than white girls, raised and trained to fulfill a woman's sole end and purpose: to love, to be beautiful, to divert; never to see a man's face hardly until brought to the ball and offered to and chosen by some man who in return, not can and not will but *must*, supply her with the surroundings proper in which to love and be beautiful and divert, and who must usually risk his life or at least his blood for that privilege. No, not whores. (p. 117)

In this remarkable passage, Charles Bon raises the Octoroon prostitutes of New Orleans above "white girls," but he stylistically links the two, equating the courtship rituals of plantation society with those of the urban bordello. Following the complex motifs of doubling whereby Faulkner demonstrates how white aristocratic appearances are sustained by repressing African American realities, the Octoroon courtesans reveal the unconscious of the white Southern belle (Irwin 1975: 9).

Just what Thomas Sutpen proposes to Rosa is what he enacts with Milly Jones just one year after Rosa flees Sutpen's Hundred in 1866. Born in 1853, Milly is only 13 or 14 when in 1867 "Sutpen takes up with Milly Jones" (1964: 380). Milly's mother, Melicent, was "rumored to have died in a Memphis brothel," and we know that the Jones family represents the poor whites marginalized by the slave economy who thus become active participants in the racial hatred essential to the caste system of the Old South. As Thomas Sutpen's abuse of the child, Milly, suggests, women are not only treated as children by this paternalistic society, they are abused as children even before they have become adults. Sutpen is a "demon" in Rosa's estimation, because he exposes the elaborate fictions that maintain all of these distinctions: white Southern belle, prostitute, African American woman, child, poor white woman. Yet in recognizing her identity with all of these other oppressed people in the South, Rosa feels neither compassion for nor solidarity with them. She is horrified and flees Sutpen's Hundred, only to return again and again to re-enact the repetition-compulsion that results from profound repression (Freud 1958: 145).

Why, then, would Faulkner implicate himself in this process by insulting Rosa with his mockery of her modest literary talents? To be sure, we could attribute the remark to Quentin – it occurs in indirect discourse – or even to the paternalism of Jefferson at large, where Rosa is gently mocked for her literary pretensions. But Faulkner *does tell the story* of the Sutpens, which Rosa, Mr. Compson, Quentin, even Shreve and Charles Bon, tell only in part and from particular perspectives. As contemporary readers of *Absalom* know, Quentin cannot claim authorship because he is already dead at the end of *The Sound and the Fury* (1929). Quentin is spectral in *Absalom*, already fictionally dead, so that Faulkner himself must be Rosa's principal competitor for the "true story."

At first glance, Faulkner's insult of Rosa seems hardly comparable with Sutpen's, which dehumanizes her as fundamentally as the slavocracy does African Americans. Faulkner's gentle mockery of Rosa's poetic talents in "ode, eulogy and epitaph," however, suggests that she deals primarily in idealizing verse or laments for the dead. Her "poetry" does little to renew or revitalize the social order, but instead merely expresses the Old South's "bitter and implacable reserve of undefeat" (1964: 11). Thomas Sutpen wants a male heir to replace Henry Sutpen and restore the honor of the Sutpen name. He seeks to revitalize his family name and presumably his claim to aristocratic privilege by using Rosa as a biological means, but his insult also encompasses his disregard for what Rosa Coldfield and her family represent in the society of Jefferson: some claim to cultural authority. It would be unthinkable, of course, for the blunt and uncultivated

Thomas Sutpen even to consider the value of Rosa's poetic contributions to the local newspaper in his marriage proposal, but Rosa knows that Thomas Sutpen's "insult" goes beyond his immodest proposal to her and encompasses his desire to use her respectable name to restore his family's tarnished reputation. Most readers recognize that one of Thomas Sutpen's major failures is his inability to *love* other people, including his children, his slaves, his two wives (Eulalia Bon and Ellen Coldfield), his fiancée (Rosa), and his mistress (Milly Jones).

Quentin concludes that Rosa tells him her part of the story to encourage him to carry on the legacy of Southern storytelling on which the social status of the Coldfields, Compsons, and DeSpains depends. To be sure, these white class pretensions are merely foolish day-dreams by 1909–10, the years Quentin attends Harvard and attempts to retell the story to Shreve McCannon. Quentin's suicide in Cambridge, Massachusetts, in 1910 ought to announce the end of a storytelling tradition that preserves the lies of the white ruling class from the antebellum to post-Civil War eras. Faulkner, then, competes not with Rosa, but with Thomas Sutpen, which is perhaps why both "insult" Rosa Coldfield.

In the tradition of avant-garde modernism in which William Faulkner certainly figures importantly, albeit eccentrically given his insistent Southern regionalism, the struggle between genealogical and cultural authority is central. T. S. Eliot's insistent trivialization of sexual reproduction in *The Waste Land* (1922) depends on his efforts to revitalize cultural values and claim his own authority. The sad, dirty liaison between the "typist" and "the young man carbuncular" in "The Fire Sermon" is "witnessed" by Tiresias only to remind us of the decadence of the modern age, but the episode is the prelude to Eliot's eulogy of Queen Elizabeth I, the Virgin Queen who represents for him the cultural vitality of England in the Elizabethan Age (Eliot 1962: 36–41). In the same section, St. Augustine (helped along by Eliot's version of Buddhism) "burns" through his youthful lust in Alexandria to achieve the sort of ascetic transcendence central to Christianity's divine love (p. 41). In response to what Eliot considers the sexual decadence of the modern age, he counsels literary sublimation and its more enduring "procreation" of enduring cultural values. Ezra Pound metaphorized the brain as a "great clot of genital fluid," and his *Cantos* work to create a complex genealogy, even kinship system, among the political and cultural "thrones" he identifies throughout history and around the globe (Pound 1922: 206;, Rowe 2002: 124–30). William Faulkner is neither a version of Eliot's Christian poet nor Pound's Fascist artist, but he resembles both of his contemporaries in his insistence upon the role of aesthetics in cultural revival and thus in social rule.

Thomas Sutpen fails in the end, killed by Wash Jones, the squatter occasionally employed by Sutpen and whose "honor" is quixotically threatened when Sutpen gets Jones's granddaughter, Milly, pregnant. Faulkner wants us to conclude that Sutpen meets the sordid end that he himself deserves for the lies he told and the secrets he tried futilely to keep. Thomas Sutpen fulfills the prophecy of the de Spains, Compsons, and Coldfields about a "new" South, even though he establishes his plantation in Yoknapatawpha County, Mississippi, in 1833, 28 years before the beginning of the

Civil War. To the heirs of the ruined Southern aristocracy, like Rosa Coldfield and Mr. Compson, Thomas Sutpen is a prophetic version of the later, hated "carpetbagger," who arrived to profit from the postbellum anarchy and socio-economic reorganization of the South after Emancipation. But "carpetbaggers" were from the North, not the West Virginia mountains, where Sutpen was born in 1807 (or 1808) before West Virginia was in fact a state, and certainly not from Haiti, where Sutpen emigrated and married the "only child of Haitian sugar planter of French descent" in 1827 (Faulkner 1964: 381).[5]

For Faulkner, Thomas Sutpen is not a Northern carpetbagger; he is the ghostly embodiment of everything behind the Southern romance of graceful plantation life and culture. What the Compsons and de Spains despise about Thomas Sutpen is the way he reveals their own lies, so that they work desperately to control his family "tragedy" in hopes of renovating their own social authority. Yet in distancing themselves from what Thomas Sutpen represents, they trivialize themselves and reduce their stories to mere gossip. In exposing the elemental truth Sutpen expresses, Faulkner tries to avoid the faded gentility that captures Miss Coldfield and Mr. Compson and drives Quentin to an early end. Yet in equating Sutpen's truth with the authority of the South, Faulkner cannot help himself from desiring, even emulating, that terrible power.

Thomas Sutpen's authority depends on the inextricable relationship he establishes between his identity and his ability to kill. Although state laws throughout the antebellum South varied considerably with respect to the authority they gave slave-owners over the lives and deaths of their slaves, the actual practices of slaveholders seem to confirm the godlike authority over life and death exercised by so many white masters. Sutpen is not an ordinary slave owner, but a philosophical abstraction of slave-owning – in short, a literary representation of its social psychology. He represents the terrifying reality of an individuality possessing philosophical being possible only as a consequence of another's lack of identity. Faulkner's Thomas Sutpen represents the beneficiary of that system in which the slave experiences "social death." As Orlando Patterson points out, the "slaveholder class" generally denied the violence of this situation by genuinely believing "that they cared and provided for their slaves and that it was the slaves who . . . had 'been raised to depend on others'" (1982: 338). Condemning both this mystification and the power behind it, critics of the slavocracy focus understandably on the terrible consequences for the African Americans who suffered its material, psychological, and sociological terrorism. But the other side of the system is just as important for us to understand, Faulkner argues, if we are ever to overcome the inherent power dynamics of such a caste system in which some people possess spiritual "being" and others are reduced legally to "chattel."

The moral center of *Absalom, Absalom!* is the story Thomas Sutpen tells General Compson about his origins in West Virginia and then Tidewater Virginia. I want to stress the fact that *Sutpen* tells his story, even if it is Quentin and Shreve who will retell it to each other in that cold Harvard dormitory room. Usually taken to be the antithesis of the Southern storyteller, Thomas Sutpen nevertheless spins a yarn that is perhaps the most riveting one in the entire novel, even if we never read precisely his version but instead some mediated account. Sutpen tells the story while he is hunting down his French architect, in an episode that reminds us that the enslavement of African Americans was shared by many other peoples, albeit usually to lesser degrees. The story Sutpen tells is Faulkner's great mythic parable of the psychological origins of slavery and its complementary class and gender distinctions. Whereas the title of the novel refers us to the biblical parable of King David and his rebellious son, Absalom, Sutpen's story offers its own version of a will-to-power that virtually "invents" slavery as an institution and legitimates the authority of the white master.

Born in the frontier wilderness that was not yet West Virginia in 1807–8, raised in a pre-agrarian hunting-and-gathering economy that seems tribal and communal, the young Thomas Sutpen appears to lack any sort of being or identity. As an adolescent – "he was eleven or twelve or thirteen now because this was where he realized that he had irrevocably lost count of his age" (1964: 228) – he moves with his family to Tidewater Virginia, identifiable with Jamestown, site of the early colony, where he confronts the true meaning of ownership and its complement, colonialism.[6] Sutpen's (or Faulkner's or Quentin's) account is aptly dream-like and vague with regard to details, and it thus has the qualities of some mythic origin story:

> He was just there, surrounded by the faces, almost all the faces which he had ever known . . . living in a cabin that was almost a replica of the mountain one except that it didn't sit up in the bright wind but sat instead beside a big flat river that sometimes showed no current at all and even sometimes ran backward, where his sisters and brothers seemed to take sick after supper and die before the next meal, where regiments of niggers with white men watching them planted and raised things he had never heard of. (p. 227)

Sutpen's family seems to repeat the famine and illness suffered by the settlers of the early Jamestown colony, which was poorly situated along a peninsula (now an island) formed by the slow-moving and marshy James River as it empties into the Atlantic.

As important to the American origin story as Plymouth Plantation, Jamestown usually invokes the redemptive myth of Pocahontas (Matoaka in Pamunkey), whose salvation of Captain John Smith and marriage to John Rolfe are used as mythic justifications of the European colonization of the South and as curious testaments to the aristocratic authority of those "First Families of Virginia," who can trace their genealogy back to this symbolic marriage of native and European Americans.[7] The adolescent Thomas Sutpen does not, however, witness these American mythemes; instead, he spies American "civilization" in the form of a master–slave tableau:

> And the man who owned all the land and the niggers and apparently the white men who superintended the work, lived in the biggest house he had ever seen and spent most of the afternoon (he told how he would creep up among the tangled shrubbery of the lawn and lie hidden and watch the man) in a barrel stave hammock between two trees, with his shoes off, and a nigger who wore every day better clothes than he or his father and

sisters had ever owned and ever expected to, who did nothing else but fan him and bring him drinks. (1964: 227–8)

Faulkner carefully sets up this moment as a critical threshold in Thomas Sutpen's transition from childish innocence to adult experience: "Because he had not only not lost the innocence yet, he had not yet discovered that he possessed it" (p. 228). Yet in working at the mystery posed by the man in the hammock, who owns everything and yet does not have to labor, Sutpen comes to adult consciousness at the cost of his innocence.

Faulkner creates a scene of literary self-consciousness in which Sutpen virtually recognizes himself in his power to kill. Descartes's *Cogito ergo sum* is effectively replaced by Sutpen's *Cogito ergo neco*, even if Faulkner's backwoods character never utters these Latin words. "I think, therefore I can kill" does seem to be Sutpen's motto from the moment he witnesses the twinned relationship of chattel slavery and landownership. Drawing on his limited experience, the young Sutpen tries to explain the man in the hammock who owns everything by analogy with a "mountain man who happened to own a fine rifle" (1964: 228), but he cannot comprehend how the chance of such possession would allow "another . . . to say to other men: *Because I own this rifle, my arms and legs and blood and bones are superior to yours* except as the victorious outcome of a fight with rifles . . ." (p. 229). Faulkner is masterful at conveying two messages at the same time: the boy's incredulity before the owner's authority and the ineluctable truth of that mastery. Faulkner achieves this effect by the rhetorical use of double negatives and a variety of other negative constructions, most of which follow the logic of psychic repression, anticipating the more famous concluding lines of the novel, in which Quentin answers Shreve's question, "'Why do you hate the South?'" with his terrible cry: "'I don't hate it,' he said. *I don't hate it* he thought panting in the cold air, the iron New England dark; *I don't. I don't! I don't hate it! I don't hate it!*" (p. 378).

Sutpen thinks by association from possession of that rifle to the possibility he can kill the white master, especially after the young man has been humiliated by the white owner's slave who tells the boy to deliver his message to the back, not the front, door of the plantation house: "*But I can shoot him*" (1964: 234). Although the young Sutpen rejects this option, he repeats it as if to keep it open:

> *But I can shoot him:* he argued with himself and the other: *No. That wouldn't do no good:* and the first: *But I can shoot him. I could slip right up there through them bushes and lay there until he come out to lay in the hammock and shoot him:* and the other: *No. That wouldn't do no good:* and the first: *Then what shall we do?* and the other: *I don't know.* (p. 235).

The mental debate represents the young Sutpen's attempt to sort out the ethical dimensions of a profound problem.

"*Because I own this rifle*" and "*But I can shoot him*" are the twin claims the young Sutpen makes in this stunning "awakening," even if he repudiates the effectiveness of these means to power. We should not forget that the young Sutpen turns to these murderous alternatives to compensate for his inability to deliver his father's message to the slave-owner:

> *He never gave me a chance to say it and Pap never asked me if I told him or not and so he can't even know that Pap sent him any message and so whether he got it or not cant even matter, not even to Pap; I went up to that door for that nigger to tell me never to come to that front door again and I not only wasn't doing any good to him by telling it or any harm to him by not telling it, there aint any good or harm either in the living world that I can do to him.* (1964: 238–239).

Communication of any sort, whether a simple message or a complex story, seems to be of no consequence in the social order glimpsed by the young Sutpen. Faulkner here seems to anticipate the more postmodern sentiments of Don DeLillo, who understands the terrorist or political assassin to have perversely assumed the social authority of the novelist (see Rowe 2003: 21–43). Long before Lee Harvey Oswald, Timothy McVeigh, and al-Qa'eda, the slavocracy refined its terrorist techniques from the Middle Passage to the colonial subjection of bodies and psyches forcibly displaced to a foreign land. With its ban on African-American literacy, its efforts to deprive poor whites, like the Sutpens, of education and economic opportunity, the Southern slave system relied on the breakdown of communication and the commodification of human relations.

Thomas Sutpen's internal dialogue continues as he lies in his bed that night, thinking:

> 'If you were fixing to combat them that had the fine rifles, the first thing you would do would be to get yourself the nearest thing to a fine rifle you could borrow or steal or make, wouldn't it?' and he said Yes. 'But this aint a question of rifles. So to combat them you have got to have what they have that made them do what he did. You got to have land and niggers and a fine house to combat them with. You see?' and he said Yes again. He left that night. . . . He never saw any of his family again.
>   "He went to the West Indies." (Faulkner 1964: 238)

Rifle, shoot, property: these are the different names Faulkner gives to the stages by which ownership of land and people becomes imaginable. They are rhetorical metonymies (literally: "changes of name") for the same activity, all of them describing in almost syntactically correct form – "I will shoot this rifle to seize what my neighbor has" – the historical process of the primitive accumulation of capital. Slavery and land landowner-ship, both of which are impossible according to any basic conception of the human and the natural, are the consequences of the usual violence. No owner can trace his rights to anything other than theft or piracy for that which cannot be properly owned. So just how "childish" is the adolescent Thomas Sutpen in his peep at Southern white "civilization"?

"He went to the West Indies" (1964: 238). *Rifle, kill, ownership, slavery, colony.* The names proliferate, but the message is the same. From seventeenth-century Jamestown, Sutpen travels back in time to Columbus's fifteenth-century Hispaniola, retracing the violent genealogy of the European colonization of the Americas and its slave economy. Faulkner's ability to tell this story, which implicates not just Southern slaveholders but all descendants of those European conquerors and slave traders, is uncanny. Of course, the terrible origin story Faulkner offers us is a testament to his rhetorical and imaginative talents, but it is also an expression of his bewildered admiration for Sutpen. Faulkner cannot even control the racial slurs that spill across the page in his account of Sutpen's fantasy. The angry adolescent Sutpen is responsible for "the monkey nigger" and "the nigger [who] was just another balloon face slick and distended with that mellow loud and terrible laughing so that he did not dare burst it" (p. 234), but Faulkner writes with a certain enthusiasm, understanding how the ugliness of these racial epithets derives from a superiority integral to the caste system of the Old and the New South.

The only African American who gets a "speaking part" in *Absalom, Absalom!* is Charles Bon, who is killed again and again in a narrative designed to expose the culture of death produced by an economy of ownership. In killing Charles Bon, Faulkner silences him, allowing his dialogue to recirculate only in the memories of his white narrators and, of course, through the author himself.[8] Sacrificial, certainly Christological, Bon figures emblematically in the narrative and thus cannot by any means be trivialized, but his symbolic power is primarily identifiable with the "tragedy" of the Sutpen family. Charles Bon is certainly a member of that family in Faulkner's narrative, even if he cannot claim a proper genealogical or even legal relationship with the white ruling class of the South. African American social inclusion, then, is ambivalently treated in Faulkner's narrative: recognition of African American identity can redeem the tragic action of *Absalom, Absalom!* by lifting the repression of the family ties (and thus community relations) that connect indissolubly black and white Southerners, but this social psychological therapy is achieved in and through white cultural mechanisms.

In sum, Faulkner does not align himself with Charles Bon or even with his son, Charles Etienne de Saint Velery Bon, who "married a full-blood negress, name unknown, 1879," and thus returns his father's and mother's ("an octoroon mistress whose name is not recorded" [1964: 383]) racial hybridity to "full-blood" blackness and the anonymity, in virtual spite of the aristocratic grandeur of his given names, achieved by his own son, the "Jim Bond," whom Shreve McCannon predicts will constitute one of a group – "the Jim Bonds" – that will "conquer the western hemisphere" (p. 378). Faulkner does not align himself with the dilettantish Rosa Coldfield, the vanished DeSpains, or the powerless Compsons – the gentility of the Old South in Yoknapatawpha – but instead with Thomas Sutpen, the parvenu and social climber who lacks utterly the "culture" and thus manners Rosa expects and yet who tells the only story in the novel to challenge Faulkner's literary authority. Even Charles Bon's comparison of the Southern (white) belles with the African-American prostitutes of New Orleans is subordinate finally to Sutpen's story of a will-to-power that encompasses not only the human and territorial conquest of the South but the legacy of European contact with the Western hemisphere. What Shreve McCannon predicts for the destiny of those "Jim Bonds" follows that logic: *another* "conquest," even if it is troublingly identified with sexual procreation: "'of course as they spread toward the poles they will bleach out again like the rabbits and birds do, so they won't show up so sharp against the snow'" (p. 378). But let there be no mistake about it, McCannon insists, "'it will still be Jim Bond; and so in a few thousand years, I who regard you will also have sprung from the loins of African kings'" (p. 378).

Faulkner's alternative to Sutpen's militarism – "Because I own this rifle . . ." – is certainly his more humane literary story, wherein author and reader *imagine* others in order to understand them. Much has been written about how Quentin and Shreve share the story of the South in the cold dormitory room at Harvard in ways that substitute communication, imagination, and finally compassion for the racial divisions and class hatreds of the slavocracy. Anyone would prefer, of course, their conversation as the metaphor for Faulkner's relationship with the reader either to Rosa's mystification or, much worse, Sutpen "wrestling" with his slaves to demonstrate ritually his physical (and psychological) superiority. Yet there is still some residual element in Faulkner's version of the story that is intended to be too encompassing, too white, too tragic, and too universal to allow him escape from the ghost of Thomas Sutpen. Literature's power is not always humane, does not inevitably redeem us, and can reveal only some truths by hiding others. Like Quentin, Faulkner has good reasons to hate the South and its storytelling traditions.

If we take seriously Shreve's prediction, then one of those reasons is profoundly racial and indicates how Sutpen's will-to-power enthralls Faulkner to the end of the novel. The "Jim Bonds" are taking over, not by virtue of their abilities to tell their stories, not through their powers to recognize their complicity in the symbolic story of the Sutpens, but by some perverse natural selection, "like the rabbits and the birds," who adapt in order to survive. Cultural work without economic, political, and psychological power, Faulkner argues, is mere dilettantism, a dying art, like Rosa's odes and epitaphs. The history of the South Faulkner represents in *Absalom, Absalom!* will repeat itself, now as a revenge cycle in which those oppressed will assume power by what appears to be a law of nature. Of course, such repetitions repudiate human history as we understand it, so that the stories told in *Absalom* will be eventually forgotten, their figured pages whitened to silence in the long view Shreve offers at the end.

In *Playing in the Dark*, Toni Morrison analyzes six "linguistic strategies employed in fiction to engage the serious consequences of blacks." (1992: 67–9).[9] It is worth noting that Morrison explicitly adapts her categories from James Snead's analysis of "the characteristic features of racial division" in literary language in his book, *Figures of Division: William Faulkner's Major Novels* (1986: x–xi). Two of Morrison's "linguistic strategies" are particularly apt to the mode of literary mystification that works so powerfully in Faulkner's *Absalom, Absalom!* "Metaphysical condensation," Morrison writes, "allows the writer to transform social and historical differences into universal differences" (1992: 68). "Dehistoricizing allegory" seems to be its proper complement, because such allegory "produces foreclosure rather than disclosure" by postponing social change to such "an unspecified infinite amount of time" that "history, as a process of becoming, is excluded from the literary encounter" (p. 68). In his effort to implicate all of us in the story told by Quentin and Shreve in New England, Faulkner allegorizes the South from a specific region into a tragic human condition. By concluding with the Canadian Shreve McCannon's prediction "that in time the Jim Bonds are going to conquer the western hemisphere," Faulkner metaphysicalizes and dehistoricizes the specific class, gender, and racial problems of the New South. By situating the complementary cultural work of storytelling (or more generally communal representation) in a white imaginary and excluding African Americans from their own self-representation, Faulkner perpetuates the Southern arts of mystification in his very effort to reveal their perversity.

NOTES

1 Of course, one of Douglass's purposes in his 1845 *Narrative* is to provide some means of overturning the symbolic power of the slavocracy. See Rowe (1997: 96–123).

2 *Absalom, Absalom!* includes a "Chronology" and "Genealogy" for the characters, but it is clear that the factual references in this section are utterly overwritten by the narrative itself, in which these mere personal details are overwhelmed by the entanglements of the characters' lives and fates represented in the novel. Faulkner thus uses the "Chronology" and "Genealogy" not simply as mnemonic devices for readers, but also as indications of the superiority of the novel over chronicle as the proper mode of historical representation for complex human events.

3 Twain's best-known parody of Julia A. Moore, the "Sweet Singer of Michigan," is "Ode to Stephen Dowling Bots, Dec'd.," in chapter 17 of *The Adventures of Huckleberry Finn* (1999: 122–3).

4 "It was schoolteacher who taught them otherwise. . . . Watchdogs without teeth; steer bulls without horns; gelded workhorses whose neigh and whinny could not be translated into a language responsible humans spoke" (Morrison 1987: 125).

5 Shreve points out to Quentin that "there wasn't any West Virginia in 1808 because – . . . West Virginia wasn't admitted." (1964: 220). Shreve's historical pedantry irritates Quentin – " 'All right,' Quentin said. . . . 'All right all right' " – but Faulkner wants us to know that Sutpen is born on the frontier, outside the legal boundaries of the United States (p. 220).

6 In the "Chronology," Faulkner is more specific about Thomas Sutpen's age at the time of the family's move: "1817 Sutpen family moved down into Tidewater Virginia, Sutpen ten years old" (1964: 379).

7 The curiosity in the myth of the First Families of Virginia that they are "descended" from Rolfe and Pocahontas is, of course, that it validates the ethnic hybridity and miscegenation that in all other respects Southern white aristocrats treated as a social taboo. On the Pocahontas myth, see Tilton (1994).

8 See my discussion of the problem of "the African-American voice" in Faulkner's fiction in *At Emerson's Tomb* (1997: 222–46).

9 The six categories are: economy of stereotype, metonymic displacement, metaphysical condensation, fetishization, dehistoricizing allegory, and patterns of explosive, disjointed, repetitive language.

REFERENCES AND FURTHER READING

Douglass, F. (1982). *Narrative of the Life of Frederick Douglass, an American Slave, Written by Himself.* New York: Penguin. (Original pub. 1845.)

Eliot, T. S. (1962). *The Waste Land and Other Poems.* New York: Harcourt. (Original pub. 1922.)

Faulkner, W. (1942). *Go Down, Moses*. New York: Random.

Faulkner, W. (1964). *Absalom, Absalom!* New York: Random. (Original pub. 1936.)

Freud, S. (1958). The "Uncanny." In *On Creativity and the Unconscious: Papers on the Psychology of Art, Literature, Love, Religion* (ed. Benjamin Nelson, trans. under the supervision of J. Riviere). New York: Harper.

Irwin, J. (1975). *Doubling and Incest/Repetition and Revenge: A Speculative Reading of Faulkner*. Baltimore: Johns Hopkins University Press.

Morrison, T. (1987). *Beloved*. New York: Random.

Morrison, T. (1992). *Playing in the Dark: Whiteness and the Literary Imagination*. New York: Random.

Patterson, O. (1982). *Slavery and Social Death: A Comparative Study*. Cambridge, MA: Harvard University Press.

Pound, E. (1922). Translator's Postscript. In R. de Goncourt. *The Natural Philosophy of Love* (trans. E. Pound) (pp. 206–19). New York: Boni and Liveright.

Rowe, J. C. (1997). *At Emerson's Tomb: The Politics of American Literature*. New York: Columbia University Press.

Rowe, J. C. (2003). The Dramatization of *Mao II* and the War on Terrorism. *South Atlantic Quarterly*, 103(1): 21–43.

Rowe, J. C. (2002). *The New American Studies*. Minneapolis: University of Minnesota Press.

Rowe, J. C. (2005). Mark Twain's Critique of Globalization (Old and New) in *Following the Equator: A Voyage around the World*. *Arizona Quarterly*, 61(1): 109–35.

Snead, J. A. (1986). *Figures of Division: William Faulkner's Major Novels*. New York: Methuen.

Tilton, R. S. (1994). *Pocahontas: The Evolution of an American Narrative*. New York: Cambridge University Press.

Twain, M. (1999). *The Adventures of Huckleberry Finn* (ed. T. Cooley). New York: Norton.

28

"The Cradle of Your Nativity": Codes of Class Culture and Southern Desire in Faulkner's Snopes Trilogy

Evelyn Jaffe Schreiber

Toward the end of William Faulkner's *The Town*, lawyer Gavin Stevens stops on the ridge beyond Seminary Hill to

> see all Yoknapatawpha . . . [,] the whole sum of [his] life. . . . First Jefferson . . . [,] stratified and superposed . . . [; the] white plantation names . . . [,] the roadless, almost pathless perpendicular hill-country . . . [,] and last on to where Frenchman's Bend lay beyond the southeastern horizon, cradle of Varners and ant-heap for the northwest crawl of Snopes. (1961: 315–17)

Stevens's equation of his life with a microcosm of his community, including the association of Varners with cradles and Snopeses with crawling ants, demonstrates the social constructionist and psychoanalytical theories that explain how people develop a sense of self through acts of recognition (and misrecognition) in social interactions with their culture. In the Southern world of Faulkner's fiction, cultural codes define people according to a social hierarchy. This patriarchal system ranks wealthy men above poor ones, landowners above tenant farmers, city folk above country people, men above women, and white women above blacks. The following discussion considers how men in Faulkner's Snopes trilogy – *The Hamlet* (1940), *The Town* (1957), and *The Mansion* (1959) – confront personal and social change in a stratified cultural symbolic order based on Southern patriarchy, operating in relationship to a signifying chain of Southern hierarchy and class. (See also Schreiber 2002: ch. 2 for a discussion of women's subjectivity and cultural change.) Individual and cultural defenses and adaptations evolve as threats to the status quo create community response. In the Snopes trilogy, Flem Snopes and his kinsmen force cultural change, while Varner, Ratliff, Stevens, and other community members attempt to adapt to a shift of power. Jacques Lacan's theory of identity will help to explain the anxiety that both produces and results from this shift and how the community recovers its balance through the psychic mechanisms of projection, along with what Lacan refers to as avoidance of the "real" and a greater awareness of master signifiers such as class and race.

Before analyzing individual and collective response to the shifts of class and power in *The Hamlet*, *The Town*, and *The Mansion*, a brief plot summary is useful. In the Snopes trilogy, Flem Snopes moves from his position of impoverished tenant farmer to a position with social power as bank president. Flem supplements his wealth with respectability by negotiating and trading with Will Varner to marry his daughter Eula, pregnant with another's child. To maintain his position, Flem must keep Eula's daughter, Linda, from leaving Jefferson with her inheritance and must ignore his wife's 18 years of infidelity with Manfred de Spain. Flem also must keep his law-breaking relatives – Mink, Byron, I.O., Montgomery Ward – out of Jefferson in order to preserve his respectability. When Eula protects Linda from scandal by committing suicide, Linda exacts revenge for her mother's death on Flem by orchestrating the release of Flem's imprisoned cousin Mink, whose sole purpose in life is to kill Flem in retaliation for the desertion that left Mink to a life sentence.

Much has been written about how Flem's actions reflect the weaknesses of his community. Kevin Railey describes how, according to the code of Southern paternalism, "the responsibility for Flem's drive to get into a business lies with Varner's and de Spain's actions. These men were exploiting farmers and demanding obedience, much as all paternalists would, but they did not feel any responsibility for the plight of the tenant in return" (1999: 152).

Further, "if power in a society is not preempted by a benevolent paternal class of rulers, dispensing largesse according to the moral deserts of the individual, then society will always fall victim to Snopesism" (1999: 148). Similarly, Noel Polk contends that the Snopeses "are not a mysterious force, separate and distinct from us. . . . If [Flem] is mindless, if he is soulless, if his heart is an electronic calculator, he is the picture of what Faulkner believed we would all become if we subscribed to those same middle-class virtues of security and conformity" (1983: 114, 116–17). Flem has learned from his community that "thievery is an unacceptable road to respectability, but hypocrisy is not" (Stroble 1980: 203). Thus, "Flem is not an alien from outside the human species: he is its creation born within its collective womb and nurtured by its hypocrisy" (1980: 205). Additionally, "Flem's journey to dominance has been one of insidious infiltration and usurpation of codes and positions already ingrained in the local psyche. . . . [H]e has adopted all the trappings of those he has displaced" (Robinson 2001: 0).

Flem comes to represent "the ways individual identity is shaped by dangerously constructed and precariously maintained cultural practices" (Towner 2000: 116). The microcosm of Yoknapatawpha earlier outlined by Stevens epitomizes Lacan's psychoanalytic theory that describes people as being born into a community discourse that socially constructs their identity. In explaining Lacan's theory, Mark Bracher outlines how what Lacan calls "'master signifiers' . . . function as bearers of our identity" (1993: 23). Further,

> Master signifiers are able to exert such force in messages because of the role they play in structuring the subject – specifically in giving the subject a sense of identity and

direction. . . . Master signifiers thus account for much of the interpellative force, both immediate and enduring, that discourses have. . . . Discourses that offer this dominance usually give us a sense of security and well-being, the sense that we have a definite identity, that we are significant, that our existence matters. (1993: 25–6)

Marshall Alcorn elaborates the interpellative nature of master signifiers by discussing Althusser's theory of "the subject's entrapment by ideology" (2002: 13). He adds that "[m]aster signifiers come to represent the subject. They 'stand in' for subjectivity, filling in the lack of subjectivity with meaning and value. Of course, this meaning and value come from the master" (2002: 70). This connection between identity and ideology accounts for the resistance of culture to forces of change.

Lacan's theory of social interaction – how subjectivity and desire stem from the Other – helps to explain much of the action in the Snopes trilogy. In brief, Lacan refers to a person's outside, social, organizing, and defining structure as the "symbolic structure," whose laws and language divide the self and establish one as a subject of lack. This outer structure is necessary for the subject to exist: "The subject sets itself up as operating, as human, as *I*, from the moment the symbolic system appears" (1991: 52). But the subject is one of lack in the sense that the symbolic structure acts as a barrier to the recognition of one's identity apart from the cultural codes that construct one. This pervasive sense of lack creates the need to establish a perceived prior state of wholeness, but the subject confronts, in a search for fulfillment, what Lacan calls the "real" or what is repressed and cannot be represented. Rather than imaginary wholeness, the "real" creates a sense of fragmentation, a sense of being a "body in pieces." The "real" is "presented . . . in the form of that which is *unassimilable* in it – in the form of the trauma" (1981: 55). This trauma represents the cut in the subject that produces the subject of the symbolic, whose experience of self is one of lack, or nothingness.

Essentially an encounter with one's "own nothingness" (1981: 92), this confrontation with the "real" often occurs through encounters with the gaze of the Other, a gaze that reduces one to a position as object by undermining a subject's illusion of control and self-knowledge through "some form of 'sliding away' of the subject" (1981: 75). But ironically, self-actualization can come from this moment of recognition as object. People can introduce cultural shifts through recognition of their lack. The unconscious cultural response to lack – in Yoknapatawpha, the hierarchical class structure – can be changed only through individual understanding of, and hence altered relationship to, lack. Interestingly, in addition to producing lack, Lacan suggests that a culture's symbolic structure – here the class system – is also a symptom that represses society's anxiety of lack. Further, Lacan theorizes that the act of repressing a sense of lack gives rise to desire, which can drive subjects to repeat obsolete behavior. Thus, desire is a response to lack, expressed in culture as "the discourse of the circuit in which I am integrated. I am absolutely one of its links. It is the discourse of my father [and] . . . I am condemned to reproduce [his mistakes] because I am obliged to pick up again the discourse he bequeathed to me" (1991: 89). For Lacan, the repetition of cultural ideology (e.g., Southern hierarchy) represents the drive's circuit as an expression of desire.

According to Lacan, "[i]t is desire which achieves the primitive structuration of the human world, desire as unconscious" (1991: 224). Further, "Desire emerges just as it becomes embodied in speech, it emerges with symbolism" (1991:234), making Lacanian desire "a perpetual effect of symbolic articulation" (1981: Miller's note 278). This articulation or cultural discourse predetermines individual desire, and the "voices" of culture dictate one's desire, representing a response to lack. One common collective response to lack is projection, a repetition of symbolic ritual that serves to protect against anxiety. For example, to preserve their own organic integrity, the people of Yoknapatawpha County will project their own weaknesses onto the Snopes clan. The psychic enjoyment that stems from the erasure of lack propels the community members to project hatred onto the Snopes family rather than question their culture. Sigmund Freud outlines projection by describing children's games as a means of converting their perceived passivity into active mastery, claiming that as "the child passes over from the passivity of the experience to the activity of the game, he hands on the disagreeable experience to one of his playmates and in this way revenges himself on a substitute" (1957: 17). The child gains control, which eases the anxiety of lack, by projecting onto this substitute. This projection serves to protect against anxiety. When people project unconscious and forbidden desires elsewhere, they protect themselves from lack and act to conserve homeostasis or constancy. Much critical attention has been given to how projection operates in Southern culture and Faulkner's work (see Irwin 1975; Jenkins 1981; Sundquist 1983; Fowler 1997). Lacan suggests that the need for repetition of cultural projection is a "form of behaviour staged in the past and reproduced in the present in a way which doesn't conform much with vital adaptation" (1991:, 89–90). Such repeated behavior on a communal level forms a culture's symbolic structure.

When the community members project their lack onto the Snopeses, they reinforce the current symbolic structure and their place in it. On the other hand, the Snopeses themselves protect against the anxiety of lack through recognition of their nothingness in the current structure. Only when this unconscious desire – the cultural code or master signifier – is understood to be the irrational desire of one's culture can one re-evaluate it in order to discover one's own desire. Lacan suggests that individuals can enact change when they become subjects, or move from being an object in the meaningless signifying chain to having a type of knowledge. Lacan describes this as a movement from S1 to S2, with S1 being a state of blindly acting out a symptom or master signifier and S2 being a state of having knowledge. This knowledge gives meaning to the symptom. For example, in Faulkner's South, S1 consists of a meaningless signifying chain expressed in the symptom of hierarchical separation. The paradox of Lacan's schema is that S1 only makes sense retroactively with the knowledge of S2. In *The Town*, Stevens summarizes this retroactive knowledge when he ponders that "the tragedy of life is, it must be premature, inconclusive and inconcludable, in order to be life; it must be before itself, in advance of itself, to have been at all" (1961: 317–18). That is, knowledge and an altered subjectivity brings into focus S1 – the symptom – retroactively. When symptoms, attachment patterns related to the past, pass into speech, they can to some extent be reconfigured in the symbolic order. Reconfiguration occurs through acknowledgment or verbalization of how the gaze of the Other makes one an object and confines one to a prescribed role in society.

Consequently, a subject can reform what has been repeated. Knowledge – desire brought forward from the unconscious – allows a subject to have the present dictate behavior, thereby breaking a pattern of repeated social interactions. In essence, a subject can reconfigure desire by refusing the demand of the cultural symbolic structure. Thus, only by reconfiguring one's relationship to desire and its implied lack can one let go of a dysfunctional system and create a new cultural or personal structure. The symptom (class structure) – repeated in the past and verbalized in the present – can, in an open-minded environment, lead to social reform or resignification. In psychoanalysis, "talk therapy" produces postanalytic subjects who are able to reconfigure their relationships to lack and the cultural symbolic so as to embrace a new signification that alters their actions.

Such reconfiguration of desire is necessary in order for the people in Faulkner's Yoknapatawpha County to accept the inevitable rise of the Snopeses and a shift of power or order. This shift stems from a two-fold anxiety: the Snopeses strive to overcome their sense of lack in response to their fixed lower-class position, and the community members battle the threat to their social order. Reactions to the Snopeses' threat include negotiation, humor, terror, and panic. Lacan's theory of lack and desire accounts for this range of response. Anxiety about displacement and class alterations produces actions that stem from the anxiety of lack, experienced through the gaze of the Other. The "invasion" of Snopeses creates communal anxiety that develops over the course of the trilogy. Ratliff (an itinerant sewing-machine salesman, confidante to all, and source of community gossip) and Stevens (the Harvard- and Heidelberg-educated Jefferson attorney), on behalf of Jefferson society, attempt to perceive, monitor, and alter the threat. The limits of their capacity to "hold" and "tote" the burden of sparing the community from this invasion plays out over time (1961: 102). In order to succeed, they must become subjects with knowledge of the Other – Lacan's S2 – and engage with the gaze of the Other, acknowledging their own desire and that of their culture. Unfortunately, the voice of their culture reinforces both Ratliff's and Stevens's positions as S1 – unknowing subjects – and curtails their ability to confront and adapt to change. Thus, although they analyze the communal interactions of Snopeses, they do not fully comprehend their own characteristics that the Snopeses reflect. As Wilson claims, the narrators "recognize evil when they see it in Snopes but not in the original perpetrators whom Flem Snopes first imitates and then excels" (1980: 433).

Thus, in the Snopes trilogy, an outmoded cultural symbolic confronts the social upheaval initiated by the Snopeses. The Snopeses serve as the "real" or the traumatic cut for Southern patriarchal culture. Flem and Mink act out a lower-class response to lack, responding to their rigid place in society by moving from objects or meaningless links in the signifying chain to subjects with agency. While patriarch Ab Snopes "just soured" into a barn burner after his interactions with the Jefferson community, Flem's culture's treatment of Ab serves as Lacan's "real" for Flem in that the intrusion of the "real" serves to unmask the illusion of self-identity produced by the external cultural codes of Southern life. That is, he sees his father's object position and what this means for himself (Faulkner 1991: 29). Skinfill describes the situation as "a historical cycle of poverty which reproduces itself with each succeeding generation of tenant farmer" (1996: 164). In this way, "class comes to overdetermine identity and destiny in their most infinitesimal capacities" (1996: 165). Flem's rejection of this position renders him a force of change that proves too strong for his community to combat or suppress; as a result, the townspeople choose to look the other way. They collectively avoid the gaze of the Other that they experience with Flem. They accommodate the Other to avoid a painful confrontation with Lacan's "real": "[Frenchman's Bend] had acquiesced to the clerk's presence even if it had not accepted him, though the Varners seemed to have done both" (Faulkner 1991: 62). By acquiescing to Flem – they marvel at and gossip about his audacity and cunning but never bar or stop him – and the threat of barn burning and the material repercussions of destroyed property, Jefferson community members keep their own subjectivity intact. They protect themselves against Flem's threat by yielding to him and thus maintain their own desire for material well-being by allowing *his* desire to dominate. As Flem becomes a subject, they assume an object position, experiencing the trauma of Lacan's "real" and thus being thrust into the repetition of the symptom of their culture – the reinforcement of class hierarchy. By reacting to the "abstract idea of the Snopeses as a polluting menace, which seems to reflect an in-group prejudice against an out-group" (Volpe 1964: 310), the community struggles to maintain its identity.

The trilogy opens and closes with the threat of the "real" in the form of the death and decay of Southern patriarchal culture. The opening description of the Old Frenchman place epitomizes the erasure of self:

> But now nobody knew what he had actually been, not even Will Varner, who was sixty years old and now owned a good deal of his original grant, including the site of his ruined mansion. Because he was gone now, the foreigner, the Frenchman, with his family and his slaves and his magnificence. His dream, his broad acres were parcelled out now. (1991: 4)

The settler's dream and pride have become nothing but dust. At the close of *The Mansion*, Mink visualizes his own return to the earth, "comfortable and easy so wouldn't nobody even know or even care who was which any more, himself among them, equal to any, good as any, brave as any, being inextricable from, anonymous with all of them" (1965: 435). Death in both cases is the great equalizer, representing the merging of the self and Other. In this way, death can come to represent peace for Mink. In essence, the lesson of the Snopes trilogy is that death comes to all, and peace comes with a certain mastery of the "real" by confronting the voices of our culture and our own desires while alive.

Varner, "chief man of the country" (1991: 5), has wealth and power, accumulated through his shrewd dealings, but he has no illusions about his place in the universe and no need to go beyond his domain. He sits on his reconstructed flour barrel, in the "fallen baronial splendor" of the Old Frenchman place, "trying to find out what it must have felt like to be the fool that would need all this . . . just to eat and sleep in" (1991: 7). He is aware that his position in the hierarchy results from his economic power over the tenant farmers. His musing on the place of actual need in the accumulation of property foreshadows Flem's representation of "a social order determined extensively by a market economy: a system of exchange in which profit rather than use determines value" (Skinfill 1996: 154). Unlike Varner, Flem sees the Old Frenchman place as "a piece of property" to be sold for profit (Urgo 1995: 457). Varner, unlike everyone else in Jefferson, realizes that he "cant beat him [Flem]" (1991: 345). As a result of this knowledge, Varner is most able to accept Flem, using him to reinforce his own desire and place in the social structure. Like others in his community, however, Varner's son Jody seeks to avert confrontations or violence with Flem, thus becoming powerless against him. Tricked by Flem into renting to him, Jody discovers too late Flem's connection with barn burning. When Jody tries to confront Flem, he cannot engage him with eye contact: "He had never been certain just when the other had been looking at him and when not" (1991: 26). Later, Ratliff is not able to engage Flem's gaze either, as there is nothing to see below "the cap save the steady motion of his jaws" (1991: 346). By not engaging with the gaze of the Other, the townspeople avoid seeing their own reflection, as Flem's actions mirror their own dominant capitalistic and material cultural desire. "Flem is not a 'force' or 'power' but merely one man adapting vestiges of the Old South's ability to manipulate the truth" (Nichol 1997: 493). To maintain their imaginary master signifiers of class superiority, the community members tolerate Flem in defense of their subjectivity.

The community is tolerant but also vigilant in its guard against Snopeses, as if being alert to cultural changes that might somehow control them: "[T]hey just watched, missing nothing" (1991: 66). Implicit in this ambivalent, fearful desire to engage the Other is the need to somehow comprehend the threat to life's necessities and the status quo. Robinson describes the narrators of Frenchman's Bend as an "interpretive community" that lacks "self-awareness," claiming that Flem "exposes the contrived and transient nature of any such community, making clear the arrogance, however unconscious, of such prescriptive assumption" (2003: 62). The townspeople pay attention to Flem, trying to decode his meaning:

> Ratliff and his companions sat and squatted about the gallery all that day and watched not only the village proper but all the countryside within walking distance come up singly and in pairs and in groups, men women and children, to make trivial purchases and look at the new clerk and go away. They came . . . completely wary, almost decorous like half-wild cattle following word of the advent of a strange beast . . . with whom . . . they would have to deal for the necessities of living. (1991: 57–8)

Initially controlling their household and food supplies, Flem will eventually infiltrate the community's well-being by controlling other local businesses and the bank. For example, he displaces the blacksmith Trumbull by replacing him with a relative, and he buys and sells with a profit at Varner's expense; "even Ratliff had lost count of what profit Snopes might have made" (1991: 74). Control of the hotel and the store follows. Flem attends church and rivals Varner by wearing a tie. In fact, Flem models himself after the "chief man" in order to become a subject, learning from his prototype, sitting "on a nail keg at his knee with the open ledgers" (1991: 67). The townspeople tell each other that when Flem took over the scale-beam, "he passed Jody," passing him a second time when he takes the "roan horse" too (1991: 66, 92). By monitoring these levels of Jody's displacement, the community projects its anxieties onto the Varners so as to avoid the implications for themselves. "Flem has grazed up the store and he has grazed up the blacksmith shop and now he is starting in on the school. That just leaves Will's house. Of course, after that he will have to fall back on you folks" (1991: 77). Flem will eventually pass Varner as well, making a profit from the Old Frenchman place (something Varner was unable to do) and taking over Varner's place in the custom-made flour-barrel chair. Varner sometimes thinks he can adapt by controlling Flem, but the "real" keeps emerging for him as Flem usurps his position as premier landowner as well as usurious lender: "any sum between twenty-five cents and ten dollars could be borrowed from him at any time, if the borrower agreed to pay enough for the commodation" (1991: 67–8). Using humor to assuage the anxiety of displacement, Bookwright quips, "Anyhow, he aint moved into Varner's house yet" (1991: 63). Humor verbalizes the threat in an attempt to accommodate the trauma of the "real."

An additional distancing tactic by the townspeople is to muse on Flem's range of manipulation. When hearing that Flem is lending blacks money, Ratliff reflects, "So he's working the top and the bottom both at the same time. At that rate it will be a while yet before he has to fall back on you ordinary white folks in the middle" (1991: 78). The belief that Flem's actions are out of their province prevails: "'What could we do?' Tull said. "'It aint right. But it aint none of our business'" (1991: 79). When Ratliff responds that there should be something they can do, Bookwright warns that Flem Snopes is too great an adversary, even for Ratliff. Flem's tricking Ratliff and Bookwright into buying the Old Frenchman place proves their vulnerability. A trader by nature turned entrepreneur, Ratliff makes a game of financial ventures, sometimes winning, sometimes losing. His failure "to beat" Flem alerts him to the precariousness of subject status, which always relies on self-knowledge in relationship to the Other. As Towner argues, "Ratliff does not understand the degree to which he himself both benefits from and is restricted by . . . cultural privileges" and lives with "an unexamined ideology" (2000: 90). "Ratliff's concern for the planting and cashing of crops complements Varner's. Both are merchants who depend for the retail of their stock on a system which leaves Southern labour with less than little on which to live" (Godden 2003: 618). Yet Ratliff's roots as a tenant farmer give him somewhat greater empathy and insight than most members of his community, enabling him to adapt to threats to the subject status of established Southern patriarchy.

The trauma attached to the Snopes invasion appears in the imagined confrontation between Jody and Flem: "'How many more is there? How much longer is this going on? Just what is it going to cost me to protect one goddamn barn full of hay?'" (1991:

74). The protection of property, and with it the position of landowning subjects, have forced the townspeople to adjust to Flem's blackmail. Ratliff verbalizes the town's sense of enormity and danger and his own inability to protect society when he tells Bookwright, "I never made them Snopeses and I never made the folks that cant wait to bare their backsides to them. I could do more, but I wont. I wont, I tell you!" (1991: 355). In this uncharacteristic outburst, Ratliff verbalizes the trauma wrought by Flem. His "community . . . is based on exploitation of itself by its members" (Urgo 1987: 179); attempts to make Flem a victim fail. Ratliff concludes, "It's hopeless. Even when you get rid of one Snopes, there's already another one behind you even before you can turn around" (1965: 349). Thus, the Snopeses become the "real" – what cannot be controlled – and a reflection of cultural weakness.

Ratliff and Stevens sense that "Snopeses had to be watched constantly like an invasion of snakes or wildcats" and that "nobody else in Jefferson seemed to recognize the danger" (1961: 106). When Stevens is away at war, Ratliff is left "to tote the whole load by himself," the "danger and the threat" (1961: 112). Like a poisonous animal that strikes without warning, the true danger of the Snopes invasion is not realized until after the fact. Members of the community embody Lacan's S1, meaningless links in the symbolic structure. Their knowledge of their own vulnerability comes too late. By avoiding confrontation with Flem and thus the "real," community members become objects as Flem usurps the subject position. Even Ratliff, who has the most self-knowledge and appears securely a subject, falters in his interactions with Flem. His gall-bladder illness serves as metaphor for his need to look inward, to protect himself from an innate weakness in the face of the "real." Thus, in his lack of knowledge of the Other, Ratliff underestimates how far a Snopes will go. He "just never went far enough" in his thinking, and his two schemes – the goat trading and the sewing-machine scam – backfire (1991: 97). Analyzing his actions, Ratliff ponders, "I reckon I was sicker than I knowed. Because I missed it, missed it clean" (1991: 96). Likewise, he is duped into buying the Old Frenchman place because he has failed to think as shrewdly as Flem or to see himself in the object position.

As Flem's power grows, so does the community's knowledge. "At first we thought that the water tank was only Flem Snopes's monument"(1961: 3). Later they realize that "[i]t was a footprint." The community slowly acknowledges the social shifting. One day Flem appears, the next he owns Ratliff's restaurant. Ratliff verbalizes this knowledge: "Just give him time" (1961: 4) and Flem will take over. Soon, "there were even more Snopeses than Varners" (1961: 5). The depth of the community's ignorance of the Other emerges when the members are shocked at Flem's becoming a superintendent of the power plant; they were unaware that such a job existed. Flem gains his power by reinscribing the symbolic structure. He creates and then occupies a new civic position with no one to challenge him. They "had not yet read the signs and portents which should have warned, alerted, sprung us into frantic concord to defend our town from him" (1961: 15). Flem's rented dress suit for the Cotillion is a red flag marking how far he has surpassed his community members with his trappings of wealth; it indicates his usurping of symbolic power, his movement from an insignificant symptomatic link in the symbolic order to a position of agency with money and class stature. Stevens realizes that in their refusal to engage with the gaze of the Other, they have "all bought Snopeses here, whether we wanted to or not" and share the burden of making him respectable (1961: 95). Trying both to avoid and monitor the "real," they adapt half blindly to Flem's manipulation. By the time they realize that Flem has become a major bank stock owner, "it was done now; too late to help" (1961: 137).

In analyzing their relationship to Flem, Ratliff realizes that Stevens has "missed it" – Flem's need for respectability – because Stevens avoids recognizing his own illusions about his society (1961: 177). His misconceptions about Flem parallel his own missed encounter with the "real." He represses his own and his community's desire for Eula, Linda, material wealth, respectability, *"reputation* and *good name"* (1961: 202) in order to keep his illusions about his culture. Varner also looks the other way for 18 years, "missing" his daughter Eula's affair with de Spain to avoid facing the fact that he swapped Eula for his own respectability, making her Flem's "twenty-dollar gold piece" (1961: 335). The townspeople similarly avoid the gaze of the Other when they silently sanction Eula and de Spain's affair. Their tolerance affirms their symbolic mantle of respectability that prohibits sexual desire and necessitates keeping it unconscious.

The community members further avoid the gaze of the Other by not firing Grover Winbush; they cannot admit that the righteous men of Jefferson wanted to see Montgomery Ward's dirty pictures. In addition, they try to avoid encounters with Old Het, but "sooner or later they would have to come out and there she would be, tall, lean, of a dark chocolate color" (1961: 231). She tells Gavin that she services Jefferson, in effect by functioning as its "real": "I serves Jefferson too. If it's more blessed to give than to receive like the Book say, this town is blessed . . . [because I'm] steady willing from dust-dawn to dust-dark, rain or snow or sun, to say much oblige" (1961: 245). Het profits from her community's need to deny its own vulnerability.

In order to maintain an ideal of purity and the illusion of wholeness, the community must get rid of Montgomery Ward, if possible "exterminate him" (1961: 165). In his zeal to do so, Stevens underestimates how much Flem wants to purge Jefferson of this shame. Ostensibly acting to save Jefferson's good name, Flem actually wants Montgomery Ward to be sent to Parchman so he can fool Mink into trying to escape. Doing so will add another 20 years to Mink's sentence, preventing his release and his killing of Flem. Stevens, who cannot be bribed, fails to read Flem's devious behavior adequately because Stevens cannot or will not think like Flem. Essentially, Flem "protects" Jefferson to avoid his own "real" – his own death at the hands of his cousin Mink. Later, when Flem relieves Jefferson of Byron's wild, animal-like children, he will begin his establishment of true respectability, and all of Jefferson bears witness to his transfer into a subject position as community member. Ratliff calls it "the end of a era. . . . The last and final end of Snopes out-and-out unvarnished behavior in Jefferson" (1961: 370). Their exodus represents the removal of the gaze of the Other, which allows society to regain its equilibrium. Gavin's nephew Chick affirms the apparent disappearance of the Other as Byron's brood boards the train never to return: "we represented Jefferson – watched them mount and vanish one by one into that iron impatient maw" (1961: 371). For the moment, the "real" is at bay and the community members, with Flem now one of their "respectable" citizens, seem to regain their subject status.

Once Flem establishes his power, he himself takes over the job of "holding and toting" for the community. As Stevens puts it, "realising that we would never defend Jefferson from Snopeses, let us then give, relinquish Jefferson to Snopeses . . . so that in defending themselves from Snopeses, Snopeses must of necessity defend and shield us, their vassals and chattels too" (1961: 44). To maintain his respectability, Flem must free Jefferson of Snopeses; the town's "real" has become Flem's as well. "Flem takes on the 'habit' of civic virtue when he abandons his 'monster-like' ability to be a cunning trader and conforms to the town's standard of behavior" (Nichol 1997: 500). Once he shares the culture's symbolic desire, Flem falls prey to its powerful narrative. Each "trade," deal, and scheme enacts the Other's desire – first to obtain money, second to obtain respectability. Flem's path to power begins at Frenchman's Bend, at Varner's knee, where he exacts the letter of the law in dismantling the existing, perhaps itself exploitative honor system and credit, exacting cash payment from store customers, including collecting from Will Varner himself for his tobacco. Wearing his bow tie and white shirts – the signification of money and class – Flem embraces the symbolic order that excludes him. In his desire for social advancement, he later dons a "black felt hat somebody told him was the kind of hat bankers wore" (1965: 65). He finds out "that the only limit to the amount of money you could shut your hands on and keep and hold, was just how much money there was" (1965: 66). Volpe observes that Flem "has one aim: to make money. . . . He has no other desires" (1964: 322), and Ownby claims that Flem "has no goals in mind for his money and he derives no enjoyment from it" (1995: 119). Amassing money for its own sake, of course, deprives Flem of true subjectivity, but it gives him a crucial foothold in this culture's symbolic order.

Flem must maintain this new position with more than money; he must gain respectability. This realization ties his mission to that of Jefferson: eradicating the "real" represented by the Snopeses. Flem will let Mink go to the penitentiary, according to Ratliff, because he "has got to cancel all them loose-flying notes that turns up here and there every now and then" (1991: 354). However, his relatives think that Flem has the power to protect them outside the law but will not do so. Byron, I.O., Montgomery Ward, and Mink all think they will be protected by Flem, but the law of the cultural symbolic must be intact for Flem to remain a subject. When Flem becomes middle-class, he shares the town's anxiety about Snopeses, not just that Mink will kill him but also that his name will be tarnished by the illegal and immoral deeds of his relatives. In effect, Flem becomes a non-Snopes and must disassociate himself from his kinsmen. He chooses furniture in Memphis to reflect his social position, and must keep up appearances by blackmailing Eula to keep Linda at home and Eula's good name intact. The truth behind Flem's domestic appearances would jeopardize his social standing. As Polk points out, "Flem is then the perfect bourgeois; his every aim in life is to meld so completely into the Jefferson community that he is indistinguishable from everybody else in it" (1983: 115). Thus he just repeats the signifying chain of culture. Flem's "respectability depended completely on Jefferson not jest accepting but finally getting used to the fact that he not only had evicted Manfred de Spain from his bank but he was remodeling to move into it De Spain's birthsite likewise" (Faulkner 1961: 348). Later, Eula's monument solidifies his facade of respectability. Although he moves from object to subject by taking a place of power in the symbolic order, Flem remains a cultural symptom on the level of Lacan's S1, a meaningless link in the symbolic chain of his social structure. His failure to pursue a desire apart from the desire of his culture keeps Flem from becoming a subject with individual agency. The voice of his culture molds his desire.

With his need for class signifiers, Flem is inscribed by culture, not free of it. He names not his own desire but that of middle-class culture. Although initially he breaks out of his object position by naming his desire to possess what the Other has – money, power, and class standing – he fails to derive individuation from his journey, and he dies a meaningless link in the chain of middle-class culture. His later desire for respectability also represents the voice of his culture. Flem never verbalizes his desire for two reasons: he never talks to anyone and he does not know his own desire. "The first man Flem would tell his business to would be the man that was left after the last man died. Flem Snopes dont even tell himself what he is up to. Not if he was laying in bed with himself in a empty house in the dark of the moon" (1991: 309). The closest he comes is when he tells the Memphis decorator that his home must look like those in the magazines. Although Flem overcomes poverty and physical impotence to attain the cultural ideal of success through his wife, daughter, position, and wealth, he dies calmly facing Mink's cocked gun, a victim of his culture's desire. Flem dies in his hat and bow tie – his symbols of subjectivity. In Lacanian terms, pure submission to the cultural symbolic is a type of death – the death of desire. By submitting to the cultural symbolic, Flem yields his desire, and without desire, he has been figuratively "dead" all along. His impotence is an apt metaphor for his subjectivity. Nichol observes that Flem's "[b]eing willing to die for an image suggests no individuality at all; it suggests a lack of courage to pursue a moral responsibility toward himself" (1997: 504). Although Flem is a major vehicle of social change, he himself does not undergo the significant change of self-knowledge. Only at his death, by facing Mink – the gaze of the Other that he might have been himself – does Flem perhaps acknowledge the "real." Perhaps in his death he perceives that he has not followed his own voice but only the voice of his culture.

In contrast to Flem, Mink moves from obeying the law of his symbolic order to becoming a subject with individual agency and naming his own desire not to be a meaningless link in the signifying chain. Although Mink abides by Varner's judgment of the fee he owes Houston and dutifully pays the price set by working it out in labor rather than take charity, Varner sees in Mink a danger that made him "afraid for the peace and quiet of the community which he held in his iron usurious hand, buttressed by the mortgages and liens in the vast iron safe in his store" (1965: 19). In response, Varner tries to pay Mink's debt so he will go back to work. Mink eyes the money but refuses to take it, asking Varner, "Have you heard any complaint from me about that-ere cow court judgment of yourn?" (1965: 19). Houston also attempts to force Mink to let him pay the debt and be done with it, confronting Mink: " 'Look at me.' He [Mink] looked up then, not pausing. Houston's hand was already extended; he, Mink, could see the actual money in it" (1965: 18). But Mink disengages, continuing to plant the fence post "that anyway looked heavier and more solid than he did" (1965: 18). In this exchange, Mink sees himself as weak object in a cultural symbolic that solidifies Houston and Varner in the subject position; the enormity of his object status appears through the "real" of Houston and Varner. Houston will come to be for Mink a literal body in pieces when he discards Houston's extremities, representing Mink's own lack of control. Likewise, while Varner perceives himself as object in Mink's response, sensing a danger and the need to re-establish equilibrium, Houston misses the warning, making the mistake of not noticing Mink " 'until he stepped out from behind that bush that morning with that shotgun' " (1965: 378). Throughout the trilogy, childlike imagery describes Mink and the perception of him as small, harmless, and invisible, reducing his threat; diminishing the gaze of the Other serves to disempower Mink. But his threat remains. Stevens encounters Mink as a "small figure . . . as slight and frail and harmless-looking as a child and as deadly as a small viper" (1965: 45). Mink was "just small, just colorless, perhaps simply too small to be noticed" (1965: 412). But for Jefferson society and for Flem, Mink represents the "real," and the "real" always returns.

Mink begins as object, blindly following the demand of his cultural symbolic, but becomes subject when he listens to his own particular, unique desire as opposed to that of his culture. In the process, he thinks how the cultural symbolic structure, which fixes his position in society, thwarts his attempts to get ahead or to find peace (he cannot farm his own land, have a roof that does not leak, or feed his family). In jail for killing Houston, Mink verbalizes his desire "Jest to get out of here and go back home and farm. That dont seem like a heap to ask" (1965: 40). And yet Mink later realizes the imprisonment of the tenant position itself and voices his fate as Other: "People of his kind never had owned even temporarily the land which they believed they had rented . . . It was the land itself which owned them . . . in perpetuity" (1965: 91). Throughout his life, Mink has accepted his lot, what he calls his "bad luck [that] had all his life continually harassed and harried him into the constant and unflagging necessity of defending his own simple rights" (1965: 7). As a meaningless lower-class cog in his community's wheel, he is at the mercy of "Them" (1965: 22), who try "him to see just how much he could bear and would stand" (1965: 16), but he hopes that at some point he will be able to "get his own just and equal licks back" (1965: 6). Mink thinks he can "beat Them" through his patience and his ability to work and wait (1965: 22). But in his scheme to salvage his barren cow at Houston's expense, he had "underestimated *them*" (1965: 16). He accepts the punishment from "Them" despite his "thin furious rage against them" until he reaches his limit (1965: 16).

Initially resigned to working hard for little profit in a system that circumscribes him, Mink submits to Varner's letter of the law. When the dollar pound fee catches Mink off guard, he tells Varner that "if that's the Law" it must be answered (1965: 29). But in fact, this fee finally pushes Mink to claim his subjectivity in the symbolic structure. Godden claims that "Mink's bull and Ab's fire are weapons in the same war, and as such, their deployment is a measure of shared class consciousness" (2003: 604). By fighting back through his violence against Houston and then later against Flem, Mink becomes a subject with agency, Lacan's S2, able to follow his own desire. Mink would have verbalized his subjectivity to Houston had there been time, would have told him that he understood the system where "all you rich folks has got to stick together or else maybe some day the ones that aint rich might take a notion to raise up and take hit away from you" (Faulkner 1965: 39). Mink exacts revenge on Houston not because he is rich while Mink is poor, but because Houston has demanded the ultimate penalty allowed by law rather than see Mink as a suffering individual and equal human being.

Mink verbalizes his desire to Stevens when he asks him what he will have to do to be free in 25 years, rejecting a new trial and the insanity plea that Stevens, in his fear of Mink, tries to convince him would be possible. Stevens experiences Mink's threat and hopes to put him away in Jackson so "we'll be safe" (1965: 46). But Mink knows that his life sentence is his way out, if his lawyer is being honest, and he must be "because there was some kind of rule" (1965: 48). Mink knows he is not crazy – he is just verbalizing his desire, which the cultural symbolic would label insane. Now Mink will submit to the law and the symbolic structure to exact his revenge; the same law that demands his imprisonment will also let him out in 20 to 25 years if he obeys the rules. By asking Stevens to have the judge verify (with "a wrote-out paper saying so") that the law will reward his patience, Mink actively seeks to control the symbolic order (1965: 44).

As long as Mink internalizes his culture's dictates regarding his identity, he cannot name his own desire. By yielding his desire to the demand of his cultural symbolic, Mink would remain a meaningless link of the signifying chain of Southern culture. However, when he is able to verbalize his own desire, he can finally act on his own rather than submit to the cultural symbolic. By recognizing the Lacanian "real" in the form of the gaze of the Other – how Jefferson views him as object – Mink reaches his breaking point, shoots Houston, and names his desire to be in the subject position. Mink "would have liked to . . . leave a printed placard on the breast itself: *This is what happens to the men who impound Mink Snopes' cattle*, with his name signed to it" (1991: 242). He verbalizes his desire to rebel against the poverty of "the paintless two-room cabin . . . which was not his, on which he paid rent but not taxes, paying almost as much in rent in one year as the house had cost to build; not old, yet the roof of which already leaked and the weather-stripping had already begun to rot" (1991: 243). His actions symbolize his desire for a place as subject in the symbolic structure that circumscribes him as impoverished object.

Mink's voicing of his desire parallels Lacan's notion that the therapeutic talk of analysis allows for the libidinal pleasure of blind repetition to give way to desire through a reconfiguration of the subject's relationship to the symbolic order. In his *Seminar, Book II*, Lacan writes that in analysis, what's important is to teach the subject to name, to articulate, to bring this desire into existence. . . . If desire doesn't dare speak its name, it's because the subject hasn't yet caused this name to come forth. That the subject should come to recognise and to name his desire, that is the efficacious action of analysis. But it isn't a question of recognising something which would be entirely given, ready to be coapted. In naming it, the subject creates, brings forth, a new presence in the world. (1991: 228–9)

Through naming the desire to reject the demand of the cultural symbolic, Mink emerges as subject at the end of the novel. That is, Mink's understanding of his symptom renders him a subject of knowledge (Lacan's S2); he links the empty repetition of his symptom (S1) to an understanding that restructures his relation to the symbolic order. He can defy the demand of separation of rich and poor, personifying his community's fear of an altered cultural symbolic.

At the end of the trilogy, Mink finds peace because he has defeated his demons by murdering Houston and Flem, a necessary acting out of his desire. While Mink asserts that he would never steal, he does commit murder to symbolically dismantle the system that renders him powerless. When he kills Flem, Mink knows he has to shoot him *"in the face"* to erase the gaze of the Other (1965: 415). "He didn't need to say 'Look at me, Flem.' His cousin was already doing that" (1965: 415). Mink becomes S2 by demanding recognition from the top representative of the symbolic structure that objectifies him. Flem resigns himself to this encounter, and "appeared to sit immobile and even detached too, watching Mink's grimed shaking childsized hands," with his eye on the pistol as it explodes (1965: 415). Ratliff observes that Mink is "free now. He wont never have to kill nobody else in all his life," indicating his understanding of the position of the lower-class Other who has had his revenge (1965: 432). Mink concurs when he thinks *"I am free now. I can walk any way I want to"* (1965: 434). When Mink learns that he is free to go and that Linda has left him money to be sent in installments, he recognizes that he has finally beaten "Them" with a "Much obliged . . . Send it to M.C. Snopes. . . . That's my name: M.C." (1965: 433). By naming himself, Mink solidifies his position as S2.

In this closing scene, Ratliff and Stevens also recognize Mink's subjectivity by aiding and abetting his escape. As participants in a changing order, they assist him with mixed motives. On the one hand, his leaving will put the era of Snopeses behind them, a gesture that protects them from the "real." At the same time, their actions acknowledge the "real" and their own precarious subject positions. The community efforts of Ratliff, Stevens, and Linda to sanction Mink's actions reflect the knowledge that Jefferson's own values created Flem, the embodiment of their own weakness. Railey notes that "allegiance to respectability – a commodity that increases one's social position – has replaced any real sense of morality" (1999: 159). As a result, Stevens "made the mistake of thinking a Snopes was a different 'kind' of human being than a Stevens" (1999: 201); the "'Snopes alarm' and their hatred and fear of Flem and his clan have been based on pure ignorance that 'Snopeses' are really no different from any other human beings, including themselves" (1999: 202). Ratliff and Stevens depart as the walking wounded:

"Gentle and tender as a woman, Ratliff opened the car door for Stevens" (Faulkner 1965: 433). Ratliff displays the need for kindness and understanding of their failings if they are to carry on, even while Stevens must verbalize his continuing effort to deny of the "real." In response to Ratliff's question about Linda's motives – "So you think she really didn't know what he was going to do when he got out?" – Stevens insists, "Yes I tell you" (1965: 429). Ratliff and Stevens verbalize the combative relationship between the Other and the social order. In this battle throughout the trilogy, Ratliff attempts to control information, Varner tries to control Flem's wealth and advancement, and Stevens strives to control Linda's future. That their efforts fail indicates the extent to which they cannot separate from the voice of their culture.

And yet their response to Mink indicates the extent to which they are "postanalytic" in that they have gained an awareness of their culture and its master signifiers. While Ratliff and Stevens will continue to live in the symbolic structure and its signifying chain, they have gained understanding and growth as individuals. They see themselves as part of a larger cultural voice and must accept their roles and place among the "poor sons of bitches" (1965: 429). Railey asserts that Mink "recognizes his place in the social order . . . [and] comes to represent also the necessity for change in this social structure" (1999: 161–3). Polk's comment that "If violence, if murder, is the only way we can deal effectively with Snopesism, if the world has to depend on the likes of Mink Snopes to save it, then we are in sorry shape indeed" (1983: 125). Yet it is through this realization that Ratliff and Stevens offer some hope of cultural change. In place of radical or revolutionary departure from master signifiers, Ratliff and Stevens experience the trauma of cultural inscription. They realize that their culture has created and destroyed Flem. As they become aware of their alienation from their existing social structure, they acknowledge the need to produce new master signifiers. A greater understanding of the system does not equate with the power to change it, but such knowledge necessarily precedes social change.

References and Further Reading

Alcorn, M. W., Jr. (2002). *Changing the Subject in English Class: Discourse and the Constructions of Desire.* Carbondale: Southern Illinois University Press.

Bracher, M. (1993). *Lacan, Discourse, and Social Change: A Psychoanalytic Cultural Criticism.* Ithaca, NY: Cornell University Press.

Faulkner, W. (1961). *The Town.* New York: Vintage. (Original pub. 1957.)

Faulkner, W. (1965). *The Mansion.* New York: Vintage. (Original pub. 1959.)

Faulkner, W. (1991). *The Hamlet.* New York: Vintage International. (Original pub. 1940.)

Fowler, D. (1997). *Faulkner: The Return of the Repressed.* Charlottesville, VA: University Press of Virginia.

Freud, S. (1957). *Beyond the Pleasure Principle.* In *The Standard Edition of the Complete Psychological Works of Sigmund Freud*, vol. 18 (trans. J. Strachey) (pp. 7–64). London: Hogarth Press and the Institute of Psycho-Analysis.

Godden, R. (2003). Comparative Cows: Or, Reading *The Hamlet* for its Residues. *English Literary History,* 70(2): 597–623.

Irwin, J. T. (1975). *Doubling and Incest/Repetition and Revenge.* Baltimore: Johns Hopkins University Press.

Jenkins, L. (1981). *Faulkner and Black–White Relations: A Psychoanalytic Approach*. New York: Columbia University Press.

Lacan, J. (1981). *Four Fundamental Concepts of Psycho-Analysis* (ed. J.-A. Miller, trans. A. Sheridan). New York: Norton.

Lacan, J. (1991). *The Seminar of Jacques Lacan, Book II: The Ego in Freud's Theory and in the Technique of Psychoanalysis 1954–1955* (ed. J.-A. Miller, trans. S. Tomaselli). New York: Norton.

Nichol, F. L. (1997). Flem Snopes's Knack for Verisimilitude in Faulkner's Snopes Trilogy. *Mississippi Quarterly*, 50(3): 493–505.

Ownby, T. (1995). The Snopes Trilogy and the Emergence of Consumer Culture. In D. M. Kartiganer and A. J. Abadie (eds.). *Faulkner and Ideology* (pp. 95–128). Jackson: University Press of Mississippi.

Polk, N. (1983). Idealism in *The Mansion*. In M. Gresset and P. Samway, SJ (eds.). *Faulkner and Idealism: Perspectives from Paris* (pp. 113–26). Jackson: University Press of Mississippi.

Railey, K. (1999). *Natural Aristocracy: History, Ideology, and the Production of William Faulkner*. Tuscaloosa: University of Alabama Press.

Robinson, O. (2001). Monuments and Footprints: The Mythology of Flem Snopes. *Faulkner Journal*, 17(1): 69–86.

Robinson, O. (2003). Interested Parties and Theorems to Prove: Narrative and Identity in Faulkner's Snopes Trilogy. *Southern Literary Journal*, 36(1): 56–74.

Schreiber, E. J. (2002). *Subversive Voices: Eroticizing the Other in William Faulkner and Toni Morrison*. Knoxville: University of Tennessee Press.

Skinfill, M. (1996). Reconstructing Class in Faulkner's Late Novels: *The Hamlet* and the Discovery of Capital. *Studies in American Fiction*, 24(2):151–69.

Stroble, W. (1980). Flem Snopes: A Crazed Mirror. In G. O. Carey (ed.). *Faulkner: The Unappeased Imagination: A Collection of Critical Essays*. (pp. 195–212). Troy, NY: Whitson.

Sundquist, E. J. (1983). *Faulkner: The House Divided*. Baltimore: Johns Hopkins University Press.

Towner, T. M. (2000). *Faulkner on the Color Line: The Later Novels*. Jackson: University Press of Mississippi.

Urgo, J. (1987). *Faulkner's Apocrypha: A Fable, Snopes, and the Spirit of Human Rebellion*. Jackson: University Press of Mississippi.

Urgo, J. (1995). Faulkner's Real Estate: Land and Literary Speculation in *The Hamlet*. *Mississippi Quarterly*, 48(3): 443–57.

Volpe, E. L. (1964). *A Reader's Guide to William Faulkner*. Syracuse: Syracuse University Press.

Wilson, R. J., III (1980). Imitative Flem Snopes and Faulkner's Causal Sequence in *The Town*. *Twentieth Century Literature*, 26(4): 432–44.

PART V
After Faulkner

29

"He Doth Bestride the Narrow World Like a Colossus": Faulkner's Critical Reception

Timothy P. Caron

Faulkner's work and reception are so irrevocably intertwined with twentieth century American literary and critical history that grappling with the text we know as "Faulkner," in all its permutations, is essential to understanding where we have been and how we got to where we are now.

D. Matthew Ramsey, "'Lifting the Fog':
Faulkners, Reputations, and *The Story of Temple Drake*"

Literary reputations rise and fall dramatically because the critics reflect not universal, but relative, literary values which are, in large measure, historically determined.

Lawrence H. Schwartz, *Creating Faulkner's Reputation:*
The Politics of Modern Literary Criticism

At the outset of his essay "Faulkner in the Twenty-First Century: Boundaries of Meaning, Boundaries of Mississippi," Michael Kreyling asks, "what Faulkner will we need, what Faulkner will endure, in the twenty-first century?" (2003: 14). The question is an important one because it acknowledges our roles as students and teachers of Faulkner in determining what exactly *Faulkner* has meant to previous readers, what that label means to contemporary students and teachers, and what it will mean to future generations of readers. A partial answer is one grounded in multiplicity. Quite simply, we no longer have *Faulkner* but *Faulkners*; rather than a single author-function that can contain the various readings, analyses, and interpretations given over to his work, we now have a plurality. The proliferation of critical approaches following the "theory boom" of the 1980s and 1990s in the US has dramatically shifted critical orthodoxies. This recalibration of our readings of Faulkner's work has done nothing to diminish his stature. Instead, the opposite is true, for, like Shakespeare, the other "colossus" of the Anglo-American tradition (and from whose *Julius Caesar* I'm borrowing my title), Faulkner's importance continues to grow with the emergence and development of each new critical methodology. We now have a psychoanalytic Faulkner, a Derridean Faulkner, a feminist Faulkner, a Lacanian Faulkner, a "race" Faulkner, a "queer" Faulkner, an eco-critical or "green" Faulkner, and a post-colonial Faulkner, to name just a few. In fact, Faulkner's work is now sought out as a proving ground for new theoretical developments and critical approaches; rather than a particular theory or approach being used to endorse or recommend his work to a wider reading audience, Faulkner's reputation now validates and gives credence to the various reading models and paradigms employed in reading and analyzing his works. I would like to keep Kreyling's question before me as I attempt to limn the broad contours of Faulkner's critical reception (emphasizing books more than essays) because an understanding and appreciation of that reception, tracing the major readings, the signal moments, and the successive waves of critical and theoretical approaches, will offer another response to Kreyling's question about which Faulkner(s) will "endure" in the coming century.

Before tracing the historical contours of Faulkner's critical reception, I'd like to offer one brief, but revealing, I hope, example of the type of interpretive multiplicity I've been talking about: the man in the red tie from *The Sound and the Fury* (1929). As most readers remember, Caddy Compson's daughter, Miss Quentin, flees the domestic turmoil and her uncle Jason's not-so-subtle leering by running away with a man wearing a red tie. To the new critics of the 1950s and 1960s, those readers whose re-evaluation of Faulkner's work was so instrumental in his canonization – critics such as Cleanth Brooks, Olga Vickery, and Michael Millgate, for example – the man in the red tie, if he were noticed at all, might reveal just how far the Compson family had fallen in social status. To a critic interested in class issues in the novel, the man in the red tie might suggest the ascendancy of a consumerist, entertainment-based economy at the expense of the paternalistic structures embodied by the once noble Compson family. More recent critics of the novel have concentrated more on the man's tie and what it might represent than on the man himself. For instance, Michelle Ann Abate's research into the sartorial semiotics of gay subculture in early twentieth-century America suggests to her that the young man's red tie – a subtle but common means for a gay man to indicate his sexual orientation to other gay men – indicates that he is gay (2001). The red tie could have other possible meanings. From Cheryl Lester (1995), we learn that supporters of the race-baiting senator from Mississippi, James K. Vardaman, wore red ties as symbols of support for their candidate; therefore, perhaps the carnival worker's red tie merely reveals his political allegiances. If such a seemingly innocuous textual detail of this incredibly rich and complex text has been made so thoroughly and completely unstable by the multitude of critical approaches brought to bear upon the novel, a reader might justifiably wonder if any element of that vast body of work we identify as *Faulkner* is stable.

Casting Long Shadows: Early Readings of Faulkner's Work

To be sure, Faulkner did have his early admirers and passionate defenders among the very first reviews of his works during the 1920s and 1930s, but there is no denying that his critical "stock" was at rock bottom early on in his career. Among the very earliest attempts to bolster his reputation and to boost his sales is George Marion O'Donnell's essay "Faulkner's Mythology," originally published in the influential journal the *Kenyon Review* in 1939 (O'Donnell 1960). As Donald Kartiganer explains, O'Donnell's essay helped to reorient the scant attention paid to Faulkner's work early on. After this, Faulkner's critics no longer felt obliged to begin their essays by defending the novels against charges of immorality, nihilism, or willful obscurantism; rather, "the action of [Faulkner's] fiction reveals itself as engaged in a great moral conflict, with Faulkner very much on the side of traditional moral values" (Kartiganer 2001). If O'Donnell's reading of Faulkner's work strikes contemporary readers as a bit too reductive in its division of all his characters into two broad categories, "Sartorises" and "Snopeses" – that is, those who valiantly hold onto the best aspects of the South's cultural inheritance and those who degrade and erode it (O'Donnell 1960: 83) – he was nonetheless successful in helping to bring about some small measure of critical acclaim at a time when Faulkner, largely because of the infamy of *Sanctuary* (1931), was seen as a pre-eminent member of the "cult of cruelty," a writer whose work was more interested in shocking, titillating, and/or offending the decent book-buying American public.

O'Donnell, however, was virtually a lone voice in the wilderness (apart from a few others such as Conrad Aiken), extolling the genius of the man from Oxford. Despite these efforts to reclaim Faulkner and his reception, his books continued to sell poorly through the 1930s and 1940s. It is difficult then, for two reasons, to overestimate the importance of Malcolm Cowley's *The Portable Faulkner*, published in 1946, in rehabilitating Faulkner's critical reception. First, as Cowley himself notes in the "Introduction" to the *Portable*, "in 1945 all of [Faulkner's] seventeen books were out of print" (1960: 96), and this collection of Faulkner's writings, carefully selected and arranged to present a coherent, chronological history of Yoknapatawpha county, began the rehabilitation of Faulkner's critical reception, sparking both a popular and a critical re-evaluation of Faulkner's work. Second, Cowley's "Introduction" offered a nuanced and complimentary rereading of the work that helped to establish the parameters of Faulkner criticism for an early generation of critics and readers. From the fiction, Cowley extracted an articulate summary of the overarching story that Faulkner seemed to be telling, what Cowley called a "legend of the South" (p. 102) in both his novels and short fiction:

> Briefly stated, the legend might run something like this: The Deep South was settled partly by aristocrats like the Sartoris clan and partly by new men like Colonel Sutpen. Both types of planters were determined to establish a lasting social order on the land they had seized from the Indians (that is, to leave sons behind them). They had the virtue of living single-mindedly by a fixed code; but there was also an inherent guilt in their "design," their way of life; it was slavery that put a curse on the land and brought about the Civil War. After the War was lost, partly as a result of their own mad heroism (for who else but men as brave as Jackson and Stuart could have frightened the Yankees into standing together and fighting back?) they tried to restore "the design" by other methods. But they no longer had the strength to achieve more than a partial success, even after they had freed their land from the carpetbaggers who followed the Northern armies. As

time passed, moreover, the men of the old order found that they had Southern enemies too: they had to fight against a new exploiting class descended from the landless whites of slavery days. In this struggle between the clan of Sartoris and the unscrupulous tribe of Snopes, the Sartorises were defeated in advance by a traditional code that kept them from using the weapons of the enemy. As a price of victory, however, the Snopeses had to serve the mechanized civilization of the North, which was morally impotent in itself, but which, with the aid of its Southern retainers, ended by corrupting the Southern nation. (pp. 102–3)

This "legend" bears more than a passing resemblance to the "mythology" that O'Donnell glimpsed within Faulkner's fiction; both O'Donnell and Cowley emphasize regional history and see Faulkner lamenting the disappearance of traditional values and community in the changing South of the early twentieth century. Faulkner garnered more and more attention following the success of the *Portable*, and following his winning of the Nobel Prize in 1950, succeeding critics used Cowley's "Introduction" as something of a template for many of their own readings.

Criticism begets criticism. Robert Penn Warren's review of the *Portable*, originally published in 1946 (Warren 1960), is strange as a review because it's more of a response to and amplification of Cowley's essay than it is a review of Faulkner's book, but it was among the first to recognize the importance of Cowley's anthology. Whereas Cowley emphasized Faulkner's genius by placing him within the regional context of the South, Warren cast his net wider, arguing for a truly "universal" quality to Faulkner's fiction. For Warren, the fiction was not to be read "in terms of the South against the North, but in terms of issues which are common to our modern world" (1960: 112). In language presaging Faulkner's Nobel Prize acceptance speech, Warren outlined why he felt that Faulkner's work was so vital in the burgeoning Cold War context:

The legend is not merely a legend of the South, but is also a legend of our general plight and problem. The modern world is in moral confusion. It does suffer from a lack of discipline, of sanctions, of community of values, of a sense of mission. It is a world in which self-interest, workableness, success provide the standards. It is a world which is the victim of abstraction and of mechanism, or at least, at moments, feels itself to be. (1960: 112)

Warren's gendered, community-based, politically conservative agrarian values are manifest in his praise of Faulkner and would become the cornerstone of the New Critics' canonization of Faulkner; the fiction's primary value becomes its ability to help us make sense of a seemingly senseless world.

Warren concludes his review of the *Portable* with an audacious claim: "The study of Faulkner is the most challenging single task in contemporary American literature for criticism to undertake. Here is a novelist who, in mass of work, in scope of material, in range of affect, in reportorial accuracy and symbolic subtlety, in philosophical weight can be put beside the masters of our own past literature" (1960: 124). This statement seems self-evident here at the beginning of the twenty-first century, but it is important to remember just how low Faulkner's critical stock was at the time: the great man of Oxford was not yet a Nobel Laureate and was in the fallow period between the publication of *Go Down, Moses* (1942) and *Intruder in the Dust* (1948). Warren not only loudly proclaimed that Faulkner should be enshrined in the pantheon of American literary immortals, but he went even further, outlining the areas of investigation that future critics should pursue as they too came to recognize Faulkner's genius. According to Warren, enterprising critics should hasten to explore Faulkner's interactions with Nature; the humor in his writing; his characterizations of "the Negro" and the "poor white"; and his fictional techniques, such as his deployment of symbols and images (1960: 114–24).

Taming Faulkner's Fiction: New Critical Readings

Following the trail blazed by Cowley and Warren came several studies, most notably Cleanth Brooks's *William Faulkner: The Yoknapatawpha Country* (1963), Olga Vickery's *The Novels of William Faulkner* (1959), Michael Millgate's *The Achievement of William Faulkner* (1966), and Edmund Volpe's *A Reader's Guide to William Faulkner* (1964), that secured Faulkner's reputation and created a critical orthodoxy that, in some respects, we are still responding to and reacting against today. Whereas a contemporary reader of Faulkner's work, one attuned to contemporary critical attitudes toward issues of class, gender, and racial inequality, for instance, will likely comment upon the fragmentary or provisional nature of many of his greatest novels, the critics who helped to canonize Faulkner in the 1950s and 1960s replicated many of the underlying principles of Cowley's "legend." Common to Cowley and Warren's understanding of Faulkner (even O'Donnell's in the 1930s) is a strain of cultural and political conservatism. Prized above all else in Cowley and Warren's readings are virtues such as "family" and "community." Both see these virtues as residing within white males, those who might be classified as belonging to or having honorary membership of the proud Sartoris clan. These "aristocratic" white men, and their diminished male scions ("integer for integer" smaller than their ancestors, as Mr. Compson might say), are engaged in a life-or-death struggle to maintain the heroic ideals of earlier generations against the social, political, and economic advances of the formerly "landless" – and slaveless – whites, epitomized by the Snopeses. The real drama of Faulkner's fiction is enacted between men of a certain (perhaps diminished) nobility. In this diagram of Yoknapatawpha, both women and African Americans lack agency and only exist in relation to white males: women are either vessels of virtue, embodying the vital elements of the South's inheritance, or fallen, and black characters are the reminders of white guilt caused by the curse of slavery.

Linda Wagner-Martin's "Introduction" to *William Faulkner: Six Decades of Criticism* lists many common assumptions carried over from Cowley and Warren's work to the New Critical Faulkner:

- . . . of course Quentin Compson honored his father's moral principles, cynical though they were;
- . . . the only power axis in Faulkner's world was drawn from one white man to another;
- . . . all of his African American characters were nostalgically stereotypical;
- . . . women characters existed only as foils for his men, or as prompts to spark action from the all-too-often passive Southern males;
- . . . the values of the South, and its attendant Christian philosophical base, were unquestioned in Faulkner's writing;
- . . . the customs of the South, regardless of the time period, were stable and judicious;
- . . . the reasonable citizens of Faulkner's country were never plagued by guilt, sorrow, or irony, so that the role of memory in his writing was that of honoring the past, never questioning it. (2002: xi)

The "central critical task" for figures such as Cleanth Brooks, an influential shaper of both the New Critical approach and the canonization of Faulkner, is "to determine and evaluate the meaning of the work in the fullness of its depth and amplitude" (Brooks 1963: 8). A "useful criticism" should "make its account of symbolic events and scenes coherent and responsible by relating the alleged symbols to the total fictional context" (p. 8). In other words, a New Critical reading will be, as much as humanly possible, a totalizing narrative, one that strives for and celebrates consistency and surface smoothness.

The real consequence of Brooks, Volpe, Vickery, and Millgate's readings, as brilliant and effective as they were in bringing new critical and popular reading audiences to the novels, was that Faulkner was tamed, for in their quest to construct Brooks's "total fictional context," their readings of certain iconic Faulkner characters became fairly homogeneous, similar to Cowley and Warren's politically and culturally conservative pronouncements. For this group of critics, Thomas Sutpen, to take but one example, is not a rapacious zealot, a sort of land-locked Ahab who replicates the racist ideology of the slavocracy, but an "innocent" whom "we must understand if we are to understand the meaning of his tragedy" (Brooks 1963: 296). When Olga Vickery proclaims that Sutpen is "the staunchest defender of the idols of the South *at a time when they most needed defending*" (1959: 93; italics mine), a contemporary reader might well wonder just what Southern "idols" she might have in mind that so desperately need to be defended —a fanatical devotion to establishing, maintaining, and policing racial purity, gender dominance, or class distinctions? In these critics' readings, Faulkner's fiction seems more like a defense of the region than a sensitive analysis and courageous exposure of the South's "peculiar" history, and their readings are sometimes obscured by a "moonlight and magnolias" mythology. If we fail to recognize their Faulkner, we should remember that Faulkner probably would not enjoy his current acclaim were it not for the pioneering efforts of Brooks, Vickery, Millgate, and Volpe, for they created a "Faulkner" that was simultaneously both celebrated as a genius and made accessible for consumption by a wide and diverse reading public. Each of their readings spans the range of Faulkner's corpus, providing, in their elegant prose styles, compellingly authoritative commentaries on every novel in the Yoknapatawpha chronicles. This impulse to regularize Faulkner's fiction finds its apotheosis in Volpe's *Reader's Guide* and its author's affection for taxonomies and various types of charts and diagrams. His emphasis upon and inclusion of maps, genealogies, plot summaries, chronologies, and a guide to temporal shifts within the Quentin and Benjy sections of *The Sound and the Fury* make Faulkner more accessible to a wide audience of students and general readers. Common to all of these critics' estimations of Faulkner is the consensus that he was an artist of great moral vision; therefore, he was worthy of inclusion in the pantheon of the West's greatest writers of all time: "Faulkner's achievement can be adequately estimated only by our seeing him as a great novelist in the context not merely of the South, or even of the United States, but of the whole western tradition" (Millgate 1966: 292).

New Directions: Bleikasten and Irwin

If one were to work backwards, tracing the various threads of contemporary Faulkner criticism in an attempt to determine how we got from the orthodox, tamed Faulkner of the New Critics and their deftly rendered totalizing interpretations to an ever-evolving multiplicity of readings, one would see that two figures smashed the well-wrought urn of Brooks and his contemporaries and, depending upon one's point of view, brought either chaos or liberation. In the 1970s, two readers revived the world of Faulkner studies: André Bleikasten and John T. Irwin. Bleikasten, writing in France where Faulkner had long been appreciated, applied contemporary European critical approaches to Faulkner's work in two books whose small size belied the huge impact they would have. In the "Preface" to the first of these, *Faulkner's* As I Lay Dying (1973), Bleikasten alludes to the towering presence of the preceding generation's great explicators of Faulkner – Vickery, Brooks, and Millgate. While acknowledging these past masters, Bleikasten begins the process of nudging Faulkner studies in new directions in his examination of *As I Lay Dying* (1930). He announces in the preface that his approach is "based on a close reading of the novel's text (from the initial stages of its composition to the final version of the published book) and on a detailed examination of its formal and technical aspects (language, style, structure, creation of character) as well as of its thematic design" (1973: viii); hardly a call to arms against the New Critics, but there are subtle but significant differences between his approach and that of his predecessors. Most notably, he probes the interiority of Faulkner's characters much more thoroughly than prior critics. In Bleikasten's reading, the members of the Bundren family seem more like complex characters with rich hidden lives filled with desires, fears, anxieties, and unarticulated longings, and less like the New Critics' rendering of them as embodiments of abstract principles like "duty" or "perseverance." Bleikasten quickly followed *Faulkner's* As I Lay Dying with *"The Most Splendid Failure": Faulkner's* The Sound and the Fury (1976), in which he fires this shot across the bow of the New

Critics: "To interpret a text is to do it violence. No criticism is innocent of distortion; no interpreter leaves a text as he found it, and the kind of transparency which critical discourse manages to achieve is always achieved through reductive procedures" (1976: viii). With this comment, Bleikasten heralds a new direction in Faulkner studies. Whereas the New Critics might characterize their readings as attempting to reveal the difficult-to-ascertain but underlying unity of Faulkner's work, Bleikasten reveals these elegant readings to be only partial truths. He was one of the first Faulkner critics to articulate a commonplace of contemporary criticism – an interpretation of a literary text, its meaning, is *constructed*, not simply received, by that text's readers. In an effort to construct his own analysis of *The Sound and the Fury*, he relied upon the methodology of the *nouvelle critique*, an eclectic blend of contemporary European thinkers, theorists, and critics such as Roland Barthes, Jacques Lacan, and Roman Jakobson. While Bleikasten adroitly blends many theoretical perspectives in *"The Most Splendid Failure"*, a strain of psychoanalytic thought runs throughout his investigation, a helpful orientation given Faulkner's fierce insistence on taking his readers deep into the various consciousnesses of the Compson brothers.

A similar emphasis upon psychoanalytic thought can be found in the other groundbreaking work of Faulkner criticism from this period, Irwin's *Doubling and Incest/ Repetition and Revenge*. Irwin's approach is to read Faulkner, Freud, and Nietzsche intertextually, "oscillating" between these texts to make all of them "more problematic, richer, and more complex" (1975: 2). The great value, then, of Irwin's investigation is the deep analogues he reveals between Faulkner's fiction and Freud's theories regarding castration anxiety, incestuous desires, Oedipal struggles, and the psyche's organization into the id, ego, and superego. If for the New Critics, Faulkner's greatness lay in his celebration of universal human virtue, which they presented in language that sometimes sounds cribbed from his Nobel Prize acceptance speech, for Irwin, Faulkner's greatness lay in his unmatched ability to explore not the depths of the human heart but, as in the following example, our human psychology:

> It is a theme that Faulkner never tires of reiterating: by courageously facing the fear of death, the fear of castration, the fear of one's own worst instincts, one slays the fear; by taking the risk of being feminized, by accepting the feminine elements in the self, one establishes one's masculinity. And it is by allowing the fear of death, of castration, of one's own instincts, of being feminized, to dominate the ego that one is paralyzed, rendered impotent, unmanned, as in the case of Quentin. (Irwin 1975: 58)

Note the neat summarization of Freud's major concerns in this passage – a whole host of demons lurk just beneath the surface of our consciousness, demanding our attention.

While Bleikasten argues for the incompleteness of any reading of a literary text, Irwin positively celebrates Faulkner's particular resistance to interpretive closure. Irwin exults that he would like "to have written [his] book in one long unpunctuated sentence, or perhaps one long unbroken paragraph" (1975: 9) in an attempt to suspend the creation of a totalizing interpretation of Quentin Compson in *Absalom, Absalom!* (1936) and *The Sound and the Fury*. This method appeals to Irwin because of the peculiar nature of Faulkner's fiction:

> There is a further reason why this continual deferment of meaning as embodied in my text is appropriate to a treatment of Faulkner's novels, for Faulkner himself seems to have understood the oscillating relationship between a narrator and his story, between a writer and his book, as embodying "the always deferredness" of meaning – as a kind of Freudian *Nachträglichkeit* [deferred action], in which the act of narration, as a recollection and reworking, produces a story that almost makes sense but not quite, yet whose quality of *almost* being meaningful seems to indicate, seems to promise, that meaning has only been temporarily deferred and that some future repetition of the story, some further recollection and reworking, will capture that ultimate meaning. (p. 8)

As this excerpt reveals, Irwin not only helped to introduce Faulkner studies to emerging critical trends from Europe, but he also introduced a freer, more playful writing style to Faulkner criticism. In his investigation of Faulkner's "deferral" of meaning, Irwin's own prose style thus takes on many of the hallmarks of Faulkner's, especially his parataxis, as Irwin rejects the staid prose of the New Critics.

Perhaps the greatest benefit of Bleikasten and Irwin's work is that together they helped to chip away many of the critical orthodoxies around Faulkner's work. Brooks and the New Critics of his generation had worked hard to defend Faulkner against a preceding generation's charges of inscrutability, excessive technical experimentation, and immorality, but they had too fully tamed Faulkner's texts. Bleikasten and Irwin restored a *force*, an energy, to Faulkner studies: the texts became much less stable, more open-ended, and indeterminate. The vitality these two helped to bring to Faulkner studies was largely due to their infusion of new critical paradigms that were just beginning to take hold in the United States. Faulkner scholars suddenly had to become conversant with the theories of European thinkers like Freud, Nietzsche, Lévi-Strauss, Barthes, Jakobson, and Lacan. However, neither Bleikasten nor Irwin took as much advantage of feminist theory as others later would, or paid as much attention to African American history or culture, or the history of the US South. For example, Bleikasten's somewhat reductive view of Addie Bundren is that she simply hates her children, and in his reading, she has many of the same qualities as the wicked stepmother of fairy tales. Today, feminist critics are much more likely to view Addie as a woman struggling with the biological determinism of motherhood. Just as Bleikasten's reading of Addie posits a character without a great deal of agency, Irwin's Caddy Compson exists only as an object of her brothers' twisted sexual desires, not as a woman who refuses to conform to societal gender expectations. Succeeding generations of critics stand upon the shoulders of their predecessors, and it would be up to subsequent Faulkner critics to respond to and amend the interpretations of these two pioneers.

From Faulkner to *Faulkners*: The "Theory Boom" and Faulkner Studies

In my chronological account of Faulkner studies so far, I've made it seem as if the signal events, key players, and major shifts in the ways we read, receive, and discuss Faulkner and his works are easily identifiable, as if this history of Faulkner studies is obvious or natural and could not have evolved in any other fashion. But such a reckoning of Faulkner's reception is a fiction, an attempt to impose an order upon a vast and contentious group of readers of and responders to Faulkner's fiction. I make this somewhat obvious admission because, during the 1980s and 1990s, Faulkner's critical reception becomes positively dizzying in its multiplicity. The first several stages in the evolution of Faulkner criticism lie far enough in the past to offer some slight historical perspective on just who has offered up which groundbreaking interpretations, carved out original interpretive space, or thoroughly and completely rebutted some critical piety or piece of received wisdom. The 1980s and 1990s, however, are more difficult to sift through, not only because of propinquity, but because the entire period seems to have been devoted to offering new and startling interpretations of Faulkner's work. If Bleikasten and Irwin can be said to have pioneered new directions in Faulkner studies, then a whole host of scholars quickly followed their lead.

This generation – what I'm referring to as "the theory boom" – is cleverly described by Terry Eagleton in his book *After Theory* (2003) as the generation of scholars, writers, and critics who follow those theorists whose names constitute the syllabi of literary theory courses at both the undergraduate and graduate level all across the United States. For Eagleton, a group of august titans make up the "golden age of theory": Jacques Lacan, Claude Lévi-Strauss, Louis Althusser, Roland Barthes, Michel Foucault, Raymond Williams, Luce Irigaray, Pierre Bourdieu, Julia Kristeva, Jacques Derrida, Hélène Cixous, Jürgen Habermas, Frederic Jameson, and Edward Said (p. 1). The "theory boom," then, is comprised of those who come *after* these towering figures who revolutionized the humanities, those who analyze, critique, and, most importantly, apply the ideas of these celebrated thinkers. "Those who can, think up feminism or structuralism," writes Eagleton; "those who can't, apply such insights to *Moby-Dick* or *The Cat in the Hat*" (p. 2). Or Faulkner's fiction. It is the "theory boom" that gives us a race Faulkner (Davis and Sundquist), a feminist Faulkner (Gwin), a deconstructive Faulkner (Matthews), a Lacanian Faulkner (Weinstein and Fowler), and a Marxist Faulkner (Godden), to name but a few of the many *Faulkners* we now have. At the heart of this explosion of new interpretations of Faulkner, however, lies a curious paradox. At the moment when our understanding of Faulkner was changing and expanding more rapidly than it ever had, in one way it remained limited. These studies almost all grant canonical status only to Faulkner's early "masterpieces," a list that usually includes only *The Sound and the Fury*, *As I Lay Dying*, *Light in August* (1932), *Absalom, Absalom!*, and *Go Down, Moses*.

Among the first studies to usher in these new approaches to Faulkner studies was John T. Matthews's *The Play of Faulkner's Language* (1982), a Derridean analysis of

Faulkner's fiction. Matthews deploys Derrida's argument "on the impossibilities of coherence, manifestation, and presence in philosophic texts" (1982: 23) to read Faulkner's novels, and his particular interest is in Faulkner's penchant for absent presences. *The Sound and the Fury, Absalom, Absalom!, Light in August, As I Lay Dying* – all of these works have at their core some central event or character that is rendered only through its absence, through the text's steadfast refusal to reveal, to name, that which is central to its very own textual existence; and Matthews's book is a masterful application of Derridean concepts to Faulkner's texts to reveal just how Faulkner is able to use this textual effect to examine issues of gender and race. If Matthews's investigation of Faulkner's fiction is one predicated upon the examination of loss and absence, then Minrose Gwin's *The Feminine and Faulkner* (1990) might be seen as a feminist application of this insight to the novels, a sort of gendered deconstructive reading of Faulkner's more notable female characters – Caddy Compson, Addie Bundren, Rosa Coldfield, and Charlotte Rittenmeyer from *If I Forget Thee, Jerusalem/The Wild Palms* (1939). The power of Gwin's reading of Faulkner lies in her provocative rereading of these female characters as agents of instability and disruption; in her analysis, these women destabilize the South's gender hierarchies, revealing the region's "cult of true womanhood" to be anything but natural or transparent. After Gwin, gender has become a primary focus of Faulkner studies, and an entire generation of Faulknerians has learned the necessity of listening for Caddy's voice.

While Matthews and Gwin could be considered leading examples of those Faulknerians who subjected the novels to increasingly close readings of Faulkner's language during this period, then Eric Sundquist's *Faulkner: The House Divided* (1983) and Thadious Davis's *Faulkner's "Negro": Art and the Southern Context* (1983) can be considered among the finest studies of the other subject that came to the fore of Faulkner studies in the "theory boom": race. Common to Sundquist's and Davis's projects is their insistence that Faulkner's work be placed within the cultural context of the South, and both critics masterfully situate him and his work within the framework of Southern race relations. Sundquist, in fact, argues that Faulkner's brilliant early experiments in high modernism – *The Sound and the Fury, As I Lay Dying,* and *Sanctuary* – were a mere prelude to the greatest achievements of Faulkner's career – *Light in August, Absalom, Absalom!,* and *Go Down, Moses.* These novels, Sundquist argues, are the pillars upon which Faulkner's reputation should stand, for they display his prodigious technical achievement in service to his greatest theme, "the combined passion, fear, and promise of racial conflict – the problem of miscegenation" (1983: ix). Sundquist's title refers, of course, to Lincoln's infamous comment on the necessity of preserving the Union because "a house divided against itself cannot stand." Perhaps the greatest contribution made by Sundquist's book is that he reveals not only the way in which the US, the South especially, is "divided" by race but also how Faulkner himself was "divided" over the issue of race relations. Davis likewise explores the ways in which the South's tortured racial history impinges upon Faulkner's fiction, and she finds that the South was so race-obsessed that he had to grapple with the issue in order to "tell about the South," because the "Negro" – that is, the dominant white culture's creation of a racial "other"

against whom it could assert its superiority – is central to the South's self-image
(1983: 25). Davis finds that

> [f]rom the beginning of his career as a novelist, then, Faulkner evidences an artistic
> dependency upon the Negro in order to enrich his fiction, to add a measure of complexity
> and ambiguity, to suggest the dimensions (depths or shallowness) of his white characters'
> humanity. . . . In an artistic sense, he is obsessed not with the Negro as a rounded char-
> acter or as part of the world of humankind, but with the Negro as an idea which impinges
> upon the white man's internal world of thought and feeling, and upon the artist's own
> imaginative world. (1983: 64)

For both Sundquist and Davis, race is key to understanding Faulkner's work because
the novels' production and content are so thoroughly enmeshed in the South's matrix
of racial attitudes and tensions.

The "theory boom" of the 1980s and 1990s in the US proliferated other *Faulkners*,
including:

- a Bakhtinian Faulkner, one who explored the paradox of language's imprecision
  and its ability to capture and give order to our lived experience, as described in
  Stephen M. Ross's *Fiction's Inexhaustible Voice: Speech and Writing in Faulkner* (1989)
  and Judith Lockyer's *Ordered by Words: Language in Narration in the Novels of William
  Faulkner* (1991);
- a Lacanian Faulkner, given to us by Doreen Fowler's *Faulkner: The Return of the
  Repressed* (1997), who understands that meaning is created by excluding possible
  meanings but that those dismissed meanings are always hovering nearby, and, as a
  result, "men and women make themselves in culture through language" (1997: 167);
- a Marxist Faulkner, as represented in Richard Godden's *Fictions of Labor: William
  Faulkner and the South's Long Revolution* (1997), who used "the Compson material to
  mount a sustained exploration of how owners owned so much, for so long, by such
  'peculiar means,' and in the teeth of partial self-knowledge and sustained opposition" (1997: 233);
- an "ideological" Faulkner, who, according to Kevin Railey's *Natural Aristocracy:
  History, Ideology and the Production of William Faulkner* (1999), emblematizes the
  South's struggle to cling to a residual ideology of paternalism toward African
  Americans and women in the face of newly emerging and dominant ideologies of
  liberalism;
- and the "performative" Faulkner in whom James G. Watson, in *William Faulkner:
  Self-Preservation and Performance* (2000), sees the ability to integrate seamlessly his
  public utterances (his fiction, his interviews, and his photographs) with his private
  expressions, such as his letters, restoring coherence to an artist with a penchant for
  play-acting and role-playing (aviator, jilted lover, bohemian, farmer, public Civil
  Rights spokesman, and loyal son of the South).

While all of these works have greatly contributed to our understanding and appreciation of Faulkner's works, Philip Weinstein's *Faulkner's Subject: A Cosmos No One Owns* (1992) stands as perhaps the most ambitious of the examinations of the "theory boom," for in his book Weinstein reveals an admirable eclecticism as he skillfully shuttles between many of the approaches popularized during the period. Realizing that Faulkner's fiction is so complex and multivalent that no single approach could possibly comprehend it, Weinstein employs Lacanian psychoanalysis; Althusser's theory of subjectivity formation vis-à-vis ideology; Derrida's theory of deconstruction; Foucault's investigation of culture's disciplinary practices; the European feminism of Kristeva and Irigaray; and Bakhtin's theories of the self's construction through dialogic engagement with other speakers and other voices. Weinstein's title, with its reference to Faulkner's "subject," puns on Faulkner's own subjectivity and the material he took as his subject, Yoknapatawpha County, the "cosmos" of which he was "sole owner and proprietor." Neither artist nor his creation, as revealed in Weinstein's study, is unified and singular; both resist a determinant, closed reading. (See Wright 1990 for a fictionalized version of this interpretive proliferation of Faulkners.)

As noted earlier, a fundamental paradox lurks at the heart of most works produced in the "theory boom": while they opened up the Faulkner canon in important ways, they continued to explore the same small subset of Faulkner's total literary production and were quick to dismiss the later novels, those written after *Go Down, Moses*, as vastly inferior to the early masterpieces. This belief is probably best summarized by Eric Sundquist when he says that

> [t]here is some irony in the fact that Faulkner's deserved public recognition came at a time (the late 1940s and on to his death) when his best work was a decade old and he was writing some of the most disappointing fiction a major novelist could conceivably write. Little that he produced after *Go Down, Moses*, including *Intruder in the Dust*, the novel that guaranteed that recognition, merits sustained attention. (1983: 3)

During the "theory boom," *The Sound and the Fury, Absalom, Absalom!, Light in August, As I Lay Dying, Go Down, Moses*, and perhaps *Sanctuary* and *The Wild Palms/If I Forget Thee, Jerusalem* were the only Faulkner novels worth reading, teaching, and writing about. How might these studies have differed had they explored his later works? For instance, if Davis and Sundquist had explored the issue of race in *The Reivers* (1962) and had not assumed that Faulkner was merely a didactic old windbag at the end of his career and life? Or if Gwin had examined Eula Varner from the Snopes trilogy (*The Hamlet* [1940], *The Town* [1957], and *The Mansion* [1959]) as part of her study of gender? Running throughout the investigations produced during the "theory boom" is a common assumption: Faulkner's earlier novels are the ones worth reading, study, and teaching because he allegedly takes more risks in them, both in terms of his formal experimentation and in his willingness to fearlessly explore the South's peculiar history and continued legacy of racial violence, gender inequality, and class conflict in a way he would supposedly abandon later. One explanation for this selection of Faulkner's works is that the aesthetic of the "theory boom" critics is not one that values didacticism. The exclusion of his later works from these important, formative studies, however, continues to have a tremendous impact upon the contours of Faulkner studies because they have shaped our valuing and ranking of his works. Only now are the later works beginning to receive the critical attention they deserve.

The Problem of Late Faulkner

The exploration of "late Faulkner" has brought about a shift just as profound in its impact on how we view Faulkner as the theory boom, for if the efforts of Faulkner scholars such as Joseph Urgo, Theresa Towner, and Doreen Fowler prove to be successful, then the Faulkner canon will be vastly expanded to include rich, complex texts deserving of further analysis, texts such as *Intruder in the Dust, Requiem for a Nun* (1951), the Snopes trilogy, and *The Reivers*. Among the first to attempt to reorient Faulkner criticism toward a consideration of the *entire* corpus of Faulkner's work was Doreen Fowler's *Faulkner's Changing Vision: From Outrage to Affirmation* (1983). Fowler responds to those Faulknerians who characterized the later works as drastically inferior in style and treatment of subject matter to the early works by emphasizing what she sees as a slow and gradual evolution in Faulkner's writerly attitudes throughout the range of his career, a shift from an emphasis upon "human limitations" in the early fiction to one upon "human capabilities" (1983: 4) in the later works. Fowler detects a consistency running throughout Faulkner's work: "All of Faulkner's novels pose the question – what meaning has human existence? The question is always the same, but the answer gradually changes. Faulkner begins in despair and ends in affirmation. What evolves in the course of his literary career is Faulkner's vantage point on the spectacle of humanity, not the spectacle itself" (1983: 65). Implicit within Fowler's work is a subtle but powerful indictment of Faulkner scholars who emphasize the early works to the exclusion of the later – perhaps the flaws reside within Faulkner's readers and not the texts themselves. In other words, maybe we as readers simply aren't asking the correct questions of these texts.

Joseph Urgo's *Faulkner's Apocrypha: A Fable, Snopes, and the Spirit of Human Rebellion* (1989) takes up Fowler's challenge. In his study, Urgo examines Faulkner's description of his fictional universe as an "apocrypha," as opposed to early characterizations by Malcolm Cowley of Yoknapatawpha County as a myth or a legend. Whereas myths and legends seek to impose order upon a chaotic universe through narrative's power to order and organize human experience, "an apocrypha aims to upset and to create a sense of *competing* accounts, not a single vision, of the real" (1989: 15). For Urgo, the three Snopes novels become the "apotheosis" of "Faulkner's apocryphal vision," the masterpiece in which "the importance of the trilogy as a trinitarian mediation" upon the flesh, the mind, and the spirit "finally emerges" (p. 168). Fowler's understated rebuke to other Faulkner scholars is more explicitly stated in Urgo's work: "it seems . . . likely that critics who prefer the intensity of the early Faulkner novels see as a falling off in creative power what is actually a shift in narrative strategy, subject matter, and literary purpose" (p. 145). More recently, Theresa M. Towner's *Faulkner on the Color Line: The Later Novels* (2000) has attempted to rescue late Faulkner from neglect, arguing that many of the later novels are just as powerful meditations upon race as earlier works like *Light in August*, *Absalom, Absalom!*, and *Go Down, Moses*. These investigations challenge the impression too frequently given in most studies that the only Faulkner worth reading and studying is the early Faulkner.

Comparative Faulkner

As some critics are doggedly determined to expand the Faulkner canon, so others are just as doggedly determined to expand Faulkner studies' intertextual scope to include not just writers from the American South, such as the Agrarians, Flannery O'Connor, Eudora Welty, and Richard Wright, but writers from Latin America and the Caribbean and his fellow Nobel Prize winner, Toni Morrison. Faulkner scholars are taking to heart Eric Sundquist's admonition in "Faulkner, Race, and the Forms of American Fiction" (1987), an essay presented at the 1986 "Faulkner and Yoknapatawpha" Conference and contained in that year's proceedings, *Faulkner and Race*, that we read Faulkner in conversation with other texts, particularly African American texts:

> Although Faulkner's novels bring to a pitch the literary confrontation with race hatred in the early twentieth century, there are, by the same token, limitations to his vision. The fictional forms achieved by other authors, both black and white, in this way engage and complete those of Faulkner, reaching beyond the world of Yoknapatawpha and giving clearer voice to black lives and to the cultural traditions of race in America. The reconstruction of these traditions, their strands of signification and revising improvisations on the past, is today the main question for Faulkner's readers. (1987: 3)

Now this call to read Faulkner intertextually is being heeded through comparative readings of Faulkner with African American authors, most frequently Toni Morrison, and with other authors from throughout the hemisphere.

Many of the comparative readings that place Faulkner within the hemispheric context of the Americas employ post-colonial theories to detect the similarities and convergences between Faulkner and his Latin American and Caribbean counterparts. As Jon Smith and Deborah Cohn point out in their co-edited essay collection, *Look Away!: The U.S. South in New World Studies* (2004), while the pairing of Faulkner with Jorge Luis Borges, Carlos Fuentes, Gabriel García Márquez, Juan Carlos Onetti, or Mario Vargas Llosa might seem peculiar at first, these New World authors have profound similarities, despite the different languages in which they write:

> Faulkner became a focal author for [Latin American] writers . . . as a result of those writers' (transferential) perception of historical and cultural affinities between the South

and Latin America (most frequently defeat in war, racial conflict, underdevelopment, and a generally difficult entrance into modernity), as well as a model for the writers' positioning of themselves vis-à-vis the cultural metropolis. (2004: 304)

This trend of placing Faulkner within a hemispheric context is part of a larger, general trend within Southern literary studies to trace continuities between the American South and writers and cultures further south, in the Caribbean and in Central and South America.

Two recent examples of this contemporary trend of reading Faulkner through the lens of post-colonial theory are Charles Baker's *William Faulkner's Postcolonial South* (2000) and Edouard Glissant's *Faulkner, Mississippi* (1999). Despite certain similarities between Baker's and Glissant's borrowings from leading post-colonial theorists, there is a basic difference in the scope of their investigations. Baker is much more interested in orienting Faulkner along the lines of power that run from the American North to the South, from the metropole, the center of the colonizer's economic and cultural power, to the now abject and defeated former Confederate states. Glissant, on the other hand, situates Faulkner's work within the hemispheric context of the New World. Faulkner critics' prose sometimes comes to bear an uncanny resemblance to Faulkner's own prose, and Glissant's *Faulkner, Mississippi* employs this critical mimicry to better effect than any work since Irwin's *Doubling and Incest/Repetition and Revenge*. In his work, Glissant reveals an encyclopedic knowledge of the range of Faulkner's fictional world, but it is perhaps his style that is the most distinctive feature of the book. Like his predecessor, Irwin, Glissant realizes that his own critical language and writing style must rival that of Faulkner himself in order to adequately convey his meaning. Glissant's post-colonial investigation of the parallels between Faulkner's Mississippi and his own home of Martinique is rendered in a style immediately recognizable to students of Faulkner — long, circuitous sentences, filled with parenthetical elements and modifications, and evocative, imagistic language that conveys a literal meaning but whose impact is often first felt on an intuitive or affective level. Glissant, like Irwin, describes Faulkner's as a type of "deferred writing," and his description is just as apt for describing his own prose: "the hidden, the described, and the inexpressible . . . are interwoven throughout a book . . . , just as they are within a chapter and sometimes within a single sentence, carrying the reader to a vertiginous unknown, which is the most precise manner of approaching what can be known." Like Faulkner's, his prose is "wandering and dense, swinging and transported, straight to the point and suspended" (1999:139). What almost all post-colonial investigations of Faulkner's work, like Baker's and Glissant's, share is, in John T. Matthews's words, a fundamental recognition "that the plantation South derives its design from new-world models, owes a founding debt to West Indian slave-based agriculture, extracted labor and profit from African-Caribbean slave trade, and practiced forms of racial and sexual control common to other hemispheric colonial regimes" (2004: 239).

In *Faulkner, Mississippi*, Glissant recalls a lecture he delivered at Southern University, a historically black college located in Baton Rouge, Louisiana, in which he argued for the relevance of Faulkner's work to the lives of the African American students in his audience, for in the novels "there was . . . an upheaval of the unitary conceptions of being, a deferral of the absolutes of identity, and a vertigo of the word" (1999: 105), qualities with which most contemporary readers could identify. Despite his high praise of Faulkner's work, Glissant, like all those who follows Sundquist's admonition to read Faulkner's work in dialogue with other writers, recognizes that Toni Morrison is perhaps uniquely qualified to amplify Faulkner's oeuvre, for then Faulkner's work will become vital to and for African Americans. Comparative readings of Faulkner and Morrison have increased with such frequency that this specific comparison might be said to comprise something of a subset of contemporary Faulkner criticism. An exploration of race is the common ground most frequently named when a comparison of the two is invoked. As Philip Weinstein notes in the introduction to *What Else But Love? The Ordeal of Race in Faulkner and Morrison* (1996), both are "major novelists of racial turmoil" (p. xix). Likewise, the editors of the essay collection *Unflinching Gaze: Morrison and Faulkner Re-Envisioned* (1997), Carol A. Kolmerten, Stephen M. Ross, and Judith Bryant Wittenberg, assert that their interest in pairing Morrison and Faulkner lies in both authors' steadfast "refusal to look away" (p. ix) from difficult issues such as race.

The best of the critical works comparing Faulkner and Morrison do not resort to influence studies. To take the example of Weinstein's *What Else But Love?* and the contributors to *Unflinching Gaze*, what these works do *not* attempt is a type of reading which merely searches Morrison's texts for echoes of Faulkner's work, an approach which runs the risk of claiming that the imaginative works of this African American author somehow derive from the literary production of this male, white predecessor, replicating the larger culture's paternalistic racism. Nor do the best of these examinations merely posit Morrison's fiction as a type of corrective to Faulkner's. Rather, the most rewarding work on Faulkner and Morrison tends to adopt an intertextual approach. As John N. Duvall explains, "Intertextuality, with its emphasis on the infinitely resonating signification of language, means that one can validly read not only Faulkner's influence on Morrison, but also Morrison's influence on Faulkner – how her fiction and literary criticism may cause one to rethink Faulkner in a fundamental way" (1997: 4). And these paired readings of Faulkner and Morrison, along with pairings of Faulkner with Latin American writers in post-colonial readings, have caused us to collectively "rethink" our views on Faulkner "in a fundamental way." Faulkner's critical reception and stature have grown outward in ever-expanding concentric circles, from his earliest detractors' claims that he was nothing more than a depraved regionalist, less talented than his contemporary, Erskine Caldwell; to his becoming the avatar of Southern literature for his earliest defenders; to his canonization as a "universal" writer for the New Critics; to his estimation as a giant of the American literary tradition during the "theory boom"; to these most recent studies which see Faulkner as one of the mainstays of international modern literature.

The Contemporary Scene: Where Are We Now with Faulkner Studies?

The proliferation of Faulkner studies does not appear likely to slow in the immediate future. For instance, simply enter "Faulkner, William" into the MLA International Bibliography database, limit your search to years 1986 to 2006, and, as of this writing, you will receive a listing of 2,453 entries, written by scholars from around the world in numerous different languages. In fact, the internet has made it even easier for this international community of Faulkner scholars to communicate with one another, by sharing insights and ideas in an online discussion forum devoted to Faulkner's books; by visiting what is perhaps the best and most comprehensive website devoted to a single author, John Padgett's "William Faulkner on the Web"; and by continuing to submit work to the always provocative and cutting-edge *Faulkner Journal*.

As further proof of Faulkner's absolute centrality to the contemporary scene of publishing, reading, and writing, three of his novels have been included in Oprah Winfrey's book club (see Young 2001 on a similar phenomenon in Toni Morrison's career), and she enlisted the services of some important Faulkner scholars to help bring these rewarding works to the widest reading audience he is ever likely to enjoy: Robert Hamblin, Thadious Davis, and Arnold Weinstein helped the members of Oprah's book club through *As I Lay Dying*, *The Sound and the Fury*, and *Light in August*. The boxed set of the novels, specially repackaged together for her book club members, is ubiquitous; it's even available in my local grocery store, right alongside traditional summer "beach reading" such as romance novels with embossed covers. Perhaps Oprah's book club (which has the potential to deliver Faulkner to an even wider audience than Cowley's *Portable Faulkner* and the Nobel Prize) will, through its faith in the American reading public, create yet another Faulkner, the one that no new critical methodology has yet succeeded in creating – a Faulkner who sits atop the bestseller list.

ACKNOWLEDGMENT

I would like to thank Bert Emerson for his help with this chapter.

REFERENCES AND FURTHER READING

Abate, M. (2001). Reading Red: The Man with the (Gay) Red Tie in Faulkner's *The Sound and the Fury*. *Mississippi Quarterly*, 54(3): 294–312.

Baker, C. (2000). *William Faulkner's Postcolonial South*. New York: Peter Lang.

Bleikasten, A. (1973). *Faulkner's* As I Lay Dying (trans. R. Little with the collaboration of the author). Bloomington: Indiana University Press.

Bleikasten, A. (1976). *"The Most Splendid Failure": Faulkner's* The Sound and the Fury. Bloomington: Indiana University Press.

Brooks, C. (1963). *William Faulkner: The Yoknapatawpha Country*. New Haven, CT: Yale University Press.

Cowley, M. (1960). Introduction to *The Portable Faulkner*. In F. J. Hoffman and O. W. Vickery (eds.). *William Faulkner: Three Decades of Criticism* (pp. 94–109). East Lansing: Michigan State University Press. (Original pub. 1946.)

Davis, T. M. (1983). *Faulkner's "Negro": Art and the Southern Context*. Baton Rouge: Louisiana State University Press.

Duvall, J. N. (1997). Toni Morrison and the Anxiety of Faulknerian Influence. In C. A. Kolmerten, S. M. Ross, and J. B. Wittenberg (eds.). *Unflinching Gaze: Morrison and Faulkner Re-Envisioned* (pp. 3–16). Jackson: University Press of Mississippi.

Eagleton, T. (2003). *After Theory*. New York: Basic Books.

Fowler, D. (1983). *Faulkner's Changing Vision: From Outrage to Affirmation*. Ann Arbor: UMI Research Press.

Fowler, D. (1997). *Faulkner: The Return of the Repressed*. Charlottesville, VA: University Press of Virginia.

Glissant, E. (1999). *Faulkner, Mississippi* (trans. B. Lewis and T. C. Spear). New York: Farrar, Straus, and Giroux.

Godden, R. (1997). *Fictions of Labor: William Faulkner and the South's Long Revolution*. New York: Cambridge University Press.

Gwin, M. C. (1990). *The Feminine and Faulkner: Reading (Beyond) Sexual Difference*. Knoxville: University of Tennessee Press.

Irwin, J. T. (1975). *Doubling and Incest/Repetition and Revenge: A Speculative Reading of Faulkner*. Baltimore: Johns Hopkins University Press.

Kartiganer, D. M. (2000). Faulkner Criticism: A Partial View. *Faulkner Journal*, 16(3): 81–98.

Kolmerten, C. A., S. M. Ross, and J. B. Wittenberg (eds.). Introduction. In *Unflinching Gaze: Morrison and Faulkner Re-Envisioned* (pp. i–xv). Jackson: University Press of Mississippi.

Kreyling, M. (2003). Faulkner in the Twenty-First Century: Boundaries of Meaning, Boundaries of Mississippi. In R. W. Hamblin and A. J. Abadie (eds.). *Faulkner in the Twenty-First Century: Faulkner and Yoknapatawpha, 2000* (pp. 14–30). Jackson: University Press of Mississippi.

Lester, C. (1995). Racial Awareness and Arrested Development: *The Sound and the Fury* and the Great Migration (1915–1928). In P. Weinstein (ed.). *The Cambridge Companion to William Faulkner* (pp. 123–45). Cambridge: Cambridge University Press.

Lockyer, J. (1991). *Ordered by Words: Language and Narration in the Novels of William Faulkner*. Carbondale: Southern Illinois University Press.

Matthews, J. T. (1982). *The Play of Faulkner's Language*. Ithaca, NY: Cornell University Press.

Matthews, J. T. (2004). Recalling the West Indies: From Yoknapatawpha to Haiti and Back. *American Literary History*, 16(2): 238–62.

Millgate, M. (1966). *The Achievement of William Faulkner*. London: Constable.

O'Donnell, G. M. (1960). Faulkner's Mythology. In F. J. Hoffman and O. W. Vickery (eds.). *William Faulkner: Three Decades of Criticism* (pp. 82–93). East Lansing: Michigan State University Press. (Original pub. 1939.)

Railey, K. (1999). *Natural Aristocracy: History, Ideology, and the Production of William Faulkner*. Tuscaloosa: University of Alabama Press.

Ramsey, D. M. (2000). "Lifting the Fog": Faulkners, Reputations, and *The Story of Temple Drake*. *Faulkner Journal*, 16(1/2): 7–33.

Ramsey, D. M. (1999). "Turnabout" is Fair(y) Play: Faulkner's Queer War Story. *Faulkner Journal*, 15(1/2): 61–81.

Ross, S. M. (1989). *Fiction's Inexhaustible Voice: Speech and Writing in Faulkner*. Athens, GA: University Press of Georgia.

Schwartz, L. H. (1988). *Creating Faulkner's Reputation: The Politics of Modern Literary Criticism*. Knoxville: University of Tennessee Press.

Smith, J. and D. Cohn (eds.) (2004). *Look Away!: The U.S. South in New World Studies*. Durham, NC: Duke University Press.

Sundquist, E. J. (1987). Faulkner, Race, and the Forms of American Fiction. In D. Fowler and A. J. Abadie (eds.). *Faulkner and Race* (pp. 1–34). Jackson: University of Mississippi Press.

Sundquist, E. J. (1983). *Faulkner: The House Divided*. Baltimore: Johns Hopkins University Press.

Towner, T. M. (2000). *Faulkner on the Color Line: The Later Novels*. Jackson: University Press of Mississippi.

Urgo, J. R. (1989). *Faulkner's Apocrypha: A Fable, Snopes, and the Spirit of Human Rebellion*. Jackson: University Press of Mississippi.

Vickery, O. (1959). *The Novels of William Faulkner.* Baton Rouge: Louisiana State University Press.

Volpe, E. (1964). *A Reader's Guide to William Faulkner.* New York: Farrar, Straus, and Giroux.

Wagner-Martin, L. (2002). Introduction. In L. Wagner-Martin (ed.). *William Faulkner: Six Decades of Criticism* (pp. vii–xvii). East Lansing: Michigan State University Press.

Warren, R. P. (1960). William Faulkner. In F. J. Hoffman and O. W. Vickery (eds.). *William Faulkner: Three Decades of Criticism* (pp. 94–109). East Lansing: Michigan State University Press. (Original pub. 1946.)

Watson, J. G. (2000). *William Faulkner: Self-Preservation and Performance.* Austin, TX: University of Texas Press.

Weinstein, P. M. (1992). *Faulkner's Subject: A Cosmos No One Owns.* New York: Cambridge University Press.

Weinstein, P. M. (1996). *What Else But Love? The Ordeal of Race in Faulkner and Morrison.* New York: Columbia University Press.

Welling, B. (2002). A Meeting with Old Ben: Seeing and Writing Nature in Faulkner's *Go Down, Moses. Mississippi Quarterly*, 55(4): 461–96.

Wright, A. M. (1990). *Recalcitrance, Faulkner, and the Professors: A Critical Fiction.* Iowa City: University of Iowa Press.

Young, J. (2001). Toni Morrison, Oprah Winfrey, and Postmodern Popular Audiences. *African American Review*, 35(2): 181–204.

30

Faulkner, Latin America, and the Caribbean: Influence, Politics, and Academic Disciplines

Deborah Cohn

As Flannery O'Connor famously stated, "the presence alone of Faulkner in our midst makes a great difference in what the writer can and cannot permit himself to do. Nobody wants his mule and wagon stalled on the same track the Dixie Limited is roaring down" (1961: 45). But for Spanish American writers such as Jorge Luis Borges, José Donoso, Carlos Fuentes, Gabriel García Márquez, Juan Carlos Onetti, Juan Rulfo, Mario Vargas Llosa, and others, Faulkner was not a paralyzing influence. Rather, as I have argued elsewhere (see Cohn 1999: esp. ch. 1), he offered a liberating inspiration to authors who were struggling under the weight of a literary tradition that was still heavily dominated by realism and regionalism through the 1940s. This chapter begins with a discussion of the Southerner's legacy to Spanish American authors, focusing on their interest in the Southern history and culture that he depicts, as well as his use of modernist stylistics; I also examine the implications of the writers' identification with Faulkner's Southern heritage. Literary influence, however, is but one of many areas where Faulkner has played a role in Latin American culture and history, as well as in the disciplines devoted to these topics. The second part of this chapter discusses the political implications of Faulkner's relationship to Latin America, in terms of both his own travels south and his influence on the region's literature. I address the concern that this relationship reinscribes neocolonial patterns of domination and cultural imperialism that have long characterized the political relationship between the US and Latin America. Finally, I analyze the current interest in studying Faulkner within an inter-American (rather than strictly US) context. Scholars are exploring commonalities shared by the South, Latin America, and the Caribbean, including the legacies of slavery and the plantation; cultural mixing and hybridity; and the experience of US colonialism and imperialism. I will discuss the nature and implications of these commonalities for Southern studies and "American" studies alike.

This chapter focuses primarily on writers from Spanish America (i.e., the Central and South American and Caribbean nations previously under Spanish colonial rule). I do not explore Faulkner's presence in Brazilian literature, although he was well known and much admired in Brazil. This topic has attracted less attention, although scholars have studied his affinities with writers such as João Guimarães Rosa and Jorge Amado, among others. As Daniel Richardson notes, "Critical works on Brazilian literature published in Brazil continue to mention Faulkner as having provided a standard for forging a new fiction in that country, by deriving narrative modalities that are not dependent on an Iberian colonial matrix, by exploring psychological . . . perspectives, and by laying open the vast interior spaces of consciousness" (2000: 15). Earl Fitz, however, argues that Faulkner's "overall influence on the evolution of Brazilian narrative is simply not as dramatic or as profound as it is on modern Spanish American narrative" because of the influence of Joaquim Maria Machado de Assis, who in the late nineteenth century revolutionized Brazilian narrative, freeing it from the realist tradition (2004: 419–25).

Faulkner and Latin American Literature

In his 1982 Nobel Prize acceptance speech, Gabriel García Márquez invoked the figure of Faulkner and his own speech:

> On a day like today, my master William Faulkner said, "I decline to accept the end of man." I would fall unworthy of standing in this place that was his, if I were not fully aware that the colossal tragedy he refused to recognize thirty-two years ago is now, for the first time since the beginning of humanity, nothing more than a simple scientific possibility. Faced with this awesome reality that must have seemed a mere utopia through all of human time, we, the inventors of tales, who will believe anything, feel entitled to believe that it is not yet too late to engage in the creation of the opposite utopia. A new and sweeping utopia of life, where no one will be able to decide for others how they die, where love will prove true and happiness be possible, and where the races condemned to one hundred years of solitude will have, at last and forever, a second opportunity on earth. (García Márquez 1982)

García Márquez both echoes and transforms the words of his "master" here, fusing them seamlessly with a rewriting of his own heart-stopping conclusion to *One Hundred Years of Solitude*. His acknowledgment of a model and source of inspiration, simultaneously coupled with an affirmation of his own originality, reflects a dynamic at the heart of Spanish American authors' relationship to Faulkner and other Western writers during the 1960s and 1970s, when García Márquez, along with Julio Cortázar, Fuentes, and Vargas Llosa rose to prominence, bringing Spanish American literature into the international spotlight at the same time that they sought to define and promote a regional identity as part of the movement known as the "Boom."

As I shall discuss in the following section, the study of Faulkner and his literary influence has long been both political and polemical from the perspective of some Latin Americanists. In recent years, Faulkner's place in Southern literature has also been dramatically reconsidered: while writers such as O'Connor spoke to the looming influence of a Great Author on the next generation of writers, African American authors and critics as well as Southernists have more recently been concerned with Faulkner's role as a "Great White Father" and have sought to reconsider the writer's place in the field. And yet, it would be wise to not disregard the author's importance as an inspiration for Spanish American writers. As Jon Smith and I have written elsewhere,

> as a resident of a dirt-poor region colonized by an industrial and imperial north, Faulkner has also, to New World creoles further south, seemed more a postcolonialist writer, the kind of "good" father who shows the way for his intellectual descendants, the writer who, more than any other, deployed and developed modernist techniques precisely to show the plight of a figuratively sterile region stalled on the tracks of modernity's post-Reconstruction, post-1898 New World order. Thus, to read Faulkner simply as "white" or "hegemonic" and thereby to question his importance to Latin American and Caribbean writers . . . is to project a largely North American black/white binary onto cultures that have, for much of the 20th century, though not always in good faith, prized their *mestizaje* [fusion of European and indigenous culture]. (Smith and Cohn 2004: 303)

Long after European and US writers had rejected realism, Spanish American prose fiction was still heavily marked by the mode. Although poets such as Pablo Neruda and César Vallejo, among others, were profoundly influenced by the avant-garde in the early 1920s, prose fiction lagged behind, dominated by the genre known as the "novel of the land," which Donoso once described as a way of writing "for [the] parish . . . [a way of] cataloging the flora and fauna . . . which were unmistakably ours . . . all that which specifically makes us different [from] other countries of the continent" (1977: 11, 15). The emphasis on the local, and on the local as difference, made it difficult for those writers who were lucky enough to be published – no small feat in Latin America for many years – to appeal and, by extension, sell to audiences beyond their own national boundaries. In 1931, however, Argentine writer Victoria Ocampo established *Sur*, a journal that disseminated contemporary European and US cultural currents throughout Latin America by publishing translations of literary and critical works. *Sur* also published the work of Argentine writers who were at the forefront of the avant-garde movement in Spanish America, including Adolfo Bioy Casares, Borges, Cortázar, Eduardo Mallea, and Ocampo herself. As Tanya Fayen has detailed, Faulkner criticism began to appear in the journal starting in the 1930s, though it was not until the 1950s that he started to receive "considerable sustained attention" in its pages (1995: 95); additionally, *Sur* published translations and reviews of his works in the 1940s, and *Sur* publishers released *Luz de agosto* (*Light in August* [1932]) in 1942 (p. 95). The journal's focus on Faulkner was key to furthering his reputation in Spanish America for, as Fayen observes, "As a magazine of considerable prestige in *the* most important cultural capital in Latin America, *Sur* exercised a considerable and important long-term effect upon literary assimilation on the continent" (p. 93). Additionally, the attention to Faulkner demonstrated by French critics further sparked the interest of Spanish American writers long before the writer became popular in the US. Several authors were inspired to tackle Faulkner's work directly: Cuban writer Lino Novás Calvo's 1934 publication of *Santuario*

(*Sanctuary* [1931]) initiated the translation of Faulkner's work into Spanish; and Borges translated *Palmeras salvajes* (*Wild Palms* [1939]) in 1940, in addition to writing reviews of *The Unvanquished* (1938), *Absalom, Absalom!* (1936), and *The Wild Palms*.

Faulkner had a profound effect on Juan Carlos Onetti and Juan Rulfo, both writers whose experimental works, along with those of Borges and Bioy Casares, played a critical role in fostering the "new narrative," a literary movement with modernist roots that was key in moving Spanish American literature away from realism in the 1940s and 1950s. It was, however, the generation of writers who began to publish in the late 1950s and who later comprised the Boom whose work was most profoundly and systematically affected by Faulkner. As Lois Parkinson Zamora has observed, Boom writers such as Cortázar, Fuentes, García Márquez, and Vargas Llosa participated in "an unprecedented literary conversation" in which they read and responded to one another's works, "emphasiz[ing] the communal nature of their literary project . . . self-consciously engaging, and in some sense also creating, a reality shared by the many countries and cultures of their region" (1989: 20–1). This "conversation" and joint effort – part and parcel of the Boom itself – was an outgrowth of the writers' support for the Cuban Revolution (1959), which brought the possibility of political and cultural autonomy to Latin America: authors considered themselves to be part of a group whose agenda included constructing and promoting a pan-Spanish American cultural identity. Their cultivation of totalizing and often allegorical novels whose implications resonated beyond the boundaries of their own nations, and their recourse to modern and modernist stylistics that had already gained currency in Western literature, made their work appeal to a broader audience, both throughout and beyond the Americas. As a result, the 1960s and 1970s witnessed a dramatic increase in the publication and distribution of Spanish American works within the region, as well as their translation and dissemination throughout the West.

Philip Weinstein has observed that

> a growing number of scholars have sought to pair Faulkner with his Latin American counterparts, not least because those counterparts have recognized his kinship and enabling influence. More, Faulkner's *modernism* is crucial in the recognition, for his experimental modes invited – through their reconfiguring the relations of subject, time, and space – a Latin American rethinking of problem and possibility outside the norms of progressive Western realism. (2004: 361)

Weinstein argues that while Faulkner can only demonstrate the breakdown of the realist plot of rational and linear behavior and mastery over one's environment, García Márquez and other post-colonial writers draw on modernist practices and representational procedures to devise new plots that accommodate the experiences of cultures that are neither Western nor white (pp. 366–7). Although Boom writers read and admired other modernists such as James Joyce and Virginia Woolf, their concern with depicting the troubled pasts and presents of their respective nations left them drawn not just to the movement's rejection of linear time and causality in general, but to Faulkner's particular use of modernist stylistics to represent a postbellum white South experiencing defeat, the breakdown of plantation society, and modernization. As I have discussed elsewhere (Cohn 1999, 2003), Faulkner's themes, images, and paradigms resonated with Spanish American authors because they saw their own national histories in the agrarian, plantation, and post-plantation societies that he portrayed, as well as in his depiction of the social order and its decline, racial tensions, underdevelopment, poverty, and marginalization. Just as importantly, they empathized with the history of the white South: many authors felt that the South's defeat in the Civil War, the stigma attached to it subsequently, its subordination to and neocolonialism at the hands of the North (another North), and the loss of its right to self-determination were akin to the experiences of their own nations. Hence Fuentes's claim that "thus we felt Faulkner's work [to be] so close to us . . . : only Faulkner . . . in the closed world of optimism and success, offers us an image common to the U.S. and Latin America: the image of defeat, of separation, of doubt: of tragedy" (1970: 65).

Spanish American writers were particularly drawn to the sagas of the Compsons, Sutpens, and Sartorises, for their depiction of societies that continued to live by the codes of the Old South, trapped in a past that history – and modernity – have left behind, closely echoed the authors' own experiences. They found models for their work in characters such as Emily Grierson, Rosa Coldfield, and Quentin Compson, who embody the theme of historical paralysis, spending their lives at an emotional impasse. Of all Faulkner's works, I believe that *As I Lay Dying* (1930) and *Absalom, Absalom!* have had the most profound and lasting impact on Spanish American writers from the new narrative to the Boom. *As I Lay Dying* provided the basic paradigm for a genre of novels in which multiple perspectives centering on a dying or dead figure offer a kaleidoscopic view of her or his life, family, and the social order. María Luisa Bombal's *The Shrouded Woman* (1938, English trans. 1948), Rulfo's *Pedro Páramo* (1955, English trans. 1959), García Márquez's *Leaf Storm* (1955, English trans. 1972) and *The Autumn of the Patriarch* (1975, English trans. 1976), and Fuentes's *The Death of Artemio Cruz* (1962, English trans. 1964) all trace some of their roots back to Faulkner's novel. While *The Shrouded Woman* follows *As I Lay Dying* in circumscribing its focus within the sphere of the experience of a woman and her family, the scope of the other novels was amplified through amalgamation with *Absalom*'s panoramic historical vision, generating a polyphonic novel of the dead in which the central figure's life recapitulates the history of an entire nation or region. Rulfo's novel refracts Mexican history from the 1880s through the 1930s through the life and death of the patriarch and the town that he destroyed. Both García Márquez and Fuentes, in turn, use the deathbed narration in conjunction with one of modernism's most powerful innovations for subverting linear narrative time, the novel-in-a-day, to telescope national history into the narrative frame of a single calendar day: *Leaf Storm* condenses 40 years of Colombian history, from the wars of the late nineteenth century through the prosperity and decline ushered in by the banana company and on up until 1928 into a mere half-hour; *The Autumn of the Patriarch* spans within a 24-hour frame the history of Spanish America from the Conquest through the twentieth century, as well as the life and death of the dictator who was considered immortal and whose reign was thought to be eternal; and Artemio Cruz, whose tale begins and ends on the day of his death, and his family likewise constitute a microcosm of Mexican history since the first stirrings for independence through the late 1950s. These deathbed and posthumously narrated novels thus served to depict the changing of ways occasioned by war, modernization, and the paralyzing legacy of authoritarian, patriarchal social structures.

The reworking of *As I Lay Dying* in conjunction with the epic scope of *Absalom* is indicative of the pervasiveness of the latter novel in modern Spanish American literature and, especially, of its vision of history and fiction. To this day, authors such as Fuentes and García Márquez invoke it as one of their favorite works. The novel's appeal is due in large measure to the fact that most of the thematic, stylistic, and structural elements that were admired in Faulkner appear together here, complementing one another. *Absalom* deploys many modernist techniques to recreate the past, most notably narrative perspectivism and the refutation of chronological order; it also draws on a non-linear strategy of delaying the disclosure of critical information. Additionally, *Absalom*'s foundational narrative essentially provided the thematic nucleus of many of the Boom's most canonical novels: first, there is a patriarch (or, in some cases, family) who is both founder and emblem of the prevailing order, whose relationship to the members of the community determines their position within it, and whose death parallels the end of the historical era; and, second, we find a historical backdrop of civil war, cycles of boom and bust, and the changing of orders. As numerous critics have observed, Thomas Sutpen's trajectory spans the heyday and decline of the plantation system, recapitulating the history of the Old South. His ascent begins with the foundational crime of original accumulation, the mythic creation "out of the soundless Nothing . . . [of] the Sutpen's Hundred, the *Be Sutpen's Hundred* like the oldentime *Be Light*" (Faulkner 1972: 8–9). The partition of the land and the financial transaction whereby he essentially purchases an appropriate wife usher in a new order grounded in economic values. His death signals the end of the plantocracy, albeit not of the racist and classist assumptions upon which it was predicated.

This template for the relationship between the founding patriarch or family and the macrocosm of national history is followed rather closely in several Spanish American novels. In Rulfo's *Pedro Páramo*, for example, the *cacique* or local boss similarly inaugurates a new order in which money is the only value: he negates all previous financial agreements, rewrites the law, and essentially buys himself a wife even as he buys his way out of honoring a debt. Historically, Pedro Páramo's centralization of landownership dates to the years of Porfirio Díaz's regime (roughly 1876–1910), which was notorious for facilitating the expansion of large estates, and Páramo's downfall takes place in the years following the Mexican Revolution but is not a product of its reforms. His trajectory allegorizes the failure of the Revolution to bring about change, resulting in the dire state that is contemporary Mexico. Fuentes's *The Death of Artemio Cruz* draws on the same paradigm to cover the first 150 years of Mexican independence. The fate of Cruz's paternal grandparents is that of the conservatives in the nineteenth century: his grandfather fought with Antonio López de Santa Anna in the mid-nineteenth century and died alongside the emperor Maximilian, "the end of a life of chance and spins of the wheel of fortune, like that of the nation itself," while his grandmother, born in 1810, the year of the first uprising for independence, experiences all of the century's subsequent upheavals, including the loss of her land to the liberals' reforms and, later, to new landowners under Díaz (Fuentes 1991: 293). Cruz himself incarnates "the new world rising out of the civil war": he is the self-made man who erases the past and sets out to map the nation's future after the Revolution (p. 44). His actions, of course, set the stage for this period: he, too, purchases a wife and, with her, her family's properties, and subsequently usurps the lands of neighboring small landowners, heralding the failure of land reform and the corruption of the new bourgeoisie. Finally, the founding of Macondo in *One Hundred Years of Solitude* entails the transformation of a virgin world "that was so new that many things still did not have names" into parcels of land owned by man (García Márquez 1967: 9). Although the initial result is a semi-utopian order where all of the houses have equal access to water and the sun, the town and the Buendía family's subsequent development encapsulates that of Colombia and Spanish America as a whole, from the development of a creole aristocracy through the nineteenth-century civil wars to the US imperialism that starts Macondo along the final path to ruin.

All of the aforementioned novels conclude with the death of the patriarch or family through whom national history is allegorized. In some cases, this signals the downfall of the way of life with which they were coextensive and opens up the possibility of change for the collectivity: the death of Artemio Cruz in 1959, the year of the Cuban Revolution, signals the end of the post-revolutionary period in Mexico and looks hopefully toward the beginning of a new order inspired by Cuba; in *The Autumn of the Patriarch*, in turn, the dictator's death awakes the city from "its lethargy of centuries," announcing "the good news that the uncountable time of eternity had come to an end" (García Márquez 1976: 1, 269). In other cases, however, it serves to underscore the permanent damage wrought by the previous power structure, a much bleaker forecast for the potential for change: the Comala of Rulfo's novel and the Macondo of both *Leaf Storm* and *One Hundred Years of Solitude*, for example, are paralyzed, condemned to extinction by their leaders and the social and political orders that they implemented. Whether the endings promise new beginnings or not, though, they are, in one way or another, pronouncements on the future by authors who were deeply influenced by contemporary debates over the nature and fate of Spanish America.

Many of these writers have also acknowledged their debt to Faulkner in tributes over the years. And perhaps some of these do reveal a bit of the "Dixie Limited" complex: García Márquez, for one, frustrated by frequent comparisons to Faulkner, has sometimes denied having read the Southerner's work until late in his career – a statement that is belied by his journalism of the early 1950s and the fact that he took a bus ride through the South in 1961 to see firsthand the world that Faulkner described. However, his homages to Faulkner – however cagily phrased – explicitly acknowledge the similarities between the regions and type of towns that each depicted, and the resulting points of contact between their works. As the Colombian observed in 1971,

I was born in Aracataca, the banana growing country where the United Fruit Company was established. It was in this region . . . that I grew up and received my first impressions. Then, many years later, I read Faulkner and found that his whole world – the world of the southern United States which he writes about – was very like my world, that it was created by the same people . . . What I found in him was affinities between our experiences, which were not as different as might appear at first sight. (quoted in Guibert 1972: 327)

Others, such as Borges, Jorge Edwards, and Vargas Llosa, invoke civil wars, struggles with underdevelopment and industrialization, and the nostalgia for an antebellum Golden Age as commonalities shared by the South and the regions that they depict. But while race and racial conflict are also mentioned in these and other homages as points of contact between Southern and Spanish American cultures, in practice they are almost absent from the writers' work.

As Jon Smith has pointed out, Spanish American authors identify primarily with Faulkner's vision of the *white* South, its version of its history as a series of frustrations, failures, and defeats, and the ensuing conquest by the North (personal communication). When they acknowledge a shared nostalgia for an idealized, long-gone past, sympathize with the South's loss of autonomy, or claim that Spanish America and the South share the experience – in Fuentes's words – "of defeat, of . . . tragedy," they accept the white South's legend of the Lost Cause, a vision of the past that was not, presumably, shared by black Southerners. As Smith has observed, Faulkner and the Boom authors alike speak from a creole subject position: the perception of commonalities between (white) Southern and Spanish American history may be at least partly attributed to the fact that the Boom authors occupy class, race, and gender positions comparable to those of Faulkner in the South. Despite the centrality of discourses of hybrid identity such as Afrocubanism, *négritude*, and *mestizaje* to official national and cultural identity politics throughout Latin America and the Caribbean from the 1920s on, the sensibility reflected in the novels that dominated the market during this period is largely creole, upper-class, and cosmopolitan. Faulkner was claimed by the Spanish Americans as one of their own, then, but his concern with race was left out of the picture. Perhaps, then, Borges was all too right when he declared that Faulkner's world is "of the same blood as this America and its history; it, too, is creole" (1985: 124).

Faulkner and Politics, the Politics of Faulkner Studies: Anti-Americanism and Inter-Americanism

If much has been written about Faulkner's impact on the Boom and on other Latin American authors, his travels to the region have received significantly less attention. Joseph Blotner (1966), for example, addresses Faulkner's foreign service expeditions and George Monteiro (1983) has translated two journalistic accounts of Faulkner's interviews during his Brazil trip. Nor have the dynamics underlying the study of Faulkner's influence on Latin American writers been addressed in detail. While these might appear to be disparate issues, they are ultimately linked by imbalances – political and academic – that have grown out of US hegemony in Latin America. In the first case, Faulkner traveled to Latin America in 1954 and 1961 at the behest and/or on the dime of the US Department of State as part of the department's efforts to cultivate goodwill through cultural diplomacy during a period of significant anti-American political sentiment. In the second, as recent debates have shown, the study of literary influence by definition places the authors and literary traditions being influenced (in this case, Latin American) in a derivative position vis-à-vis the vectors of influence (in this case, a writer from the US).

In 1950, when Faulkner was awarded the Nobel Prize, he initially declined to travel to Stockholm to pick up the award. The US ambassador to Sweden sent an urgent cable to Secretary of State Dean Acheson expressing his concern at the situation; ultimately, Muna Lee, Southern poet and State Department official, was recruited to convince Faulkner to go to Stockholm and avoid international embarrassment for the US (Blotner 1974: 1347–8). The result was, of course, a great success, and over the next few years, Faulkner was persuaded numerous times to serve as a goodwill ambassador for the US in Japan, the Philippines, Greece, Iceland, Latin America, and elsewhere. On his trips, he taught, spoke about his work, and commented on race relations in the US. Both his words and his own presence testified to the achievements of the US in nations hostile toward the US, and he was instrumental in tempering this sentiment (see Oakley 2004).

Even before the Cuban Revolution of 1959, Latin America had begun to experience a surge in leftist activism that brought it into conflict repeatedly with the US, which was, of course, firmly under the sway of Cold War politics at this point. The US had long supported repressive but anti-Communist dictatorships in Latin America, as well as neocolonial enterprises such as the United Fruit Company, and had intervened in governments whose politics leaned too far to the left (as was the case in the Guatemalan coup of 1954). The McCarran-Walter Act of 1952, which was used to restrict visas on ideological grounds (preventing authors with socialist sympathies, including Fuentes, García Márquez, Neruda, and others from entering the US), and, later, the Alliance for Progress also generated further anti-American sentiment.

That the State Department would look to Faulkner as a cultural emissary is hardly an anomaly; he was, in fact, one of many cultural figures, including Elizabeth Bishop, Robert Frost, Robert Lowell, Katherine Anne Porter, and others, whose trips to Latin America were sponsored by the State Department as part of a concerted campaign that used cultural diplomacy to improve relations with the region. In general, the 1950s and 1960s were an era of government funding of cultural and educational projects such as the clandestinely CIA-funded Congress for Cultural Freedom (see Coleman 1989 and Saunders 1999 for the organization's history); the National Defense Education Act of 1958; and numerous other programs sponsored by the State Department and the US Information Agency (USIA) that sought to promote cultural and intellectual exchange between the US and other nations. In addition to promoting US cultural achievements abroad, such programs were also inspired by the liberal belief that greater understanding of and respect for the cultural production of other countries would ultimately benefit national security. Michael Bérubé's recent analysis of the Congress for Cultural Freedom, which also holds true for official programs directed at Latin American intellectuals, effectively sums up the official motivations behind the funding of cultural programs at home and abroad:

> in a perverse yet entirely unremarkable sense, the years of the Cold War were the good old days for American artists and intellectuals – the days when . . . "the CIA was the NEA [National Endowment for the Arts]." Imagine . . . a time when the work of abstract expressionists and twelve-tone composers was considered vital to national security, a time when the establishment of the pax Americana required the funding and nourishment of a noncommunist left with high-modernist tastes in arts and letters. It is hard to tamp down a sense of nostalgia. (2003: 107)

The State Department sponsored two trips by Faulkner to Latin America: the first in 1954, when he visited Brazil and, briefly, Peru and Venezuela; and the second in 1961, when he returned to Venezuela (see Blotner 1974: 1503–7, 1777–87). Both trips were urged by State Department officials as public relations moves designed to offset criticism of the US in the local press and to improve the US's relationship with the Latin American nations, as well as its image in general. As Helen Oakley writes,

> it is surely not coincidental that the visit to Brazil took place in 1954, the year in which the CIA offensive to wipe out the threat of Communism in Guatemala had reached its most intense stage. In this sensitive climate, the importance to the U.S. government of promoting good relations with other Latin American countries would have been paramount, and the use of culture as an ideological tool was an indirect way of doing so. Additionally, U.S.–Brazilian relations in the early 1950s had been rather strained . . . The intensive drive on the part of the U.S. government to root out Communism in Latin America had the effect of risking the economic neglect and subsequent alienation of many countries. (2002: 64)

Always reluctant to travel, Faulkner was persuaded to go to Latin America the first time by Lee's appeals to his patriotism and her belief that the trips would be "an important contribution to inter-American cultural relations."[1] And so they were. Lee wrote after his visit to Peru that "Here at Washington we are still a little dazed and dazzled by the extraordinary achievement of the Embassy at Lima in making a complete Public-Relations success of the brief visit of one of the world's most illustrious, most withdrawn, and least loquacious novelists, William Faulkner" (note to Harold H. Tittman, Jr., September 2, 1954, MSS 7258 a).

From Lima, Faulkner traveled to São Paulo, Brazil, to attend an International Congress of Writers that marked the quadricentennial of the city's founding. One official, Philip Raine, urged the State Department to support Faulkner's trip as a means of counterbalancing

the flood of adverse publicity which the Department received because of alleged indifference and non-support of the U.S. exhibits in the International Exhibition of Modern
Art which was a pre-Quadricentennial event inaugurating the series of festivities. We are
still receiving and answering letters of protest on that score. A further reason for officially
sponsoring our Nobel Prize winner is the bitter criticism made of us in the Brazilian
press when the Brazilian writer, Joao Lins de Rago [sic], was temporarily denied a U.S.
visa [presumably under the McCarran-Walter Act] because of alleged connections
with political fellow travelers and favorable reviews of his work in some leftist papers.
Although hewas [sic] later given his visa, the incident coulded [sic] our cultural relations
with Brazil to some extent. (Philip Raine, unsigned typed copy of note to Mr. Riley, no
date, MSS 7258 a)

Raine also wrote that "the Public Affairs staff and the Brazil desk . . . are in complete
agreement that it would definitely further the interests of the US for William Faulkner
to participate in the International Writers' Congress" (memo to Mr. Riley, June 22,
1954, MSS 7258 a). Unfortunately, Faulkner missed most of his official engagements
at the conference because of excessive drinking, leading US officials to conclude that
"the fruits of his visit were not commensurate with the financial investment made by
the US Government in order to make possible his visit in São Paulo."[2] His return flight
included a brief stop in Caracas, where he agreed to an impromptu and successful
interview (see Blotner 1974: 1507). Despite his behavior in Brazil, Faulkner was, on the
whole, keenly aware of the impact of his presence on local audiences during these trips:
he wrote to one official afterwards that "I know now something of the problems the
US has to cope with in Latin America, and the problems which the State Department
has to face in order to cope with them" and he promised to make himself available to
the Department as needed (letter to Mr. Howland, August 15, 1954, MSS 7258 f).

In 1960, the North American Association of Venezuela invited Faulkner to Caracas
to meet with writers and educators as part of the hundred and fiftieth anniversary celebration of the nation's independence. The Association was headed by US businessmen
living in the country; it sponsored programs meant to improve relations between the
two nations and offer a positive image of the US to the Venezuelan public. Though
technically not a government organization, it frequently coordinated both its goals and
activities with the United States Information Service (USIS) office in Caracas, and
several USIS officers were on the Association's committees. US officials had high expectations for Faulkner's visit. In 1958, Vice President Richard Nixon's trip to the city had
provoked one of the first major demonstrations in Latin America of organized mass
hostility toward the US: while there had been protests at several of his other stops on
his trip to South America, crowds in Caracas went a step further and attacked his
motorcade (see McPherson 2003: ch. 1; Rabe 1988: ch. 6). Anti-Americanism had been
on the rise in Venezuela: Marcos Pérez Jiménez, the dictator whom the US had decorated
for his anti-Communist efforts and whom it was now harboring, had recently been
ousted; and the US government had limited crude oil imports from the nation, prompting great concern about negative effects on the local economy (see McPherson 2003:
28; Rabe 1988: 102). And yet, as Alan McPherson writes, "The [Nixon] ordeal

triggered no deep questioning of the impact of U.S. influence in Latin America. Rather, it simply revitalized the public relations approach to anti-Americanism" (2003: 26). Faulkner's trip to Venezuela, which also coincided with heightened tensions with Cuba and the Dominican Republic, fit in rather well with this strategy. As Lee wrote to the USIS Public Affairs Officer in Caracas, although Faulkner's visit was not official, "I know you will do what you can to help make his visit a success and to have it redound to the greater glory of the United States of America (So will he.). Hence this budget" (memo to Charles Harner, November 29, 1960, MSS 7258 f).

The timing of the visit was right, for relations with Venezuela had improved since Rómulo Betancourt, a democratic reformer, was elected president on an anti-Communist platform and had shown himself to be friendly to the US. During his stay, Faulkner met several times with Betancourt and former President Rómulo Gallegos, both of whom were also writers, and the latter decorated him with the order of Andrés Bello, Venezuela's highest civilian honor. Afterwards, the visit was hailed as "one of the greatest boons to US–Venezuelan relations that has happened for a long time" (C. Allan Stewart, quoted in a Muna Lee memo to Mr. Colwell, May 2, 1961, MSS 7258 a). According to the Embassy's cultural affairs officer,

> I don't think any other living North American could have affected the minds and hearts of Venezuelans as he did during his two weeks here . . . The most hardened press elements, the politically unsympathetic, all fell before his charm and his unwavering integrity. Even if nothing else of cultural note happens to us, we will be able to feed upon the effects of his visit for a long time to come. (Cecil Sanford, quoted in a Muna Lee memo to Mr. Colwell, May 2, 1961, MSS 7258a)

Hugh Jencks of the North American Association similarly claimed that

> The cultural leaders of Venezuela, many of whom are pre-disposed to take an anti-U.S. attitude on all international issues, include writers, artists, newspaper commentators . . . educators and people in government . . . [as well as] many on-the-fencers. Its members tend to agree with the Communist tenet that the U.S. is grossly materialistic, with no cultural achievements. To bring a literary figure of the stature of Faulkner was an effective refutation of this view. . . . The leftist extremists, who certainly would have exploited the visit for anti-U.S. attacks if they felt they could have made hay, remained silent. Mr. Faulkner's evident popularity was too great for them to make the pitch.[3]

Faulkner's visits helped to ease tensions in relations between Latin America and the US by bringing tremendous positive publicity to the US and its accomplishments. He was warmly welcomed by intellectuals who, though often anti-US, were receptive to his work and had themselves been influenced by him. Their stamp of approval may not have always won over the hostile journalists who occasionally sought to ambush him, but it did neutralize their effects, while Faulkner's charm won the public over. Characterized, respectively, as "one of the great events in inter-American cultural relations"[4] and "one of the most successful of all cultural approaches by the United States to

Venezuela,"[5] Faulkner's visits fulfilled the wildest dreams and underlying political agenda of the government that sponsored his travels by "further[ing] understanding and good will" between the US and Latin America.[6]

Faulkner returned from his travels vowing to learn Spanish and planning to return to Latin America. Also, his sympathy engaged by writers' stories about the difficulties in publishing in the region, in 1961, he set up the Ibero-American Novel Project, a competition that sought to choose the best recently written novels and assist in the process of finding publishers and translators for them in the US (see Cohn 2004; Oakley 2004). Although the competition ultimately fell short of its goals, it did succeed in gaining publicity for Latin American literature during the period when interest in authors such as Borges, Donoso, Fuentes, García Márquez, and Vargas Llosa was on the upswing in the US and Europe. It also generated great interest and goodwill among Latin American intellectuals, who felt that it introduced their work to the North and offered an opportunity to establish dialogues between intellectuals from the North and South. While US authors such as Ambrose Bierce, Waldo Frank, and Katherine Anne Porter, among others, had long taken an interest in the region, visiting and incorporating their experiences into their own works, Faulkner's project marks one of the few times that a US writer took an active role in promoting Latin American literature. Faulkner was, in effect, carrying on his State Department mission, in his own way and on his own terms.

Although inter-American political relations were tense during the 1960s and 1970s, Faulkner's Novel Project is representative of the generally positive attitude in US cultural activity toward Latin America: publishers expanded their lists of fiction from the region, and organizations such as the Center for Inter-American Relations (now, the Americas Society), with tremendous financial support from the Ford and Rockefeller Foundations, worked with publishers, periodicals, translators, and academics in the US to develop publicity campaigns to bring attention and critical success to Latin American authors and their work. In academia, however, inter-American dialogue and collaboration have, until recently, lagged far behind. The study of Faulkner's legacy, as well as that of Edgar Allan Poe, John Dos Passos, Ernest Hemingway, and other writers who also inspired Latin American authors, has long been key to Latin Americanists trying to understand the region's literary history. Some scholars, though, have viewed these studies with suspicion. Some see influence as a sign (or accusation) of a lack of originality. Additionally, there is a power imbalance implicit in the very notion of influence: the privileging of one author or tradition – and even of one discipline – over another may both reflect and reinscribe unequal power relations. As Jay Clayton and Eric Rothstein have observed,

> At its worst, discovering parallels between the literature of two nations was put to the service of a crude cultural imperialism; a work, a movement, or an entire national literature was exalted to the degree that it was able to exert a hegemony over the literature of other countries, so that twentieth-century scholars such as René Wellek or Claudio Guillén saw its improper use as a major stumbling block to the field of comparative literature as late as the 1950s. (1991: 5)

Clayton and Rothstein's assessment pertains to influence studies in general, but it is especially apt to the field of inter-American literary studies – well past the 1950s, at that – when one takes into account the geopolitical relations between the US and Latin America, relations that simply cannot be separated from the study of the latter region. Within this framework, the study of Faulkner's influence, as well as that of other US writers, has been criticized both for reduplicating the United States' efforts at hegemony over Latin America in the field of literary criticism and for putting the region's literature in a derivative, and therefore subordinate, position vis-à-vis that of the US. (This concern about the relationship between influence and hegemony is by no means limited to the sphere of foreign relations. African American authors have similarly struggled to position themselves in relation to Faulkner and his work, both affirming and resisting his pull. Critics, too, have engaged with this question, with John Duvall observing that "To speak of a possible Faulknerian influence on [Toni] Morrison's work runs the risk of calling up memories of racial and sexual abuse in the American past. Does not positing such an influence imply that without a white man's seminal text, those of the African-American woman would never have come to fruition?" [1997: 3].[7])

Additionally, over the years, inter-Americanism – the echo of "orientalism" is deliberate – in the US has, on occasion, been adjunctive to efforts to bring Latin American literature and studies within the sphere of US politics and national interests. Sophia McClennen recently noted that inter-American studies has burgeoned at a time when "Latin Americanism becomes increasingly more powerful in the academy," prompting the question of whether "Inter-American Studies represent[s] the latest variation on the Monroe Doctrine of policing [Latin America]" (2003). What Walter Mignolo calls the "locus of enunciation" (1993: 120) – whether of theories of influence or formulations of literatures of the Americas – is key here, for critical models and approaches generated in the US, or the metropolis, have been applied to Latin American cultures traditionally deemed peripheral, reinforcing inequalities between institutions and their role in the production of knowledge.[8] Recently, though, the questioning of nationalism as the basis for constituting the field and political boundaries of (US) American studies has sparked fruitful inquiries into commonalities bridging North and South America and the Caribbean. George Handley is right to warn that the "enterprise of rethinking American studies has yet to demonstrate how it will avoid a neoimperialist expansion into the field of Latin American studies" (2000: 28). And yet, scholars are carefully trying to take advantage of this disciplinary sea change, along with the concomitant acknowledgment of shared histories of plantations, slavery, and imperialism, to transform the relations between (US) American studies and Latin American studies, and dialogues and collaborative projects have developed that take into consideration the cultural and political interactions between the two regions without privileging the North.

Reconsidering Faulkner, Reconsidering the South

Comparative approaches to the black presence in the Americas were an integral part of African diaspora studies long before (US) American studies began to move toward a more transnational perspective (consider, for example, Paul Gilroy's *The Black Atlantic*, and *Callaloo*'s early special issues on Puerto Rico, as well as more recent ones on Afro-Brazilian writers and Caribbean writers such as Wilson Harris and Maryse Condé). As Mae Henderson has stated, the field of Black studies, which became a force in the academy during the late 1960s and 1970s, must be reclaimed "as a multidisciplinary, cross-cultural, and comparative model of study which places into juxtaposition the history, culture, and politics of blacks in the U.S., Caribbean, and Africa" (1996: 64). Recently, Southernists have begun to bridge African diaspora studies and US Southern studies in an effort to redefine the latter field within a transnational, inter-American context; claims to Southern exceptionalism have been reconsidered, while studying the historical and cultural legacies that the region shares with Latin America and the Caribbean has become an important area of research.[9] Fred Hobson's observation that the term used to identify the Southern United States has recently evolved in (US) American studies from "the South" to "the American South" to "the U.S. South" (2002: 1) reflects a growing awareness and acknowledgment of the region's position within Plantation America, and within an "America" that refers not just to the US but to the "New World" as a whole.

I noted previously how Boom authors, despite their general references in homages to Faulkner to racial difficulties common to the US South and Latin America, do not for the most part engage with the question of race in their work. However, as Handley's impressive *Postslavery Literatures in the Americas* (2000) demonstrates, the matter has long been a primary concern for writers from the Caribbean (and Brazil, too), where slavery was not abolished until the late nineteenth century. It is not surprising, then, that Faulkner's depictions of race, racial conflict and trauma, and post-slavery society have often been acknowledged and appropriated by writers from the Caribbean. As Handley shows, Alejo Carpentier's *Explosion in the Cathedral* (1962, English trans. 1963) reworks not just the incestuous menage à trois from *Absalom, Absalom!*, but also the novel's questions about the origins, nature, and fate of plantation society; its representation of the relationship of the plantocracy to the French Revolution and Haiti; and its treatment of US imperialism in the Caribbean (Handley 2000: ch. 4). In *Sweet Diamond Dust* (1986, English trans. 1988), Puerto Rican writer Rosario Ferré merges a Snopesian tale of the decline and replacement of a postbellum plantocracy by an upwardly mobile, materialistic bourgeoisie with a reappropriation of the miscegenation motif that led Charles Bon to his death in *Absalom, Absalom!* (see Cohn 1999: 191–3). And Barbara Ladd has demonstrated how Martinican essayist and novelist Edouard Glissant is attracted to Faulkner on the one hand because of his thematic connections to other writers of the plantation and post-plantation Americas and, on the other, because of his inclusion of the voices of the dispossessed and colonized of the "Other America" and his privileging of hybridity – key elements of Glissant's own *poétique de la Relation* (a cross-cultural poetics or creole aesthetic) (Ladd 2003: esp. 34–5). As Glissant himself states in *Faulkner, Mississippi*, Yoknapatawpha County "is linked with its immediate surroundings, the Caribbean and Latin America, by the damnation and miscegenation born of the rape of slavery – that is, by what the country creates and represses at the same time" (1999: 88).

Comparative studies of Faulkner and Latin American and Caribbean authors have traditionally focused on shared themes, motifs, and structural elements. Recently, however, these commonalities have themselves been treated as points of departure for exploring broader political, historical, and cultural issues. Weinstein (2004), for example, studies García Márquez's transformation of Faulkner's work as a post-colonial strategy for reconfiguring Western patriarchal social structures, while Dane Johnson (2004) explores these authors' use of a non-cosmopolitan aesthetic to represent their own culture to a metropolis that views their regions as "provincial" or "third world." Also, rather than studying influence per se, authors are read to see how they shed light on one another, as well as on their broader contexts: in what ways do these other writers respond to Faulkner, and how does reading the work of the former change or reformulate one's understanding of the latter? What aspects of the culture and history of plantation America are illustrated in the works of authors from both South and North? (These questions echo those posed in several of the essays in *Unflinching Gaze* [Kolmerten et al. 1997], which address the same issue with regard to the relationship between Morrison and Faulkner.)

Some of the most exciting scholarship in recent years has taken a new approach to the comparativist perspective by situating Faulkner's work within the context of post-plantation society and discussions of race throughout the Americas, foregrounding the inherently inter-American dimension of the author's production. Valerie Loichot, for example, reads *Light in August*'s Joe Christmas "as an individual projection of the collective African Diaspora's experience of the origin" – that is, of the loss of the origin and genealogy that might have allowed both Christmas and displaced Africans to achieve social legitimacy (2003–4: 101). Scholars such as Ladd, Richard Godden (1997), and John T. Matthews (2004) have explored the formative influence of Haiti – in particular, the island's slavery and post-slavery racial codes and laws – on *Absalom*'s Thomas Sutpen, as well as the "ripple effect" of fear that the Haitian Revolution and the subsequent formation of a mulatto government sent through the Southern plantocracy and the US as a whole. Randy Boyagoda, in turn, attributes the suitability of Haiti to Sutpen's design to the island's "having a plantation system similar to that of the American South," even as the miscegenation that characterizes both systems is ultimately responsible for Sutpen's inability to establish a pure lineage, bringing his plans, dynasty, and house tumbling down (2003–4: 71–2).

Ladd also contrasts the racial systems of Louisiana and the US, noting the tensions that arose from the incorporation of the former French colony. Through the figure of Bon and Faulkner's descriptions of New Orleans, Ladd reveals the anxieties about assimilating Louisiana's non-white and miscegenated populations – some of whom had, under the French colonial system, been afforded legal and social privileges not granted to US blacks – into a national body "imagined as Anglo-Saxon" (Kaplan 2002: 27). As there was also concern about the fitness for self-rule of the white creoles who had lived in close proximity and granted privileges to the blacks, affirmation of white racial purity became the key to maintaining power in the new national framework (Ladd 1995: 348–50). And, as Ladd observes, Reconstruction of the white Southerner once again invoked many of these issues: "race and nationalism, assimilation and segregation . . . the moral 'contamination' of the slaveholder by the slave, as well as the cultural effects of racial hybridization or amalgamation versus what might be termed racial purity [or] homogeneity" (1995: 352).

While Ladd demonstrates how US expansion into Louisiana and the South was coextensive with a renewed consecration of the color line to assuage anxieties about prior racial mixing, José Limón (1998) identifies a similar process following the Mexican–American War and the annexation of Texas. Suzanne Bost's arguments concur with those of Limón: she observes that after acquiring the New Mexico territories, "*mestizos* of the Southwest were racially unintelligible in a system designed to support the racial hierarchies of US slavery and whose 'criteria of intelligibility' were, in the 1850 and 1860 censuses, 'white,' 'black,' and 'mulatto' " (2003: 648). This leads her to conclude that "nineteenth-century census forms suggest that US national interests demanded the exclusion of Mexican or Latin American identity from the borders of the American body" (p. 649). Handley and Amy Kaplan, in turn, study the international deployment of US racial discourses in the nation's movement into the Caribbean following the Spanish–American War. As Handley argues, "plantation discourse, always dependent on structures of colonialism, wedded itself to the growth of US imperialism after emancipation" (2000: 5). In the Southern US and the Caribbean, racial discourse was inextricably interwoven with imperial expansion and notions of citizenship, prompting the questions of who could be(come) an "American," what does "America" ultimately mean, and whom does the designation represent?

Studying Faulkner in an inter-American context thus brings to light issues that are at the heart of the transformation of "American" studies today even as this approach points to current reconfigurations of the South and its borders: is the South a marginalized region within the national body? Progenitor of racial discourses that both motivated and justified the US's imperialist expansion into the Caribbean in the late nineteenth and early twentieth centuries? Part of or apart from plantation America? Or, perhaps, a bit of all of the above?

ACKNOWLEDGMENT

Sections of this chapter appeared in "William Faulkner's Ibero-American Novel Project: The Politics of Translation and the Cold War," " 'Of the same blood as this America and its history': William Faulkner and Spanish American Literature," and "Faulkner and Spanish America: Then and Now," and are used with the permission of the publishers. I am also indebted to the National Endowment for the Humanities for the fellowship that has given me time to prepare my research; any views, findings, or conclusions expressed in this publication do not necessarily reflect those of the NEH. I also received a Franklin Research Grant from the American Philosophical Society, as well as a grant from McGill University, to travel and conduct this research. I am grateful to the University of Virginia Library's Special Collections Department, where I conducted research on this project, and to Regina Rush for her assistance. Thanks to George Handley and Jon Smith for their thoughtful comments on this chapter.

NOTES

1   Muna Lee, office memo to Thomas Driver, July 26, 1954, box number MSS 7258 a, Joseph Blotner-William Faulkner Collection, Special Collections, University of Virginia Library. Subsequent references to materials in this collection will be identified by the prefix MSS followed by the box number.

2   John W. Campbell, Public Affairs Officer USIS-São Paulo, to the Department of State, Washington D.C., September 17, 1954; 511.203/9–1754; Central Decimal Files, 1950–1954; General Records of the Department of State, Record Group 59 (RG 59); National Archives at College Park, College Park, MD.

3   Report to the North American Association on the Visit of Mr. Faulkner, May 10, 1961, MSS 7258 a.

4   Muna Lee, memo to Mr. Mattison, August 30, 1955, MSS 7258 a.

5   Muna Lee, memo to Mr. Colwell, May 2, 1961, MSS 7258 a.

6   Muna Lee, note to Harold H. Tittman, Jr., September 2, 1954, MSS 7258 a.

7   See the essays collected in *Unflinching Gaze: Morrison and Faulkner Re-Envisioned* (Kolmerten et al. 1997) for further discussion of the question of the implications of influence and the relationship between Faulkner and Morrison.

8   See Hosam Aboul-Ela (2003–4) for a discussion of the need for the discipline devoted to the study of literature of the Americas to acknowledge "the spatial inequalities within the hemisphere" (p. 56).

9   See Jon Smith's "Postcolonial, Black, and Nobody's Margin: The US South and New World Studies" (2004) for a discussion of the recent developments in the conceptualization of Southern studies.

REFERENCES AND FURTHER READING

Aboul-Ela, H. (2003–4). The Political Economy of Southern Race: *Go Down, Moses*, Spatial Inequality, and the Color Line. *Mississippi Quarterly*, 57(1): 55–64.

Bérubé, M. (2003). American Studies Without Exceptions. *PMLA*, 118(1): 103–13.

Blotner, J. (1966). William Faulkner: Roving Ambassador. *International Educational and Cultural Exchange*, Summer: 1–22.

Blotner, J. (1974). *Faulkner: A Biography. Vol. 2.* New York: Random House.

Borges, J. L. (1985). Review of *The Unvanquished*, by William Faulkner. In E. R. Monegal (ed.). *Ficcionario* (pp. 123–4). México: Fondo de Cultura Económica.

Bost, S. (2003). West Meets East: Nineteenth-Century Southern Dialogues on Mixture, Race, Gender, and Nation. *Mississippi Quarterly*, 56(4): 647–56.

Boyagoda, R. (2003–4). Just Where and What Is "the (Comparatively Speaking) South"? Caribbean Writers on Melville and Faulkner. *Mississippi Quarterly*, 57(1): 65–73.

Clayton, J. and E. Rothstein (1991). Figures in the Corpus: Theories of Influence and Intertexuality. In J. Clayton and E. Rothstein (eds.). *Influence and Intertextuality in Literary History* (pp. 3–36). Madison: University of Wisconsin Press.

Cohn, D. (1999). *History and Memory in the Two Souths: Recent Southern and Spanish American Fiction.* Nashville: Vanderbilt University Press.

Cohn, D. (2002). "Of the Same Blood as this America and its History": William Faulkner and Spanish American Literature. In B. Buchenau and A. Paatz (eds.). *Do the Americas Have a Common Literary History?* (pp. 301–25). Frankfurt: Peter Lang.

Cohn, D. (2003). Faulkner and Spanish America: Then and Now. In R. Hamblin and A. Abadie (eds.). *Faulkner and the Twenty-First Century: Faulkner and Yoknapatawpha, 2000* (pp. 50–67). Jackson: University Press of Mississippi.

Cohn, D. (2004). William Faulkner's Ibero-American Novel Project: The Politics of Translation and the Cold War. *Southern Quarterly*, Winter: 5–18.

Coleman, P. (1989). *The Liberal Conspiracy: The Congress for Cultural Freedom and the Struggle for the Mind of Postwar Europe.* New York: Free Press.

Donoso, J. (1977). *The Boom in Spanish American Literature: A Personal History* (trans. G. Kolovakos). New York: Columbia University Press.

Duvall, J. N. (1997). Toni Morrison and the Anxiety of Faulknerian Influence. In C. A. Kolmerten, S. M. Ross, and J. B. Wittenberg (eds.). *Unflinching Gaze: Morrison and Faulkner Re-Envisioned* (pp. 3–16). Jackson: University Press of Mississippi.

Faulkner, W. (1972). *Absalom, Absalom!* New York: Vintage Books. (Original pub. 1936.)

Fayen, T. (1995). *In Search of the Latin American Faulkner.* Lanham: University Press of America.

Fitz, E. (2004). William Faulkner, James Agee, and Brazil: The American South in Latin American Literature's "Other" Tradition. In J. Smith and D. Cohn (eds.). *Look Away!: The U.S. South in New World Studies* (pp. 419–45). Durham, NC: Duke University Press.

Fuentes, C. (1970). *Casa con dos puertas.* México: Joaquín Mortiz.

Fuentes, C. (1991). *The Death of Artemio Cruz* (trans. A. MacAdam). New York: Noonday Press.

García Márquez, G. (1967). *Cien años de soledad.* Barcelona: Bruguera.

García Márquez, G. (1976). *The Autumn of the Patriarch* (trans. G. Rabassa). New York: HarperPerennial.

García Márquez, G. (1982). http://nobelprize.org/literature/laureates/1982/marquez-lecture-e.html, accessed September 29, 2004.

Glissant, E. (1999). *Faulkner, Mississippi* (trans. B. Lewis and T. C. Spear). New York: Farrar, Straus, and Giroux.

Godden, R. (1997). *Fictions of Labor: William Faulkner and the South's Long Revolution.* Cambridge: Cambridge University Press.

Guibert, R. (1972). *Seven Voices: Seven Latin American Writers Talk to Rita Guibert* (trans. F. Partridge). New York: Alfred A. Knopf.

Handley, G. B. (2000). *Postslavery Literatures in the Americas: Family Portraits in Black and White.* Charlottesville, VA: University of Virginia Press.

Henderson, M. (1996) "Where, By the Way, Is This Train Going?" A Case for Black (Cultural) Studies. *Callaloo,* 19(1): 60–7.

Hobson, F. (2002). Introduction. In F. Hobson (ed.). *South to the Future: An American Region in the Twenty-first Century* (pp. 1–12). Athens, GA: University of Georgia Press.

Johnson, D. (2004). "Wherein the South Differs from the North": Tracing the Noncosmopolitan Aesthetic in William Faulkner's *Absalom, Absalom!* and Gabriel García Márquez's *One Hundred Years of Solitude.* In J. Smith and D. Cohn (eds.). *Look Away!: The U.S. South in New World Studies* (pp. 383–404). Durham, NC: Duke University Press.

Kaplan, A. (2002). *The Anarchy of Empire in the Making of U.S. Culture.* Cambridge, MA: Harvard University Press.

Kolmerten, C. A., S. M. Ross, and J. B. Wittenberg (eds.) (1997). *Unflinching Gaze: Morrison and Faulkner Re-Envisioned.* Jackson: University Press of Mississippi.

Ladd, B. (1995). "The Direction of the Howling": Nationalism and the Color Line in *Absalom, Absalom!* In M. Moon and C. Davidson (eds.). *Subjects and Citizens: Nation, Race, and Gender from Oroonoko to Anita Hill* (pp. 345–72). Durham, NC: Duke University Press.

Ladd, B. (2003). William Faulkner, Edouard Glissant, and a Creole Poetics of History and Body in *Absalom, Absalom!* and *A Fable.* In R. Hamblin and A. Abadie (eds.). *Faulkner and the Twenty-First Century: Faulkner and Yoknapatawpha, 2000* (pp. 31–49). Jackson: University Press of Mississippi.

Limón, J. E. (1998). *American Encounters: Greater Mexico, the United States, and the Erotics of Culture.* Boston: Beacon Press.

Loichot, V. (2003–4). Glissant, Yoknapatawpha. *Mississippi Quarterly,* 57(1): 99–111.

Matthews, J. T. (2004). Recalling the West Indies: From Yoknapatawpha to Haiti and Back. *American Literary History,* 16(2): 238–62.

McClennen, S. (2003). Inter-American Studies: Latin Americanism's Imperial Threat? Paper given at MLA Convention. Marina Marriott, San Diego, December 28.

McPherson, A. (2003). *Yankee No! Anti-Americanism in U.S.–Latin American Relations.* Cambridge, MA: Harvard University Press.

Mignolo, W. (1993). Colonial and Postcolonial Discourse: Cultural Critique or Academic Colonialism? *Latin American Research Review,* 28(3): 120–34.

Monteiro, G. (1983). Faulkner in Brazil. *Southern Literary Journal*, 16(1): 96–104.

Oakley, H. (2002). *The Recontextualization of William Faulkner in Latin American Fiction and Culture*. Lewiston, New York: Edwin Mellen Press.

Oakley, H. (2004). William Faulkner and the Cold War: The Politics of Cultural Marketing. In J. Smith and D. Cohn (eds.). *Look Away!: The U.S. South in New World Studies* (pp. 405–18). Durham, NC: Duke University Press.

O'Connor, F. (1961). The Grotesque in Southern Fiction. In S. Fitzgerald and R. Fitzgerald (eds.). *Mystery and Manners* (pp. 36–50). New York: Farrar, Straus, and Giroux.

Rabe, S. (1988). *Eisenhower and Latin America: The Foreign Policy of Anticommunism*. Chapel Hill, NC: University of North Carolina Press.

Richardson, D. C. (2000). Towards Faulkner's Presence in Brazil: Race, History, and Place in Faulkner and Amado. *South Atlantic Review*, 65(4): 12–27.

Saunders, F. S. (1999). *Who Paid the Piper? The CIA and the Cultural Cold War*. London: Granta Books.

Smith, J. (2004). Postcolonial, Black, and Nobody's Margin: The US South and New World Studies. *American Literary History*, 16(1): 144–61.

Smith, J. and D. Cohn (2004). William Faulkner and Latin America. In J. Smith and D. Cohn (eds.). *Look Away!: The U.S. South in New World Studies* (pp. 303–9). Durham, NC: Duke University Press.

Weinstein, P. (2004) Cant Matter/Must Matter: Setting Up the Loom in Faulknerian and Postcolonial Fiction. In J. Smith and D. Cohn (eds.). *Look Away!: The U.S. South in New World Studies* (pp. 355–82). Durham, NC: Duke University Press.

Zamora, L. P. (1989). *Writing the Apocalypse: Historical Vision in Contemporary U.S. and Latin American Fiction*. Cambridge: Cambridge University Press.

31

Faulkner's Continuance

Patrick O'Donnell

How can we think through Faulkner's relation to modernism, save as an after-effect, something we view from the historical moment of postmodernism? The question, itself, assumes that both modernism and postmodernism are comparatively "settled," epochal formations whose relation to each other is a matter of negotiation between separable clusters of equally separable ideological, thematic, economic, and aesthetic strands. Moreover, we must ask what is at stake in thinking about Faulkner as a prototypical modernist or as a precursor to postmodernism; as an author whose historical and thematic concerns and whose narrative strategies somehow inform the writing of the last fifty years, taking place under the variable rubrics of late capitalism, postmodernism, post-colonialism. All of these questions assume that literary history works in an evolutionary fashion, as we move from one "stage" to the next, one author to the next, albeit with the ironic recognition that "modernism" and "postmodernism" are critical constructs, formulated in the wake of the writing that these constructs seek to explain or encompass. In a sense, we are always at a future remove in considering a body of writing within the framework of an epoch, and especially when we consider the work of a modern writer in terms of its relation to postmodernism, whether authorial, historical, or aesthetic, we are attempting to understand and anticipate the future of writing per se. In attempting to address Faulkner's relation to postmodernism, then, we recognize that this relation is not necessarily important simply because it enables us to pigeonhole Faulkner historically, or to evaluate the "evolution" of narrative, or to denote a major writer's influence on writers to come. The importance of this relation occurs because it allows us to better understand ourselves as readers of Faulkner within an historical horizon and a temporal continuum that bridge epochal movements ("modernism" and "postmodernism") in which the very notions of futurity and continuum "at the end of history" (or in the face of a time when the end of history could be conceived) have been negotiated.

Within the terms of these questions, Faulkner's deep thematic concerns with temporality and history become paramount in understanding his continuity as a writer and the continuum of writing across modernism and postmodernism. For Faulkner shares, at the outset, the sense of "modernity" and the relation of subjects to history within modernity described by Henri Lefebvre in the *Introduction to Modernity*:

> [Under modernity] instead of the past being clarified by the present, and vice versa, it becomes a glass in which the present seeks its own image. . . . The result is contradictory: at one and the same time an ignorance about becoming and about the lessons of this historical past, and an extraordinary overloading of culture and consciousness. Like other knowledge . . . knowledge about the past accumulates. . . . Nostalgic memories are evoked for anxieties about what is possible, but they provide no clear-cut answers. We are overloaded with fragmented pieces of unarticulated information, the debris of the past, knowledge as a scrapyard. Nevertheless, the objective of history as an object of methodical knowledge and highly precise techniques is constantly being questioned. Now it appears as a limit, now as a lure, and now as a pretext for mystifications. (1995: 225)

For the notion of the historical present as the place where the "debris of the past" accumulates, Lefebvre is clearly relying on Benjamin's notion of the "Angelus Novus," the "angel of history" who surveys the totality of historical progress with its back turned toward the future as "one single catastrophe which keeps piling wreckage upon wreckage" in a seemingly eternal present that merely serves as a catchment for these anterior "fragments shored up against [the] ruins" of history. (Benjamin 1968: 257). As the reference to *The Waste Land* (1922) indicates, both Benjamin and Lefebvre share T. S. Eliot's modernist sense of the present as a historical watershed preceding an apocalyptic future, and history per se as an unredeemed, ironic totality condemned to be mired in this present. Like Benjamin, Lefebvre views history as a totality which we cannot properly grasp or perceive in the present moment, because the "proper," progressive relation between past and present has been transformed into a form of narcissistic repetition that converts the past into, merely, a "glass" (or, perhaps more accurately, a kaleidoscope) "in which the present seeks its own image." Like shards of a mirror, historical totality is fragmented in this view, the past casting a thousand reflections that provide myriad narratives and representations of what the past was only in terms of a present that sees the past in pieces, randomly, as an array of contingencies only partially and accidentally connected.

This post-epochal sense of the past as crazy-quilt, and history – to the extent that it is narratable at all – as reflexive fabrication, is surely shared by Faulkner, who writes in the infamous passage where Mr. Compson communicates to Quentin his ironic recognition that the story of Thomas Sutpen, in the end, simply does not add up:

> we have a few old mouth-to-mouth tales; we exhume from old trunks and boxes and drawers letters without salutation or signature, in which men and women who once lived and breathed are now merely initials or nicknames out of some now incomprehensible affection which sound to us like Sanskrit or Chocktaw; we see dimly people, the people in whose living blood and seed we ourselves lay dormant and waiting, in this shadowy attenuation of time possessing now heroic proportions . . . They are there,

yet something is missing; they are like a chemical formula exhumed along with the letters from that forgotten chest . . . you bring them together again and again and nothing happens: just the words, the symbols, the shapes themselves, shadowy inscrutable and serene, against that turgid background of a horrible and bloody mischancing of human affairs. (1986: 80)

For Mr. Compson, the relation between past and present is compromised by contingency as such, and a belief that the present is "all" contingency, and all that there is of the totality of history. What provides for many of Faulkner's readers a joyful occasion for rejecting the perceived apodictic excesses of realist narrative and historiographic conventions is, for Mr. Compson, in his recognition that all that we have of the past in the present are fragments and shadows, a reaffirmation of that form of romantic irony that nostalgically posits a historical continuity and totality that never existed but whose ongoing presence, illogically, is "proved" by the existence of the past's remnants in "old mouth-to-mouth tales," faded signatures, and ancestral shadows. Mr. Compson wishes to detect the ghostly trace of an epic, monumental past in the fragments of narrative that circulate through Yoknapatawpha in the form of gossip, faded letters, worn engravings on headstones, just as he implicitly hopes that there is still a community of tellers and listeners that forms itself around transmission of these material embodiments of historical process. Conversely, his recognition that "you bring them together and nothing happens" suggests that he has "given up" on the past, and the possibility of dwelling in a historical continuity that gives shape to change and meaning to contingency.

But, assuredly, we do not want to equate Faulkner's view of history, historical continuity, and the relation between past and present with that of Mr. Compson. Nor should we, at this moment, simply leave the field to Mr. Compson or whatever distinctions we might draw between Faulkner's character and the philosophy of history to be derived from his work, especially given that we have available to us not only myriad critiques of the colonialism that Sutpen's story typifies and of the reflexive modernism that underwrites the means of its telling, but also ample evidence of the effect of Faulkner's writing on post-colonial and postmodern writers. However true it may be that this key passage from Faulkner's most reflexive novel provides us with a means of understanding how Faulkner regards his own writing, it is equally true that it allows us, perhaps from a perspective beyond that of "Faulkner," to see the extent to which *Absalom, Absalom!* (1936) – first among many of his novels in this respect – engages the question of how such post-tragic writing is part of a historical continuum that allows us to see the limits and beyond the limits of ego, nation, and empire as the elemental components of the "historical," personal or worldly (see especially Matthews 1982; Kartiganer 1979; Irwin 1996; Bleikasten 1990). To put the question in slightly different terms, how might we see the place of Faulkner's writing historically if we insist on understanding history – personal and communal – in terms other than those of Mr. Compson's vainglorious fatalism, based upon an imagined fall *from* History (the monumental, epic past) experienced as a waning of the past amidst the debris of the present?

An alternative perspective has been provided for us by Edouard Glissant, the Martinican novelist-critic whose *Faulkner, Mississippi* (1999) is dedicated not to "preserving" Faulkner for the ages, nor to detecting his influences, but rather to understanding both his investments in and departure from a conception of history that would inscribe foundational origins of identity in a narrative that is evolutionary, progressive, and total. We might regard Glissant's project in reading Faulkner as opposite to that of Malcolm Cowley, who, in framing and organizing excerpts from the novels and stories in *The Viking Portable Faulkner* (1946), posited the notion of the "world" of Faulkner's Yoknapatawpha emerging *in toto* out of the assemblage of overlapping and disconnected "mouth-to-mouth tales." Glissant, whose view of history is generally Hegelian, regards Faulkner, in contrast, as part of and contributing to the "world-totality" to which all people, literatures, and languages stand in relation. Faulkner's work in itself, taken as a whole, does not figure *a* world, but stands in relation as a partiality to *the* world.

The difference is crucial, in Glissant's view: for him, Faulkner's fiction is essentially anti-foundational (despite the desire for permanent and uncontaminated foundations and origins to be found in Faulkner's characters), as a form of "deferred writing" based upon a "presupposition" that is never reached: "In Faulkner's works, the narration's presupposition – the illegitimate foundation of the South – is never formally expressed. The writer's task is to reveal this presupposition while revealing its painful parallels in the present and also making it clear that the true revelation will be put off indefinitely" (1999: 139). Tellingly, Glissant does not name "the illegitimate foundation of the South" as an *authorial* presupposition: in fact, the "writer's task," as he sees it, is to expose the narration's illegitimate foundational presuppositions, but not necessarily to posit their origins, endorse them, or (impossibly, in Glissant's view) manifest or reveal their "ends" in some epiphanic future. This places Faulkner in ironic relation to his own "deferred" writing, for in Glissant's terms, "narration," in effect – and specifically the anti-foundational narrative revealing the illegitimate foundation of the South – runs under its own steam, and is so deeply implicated in historical process that its "origins" can only be mythologized in racist terms and its "ends" can only be posited as an endlessly delayed, obscured revelation. Within this framework, Faulkner, the writer, works to expose the illegitimacy of his own narrative, or more precisely, the illegitimacy of the historical narrative that he is compelled to represent, both as a totality that welds a mythic past to an apocalyptic future and as a partiality, a rag-tag assemblage of "tales" (the quanta of Faulkner's fiction) that add up to an endless delay of history's end, a metonymization of its ultimacies. The irony of Faulkner's fiction can be viewed in the ratio between the narrative drive to encompass the "whole" of history in the "little postage stamp of native soil" and the disruption of that drive in the form of "mouth-to-mouth tales," "words," "symbols," "shapes", the "horrible and bloody mischancing of human affairs."

In *Faulkner, Mississippi*, Glissant suggests that Faulkner's writing is a writing of the future that finds its fullest expression and fulfills its fatal logic (but only, always, partially) in the present. Of that present, where national and transnational socio-political forms contend – a contention that finds one of its epistemological counterparts in struggles over individual and communal authorities and truths – Glissant writes: "We are living in the moment when an indivisible world harmony and the conceptions it suggests are breaking up, a time when partial harmonies arise everywhere and converge toward a generalized disharmony, something the writer feels strongly he cannot first explore without first renouncing this indivisibility that established him, sovereign and seer, in his place and words" (1999: 4–5). The authorial renunciation of indivisibility that Glissant invokes is consonant with the ironic temporal relation in Faulkner's fiction between contingency and totality, where, under the sign of the former, past and future are linked in the present through narrative seriality and deferred revelation, and, under the sign of the latter, past and future are welded into the "indivisibility" of mythic origin always in the process of becoming historical apocalypse.

For Glissant, the renunciation of indivisibility involves a renunciation of authorial rights and privileges over the narrative as such as "sovereign and seer," that is, as one who ordains a world and provides particular insights about its elements, origins, and ends. The writer, in this view, becomes an embodiment of her own ironic relation to a work that she has brought into being, for which she has served as filter, medium, and transmitter of specificities amidst the welter of worldly disharmonies, contingencies, objects, and semes, but over which she has no final say as to its place in time and history or the status of its revelations and reception – that is, no control over its continuance and temporalization. Glissant views Faulkner as *the* precursor to the present moment of writing amidst a "generalized disharmony" (geopolitically, the "moment" of post-colonialism) because he incorporates this irony in his fiction thematically and structurally. Faulkner is, at once, the author who drew maps to the fictional "world" he created, and yet whose novels (as Mr. Compson complains about what is available to him as would-be master storyteller) have been both praised and attacked for providing, always, only partial, disjoined, unfinished narratives, the totality of his work palimpsestic rather than epic. In Faulkner's narrative, the paradoxical affect generated by the collision of totalized and "disharmonized" senses of writing and history is that of nostalgia and its temporal consequences – a cynicism regarding the ends of history, an anxiety that the future is the site not of historical progression toward the fulfillment of human destiny, but of the collapse of history and the disappearance of the human. In Glissant's view, Faulkner's capacity for negotiating these historical and temporal antinomies is what ensures his role as the precursor to our "moment" and the continuance of his writing.

Examples of the ironic relation and affect that subtend Faulkner's anti-foundational writing can be found throughout his fiction, but perhaps nowhere more starkly than in those moments in such novels as *Absalom, Absalom!*, *Go Down, Moses* (1942), and *Light in August* (1932) where historical temporality is, rhetorically, put to the test of the future. In such moments, we can observe what Paul de Man characterizes as the ironic "substance" of modern temporality unfolding within a detotalized, post-foundational "History" comprised of "a temporal sequence of acts of consciousness which is endless" (1983: 220). De Man describes the epoch of modernity as working under the sign of "Irony" that, rhetorically, is the means for negotiating the relation between a lost past viewed as total and organic, the present of "generalized disharmony" that Glissant represents as "our moment," and a radically open future repeatedly traversed by "consciousness which is endless":

> irony . . . reveals the existence of a temporality that is definitely not organic, in that it relates its source only in terms of distance and difference and allows for no end, for no totality. Irony divides the flow of temporal experience into a past that is pure mystification and a future that remains harassed forever by a relapse into the inauthentic. (1983: 222)

For de Man, the "inauthentic" is the failure of consciousness to ever catch up with its own full self-reflection in history. For Faulkner, this inauthenticity (paradoxically, that which, for Glissant, underscores the relevance, authenticity, and continuance of his narrative) is realized in what can be termed the metonymization of human destiny, the multiplication and mutability of stories and persons to the extent that the totalities of history and ego simply evaporate in the reach of time.

In the penultimate chapter of *Go Down, Moses*, "Delta Autumn," we read old Uncle Ike McCaslin's reflections on the changes in the Delta that have taken place over his long lifetime, and the imagined transformations to come in an illimitable future:

> At first there had been only the old towns along the River and the old towns along the hills from which the planters with their gangs of slaves and then of hired laborers had wrested from the impenetrable jungle of water-standing cane and cypress, gum and holly and oak and ash, cotton patches which as the years passed became fields and plantations. . . . Now a man drove two hundred miles from Jefferson before he found wilderness to hunt in. Now the land lay open from the cradling hills on the East to the rampart levee on the West, standing horseman-tall with cotton for the world's looms – the rich black land . . . which exhausted the hunting life of a dog in one year, the working life of a mule in five and of a man in twenty . . . the land across which there now came no scream of panther but instead a long hooting of locomotives: trains of incredible length and drawn by a single engine, since there was no gradient anywhere and no elevation save those raised by forgotten aboriginal hands as refuges from the yearly water and used by their Indian successors to sepulcher their fathers' bodies. (Faulkner 1990: 324–5)

Tracing the evolution of the Mississippi Delta to its origins as a "jungle" first inhabited by paternal, aboriginal ancestors who marked the land with the graves of their fathers, then colonized by plantation owners, McCaslin constructs a "now" in which, paradoxically, the industrialized landscape is both open geographically and geopolitically (its bounty available to the world), yet completely mapped and surveyed, criss-crossed by roads, furrows, and rails, its topography now rendered by human constructions that serve to convert the secreted, "aboriginal" past into the temporal, human order of the present. In some senses, the geographical "progress" that McCaslin traces here – from a closed, totalized, "aboriginal" past to a present in which the land is opened, cut up, and traversed by humans marking the time of their labor – mirrors the movement from epic time and consciousness to novelistic temporality and self-consciousness that Lukács traces in *The Theory of the Novel* (1971). Like Lukács, Faulkner represents this movement as fundamentally historic, that is, as taking place within a history which is the narrative of this progression. But unlike Lukács, as we shall see, Faulkner regards the opening out of history onto the future as profoundly ironic as it moves not toward a reinstantiation of a utopian totality with the end of class division and struggle, but toward a multiplication of conflicted and hybrid identities, narratives, and histories that populate the landscape of "generalized disharmony" (Lukács 1971: 56–69).

For McCaslin, it seems important, however much it may be plowed under, traversed, and covered over by tracks in the "now", that the openness and flatness of the Delta's topography still be marked by the "elevations" of ancestral remains that signify a remainder (and reminder) of prehistoric origins in the form of obstructions and occlusions. This is to view the past in the ironic mode that de Man describes as "pure mystification," separated off from a present streaming into a future "that remains harassed forever" by a relapse into the inauthentic." Yet, *pace* de Man, for Faulkner the separation is never complete; or more precisely, the mystifications of the totalized past are realized in McCaslin's ironic "now" as decomposing remnants that dot the landscape given entirely over to time and contingency, thus giving the lie to the aboriginal and ancestral as pure, undefiled, before time. For Faulkner, the "harassment" of inauthenticity occurs *from the beginning and at the origin of things*, and it is precisely in McCaslin's positing an origin or a "time before" that the ironic truth of time and history as always already detotalized becomes the transparent "fact" of our continuum.

But things are not simply left here, with McCaslin's nostalgic view of a landscape framed within the larger recognitions provided by the Faulknerian irony that saturates the temporalizing of this nostalgia. For McCaslin, tracing the imaginary progression from prehistory to the historical present, constitutes the "now" as a form of continuance moving into an incomprehensible future where (in his racist reflections) "all" will become "one":

> This Delta, he thought. This Delta. *This land which man has deswamped and denuded and derivered in two generations so that white men can own plantations and commute every night to Memphis and black men own plantations and ride in jim crow cars to Chicago to live in millionaires' mansions on Lakeshore Drive, where white men rent farms and live like niggers and niggers crop on shares and live like animals, where cotton is planted and grows man-tall in the very cracks of the sidewalks, and usury and mortgages and bankruptcy and measureless wealth, Chinese and African and Aryan and Jew, all breed and spawn together until no man has time to say which one is which nor cares.* (Faulkner 1990: 347)[1]

McCaslin's mental rant on the devolutionary history of the Delta moves frantically through a series of constructed binaries (white/black, rich/poor, human/animal, nature/culture, country/city). He is anxious about the collapse of these cultural binaries as the present moves toward the future into a singular totality where race, class, and "humanness" itself become indistinguishable. Yet the very multiplicity and hybridism that he so fears serve to redress the racist logic that underlies a view of time and history moving from one totality to another, from an imagined purity of origins (only available in the form of defiled remnants) to an equally imagined apocalypse of singularity that parodies, in its hysterical affect, both the idea of uncontaminated (white) beginnings and the "dystopia" of the genetic melting pot. Infiltrating Ike's vision, lurking in the interstices of its constructed binaries mediating the totalities of prehistorical origin and post-historical end, is a set of contingent disparities that reveal, for Glissant, Faulkner's contemporaneity. The disparate ratios that exist between "Chinese and African," as if these continental designations were meant to encompass all racial difference; everyone (and everything) that exists somewhere between the projected "extremities" of millionaire blacks and poor white sharecroppers, as if "rich/poor" and "white/black" were simply interchangeable terms in a totalized racio-economic linguistic system whose very interchangeability was the sign of meaninglessness; the infinite variations of topography, contesting growth, and life that exist between a land "rivered" and a land "derivered" – all are glossed over, yet invoked, in Ike's jeremiad. In his enunciation, we can observe what might be viewed as a historical and narrative anxiety produced in the face of the "now" that Glissant describes as a time when "partial harmonies arise everywhere and converge toward a generalized disharmony." Faulkner's notation of this "disharmony" is registered in Ike's terror at genetic hybridization and a collapse of social and cultural binaries, and in Mr. Compson's recognition that the stories of the past cannot be combined into a totalized historical narrative that would explain the present and predict the future. This notation, I have argued, ironically registers as well Faulkner's own deferred, hesitant, and conflicted renunciation of indivisibility as an author writing in his time and for the future.

We began with a consideration of Faulkner's place in the seam between modernism and postmodernism, but viewed through Glissant's perspective, it now appears that figuring out the relation or difference between modernism and postmodernism, in epochal terms or in terms of Faulkner's writing, may be irrelevant to the actuality of that writing as a form of continuance. Faulkner writes of temporality – the relation of the "then" to the "now," the writer's commerce with stories of the past, the dystopic projections that inhere in tracing historical "progress" and the filiations of the social order – but as we have seen, he does not regard temporality as something that can be "settled" within an (impossibly) totalized narrative or a view of historicity founded on a "harmonic" relation between past, present, and future. Instead, when temporal relations are narrativized in Faulkner's writing, they are inevitably marked as disjunct, uneven, "only in terms of distance and difference [that] allows for no end, for no totality." For Glissant, this ensures Faulkner's continuity, his ongoing presence in a world of historical contingency and brutal contact, whose narrative is a multiplicity of conflicting and converging narratives. This is to regard narrative as dangerous, for, if narrative is detotalized, bereft of "authenticity" in de Man's terms, and in an ironic relation to its sources of authority, who is to say which "mouth-to-mouth tales" get inscribed as bearing some element of historical truth? Which ones embody the gesture to the future that will become the future? Which ones explain our current situatedness? Faulkner's writing addresses these questions, in its own terms, as a matter of how history and bodies in history can be regarded, and this, for Glissant, ensures the ongoing relevance of Faulkner's work in a time of general disharmony that, for Glissant, is the post-colonial moment. Faulkner's writing inhabits this moment even as, residually, regarded through the eyes of the post-colonial subject, it is a/part from/of it. As a form of deferred and dislocated writing, it does not remain comfortably in any epochal construct we might name, any historical "home" we might give it, and therein resides its continuance.

NOTE

1 I am extending here my earlier reading of this passage as a reflection on futurity within the context of Agamben's notions of modernity and temporality (O'Donnell 2003).

REFERENCES AND FURTHER READING

Agamben, G. (1993). *Infancy and History: Essays on the Destruction of Experience* (trans. L. Heron). New York: Verso.

Benjamin, W. (1968). Theses on the Philosophy of History. In *Illuminations* (ed. and intro. H. Arendt) (pp. 253–64). New York: Schocken.

Bleikasten, A. (1990). *The Ink of Melancholy: Faulkner's Novels from* The Sound and the Fury *to* Light in August. Bloomington: Indiana University Press.

de Man, P. (1983). The Rhetoric of Temporality. In *Blindness and Insight: Essays in the Rhetoric of Contemporary Criticism* (2nd edn rev.). Minneapolis: University of Minnesota Press.

Derrida, J. (1994). *Specters of Marx: The State of the Debt, the Work of Mourning, and the New International* (trans. P. Kamuf). New York: Routledge.

Faulkner, W. (1986). *Absalom, Absalom!* New York: Vintage. (Original pub. 1936.)

Faulkner, W. (1990). *Go Down, Moses.* New York: Vintage. (Original pub. 1942.)

Glissant, E. (1999). *Faulkner, Mississippi* (trans. B. Lewis and T. C. Spear). New York: Farrar, Straus, and Giroux.

Irwin, J. T. (1996). *Doubling and Incest/Repetition and Revenge: A Speculative Reading of Faulkner* (2nd edn). Baltimore: Johns Hopkins University Press.

Kartiganer, D. (1979). *The Fragile Thread: The Meaning of Form in Faulkner's Novels.* Amherst: University of Massachusetts Press.

Lefebvre, H. (1995). *Introduction to Modernity: Twelve Preludes September 1959–May 1961* (trans. J. Moore). New York: Verso.

Lukács, G. (1971). The Epic and the Novel. In *The Theory of the Novel* (trans. A. Bostock) (pp. 56–69). Cambridge, MA: MIT Press.

Matthews, J. T. (1982). *The Play of Faulkner's Language.* Ithaca, NY: Cornell University Press.

O'Donnell, P. (2003). Faulkner's Future Tense: A Critique of the Instant and the Continuum. In R. W. Hamblin and A. J. Abadie (eds.). *Faulkner in the 21st Century* (pp. 107–21). Jackson: University Press of Mississippi.

Index

Page numbers in *italics* refer to illustrations.

Absalom, Absalom!, 8, 20, 29, 34, 38–9, 55, 88–9, 94–5, 99, 109, 120–7, 135, 159, 166–7, 172–9, 180, *181–3*, 184, 189, 191, 193–6, 210, 212, 233, 241–4, 246, 250, 252–3, 257–60, 266, 271, 302, 307, 322, 327, 336, 343–5, 352, 355–6, 368, 371, 373–5, 378–9, 381, 384–9, 395, 401, 422–4, 445–9, 451–2, 455–7, 487–9, 491, 493, 502–5, 513–14, 520–1

Across the Creek: Faulkner Family Stories (Jimmy Faulkner), 110

Adorno, Theodor, 72–3, 85, 97–8, 100, 290, 305, 355

African American studies, 141: *see also* Black studies

"Afternoon of a Cow," 162

Agnew, John, 204–6

Agrarians, 31–3, 50, 171, 270, 359–61, 370, 482, 493, 503

Agricultural Adjustment Act (AAA), 11–12, 18, 20, 203

Aiken, Conrad, 324, 327, 329, 365, 481

Althusser, Louis, 85, 95, 357n, 461, 488, 491

"Ambuscade," 135, 403; *see also The Unvanquished*

"American Drama: Inhibitions," 329

American Indians, *see* Native Americans

"And Now What's To Do," 324

Anderson, Sherwood, 54, 322, 324, 328–30, 332, 395, 397, 414, 443n

androgyny, *see* gender

anti-Semitism, 192, 224, 237, 265, 525

"Appendix: Compson, 1699–1945," 12, 70, 189, 191, 335

art, 44, 54, 65–83, 105, 109, 111, 148–50, 153, 155, 158–9, 279, 301–16, 321, 326, 328, 342, 359, 361–3, 376, 379, 413–14, 416, 429–30, 441, 456, 509

As I Lay Dying, 33, 55, 93, 109, 130, 166–72, 175, 177–9, 252, 302, 306–7, 322, 326, 334–5, 346, 357n, 360, 370, 373, 398, 424, 429–43, 485, 488–9, 491, 496, 503–4

avant-garde, *see* modernism

Baird, Helen, 54, 365

Baker, Charles, 494

Bakhtin, Mikhail, 25n, 85, 127, 490–1

Baldwin, James, 42–3

Balzac, Honoré de, 310, 361

"Barn Burning," 58, 89–90, 332, 395, 402, 464

Barthes, Roland, 486–8

"The Bear," 90, 152, 247, 265, 404–5, 447; *see also Go Down, Moses*

"A Bear Hunt," 402

Beardsley, Aubrey, 54, 152, 326

"Beer Broadside," 337–8, 415, 417

Benjamin, Walter, 297, 520

"Beyond," 401

The Big Sleep (Hawks), 307, 373

Big Woods, 327, 407

Bildungsroman, 231

The Birth of a Nation (Griffith), 99, 287–99

bisexuality, *see* sexuality

Bishop, Elizabeth, 507
Bitterweeds: Life with William Faulkner at Rowan Oak (Franklin), 110
"Black Music," 401
Black studies, 513; *see also* African American studies
blackface, *see* minstrelsy
Blanchot, Maurice, 284, 286–9, 295, 297–9
Bleikasten, André, 87, 92–3, 237–8, 356n, 369, 485–8, 521
Blotner, Joseph, 107–11, 148, 279, 287, 323–9, 333, 362, 425, 506
Borges, Jorge Luis, 258, 493, 499, 501–2, 506, 511
Bradley, David, 145
Brodsky, Louis, 109–11, 336
Brooks, Cleanth, 47, 270, 274, 360, 363, 365, 369–70, 480, 483–5, 487
Brown, Calvin, 205–6, 218
Brown v. Board of Education, 28, 39–41, 44, 45n, 216, 230, 233
Butler, Judith, 8, 86

Cabell, James, 326, 365
Cain, James, 72
Caldwell, Erskine, 495
Camus, Albert, 337
"Carcassonne," 331, 363–5, 400
Caron, Tim, 270, 272
Carpenter, Meta, *see* Wilde, Meta Carpenter
Carpentier, Alejo, 513
Carr, Duane, 168–9
Carr, John, 373
Carter, Hodding, 337
Carvill, Caroline, 62n
The Catcher in the Rye (Salinger), 339
"Centaur in Brass," 402; *see also The Town*
Chandler, Raymond, 333, 373
cinema, *see* film
Civil Rights Movement, 28–33, 39–44, 92, 141, 145–6, 203, 215–17, 220, 222, 230, 232, 419, 490; *see also Brown v. Board of Education*
Civil War, 9, 88, 119, 133, 135–42, 153, 176–7, 180, 184–8, 195, 208, 211, 217, 239, 241–3, 253, 259, 270–1, 292, 297–8, 331, 345, 353, 362, 381, 388, 396, 401, 403, 416, 450–1, 481, 503–6
Cixous, Hélène, 86, 488
Clarke, Deborah, 91
class, 9–13, 16–18, 20, 24, 29–32, 48–9, 51–3, 55–61, 87–95, 97, 120, 149, 154, 156–7,

160, 163n, 165–79, 180, 193–4, 200, 209, 238–9, 242–5, 250, 282, 284, 305, 308, 351–2, 368–9, 399, 432–3, 446–57, 459–74, 480
Cold War, 28, 32, 65, 71, 97, 337, 411–12, 482, 506–11
Collected Stories, 331, 402, 405–7
colonialism, 9, 178, 212, 242, 252–67, 452–6, 480, 493–5, 499–515, 519, 521, 523, 527; *see also* post-colonialism
Commins, Saxe, 70, 423, 425
Communism, *see* Cold War
Conrad, Joseph, 108–9, 129, 242, 254–5, 342–5, 347, 356, 361, 397, 445
consumer culture, 31, 49, 58, 72, 75, 98, 169–71, 176, 214, 223, 225, 229, 233, 305, 313, 380, 480, 484, 496
Cook, Sylvia, 169, 433
Cowley, Malcolm, 53, 69, 104, 138, 184, 202, 204, 207–8, 218n, 315–16, 327, 335, 337, 395, 405–6, 415, 481–4, 492, 496, 522; *see also The Portable Faulkner*
crime genres, 67, 71–2, 74, 79–81, 226–31, 233, 238, 245, 301, 313, 315, 322, 333–4, 359, 367, 373–92, 401–3, 405–6
cubism, 109, 359, 441

Davis, Thadious, 92, 134, 142–3, 210–11, 260, 262, 267, 278–9, 488–91
de Beauvoir, Simone, 86
de Man, Paul, 523–6
deconstruction, 92, 94, 352, 488–9, 491; *see also* Derrida, Jacques
DeLillo, Don, 97, 454
"Delta Autumn," 90, 142, 145, 264, 404–5, 524; *see also Go Down, Moses*
depression (economic), 11–12, 29–30, 171, 208, 220–2, 226–30, 245–6, 335–6, 369
depression (psychological), 107, 410
Derrida, Jacques, 85, 479, 488–9, 491; *see also* deconstruction
detective fiction, *see* crime genres
"Divorce in Naples," 48, 54, 400
Doctor Martino and Other Stories, 401, 406
Douglass, Frederick, 91–2, 445–6, 457n
drama (Faulkner), 279, 322, 326, 331, 336–7; *see also The Marionettes; Requiem for a Nun*
drawings (Faulkner), 54, 150–2, *181*, 258, 266, 321, 326–7, 329, 331, 523
"Dry September," 34, 399–400
Du Bois, W. E. B., 8, 30, 42

Dussere, Eric, 94, 96
Duvall, John, 72–3, 91, 270, 381, 495, 512

Eliot, George, 342–4
Eliot, T. S., 104, 322, 324–5, 327, 342–3, 345–7, 450, 520
Ellis, Havelock, 52, 155–7, 163n
Ellison, Ralph, 32, 39–42, 44, 134–5, 141–2
Ellmann, Richard, 106
Emancipation, 8, 17, 135, 138, 140–2, 146, 288, 418, 451, 515
"An Error in Chemistry," 333, 405; *see also Knight's Gambit*
Erskine, Albert, 423, 425
essays (Faulkner), 33, 40, 98–9, 104–5, 322, 333–5, 410–19, 430; *see also* individual titles

A Fable, 55, 282, 336–7, 352–3, 407, 422, 492
Fadiman, Regina, 361–2, 368
Falkenberg, Pamela, 81–3
Falkner, John, 105
Falkner, Murry, Jr., 105, 287
Falkner, Murry, Sr., 190
Falkner, Col. William, 109, 184–8
family, 9, 12, 17, 34, 38, 47, 50, 53, 68, 86, 91, 104, 107, 109–10, 119, 126, 130, 133, 138, 141, 144–5, 167, 172, 175–6, 180–200, 202, 223–6, 236, 238, 245–7, 250, 253, 260, 267, 272, 278, 280, 287–8, 321, 328, 331–2, 335, 337, 351, 353–4, 385, 391, 398, 406, 417–19, 429–31, 433–43, 446–57, 462, 464, 471, 480, 483, 485, 503–5
fascination, 47, 99, 137, 139, 157, 227, 237, 250, 253–4, 257, 270, 272, 284–99, 445
Fascism, 34, 66, 83, 97–100, 192, 239, 450
"Father Abraham," 397, 401, 431–3
Faulkner: A Biography (Blotner), 107–11, 425
Faulkner, Jill, *see* Summers, Jill Faulkner
Faulkner, Jimmy, 110
Faulkner: The Man and the Artist (Oates), 108
The Faulkner Reader, 333, 413
Faulkner: The Transfiguration of Biography (Wittenberg), 108
Faulkner's works:
    Absalom, Absalom!, 8, 20, 29, 34, 38–9, 55, 88–9, 94–5, 99, 109, 120–7, 135, 159, 166–7, 172–9, 180, *181–3*, 184, 189, 191, 193–6, 210, 212, 233, 241–4, 246, 250, 252–3, 257–60, 266, 271, 302, 307, 322, 327, 336, 343–5, 352, 355–6, 368, 371, 373–5, 378–9, 381, 384–9, 395, 401,

422–4, 445–9, 451–2, 455–7, 487–9, 491, 493, 502–5, 513–14, 520–1
"Afternoon of a Cow," 162
"Ambuscade," 135, 403; *see also The Unvanquished*
"American Drama: Inhibitions," 329
"And Now What's To Do," 324
"Appendix: Compson, 1699–1945," 12, 70, 189, 191, 335
As I Lay Dying, 33, 55, 93, 109, 130, 166–72, 175, 177–9, 252, 302, 306–7, 322, 326, 334–5, 346, 357n, 360, 370, 373, 398, 424, 429–43, 485, 488–9, 491, 496, 503–4
"Barn Burning," 58, 89–90, 332, 395, 402, 464
"The Bear," 90, 152, 247, 265, 404–5, 447; *see also Go Down, Moses*
"A Bear Hunt," 402
"Beer Broadside," 337–8, 415, 417
"Beyond," 401
The Big Sleep (Hawks), 307, 373
Big Woods, 327, 407
"Black Music," 401
"Carcassonne," 331, 363–5, 400
"Centaur in Brass," 402; *see also The Town*
Collected Stories, 331, 402, 405–7
"Delta Autumn," 90, 142, 145, 264, 404–5, 524; *see also Go Down, Moses*
"Divorce in Naples," 48, 54, 400
Doctor Martino and Other Stories, 401, 406
drama, 279, 322, 326, 331, 336–7; *see also The Marionettes*; *Requiem for a Nun*
drawings, 54, 150–2, *181*, 258, 266, 321, 326–7, 329, 331, 523
"Dry September," 34, 399–400
"An Error in Chemistry," 333, 405; *see also Knight's Gambit*
essays, 33, 40, 98–9, 104–5, 322, 333–5, 410–19, 430; *see also* individual titles
A Fable, 55, 282, 336–7, 352–3, 407, 422, 492
"Father Abraham," 397, 401, 431–3
The Faulkner Reader, 333, 413
"The Fire and the Hearth," 142, 145, 247, 262, 404; *see also Go Down, Moses*
Flags in the Dust, 184–5, 212, 366, 424, 430, 435, 442
"Fool About a Horse," 401; *see also The Hamlet*
"Foreword" to *The Faulkner Reader*, 334, 413
"Go Down, Moses" (story), 145, 247, 405; *see also Go Down, Moses*

Go Down, Moses, 8, 21–5, 25n, 55, 90, 92, 134–6, 139, 142–5, 152–3, *154*, 162, 163n, 189, 196–9, 246–7, 250, 253–4, 260–7, 282, 322, 331–2, 336, 353, 368, 371, 402–5, 447, 483, 488–9, 491, 493, 523–6

"A Guest's Impression of New England," 99, 415

The Hamlet, 47–8, 58, 90, 123–7, 130, 244–6, 250, 302, 307, 332, 336, 356, 394, 397, 401–2, 420–2, 432–3, 459–74

"Hand Upon the Waters," 405; *see also Knight's Gambit*

Helen: A Courtship, 321

"Hell Creek Crossing," 407; *see also The Reivers*

"Hermaphroditus," 155, 161

"The Hill," 396–7

"His Name Was Pete," 417

"The Hound," 401; *see also The Hamlet*

If I Forget Thee, Jerusalem, 26n, 65–83, 111, 212, 307–8, 312, 322, 324, 326, 333, 336, 378–81, 424, 489, 491, 502

"If I Were a Negro," 40, 412

"Impressions of Japan," 415–16

"An Innocent at Rinkside," 99, 416–17

introduction to *The Faulkner Reader* (Random House), 333

introduction to *Sanctuary* (Modern Library), 226, 334–5

introductions to *The Sound and the Fury* 16, 88, 301, 360–1, 366

Intruder in the Dust, 55, 135, 206, 210, 230–3, 307, 322, 331, 337, 368, 373–7, 379, 381, 389, 425, 483, 491–2

"A Justice," 189, 266, 400

"Kentucky: May: Saturday," 322, 416–17

"The Kingdom of God," 188

Knight's Gambit, 322, 333, 373–4, 377–9, 401–2, 405–6

"Landing in Luck," 54, 327, 331, 396

"L'Apres-Midi d'un Faune," 324, 365

"The Leg," 59, 401

"A Letter to the Leaders of the Negro Race," 411

"A Letter to the North," 39–42

"Letter to a Northern Editor," 29, 411

letters, 28–9, 33, 39–41, 54, 70, 98, 100, 106–8, 110–12, 121, 129, 138, 184, 253, 321–3, 325–6, 329–31, 337–9, 353, 384, 407, 411, 415, 417, 421–2, 429, 490, 509, 520–1

Light in August, 34–9, 44, 48, 55, 109, 127–30, 135, 206, 212, 236, 239–41, 244, 246, 250,

252, 254, 270–1, 273–4, 276, 282, 284–99, 302, 307, 322, 335, 360–2, 368–71, 373–5, 378–82, 384, 388–9, 391, 398, 488–9, 491, 493, 496, 501, 514, 523

The Lilacs, 321, 325

"Lion," 189, 197, 260, 402; *see also Go Down, Moses*

"Lizards in Jamshyd's Courtyard," 401–2; *see also The Hamlet*

"Lo," 402

"Love Song," 325

The Mansion, 126–7, 190, 332, 360, 407, 421, 459–74, 491

maps, 190, 233, 252–60, 266–7, 327, 485, 523

The Marble Faun, 321, 325, 328, 330, 360, 365–6

The Marionettes, 149–51, 154, 163n, 322, 326–7, 331, 365–6

Mayday, 322, 324, 326–7, 330–1, 365–6, 397

"Mirrors of Chartres Street," 330

"Mississippi," 40, 413, 418–19

Mississippi Poems, 321

"Mistral," 400

"Monk," 405; *see also Knight's Gambit*

Mosquitoes, 33, 148–63, 324, 326, 335, 353, 360, 366, 443n

"A Mountain Victory," 401

"Mule in the Yard," 402; *see also The Town*

"Naiad's Song," 324

New Orleans Sketches, 213

"A Note on Sherwood Anderson," 414

Notes on a Horse Thief, 337

"Nympholepsy," 324, 364–5, 368, 397

"An Odor of Verbena," 140, 142, 403; *see also The Unvanquished*

Old Man, 66–73, 77, 333, 424; *see also If I Forget Thee, Jerusalem*

"The Old People," 145, 404; *see also Go Down, Moses*

"On Fear: Deep South in Labor: Mississippi," 97, 411

"On Privacy," 98, 104

"Orpheus and Other Poems," 321, 325

"Pantaloon in Black," 21–4, 247, 250, 263, 265, 371, 404; *see also Go Down, Moses*

poetry, 33, 54, 105, 107, 112, 115, 149–51, 155–6, 161–2, 180, 310, 321–31, 336, 339, 342, 345, 360, 363, 365–6, 394, 397, 400, 410, 440–2, 448–50, 501, 507; *see also* individual titles

Faulkner's works: *(cont'd)*
 The Portable Faulkner (ed. Cowley), 204, 207,
  252, 266–7, 315, 335, 481–3, 522
 Pylon, 55, 98, 336, 422–3
 "Race at Morning," 407
 "Raid," 403
 The Reivers, 46, 48, 55–61, 83, 220, 236,
  247–50, 322, 332, 407, 491–2
 Requiem for a Nun, 53, 208, 212, 269–70,
  279–82, 322, 336–8, 407, 422, 492
 "Retreat," 135, 403; *see also The Unvanquished*
 reviews, 329, 414
 "Riposte in Tertio," 403; *see also The*
  Unvanquished
 "A Rose for Emily," 315, 330, 398, 400
 Sanctuary, 34, 46–8, 59, 62n, 117–19, 130,
  162, 204, 212, 226–30, 234, 236–9, 244,
  246, 250, 302, 306–15, 322, 326, 334–7,
  350–1, 360, 366–8, 373–5, 388–92, 398,
  421, 430, 481, 489, 491, 502
 Sartoris, 33, 130, 184–8, *186*, 212, 233, 271,
  335, 366, 424, 430
 Sherwood Anderson and Other Famous Creoles, 414
 short stories, 34, 48, 54, 58–9, 69–71, 78, 89,
  106, 108, 111, 135, 162, 180, 185, 189, 191,
  204, 207, 227, 247, 260–1, 266, 287, 301–2,
  307, 315, 322–3, 327–36, 362–3, 365, 369,
  371, 373, 375, 379–80, 394–408, 420, 441,
  447, 522; *see also* individual titles
 "Sinbad in New Orleans," 330
 "Skirmish at Sartoris," 142, 403; *see also The*
  Unvanquished
 "Smoke," 401, 405; *see also Knight's Gambit*
 Snopes trilogy, 123, 126, 250, 332, 337, 357n,
  360, 368, 397, 421, 459–74, 491–2; *see also*
  The Hamlet; The Mansion; The Town
 Soldiers' Pay, 33, 55, 212, 220, 315, 322, 330,
  335, 366, 397, 443n
 The Sound and the Fury, 8, 12–17, 29, 33–4, 47,
  52–3, 55, 61, 70, 86, 88–90, 109, 115–16,
  118, 124–5, 137, *154*, 162, 184, 188–93,
  204–6, 223–6, 230, 236–8, 244–6, 252–7,
  259, 269–70, 277–81, 301–2, 306–7, 322,
  324, 326–7, 330, 334–5, 344–6, 352–3,
  356, 357n, 359–61, 365–7, 373–4, 395,
  397–8, 420–2, 424, 429–30, 433, 435,
  441–2, 449, 480, 485–9, 491, 496
 speeches, 28, 71, 306, 322, 337–9, 353,
  410–11, 482, 486, 500
 "Sunset," 204, 213; *see also New Orleans Sketches*
 "That Evening Sun," 395, 399–400

 "There Was a Queen," 185, *186*
 "Thrift," 402
 "To the Youth of Japan," 416
 "Tomorrow," 405; *see also Knight's Gambit*
 The Town, 43–4, 83, 206, 337, 402, 407, 421,
  459–74, 491
 "Turnabout," 48
 Uncollected Stories, 365, 402, 406
 "The Unvanquished" (story), 403
 The Unvanquished, 47, 119, 135–42, 144, 185,
  218n, 307, 327, 331, 336, 394, 402–6, 502
 "Vendée," 403; *see also The Unvanquished*
 "Victory," 399–401
 "Vision in Spring," 321, 325
 "Wash," 401
 The Wild Palms, see If I Forget Thee, Jerusalem
 The Wishing Tree, 331
feminism, 54, 62n, 71–2, 85–6, 148, 238, 364,
  480, 487–9, 491
Ferré, Rosario, 513
Fiedler, Leslie, 301–6, 308, 315–16, 369
film, 53, 55, 65–8, 72–83, 99, 172, 226–7, 229,
  241, 284–97, 309, 311, 331, 333, 335–6
film noir, *see* crime genres
"The Fire and the Hearth," 142, 145, 247, 262,
  404; *see also Go Down, Moses*
Fitzgerald, F. Scott, 111, 329, 395
Flags in the Dust, 184–5, 212, 366, 424, 430, 435,
  442
"Fool About a Horse," 401; *see also The Hamlet*
"Foreword" to *The Faulkner Reader*, 334, 413
Forrest, Leon, 145
Forster, E. M., 254–5
Foucault, Michel, 85–6, 229, 488, 491
Fowler, Doreen, 62n, 93, 144, 462, 488, 490, 492
Frankfurt School, 97–101
free indirect discourse, 25n, 125
Freeman, Barbara, 364
Freud, Sigmund, 19, 25, 52, 85–101, 108, 152,
  155–6, 244, 274–5, 342–7, 353, 377–8,
  385–7, 434–6, 439, 442, 443n, 449, 462,
  486–7
Friedan, Betty, 86
Frost, Robert, 106–7, 507
Fuentes, Carlos, 493, 499–507, 511

Gaines, Ernest, 145
García Márquez, Gabriel, 493, 499–500, 502–7,
  511, 514
gangster fiction and film, *see* crime genres
gay sexuality, *see* sexuality

gender, 12, 24, 26n, 46–61, 62n, 71–2, 75–7, 81, 86, 90–1, 93–5, 99, 133–4, 148–63, 165, 180, 192, 198, 209, 212, 224–6, 239–40, 245, 282, 324, 334, 351–2, 360, 365–9, 374, 377–8, 381–3, 391–2, 446, 448–50, 452, 457, 482–4, 486–7, 489, 491, 506; *see also* sexuality

ghosts, 21, 61, 145, 187–8, 213, 242, 271, 296, 332, 356, 388, 441–2, 451, 456, 521

Giddens, Anthony, 256–7

Glissant, Edouard, 178, 494–5, 513, 522–7

"Go Down, Moses" (story), 145, 247, 405; *see also Go Down, Moses*

Go Down, Moses, 8, 21–5, 25n, 55, 90, 92, 134–6, 139, 142–5, 152–3, *154*, 162, 163n, 189, 196–9, 246–7, 250, 253–4, 260–7, 282, 322, 331–2, 336, 353, 368, 371, 402–5, 447, 483, 488–9, 491, 493, 523–6

Godard, Jean-Luc, 65–8, 74, 77–83

Godden, Richard, 62n, 72–4, 88–9, 120, 466, 472, 488, 490, 514

Gone With the Wind (Mitchell), 242, 302

gothic, 253, 271, 359–71

Gray, Richard, 13, 68, 109–11, 118, 121, 125, 210

Great Migration, *see* migration

Great War, *see* World War I

"Green Bough," 155

Gresset, Michel, 87, 286, 295

grief, 21–5, 46, 65–7, 71, 76–7, 83, 90, 100, 141–5, 155, 158, 190, 193, 196–9, 247, 253, 261, 263–5, 437

Gubar, Susan, 153

"A Guest's Impression of New England," 99, 415

Gwin, Minrose, 72–3, 93, 148, 161, 488–9, 491

Haiti, 120, 166–7, 178, 193–4, 242–3, 252, 343, 446–7, 451, 513

Hamblin, Robert, 62n, 336, 496

The Hamlet, 47–8, 58, 90, 123–7, 130, 244–6, 250, 302, 307, 332, 336, 356, 394, 397, 401–2, 420–2, 432–3, 459–74

Hammett, Dashiell, 226, 333, 373

"Hand Upon the Waters," 405; *see also Knight's Gambit*

Hannon, Charles, 92, 94

Hanson, Philip, 223

hard-boiled detective, *see* crime genres

Harris, George Washington, 332

Harris, Oliver, 286, 289–92, 295–7, 299

Hawks, Howard, 68, 79–80

Hegel, G. W. F., 7–8, 90, 522

Helen: A Courtship, 321

"Hell Creek Crossing," 407; *see also The Reivers*

Hemingway, Ernest, 71, 77, 111, 242, 328, 334, 338, 351–3, 395, 414, 511

"Hermaphroditus," 155, 161

heterosexuality, *see* sexuality

"The Hill," 396–7

"His Name Was Pete," 417

Hollywood, 34, 46, 54, 68, 72, 74–81, 110, 112, 226, 301, 306, 315, 327, 331, 335–6, 398, 406

homoeroticism, homosexuality, *see* sexuality

Horace (Roman poet), 301, 309–10

horse-racing, 58, 60–1, 189, 266, 416–17; *see also* sports

"The Hound," 401; *see also The Hamlet*

Housman, A. E., 324, 327, 363, 365

Huyssen, Andreas, 71, 303–4

ideology, 52, 54, 72, 83, 86, 88–92, 95–9, 133–5, 142–5, 153, 166–79, 211–12, 220–5, 227–9, 230–4, 239, 253, 257, 259, 262, 265–7, 269–82, 290, 345, 357n, 376, 379, 460–74, 484, 490–1, 507–8, 519

If I Forget Thee, Jerusalem, 26n, 65–83, 111, 212, 307–8, 312, 322, 324, 326, 333, 336, 378–81, 424, 489, 491, 502

"If I Were a Negro," 40, 412

immigration, *see* migration

"Impressions of Japan," 415–16

incest, 13–17, 87, 152, 159–60, 178, 180, 192, 194–6, 199, 243–4, 265, 346, 361, 446–7, 486, 513

Indians, *see* Native Americans

industrialization, 13, 21–3, 31, 41, 48–50, 68, 72–6, 78–82, 87–9, 97–8, 105, 169–71, 209, 214–15, 221–2, 225, 230, 290, 301, 305, 333, 335, 359, 361, 370, 501, 506, 524

"An Innocent at Rinkside," 99, 416–17

introduction to *The Faulkner Reader* (Random House), 333

introduction to *Sanctuary* (Modern Library), 226, 334–5

introductions to *The Sound and the Fury* 16, 88, 301, 360–1, 366

Intruder in the Dust, 55, 135, 206, 210, 230–3, 307, 322, 331, 337, 368, 373–7, 379, 381, 389, 425, 483, 491–2

Irigaray, Luce, 86, 488, 491

Irwin, John, 86–7, 155–6, 243–4, 282, 356n, 377–8, 485–7

James, Henry, 109, 129, 343, 361
Jameson, Fredric, 85, 290, 488
Jehlen, Myra, 88, 94, 165, 246
Jenkins, Lee, 139, 198, 462
Joyce, James, 106, 109, 111, 257, 302, 322, 324, 329, 342, 346–7, 502
"A Justice," 189, 266, 400

Kafka, Franz, 347, 351, 353–6, 357n
Karl, Frederick, 38, 108–9, 111, 152
Kartiganer, Donald, 199, 270, 295, 298, 437, 481, 521
Kawin, Bruce, 65–7, 78, 81, 322, 333, 336
Keats, John, 36, 197, 365–6, 413
"Kentucky: May: Saturday," 322, 416–17
King, Martin Luther, Jr., 43
King, Vincent, 74, 121, 308
"The Kingdom of God," 188
Kinney, Arthur, 131n, 184–5
Kipling, Rudyard, 254–5
Kline, T. Jefferson, 66–8, 81, 83
Knight's Gambit, 322, 333, 373–4, 377–9, 401–2, 405–6
Kreiswirth, Martin, 206–7
Kristeva, Julia, 86, 368, 488, 491
Ku Klux Klan, 41, 88, 239, 286–8, 292, 298

labor, 7–25, 28, 30, 32, 49–51, 73, 80, 87–91, 93, 100, 107, 168, 171, 203, 211, 213, 224, 279, 281, 286, 351, 370, 374, 387, 437, 453, 470, 490, 494, 524
Lacan, Jacques, 85, 95–6, 459–74, 480, 486–8, 490–1
Ladd, Barbara, 178, 513–15
"Landing in Luck," 54, 327, 331, 396
language, 16, 19–20, 35, 51–2, 56, 73, 91–2, 94, 96, 109–10, 115–17, 119, 122, 127–30, 131n, 133, 245, 249–50, 262, 276, 279–80, 308, 321, 324, 327, 343, 345, 354, 360–1, 363, 366, 369, 379, 388, 399, 413, 415, 440–1, 456, 457n, 461, 482, 485–6, 489–90, 493–6; *see also* ideology
"L'Apres-Midi d'un Faune," 324, 365
Latham, Sean, 173, 178–9, 253
"The Leg," 59, 401
lesbian sexuality, *see* sexuality
Lester, Cheryl, 88, 204, 480
"A Letter to the Leaders of the Negro Race," 411

"A Letter to the North," 39–42
"Letter to a Northern Editor," 29, 411
letters (Faulkner), 28–9, 33, 39–41, 54, 70, 98, 100, 106–8, 110–12, 121, 129, 138, 184, 253, 321–3, 325–6, 329–31, 337–9, 353, 384, 407, 411, 415, 417, 421–2, 429, 490, 509, 520–1
liberalism 28–45, 90–1, 99, 130, 171–9, 220–34, 342, 419, 490, 505, 508
The Life of William Faulkner: A Critical Biography (Gray), 109–11; *see also* Gray, Richard
Light in August, 34–9, 44, 48, 55, 109, 127–30, 135, 206, 212, 236, 239–41, 244, 246, 250, 252, 254, 270–1, 273–4, 276, 282, 284–99, 302, 307, 322, 335, 360–2, 368–71, 373–5, 378–82, 384, 388–9, 391, 398, 488–9, 491, 493, 496, 501, 514, 523
The Lilacs, 321, 325
"Lion," 189, 197, 260, 402; *see also* Go Down, Moses
"Lizards in Jamshyd's Courtyard," 401–2; *see also* The Hamlet
"Lo," 402
Lost Cause, 29, 89, 141, 270, 396, 442, 506
Lott, Eric, 153
"Love Song," 325
A Loving Gentleman (Wilde), 46, 110
Lowell, Amy, 324–5
Lowell, Robert, 507
Lukács, Georg, 524–5
Lurie, Peter, 62n, 73–5, 97, 99, 309, 311–12, 316
lynching, 21, 24, 30–1, 33–6, 39, 46, 52, 90, 180, 199, 229–30, 238–9, 271, 275, 287, 293, 299, 362, 367–8, 371, 389, 418
Lyotard, Jean-François, 364

Macherey, Pierre, 117
Maclean, Nancy, 202–3
Mallarmé, Stéphane, 324, 327, 365
Mann, Thomas, 302, 351, 353
The Mansion, 126–7, 190, 332, 360, 407, 421, 459–74, 491
maps, 184, 190, 233, 252–60, 264, 266–7, 327, 485, 523–4
The Marble Faun, 321, 325, 328, 330, 360, 365–6
Marcuse, Herbert, 85, 97–101
The Marionettes, 149–51, 154, 163n, 322, 326–7, 331, 365–6
Marshall, Thurgood, 32, 39–42
Marx, Karl, 77, 85–101, 488, 490
Marxism, *see* Marx, Karl

mass culture, *see* popular culture

Matthews, John, 72, 89–92, 94, 97, 150, 175–6, 178, 224, 279, 316, 356n, 488–9, 494, 514, 521

Mayday, 322, 324, 326–7, 330–1, 365–6, 397

McCoy, Horace, 72

McHaney, Thomas, 69–72, 74–5, 81, 90, 207, 311, 323, 328–9, 332, 334–5

melodrama, 68, 73, 75, 77, 80–1, 292

migration, 10–11, 18, 24, 48, 88, 136, 146, 171, 184, 190, 203–4, 212–14, 218n, 286, 296, 451

Millgate, Michael, 105, 239, 395, 483–5

Miner, Ward, 207–11, 218n

minstrelsy, 41, 148–63, *154*, 293

Minter, David, 108, 135, 196, 303, 307

"Mirrors of Chartres Street," 330

miscegenation, 16–18, 38, 44, 90, 109, 152, 159–60, 163, 180, 182, 195–6, 199, 287, 265, 447, 457n, 489, 513–14

"Mississippi," 40, 413, 418–19

Mississippi Poems, 321

"Mistral," 400

Mitchell, Juliet, 86

modernism, 54, 66, 71, 73, 77, 85, 104, 108–9, 150, 153, 223, 245–6, 256, 261, 269, 273, 282, 302–3, 305–7, 309–11, 315–16, 321–2, 342–57, 365, 373, 379, 389, 411, 419–50, 489, 499, 501–4, 519–27; *see also* postmodernism

"Monk," 405; *see also Knight's Gambit*

Moreland, Richard, 89–90, 231, 245, 280, 356n

Morrison, Toni, 92, 146, 153, 448, 456, 457n, 493, 495–6, 512, 514, 516n

Mosquitoes, 33, 148–63, 324, 326, 335, 353, 360, 366, 443n

"A Mountain Victory," 401

movies, *see* film

"Mule in the Yard," 402; *see also The Town*

mystery fiction, *see* crime genres

"Naiad's Song," 324

narrative form, 19, 25n, 36, 42, 48, 50, 55, 66, 69–73, 76–8, 82, 87, 90–2, 101, 105–6, 108, 110, 117–30, 135, 138–46, 149, 160, 166–7, 172, 176–80, 195, 204, 207–8, 215, 223, 228, 231–3, 241–4, 249–50, 252–7, 260–2, 264–5, 267, 273–4, 282, 288–9, 291, 297–9, 322, 326, 331, 336, 338, 343–57, 359, 362–3, 365, 367–71, 374, 377, 381–2, 384, 389–91, 394–401, 404, 406–7,

421, 429, 431, 433–5, 444–57, 469, 484, 492–3, 500, 502–4, 519–27

Native Americans, 50, 156, 178, 189, 212–13, 258, 263–4, 396, 400, 402, 405–6, 481, 524; *see also* colonialism

Naylor, Gloria, 145

Neruda, Pablo, 501, 507

New Criticism, 105–6, 423, 479–80, 482–7, 495

New Deal, 9–11, 18, 20, 30–3, 220–2, 230, 338

New Orleans Sketches, 213

New South, 88, 169, 171, 375, 445, 455, 457

Nobel Prize, 39, 69–71, 83, 104, 306, 322–3, 334, 336–7, 339, 406, 410, 413, 425, 482–3, 486, 493, 496, 500, 507, 509

non-violence, 28, 36, 412; *see also* violence

"A Note on Sherwood Anderson," 414

Notes on a Horse Thief, 337

"Nympholepsy," 324, 364–5, 368, 397

Oates, Stephen, 108

O'Connor, Flannery, 396, 493, 499–500

O'Donnell, George, 359, 481–3

"An Odor of Verbena," 140, 142, 403; *see also The Unvanquished*

Old Man, 66–73, 77, 333, 424; *see also If I Forget Thee, Jerusalem*

"The Old People," 145, 404; *see also Go Down, Moses*

Old South, 88–9, 119, 173, 447, 449, 455, 465, 503–4

Oldham, Estelle, 46, 54, 429

"On Fear: Deep South in Labor: Mississippi," 97, 411

"On Privacy," 98, 104

One Matchless Time: A Life of William Faulkner (Parini), 110–12

oratory, 138–41

"Orpheus and Other Poems," 321, 325

"Pantaloon in Black," 21–4, 247, 250, 263, 265, 371, 404; *see also Go Down, Moses*

Parini, Jay, 110–12

pastoral, 29, 44, 302, 308, 310–11, 314, 324, 359–71

paternalism, 9, 42, 90, 172–9, 197, 244, 262, 376–7, 449, 460, 480, 490, 495

Patterson, Orlando, 18, 451

Peek, Charles, 62n

performance, 44, 48, 117, 133, 148–63, 228, 233–4, 279, 295, 303, 321, 335, 339, 363, 374, 391, 400, 431, 490

Pierrot, 149–52, *154*, 163n, 326, 365–6

place, 23–5, 29, 31–2, 35, 39, 42–3, 50, 52, 73, 76, 88, 93, 140, 145, 160, 166, 170–1, 173, 175, 202–18, 256–8, 263, 277, 354–67, 395–6, 462–5, 470, 472, 474, 523; *see also* space

plantation novel, 8, 138

plantations, 7–25, 50, 89, 94, 137, 139–51, 166, 172–9, 184, 193–7, 202–3, 208–9, 214, 217, 241–4, 246–7, 258, 261–3, 265–7, 293, 385–6, 396, 405, 431, 447, 449–53, 459, 494, 499, 503–4, 512–15, 524–5

poetry (Faulkner), 33, 54, 105, 107, 112, 115, 149–51, 155–6, 161–2, 180, 310, 321–31, 336, 339, 342, 345, 360, 363, 365–6, 394, 397, 400, 410, 440–2, 448–50, 501, 507; *see also* individual titles

politics, 18, 28, 30, 32–4, 37–8, 41, 47–8, 50–1, 72, 80, 83, 86–7, 90–4, 96, 97–100, 130, 174, 184, 187, 190, 203–4, 209–10, 215–17, 220–34, 236, 239, 245, 249, 270, 275, 282, 287–8, 290, 293, 305, 336, 364, 367, 374, 412–13, 418, 432, 446, 450, 454, 456, 479–80, 482–4, 499–500, 502, 505–7, 509–15, 522–4; *see also* the state

popular culture, 28, 53, 56, 65, 68, 71–2, 77, 81, 83, 97–101, 118, 153, 176, 226–30, 286–7, 290, 298, 380, 387–99, 301–16, 321–2, 330–1, 333, 379, 407, 481, 484

The Portable Faulkner (ed. Cowley), 204, 207, 252, 266–7, 315, 335, 481–3, 522

Porter, Carolyn, 95, 100, 295

Porter, Katherine Anne, 507, 511

post-colonialism, 252–67, 480, 493–5, 499–515, 519–27; *see also* colonialism

postmodernism, 85, 301, 305, 316, 364, 454, 519–27

Pound, Ezra, 322, 342, 352, 450

primitivism, 148–63, 169, 187, 257, 264, 383, 454, 462

progress, 49, 221–2, 169, 171, 214–15, 232, 344–5, 399, 414–15, 433–4, 520, 522–7

prostitution, 13, 46, 51–2, 55–60, 149, 159–60, 240, 249, 279, 281, 333, 448–9, 455

Proust, Marcel, 257, 302, 344, 347–51

puns, 16, 18–20, 77, 82

Pylon, 55, 98, 336, 422–3

race, racism, 9–25, 28–44, 49–59, 88, 94, 99, 120, 129–30, 133–46, 149–63, 165, 173–80, 193–200, 205, 216, 231–3, 237, 239, 244, 247, 254, 265, 267, 270, 272, 275–9, 281–2, 284–99, 308, 337, 339, 353, 360, 367–71, 374–88, 396, 400, 403, 405, 410–13, 417–19, 431, 441, 445–57, 460, 480, 484, 488–91, 493, 495, 504, 506–7, 513–15, 522, 525–6

"Race at Morning," 407

"Raid," 403

Railey, Kevin, 90, 165, 171–2, 174, 178, 460, 473–4, 490

rape, 39, 46, 48, 52, 90, 160, 178, 195–7, 227–9, 236, 238–9, 241–2, 247, 281, 293, 299, 310, 350, 367–9, 391–2, 400, 447

realism, 73, 79, 116, 192, 197, 240, 243, 252, 290, 292–3, 298, 332, 342, 345, 347–8, 350, 379, 429, 500–2, 521

Reconstruction, 9–10, 20, 141–2, 185, 193, 202, 260, 286–7, 292, 298, 331, 376, 381, 416, 501, 514

region, 9, 11–12, 25, 28–33, 40–3, 48–53, 61, 62n, 88, 90, 109, 119, 138, 141, 146, 166–7, 178, 216–17, 223, 246, 256, 287–8, 322, 337–8, 353, 360–2, 370, 395, 445, 450, 457, 482, 484, 489, 495, 499–503, 405–7, 511–15

The Reivers, 46, 48, 55–61, 83, 220, 236, 247–50, 322, 332, 407, 491–2

religion, 35–8, 47–8, 57, 98, 128, 199, 229, 239, 246, 269–82, 304–5, 310, 345–6, 382, 415; *see also* spirituality

Requiem for a Nun, 53, 208, 212, 269–70, 279–82, 322, 336–8, 407, 422, 492

"Retreat," 135, 403; *see also The Unvanquished*

reviews (by Faulkner), 329, 414

reviews (of Faulkner), 47, 480–2, 502

Richardson, H. Edward, 105

"Riposte in Tertio," 403; *see also The Unvanquished*

Roberts, Diane, 72, 91

Rogin, Michael, 153, 293, 296

romanticism, 50, 59, 71, 79, 109, 112, 145, 185, 242, 321, 323, 333, 342, 359–71, 377–8, 423, 521

Roosevelt, Eleanor, 31

Roosevelt, Franklin D., 30, 221–2

Roosevelt, Theodore, 221

"A Rose for Emily," 315, 330, 398, 400

Rose, Jacqueline, 86

Ross, Stephen, 490, 495

Rulfo, Juan, 499, 502–5

rural society, 11, 20, 50, 134, 167, 169–71, 175, 203, 213–14, 246, 294, 302, 366, 396

Said, Edward, 253–4, 256, 260, 266, 488

Sanctuary, 34, 46–8, 59, 62n, 117–19, 130, 162, 204, 212, 226–30, 234, 236–9, 244, 246, 250, 302, 306–15, 322, 326, 334–7, 350–1, 360, 366–8, 373–5, 388–92, 398, 421, 430, 481, 489, 491, 502

Sartoris, 33, 130, 184–8, *186*, 212, 233, 271, 335, 366, 424, 430

Sartre, Jean-Paul, 69, 256, 345

Saussure, Ferdinand, 116

Sayers, Dorothy, 333, 373

Schwartz, Lawrence, 97, 100, 479

segregation, 16, 29, 44, 133–46, 202–3, 205, 210–11, 217, 277

Sensibar, Judith, 324–5

sexuality, 13–18, 23, 24–5, 46–61, 62n, 71–2, 75, 82, 86, 93, 108–9, 148–63, 163n, 212, 227, 236, 238, 240–1, 243, 246–7, 249, 273–4, 282, 287–8, 292, 307, 315, 325, 348–9, 367–8, 370, 383, 397, 434–8, 442, 450, 456, 468, 480, 487, 494, 512; *see also* gender

sharecropping, 9–12, 30, 202–3, 209, 214, 244–5, 332, 525–6; *see also* tenant farming

Sherwood Anderson and Other Famous Creoles, 414

Shiner, Larry, 303–4

short stories (Faulkner), 34, 48, 54, 58–9, 69–71, 78, 89, 106, 108, 111, 135, 162, 180, 185, 189, 191, 204, 207, 227, 247, 260–1, 266, 287, 301–2, 307, 315, 322–3, 327–36, 362–3, 365, 369, 371, 373, 375, 379–80, 394–408, 420, 441, 447, 522; *see also* individual titles

Simpson, Lewis, 360

"Sinbad in New Orleans," 330

"Skirmish at Sartoris," 142, 403; *see also The Unvanquished*

slavery, 7–10, 16–20, 25n, 39, 42, 50–1, 53, 58–9, 87–8, 109, 120, 133–40, 142, 157, 159, 167, 172–9, 193–4, 196–7, 202–3, 208–9, 217, 218n, 232, 239, 247, 253, 259–60, 262–3, 272, 287–8, 293, 296–8, 353, 369, 371, 381, 385–8, 396, 418, 445–56, 464, 481–3, 494, 499, 512–15, 524

Smith, Hal, 429–30, 443

Smith, Harrison, 252

Smith, Jon, 493, 501, 506

Smith, Lillian, 41, 52, 61

"Smoke," 401, 405; *see also Knight's Gambit*

Snead, James, 90–2, 100, 129–30, 456

Snopes trilogy, 123, 126, 250, 332, 337, 357n, 360, 368, 397, 421, 459–74, 491–2; *see also The Hamlet; The Mansion; The Town*

Soldiers' Pay, 33, 55, 212, 220, 315, 322, 330, 335, 366, 397, 443n

The Sound and the Fury, 8, 12–17, 29, 33–4, 47, 52–3, 55, 61, 70, 86, 88–90, 109, 115–16, 118, 124–5, 137, *154*, 162, 184, 188–93, 204–6, 223–6, 230, 236–8, 244–6, 252–7, 259, 269–70, 277–81, 301–2, 306–7, 322, 324, 326–7, 330, 334–5, 344–6, 352–3, 356, 357n, 359–61, 365–7, 373–4, 395, 397–8, 420–2, 424, 429–30, 433, 435, 441–2, 449, 480, 485–9, 491, 496

space, 16–17, 23, 29, 32–3, 35, 37–40, 43–4, 59, 61, 72, 90, 117–18, 138, 145–9, 161, 166, 170, 173, 175, 206, 210, 215, 217, 222, 229, 231, 233, 245, 252–67, 273, 277, 291, 294, 345, 347, 350, 355, 380–1, 385, 387, 391, 404, 411, 502; *see also* place

speech, 13, 15, 19, 130, 181n, 138–9, 245, 278, 280, 311, 350, 376, 462

speeches (Faulkner), 28, 71, 306, 322, 337–9, 353, 410–11, 482, 486, 500

spirits, *see* ghosts

spirituality, 35–8, 50, 110, 142, 157, 208, 210, 269–82, 303–4, 310, 337, 451, 492; *see also* religion

sports, 99, 245, 322, 416–17

Spratling, William, 54, 152, 330, 414

Stanchich, Maritza, 178

the state, 20, 30, 40–1, 86, 97–8, 100, 133, 179, 185, 189, 209, 211, 215, 217, 220–34, 258–9, 261–2, 281, 286, 292–3, 304, 312, 337–8, 357n, 415, 451, 457n, 494, 507–13

Stone, Phil, 54, 104, 110, 321, 323–5, 328–30, 332

Stout, Rex, 333, 373

sublime, 35, 304, 346, 359–71

Summers, Jill Faulkner, 110, 410

Sundquist, Eric, 13, 36, 176, 226, 231–2, 247, 360, 462, 488–91, 493, 495

"Sunset," 204, 213; *see also New Orleans Sketches*

Sur, 501

Swinburne, Algernon, 324, 327, 329

Symbolists, 321, 324, 326, 360, 365

Taylor, Herman, 215–17

technology, 48, 97, 171, 294, 338, 414–15

tenant farming, 9–12, 18, 30, 202–3, 245, 431–3, 459–60, 464–6, 471; *see also* sharecropping

texts (Faulkner), 69, 420–5
"That Evening Sun," 395, 399–400
"There Was a Queen," 185, *186*
Thomas-Houston, Marilyn, 215–17
Thompson, Alan, 227
Thompson, Lawrance, 106–7
"Thrift," 402
To Have and To Have Not (Hawks), 307
"To the Youth of Japan," 416
"Tomorrow," 405; *see also Knight's Gambit*
Torgovnick, Marianna, 152–3
The Town, 43–4, 83, 206, 337, 402, 407, 421,
    459–74, 491
Towner, Theresa, 91–2, 231–2, 460, 466, 492–3
trauma, 44, 89–91, 96, 174–5, 216, 238, 253,
    272, 275, 280, 288, 297–9, 344, 349,
    351–3, 373–92, 438, 461, 463–4, 466–7,
    474, 513
travel, 54, 108, 112, 137, 214, 217, 314, 322,
    328–30, 387, 397, 415–16, 454, 499, 506–9,
    511
Trilling, Lionel, 99
"Turnabout," 48
Twain, Mark, 25n, 231, 302, 332, 445, 448, 457n

Uncollected Stories, 365, 402, 406
"The Unvanquished" (story), 403
The Unvanquished, 47, 119, 135–42, 144, 185,
    218n, 307, 327, 331, 336, 394, 402–6, 502
Urgo, Joseph, 97, 99–100, 214, 316, 465, 467,
    492–3

"Vendée," 403; *see also The Unvanquished*
Vickery, Olga, 480, 483–5
"Victory," 399–401
violence, 19, 24, 28–9, 33–4, 36–7, 39–40, 43–4,
    45n, 46, 57, 88–9, 109, 145, 153, 174, 176,
    178, 193, 226–9, 236–50, 253, 259–66,
    270–1, 273–7, 281–2, 285–7, 292, 294,
    296–9, 307, 310–11, 313, 315, 337–8, 344,
    351, 353, 362, 368, 375–7, 381, 383, 396,
    412, 418, 435–9, 451, 454–5, 465, 472, 474,
    486, 491; *see also* non-violence
"Vision in Spring," 321, 325
Volpe, Edmund, 464, 469, 483–5

Wagner-Martin, Linda, 260, 483–4
Warren, Robert Penn, 323, 331–2, 338–9, 482–4

"Wash," 401
Washington, Booker T., 30, 412
Wasson, Ben, 110, 150, 152, 424
The Waste Land, see Eliot, T. S.
Watson, James, 279, 490
Watson, Jay, 91, 229
Weinstein, Arnold, 496
Weinstein, Philip, 87, 91, 135, 149, 232, 237,
    253–4, 267, 356, 488, 491, 495, 502,
    514
Wells, Ida B., 52
Welty, Eudora, 322, 327, 395, 493
Werner, Craig, 136, 145–6
whiteface, *see* minstrelsy
The Wild Palms, see If I Forget Thee, Jerusalem
Wilde, Meta Carpenter, 46, 68, 76, 108, 110–11,
    327
Wilde, Oscar, 53–4, 152, 365
William Faulkner: American Writer (Karl), 108–9,
    111
William Faulkner and Southern History
    (Williamson), 109
William Faulkner: His Life and Work (Minter),
    108
Williams, Joan, 108, 110
Williams, Leonard, 222
Williams, Raymond, 85, 89, 91–8, 168–71,
    211–15, 221, 366, 370, 488
Williams, Sherley Anne, 145
Williamson, Joel, 10, 12, 109, 133, 141, 185,
    239
Wilson, Charles, 270–1, 276
Winesburg, Ohio (Anderson), 395
The Wishing Tree, 331
Wittenberg, Judith, 108, 495
Woolf, Virginia, 111, 257, 322, 351–2, 502
World War I, 10–11, 25n, 34–5, 187, 213, 217,
    221, 223, 324, 326, 345, 351–3, 396,
    399–402
World War II, 32, 50, 66, 78, 202, 209–10, 212,
    220, 304, 336, 352–3, 416
Wright, Austin, 491
Wright, Richard, 210–11

Yeats, William B., 106, 324, 365
Young, Stark, 54, 152, 328–9

Zender, Karl, 88, 97, 99, 279–80

PS 351
A 86
Z 7585
2007